BY WOMEN
POSSESSED

BY WOMEN POSSESSED

A Life of Eugene O'Neill

ARTHUR GELB AND BARBARA GELB

A MARIAN WOOD BOOK

Published by G. P. Putnam's Sons

an imprint of Penguin Random House

New York

PUTNAM

G. P. PUTNAM'S SONS
Publishers since 1838
An imprint of Penguin Random House LLC
375 Hudson Street
New York, New York 10014

Library of Congress Cataloging-in-Publication Data

Names: Gelb, Arthur, 1924–2014. | Gelb, Barbara.
Title: By women possessed : a life of Eugene O'Neill / Arthur Gelb and Barbara Gelb.
Description: New York : G. P. Putnam's Sons, an imprint of Penguin Random House,
2016. | "A Marian Wood book." | Includes bibliographical references and index.
Identifiers: LCCN 2016008421 | ISBN 9780399159114 (hardback)
Subjects: LCSH: O'Neill, Eugene, 1888–1953. | O'Neill, Eugene, 1888–1953—Relations
with women. | Dramatists, American—20th century—Biography.
BISAC: BIOGRAPHY & AUTOBIOGRAPHY / Entertainment & Performing Arts. |
BIOGRAPHY & AUTOBIOGRAPHY / Literary. | BIOGRAPHY
& AUTOBIOGRAPHY / General.
Classification: LCC PS3529.N5 Z6527 2016 | DDC 812/.52–dc23
LC record available at http://lccn.loc.gov/2016008421
p.   cm.

Printed in the United States of America
1   3   5   7   9   10   8   6   4   2

BOOK DESIGN BY NICOLE LAROCHE

For our sons, Michael and Peter

our grandchildren, Daniel, Sarah, David, Matthew

and our great-granddaughters, Hannah and Emma,

with love forever and a day

This is Daddy's bed time secret. Man is born broken. He lives by mending. The grace of God is glue!

—*The Great God Brown*, Act IV, Scene 1

CONTENTS

PREFACE

Arthur Gelb, my husband and collaborator of sixty-eight years, did not live to see the publication of *By Women Possessed*. He died on May 20, 2014, just as we were wearily polishing the last few pages of our seven-hundred-page final draft. Together, we'd been wrestling with the book's research and writing for almost a decade.

Semi-emerging some months later from a grief-stricken languor, I found myself, alone and tearful, tweaking those last pages (which, in the event, we'd already rewritten half a dozen times). Arthur's ghost was looking over my shoulder. I nervously changed a semicolon to a period, hoping he'd approve. This was, after all, his book as much as mine.

As for this preface, he'll just have to trust me on my own. I hope he'll be okay with it.

It's hard to believe it was more than half a century ago that Arthur and I had the audacity to tackle the writing of the first full-scale biography of Eugene O'Neill. I was thirty and Arthur was thirty-two. The year was 1956, three years after O'Neill's death at sixty-five. His last new play on Broadway—after a silence of twelve years—had been *The Iceman Cometh*, in 1946. The play was ahead of its time, the production was flawed, and it didn't have an impressive run.

Arthur and I had both been avid theatergoers since childhood, and he had recently been appointed as an assistant drama critic (covering Off-Broadway) for *The New York Times*. We were too young to have seen any of the original productions of O'Neill's earlier plays, but we had read many of them. We well knew that O'Neill had once been a blazing, larger-than-life presence on the American stage—that, in fact, during the 1920s and '30s, he was the acknowledged architect of a grown-up American theater, a literary theater—paving the way for such later innovators as Tennessee Williams, Arthur Miller, and Edward Albee.

But after a humiliating Broadway failure (*Days Without End*) in 1934, O'Neill had retreated into silence. His earlier successes were rarely revived during the ensuing decade, and by the mid-1950s, he was an all-but-forgotten man.

The picture changed dramatically when *Long Day's Journey Into Night* exploded on Broadway on November 7, 1956, having been preceded six months earlier by a brilliant revival of *The Iceman Cometh*. O'Neill, once again, was being hailed as his country's greatest playwright, and the publishing world suddenly got the message that it was time for an O'Neill biography.

Harper & Brothers, one of the most respected publishing houses of the day, wanted Brooks Atkinson to take on the job—surely an appropriate choice. Atkinson was the powerfully influential drama critic of *The New York Times*. He had written many thoughtful reviews of O'Neill's plays and had eventually formed a warm friendship with both the dramatist and his wife.

But Atkinson demurred. At sixty-two, he said he was too old to take on so demanding a subject while also continuing as a critic for the *Times*.

And that's when Arthur and I came into the picture.

Atkinson managed to persuade Harper's editor in chief to give us the assignment in his stead. He introduced Arthur to the editor as his colleague and protégé in the *Times*'s drama department, praising him as a knowledgeable theater reporter and critic.

And he explained that since the *Times* did not give reporters leaves of absence to write books, Arthur would need the assistance of his wife,

Barbara, with whom he had collaborated on numerous magazine articles and a recent well-reviewed book about Bellevue Hospital.

Atkinson also pointed out that as the stepdaughter of the playwright S. N. Behrman, a contemporary of O'Neill's, I had the advantage of having grown up with a theater background.

What probably clinched the argument was Atkinson's promise that he, himself, would smooth our way with O'Neill's widow, the former stage actress and once-renowned beauty Carlotta Monterey. He said Monterey was a vital repository of information, but she was a woman of mercurial moods. She could be contentious, and he foresaw that she would require diplomatic handling.

The upshot was that Harper's offered Arthur and me the assignment—at a considerably lower royalty than they'd offered Atkinson, of course—and we accepted.

How could we not?

For one thing, we were dying to know—along with many other theatergoers—how much of *Long Day's Journey* actually was based on O'Neill's own life.

Was his mother really a morphine addict?

Was his actor-father the heavy-drinking, intermittently unfeeling skinflint portrayed in the play?

Were O'Neill and his brother truly locked into the virulent sibling rivalry depicted in *Long Day's Journey Into Night*?

I know it's hard to believe—in light of the ocean of information we now have about O'Neill—that, in those days, so little was known of his personal life.

It's true that he'd given several long magazine interviews during his lifetime, and also (reluctantly) authorized a short, dry biography by the critic Barrett H. Clark, but the interviews dealt mostly with his work philosophy and with his early seafaring and derelict days, of which he was inordinately proud.

It also was generally known that he'd left his second wife, Agnes Boulton—the mother of his two children, Shane and Oona—to marry the thrice-divorced Carlotta Monterey. And in 1943 there had been the well-publicized scandal—in the midst of World War II—of his daughter Oona's marriage, at eighteen, to the womanizing Charlie Chaplin, who was O'Neill's own age.

As for his plays, devotees were, of course, aware that many of them were inspired by the tragedies of the ancient Greeks and Shakespeare, along with biblical lore.

But only his most intimate friends were aware that the plays also sprang from O'Neill's own spectacularly dysfunctional family history—a history that, as we now know, included betrayal, adultery, unresolved oedipal yearning, violent alcoholism, drug addiction, suicide, bipolarity, and doomed spiritual striving among other bedevilments.

ARTHUR AND I had no inkling that our own lives were about to become obsessively and permanently entangled with the tormented, enigmatic O'Neill. And not only Arthur and me, but—to some degree—the two little boys we were raising.

We had converted the living room of our two-bedroom apartment in Manhattan into an office. It would be awash, for the next six years, in notebooks crammed with interview notes, copies of letters, and cartons of photographs. Our boys were used to hearing Arthur and me in endless discussions about our research. They had begun to feel possessive about O'Neill; indeed, they regarded him as a member of the family.

The younger of the two, Peter, who grew up to be the general manager of the Metropolitan Opera, already fancied himself a cultural expert at the age of four.

One day, I took Peter and his six-year-old brother, Michael, to the Shakespeare Garden in Central Park and pointed out Shakespeare's bust, explaining that he was commemorated here as the world's greatest playwright.

To Michael's and my amazement, Peter indignantly demanded, "Oh yeah? What about Gene O'Neill?"

In 1962, after publishing *O'Neill*, our 964-page biography (which we updated and revised several times during the next dozen years), Arthur and I went on to other interests: he, at the *Times*, climbing from investigative reporter and theater critic to metropolitan editor—where he also supervised the paper's cultural coverage—and ultimately to managing editor. During that period, he cowrote (with *Times* executive editor A. M. Rosenthal), *One More Victim: The Life and Death of a Jewish Nazi* (1967) and also coedited several news-related books based on *Times* reporting.

After his age-mandated retirement from the newsroom, Arthur headed the New York Times Foundation and, later, the paper's college scholarship program. He also found time to write a memoir of his newspapering years, called *City Room* (2003).

And I continued to write magazine articles and books, including the biography *So Short a Time* (1973), about John Reed and his wife, Louise Bryant, who had been among the fellow founders, with O'Neill himself, of the Provincetown Players, in 1916. Shifting gears somewhat radically, I spent the next couple of years with an elite New York City Police Department homicide squad. The resulting book was *On the Track of Murder* (1976) and I followed that with one about the politics of New York City's police hierarchy, *Varnished Brass* (1983).

A bit later, encouraged by Colleen Dewhurst, I wrote *My Gene*, a one-woman play about the widowed—and slightly mad—Carlotta Monterey O'Neill, which was produced at Joseph Papp's Public Theater in 1987. But even when O'Neill was only marginally in our lives, Arthur and I lectured about him and wrote program notes and articles related to revivals of his plays.

We both turned our full attention back to O'Neill in the late 1990s, when a trove of new material revealing the background of the O'Neill family was unearthed in Ireland. We had previously written of how

O'Neill's actor-father, James O'Neill, threw away a promising career as a Shakespearian actor (and presumed successor to Edwin Booth) in order to grow rich touring in his ever-popular vehicle, *The Count of Monte Cristo*. It was a decision he would come to regret, ultimately condemning himself as a failure.

The newly revealed data from Ireland enlarged our understanding of James O'Neill and the major influence he had on his son's plays; and this data was the impetus for our writing *Life with Monte Cristo* (2000).

Next, we cowrote, with Ric Burns, his documentary *O'Neill*, which was aired by PBS in 2006. During our research for the documentary, we were astonished by how much new information (apart from James O'Neill's early history) had emerged since the last time we'd updated our original biography. We felt an irresistible urge to acquire the lowdown. And, while we were at it, we thought we'd take one more look—a deeper and more nuanced look—at the haunted dramatist by whom we had for so long been possessed.

We had, in fact, grown to believe that in our earlier writing we hadn't delved deeply enough into the impact Ella O'Neill had on her son's life and work—considerably greater than her husband's, when we came to think of it. We felt we'd really be remiss if we failed to reassess the evidence of O'Neill's unabashed, lifelong yearning for a loving, all-embracing mother, as so graphically expressed in both his life and his plays.

THIS TIME AROUND, Arthur and I were approaching our eighties, and we did not plan to do the kind of exhaustive research we'd done in our thirties. But we did examine much of the relevant new material that was out there. We also searched back through our original file notes, recalling that among the more than four hundred people we'd interviewed for our 1962 *O'Neill*, there were several who had agreed to talk to us with the proviso that certain of their comments be withheld until after Carlotta O'Neill's death. Well, she'd outlived her husband by seventeen years, but she was long gone now.

In *By Women Possessed*, we've tried to interweave these long-withheld items of lore with the newly revealed chunks of information. After all these years of living in O'Neill's head, we hope we've managed to cast a newly insightful perspective on the O'Neill family dynamic.

WHEN, AS AN ADOLESCENT, Eugene O'Neill realized that his mother, Ella Quinlan O'Neill, blamed her morphine addiction on his birth and confessed that she wished him unborn, she betrayed him in a way he could never forgive or forget.

His love-hatred of his mother was one of the many conflicts between O'Neill's two selves. He himself was aware of the sharp contradictions in his character. But they were out of his control. He was the ultimate example of a god with feet of clay.

He could, when he chose, display the most exquisite manners and could charm both friends and lovers—many of whom were devoted to him to the end of his life. They included his theater colleagues, the doctors who strove to alleviate his various illnesses, and the old, disreputable cohorts of his past, to whom he gave endless handouts.

But he also had a violent and destructive temper—especially when he was on a drinking binge. At those times, he didn't hesitate to manhandle his lovers—as both Agnes Boulton and Carlotta Monterey have vividly described.

As for his drinking, in this new book we have corrected a long-held belief that O'Neill gave up drink in his late thirties, after submitting to a sort of abridged psychoanalysis. In fact, he had a number of relapses, several of them prolonged. We became convinced, also, that—in spite of O'Neill's oft-quoted denial that he never attempted to write when drunk—he wrote much if not all of *The Great God Brown* while under the influence of alcohol.

Perhaps even more of a character flaw than O'Neill's convoluted relations with women was his unconscionable neglect of his two children with his second wife, Agnes. Once he was divorced from their mother, he rarely condescended to see his son, Shane, or his daughter, Oona. His justification was his work. He was unable to tolerate any distraction from his writing. He grudgingly paid for their support, and at the same time he regularly complained of the way Agnes was raising them. Whenever word reached him that either of his children was behaving in a manner of which he disapproved, he would fire off bitter, denunciatory letters to them.

Shane was a shy, oversensitive, insecure boy who bounced from school to school, married young and irresponsibly, and drifted into drugs. Oona, encouraged by her mother, sought a life of debutante glamour, infuriating O'Neill by trading on his name. When, seeking the father she'd never had, she married Chaplin at eighteen, O'Neill disinherited her.

But, whatever O'Neill's personal failings, there is no denying that, as an artist, he stood tall. He possessed a work ethic and a professional integrity that we rarely encounter these days. An idealist and a visionary, he bravely endured his years of struggle, demanding to be accepted on his own terms as a dramatist. And—though he raged inwardly—he mostly took it in stride when a play into which he had poured his heart and soul was deemed a critical failure.

He never wrote with an eye on the box office. He never deigned to shape a character for a particular star. (And while happy to cast one if deemed suitable, the star's performance rarely met O'Neill's expectations, nor did he hesitate to say so.) He always spoke truth as he saw it: in his greatest plays, it is a universal truth that promises to resound for generations to come.

And, despite his unwaveringly tragic outlook, O'Neill sometimes startled and delighted Arthur and me with his outbursts of sardonic humor, in both his plays and his personal life. We've sprinkled examples of that humor throughout our text, including our all-time favorite—his response to the dismissive comments made by various critics about some of his plays: "I love every bone in their heads."

———————

IN *BY WOMEN POSSESSED* we have expanded the story of O'Neill's final wrenching years. They were years of increasing ill health and wrathful battles with Carlotta, who, herself, was not well, either physically or emotionally.

During Arthur's and my numerous interviews with Carlotta for our 1962 *O'Neill*, she had elided details of the harrowing confrontations of those years. We had, nonetheless, contrived to stitch together the facts (and factoids) from various sources: the doctors and nurses who tended to both O'Neills; hospital, police, and court records; lawyers; close friends; and the observations of domestic help.

The version we ended up with made Carlotta look like a monster. It was a version whispered abroad, with relish, by Carlotta's disparagers—that is to say, those of O'Neill's friends she had cut off, who believed she had kept O'Neill a virtual prisoner during his later years. She had once acknowledged to Arthur that she knew all about these whispers but didn't know how or where to begin defending herself, and preferred to remain silent.

But—at almost the last moment before our 1962 book was scheduled to go to press—Arthur finally convinced Carlotta that our biography offered her the best chance to tell her side of the scandalous story and that she owed it to herself and to posterity. She agreed to sit for a recorded interview in the hotel suite that was her home.

"Can you come over at once?" she demanded.

My ever-resourceful Arthur immediately flung himself into a cab, lugging the thirty-pound reel-to-reel recording machine that was the tool of choice in those ancient times.

In her living room at the Carlton House, Carlotta drew the heavy drapes. She allowed Arthur only a small table lamp by which to manipulate the clumsy tape recorder. In the darkened room he switched it on and began softly asking questions.

Carlotta appeared to fall into a trance. After leading her into the subject of her retreat with her husband to Marblehead in the fall of 1948, Arthur—gently but firmly—got her talking about the climactic night of February 5, 1951. In her theatrically inflected voice, now low and halting, Carlotta recounted her hazy memories of that night when O'Neill rushed from their isolated home on Point O'Rocks Lane and when—by all accounts—she let O'Neill lie in the frozen snow of his front yard, moaning in pain with a broken leg.

Her recorded version differs in its details from the one we had assembled. It differs as well from a version Carlotta herself left behind in one of her diaries. These diaries, for many years locked away, presumably at Carlotta's own request, are now available to scholars and made use of in *By Women Possessed*.

LOOKING BACK—a very long way back—Arthur and I reflected on the striking contrast between his tape-recorded session on November 28, 1961 (which turned out to be his final meeting with Carlotta) and our very first meeting with her, five years earlier. It had been arranged by Brooks Atkinson, who briefed us in advance. He cautioned us not to be put off by Carlotta's theatrical posturing; we should bear in mind that she was a former actress and that she was always onstage. And as O'Neill's wife and widow, she was accustomed to the role of grande dame and expected deference.

Atkinson also suggested we not take notes in front of Carlotta. He told us he had hinted to her that we might, at some point, like to write about O'Neill. But he believed Carlotta would be more relaxed and forthcoming if she could regard this first meeting as a social occasion: We were two ardent admirers of O'Neill's heroic artistry who wished to pay their respects to his widow, over an informal lunch—a lunch to which she had invited us at Atkinson's suggestion.

Carlotta certainly lived up to Atkinson's description.

It turned out to be a quite elaborate lunch. We met at Quo Vadis, the restaurant adjoining the Lowell Hotel, where Carlotta was then staying.

She quickly invited us to join her in what she said was her "usual" drink, pointing out, with a throaty laugh, that it was listed on the menu as a "Monterey Cocktail"—a mix of gin and Cointreau.

Carlotta Monterey O'Neill was then sixty-eight. She had given up dieting and was no longer the slender beauty of her photographs. But she still had the bearing of a queen, and she throbbed with vitality.

She was exquisitely groomed and dressed all in black, down to her onyx jewelry. Her hair was a smooth steel gray, cut short, and swept back from her face, which was pearly white and almost unlined.

She wore tinted glasses because (as she hastened to tell us) she had ruined her eyes over the years, deciphering O'Neill's minuscule handwriting while she typed his playscripts.

We both suspected, from what Atkinson and others had already told us, that Carlotta tended to blend history and histrionics and was given to bursts of self-serving hyperbole. She did, most certainly, see herself as the final, tragic O'Neill heroine. Nevertheless, Arthur and I found her not only informative but often funny.

It was hard to resist taking a note or two, but we both (at that time) had excellent memories, and the minute we got into a taxi after leaving the restaurant, we each scribbled down every word we remembered of Carlotta's conversation. And, I must confess, that is what we did at the end of all our other interviews—except for that final one Arthur recorded. Atkinson had been right. Carlotta soon began to trust and confide in us—at least up to a point.

It wasn't long before she was giving us her melancholy version of O'Neill's final years as a sick and forgotten man, and of the isolated life she had lived with him, nursing him in the suite of a Boston hotel.

O'Neill hated hotels, she told us, because he had been born in one and had spent the first seven years of his life traveling from hotel to hotel while his father toured the country with his acting company, reluctantly accompanied by his morphine-addicted wife. Carlotta repeated what she claimed were O'Neill's last words, uttered on November 21, 1953, three days before his death.

O'Neill, she said, "clenched his fists, raised himself slightly in his bed, and gasped, 'Born in a hotel room—and God damn it—died in a hotel room!'"

Of course, we reported that verbatim in our 1962 *O'Neill*.

But at the time of her telling, Carlotta had evidently forgotten an entirely different version in the diary she'd kept during the year of O'Neill's death. In that 1953 diary, which was among those eventually made available to researchers, there is no entry for November 21. Indeed, there are no entries at all from September 29 through November 24. And her entry on the twenty-fifth noted that O'Neill, after trying but failing to speak to her, mumbled something incoherent, then fell back onto his pillow and never spoke again.

To do Carlotta justice, it's more than likely that O'Neill—at some point during his final days, if not on his actual deathbed—did utter those "last" stricken words about dying in a hotel room. They certainly make for a splendid curtain line, and one can hardly blame Carlotta for juxtaposing them. We felt obliged to correct this quirky, if minor, inaccuracy that has so often appeared in print.

In February 2014, as we approached the end of our final draft, Arthur turned ninety. Although we'd been telling ourselves since embarking on our eighties that henceforth we were living on borrowed time, neither of us had ever really felt our age.

But it was not a good time to be writing our last chapter, which goes into fairly graphic detail about O'Neill's ever-worsening health. Arthur (inevitably, I guess) began overempathizing with O'Neill's medical issues.

It didn't help when he, himself, suffered a slight stroke that, eerily, left him with some of the same symptoms suffered by the debilitated sixty-four-year-old O'Neill: severe tremors of the hand, difficulty walking, an episode or two of anxiety and depression.

Arthur's mind was as sharp as ever, and he was determined to finish polishing those last few pages of that final chapter. But he was rapidly losing ground, and soon he had to give in to his increasing physical frailty. He told me that, much as he wanted to be around to celebrate the publication of *By Women Possessed*, he knew he wasn't going to make it.

Surely O'Neill was awaiting him. Arthur chuckled weakly as he recalled the Black Irishman's mocking suggestion for his epitaph:

There's something to be said
For being dead.

Arthur keenly felt the irony of his situation. "O'Neill is having the last laugh," he said.

PART I

UPHEAVAL

1

Although it is only five o'clock on the winter-dark afternoon of January 30, 1928—three and a half hours earlier than the customary eight-thirty Broadway premiere—first-nighters are spilling from limousines and taxis in front of the new John Golden Theatre. As they step onto the roped-off sidewalk, they are surrounded by a crush of celebrity-oglers who are being pressed back by a cadre of mounted police. The celebrities themselves blithely jostle their way to their seats, undaunted by the prospect of sitting through a performance that is double the length of a conventional play.

They are here for the season's most trumpeted theatrical event, Eugene O'Neill's *Strange Interlude*.

The author, globally heralded as the pioneer of American stage tragedy and the recipient (so far) of two Pulitzer Prizes, will not be present. Chronically nervous and wary of crowds, he usually sends his wife, Agnes Boulton, as his emissary on opening nights.

Boulton, however, has her own good reasons for staying in Spithead, the Bermuda home where O'Neill, craving isolation, has settled near the sea that has called to him since childhood. Tonight O'Neill has designated as his emissary Carlotta Monterey, a former actress who is better known for her sultry beauty than for her talent. During the past year and a half, O'Neill has been twisting in the tempest of his on-and-off love affair with her.

At thirty-nine, O'Neill is as handsome as Apollo, as haunted as

Oedipus, and as conflicted as Hamlet. Although long a religious apostate, he was born and raised a Catholic, and his adultery torments him.

"It's this and that, the this-that desire—more than desire, need!—that
slow-poisons the soul with complicated contradictions," he lamented in
a letter to his closest confidant, Kenneth Macgowan, the theater critic
and author. "And do not mistake my nebulous cries for whinings. Beauty,
either here or there, is worth whatever price one has to pay for it, here or
there . . . Oh very much so!"

Carlotta Monterey, who has recently ended an unhappy marriage, is
O'Neill's age but, like Shakespeare's queen, age cannot wither her; a
jazz-era Cleopatra, she glides down the aisle to her seat, warmly greeted
by friends and stared at by strangers.

She is escorted by James Speyer, a sixty-seven-year-old widower and
powerful international banker and philanthropist. Carlotta's senior by
twenty-seven years, Speyer is an elegant, sophisticated, undemanding
man with whom she has had an intermittent love affair both before her
marriage and following her divorce. Monterey, who affectionately calls
Speyer "Papa," has led O'Neill to believe he is merely a fatherly friend.
Speyer is so fond of her that he has long since secretly settled a sizeable
annual income on her—with no strings attached. To O'Neill she attributes the money to a bequest from a childless aunt who raised her.

Monterey's bearing is haughty, but her nose-in-the-air carriage stems
from severe nearsightedness. Pointed and slightly overlong, her nose,
together with a chiseled chin and a complexion both pearly and flawless,
completes the veneer of aloof entitlement. Tonight she wears her hair—
thick, lustrous, and black—drawn into a smooth coil at the nape of her
long, slender neck; she is sometimes referred to in print as "The Swan."
But it is her dark, deep-set eyes, feathered with long lashes, that are
her most striking feature; "Shadow Eyes," O'Neill calls her, quoting
Baudelaire.

Her close friend, the actress Ilka Chase, describes her as "kind and
funny"—even, on occasion, "ribald"—although Monterey herself insists
she is "innately shy." Chase admires her immaculate grooming and cites

her predilection for couture suits and dresses. Her accessories, Chase notes, are "of the finest material, her shoes made to order of special leathers at great cost" and sometimes sewn with jewels.

Monterey's recent divorce from her third husband, Ralph Barton, has been much gossiped about. He is a prestigious artist and a bon vivant—jaunty, openhanded—with unlimited entrée; his caricatures appear prominently in *The New Yorker* and his renderings of Carlotta and his fellow Brahmins are also vied for by the editors of *Vanity Fair, Life, Judge,* and *Harper's Bazaar,* all of whom pay him exorbitant fees. He has been acclaimed for his witty illustrations for *Gentlemen Prefer Blondes,* Anita Loos's best seller parodying the social and sexual excess of what is now the tail end of the Roaring Twenties. Barton adored Carlotta and she adored him. But she could not forgive his compulsive philandering.

OPENING-NIGHTERS WHO HAVE BEEN following the chitchat about *Strange Interlude* in the newspapers anticipate an uninhibited probing of Modern Woman's psychic and sexual yearnings. Contemporary American novelists have explored this territory, but American playwrights have tended to sidestep any intense delving into the messy subject of sex. Not O'Neill.

Strange Interlude is O'Neill's nineteenth attempt in twelve years to soar beyond the limits of traditional theatrical creativity. He has confided to Carlotta, who has read the script, that the play is embedded in his own life: "Of course, there's almost everything in it that makes people mad with rapture or tortured beyond belief. . . . This whole play is I, my experience, you might say."

Carlotta has asked O'Neill if she has correctly recognized aspects of herself in Nina Leeds, the play's protagonist, and he has allowed that "there is a lot of you in the woman, I think . . . and yet, wholly unlike you." He hesitates to admit just how deeply he has blended her into the multifaceted Nina Leeds, but in truth his agonizing fixation on Carlotta was seldom out of his mind during the long months he labored over the play.

As for O'Neill's own essence in *Interlude*, it is expressed in the character of the virile psychologist, Dr. Darrell, whose first name, significantly, is Edmund (the name O'Neill will later use to represent himself in his openly autobiographical *Long Day's Journey Into Night*). Darrell, like O'Neill, is "handsome and intelligent," his "dark eyes are analytical," and there is "a quality about him, provoking and disturbing to women, of intense passion." Illicitly in love with Nina, Darrell struggles against this passion.

"Sometimes I almost hate her!" Darrell says in an aside, adding that if not for her, he'd have kept his "peace of mind"; he berates himself for being "no good for anything lately." And then O'Neill, surely thinking of his own early effort to evade Carlotta's conquest, causes Darrell to muse: ". . . got me where she wants me! . . . I'm caught . . . she touches my hand, her eyes get in mine, I lose my will." He vows to go away and "forget her in work!" But in the end, Darrell succumbs to Nina (foreshadowing O'Neill's own surrender to Carlotta).

Nina Leeds is O'Neill's Everywoman. She is the emotional and psychological aggregate of all the tragic heroines of his previous plays. She embodies for O'Neill both the darkest and most seductive characteristics of her sex—qualities that O'Neill attributes not only to the cluster of women with whom he's had unhappy love affairs, but also to the unstable, withholding mother who had wished him unborn.

The opening-night audience sits entranced by the play's convoluted and ever-more-lurid plot. It seems that Nina, the pampered, middle-class daughter of a widowed college professor, had sanctimoniously refused to sleep with her lover, Gordon Shaw, before he went off to war. Now, he has been killed in action, and Nina, crazed by guilt, hurls herself into a nursing career and sleeps with every wounded soldier who desires her. To save Nina from her self-destructive behavior, Dr. Darrell advises her to marry the dead Gordon's best friend, Sam Evans, who worships her. Although she does not love Sam, she agrees, believing she will thereby atone for having allowed Gordon to die unfulfilled.

Dutifully pregnant with Sam's child, Nina abruptly learns that (unknown to Sam) there is insanity in his family and secretly undergoes an illegal abortion; unwilling to hurt Sam, she pretends she has had a miscarriage. Sam sinks into a deep depression, and Nina—intent on providing him with his longed-for child—persuades Darrell to impregnate her. A son is born, Nina presents him to her unsuspecting husband as his own, and Sam comes joyously back to life.

Nina, meanwhile, has fallen in love with Darrell (who is equally smitten) and won't give him up. But Darrell finds it harder and harder to live with the guilt of betraying Sam and struggles to end his affair (as O'Neill is struggling to give up Carlotta).

Time goes by. Lots of time. This, after all, is a five-hour, nine-act drama that unfolds over twenty-five years and has all the elements of a novel.

Nina's affair with Darrell eventually cools; she loses the son she adores to a daughter-in-law she loathes; Sam's prosperous, happy life is cut short by a heart attack; and Nina allows herself to sink into a comfortable, asexual relationship with an old family friend, an elderly, timid mama's boy, who has always secretly loved her. At play's end, the widowed Nina longs for nothing more than to "rot away in peace."

FOR ITS DAY, *Strange Interlude* was an audacious and triumphant challenge to the Broadway showplace. O'Neill's daringly raw scenes of sexual lust—not to mention his reference to the taboo topic of abortion—were years ahead of their time not only for the American stage but also for much of contemporary American fiction.

"Even the best of modern novels [are] padded with the unimportant and insignificant," and their authors are "mere timid recorders of life," O'Neill has complained to the critic Joseph Wood Krutch. Carlotta, herself at home in the theater, knows O'Neill scorns most of his fellow dramatists (in some of whose plays Carlotta has appeared) as scramblers after easy success; they wedge their characters into artificial situations and then melodramatically extricate them—all in the cause of sending their audiences home in a glow of happy endings.

O'Neill himself has never stooped to crowd-pleasing; none of his previous successes had happy endings—not *The Hairy Ape*, *The Emperor Jones*, or *Desire Under the Elms*; nor the two for which he won the Pulitzer Prize, *Beyond the Horizon* and *Anna Christie* (although some of his critics, to O'Neill's dismay, misread the latter play's conclusion).

In all his writing, O'Neill was obsessed with man's battle against fate, a battle he inevitably loses. It is the bedrock of his creativity and he has never flinched from expressing it.

"Most modern plays are concerned with the relation between man and man. But that does not interest me at all," he has declared. "I am interested only in the relation between man and God."

In *Strange Interlude*, O'Neill has chosen to focus on the relationship between *woman* and God; Nina Leeds is every bit as God-forsaken and afflicted as any of O'Neill's earlier suffering male protagonists.

THE KNOWLEDGEABLE OPENING-NIGHT audience is quick to realize that *Strange Interlude* is O'Neill's most ambitious effort to date, offering a feast of insights into the psyches of his characters—particularly when they voice their sometimes startling inner thoughts in spoken asides. He makes no apology for borrowing this archaic device; he is just as ready to pinch Elizabethan technique, when he thinks it will work, as he is to appropriate stagecraft from the ancient Greeks.

He is, however, quick to deny that he has been influenced by Freudian gospel, as some of his critics will assert (this being, after all, the dawn of psychoanalytical enlightenment). He has more than once insisted that every creative artist since the beginning of time is an instinctive psychologist and doesn't require Freud's assistance.

———————

As the curtain rises (shortly after five fifteen) on part one of *Strange Interlude*, Carlotta is in a flutter. She and O'Neill have made plans to secretly slip away to Europe in ten days, and if the play is a hit—as she suspects it will be—his freshly garnered notoriety will make it all but impossible for them to maintain their privacy. As she strains to sense the audience's reaction, she doesn't know if she's more terrified or thrilled by what awaits her. Forewarned that the five-hour performance will break for a dinner intermission at a quarter to eight, many playgoers plan to return home to change into the black-tie attire that is de rigueur for a premiere (but gauche at five in the afternoon), before reclaiming their seats for the play's second half, at nine o'clock. Others, more interested in nourishment than fashion, are already in formal attire and scurry to nearby restaurants.

The Golden Theatre, somewhat isolated (on Fifty-eighth Street near Central Park) has fewer dining choices than the pulsing midtown theater district, but the nearby Park Central has tailored a "Dinner Interlude" between seven forty-five and nine for the *Strange Interlude* audience, and the Au Grande Vatel promises (in the *Playbill*), "You Will Be Repaid by Walking Three Blocks South on 7th Avenue for Your Intermission Dinner," which (including dessert and coffee) is available "from 75 cents to $1.75." It will be a shivery walk, though, with the temperature in the low twenties.

Carlotta is among those who forgo dinner. She is driven to her Upper East Side apartment where, before changing into an evening gown, she telephones a jittery O'Neill at the Wentworth Hotel on Forty-sixth Street near Broadway.

The audience is savoring the play, she reports, and she pictures her lover's rare smile of pleasure, the light in his piercing dark brown eyes. His image is seldom out of her mind—his silky brown hair and mustache, the lean muscular body of the habitual swimmer. She thinks of the moments shared with him at the back of the dark, near-empty theater during rehearsals, watching his play evolve, her hand enclosed in his long-fingered grip.

In looks, he is her perfect male counterpart; they relish posing together for portrait photographers, all of whom are sworn to withhold the photos until after their marriage. While she speaks to O'Neill on the phone, she imagines him pacing his two-room suite, tense about his newest work, wishing it were over, missing her, fighting his anxiety and guilt.

O'Neill also gets a favorable report from Lawrence Langner, his producer and the principal founder of the Theatre Guild. During intermission, Langner ducks into a nearby drugstore phone booth to give O'Neill "a blow-by-blow account" of how the play is being received.

Unknown to Carlotta, O'Neill—in a characteristic gesture of nostalgia for his vagabond youth—has chosen to wait out the evening in his suite with Bill Clarke, a former circus daredevil known as "Volo the Volitant," who once turned loops in the air while riding his bicycle down a precipitous incline at Madison Square Garden. (O'Neill will later partly base the character of Ed Mosher, "one-time circus man" in *The Iceman Cometh*, on him.) O'Neill has invited Clarke to join him for dinner.

"Well, everything seems to be going all right," he remarks to Clarke after receiving his two phone calls. Then, in a voice of profound sadness, he adds, "It would be nice to have Jamie here now." O'Neill is referring to his older brother, who died of alcoholism five years earlier, at forty-five, and who often used to accompany O'Neill and Clarke on whiskey-soaked sprees from which O'Neill emerged in need of sympathetic tending. "You were good to me in the old days, Clarkie," O'Neill says. "I've never forgotten it."

O'Neill hasn't mentioned Clarke's presence to Carlotta, knowing she is something of a social snob and would disapprove. She has been trying to nudge O'Neill away from his attachment to his bohemian past, to live up to her own (acquired) standard of upper-class elegance.

STRANGE INTERLUDE STARS Lynn Fontanne, whose husband, Alfred Lunt, happens also to be appearing on Broadway in an O'Neill play, *Marco Millions*, which opened at the Guild Theater three weeks earlier.

(It isn't the first time that the prolific O'Neill has had two new plays running simultaneously in New York.) *Marco Millions* is a satirical pageant about Marco Polo, whose adventures as a thirteenth-century Venetian merchant perfectly parallel O'Neill's concept of the twentieth-century rich American businessman—his symbol of American greed. O'Neill sees Marco as an arid-souled materialist, destructive of the beauty and poetry in life.

The play, in a clumsy production that disappointed O'Neill, has received only lukewarm reviews (but manages a run of ninety-two performances). Lunt and Fontanne, both established stars in their own right, are poised to emerge as Broadway's reigning royal couple, and their quips and comments quickly become gossip items.

Lunt is widely quoted as having ridiculed *Strange Interlude* as "a six-day bisexual race"—a reference to the six-day bicycle races that are a popular Madison Square Garden draw. Fontanne's attitude toward the play is no better calculated to endear her to O'Neill. (Eight years earlier she had appeared in the failed out-of-town tryout of his *Chris Christophersen*, later rewritten as *Anna Christie*, and although he'd kept his distance from that production, he'd had derogatory reports about Fontanne's performance both on- and offstage.)

"There were a good many lines intended by O'Neill to be taken seriously, that I thought would get belly laughs from the audience," recalls Fontanne, disparaging the play's spoken asides. "It would have hurt the play. For instance, I would have to say in an aside something like, 'Ned [Edmund Darrell] has the bluest eyes I ever saw; I must tell him so.' Then I would go to Ned and tell him he had the bluest eyes I ever saw.

"I felt it was unnecessary to say this twice. I told O'Neill it would be better if I looked at Ned's eyes with admiration the first time, silently, instead of saying the line as an aside. I asked him if I could cut the line. He said, 'No, you can't. Play it as I wrote it.'

"But the play was so long I felt O'Neill wouldn't realize if I cut a line here and there, so, with fear and trembling, I cut a few of those horse-laugh lines. O'Neill never knew about this sly business of mine."

As the son of the actor James O'Neill, a widely celebrated matinee idol of his day, Eugene believed he knew all too much about actors' wiles. Only recently, he'd complained to an interviewer for the *World*, "Actors generally get between me and the performance. That is, I catch myself recognizing the technique all the time. I don't mean that I blame them, but having been brought up among actors I recognize what they are doing when they put over a point. The mechanics of acting stop me from seeing the play."

To Lawrence Langner, more bluntly, an exasperated O'Neill grumbles, "If the actors weren't so dumb, they wouldn't need asides. They'd be able to express the meaning without them."

Shortly before rehearsals began for *Marco* and *Interlude*, O'Neill confided his disdain for the stars of his two plays to Agnes (from whom he had not yet formally separated): "I haven't met either Lunt or Fontanne yet. From what I hear they are both pretty dull in the old bean—but that hardly astonishes me."

WHEN THE FINAL curtain drops on *Strange Interlude* shortly after eleven o'clock, Carlotta Monterey, reveling in the animated audience response, joins O'Neill—now alone at the Wentworth—and assures him the play is a hit. The next day's reviews confirm her judgment. O'Neill—who has long since stated his goal of matching on the stage the achievements of America's most innovative novelists—especially appreciates the appraisal in the *World*, which calls *Strange Interlude* "not only a great American play but the great American novel as well."

That assessment is by Dudley Nichols, a twenty-seven-year-old star reporter who—just an hour before curtain time—was asked by the paper's editor, Herbert Bayard Swope, to replace its established critic, Alexander Woollcott. Woollcott had behaved unethically, said Swope, in writing a condemnation of *Strange Interlude* for the February issue of a rival publication, *Vanity Fair*, which came out a week before the play's opening. (Woollcott had read a script, rumored to have been smuggled to him by Lynn Fontanne, and—convinced the play would be a spectacular flop—had been holding forth at dinner parties, deriding *Strange Interlude* as "the Abie's Irish Rose of the pseudo intelligentsia.")

An immediate hit, the play is soon the center of controversy—nothing new for O'Neill. The powerful Shubert theater organization complains to the Manhattan district attorney that *Strange Interlude* is "of a low moral tone" and demands of the play's producers, "Why does not the Theater Guild . . . come down from the pedestal of art and virtue upon which it has been posing . . . and declare frankly that it is out for every dollar that it can tease into its coffers?"

The Shuberts plainly are envious of their competitor's success and the Theatre Guild can afford an enigmatic smile; as the American producers of *Saint Joan*, George Bernard Shaw's great succès d'estime, the Guild is secure in its record of "art and virtue."

The D.A. responds that he will have the police commissioner investigate the play's moral tone. But the commissioner reports that his investigator "has been unable to buy tickets for any performance earlier than May 28"—hardly a statement to placate the Shuberts. The investigation comes to nothing. (Some months later, O'Neill runs into Lee Shubert in Spain, and reports to a friend, "We shook hands smilingly as though neither had ever heard of a play called *Strange Interlude*. It was a funny scene.")

STRANGE INTERLUDE LOOKS to be O'Neill's biggest hit to date. For seventeen months, it will play 426 performances to capacity audiences in New York, and generate two road companies. It will earn O'Neill more money—$275,000, a fortune in this era of low taxes—than he has ever made before.

When published soon after its Broadway opening, the playscript becomes a best-selling book—one hundred thousand copies—and wins O'Neill his third Pulitzer. It's made into a movie starring Clark Gable and Norma Shearer.

O'Neill is, of course, gratified. But well beyond its artistic and material rewards, *Strange Interlude* signals for him the start of a colossal upheaval, both personal and professional. About to make a radical change in the way he lives, he is uneasy about his ever-increasing fame.

At the moment, he'd very much prefer not having the newspapers delving into his private life.

2

The first face-to-face meeting between Carlotta Monterey and Eugene O'Neill hardly signaled their explosive entanglement to come.

Carlotta had taken over the small but crucial role of Mildred Douglas in *The Hairy Ape* when it moved to Broadway's Plymouth Theatre from the Provincetown Playhouse in mid-April 1922. O'Neill, to her chagrin, barely acknowledged her presence in the cast.

Carlotta ceased to be troubled by O'Neill's indifference, however, when Ralph Barton, infatuated by her beauty after he saw her onstage, presented himself as her impassioned suitor. Barton at thirty-one is three years younger than Carlotta. He dresses like a dandy, has charming manners, and denies himself little in the way of fine food, wine, and revelry. He is married to his second wife, Anne Minnerly, a model—very pretty, but no match for Carlotta.

Until she meets Barton, Carlotta—with two failed marriages behind her—has all but despaired of finding her ideal mate. Moreover, in spite of her role in a prestigious O'Neill play, she is disillusioned with her career, complaining to friends that rarely has she been cast as anything but "the bitch or the vamp."

Indeed, she is fed up with the theater and, for some time now, has envisioned a different career. As she wandered from one vapid melodrama to another in just the sort of glib, happy-ending trivia O'Neill loved to disparage, she never grew as an actress. What Carlotta now longs for— what she believes is her destiny—is to be muse and ministering angel to a creative genius; in spite of her allure, though, it hasn't been easy to track and capture that creature of her dreams.

One night in early May, after a performance of *The Hairy Ape*, she is introduced to Barton at a party. Barton doesn't leave her side and she's quick to recognize him as the trophy she has been hunting. Hunter and prey soon are in bed together. It isn't long before Minnerly files for divorce (and soon after marries the poet who famously signs himself e.e. cummings).

Two months go by, and Barton is sketching a magazine caricature of Carlotta. "I cannot visualize your nose satisfactorily," he tells her in a note, adding he has been forced instead to concentrate on her eyebrows. His note addresses her as "Semiramis; Ninon; Carlotta"—linking her name to two fabled courtesans, one mythological, the other seventeenth-century French. Surely meaning to flatter, Barton is delighted to have spotted the courtesan in Carlotta.

During their four years together, Carlotta dedicates herself to Barton, swooning over his work, micromanaging his household, assuming secretarial duties, and pleasurably sharing his sybaritic lifestyle. She and Barton are inseparable. Carlotta excels as the hostess of sumptuous all-night parties. The popular portrait photographer Nickolas Muray, for one, is amazed by the bounty of the Barton salon with its inexhaustible flow of food, bootleg liquor, and entertainment. Among the guests—always formally attired—were the handsome, raffish mayor of New York, Jimmy Walker, and Barton's closest friend, Charlie Chaplin, who, Muray recalled, would give impromptu performances, sometimes spouting "double-talk in half a dozen languages."

The Barton-Monterey relationship is stormy and passionate, according to Ilka Chase. Plagued by insomnia and restlessness, Barton is often irascible and, at moments when he feels suffocated by Carlotta's relentless nurturing, he turns on her. "Carlotta would arrive at the theater in a seething, emotional turmoil and pour her misfortunes into my willing ears," recalled Chase. "As she was very beautiful, Ralph was not the first man who had made her unhappy."

In spite of their persistent bickering, Carlotta and Barton are in love and, after living together for nearly three years, she elicits from him a promise of monogamy. They marry on March 17, 1925.

"Carlotta was mad about Barton," observed Carl Van Vechten, the novelist and photographer. But, like his dear friend Chaplin, Barton is a compulsive philanderer; he is also—although the symptoms apparently are not yet pronounced—a manic depressive. One evening, after dinner with the Bartons, Van Vechten listens to Carlotta and Barton as they debate, for three hours, whether they will "live together any more."

They come to no conclusion that night. But Carlotta has begun to doubt Barton's vow of monogamy and he chafes under her accusations. They have taken to quarreling in front of friends; it's apparent the marriage is unraveling. Carlotta, at thirty-seven, is not happy at the way her life is turning out.

Born Hazel Nielsen Tharsing on December 28, 1888, in Oakland, California, Carlotta has borrowed her stage surname from the California resort city of Monterey. "Carlotta" completes the exotic effect, but no Spanish blood flows through her veins.

Her father, Christian Nielsen Taasinge, was born in Denmark (slightly altering his surname after arriving in the United States). A seaman in his youth, he eventually settled as a fruit farmer in California's Yuba County, where he raised apricots and peaches. His daughter liked to describe him rather grandly as a "horticulturist."

The former Hazel Tharsing is proud of her mixed-European heritage. Her mother, Nellie Gotchett, is a high-spirited woman of Dutch and French-Alsatian descent. In 1853, Nellie's parents left their home in Saint Louis, traveling by covered wagon to Yuba County, where eighteen-year-old Nellie met Tharsing. Yearning to escape from her restrictive family, she married him. But he was some twenty years her senior, and the marriage was not compatible.

Hazel's parents divorced when she was not quite five. An only child, she was placed with her mother's parents so that Nellie, who had a head for business, could forge an adventurous life as an independent woman. She opened the first of several boardinghouses in San Francisco (not a "bawdy" house, as some malicious rumor had it); after renovating it, she sold it at a profit and went on to the next, enabling her to contribute generously to Hazel's upkeep. All the while, disdainful of convention, she flitted from one man to another, several of them wealthy and influential.

When Hazel turned eight, Nellie sent her to a married sister, Mary Shay, who, with her husband, John, was raising two sons in San Francisco. Hazel was an introverted girl who loved to read but was tormented by severe myopia. An incompetent eye surgeon evidently worsened her condition to the point that in later life she had difficulty focusing her eyes, causing severe headaches.

At fourteen, although her parents were Protestant, Hazel enrolled in a Catholic boarding school: St. Gertrude's Convent Academy in Rio Vista, about forty miles from Oakland. The school was supervised by German nuns who praised her skills in piano and singing.

Reminiscing decades later, Carlotta Monterey stressed a quirky aspect of her life in the convent: her sense of the theatrical, she recalled, was roused to such a degree that the Mother Superior was obliged to scold her for spending so much time in chapel genuflecting. The music, color, and drama of church ritual that cast their spell on Hazel Tharsing lingered with her as Carlotta Monterey.

(In fact, her convent background would later embellish O'Neill's portrait of his mother as Mary Tyrone in *Long Day's Journey Into Night*. Like Mary, Carlotta had wanted to be a nun; and like Mary, she had been told by the Mother Superior to go home and think it over for a year before making a decision.)

Young Hazel, with her burgeoning tug toward self-dramatization, was growing ever more beautiful, and her thriving mother conceived a long-range plan to find her a substantial husband. Nellie's real estate holdings had flourished, helped by her liaison with Melvin C. Chapman, a prominent attorney and former mayor of Oakland.

When Hazel, at seventeen, graduated from the convent school, Nellie took her to London and established her in a town house in Torrington Square among a colony of proper and rich American girls studying for careers in the arts. Hazel was provided with a singing coach and enrolled in Sir Herbert Beerbohm Tree's Academy of Dramatic Art (which later became the Royal Academy of Art). The last thing Nellie wanted for her daughter was a stage career; but she believed the training would teach Hazel to be a well-spoken, socially graceful young lady who, aided by her beauty, might attract an upper-crust husband.

The strategy began to work almost at once. Hazel was noticed by the London correspondent for the San Francisco *Sunday Call*, who wrote that wherever mother and daughter went, people stared at the daughter. One night, as they entered the dining room of the Clarendon Hotel, the reporter, Herbert Williams, noted:

"The object of all eyes was Hazel. There was no doubt in my mind that she was really the fairest of California or the fairest woman anywhere. I had never seen anyone so radiantly beautiful."

Yet Hazel knew better than to carry herself like an acclaimed beauty, for the nuns had taught her modesty; that was part of her charm. In one posed photograph, dressed in a stylish evening gown, her silky dark hair arranged in an elaborate coiffure, Hazel looks demure and pensive rather than glamorous.

Nellie engaged a chaperone for her daughter and then returned to California. Hazel was left to pursue her self-improvement. Two years later, on receiving a recent photograph of her daughter, Nellie impulsively submitted it to the Miss California Beauty Contest of 1907. Hazel, declared by the judges—two painters and a sculptor—to be "California's most beautiful woman," was chosen Miss California.

When the San Francisco *Call*, sponsor of the contest, cabled Hazel with the news and asked for an interview, she cabled back, "Mother thinks I am better looking than I am." She added: "Be sure to let the sisters at Rio Vista Convent know about this. They will be pleased."

The *Call* asked her to take the first steamship to New York, at the newspaper's expense. Her mother would be waiting at the pier to accompany her to Chicago for the Miss America Pageant. Hazel won second place, and it was only a few months later, after she'd returned to London, that Nellie's labors paid off. Nineteen-year-old Hazel accepted a proposal of marriage from John Moffat, a twenty-eight-year-old Scotsman, whose highborn and enormously wealthy family owned several grand estates in Scotland.

Hazel and Moffat had met at the Royal Academy, where both were enrolled in a fencing class. "Well, sometime ago I met a very charming Californian girl and fell madly in love with her," wrote Moffat to his sister, Edith. After swearing Edith to secrecy, he confided he had proposed, "but the Mother said she was too young, & has sent her to a finishing school in Paris. . . . In 18 months she leaves & if we are then both of the same mind we will be allowed to announce our engagement."

Hazel, continued Moffat, was "very sweet, lovable &, I should think, easily influenced by kindness." Young and naive as he was, Moffat added, "I don't want anyone to know about my attachment as I don't wish to be laughed at if it falls through."

It did not fall through. Hazel, doubtless urged on by her mother, permitted Moffat to introduce her to his mother at one of the Moffat estates. Mrs. Moffat asked Hazel why she wanted to marry her son, and Hazel's disingenuous reply was "I like Jack." Moffat's mother, nothing if not the pragmatic British aristocrat, accepted the obvious fact that the beauteous Hazel was not in love with her son.

With perfect sangfroid, she assured Hazel that she would almost certainly find some other man to whom she was physically attracted; and that whatever she did about that would be all right, as long as the affair did not become public. If it did, she would disown her daughter-in-law; but as long as it remained a secret, she would have no objection.

At twenty-three, Hazel accepted these terms with equanimity. She and Moffat were married in New York in 1911 and then returned to Europe. Years later she conceded they were both inexperienced sexually, that Moffat sought medical aid for what he believed was impotence, and that the marriage was platonic. Nonetheless, they carried on.

Despite the marital problems, Carlotta in later life boasted that she had "the best things in Europe as a young bride—the best of everything—clothes, servants, admiration." She did not exaggerate; her mother-in-law's wedding gift was a Rolls-Royce; Moffat proffered jewels. When not traveling the Continent they lived at one or another of the family estates—one of them so vast its upkeep required forty groundskeepers.

Moffat's mother swept Hazel under her wing, instructing her in the rituals of the formal dinner party, the handling of servants, and even the etiquette of fox hunting. Under her mother-in-law's tutelage, Hazel learned to suppress her shyness. Seated at dinner parties next to prominent men, she was schooled, as she once recalled, in "how to be a conversationalist."

The marriage broke up after three years, when the Moffats experienced a series of financial setbacks and "the best things" began to vanish. Hazel gave back the Rolls-Royce and the jewelry, and returned to America.

"I divorced Moffat, but he forgave me," Carlotta quipped many years later. She and Moffat continued to correspond. He addressed her as "my dear child," and once declared, "I love Carlotta, I'll always love Carlotta." No question, she was a born Circe.

Hazel decided to pursue a stage career even though Nellie abhorred the idea of her daughter entering the Broadway arena "in the company of whores," as she put it. Nellie said she would shoot her if she used her real name. It was then that Hazel Tharsing became Carlotta Monterey.

In 1914, before trying for a role on Broadway, Carlotta toured the English provinces in a trivial play, *The Geisha*. The following year, determined to make her reputation in New York, she was in the office of Chamberlain Brown, a major talent agent, when he took a call from the Broadway mogul Lee Shubert, who was seeking "a dark-haired girl of decidedly Continental appearance."

Shubert hired Carlotta at $350 a week to play opposite the debonair thirty-three-year-old star Lou Tellegen in a farce called *Taking Chances*. (Tellegen, born in Holland as Isidor Louis Bernard Edmund van Dommelen, had been Sarah Bernhardt's leading man in Paris and, during that time, he'd earned a reputation as a Casanova.)

Carlotta, who appeared in the last act of *Taking Chances* draped in a nearly transparent negligee, drew praise as an ingénue fatale when the play opened in early March 1915. It ran for eighty-five performances, constituting a hit for that era. In a photograph for *Vogue*, Carlotta, exquisite in profile, is seated on a table, coyly proffering her unclad foot to a sleekly handsome Tellegen, who is gallantly slipping on her shoe.

Inevitably, rumors circulated of a love affair between Carlotta and Tellegen. True or not, he advised her to have a child, cautioning she would never be a good actress until she had experienced motherhood. He, however, had decided to marry the internationally renowned opera diva, Geraldine Farrar.

Carlotta was left to find someone else to father her child, but before taking that step, she joined a road tour, playing a Hawaiian princess in a maudlin trifle called *The Bird of Paradise*. By the time the tour reached San Francisco, Carlotta, more than ready to take a vacation from acting, quit the show and rejoined her mother in Oakland.

Nellie Tharsing was still living with ex-mayor Chapman, and Carlotta took the opportunity to flirt with Chapman's twenty-year-old son, Melvin Jr., whom she'd known since childhood; he was working as a housepainter while planning to attend law school. Carlotta, by now twenty-eight and mindful of Tellegen's advice, assessed Melvin Jr.—six feet six inches and handsome, with an athletic build—as eugenically suited to father her child.

They were married on October 12, 1916, and Carlotta discovered on their wedding night that Melvin was a virgin. She gave him the benefit of her own experience (presumably with Tellegen) and, ten months later, on August 20, 1917, the Chapmans produced a daughter, Cynthia Jane.

Carlotta almost immediately handed off her baby to Nellie, so that she could pursue her career unencumbered—just as Nellie, two decades earlier, had handed off Carlotta to her aunt Mary Shay. Carlotta and Chapman were soon divorced.

Motherhood did not noticeably improve Carlotta's acting, but her beauty continued to bring her roles, and magazines pressed her to pose for photo layouts. It was in the fall of 1918—shortly before the end of World War I—that Carlotta landed a more or less literate role in a comedy called *Be Calm, Camilla*, one of the 126 plays that had opened on Broadway since the beginning of 1917. (The play was significant because its producer, Arthur Hopkins, and its designer, Robert Edmond Jones, both highly respected in theater circles, were soon to be associated with the as-yet-little-known O'Neill.)

DURING THE NEXT four years, Carlotta went on to perform in a dozen plays, most of them short-lived; almost invariably she was singled out by the critics for her seductive presence and extravagant costumes. The marquees flashed titles like *The Ruined Lady*, *The Sacred Bath*, *The Other Rose*, *Fashions of New York*, and *The Sable Coat*.

In February 1922, Arthur Hopkins cast Carlotta in something called *Bavu*; it was a flop, but Hopkins had taken a professional liking to her and cast her as the effete society girl in O'Neill's *The Hairy Ape* when he daringly moved that experimental play from downtown to Broadway's Plymouth Theatre on April 17, 1922. It ran for 120 performances—and Carlotta at last found herself basking in a respectable play.

Her final Broadway role was in *The Man in Evening Clothes*, which opened on December 5, 1924, and closed eleven days later. She had been on the stage since 1915 and—after nine years—she was only too aware of her limitations.

It was then that Carlotta Monterey, having at last persuaded Ralph Barton to promise fidelity, decided to marry him. One afternoon in November, only eight months after their marriage, Carlotta returned to their apartment earlier than expected and surprised Barton in bed with a woman she happened to know. Staggered by Barton's betrayal, she walked out, weeping uncontrollably.

She had schooled herself to be in all ways his intellectual and social soul mate. She had hung on his ironic pronouncements about art and artists. She'd indulged his passion for museums and galleries—in New York as well as in London and Paris, where he was known to everyone who mattered. She'd gone out of her way to be gracious to his eminent friends, even those she disliked. Indeed, she had turned cartwheels to surround him with an esthetically serene environment in which to work and play.

Barton pleaded for forgiveness. He begged her to come back. But Carlotta, by then snugly established in her own Upper East Side apartment, was adamant. Four months later, in March 1926, she sued Barton for divorce. It was only after she'd left him that Barton, ever careless of the women in his life, realized he had been—in his own words—"a blithering idiot."

Accustomed to subservience, he had not only taken Carlotta's devotion for granted but had chafed under it—even at times lashing out at her. He had poked fun at her narrow comprehension of modern painting and seldom acknowledged her obeisance to his own art. He seemed indifferent to the care with which she had organized his household—and he rarely expressed the rapturous gratitude she expected for the sexual pleasure she lavished on him. It was, all in all, his insensitivity that finally wrecked the marriage.

When Carlotta received her interlocutory divorce decree, she told friends she'd asked for nothing of the court but to drop the name Barton. She was not inconsolable, for she knew there would always be men in her life. She was still one of the most photographed women of her day, even though she had quit the stage. Like most of her hedonistic circle of actors, writers, and artists, she was vain of her sexual allure. The photographer Ben Pinchot recalled a session with Carlotta when she undressed in his studio to change into a costume. "What do you think of my pussy?" she asked the nonplussed photographer. (Pinchot's opinion of Carlotta's genitalia is unrecorded.)

Ilka Chase, writing of Carlotta's other personal attributes, pointed out rather unkindly that she had "large hands and feet"—implying that Carlotta, in some respects, was physically more peasant than duchess. True, she liked to eat well, and had a problem with fluctuating weight; she sternly watched her diet, determined to maintain a lissome figure; one thing she did not have to worry about was the lusciously rounded bosom any woman would have been happy to possess.

3

On the brink of his elopement with Carlotta, set for February 10, 1928, a week and a half after the opening of *Strange Interlude*, O'Neill is still trying to justify to himself the fearsome decision he has made.

All during the late fall and early winter of the previous year, while laboring to ready *Strange Interlude* (and *Marco Millions*) for Broadway production, he has been shuttling back and forth between Bermuda and New York by steamship (a two-day voyage each way). He is still waffling between Agnes, the devil he knows, and Carlotta, the bewitching but possibly dangerous rescuing angel.

A successful pulp-fiction writer before her marriage to O'Neill, Agnes Boulton had enthusiastically agreed to share with him a life dedicated to writing and mutual devotion. They would allow nothing ever to disturb the sanctity of their love or their work. But Agnes's fervor for her writing was no match for O'Neill's total creative immersion. As his career prospered, he found himself fretting over the disparity between their ideas of a workable partnership.

He needed seclusion and a quiet, orderly environment in which to work, and he demanded a wife's single-minded attention during his free time. They had vowed not to have children, but within five years there were two—and once the children were there, Agnes fretted at her husband's evident inability to interact with them. O'Neill shrank from casual socializing, but Agnes enjoyed parties and gossip. She longed for a more relaxed marital give-and-take. He resented her for wanting it.

For the nearly ten years of their marriage, O'Neill and Agnes have alternately adored and goaded each other.

Now, having (however guiltily) succumbed to Carlotta, O'Neill has at last told Agnes he is leaving her.

Because O'Neill has, for the past few months, isolated himself from most of the friends he shares with Agnes, he seeks the companionship of two new friends when he feels a compulsion to talk about Carlotta and his romantic quandary. They are Robert Rockmore, a lawyer with theater clients, and Norman Winston, a prosperous builder who had helped finance the operation of the Provincetown Playhouse in Greenwich Village, where O'Neill's earliest plays were produced.

Rockmore, who frequently visits O'Neill in his suite at the Wentworth Hotel, particularly recalls an afternoon in November 1927, when O'Neill answers his knock and, says Rockwell, seems "lost in a daze."

"What breasts! What breasts!" O'Neill rhapsodizes, by way of greeting, looking past Rockmore into the hall. According to Rockmore's amused recollection, it took several moments before O'Neill returned to reality. Rockmore didn't press him, but he was certain he had recognized a veiled Carlotta as she passed him in the hotel lobby on her way out.

O'Neill appreciates that Rockmore and Winston take his celebrity in stride; he trusts them as down-to-earth, both sensible and candid and, truth be told, he needs to escape now and again (as did Barton) from Carlotta's smothering presence.

Winston recalls several occasions on which O'Neill drifted back to his youthful tribulations: "Sometimes he would tell me a little about his family. But he seemed incapable of finishing his thoughts. He would say, 'Our family . . . there was a great deal of tragedy . . . we drifted apart . . . my mother . . .' He seemed to be bearing a cross, quietly. But he did say, several times, that one day he would write the tragic story of himself and his family."

Toward the end of November, O'Neill made an overnight visit to Winston's Long Island home; strolling with his host to the edge of the Sound that evening and watching the moon's reflection on the water, he confided a fantasy:

"If I were thinking of suicide, I'd swim along that reflection until I was exhausted and couldn't swim anymore." Is he thinking of suicide? Winston asks, and O'Neill says no, but if he ever decides to do it, that would be a good way.

He does not mention his actual suicide attempt (with sleeping pills) sixteen years earlier, nor does he tell Winston that the idea of swimming to his death derives from his literary hero, August Strindberg; in *The Dance of Death*, a young woman thwarted in love speaks of killing herself by swimming with her lover out into the sea until they drown. "There would be style in that," she says.

AFTER HIS OVERNIGHT VISIT with Winston, O'Neill is happy to rejoin Carlotta in New York and to have her at his side during rehearsals of *Strange Interlude*. He tries to forget his domestic troubles in the swirl of production problems. He introduces Carlotta to Philip Moeller, the play's director, and Carlotta, aware of O'Neill's respect for Moeller's artistic dedication, tries her winsome best to make a friend of him. In his late forties, Moeller has recently raised the role of director to artistic prominence in the American theater with his staging of Shaw's *Saint Joan*, Molnár's *The Guardsman*, and Sidney Howard's *They Knew What They Wanted*.

Moeller finds it difficult to draw close to O'Neill. "He seemed so lonely, always looking for happiness," Moeller recalls. "He was an outsider; everything was bitter and wrong for him. But there was no small meanness about Gene. He had tremendous integrity, was one of the most honest human beings I've ever known. And of all the people I've known, he possessed the most intense dramatic sense."

O'Neill submits to most of his director's cuts. He even volunteers cuts of his own that exceed Moeller's concept and dismay him. Co-producer Lawrence Langner is amazed that "Time after time, Gene insisted on cutting out comedy lines or 'laughs' when, in his opinion, they interfered with the emotional build of a scene."

Moeller adores the comedy and, by Langner's account, every time O'Neill solemnly cuts an amusing line, Moeller pleads for its return. "I hope he doesn't realize that line is funny," Moeller once remarked to Langner, "for if he does, out it'll go."

George Jean Nathan, the critic who has been O'Neill's major booster and solicitous guide since his earliest writings, attends a rehearsal during which Moeller asks O'Neill to insert a line of comedy. Nathan later quotes O'Neill's exasperated response:

"I'll tell you what to do. Just turn slowly around after the character has spoken, drop your pants, and disclose to the audience your backside painted an Alice blue. That should do it."

Shortly before the opening of *Strange Interlude*, O'Neill reveals to the magazine essayist Elizabeth Shepley Sergeant that his marriage to Agnes has collapsed. He and Sergeant have been friends since the summer of 1926, when she first interviewed him.

Earlier, when first reading Sergeant in *The New Republic*, O'Neill had been struck by her probity and acuity. Stylistically ahead of most of her peers, Sergeant was intent on interpreting essences and conveying nuanced literary impressions rather than recording bald facts. Her "personality studies," as she called them—of such figures as Willa Cather, H. L. Mencken, Oliver Wendell Holmes, and Robert Frost—had won her O'Neill's admiration and confidence, and led to the 1926 interview.

Sergeant's resultant profile, published in *The New Republic*, was called "The Man with a Mask."

"You cannot be near O'Neill without recognizing in him a unique temperament with a unique power of concentration," wrote Sergeant, adding that there is "nothing crystallized about him," and going on to describe him as "a man in a state of growth, a man in a state of progression." There are, she writes, no limits to the "range of his imagination," and "he gives the impression of being still at the very beginning of a career which is incalculable, except that it will be precipitate, fertile, concentrated, and solitary." O'Neill loved every word of it.

He now trusts Sergeant enough to confide in her about his resentment of Agnes for having violated their vow to have a childless marriage and to devote themselves entirely to their work and to each other. And, after speaking of his hesitancy, despite all his grievances, to make a decisive break with Agnes, he confesses his affair with Carlotta.

Certainly aware he's not the first man ever confronted with a choice between wife and mistress, O'Neill nonetheless persuades himself the dilemma is uniquely and tragically his own. Sergeant listens sympathetically. Of course, she will keep his confidence—at least while he is alive—but she keeps private notes of their conversations.

Later, when introduced by O'Neill to Carlotta, Sergeant concludes that she is "more in love with the Great Dramatist than she is with Gene"; she finds Carlotta "charming and enormously poised, a woman of the world, at home anywhere, completely in command."

Sergeant believes that Carlotta's private income (the secret income from Speyer disguised as a legacy from her aunt) is what gives her "standing in Gene's eyes." But there is more to it than that. Carlotta has offered O'Neill the possibility of an alternative life centered on his writing, free of domestic disturbances, served by a selflessly devoted partner—a life that his creative genius deserves; in short, a life that Agnes is unwilling to indulge. Carlotta slyly encourages O'Neill to exaggerate his list of grievances against Agnes—among them her refusal to give up all drinking.

Agnes has pointed out that, unlike O'Neill, who is an alcoholic, she can control her intake (which at this point she still can). Carlotta gently reminds O'Neill that she herself, on the other hand, is prepared to join him in total abstinence if it will help him in his ongoing struggle to stay sober.

Carlotta's annual love-gift from Speyer of $14,000 (the equivalent today of roughly $125,000) will enable her to share their living expenses; to O'Neill, always worried about money, this is no small consideration.

When Carlotta informs Speyer that she wants to marry O'Neill because he needs her, Speyer, in his role as protective father, gives her his blessing; it is then that he assures her he will continue providing her with financial guidance, along with a lifetime income.

Reassured, Carlotta feels safe in disingenuously introducing "Papa" Speyer to O'Neill as her surrogate father and financial adviser, and telling him Speyer understands and supports her love affair with O'Neill. O'Neill accepts Carlotta's story.

WHILE CARLOTTA IS congratulating herself on Speyer's approval of her challenging liaison with America's foremost dramatist, O'Neill encounters an amateur clairvoyant from whom he receives a startling prophecy about that liaison.

One evening in mid-December 1927, he visits Benjamin De Casseres, a poet, philosopher, and essayist with whom he has begun a friendship. De Casseres introduces O'Neill to his wife, Bio, who listens intently while the two men talk theater and art. Known to have an affinity for the occult, Bio is referred to affectionately by her husband as an "Effulgent Spirit of Affirmation." She takes herself seriously as an amateur practitioner of palmistry.

Bio has not met O'Neill before. But she knows his plays, has read about him in newspapers and magazines, and her husband has sketched a picture for her of his uneasy life with Agnes in Bermuda—from all of which Bio has intuited possibilities she thinks might interest O'Neill.

On impulse, during a lull in the conversation, Bio turns to O'Neill. "I would like to look at your palm. May I?" With a wan smile, he extends his hand. She has sized him up correctly. O'Neill, the lapsed Catholic, is manifestly superstitious and receptive to mystical prognostication.

Bio is seized with an unfathomable source of "inner illumination," as she later describes it. "You are never going back to Bermuda," she predicts, as she begins to read his palm. "You will live in Europe and San Francisco. You have a long journey before you. You are leaving your wife. Another woman is in your life now. You met her five years ago. There will be a great deal of publicity and you will have a struggle for a divorce before you are able to marry her. Your plays will be successful. You will live for twenty-five years." (Except for being off by one year as to the date of O'Neill's death—he died in 1953— Bio was spot on.)

Early the next day, O'Neill invites De Casseres to lunch to tell him he is stunned by his wife's predictions. Only a few close friends, he says, know he and Carlotta are planning to go abroad together; he has not yet disclosed his decision even to Agnes.

After informing Elizabeth Sergeant that he and Carlotta have chosen February 10 for their elopement, O'Neill lets Norman Winston in on the secret and asks what he thinks of the plan. Although Winston has his doubts, he endorses the idea. "If it doesn't work out," he says, "you can break up for good." O'Neill then asks Winston how he and Carlotta can slip away without attracting attention. Winston helps them book separate cabins under false names on the ocean liner they have selected.

Three days before sailing, O'Neill writes to Agnes in Bermuda. Although she has by now halfheartedly agreed to divorce him, he feels compelled to tell her that he doesn't trust her good faith. During recent weeks, he writes, "so many ugly rumors" have reached him "about what you said to this one and that about how you were going to 'wait me out' . . . that I have felt anything but secure."

Harshly, he scolds, "It isn't that I don't trust you to keep your word— when you're yourself, the fine, honorable woman you are at bottom." But, he adds, he has heard she has begun to drink excessively, and when she drinks, she is "neither fine nor honorable."

Conceding he was equally to blame for their discord, he rationalizes, "It is what life does to love—unless you watch and care for it. This time I am going to watch and care. And when you fall in love—as I am sure you soon will—you better bear that in mind, too."

Still, O'Neill is suddenly suffering squalls of guilt toward the two children he has fathered with Agnes—eight-year-old Shane and two-year-old Oona—whom he is abandoning. Always ambivalent about his fatherhood, he now attempts to justify his desertion with a letter to his son that is, in effect, a protracted moan of self-pity; meant for Agnes's eyes, it includes misleading information about his destination.

He "explains" to Shane that he must travel to California for the production of a new play and goes on to say it probably will be a long time before he sees him and Oona again and he will miss them "very much."

"I often lie in bed before I go to sleep—or when I can't go to sleep— and I picture to myself all about Spithead and what you both have been doing all day and I wonder how you are—and then I feel very sad and life seems to me a silly, stupid thing even at best when one lives it according to the truth that is in one . . . always remember that I love you and Oona an awful lot—and please don't ever forget your Daddy."

CARLOTTA IS BUSY with last-minute packing and, since she and her lover plan to arrive separately at the pier, O'Neill elects to spend February 9, his final evening in New York, with Winston and Rockmore. "This is the worst struggle I've ever had against taking a drink," he tells them, "but if I have one, I'm off." He didn't have one.

The following morning O'Neill, bolstered by reports of a box-office surge for *Strange Interlude*, boards the S.S. *Berengeria*, followed soon after by Carlotta, for their seven-day voyage to London. They will not return to the United States for three years.

James Speyer sees them off, bringing flowers for Carlotta. Seated in her spacious double cabin, attended by her personal maid, Carlotta makes a diary note just as the ocean liner pulls away:

"Am nervous, afraid (of *what* I don't know) and feel terribly alone! Gene arrives *looking* as I *feel*! He looks out the porthole at the part of New York he used to know so well in his youth. Is emotionally disturbed as I am—, finally, takes me in his arms, holds me very close—says 'I love you—' kisses me on the forehead and leaves!"

O'Neill's own terse comment, noted in his Work Diary: "N.Y. Exit— S.S. 'Berengeria'!"

Traveling incognito in separate cabins, both O'Neill and Carlotta are tense and apprehensive about the days ahead. "The ship is rolling—cold & damp—to me everything has an unreal quality," Carlotta writes. And in a moment of what is either panic or clairvoyance, she calls upon the deity: "God help us both!"

Carlotta is sanguine about at least one aspect of their risky undertaking; she is a self-assured traveler in Europe. O'Neill is not. The one time he was in Europe—as a seaman, with his ship in dry dock at Southampton to undergo nearly three weeks of repairs—he spent his shore leaves hanging around the waterfronts of Southampton and Liverpool with his brother sailors, not venturing farther afield.

That was a year after he'd shipped out to Buenos Aires as an apprentice seaman (his fare paid by his father) on the *Charles Racine*, a Norwegian bark, one of the last of the clipper ships to compete with steamers at the end of the nineteenth century. For O'Neill, at twenty-one, climbing the rigging amid a churning sea was the apotheosis of Romance. (In a naively derivative poem entitled "Free," written on the ship's deck in 1910, he attempted to convey his sense of oneness with the sea:

> Then it's ho! for the plunging deck of a bark, the hoarse
>   song of the crew
> With never a thought of those we left or what we are
>   going to do
> Nor heed the old ship's burning, but break the shackles
>   of care
> And at last be free, on the open sea, with the trade wind in
>   our hair.

It was being at sea and living the life of a sailor that mattered. He often spoke of that period as the most exalting of his life. Shipping out at that time was an attempt to free himself from circumstances that were suffocating him—as it is on this present voyage of escape from a strangling marriage.

Maintaining a low profile, Carlotta and O'Neill take their meals in Carlotta's cabin, only occasionally venturing on deck for a walk. O'Neill chain-smokes and Carlotta is gratified to see him using the cigarette case she bought him in New York. ("I asked him if he had ever wanted something that was quite unnecessary," she once noted. "He looked at me & smiled that charming smile of his," and replied, 'I always envied a man who could reach into his pocket & nonchalantly pull forth a long, thin, plain, solid gold cigarette case!'" O'Neill laughed and almost blushed, according to Carlotta. "I got him the case—& he was flabbergasted!")

CARLOTTA IS KEENLY conscious that from this time on, O'Neill's writing and his life will be in her care; and O'Neill is thankful he has at last found his ultimate earth mother, the woman who will give him the unconditional love and nurturing that his unstable mother could not provide.

Once it had been Agnes who satisfied O'Neill's voracious need for mothering. "You are wife of all of me but mother of the best of me," he wrote to her when they were briefly apart soon after the birth of their first child. And a month later, when they were again apart: "In a few days I'll be back in your arms, My Own, and be your other—and firstborn!—baby again!"

O'Neill's craving for maternal nurturing was of long standing. While staying with his parents in their vacation home in New London, Connecticut, in the summer of 1914, he'd fallen in love with the nineteen-year-old Beatrice Ashe, a spirited brunette who played at being a free spirit. That fall, as a twenty-six-year-old student at a playwriting workshop at Harvard, O'Neill wrote an infatuated letter to Beatrice begging for her mothering:

"I feel the impulse of the tired child who runs to his mother's arms and lays his head upon her breast, and sobs for no reason at all. Be my Mother!"

O'Neill frequently left Cambridge for visits to New London, where he attempted, unsuccessfully, to bed the provocative Beatrice; but she, the daughter of the respectable superintendent of New London's trolley-car system, was actually as conventional-minded as her father, and the affair was never consummated.

Now, it is Carlotta to whom O'Neill clings. And she is more than merely maternal. To O'Neill, she is the ultimate fulfillment of a concept that has bedeviled his life—a fusion of mother/mistress/wife. In his eyes, she is almost too perfect. There is, of course, her great beauty. Worldly and resourceful, she is a sophisticated traveler, willing to take on all the responsibility involved in planning a complicated journey; her substantial private income enables her not only to dress exquisitely but also to pay for whatever service or luxury she requires, including a personal maid. She is well-read (if sometimes appallingly misguided, narrow-minded, and self-righteous). And O'Neill is convinced she is prepared to protect his privacy to write while lavishing on him her dedicated and unconditional love.

As mistress and wife-to-be of America's icon of theatrical tragedy and, despite the goblins she will have to sweep from her stage, Carlotta finds herself, at last, in a role that suits—a role she will play to the hilt.

4

Still relying on assumed names, O'Neill and Carlotta check into separate rooms at the Berkeley Hotel in London on February 18. It has been less than a month since O'Neill embraced the dream he'd once thought hopeless and he can barely wait to share his jubilation with his confidant Kenneth Macgowan.

Macgowan, having suffered through many of the battles between O'Neill and Agnes, had come to view her as a negative influence on her husband's work. He was the first person in whom O'Neill had confided his love for Carlotta.

"I'm simply transformed and transfigured," O'Neill now writes to Macgowan. Aflame with boyish rapture, O'Neill pummels his friend with the wonderment of his new love: "I wander about foolish and goggle-eyed with joy in a honeymoon that is a thousand times more poignant and sweet and ecstatic because it comes at an age when one's past—particularly a past such as mine—gives one the power to appreciate what happiness means and how rare it is and how humbly grateful one should be for it."

He has been rendered putty in Carlotta's hands and is unable to restrain his ardor. "We 'belong' to each other!" he warbles. "We fulfill each other!"

The two men have been friends since 1920, when Macgowan, then a critic for the New York *Globe*, reviewing *Beyond the Horizon*, extolled its author as a genius who "seems incorruptible"; four years later they started working together to rescue the theater in Greenwich Village that had given O'Neill his start in 1916—the by-then-faltering Provincetown Playhouse.

As for Carlotta, she writes like a lovesick and barely articulate schoolgirl to Elizabeth Sergeant four days after their arrival:

"I am so happy I could die! . . . this extraordinary exaltation—this divine spiritual thing with its understanding, gentleness and warmth . . . being loved and loving is almost too much for me! Gene is an angel—despite his need of solitude, sunshine & exercise he is smiling & laughing! He is letting go." To this effusion, O'Neill adds a postscript: "I will go Carlotta one better and say that I am so happy I can live!"

Part of Carlotta's pleasure lay in having enticed O'Neill into visiting the smart tailor and boot maker she remembers from shopping jaunts with her first husband, John Moffat, as well as with Ralph Barton. She is still intent on molding O'Neill into a model of sartorial panache and O'Neill, of two minds about her attempted makeover, is trying to comply.

She began several months ago in New York, when she presented him with a mink-lined overcoat similar to one she had bought for Ralph Barton, and O'Neill began wearing it somewhat abashedly. Like a newly anointed princeling not quite certain of his bona fides, O'Neill has singled out several friends to view Carlotta's resplendent gift, as though seeking reassurance that he deserves it. Among them is Jo Mielziner, who has designed the sets for *Strange Interlude*.

"O'Neill was always interested in the technical problems of design and lighting and often made perceptive comments about them," recalls Mielziner. "But this time he had an ulterior motive. He phoned very early in the morning and said he'd be over right away. Would I lean out of my window—I was living on the top floor of a brownstone in the East Sixties—and watch for him as he got out of the taxi?"

Puzzled but accommodating, Mielziner did as requested and beheld O'Neill and his coat as they emerged from the taxi. O'Neill entered Mielziner's apartment with the coat flung open to reveal the lining. "He was beaming," recalled Mielziner. After showing off the coat, he dropped it on the floor in a mock repudiation of its grandeur.

A few days later, O'Neill attempted a similar gesture but was unable to carry it through. He asked Norman Winston to accompany him on a visit to Joe Smith, one of his black friends in the Village. O'Neill was wearing his mink-lined coat.

Smith lived on a small pension from a company that had once employed him as a night watchman—a pension supplemented, it was rumored, with a pair of loaded dice. Smith, like the circus performer Bill Clarke, dated to O'Neill's derelict days, when he often drank himself insensible; in those days Smith would take him home to his sister, who nursed him back to (temporary) sobriety.

Smith is among several old drinking cronies to whom O'Neill now gives handouts. (Like Clarke, Smith will loan part of his persona to yet another character in *The Iceman Cometh*, Joe Mott, the operator of a gambling house.)

"At the last minute Gene didn't have the nerve to appear before Joe in The Coat," Winston remembers. "He was truly too embarrassed to display it. He stopped in the dark passageway leading to Joe's upstairs flat and found a hook near the basement door; he hung his coat there before knocking on Joe's door."

Carlotta—to give her her due—is as much concerned with O'Neill's comfort as with his facade. As she notes in her diary, "He wore shoes that didn't fit properly and caused his toes to curl up." Persuading him to buy new shoes, she congratulates herself: "I never knew a human being to fight so against well made clothes! But, as his wardrobe grew & he could pick & choose—he was like a happy child—all smiles and pleasure."

FULFILLED IN LOVE and fashionably dressed though he might be, O'Neill soon finds his blissful honeymoon soured by a letter from an irate Agnes, prodding him about the domestic muddle he has left behind.

The letter, which doesn't reach O'Neill until early March—when he and Carlotta have already left England for France—was written shortly after he'd sailed from New York; Agnes, unaware of O'Neill's whereabouts, has sent it in care of his attorney, Harry Weinberger, who has forwarded it. It's a response to the accusatory letter O'Neill wrote her before his departure, and it's no less acerbic than his own.

Accusing O'Neill of having left New York with everything unsettled, Agnes goes on to warn him to cease his jibes about her drinking. "Lots of other men—though few who were such drunkards as you, I admit—have cut out drinking without selfishly insisting that their wives, to whom it did no harm, cut it out absolutely too."

Rather than answer Agnes, O'Neill spends hours complaining about her to Weinberger. He doesn't think his attorney is pushing her hard enough to accept the financial arrangement they discussed before he left for Europe. He wants Weinberger to hasten Agnes's departure to Reno for the divorce.

At the Hotel du Rhin in Paris, Carlotta attends to O'Neill's personal needs with the same fervor she once bestowed on Ralph Barton. More efficient even than a Parisian concierge, she arranges train, car, and hotel accommodations for the next phase of their prenuptial voyage.

"Gene, at times, like a child, so astonished at being done for, & not asked for anything in return," she bubbles in her diary. Overcome by her own "polite" and "unselfish" treatment of him, she expresses the hope that he will learn to respond in kind.

So far, so good.

Although neither O'Neill nor Carlotta can quite shake off a sense that their rapturous new life is fated soon to hit some rocky terrain, they begin their hunt for an idyllic (if temporary) retreat. They explore the Basque countryside along the Bay of Biscay, seeking both serenity and seclusion for O'Neill's long-interrupted writing. In mid-March, they find what they've been seeking: the Villa Marguerite in the village of Guéthery, five miles south of Biarritz near the Spanish border; they sign a six-month lease.

Their combined income has sizeable stretch in France in the late 1920s, and Carlotta staffs the villa, which has a tennis court and a private beach, with a cook, two housemaids, and a handyman—all these in addition to her personal maid, Tuwe Drew, who has traveled with her since leaving New York.

"A new life, a really new one!" Carlotta writes to an old friend. "And to say that at my age means *something*. I have with me, in all this, a lovely soul—a keen brain & a beautiful person. And altho' our address must *not* be told now—when all this mess is over I will be proud & happy to scream it from the housetops."

In Guéthery, O'Neill, at least for the moment, feels emotionally stable enough to resume work on *Dynamo*, a play he began writing a year earlier. But his work frequently is interrupted by letters from Agnes (forwarded by Weinberger), as well as by letters from Weinberger himself.

While O'Neill continues to withhold his address from Agnes, his letters to her vacillate between placatory/amiable and accusatory/hateful. On March 10 he tells her he will pay her expenses for the next six months, including her trip to Reno, where it has been agreed she will establish the necessary residence to qualify for a divorce. And he assures her he won't sell Spithead as long as she wants to live there. But he suggests she could live more cheaply in Europe—ignoring the fact that she would be entirely friendless abroad. He cautions her to be economical because his current unprecedented success with *Strange Interlude* might well be followed by leaner years.

It's evident he's baffled about how best to prod Agnes into getting on with the divorce. In one breath, he goads her, writing that he is "happy and quite sure of the lasting fundamental value" of what he is doing; in the next breath, he hypocritically signs his letter, "All deepest friendship always, dear!"

Later that month, after receiving another two letters from Agnes contesting his terms, O'Neill grows outright hostile and berates her for being greedy and thoughtless. "Don't think you can frighten me by threatening to sue," he blusters in a four-page manifesto. "Outside of the fact that I should hate you for dragging such a nasty mess of notoriety around our children's ears, when, if you weren't so eager to get all you can, everything could be arranged quietly on a decent human basis."

Admonishing her for spending lavishly on renovations at Spithead that he never agreed to, he threatens to cable the Bermuda papers to say he won't be responsible for such debts. "If you're determined to act like an enemy, you can't expect me to take it lying down."

He issues a warning that must sound hollow even to his own ears: if Agnes continues to harass him with exorbitant financial demands, he will be too distraught to write and earn money for her to "throw away." He then stoops to repeating malicious gossip he's heard by mail about her "drinking and promiscuity." Although conceding he has "no right" to tell her "not to have lovers, or not to drink—except in our children's names," he says that nonetheless such reports upset him.

Placatingly, he then asserts that he still loves and respects her "as my partner of ten long years in which we both managed to remain fairly clean." But after apologizing for sounding bitter, he renews his self-justifying tirade:

He resents Agnes's implication that it is she who is "doing all the suffering." Doesn't she think he suffers, too? "If you don't, Agnes, you're a damn fool! Sometimes—and often!—when I think of Shane and Oona I suffer like hell from a sense of guilt toward them, and a deep sense of guilt because I've made you suffer."

O'Neill clinches his argument by laying the blame for his leaving on her, maintaining he gave her "every chance a man of honor could give" to save the marriage. He reminds Agnes that he reached for her "understanding, sympathy and help" during his early involvement with Carlotta. He chides her for having been "deaf and blind and dumb" to his need until it was too late to disentangle from Carlotta. He is in effect telling Agnes that if she had fought to keep him she could have saved the marriage. Possibly he believes this.

By now O'Neill, despite wrapping himself in his work, has sunk into what Carlotta calls "a deep depression"; he tells her that Agnes's dalliance over the divorce is poisoning his life. Carlotta silently wonders how

O'Neill could have failed, early on, to recognize Agnes's defects; she spitefully sputters in her diary that "Even a breeder of horses, dogs, pigs, etc.—is *most* careful.

"So, it goes—the artist hasn't time for such 'middle-class' thoughts—but it really *isn't* 'middle-class!'" Promising herself she will "stick" and do her best to help O'Neill, she can't suppress a whimper: "I will be the one to take the *beating* for all this!!"

Carlotta is as outraged as O'Neill to learn of Agnes's most recent ploy; she claims to be pregnant with O'Neill's child. O'Neill thinks the pregnancy might be a bluff but, in any case, he knows the child cannot be his—and he explodes to Harry Weinberger: "I'm a mild man but there is a limit and being blamed for other men's children is that limit. I don't give a damn how many lovers she may have. That's her privilege, naturally. But I don't want them bringing O'Neills into being. I have my little Puritan prejudices!"

That is only the beginning of a nine-page letter in which he declares all-out war on Agnes. Until now he has continued to hope she would agree to free him in a timely fashion. It dawns on him at last that he has miscalculated and he fulminates to Weinberger that Agnes is sabotaging him with her greed and dishonesty.

Sounding almost unhinged, he rants about what he calls "the plain facts" of the case, hurling a litany of venomous accusations against Agnes. (Perhaps it doesn't occur to him that Agnes might someday sell this letter to a university, for all the world to scrutinize; but even if it does occur to him, he simply can't control the self-justifying temper that compels him to spew his rage in this and subsequent letters to Agnes.)

O'Neill goes on to deride Agnes as a woman whom he accepted when she was "a shabby hanger-on" in Greenwich Village, "an unsuccessful cheap fiction writer, with no status of any kind." And he dredges up a long-ago episode of Agnes's past: it was not long after they'd met in the winter of 1917, writes O'Neill, that he first learned Agnes had a nearly four-year-old daughter who was being raised away from New York by her grandparents. At the time, Agnes had given O'Neill a vague account of a wartime marriage in England in early 1915, where she was then living with her parents, followed almost at once by pregnancy and widowhood.

O'Neill had not pressed her for details at the time. Now, however, digging for grounds to counter Agnes's demands during divorce proceedings, he unfurls his long-suppressed suspicion and wrath.

Agnes, he writes, had averred her child was "born in wedlock (but no shred of proof of her having ever been married before was ever brought forward)." Moreover, he says, before she married him, she had readily agreed that he "would never have to support that child"; nevertheless, he "always had partly supported her."

He then takes Agnes to task for "violating in both letter and spirit" their quixotic agreement that "if ever either came to the other and said they were in love with someone else that automatically a divorce would be given and no alimony asked." And he dismisses as "a grotesque fiction" Agnes's claim that she helped him in his work, insisting she was actually envious of his work "as compared to what she could do," and even, at times, "did her best to hamper it."

Agnes, he contends, allowed his father to support her early in their marriage; and she accepted from his mother "the only decent furs and clothes she had ever had up to then." What's more, he contends, she is a woman who was slackly raised in near poverty, to whom he gave "three fine houses" (their summer home on the Provincetown dunes, an estate in Connecticut, and Spithead, their recently purchased beachfront house in Bermuda).

Continuing to tally Agnes's treacheries, he sounds as paranoid as Othello. In conclusion, he snarls, Agnes, after squandering his money, dares to blackmail him while she entertains a lover at his expense. "Oh no! It's a bit too thick! I am bitter and I am mad. . . . I'll gladly blow up the works no matter who it crushes so long as it crushes her."

O'Neill is so furious that Agnes has not responded rationally and agreeably to his own irrational and disagreeable behavior that he abruptly shifts into reverse, informing Weinberger that he and Carlotta have decided to adopt an entirely new strategy.

They no longer care whether Agnes obtains the divorce. If it's a case of his being blackmailed for more than he can afford, he says, he and Carlotta will forgo marriage and "come out in the open and tell the world we're living together because my wife is charging too high for a divorce."

He instructs Weinberger to inform Agnes that he and Carlotta have sufficient money to live comfortably in Europe for the rest of their lives; he will have his future plays produced abroad and limit his income in America to royalties from already published work; he can no longer write, and will not try to, until his problems are settled. Agnes, he winds up in a frenzy of frustration, is "a skunk!"

It took O'Neill a day to cool down. Acknowledging to Weinberger that his previous letter about Agnes was "a bit hectic," he says he has grown "calmer about the hatred stuff," although he's still opposed to Agnes's conditions for granting a divorce.

What he now wants from Weinberger is a statement to the press that will put a stop to the rumors and speculation about his whereabouts and—most important—will protect Carlotta's reputation. He says he can't work with the specter of a tabloid scandal hanging over his head "like an unexploded bomb."

He suggests that they follow Sinclair Lewis's example and stop shrouding their divorce in secrecy. Lewis's recent divorce, he points out, attracted no salacious public attention, even though he was living with a woman not his wife, because all the facts were out in the open. It was simply announced in the papers that Lewis and his wife had separated and that she was divorcing him on the grounds of desertion; nothing more was announced until the divorce was granted.

Forgetting that it was he himself who chose to cloak his departure from his home and family in secrecy, O'Neill now demands to know why his own divorce cannot be managed like Lewis's. The "secrecy business," he says, "will eventually result in my being sought out over here and involved in a terrible mess."

O'Neill wants Weinberger to tell the press that he and Agnes have separated simply because they have grown incompatible. And he stresses there is no reason why there needs to be any mention of a third party. He instructs Weinberger to ask Agnes to corroborate the statement; she should say she is going to Reno and that "there is no question of any correspondent, that we simply cannot hit it off together anymore, etc."

O'Neill then offers Agnes the same advice: "Once they get it from your lips that we're definitely separated for good," he says, "they'll lay off of us for good." Airmail is new and erratic in 1928, and O'Neill's letter about abandoning secrecy has not yet reached Agnes—nor, presumably, Weinberger—when, on April 27, the *World* publishes an "authorized interview" with Agnes, purporting to "clarify her situation."

Rather than clarifying, Agnes distorts, perhaps stalling for time to gain a better settlement; or perhaps she's hoping O'Neill will tire of Carlotta and return to her, even though, as she has confided to friends, she herself has begun to find her marriage burdensome.

Agnes informs the *World* she is not seeking a divorce or separation. Instead, she is planning to join her husband soon in London. She doesn't know where Miss Monterey is, says Agnes, but she is aware that her husband is traveling in France with friends to escape the noisy repairs in progress at their Bermuda residence.

"Mrs. O'Neill said she hopes her husband is enjoying himself," according to the interview. "She refused to say that her failure to leave for Europe with him had constituted what other celebrities have referred to as a 'marital vacation.' Nevertheless, she believes in an occasional change of air—'for the man' she added quickly."

Based on Agnes's blithe prevarication, the baffled *World* reporter theorizes: "If Miss Monterey were one of the friends who had been with [O'Neill] he had never informed her of it. Harry Weinberger, for many years Mr. O'Neill's lawyer, paid a recent visit to Mrs. O'Neill in Bermuda, strengthening the old reports of marital disagreement. But the wife explained that this was a business visit purely, in connection with a mortgage on a house or something of that kind."

Agnes, of course, is equivocating. The Weinberger visit to Bermuda was mainly intended to gather and remove O'Neill's personal documents—an attempt thwarted by Agnes. O'Neill believed that the files containing some early playscripts and other memorabilia that he had left in his Bermuda home when he departed for London in 1928 ultimately "were either destroyed or stolen." That is what he told officials of the Princeton University Library fifteen years later, when an exhibit of his manuscripts and letters was being planned. (But the contents of those files were, in fact, sold by Agnes after his death, along with O'Neill's letters to her.)

Carlotta soothes O'Neill's distress over the published interview. In her diary she congratulates herself for being who she is. "He is like my child! And *knows I will take care of him*! He has gained, at last, a real mother—combined with mistress!"

"I'm sorry you gave the interview," O'Neill writes Agnes a few days later, sounding more sympathetic than angry and aware she had not received the letter in which he asked her to be forthright about their reasons for separating. He stresses that a simple divorce announcement would have better served to kill the press's "hope for a scandal." As it is, he says, they know Agnes is lying and probably wonder what she is concealing. He urges her once again to accept his terms and to leave for Reno.

"It is funny how soon an aching heart turns into a greedy gut!" O'Neill writes to Macgowan. He grumbles about the influence exerted on Agnes in Bermuda by her "worthy Society drunken neighbor-friends," who are advising her "to take me for all I've got." He is "too old to start in being a sucker," he adds.

He has written to Weinberger to tell Agnes that if she won't take what he has offered, she can "go to hell." The offer amounts to an income for Agnes—based on O'Neill's earnings—that might fluctuate annually between $6,000 (roughly equivalent to today's $80,000) and $10,000 (today's $130,000) and which, O'Neill has reminded Agnes, is an agreement more generous than Sinclair Lewis's wife got from him, "considering he must have been making three times my income!"

On May 1, O'Neill's mood briefly lightens. Upon receiving word he has been awarded the Pulitzer Prize for *Strange Interlude*, he becomes the only playwright at that point to have racked up three (the first for *Beyond the Horizon*, the second for *Anna Christie*). He instructs his agent to donate the prize money of $1,000 to the Author's League Fund for Needy Writers.

Somewhat cheered, O'Neill returns to his routine at the Villa Marguerite. He swims daily in the Bay of Biscay, plays tennis with Carlotta, and takes long walks with her on the beach. From the terrace of their villa, they admire what Carlotta describes as "divine sunsets." They tour the countryside; Carlotta shops for dresses and shoes and—ever the meticulous housekeeper—for domestic embellishments.

Through it all, Carlotta rarely mentions her daughter, Cynthia, still in the care of her grandmother Nellie in San Francisco. And O'Neill doesn't speak much to Carlotta about his children. But he does write to Agnes about them.

He misses Shane and Oona "like hell at times," he says. "Don't sneer! I love them as much as you do—perhaps more—in my oblique, inexpressive fashion." Believing his own words, he insists, "they will find out I have been a good father . . . when they are old enough to understand all that has happened and when they really come to know me and about me."

To Weinberger, in a burst of pathos and self-delusion, he insists he can make it up to the children later for the damage he believes Agnes (never he himself) has done to them. And to Ben De Casseres he writes that—despite his disgust with Agnes and his fear of being "smoked out" by the local press—"inside" he is "deeply at peace and happy and confident of the future," even though it is "hell on the nerves" and "it's raining boxing gloves!"

A week later O'Neill expresses his newly felt depth of happiness to Carlotta when he inscribes a copy of *Strange Interlude* to her: "My life moving in you—your life moving in me—the world is whole and perfect. I am your lover!"

Yet O'Neill's "perfect" world is ever subject to distressing bulletins about Agnes's intentions, as well as to concern for Carlotta's discomfort (in spite of her bravado) with her ambiguous relationship to him.

By mid-May 1928 the tension is too much for O'Neill. Carlotta has her first encounter with his full-blown, black-Irish rage.

5

A man named Kantor wires *he's arriving day after tomorrow!*" Carlotta complains to her diary on May 11, 1928. O'Neill tells her he knows the man only slightly. "This," writes Carlotta, "is a horrible and unkind thing to do." She is embarrassed, in her role as a married man's mistress, at having to play hostess to a stranger, and is *"dreadfully* unhappy!"

The unwelcome visitor to Villa Marguerite is a former reporter for the New York *Tribune* and a freelance contributor to *The New York Times*, who writes sometimes under the byline Louis Kantor and sometimes under the pseudonym Louis Kalonyme. As to knowing Kantor "only slightly," O'Neill has lied to Carlotta. Kantor is actually a hard-drinking crony from O'Neill's Provincetown and Greenwich Village days.

Carlotta has cautioned O'Neill to shun all his old sidekicks. Not only is she committed to keeping O'Neill abstemious for the sake of his writing, she is eager to bury any lingering notion of him as Agnes's drunken bohemian husband. Along with restyling his wardrobe, she's determined to reshape his image as a man who is temperate and aloof—in short, a dedicated artist who is worthy of her as his protector and muse.

She is rightfully suspicious of Kantor, who endeared himself to O'Neill in the early 1920s by writing adulatory articles about the then rising young playwright.

At the time, O'Neill was living with Agnes in Provincetown in a converted Coast Guard station at the edge of the Atlantic; known as Peaked Hill Bars, it had been purchased for him by his father as a wedding present. He had impulsively welcomed Kantor to an intimate friendship and even had a shack constructed close by his own dwelling.

Kantor became an acolyte—sycophant is perhaps more accurate; he would follow O'Neill about, concealing a pint of bootleg booze under his shirt, proffering the bottle when requested. He claimed he had begun to drink during the summer of 1920 "to keep up with O'Neill," and boasted, "Though I started drinking because of Gene, I became a better drinker than he, because I had a stronger stomach."

One day in Provincetown, some well-meaning friends of O'Neill's, who wanted to make sure he would sleep off the effects of a drunken binge, locked him in a room at a local hotel. Twelve hours later the proprietor, checking on the prisoner, found him still drunk. Baffled, he searched the room but discovered no liquor.

After feeding O'Neill, he warned him to behave and locked him back in. O'Neill was still drunk the following day, and this time the proprietor caught Kantor, who had climbed up the fire escape, handing O'Neill a bottle through the window.

The day Kantor is expected, May 14, O'Neill is not well. He sends Carlotta, who does not drive, in their chauffeured car to fetch her unwanted guest from the train station. "I don't know *where I am or what to do*!" Carlotta scribbles in her diary on her return. "But I *do* know a dreadful *stranger* is in our house."

Kantor finds O'Neill on edge because of recent unwanted attention from the local press, and it isn't long before the reason for Kantor's presence at the villa becomes clear; O'Neill and Kantor drive to a nearby village to buy whiskey. Returning to the Villa Marguerite and ignoring Carlotta, the men proceed to drink themselves insensible; a furious Carlotta later discovers them collapsed on beds in one of the villa's guest rooms.

The following day, she notes, "A terrible night—The good Black Irish comes to the front—hand in hand with sadistic joy in trying to kill everything in me that spells love, loyalty, devotion and decency. I nearly died!"

She watches in alarm a day later as O'Neill secludes himself in his bedroom with Kantor. She hears them rowdily reminiscing late into the night. "Things getting worse!" Carlotta records the next morning, May 17. "He starts to drink with our guest! The alcohol does *horrible* things to his brain. He *mustn't* drink—He should realize this is just what A. wants him to do."

Fearful that O'Neill's drinking will lead to "some dreadful scandal," she writes, "Things seem utterly hopeless! I don't know what to do . . . I have tried to make a good home . . . give *all of myself*, & my worldly goods! I am *frightened!*"

This is O'Neill's first stumble since he swore off alcohol two years earlier, after his psychoanalyst warned him if he continued drinking, his brain would turn into "the white of an egg" and sabotage his ability to write.

It's probable, as Kantor later theorized, that O'Neill's fall from the wagon has been triggered in part by a fresh pang of guilt over the children he has deserted. While he doesn't mention Kantor's arrival on May 14 in his Work Diary, O'Neill—with his children on his mind—does note "Oona's Third Birthday."

On the fifth day of O'Neill's bender, with no sign of Kantor's imminent departure, Carlotta braces herself to leave O'Neill. She makes her impetuous exit from the Villa Marguerite at eight in the morning in a hired car, heading for Bordeaux, where she plans to board a train for Paris. But when she reaches Bordeaux, she's unable to go on.

"I can't leave him there to God knows what! I love him!" she writes. She has herself driven back, weeping all the way, not stopping for food, and reaches the villa at nightfall. Staggering into the house, she is appalled to find that O'Neill has thrown black coffee all over the blue satin walls of the salon, staining them so badly she later is obliged to have the walls redone. Once again, she finds O'Neill and Kantor sprawled in a drunken stupor in the guest room. "So, this is genius—this is love! God help us!" she explodes.

The next morning, no one speaks. Carlotta describes O'Neill as looking like a ghost. He finally breaks his silence, morphing into a little boy begging forgiveness from his mother. Kantor echoes his plea and Carlotta, relieved that her ordeal is over, forgives them both—and even sanctions a "loan" to Kantor of $500 when at last, on May 21, he leaves the villa.

Soon after Kantor's departure, O'Neill falls seriously ill with what Carlotta describes as "a bad nervous breakdown," and suddenly she is overcome with a need to rationalize her involvement with the volatile genius to whom she has chosen to devote her life.

She records a pathetic mantra that she doubtless longs to throw in O'Neill's face (if only she dared); it is a tract she periodically trots out in exasperated self-defense, and it is replete with non sequiturs: She wasn't brought up to live the sort of life O'Neill has foisted on her; her father, "a brilliant Dane, was educated in Denmark, France, Germany & China"; she herself was educated in Europe and given "the *strictest* sort of up-bringing"; she was "taught to respect others—& to have self respect" and to be "honest, loyal, unselfish & decent"; and finally, irrelevantly, "to remember I was a woman!" With all her rationalizing, she has decided to forgive O'Neill.

BY THE END OF MAY, O'Neill and Carlotta have recovered their equilibrium. Compared with Carlotta's scribbled outbursts, O'Neill gives barely a hint of the past month's disturbances in his Work Diary. As is his wont, he sums up, under the heading "Memoranda," the number of days during which he did "creative work." In April, the first month he settled in Guéthery, he had noted twenty-eight work days on *Dynamo* and two days "blank." By contrast, in May, he recorded only twelve days of "creative work" and nineteen days "blank."

His chief concern, however, is not the lost work time, but his fear, replicating Carlotta's, that his having fallen off the wagon will become a source of gossip, providing Agnes with new ammunition. "Be forever silent," he cautions Kantor in a letter referring to the drinking episode and apologizing for his "stupidity." More than two months later, with Agnes still refusing to proceed with the divorce, O'Neill again refers to the drinking episode.

"Remember," he writes to Kantor, "to forget that incident of May! It had no meaning." And, he says, in justification, it "was really a damned good thing in its effect on my future, by way of a final K.O. to an old mistake. But how A. & Co. would love to get hold of it!"

After Kantor repeats his own apology in a letter to Carlotta, she cannily turns him into an ally who can be of service to her and O'Neill. During the next several months, she will write Kantor seventeen letters filled with intimate chitchat about the joys of her relationship with O'Neill, which she hopes he will pass on to acquaintances in New York. And she relays various requests from O'Neill for small errands; for example, she encloses postcards O'Neill has written to friends and asks Kantor, who is spending some time in Germany, to mail them from that country—the intention being to mislead those friends as well as the press as to O'Neill's whereabouts.

Despite Agnes's relentless recalcitrance, O'Neill and Carlotta have somehow managed to resume a relatively peaceful existence—so much so that by early June Carlotta can frivolously welcome the arrival of a pair of exorbitantly expensive red shoes ordered from Paris, after which she and O'Neill celebrate the delivery of their new Renault.

Although O'Neill will eventually hire a full-time chauffeur, for now he drives himself, and he and Carlotta resume touring the countryside, often motoring into the lower Alps. That month, O'Neill devotes sixteen days of work to *Dynamo* and two weeks to sightseeing and shopping.

Before leaving on the June motor trip, he writes to Theresa Helburn, a co-producer at the Theatre Guild. Pledging her to secrecy about his whereabouts, he describes his progress on *Dynamo*, which he expects the Guild to produce—although he will not venture to predict when it will be completed.

The play, inspired by O'Neill's visit to a hydroelectric plant near the home in Ridgefield, Connecticut, that he once shared with Agnes, tells the story of a teenage boy who revolts against the religious teachings of his childhood and instead embraces "the religion of electricity."

O'Neill believes he has reached a new plateau from which to challenge the fundamental maladies of modern society. As he describes *Dynamo* in a letter to the critic George Jean Nathan, the play is "a good symbolical and factual biography of what is happening in a large section of [the] American (and not only American) soul right now." It will "dig at the roots of the sickness of Today," as he experiences it.

As a true visionary, he will continue to deplore the world's current maladies for the rest of his writing life. And what he expresses as the spiritual and moral "sickness of Today" foretells all too aptly the overwhelming materialism of Tomorrow.

To Nathan, O'Neill expresses his conviction that "anyone trying to do big work nowadays must have this big subject behind all the little subjects of his plays or novels, or he is simply scribbling around on the surface of things and has no more real status than a parlor entertainer."

One evening after dinner, O'Neill reads aloud to Carlotta from the nearly completed script of *Dynamo*. She has qualms, but she entrusts them only to her diary: the play is "interesting" but, she notes, it needs cuts and revision. "He is too worried to do his best—but so anxious to prove to A. he can work in spite of her & the worry she is causing him! Of course that is all wrong—but I dare *not* offer any suggestions."

In early July, O'Neill wrenches himself from *Dynamo* long enough to launch another vicious attack on Agnes. Answering a letter from Weinberger, who has raised the old question about Agnes's first marriage, O'Neill says he has never pressed her for details, but she was always vague about her past. He is now convinced she lied about the circumstances of her daughter's birth. He sneers at her story that while in London, before the war began, she married an English newspaperman named Burton, who was killed in Belgium shortly thereafter.

"What he was doing in that country she doesn't exactly remember," O'Neill jeers to Weinberger, "but he wasn't in the army and he wasn't a correspondent. The whole story is pretty ridiculous, what? At any rate he got her with child before leaving and she came back to a Connecticut farm and had [her daughter] Barbara. That is all she has ever told me."

She has no marriage certificate, O'Neill informs his lawyer, nor has he ever heard any of her family mention the marriage. There is good reason, he adds, to suspect that "no such marriage ever took place."

O'Neill guesses Barbara's father was a Polish farmer then living near Agnes and her family in the Connecticut town of Cornwall Bridge. He tells Weinberger that Agnes, in a brief confessional moment, told him the farmer was her mother's lover as well as her own. "A nice mess, what? And people think my *Desire*, for example, is too sordid to be real!" (He is, of course, referring to *Desire Under the Elms*, produced in 1924, in which a son's jealous desire for his father's young bride leads to a sequence of incest and infanticide.)

O'Neill proposes that Weinberger hire a private detective to look into Agnes's past in Cornwall Bridge. "I am sure the whole secret is there." He also suggests that the detective tail Agnes, so that she can be "caught in flagrante," which would give him "a weapon" that would enable him "to dictate terms."

While O'Neill's accusations are mean-minded and vengeful, research conducted years later turns up clues that somewhat justify his suspicions. It seems that the father of Agnes's child could quite possibly have been Courtland Young, the well-off editor of *Young's Magazine*, who owned a 230-acre farm in Cornwall Bridge, Connecticut, and to whom Agnes had sold some of her pulp fiction. Young ceded the farm to "Agnes B. Burton" on December 30, 1915, soon after Agnes's daughter Barbara was born.

While O'Neill plots, Agnes stonewalls. She dismisses his plea that the divorce proceeding be announced publicly in the manner he has suggested—and she is still in no hurry to leave for Reno. Meanwhile, Carlotta has changed her mind about living openly with a married man.

For the time being, she and O'Neill accept the fact that their relationship must remain secret. "If only our hearts were at peace!" she sighs in her diary on July 14. They have decided to continue living in Europe as quietly as possible for at least the next two years. But before settling down, they will fulfill O'Neill's long-held yearning to explore the Far East.

It is a yearning that dates back to his mid-twenties, when he discovered that his early idol, August Strindberg, had been so fascinated a scholar of Oriental wisdom that he had learned both Chinese and Japanese. O'Neill was further drawn to the mysticism of the East when, at twenty-eight, he read *Light on the Path,* a treatise crammed with Hindu, Buddhist, and Taoist wisdom compiled by the mid-nineteenth-century romance novelist Mabel Collins. And, at thirty, he had expressed his yearning to visit the Far East through the character of Robert Mayo, a partial stand-in for himself, in *Beyond the Horizon.* Here is Mayo, attempting to explain to his brother why he is drawn to the Orient:

> Supposing I was to tell you that it's just Beauty that's calling me, the beauty of the far off and the unknown, the mystery and spell of the East, which lures me in the books I've read, the need of the freedom of great wide spaces, the joy of wandering on and on—in quest of the secret which is hidden just over there, beyond the horizon?

O'Neill continued to delve into Far Eastern culture, and in 1923, he began work on his ambitious pageant of the East, *Marco Millions.* By 1925, he was describing himself as "a most confirmed mystic." And, shortly before leaving with Carlotta for Asia, he explains to his agent, Richard Madden, why the voyage means so much to him: "It's been the dream of my life to live there for a while and absorb a bit of that background. It's going to be infinitely valuable to me in its bearing upon my future work."

Carlotta busies herself with inquiries about passage to Hong Kong, and in late July, she and O'Neill commit to sail on October 5 from Marseilles on the *André le Bon.* But Carlotta is not sanguine about the voyage. "I am, for some idiotic reason, fearful of going to China under present conditions—six weeks is a very long time for Gene to be caged up—worrying about so many things—& I am in a humiliating position."

O'Neill prods himself into finishing *Dynamo* and, on August 18, he notes in his Work Diary that the play is complete except for revisions. "We celebrate!" rejoices Carlotta in her own diary.

On August 24, during a weeklong motor trip through the French countryside, Carlotta writes that O'Neill is "already beginning to relax—we are away from his past! My darling tries to tell me how much he loves me! It is like getting out of hell! (This price I have to pay!)"

She is right about O'Neill's evident euphoria. To George Jean Nathan he writes, two days later, that he finds himself blissfully at home and at peace in the Basque country and plans to settle here "for the rest of my days." For the first time "in God knows how long," he says, "I feel as if life had something to give me . . . quite outside of the life in my work." He has even stopped worrying, he says, about Agnes's spreading nasty rumors about him and Carlotta.

"As I approach my fortieth birthday I feel younger and more pepped up with the old zest for living and working than I've ever felt since I started writing. . . . I feel as if I'd tapped a new life and could rush up all the reserves of energy in the world to back up my work. Honestly, to me it is a sort of miracle."

Carlotta's mood, however, gradually darkens. Toward the end of August, she has "a strange presentiment" that before their return from Asia she will have gone through hell. "Gene will crack someday—he can't bear all this nervous strain much longer," she predicts. "And then, what about me, his mistress?"

Their lease on the Villa Marguerite expires at the end of September, and when they return from their motor trip on August 30, Carlotta will have ample time to pack. But confronted in the villa by stacks of mail from the United States, she sighs, "My honeymoon is over!" One letter informs O'Neill that no record has been found in Somerset House— where all marriages in England are registered—of a union between Agnes Boulton and Burton. Carlotta's comment: "So Barbara's papa didn't come from where he was supposed to come. Poor Barbara!"

After O'Neill receives yet another cable from Weinberger listing Agnes's dissatisfaction with the proposed financial arrangement, Carlotta rails, "This woman is something beyond all imagination! Without any honor, self respect or common decency. Gene is sunk in depression all day."

She is cheered on September 17, in the midst of her diligent shopping and packing, to receive from O'Neill a gift she will cherish throughout their years together. It is a stuffed, scrawny, hairy, grotesquely comical stuffed monkey that looks almost alive—a reference to their shared memories of *The Hairy Ape*. The first gift O'Neill has ever given her, the monkey has long arms, "like Gene," as Carlotta recalled years later.

O'Neill christens the monkey Esteban, in memory of a young Spanish nobleman he met in Buenos Aires in 1910, after he'd sailed there as an apprentice seaman. (While O'Neill drifted and drank on the waterfront, the Marquis Esteban de Gonzales, Grandee of Spain, ruined himself with drugs.) Leering wickedly through his whiskers, Esteban is destined to perch in a corner of a sofa or armchair or on a bed in every home Carlotta occupies, until shortly before her death in 1970.

Three weeks before leaving for China, O'Neill mails Richard Madden a typescript of the completed *Dynamo*, informing him he'll be gone for a year and asking him to have copies made for several friends, including Nathan and De Casseres. Madden takes his time arranging for the copies—which is just as well, because both men will ultimately scorn it, and with good reason.

Doubtless O'Neill's aim is lofty. But the play is a muddled diatribe of misapprehension, malevolence, and misogyny, its cast verging on caricature.

As O'Neill himself describes the action of his all but incomprehensible plot: Reuben Light, the befuddled seventeen-year-old protagonist, "electrocutes his bullying father's God, finds his dead mother again in the dynamo—a mother deified into God this time by the aid of pseudoscience—and is even driven to sacrifice the girl he loves in the flesh, whom his mother was jealous of and hated, to achieve the final return to the mother after he has been unfaithful to her."

(It's tempting to regard O'Neill's description as self-parody. As Alice observes of the Jabberwocky's poem, "It seems to fill my head with ideas—only I don't exactly know what they are!")

Although O'Neill is eager to have the approbation of De Casseres and Nathan, the play's fate right now is not uppermost in his thoughts as he tries to cope with the flurry of letters and cables that keep arriving from New York, bringing more aggravating news about Agnes.

He's also absorbed in Carlotta's animated preparations for their voyage, and he can hardly help noticing the presence in his home of the costly Louis Vuitton wardrobe trunks—a must for the well-heeled traveler of the era—that Carlotta has bought and is packing with the stylish suits, shirts, silk pajamas, and dressing gowns she's helped him select. (A far cry from the day when—as an almost penniless twenty-two-year-old apprentice sailor—O'Neill stuffed his meager belongings into a battered sea chest and clambered aboard the *Charles Racine*.)

With the packing done and the trunks sent on ahead to Marseilles, Carlotta develops what she calls "the shakes." On September 24, she notes, "Gene holds me in his arms all night! Says it helps him, too!!—Bless him!" The day before departing Guéthery, she pleads, "We are off on our pilgrimage—dear God—guide us."

On September 27, after a leisurely sightseeing car trip to Paris, they check into the Hotel du Rhin, where they will stay until it's time to head for Marseilles and their October 5 departure. Both make an effort to appear at ease, although they're apprehensive about what Carlotta views as the possible "treachery" that Agnes might choose to wreak during their journey.

"Why can't we live as other people?" Carlotta ponders. "All men make mistakes in their youth . . . why must he be tormented and made ill?" She is comforted by a letter from James Speyer in New York, conveying his hope that when she and O'Neill board the *André le Bon*, "it will be Le Bon all the way on your journey."

"I really do wish I could have gone with you," he adds, "especially as I have really seen very little of this world and am getting older every day & I feel it. This is only natural and I am not complaining. I cannot tell you

how happy I feel that you are so much interested in Gene's work & doings."
He assures Carlotta she "will be of great constance [sic] and encouragement" to O'Neill in many ways, even if sometimes she "may have a mau-
vais quart d'heure."

Speyer ends with a hope that the divorce will have become "another
historical fact" by the time their voyage is over. He signs his letter, "With
love as ever, James." But Speyer's letter does not divert Carlotta from her
fury with Agnes. "I can't understand any woman *asking for money because
she lived with a man*! Where is her *pride, her self-respect*? *Whores* are paid
for their bodies,—*not wives!*" Her own arrangement with Speyer has perhaps slipped her mind—although she can readily rationalize that she did
not ask for the income Speyer has bestowed on her.

Before sailing, O'Neill writes to Shane, who will be nine on October
30. Apologizing for not having responded to a recent letter from his
son, he explains how hard he's been working on *Dynamo* and chats sympathetically about his son's various activities.

"I'm sorry but I won't be able to come back soon," O'Neill says, "although I miss you and Oona an awful lot and think of you all the time.
I've got to go on a long voyage on a ship about some plays I want to
write." He mentions India, Java, China, and Africa as places he might
visit, and promises to write to Shane about what he sees and does.

Enclosing a check for his son's ninth birthday, he says he has given
instructions to his lawyer to turn over his own bicycle and kayak to Shane
for his tenth birthday and Christmas. "Kiss Oona for me. I'm writing her
a letter too but not such a long one because she's only little compared to
you." He ends, "Much deep love to you, my son, from Your Daddy."

On October 3, two days before boarding their ship in Marseilles, Carlotta again vents her anxiety: "All night we hang on to each other—as
though we were in deadly danger!"

6

Aboard the S.S. *André le Bon* on October 5, 1928, O'Neill learns by cable that the Theatre Guild has accepted *Dynamo* for production next season. In a surge of optimism, he sets to work in his cabin, undeterred for the moment by the worsening heat.

As always his mind shimmers with possibilities. Some dramatic concepts will survive in his bulging work diaries merely as titles, others will be described in a sentence or two and later discarded; still others will be outlined and then aborted. But a few will germinate and flower, as in the most striking example—a modern version of Aeschylus's Oresteia trilogy.

"Germ idea use Greek Tragedy plot in modern setting," he had noted two and a half years earlier. Now, he makes another note for his Greek tragedy, which will emerge three years later as his most impressive work to date, the trilogy *Mourning Becomes Electra*.

It will be several months, however, before O'Neill brings full focus to this project. As the *André le Bon* glides from the Mediterranean into the Red Sea (Africa on one side, Arabia on the other), he throbs with ideas for future plays. *Without Endings of Days*, for which he makes only two brief notes in his Work Diary in October, will evolve five years later as *Days Without End*, an overwrought religious tract inspired chiefly by his exalted love for Carlotta. He also tinkers with another inspiration, "It Cannot Be Mad," which will linger in his mind for four years.

On the *André le Bon*, Carlotta (who shares a double-cabin with her personal maid), is enthusiastic over O'Neill's absorption (in his adjoining cabin) in what he is writing. More than ever, as she assures her diary, she has come to realize that *"His work is him & he is it."* But even with all her empathy, she will never entirely grasp what O'Neill's writing means to him, how much more necessary it is to him than even her love.

Writing serves him "as a suit of armor" against life's worries, O'Neill once told a young author, when he had begun to make a name for himself at thirty with *Bound East for Cardiff, The Long Voyage Home, The Moon of the Caribbees,* and other one-act plays of the sea. To a doctor's questionnaire asking how much time out he needed for vacations, O'Neill replied he didn't need vacations. "Writing is my vacation from living."

It was a truth that had been revealed to the twenty-four-year-old O'Neill at the Gaylord Farm Sanatorium in Wallingford, Connecticut, when he was diagnosed with tuberculosis—in those days often regarded as a death sentence. While his illness turned out to be treatable, it jolted him into an acute self-examination of the savagely destructive life he'd heretofore condemned himself to live.

He discovered he could vent his anger against his devils by writing about them as imaginary characters, rather than going head-to-head with them in his daily life. It was during his six-month stay at the sanatorium that he began writing one-act plays and, at last, found his justification for existence. He proclaimed his recovery from tuberculosis and his newfound mission as his "re-birth."

Carlotta has no inkling of what can happen when O'Neill is thwarted in his writing. Despite having experienced his recent drunken episode in France, she is yet to discover that when he can't write (and is unable to manipulate the creatures of his invented universe), he hurls himself into perverse physical behavior.

O'Neill's mood starts to darken on October 16 when the *André le Bon* docks briefly in the unrelenting heat of the port of Aden. Carlotta tries to assume a cheerful air, for it is O'Neill's fortieth birthday. "Rise at nine & give Genie his presents," she notes. By day's end, however, malaise has overcome her. She drifts off to sleep and is jolted awake by a nightmare: she's had a baby and O'Neill has left her.

By now at sea for eleven days and dazed by the heat, O'Neill has been unable to write. Worried that his grand tour of Asia will be a flop, he's having waking nightmares of his own. In port at Colombo, Ceylon, he and Carlotta drag themselves ashore and O'Neill, who feels deprived even in moderately warm weather when unable to swim, unnerves Carlotta by impetuously diving into water she regards as dubious.

They again leave the ship when it reaches Singapore on October 28, and O'Neill, once more desperate for a swim, hurls himself into a stream that Carlotta fears is polluted. A few days later in Saigon, he insists on immersing himself in "a mud hole," as Carlotta disgustedly describes it.

"I am certain we are en route to Hell," she writes. But on her way there, she manages a detour to purchase several yards of the black satin-silk she knows is unique to Saigon. After a brief stop in Hong Kong, she and O'Neill are afloat on the China Sea, en route to Shanghai.

Plagued by weak lungs ever since his bout with TB, O'Neill begins to suffer from one of his periodic respiratory infections—what he calls "flu"—and both he and Carlotta are once again "in awful state of nerves."

On reaching Shanghai, O'Neill agrees to take a break in their voyage and Carlotta, much relieved, settles him in bed at the Palace Hotel. "Am back at my old job of being a nurse," she writes on November 11. The hotel doctor, Alexander Renner, gives O'Neill a shot against his respiratory infection, and a second shot to calm his nerves. Carlotta grumbles that O'Neill's swims in the foul tropical waters "didn't do him any good."

Dr. Renner visits daily, and by November 15, O'Neill has recovered sufficiently to walk about his room. During the next few days, he is strong enough to do some sightseeing, but his Work Diary entry for those days says only "November 14-21 Shanghai (Palace) 'Flu.'"

He doesn't mention to Carlotta that he has run into an old acquaintance from his Greenwich Village days—Alfred Batson, a twenty-eight-year-old Canadian, now a reporter on the *North China Daily News*; at first O'Neill is alarmed, but Batson assures him that his paper, with a circulation of only 7,500, won't be interested in O'Neill's presence as a tourist in China. At O'Neill's request, Batson leads him on tours of the city. "He particularly loved the Police Museum," Batson recalled years later, "where they had an exotic display of torture items confiscated from the Chinese."

On November 18, O'Neill and Carlotta attend a dog race as guests of Dr. Renner and his wife. Instead of inspiriting O'Neill, the outing, in Carlotta's words, leaves him "exhausted and depressed," and on the following day he is withdrawn and silent. Carlotta shudders as she recalls the Louis Kantor drinking episode. Suspicious of Batson, she thinks she recognizes the signs.

The first glow of O'Neill's rapturous love for Carlotta has dimmed. He has stopped writing and has too much time to brood about how he has walked out on his children and how badly he and Agnes are treating each other. Even more pressing, he is stewing about what Agnes's thirst for revenge is likely to cost him. With large sums still accumulating from *Strange Interlude*, he feels he has earned the freedom to write at his own pace and to live comfortably without rushing to put a new play into production.

He simply cannot stomach the idea of being forced to generate income for the living expenses of an ex-wife. As he'd written to Elizabeth Shepley Sergeant before leaving for China, he is infuriated that Agnes's lawyers are "trying to hold me up for an agreement that would make me her financial slave for life."

Carlotta has correctly read the signs of O'Neill's sense of entrapment. He begins to drink.

On November 21, well-started on a drunken binge, he offhandedly agrees to let Batson interview him in his suite, after which, saying nothing to Carlotta, he leaves the hotel. She waits alone in their suite, hour after hour, in a panic about her lover's whereabouts.

As she later records: "About 1 a.m. Gene comes in the sitting-room— sees me—& weaves over to me (*filthy*, Black-Irish drunk) & says, 'What the h___ [sic] are you doing here?'

"When I could talk I said, 'I was waiting for you—I was frightened.' He drew back & said, 'No———[sic] is going to keep tabs on me!' And he knocked me flat!" (O'Neill had called her a "God-damned whore," she later told José Quintero, the director to whom, after O'Neill's death, she consigned the Broadway premiere of *Long Day's Journey Into Night*.)

Carlotta manages to continue her diary account at 1:10 a.m. She notes that Tuwe—hearing O'Neill stumble out of the suite's sitting room—comes running to help her: "I was shaking so I could hardly stand. I was terrified." She says she "wept like a fool."

Tuwe washes Carlotta's face and Carlotta calls the hotel's night manager. She asks him to get her a room in the best hotel that will take her immediately. She changes her clothes, makes sure she has her checkbook, and, taking only some hand luggage, leaves the Palace for the Hotel Astor.

She instructs Tuwe to keep an eye on O'Neill and to call Dr. Renner. She begins to wonder if O'Neill "knocked A. about." And she vows, "He'd not do that to me again—drunk or sober!" In the late morning, Carlotta instructs Tuwe to pack her trunk and send it to the Hotel Astor. The next day, November 23, Carlotta notes she is ill, weak, has a sore throat, and has been ordered by Dr. Renner to stay in bed.

According to Batson's later account, O'Neill telephones him to come to the Palace Hotel. He says Carlotta has left him. Drunk and maudlin, he tells a rambling story about her departure: he and Carlotta had an argument when he refused to leave his room, where he was quietly and happily getting plastered. He'd become jealous because Carlotta, requiring an escort, had asked the respectably married assistant hotel manager to be her guide on a sightseeing expedition. "I hit her when she got back," he confesses.

Much later—at about 10:00 p.m.—O'Neill and Batson go out on the town, drinking in a dance hall until two in the morning. When they leave the dance hall, O'Neill stumbles after walking a few feet, then sits down on the curb and begins to weep. Needing an excuse for his bathetic behavior, he mumbles that he has been "a son of a bitch to Agnes, and a terrible father"; he's not about to confess to Batson his fear that the divorce will cost him the financial security he'd recently attained, and perhaps diminish Carlotta's worshipful love for him.

Batson manages to get O'Neill back to his hotel at around 4:00 a.m. He's in terrible shape, shaking and sweating. Batson, frightened, rouses Dr. Renner, who gives O'Neill something to quiet him. Batson leaves after the doctor assures him he'll arrange for O'Neill to be admitted to the British hospital, and will notify Carlotta.

Carlotta snappishly notes on November 24 that O'Neill drank himself into a coma "or some such!" and is in the hospital; "His newspaper friends can look after him!" As for herself, she plans to return to France—alone.

Dr. Renner calls on Carlotta the next day at the Astor Hotel. Although still fuming, she yields to the doctor's plea and accompanies him to the hospital. "There the beauty is," she sneers to her diary, "turning on all the Irish charm & looks terrible!" She protests she doesn't want to give her life "to a man that knocks women down," and that she will never feel for him as she once did.

"I do not trust him!" she cries. Nonetheless, messengers carry notes back and forth during O'Neill's six-day hospital stay. "I love you—always and forever!" O'Neill writes. "Forgive me! I'll be a good 'un in future— do my damnedest best to! A million kisses, Blessed!"

It now occurs to Alfred Batson that while O'Neill, as a tourist, was not news, the famous and reclusive American dramatist lying ill in a Shanghai hospital bed is a scoop. Trying to accommodate both his loyalty to his paper and his friendship for O'Neill, he files a quiet story about the playwright's hospitalization, stating (although he knows better) that O'Neill is "recuperating from a severe indisposition contracted by underestimating the force of the sun's rays while bathing."

O'Neill, normally a prolific letter-writer, corresponds with barely anyone during the nearly four months of his Far Eastern voyage. When he does write to his friend and former dentist, Saxe Commins, he makes no mention of the turbulence he has been undergoing; he simply growls, "The climate is enervating—bad for work," and adds, "Tropics wore me out."

Ever reticent about the episode, O'Neill, even eighteen years later, dissembled. In an interview with Elizabeth Sergeant for a proposed biography (never written), he told her: "Had a touch of sun at Singapore because did what Englishmen and mad dogs did—bathed at noon."

It isn't long before correspondents for the American papers are chasing the story in Shanghai—just one more hurdle to jump for the put-upon Carlotta. "The ghastly heartache of it all!" she laments in her diary on November 27. "Serves me right."

Although still angry, she consents to a reconciliation after O'Neill agrees to abort their Asian tour. On December 1, O'Neill joins her at the Astor House Hotel to convalesce and she resigns herself, once again, to looking after him.

He seems remorseful, but Carlotta, far from reassured, scribbles her bleak thoughts about the future and deplores the recent past. With scant knowledge of what triggers the alcoholic psyche, she despairs, "Why drink when you know you are not sane with alcohol in you—literally not sane!"

After retrieving O'Neill's luggage from the Palace Hotel, Carlotta books passage to Europe for December 12 on the S.S. *Coblenz*, again under assumed names: "James O'Brien" for O'Neill and "Mrs. and Miss Drew" for herself and Tuwe.

By now, the reporters are swarming. On December 9, one of them tries to make his way into Carlotta's hotel room while she's in her bath. "I can't go on [in] this cheap, insane way!" she agonizes. Although O'Neill pleads with her to forget "all the hell" they've been through, Carlotta suspects that this is "just the beginning!"

O'Neill cables Weinberger, instructing his lawyer to misinform the press that he is planning to sail for Honolulu and will spend the winter there. *The New York Times* will report this "news" on December 13, adding that O'Neill is "extremely reticent and inclined to view the public's interest in his health with disfavor." But the international press continues to speculate about O'Neill's health and whereabouts.

As prearranged, Carlotta (with her loyal Tuwe) boards the S.S. *Coblenz* in the early morning of December 12. She places a note in O'Neill's empty cabin on her way to her own: "Darling, Let us try to start again—a new existence loving each *other* more than ourselves!" She invokes her wayward lover to throw off "the poison of an outside world that has crept into our lungs and hearts," and find again beauty, health, rest, and happiness. "Let us be such *good friends* now dearest . . . I love you."

About an hour later, Dr. Renner ushers O'Neill to his cabin. Perhaps O'Neill reads the note, perhaps not, but shortly after the doctor leaves, O'Neill "snaps" (in Carlotta's phrase) and swallows a large dose of his sedative. She can once again see "the danger signals"; after trying to minister to him and being rebuffed, she writes: "My illusion that *all will* be *well* smashed—things seem blacker—his brain befogged!"

O'Neill continues to drink despite his promises. Three days out to sea, Carlotta is dismayed when, instead of joining her for lunch in the dining salon, he orders a Scotch sent to his cabin. More and more, Carlotta fears she has made a dreadful mistake in eloping with O'Neill. She determines yet again to leave him, promising herself she will depart the ship when it reaches Hong Kong. But before it does, O'Neill assures Carlotta he will regard the remainder of their trip as "a cure," and he makes what appears to be a genuine effort, taking regular meals for a time and apparently foreswearing alcohol.

Carlotta decides to give him another chance but again the effort is short-lived. Indeed, the voyage back to Europe is turning into a gallows farce. Their liaison has already become a boilerplate for all the notorious and salacious love affairs to be blazoned in the press in years to come.

In Manila, on December 18, reporters board the *Coblenz* en masse. "Interminable interviews," Carlotta notes. "I am nearly frantic. Newspaper men after Gene everywhere—& keep after him until the boat sails." She is horrified to discover that some of the reporters are searching for her. The ship's engineer comes to her rescue, locking her into her cabin and keeping the key until the reporters have left.

O'Neill grows overwrought after receiving concerned cables from friends in New York. By now he has found a new drinking companion, an American newspaperman named F. Theo Rogers, who happens to have the cabin next to Carlotta's.

On Christmas day, O'Neill, somewhat perfunctorily, gives Carlotta an inscribed script of *Dynamo* and begins writing her a poem for her approaching fortieth birthday on the twenty-eighth—which he never finishes.

On her birthday, she encounters a drunken O'Neill, who neglects to wish her happiness. She takes it upon herself, with Tuwe's help, to search his cabin and, in a futile gesture, they remove the liquor they find. "Gene is off again and it won't be pretty this time because he has found a drunk to drink with him," Carlotta notes.

The following day, O'Neill bursts into Carlotta's cabin in a fury, demanding his liquor back. He is, in Carlotta's underlined words, "<u>Gone! Ghastly! Drunk!</u>" All but defeated, she gasps, "If I had the guts, I'd kill myself!" By now, O'Neill's identity is no longer a secret and many of the ship's crew, as well as some of the passengers, are aware of the friction between the celebrated American playwright and the famously beautiful actress who is his mistress.

On New Year's Eve, Carlotta admits defeat. She has learned that O'Neill has abandoned his own cabin and is now drinking and sleeping in Rogers's. "Gene has behaved abominably—& I can't take any more," she notes. "What a filthy mess! How this would please A. and well it might. She wins! *We are what we are!*" At her wit's end, she asks the ship's purser to assist her in leaving the *Coblenz* at Colombo, their next stop, on New Year's Day.

Early on the morning of January 1, 1929, Carlotta, with Tuwe's aid, leaves the *Coblenz* in the ship's launch. She books a room at the Grand Oriental Hotel in Colombo and then—fearing her desertion will result in ever more destructive behavior on O'Neill's part—she sends Tuwe back to the *Coblenz* to look after him for the duration of his voyage.

Numb with despair and groggy from medication given her by the ship's doctor, she sits on her hotel veranda at dusk and watches the *Coblenz*, with O'Neill on board, sail out of the harbor. "I feel as if she were pulling my entrails with her," Carlotta writes in her desolation.

With her know-how and ready money, Carlotta has little trouble booking a spacious cabin on a liner called the *President Monroe*, sailing for Europe on January 2. After receiving a radiogram from Tuwe, reporting that O'Neill is "still sleeping heavily" in Rogers's cabin, she cashes a check for $1,000—a sizable chunk of it earmarked for the generous tips with which she routinely smooths her way—and boards the *President Monroe*. "Again on my way!" reads her stoical diary entry.

As she worries about O'Neill, she receives another radiogram from Tuwe, this time reporting that he is still drinking, and that he is furious with Carlotta—who calms herself with a haircut, shampoo, and massage. On January 5, in answer to a request for news of O'Neill, Tuwe reports from the *Coblenz* that he hasn't stopped drinking and is still furious.

"PLEASE DO ALL YOU CAN TO HELP HIM," Carlotta radios back—and at last receives a somewhat reassuring answer from Tuwe: "DR. HAS VISITED HIM AND HE WILL STOP DRINKING IF YOU JOIN HIM IN EUROPE." Carlotta responds, "IF HE STOPS DRINKING AND GETS WELL I WILL." But she feels "shaken and weak," asking herself what are the "*wise*," the "*decent*," the "*fair*" things to do—"What would be *best for him*?"

On January 6, Carlotta receives a radiogram from the *Coblenz*'s doctor, reporting on a long talk he has had with O'Neill and enclosing a message from O'Neill himself:

DEAREST FORGIVE ME BUT NEED YOUR HELP MORE
THAN EVER BEFORE BECAUSE I AM HALF MAD WITH
UTTER LONELINESS WITHOUT FRIENDS PLANS OR
HOPES . . . I LOVE YOU.

After adding that he had promised the doctor to stop drinking, he asked,

HOW ARE YOU I FEEL SO TERRIBLY WORRIED
ABOUT YOU.

The next days unroll as a series of scenes from a Frank Capra comedy: Carlotta and O'Neill, both heading for Europe, separately afloat on the Red Sea, send radio messages back and forth between the *Coblenz* and the

President Monroe. The messages on both sides are loving, but Carlotta is gnawed by doubt. Has she the strength, she asks her diary on January 8, to live with O'Neill's unpredictable, nerve-racking foibles? And does she really love him "that unselfishly & that deeply?" She answers herself: "I'm afraid I do!"

That same day, O'Neill radios her that there's a good chance his ship will dock at Port Said at approximately the same time as hers—a coincidence Capra couldn't have improved on. O'Neill begs his "DEAREST ONE" to help him arrange for the two of them to "TALK SOMEHOW IF ONLY FIVE MINUTES"; it will mean "EVERYTHING IN THE WORLD" to him. Later that day he vows, "I WILL BE THERE IF I HAVE TO SWIM."

Three more days elapse before Carlotta fully regains her "faith and belief in Gene." And then, with her encouragement, O'Neill makes arrangements to hop from the *Coblenz* to the *President Monroe*, which will enable them to spend the final two weeks of their voyage back to Europe together.

Both ships at last drop anchor at Port Said, albeit at some distance from each other. Several suspenseful hours ensue, with messages flying between the two ocean liners. At last, at two in the morning on January 14, a police launch bearing O'Neill pulls alongside the *President Monroe.* He gives Carlotta a sheepish kiss and mumbles, "I'm sorry, I love you."

For the third time since their elopement, Carlotta's mothering instinct gets the better of her. Recording their anticlimactic reunion, she notes, "He is the man I've loved—and *always will love!* Oh, God—oh, God." O'Neill's recorded reaction is no less rapturous: "Carlotta again!—and happiness!"

Carlotta is amazed to find O'Neill "calm, sure, gentle, understanding"—and planning a solid future. "Genie has come home!" she marvels. "My dreams have come true."

At forty, O'Neill is convinced he has at last locked himself securely into his suit of armor and thrown away the key. He believes himself heroically headed for a lifetime of sobriety, his faith in his own genius unshakable. But it is the rare alcoholic who never again slips.

In any case, his bone-deep knowledge of the drunkard's plight will not go to waste; he will compulsively revisit the alcoholic landscape he himself is trying to flee, transmuting that knowledge into art in a final quartet of autobiographical tragedies in which he will repeatedly summon the device of drunkenness as a truth serum, freeing his characters (and himself) to reveal their tormented souls.

"I may be drunk enough to tell you the truth," says Jamie Tyrone, the soul-dead older brother of *Long Day's Journey Into Night*, poised to reveal his malevolent wish to destroy his younger brother's future.

"He'll promise you anything when he's full of whiskey," the tragic Josie Hogan despairs to her father in *A Moon for the Misbegotten*, believing herself betrayed by that same Jamie Tyrone.

"It's the liquor talking," says Con Melody, the self-pitying protagonist of *A Touch of the Poet*, defending his indefensible malice toward his wife and daughter.

As for *The Iceman Cometh*, it is the American theater's definitive and devastating portrait of drunken delusion—O'Neill's gigantic gasp of gratitude for the fate he finally, miraculously circumvented.

7

"What a joy to be away from a boat—and in Europe again," writes Carlotta on January 21, 1929, the day she and O'Neill disembark at Genoa and begin to make their way, by hired car, back to France. Within a week, they have rented the Villa Les Mimosas on the Riviera's Cap d'Ail.

In his Work Diary, O'Neill glumly records that he spent zero "creative work days" in January. He resolves that this will not be the case in February, telling himself his attempt at a Far East voyage, despite its tragicomic snags, has been worthwhile; "a million impressions" have been jammed into his brain, he writes to a few close friends.

To nine-year-old Shane and his three-year-old sister, Oona, O'Neill composes the carefully worded letter he knows Agnes will read: "I think of you both a lot and sometimes I want to see you so much that I feel like taking the first boat to America—but I have such important business to attend to over here that I have to stay for a while longer."

Responding to Harry Weinberger's news that Agnes had been ill, O'Neill asks Shane and Oona to tell their mother he is "damned sincerely sorry"; he goes on to claim that when he himself was sick in the hospital in Shanghai, "all the bitterness got burned out of" him and "the future years will prove this."

He tells his two young children that he loves them both very dearly and, as always, he asks them not to forget their "Daddy." And to almost-nineteen-year-old Eugene Jr., the son from his first marriage, he confides that "the whole trip, in spite of sickness and the lousy publicity I ran into, was a wonderful, stimulating experience that I wouldn't have missed for a million."

Dreading the Broadway opening of *Dynamo*, O'Neill rereads his script and regrets there isn't sufficient time to rewrite the entire play. To an old theater colleague he later explains that *Dynamo* was written at a time when he "shouldn't have written anything" because he was in "a continual inward state of bitter fury and resentment" and his "brains were woolly with hatred" for Agnes.

What he's embarrassed to admit is that his brains had been woolly not only with hatred for Agnes, but from his reckless return to alcohol—a lapse that nearly cost him Carlotta.

When *Dynamo* opens on February 11 at the Martin Beck Theatre, the *Times*'s Brooks Atkinson charitably discerns in the play "a lashing, poetic fury." Most of the other critics dislike it.

What bothers O'Neill the most is the disapproval of George Jean Nathan, who tells him that *Dynamo* is "far, far below you." Since Nathan has always been an ardent booster of his work, O'Neill is rattled. Nathan's enthusiasm dates from 1917, when he and H. L. Mencken were editing *The Smart Set*—which they modestly styled "a magazine of cleverness." They had the vision then to publish three of O'Neill's early one-act sea plays—*The Long Voyage Home*, *'Ile*, and *The Moon of the Caribbees*. O'Neill couldn't believe his good luck; seventy-five dollars per play, at a time when he was barely able to support himself. His first serious recognition, it marked the start of his long-lasting friendship with Nathan.

The jabs at *Dynamo* keep coming. "A womb with a view," Noël Coward calls it. And *The New Yorker*, to accompany Robert Benchley's negative critique, publishes a ditty: "Eeny, Meeny, Mynamo / I have been to *Dynamo*. / All except the girl in red / It was worse'n what you said!" The girl in red is a young Claudette Colbert—in the role of the seductive flapper Ada—whose legs attract considerable attention and help launch her on a robust movie career.

O'Neill's sense of humor eventually comes to his aid. "Henceforth," he tells Nathan, "I cast not only actresses but legs." More serious, O'Neill writes to De Casseres that the play would have greatly profited from his presence during rehearsals: "I had no right to let it go on without being there. . . . No one knows what I see in my stuff during rehearsals, or the changes I suggest or veto."

To take O'Neill's mind off *Dynamo*, Carlotta coaxes him into spending an evening dancing to records on their new Victrola. O'Neill sings along. He is thoughtful and tender and, as she remarks in her diary, "all self-consciousness is gone!"

Eager to know how long it will be before he and Carlotta can marry, O'Neill, succumbing once again to superstition, writes to De Casseres, requesting the help of his clairvoyant wife, Bio. O'Neill's request is off-the-wall. He proposes to telephone Bio at eleven thirty on the night of April 1 (which he may or may not realize is April Fool's Day); at that time he wants her to concentrate on his hand. He will hold it out and imagine her looking at it, and she will tell him when that promised peace is coming.

"Believe me," he vows, "I can do with it!" (A day after sending the letter, O'Neill and Carlotta read in the Paris *Herald* that Agnes has gone to Reno, but it will turn out the news is premature; Agnes has yet again delayed her departure.)

On April 1, at the specified hour, O'Neill makes his phone call and trustfully holds out his hand. Bio, obediently concentrating, tells him July is the month when he will find peace; she advises him to curb his impatience. He writes to her on May 10 that her "benign prophecy was most welcome." Agnes, he has learned, left for Reno earlier that month to begin her required six-week residency.

O'Neill also tells Bio she has "just about hit the facts on the head as to time and the relief and peace that will then be mine"; and he reminds her that on his last night in New York she predicted he was destined to turn forty-one before his "new era" began. Now five months from his birthday, he's convinced it will be then that his "inner self" will be "freed from the dead" and he will be "liberated and reborn."

ALTHOUGH DREADING AGNES might yet change her mind, Carlotta and O'Neill make tentative plans for a wedding in July. Since April, they have been house-hunting in Touraine, in the Loire Valley—the home, as O'Neill is happy to acknowledge, of Rabelais and Balzac.

A real estate agent guides them from one château to another—some, in Carlotta's view, "too grand," others "too run down for decent house-keeping." Ever since their journey to the Far East, Carlotta has longed for permanent domestic tranquillity. By that she means that her home—castle or not—must have a clean kitchen and a warm, comfortable environment where O'Neill will feel "loved—so he can *work*."

When they finally approach a château that looks suitable to Carlotta, O'Neill refuses to inspect it. "O.K., you look at it," he says. "I'll sit in the car." She coaxes him into accompanying her.

"We see *'Plessis'—just right!*" Carlotta trumpets in her diary. But the château will require considerable fixing up before it suits her. Although it has "lovely stone walks and romantic tourelles," it has no electricity, is heated only by fireplaces, and has but one toilet for its forty-five rooms; moreover, as Carlotta notes, there are "no baths (as Americans know them)."

O'Neill asks Carlotta, "Didn't they take baths?" Amused, she calls his attention to the bidet. "*I loved this place!*" she enthuses, relieved that "strangely enough, so did Gene!"

They decide on April 19 to sign a three-year lease for the formally named Le Plessis, which through the centuries has been owned by the family of the Marquis du Plessis. Carlotta asks the owners' permission to create a proper bathroom from one of the forty-five rooms; she also asks if she may install a swimming pool, having found a suitable site on the grounds. Since the château has no electricity, they will make do with oil lamps and candles; for heating they will rely on the many fireplaces.

Because Le Plessis has never been rented and is all but buried in dust, mold, and dead moths, the annual rent of $1,200 is ridiculously low.

Carlotta is flush enough to place orders for engraved silver flatware from Cartier, together with an individually designed china service, as well as monogrammed linens—all part of what it pleases her to call her "dot" (dowry). Carlotta informs James Speyer, with whom she has been in constant correspondence, of their plans, and he asks if she needs an advance on her income. She thanks him, but says no.

When reminiscing years later about her life at Le Plessis, Carlotta liked to stress that "Gene had never lived in a chateau," loftily implying that she, unlike the deprived O'Neill, was quite accustomed to the palatial life, having inhabited the grand Scottish estate that was her home during her marriage to John Moffat.

"Gene thought the idea of living in a chateau [was] very chichi and putting on airs. But I said, No, I will show you how simple chateaux are. And Gene saw that you could really be polite and live in a charming place and you didn't have to be ridiculous. I made him very comfortable."

What O'Neill thought of his château he conveyed to Kenneth Macgowan with much the same enthusiasm he'd expressed, respectively, for his homes in Provincetown, Connecticut, and Bermuda. The property encompassed seven hundred acres with "wonderful old woods attached," and, he said, "I feel soundly at home here." It was the sort of house, he told Macgowan, he'd always dreamed of, but could never have afforded in the United States.

He went on to brag about his "corking study" in one of the château's tourelles, pointing out that the price "of all this grandeur" was only a little more than one thousand dollars a month, which he and Carlotta were splitting. The estate, he added, required numerous servants, but wages were low in the French countryside and taxes were minimal. "Altogether the grandest bargain—this Le Plessis—that I've ever heard of!"

Carlotta has managed to convince herself that O'Neill, during his marriage to Agnes, lived in one hovel after another, even though she is well aware of their baronial sea-front house in Bermuda and the thirty-acre, fifteen-room estate they had owned in Ridgefield, Connecticut.

But to acknowledge that he had ever lived in comfort would diminish her own achievement.

Carlotta's vision of the aristocratic lifestyle, adopted during her marriage to her blue-blooded Scotsman, calls for separate bedrooms for herself and her mate. There are frequent references in her diary to O'Neill slipping from his bedroom to hers, seeking solace during the night.

On April 4, however, while still living in Villa Les Mimosas, Carlotta notes she and O'Neill have decided to try sleeping overnight in the same bed: "We are less nervous and rest better!" She does not specify sex but, according to the former curator of the O'Neill archives at Yale, Carlotta (after O'Neill's death) removed from her diaries "an occasional comment on their love-making sessions." About the closest she gets to describing sensual pleasure (at this juncture) is her frequent mention of shampooing O'Neill's hair and giving him what she calls "oil rubs."

While awaiting the completion of repairs to Le Plessis (scheduled for the first week in June), she and O'Neill continue to live at Villa Les Mimosas. They go sightseeing and indulge in lunches and afternoon teas on the terraces of various scenic inns; and they shop. Carlotta is being fitted at Molyneux for additions to her wardrobe; the high-fashion couturier who dresses Garbo and Gertrude Lawrence—along with the social elite of two continents—has recently opened a fashion house in Monte Carlo, within walking distance of Villa Les Mimosas.

Nor does O'Neill stint himself. A tailor comes to the villa to measure him for suits and he trades his Renault for a Mercedes. A month later, he decides he doesn't want the Mercedes after all and buys a red Bugatti. Carlotta surely can congratulate herself on having transformed her "tough mick," as she sometimes mocks him, into a proper aristocrat.

Despite his days of sightseeing and shopping, O'Neill, during April and May, devotes twenty-six "creative work days" to making notes for the visionary project he first conceived in 1926 and that eventually will compensate for the dismal failure of *Dynamo*. Variously referring to it as his "Greek tragedy plot idea," his "Life of Aeschylus idea," and his

"Electra idea," it has come increasingly to preoccupy him. In bed with Carlotta on May 11, he spreads his concept before her like a sacred offering. After providing her with his blueprint, he announces, "This will be your play." She is so moved, she can't speak.

No MATTER HOW HARD O'Neill tries to isolate himself for his writing, he seems unable to avoid intrusions. When he isn't the focus of marital scandal, he's incurring the wrath of censors and periodically getting himself banned in Boston. Now, in late May, amid his sybaritic and painstakingly acquired seclusion in France, he finds himself the victim of a widely publicized lawsuit in the United States.

Already worn down from legal battles over his divorce, he is driven to defend himself against a charge of plagiarism. While *Strange Interlude* is in the second year of its Broadway run, and with touring companies successfully launched, a woman using the pen name Georges Lewys sues O'Neill in New York's Federal Court, demanding $1.25 million in damages and an injunction against the play as both acted and published. She alleges that O'Neill stole *Strange Interlude* from her 1924 novel, *The Temple of Pallas-Athenae*.

"Woman is fool or crook or both!" an exasperated O'Neill writes in his Work Diary on May 28. Carlotta, reading about the lawsuit in the Paris *Herald*, is outraged. "What is all this?" she moans. "Are we cursed?"

O'Neill's lawyers send him the list of Georges Lewys's purported instances of plagiarism, which are blatantly absurd, and he is furious about the time and money it will cost to defend himself from the bogus charges.

"Some blackmail! Some Gal!" he fumes to his publisher. "She's crazy, but—she's crazy like a fox! A million dollars' worth of publicity for nothing! I lose no matter how I win! It's a grand law that permits such stunts to get by!" (The lawsuit will drag on until April 1931, and ends with O'Neill being awarded $7,500 in costs, which he's unable to collect from the bankrupt Lewys.)

In anticipation of his marriage in July, O'Neill tries to shrug off his irritation with the lawsuit. He doesn't want to dim Carlotta's happiness.

While it's true Carlotta is aglow, she has not forgotten her anger at those of O'Neill's friends she deems false, and is plotting to cut them off once she is Mrs. Eugene O'Neill. She turns for help to Saxe Commins, who by now has been added to her list of best friends. Carlotta regards Commins as absolutely loyal, even though she is aware he once participated with O'Neill in the bohemian lifestyle she detests. Commins, a would-be writer and devotee of the arts, and recently married to Dorothy Berliner, a concert pianist, is soon (in 1933) to become the editor of O'Neill's published plays at Random House.

Carlotta asks the Comminses' help in weeding out those false friends. If either of them have heard any recent slanders of O'Neill or herself, would they share them with her, for it would help—as she phrases it—in their "elimination." This, says Carlotta, would give her and O'Neill "more time for those we love—& who really love us!"

Writing trustfully to Commins, Carlotta warns him not to disclose O'Neill's French address to anyone. And if anyone says she is "ruining" O'Neill and "spending all his money—say 'yes'—and that I'm planning to *eat* his children & my own!"

In Carlotta's mind, it is actually Agnes who is spending O'Neill's money and ruining her own children. Although the divorce seems assured, Carlotta regards Agnes as spiteful and treacherous enough to do an about-face, even now.

As she tells Commins, Agnes "has never been known to keep her word in anything," and she "cannot distinguish a lie from the truth."

PART II

ABOUT AGNES

8

Agnes Boulton checked into a dude ranch outside Reno in early May 1929. Away from her children, isolated from her friends, she had time enough to ponder her failed marriage.

She knew O'Neill had come to loathe her, as only a man can who was once possessed by love. And, in truth, she herself had come to feel little but contempt for O'Neill. Yet his leaving rankled. Aware she could have been the heroine of one of her own pulp-fiction romances, she marveled that her once-ardent, utterly dependent Gene could have wiped from his mind the nearly ten years of their partnership, those exciting (if sometimes trying) years when he was striving for recognition.

She had been his lover, his bedrock, his shield; together they had celebrated his triumphs, commiserated over his failures. She had shared his grief during his father's agonizing final illness, his shock at his mother's sudden death, the torment of his brother's ultimate alcoholic disintegration.

It seemed incredible that her Gene could erase from memory all the hours she had devoted to nursing, reassuring, and mothering him during his own frequent illnesses, both physical and emotional. How could he have stonily turned his back on her and their children? Was it true, as he'd hinted, that she could have held him if she'd put up a fight? But did she, after all, really regret that the marriage was over?

Her writer's instinct surely told her this was a story any number of magazines would pay for generously—but O'Neill and his lawyers had anticipated that possibility and, under the terms of the divorce agreement now before the Reno court, Agnes has been prohibited from profiting in any such way.

AGNES WAS TWENTY-FOUR, five years younger than O'Neill, when they first met in Greenwich Village in 1917. A young woman with a sure sense of her own allure, she had large blue-gray eyes and high cheekbones and she wore her smooth brown hair in a bun, sometimes concealing it under a becoming cloche. She had come to New York on one of her excursions from the Connecticut dairy farm she shared with her family, which included three younger sisters who, like her, inherited their bohemian outlook from their parents.

Her father, Edward (Teddy) William Boulton, was a gentle, blue-eyed, white-mustached landscape and portrait painter from an upper-crust Philadelphia family. Her mother, Cecil, an early feminist with a mystical bent, believed in free love, nude sunbathing, and smoking in public for women, and she had occasionally posed in the nude for her husband's painter-colleagues at the Philadelphia Art Students League.

A Catholic convert, she raised her four daughters in the Church, but evidently saw no conflict between her religious beliefs and her feminist views—nor between her feminism and her devotion to domesticity, which included baking for her husband.

Teddy's fees, although he was praised as an artist, were not always sufficient to support his family, and Agnes helped out with her modest earnings from the romance stories she sold to pulp-fiction magazines. She also sold the milk from her cows, but the dairy business was in a slump. Her current excursion to New York was to find part-time work in a factory, while also meeting with prospective editors in an effort to further her writing career.

Agnes hoped her family would be "happy on the farm," as she recalled offhandedly in *Part of a Long Story*, her memoir of the first three years of her involvement with O'Neill, published nearly thirty years after their divorce and five years after O'Neill's death. "I had to go to New York for their sake and mine, to make more money, and I would return! But I did not return—not until many years later."

Agnes could clearly recall the night in November 1917 when she first encountered O'Neill. It was a casual meeting, typical of its time and place. Clutching her savings of a hundred dollars (a substantial sum equal to more than $2,000 today), Agnes had checked into the reasonably priced Brevoort Hotel at Fifth Avenue and Eighth Street. A gathering place for young Village artists, it had been recommended by Mary Pyne, a fledgling actress. Pyne and her husband, Harry Kemp (labeled the "hobo poet" by the press), were friends of Agnes's mother, who had invited them to stay on the Boulton farm the previous summer.

From the Brevoort, Agnes telephoned Christine Ell, with whom she had a slight acquaintance from previous visits to New York. It was Christine who, on one of those visits, mentioned the sought-for factory job and Agnes now hoped for more specific information.

Christine and her husband, Louis Ell, owned the intimate restaurant above the Playwrights' Theatre at 139 Macdougal Street, run by the Provincetown Players. She invited Agnes to meet her at ten thirty that night (after closing time at her establishment) at a nearby saloon called the Golden Swan.

Christine cautioned that the saloon, on the southeast corner of Sixth Avenue and Fourth Street, in no way lived up to its fancy name and, in fact, was known to its boozing denizens as the "Hell Hole." Promptly at ten thirty, Agnes, as instructed, entered by the side door that led to the ladies' section of a typical Irish saloon, separated by swinging doors from the men's barroom.

Agnes seated herself in the dingy, dimly lit space that smelled of beer and tobacco smoke. Christine had not yet arrived, and Agnes, glancing about uneasily, noticed a dark-haired man wearing a seaman's sweater under his jacket staring at her from a table in a far corner. When

Christine at last arrived, she embraced Agnes and greeted the man in the seaman's sweater, who silently joined them at their table. Christine introduced him: "This is Gene O'Neill."

Christine was a strapping woman, with outsized hips and breasts and a tumble of red-gold hair. O'Neill, long since drawn to her earthy warmth, once referred to her as "a female Christ." Christine was the illegitimate daughter of a Danish army captain and a peasant girl, who brought Christine as a young child to America, where her stepfather raped her when she was fourteen.

After a miserable life as a domestic and a factory worker, and innumerable humiliating short-lived love affairs, Christine was inspired by a speech in which Emma Goldman held forth on society's wrongful neglect of such people as herself, and she pulled herself together. (Three years later, Christine would serve as a part model for O'Neill's Swedish-born Anna Christie, and—with far greater poignancy—she would spark the compassionate, self-mocking giantess, Josie Hogan, in O'Neill's final play, *A Moon for the Misbegotten*.)

Both Christine and her husband—a sometime carpenter for the Provincetown Players—cooked at her restaurant and, although she claimed to be madly in love, she was routinely unfaithful to him. A generous friend and an enthusiastic matchmaker, she had decided to watch over Agnes in the Village.

Agnes was marginally aware of the existence of the Provincetown Players, who only the year before had established the Playwrights' Theatre, with O'Neill as resident wunderkind. But having little interest in the theater, she had never heard of the wunderkind himself.

When O'Neill left the table to fetch another drink, Christine told Agnes he was awaiting his brother, Jamie, because he was broke, and Jamie had promised to show up with some money. "Jamie makes love to every woman he meets," Christine warned Agnes, implying Christine herself was one among them.

Jamie soon arrived. As Agnes remembered, he was wearing a suit of loud black-and-white checks and a bowler hat, a topcoat slung over his arm, a small carnation in his buttonhole. "What ho!" he boomed, in the carrying voice he'd inherited from his actor father. He immediately began flirting with Agnes (and would later quip that he wished he had seen her first).

When the O'Neill brothers repaired to the men's barroom for a private talk, Christine told Agnes that the factory she'd spoken of the year before had closed. It was clear to Agnes she would have to sell a new pulp romance soon; her hundred dollars would not support her for long. But at the moment she was distracted by the yearning gaze she'd seen in Gene O'Neill's dark eyes.

She was startled to learn from Christine that Eugene not only did much of his drinking in the Hell Hole, but that also he actually lived in one of the second-floor rooms rented out by the owner, Tom Wallace. Himself an alcoholic, Wallace often drank with O'Neill and other of the Hell Hole's resident cronies into the early hours of the morning. (Wallace was resurrected by O'Neill years later as part model for the saloon keeper Harry Hope in *The Iceman Cometh*.)

The Hell Hole was an oasis for shady politicians, gamblers, corrupt cops, touts, pimps, and whores, not to mention a number of O'Neill's own friends, many of them struggling writers like himself, along with young actors, painters, and newspapermen.

It was in the Hell Hole, in whose dreary depths O'Neill felt at home, that he was adopted by a brutish Irish street gang, the Hudson Dusters; impressed with him as an Irishman and a coming writer, they called him "the kid."

O'Neill liked to tell a story of how they looked after him, citing a time when he was sleeping off a drunk in the back room. "I woke to find I had been robbed of all my pocket money, ten dollars and a silver watch, which my mother had given me. I told the bartender about it. Next day when I came in he called me aside, handed me the watch and the money and said: 'Nothin' happened. See?'" O'Neill saw.

Observing O'Neill's evident interest in Agnes, Christine murmured, "Well, he's fallen for you, darling. I can see that." Bewildered, Agnes asked Christine what O'Neill worked at. He wrote plays, said Christine, to which Agnes replied she didn't care about the theater. But she was interested to know why, with America ten months into the war, O'Neill hadn't yet been drafted. Christine told Agnes he'd registered for the draft in June; but he was an outspoken opponent of the war and, luckily for him, he'd been deferred because of his earlier bout with tuberculosis.

The hard-drinking, pacifist playwright had aroused Agnes's interest and she accepted his offer to accompany her across Washington Square to her hotel.

"Gene said nothing until we reached the steps in front of the Brevoort," she later recalled, "and I put out my hand to say goodnight." Then he began to talk drunkenly.

"I wish I could remember what he said, but I can't," wrote Agnes. "I don't think I quite knew—even then." She said she "must go upstairs"; but she lingered.

At last, in a low voice, O'Neill declaimed: "I want to spend every night of my life from now on with you. I mean this. Every night of my life." Agnes was stunned: "I thought him the strangest man I had ever met."

Unlike some other parts of Agnes's story, this first meeting, as she later described it, has the ring of truthful recollection. Written in her late sixties when she was in frail health from years of uncontrolled drinking, her story often seemed to be composed in a haze of suppressed resentment and anger as she "remembered"—or alternately took slapdash guesses at—the events she depicted.

Kenneth Macgowan, who knew O'Neill and Agnes more intimately than most of their other contemporaries, appraised Agnes's memoir, *Part of a Long Story*, as a contradictory mixture. In a letter to the authors of this biography written shortly after the memoir's publication, Macgowan wrote, "She gets some things about Gene very clear indeed—fearing to meet people and issues, desire for torture, drive to work, a kind of cumbersome sentimentalism. But she pours on the romance and remembers too much and too little."

There is, however, enough substance in her memoir to form at least a sketchy landscape of her early life with O'Neill. According to Agnes (and others), within a few days of her first meeting with O'Neill, she learned from Christine that the man who had just declared his wish to spend every night of his life with her—the moody, habitually drunk, and always unpredictable Gene O'Neill—was the beacon around which the Provincetown Players fervently clustered.

Shortly before Agnes's arrival in the Village, his one-act play *The Long Voyage Home* had captivated a discerning opening-night audience at the Playwrights' Theatre. The play depicted a Swedish seaman who is shanghaied as he is about to return to his longed-for life on a farm. Opening on November 2, it had followed the previous year's one-act triumph, O'Neill's *Bound East for Cardiff,* which inaugurated the Players' first New York season on November 3, 1916. *Cardiff,* powerfully realistic, stripped bare the sentiments of a dying, rough-hewn sailor reliving—and regretting—his wasted life at sea.

Some days after meeting O'Neill, Agnes, baffled at not having heard from him since he'd made his drunken vow, arrived at a party hosted by Christine at her restaurant. Agnes was hoping O'Neill might be there and suddenly she saw him enter the crowded room. She realized he was deliberately ignoring her and, after watching him gulp from a pocket flask, she walked up to him and said, "Hello! Remember me?" There was a brief exchange of empty pleasantries, and then he was gone. A few moments later, he climbed onto a chair to reach a clock hanging on the wall above a mantelpiece.

He glared at the hushed partygoers and twisted the hands of the clock backward, chanting the lovelorn lyrics of a currently popular Irish ballad: "Turn Back the Universe and Give Me Yesterday." His performance was greeted with embarrassed laughter.

Agnes, bewildered, feeling out of the know and out of place amid the room's gossipy (but to her incomprehensible) murmurings, began walking to the door. Glancing back at O'Neill, she saw him staring at her; she felt he was gloating over her discomfort.

At last, Agnes learned from Christine what many of O'Neill's friends had come to realize: that she bore a pronounced resemblance to Louise Bryant, a Greenwich Village habitué for whom O'Neill was known to be carrying a torch. Louise, just as youthfully appealing as Agnes (although seven years older), had broken O'Neill's heart when she chose to leave him that August, three months before Agnes's arrival in the Village. Bryant had gone off with O'Neill's good friend John Reed, one of the savviest and most courageous political and foreign correspondents of his day, to report on the Russian Revolution.

Christine told Agnes it was Louise's betrayal that had propelled O'Neill on the protracted drunk in which he was currently doing his best to drown himself. It was sometime later that Agnes learned the full story of the O'Neill-Bryant-Reed triangle that had begun in the summer of 1916.

Reed had fallen in love with Louise on a visit to his native Portland, Oregon, in 1915. The freest of free spirits, she was living in a houseboat on the Willamette River with her husband, a dentist, who was beginning to bore her—as was her job as the society reporter for a local newspaper; ambitious for a career in journalism, she managed to introduce herself to Reed and they were both instantly smitten.

Bryant followed Reed to the Village and moved into his apartment, where she awaited a divorce from her accommodating husband. In the summer of 1916, she shared a cottage with Reed in the old whaling community of Provincetown, Massachusetts. Reed and Bryant participated in the experimental presentations of the Wharf Theatre, founded the year before, and it was Reed, during an evening at the Hell Hole, who had persuaded O'Neill to showcase his early work at the Wharf.

Reed, Bryant, and O'Neill were frequently together during those summer days and evenings of rehearsals and performances. But Reed was often absent on magazine and newspaper assignments and Louise, herself dreaming of journalistic acclaim (although for the moment limiting herself to writing unpublished poetry), grew restless; she amused herself by seducing O'Neill, who fell violently in love with her.

O'Neill was torn between guilt and passion until Louise told him that she and Reed lived together as brother and sister because he suffered from a chronic kidney ailment that precluded sexual activity. O'Neill believed her. He also knew that both Reed and Bryant, along with many of their friends, accepted the notion of free love and open marriage, and Reed seemed unperturbed by Louise's fling with his good friend.

But O'Neill, fiercely jealous and possessive, wanted Louise to himself—even though there seemed to be no question that she had committed herself, for better or for worse, to Reed. O'Neill, for the next year, stewed in a kind of limbo, making love to Louise during Reed's absences, waiting for Louise to break with his friend. But Louise had no such intention; she wanted both men, and was content to lie to each for as long as necessary.

In August 1917, learning that Reed planned to go to Russia to cover the Bolshevik upheaval, Bryant wheedled an assignment from the Bell Syndicate, enabling her to accompany him. She believed that with Reed paving her way into one of the greatest stories of the era, she could at last make her reputation. It was then that she abruptly dropped O'Neill.

Just past thirty, Reed—six feet tall and ruggedly handsome—was a fearless, socially conscious journalist, gifted with a flair for stark imagery. At twenty-six, he had transported readers of the New York *World* and the *Metropolitan Magazine* to terrifying scenes of Pancho Villa's bloody revolutionary march across Mexico. His fame matched that of the *Tribune*'s superstar, Richard Harding Davis.

With the onset of the war in Europe, however, Reed became less a reporter and more an activist. He found both sides cynical and callous, and in his reports from the front he didn't hesitate to say so. His fiery antiwar stance didn't sit well with a generally pro-war American public.

By the time he was ready to leave for Russia, he could find no mainstream publication to trust him for the kind of unflinching coverage on which he'd built his reputation. Reed determined to deliver his own impassioned eyewitness account of the revolution in book form. The result would be *Ten Days That Shook the World*, an instant best seller when it was published in March 1919, and a subsequent classic.

Just before leaving with Reed for Russia, Louise, with her habitual insouciance, assured O'Neill of her constant love; she promised to write often and to return to him soon. But after hearing nothing from her for a month, O'Neill wrote to her on September 19 in care of the American vice-consul in Petrograd. He addressed her as "Sweetheart Mine":

> *I am sure hoping to get a bunch of letters from you . . . at least by the first of next month. If I don't I think I shall tie a large stone around my neck and practice perpetual submerging. It's so long, and I'm so worried!*
>
> *I love you! love you! love you! That isn't news for you but it's all in the world that I can find worth writing to you. Come back soon! I am waiting! Please Louise!*

Louise did finally write, but her letters were not the loving missives O'Neill expected, nor did she promise a timely return. O'Neill had trusted in her professions of love for him before she left New York; he hadn't realized the extent of her overarching ambition. Her exhilaration as a foreign correspondent at Reed's side far outstripped the satisfaction of being O'Neill's stay-at-home lover.

It's true she felt sure O'Neill was on the road to success, but Reed was already there, and able to further her career. At least for the time being, Reed seemed the judicious choice. Unwilling to relinquish O'Neill altogether, and confident of his adoration, she felt safe in setting him temporarily aside.

While unaware of O'Neill's ongoing correspondence with Louise, Agnes could hardly avoid the persistent Village gossip about the love affair. "When Louise touches me with her fingernail, it's like a prairie fire," O'Neill confided to an indiscreet friend, who couldn't resist broadcasting the remark.

Agnes also learned of the love poems exchanged between O'Neill and Louise, and about the stir caused when, during the Provincetowners' 1916 season, O'Neill cast himself in his one-acter *Thirst*, solely to play a steamy love scene with Louise. And everyone knew about Louise's efforts to advance O'Neill's career by persuading Waldo Frank, co-editor of the literary magazine *The Seven Arts*, to publish O'Neill's short story, "Tomorrow."

The story, inspired by Joseph Conrad, was set in a saloon for down-and-outers called Jimmy the Priest's near the Battery. Frank read it out of respect for Reed, and after O'Neill (at Frank's insistence) made some changes, it was published in June 1917. *The Seven Arts* paid O'Neill fifty dollars, the first respectable money he'd earned for creative writing.

"I thought it was pretty devastating stuff at the time," O'Neill reminisced many years later, adding that he doubted the magazine's editors "were as overwhelmed by its hideous beauty as I was."

9

In the days following O'Neill's ostentatious flourish with the clock on the wall of Christine's restaurant, Agnes could not understand why he was keeping her at a distance, for she sensed he was as much attracted to her as she to him.

What she did not know was that he had made a vow of chastity to the faithless Louise, and he had been in a state of ambivalence about Agnes ever since his drunken declaration on their first meeting that he wanted "to spend every night" of his life with her. Now, as his attraction to Agnes ripened, and Louise's letters to him held no assurances of love and no date for her return, it dawned on him that his vow of chastity had become a sham.

"I waited until November," he glowered in a letter to Louise. "Then I gave you a month's leeway. You didn't come. Your letters were cold and indefinite. Then I cracked. No one can say I was unfaithful to you before then. But by then . . . my cross had become too heavy to bear."

It was not until late December that O'Neill struggled out from under his cross and—although still wary—turned to Agnes. While his Greenwich Village friends were certain Louise would easily reclaim him when she returned from Russia, Agnes wanted to believe Louise no longer possessed him. The first night she and O'Neill spent together was not reassuring.

It was a spectacularly cold night in early January 1918 and the circumstances were anything but romantic. In fact, the date was noteworthy chiefly because it was the first time Agnes encountered O'Neill's drunken, jealous fury. (Like Carlotta years later, she felt impelled to record the shocking details.)

That night, Agnes and O'Neill found themselves in an untidy, cramped two-room apartment whose owner was absent. In the sort of indeterminate social encounter common to the bohemians of the Village, she and O'Neill had agreed to meet there with Hutch Collins, an actor with the Provincetown Players.

Hutch had grown up with O'Neill in New London, Connecticut, where they had been best friends, united by their boyhood rebellion against the stuffy narrow-mindedness of their small town's leading citizens and their shared passion for such scandalous writers as Shaw, Ibsen, Wilde, and Swinburne. As O'Neill once put it, he and Hutch were "twin disreputables in the village gossip," which bound them "hilariously together."

After the three had sat drinking, talking, and shivering in the living room, Hutch went into the bedroom, where he lit a can of Sterno to produce some warmth. Agnes, as she recalled in her memoir, joined Hutch. She had seated herself beside him on the bed when she was suddenly confronted by O'Neill, whom she described as "tall and menacing," standing in the doorway between the two rooms.

Roughly pulling Agnes to her feet, he shoved her back into the living room and reseated himself. Standing there in a daze, Agnes concluded that O'Neill was smoldering with jealousy over what he evidently construed as a flirtation between his girl and his best friend. According to Agnes, Hutch took no notice of the incident; he soon left the apartment, and O'Neill, without a word, reentered the bedroom and threw himself, fully clothed, onto the unmade bed, apparently settling in for what was left of the night.

It wasn't long before O'Neill peremptorily ordered Agnes to join him on the bed, which she did, also fully clothed, even to her overcoat. He turned his back to her and she huddled against him for warmth. By now, it was close to dawn.

When Agnes awoke, still pressed against the soundly sleeping O'Neill, it was daylight. She was eager to return to her hotel but she wished to say a word before parting. As she hesitated, O'Neill awoke—and immediately downed a shot of whiskey. He then began to berate her in what she described as "a tirade" that was "couched in language that he had learned at sea and in the dives of the waterfront." She listened for a while, at first dumbstruck, and then, outraged, left the apartment.

Agnes's distress was washed away when, later that day, a package was delivered to her at the Brevoort. It was the manuscript of O'Neill's poetic mood play *The Moon of the Caribbees*, that completed his cycle of four early one-act sea plays later collectively produced as *S.S. Glencairn*.

The Moon of the Caribbees was inspired, O'Neill once explained, by an evening he spent on shipboard off Trinidad during his sailing days, when the moon shone and the strange songs of the natives coming over the waters mingled with the sounds aboard ship. It was plotless, as he once noted, but poetic, his "first real break with theatrical tradition." *The Moon of the Caribbees*, he later added, was his "favorite short play."

Instead of shunning O'Neill, as she had planned, Agnes hurried to the Hell Hole to tell him how moved she had been by his script. Evidently, she had passed a crucial test. O'Neill often carried the script with him, allowing friends to read it as a mark of his trust and as proof of their sensitivity. According to Agnes, O'Neill apologized to her somewhat obliquely for his earlier behavior. He confirmed what she had intuited— that when he saw her sitting on the bed, talking to Hutch, he felt a furious surge of jealousy.

Agnes managed to reassure O'Neill that it was him she was in love with. Mollified, he explained that he'd been both beguiled by and suspicious of Agnes from their first meeting. Christine, hoping to encourage his interest in Agnes, had given him a year-old clipping she'd saved from the *World* featuring an appealing photo of Agnes. The clipping had scarcely had the desired effect.

O'Neill told Agnes the photo made her look like "a washed-out nincompoop!" and went on to mock the story's wordy headline, "Woman Dairy Farmer Who's Made a Brave Fight," with its subhead explaining that there was "No Money in Milk Cows." Reading from the article and glancing up to glare at Agnes, he quoted, "'Woman dairy farmer'— Ye gods! 'Down in New York to help the poor farmers win a milk strike—young widow has supported herself, a baby and a herd of cows by her pen.'"

There ensued a lengthy soliloquy on the state of his soul, which bewildered Agnes and left her speechless. Ranting on, O'Neill at last told her of his recent turbulent love affair with Louise Bryant, bemoaning the terrible wound Louise had inflicted by her departure with Reed.

To Agnes's reasonable response that Reed did, after all, seem to have first claim on Louise's love and loyalty, O'Neill replied that Agnes didn't understand. He rattled off the fiction Louise had fed him about living with Reed as brother and sister because of Reed's impotence.

Agnes, unwilling to disillusion O'Neill, did not dispute the story, although she instinctively disbelieved it, and, of course, she was right. The truth was that while Reed did suffer from a chronic kidney ailment, sex was not proscribed; in fact, he cheerfully confessed to casual affairs in letters to Louise during his work-driven absences.

And now, although O'Neill professed to care greatly for Agnes, he told her he was not "absolutely sure" whether he was still in love with Louise. (According to O'Neill's own later account in a letter to Louise, "Agnes knew this feeling of mine and accepted it.") Ending his tirade, O'Neill declared he had no intention of ever again going through anything like his turmoil with Louise.

Agnes was growing inured to O'Neill's mood swings, which she attributed to his erratic drinking. And she was flattered by his jealousy even while fearful of it. She listened meekly as O'Neill, with strangled fury, charged her with the follies of her earlier life—particularly her marriage and the child with whom she was now burdened.

Gradually, however, O'Neill allowed Agnes to convince him that she had indefinitely ceded her child to the care of her farm-bound parents and sisters. Indeed, Agnes appeared to have given scant thought to her infant daughter; "my little girl was doing fine and hadn't even seemed to miss me," she remarked casually in her memoir, after having received a report from her mother around this time.

Satisfied that Agnes was unfettered, and never mentioning his own earlier marriage and vaporized child, O'Neill expounded to Agnes what it was that he wanted from her: for her to feel deeply at one with him, "not you and me, but us, one being, not two." That, he insisted, must be their life from now on.

Then, to Agnes's surprise, he told her he would soon be going back to Provincetown to focus on his writing. He had given up waiting for Louise to return from Russia, he said, and he was eager to develop an idea for a full-length play that was nagging at him, along with several possible one-acters.

O'Neill knew that his theater colleagues, having often heard him complain he couldn't work amid the distractions of New York, were eagerly waiting for him to leave. They needed a new O'Neill play—better still, two or three. By mid-January, the Provincetown Players were holding their collective breath.

It was then that O'Neill asked Agnes if she would come with him to Provincetown. She said yes.

O'NEILL IMMEDIATELY SET about obtaining accommodations for himself and Agnes. On January 16, he wrote to John A. Francis, the amiable owner of a general store in Provincetown who also rented studio apartments, asking him to make the arrangements. While waiting to leave, Agnes moved from her cramped hotel room to a two-room apartment on

Waverly Place, where O'Neill could show up and make himself comfortable when he chose.

He was postponing his departure until after Louis Holladay returned to the Village. Holladay, who, after Hutch Collins, O'Neill counted as his most intimate friend, had been working on a fruit farm in Oregon. He and Holladay had met at Princeton in 1906 during O'Neill's freshman (and only) year there. Although Holladay did not attend Princeton, he had several friends among O'Neill's classmates, whom he often visited.

When one of them had chanced to introduce Holladay to O'Neill, they quickly recognized each other as kindred souls—both social rebels, both avid readers, both content to live like gypsies, and neither able to go for long without a drink. Their bonding continued after O'Neill was dismissed from Princeton by the Committee on Examinations and Standings "for poor scholastic standing." (Eugene, convinced he could learn more out of college than in, wanted no Ivy-stamped niche in life; like Shaw and O'Casey, he ultimately demonstrated that a college education was not essential to the writing of great plays.)

In New York, Holladay and O'Neill explored the city's dives together, living off odd jobs and handouts from their families. Holladay was "the most loved man friend Gene ever had," as he told Carlotta years later.

There is good reason to believe that in 1910, when both were twenty-two, Holladay accompanied O'Neill as a paying apprentice seaman aboard the clipper ship *Charles Racine*, bound for Buenos Aires. O'Neill, romanticizing his episode at sea in the many interviews he gave when he became famous, never mentioned a companion, probably because it would have made him sound less heroic. But he did tell Nina Moise, soon to direct his play *The Rope*, and in whom he often confided during his early Greenwich Village days, that Holladay had accompanied him on the Norwegian clipper ship. (Both of their passages had been paid by O'Neill's father.)

Five years after the trip, O'Neill and Holladay were bumming around together in Greenwich Village, where Holladay's sister owned a popular restaurant called Polly's, and where Holladay himself had opened a restaurant called The Sixty.

Holladay had borrowed the money for the restaurant from Louise Norton, who became Holladay's lover. But Holladay began drinking heavily and forgot to apply for a liquor license and the police closed the restaurant.

His romance with Louise Norton, whom he wanted to marry, was beginning to falter as well; she said she would not marry him unless he demonstrated he could stay sober, and he agreed to go out to the Northwest and establish himself as a fruit farmer while curing himself of his drinking habit.

Now, some months later, he had written to assure his Louise he'd achieved his goal; he'd quit drinking, had grown fit and happy at his labor, and had saved enough money to keep himself and a wife. He asked his friends to stand by for a celebration, and on January 22, O'Neill, Agnes, and a number of others gathered at the Hell Hole.

As Agnes remembered, that night of confusion and fear began joyfully. She, O'Neill, and others in their group greeted Holladay, who was triumphantly cold sober; when Louise Norton arrived, the two sat together at a small table, talking privately. Agnes, watching them, recalled that she felt an unsettling if vague uneasiness. It was now after midnight and she decided to leave; O'Neill accompanied her to her Waverly Place flat and then left, telling her he wanted to return to the Hell Hole to be with Holladay.

Friends later reported differing versions of the night's events. According to one account, Louise Norton left the party shortly after Agnes, and it soon became evident to those gathered at the Hell Hole that there was something amiss. Almost everyone later agreed, however, that Holladay suddenly began ordering drinks for himself as well as his friends. Eventually he was drunk enough to announce that Louise had told him she'd fallen in love with someone else. Holladay had always been a quiet man and he quietly did what he felt he had to do.

Although no one later wanted to be specific about it, word circulated that while the party was still in full swing, Holladay asked his old friend Terry Carlin to conjure up some heroin, and Carlin obligingly put out a street order. Himself a known user of narcotics, he had no qualms about obtaining drugs for a friend. And it was against Carlin's personal code of ethics to try to prevent anyone from overdosing—which it soon appeared was what Holladay had in mind.

Carlin, a disillusioned anarchist, had first met Holladay, as he had O'Neill, in a bookstore run by the philosophical anarchist Benjamin Tucker. Unkempt by choice and relying entirely on the Irish charm and eloquence he could summon at will, Carlin always found someone to keep him in liquor and the scant amount of food he required. Even such practiced storytellers as Jack London and Theodore Dreiser had been enraptured by the mythic quality of Carlin's yarns.

In the years when O'Neill battled despair, when he had cut himself off from his family and was all but penniless—before he was discovered by the Provincetown Players—he had clung to Carlin. Carlin's career as a perpetually homeless parasite had taught O'Neill innovative survival techniques.

They often stayed up all night, sometimes joined by Holladay, alternately drinking and napping with their heads on a backroom table at the Hell Hole. They subsisted on the saloon's free lunch and, with handouts from friends, they bought oysters cheaply by the sack at the Fulton Fish Market. From time to time, they jimmied their way into one or another unoccupied Village flat, sleeping on the floor on cast-off mattresses.

CARLIN AND THE REST of the now-blighted Holladay party moved from the Hell Hole to another favorite Village hangout, Romany Marie's. On the third floor of a building at Washington Place, the restaurant was reached by climbing one outside staircase and two interior ones.

MARIE'S SPECIALTY WAS Turkish coffee; she served no liquor and fed her patrons even when they couldn't afford to pay. A buxom woman with a throaty, heavily accented voice, she came from a family of conservative Romanians. Although respectably married to a businessman named Damon Marchand, she posed as a Gypsy, wrapping herself in floating silky layers embellished with fake jewels.

Shortly after Holladay and his party arrived at her place, according to Romany Marie, he began to look ill, probably having dosed himself at the Hell Hole. Village gossip for weeks afterward held that Holladay had snorted his heroin at Romany Marie's, but what actually happened is impossible to pin down, since everyone involved was terrified of being implicated in what might become a criminal investigation.

Although Agnes had long since gone home, she later recorded a fuzzy account, partly derived from O'Neill. In her version, when O'Neill learned about the heroin, he'd grown ill with shock; he'd fled the restaurant, hurrying back to Agnes's flat for solace. Predictably, he then began a weeklong drunk.

Not long after O'Neill left the restaurant (according to Agnes), a member of their group, Dorothy Day—a twenty-year-old reporter for the socialist magazine the *Call*—arrived at Agnes's flat with shattering news: Louis Holladay was dead. He had collapsed at a table at Romany Marie's, Day said. She had tried to revive him, while Romany Marie called for an ambulance. But he had stopped breathing before the ambulance arrived.

When Holladay's sister Polly was summoned, she informed the ambulance medics that her brother suffered from a weak heart, and they apparently pronounced the death as due to "chronic endocarditis." The police, arriving a short time later, accepted that finding.

Still according to Agnes, Dorothy Day told her that Holladay had died in her arms. Those who knew—or claimed they knew—about the heroin Carlin had obtained for Holladay were incredulous that no mention of narcotics was entered into the official record. (It's probable that someone had surreptitiously pocketed the remains of the heroin.)

To many of his friends—O'Neill among them—the senseless death of a young man whose life had seemed full of vitality and hope became an augury of disaster. The Villagers felt suddenly mortal and threatened. The painter Charles Demuth, according to the writer Hutchins Hapgood, "looked like a crazy man" who "literally seemed a being in hell." Christine Ell wept unstoppably.

It was a milestone as well in the life of Dorothy Day. Self-sufficient and uninhibited, she had come to the Village after attending schools in Oakland and Chicago, choosing to follow her father's career in journalism. Both she and her lover, Michael Gold, later a leading writer and editor for the Communist Party newspaper the *Daily Worker*, were close friends of O'Neill, and they often played and drank with the crowd.

"Everyone table-hopped," Day recalled many years later. "We were very happy and very young." But she had a hidden side, as unfathomable and untouchable as O'Neill's own dark reserve, which perhaps explained their mutual attraction.

Day's parents were Protestant, but she felt a mystical tug toward the Catholic Church. Her "first real link to Catholicism," she later acknowledged, was O'Neill's drunken recitation in the Hell Hole of "The Hound of Heaven" by the ardently Catholic poet Francis Thompson. She was fascinated by O'Neill's own religious ambivalence; it seemed to her that the further O'Neill withdrew from his Catholic roots, the more keenly he felt both the terror and exhilaration of his flight.

I fled Him, down the nights and down the days;

I fled Him, down the arches of the years;

I fled Him, down the labyrinthine ways

Of my own mind. . . .

Thus begins the Thompson poem, of which O'Neill had memorized all 183 lines. The idea of God's pursuit fascinated Dorothy Day; someday, she knew, she would have to pause in her own flight. "I used to ask Gene to recite it over again," she said. "He didn't need any urging."

After a night spent boisterously in the Hell Hole, Dorothy Day often would find herself drawn to St. Joseph's Church on Sixth Avenue. There, in the icy dawn, possessing scant knowledge of the tenets of Catholicism, she would kneel during early-morning Mass.

Following Holladay's death, Day fled the Village and threw herself into a nursing career. Very probably it was Day's precipitous action that suggested O'Neill's depiction, in *Strange Interlude*, of Nina Leeds's sudden, frenzied nursing career as expiation for her guilt over her fiancé's death.

A decade later, Day converted to Catholicism and eventually became the selfless founder of the Catholic Worker Movement. At her mission house in lower Manhattan, the destitute men and women who lined up daily to be fed and clothed would grasp at her hand, attempting to kiss it with the reverence tendered a saint.

Four years after O'Neill's death in 1953, Day reflected at the mission on the O'Neill she knew. "Gene was single-minded in his objective," she said. "Nothing could distract him. Nothing could devour him. In that sense there was a kind of purity in him. He was not attracted to evil, but to darkness. He was absorbed by death and darkness."

"One day recently when I was saying the rosary, I noticed a candle dripping, and I was suddenly reminded of a line from 'The Hound of Heaven'—'Life's dripping taper.' It made me think of Gene. I pray for him even now." Referring to a fundamental principle of Christian doctrine that holds that with an eternal God there is no past, present, or future, Day concluded, "There is no time with God. All the prayers said for [O'Neill] after his death would be of avail at the moment of his death. I pray that Gene turns to the light."

When O'Neill finally roused himself from his weeklong drunk at the end of January 1918, he had come to a decision. His colleagues at the Playwrights' Theatre quietly congratulated themselves when he packed his bags and left for Provincetown. What startled many of them was that he took Agnes with him.

10

A different Gene" was how Agnes Boulton remembered the brooding lover who hurried her off to Provincetown that frigid winter of 1918. During their first week together in February, she found her ardor deepening and she was convinced O'Neill now returned her love in kind. She was enraptured by his "charm," "his expressive great dark eyes"; never had she "seen or touched such beautiful hair."

With slender means and little concern for creature comforts, Agnes and O'Neill lived randomly in the twin studios that John Francis had prepared for them. Francis was a pushover when it came to his tenants, many of whom, like O'Neill, were artists living on the edge of poverty. Himself the uneducated son of a Portuguese fisherman, Francis respected their creative strivings and often allowed them to put off paying their rent for months. O'Neill, who had rented from him in the past, was among his favorite charities.

In his letter reserving a studio, O'Neill had asked if it could be adequately heated. Francis's reply—spontaneous, misspelled, ungrammatical, and generous—was a defining example of the man's character: "If the war keeps on I be lucky to have a shirt to put on anyway you can take the stove I have had to do with the one in the front shop to save fuel . . . you will have no trouble to get small quantities of coal and wood the same you can have the studio for $75. to Dec 31 this year and I will pay the water bill only be careful and report any leak." Francis threw in the adjacent studio at no extra cost.

Agnes was a casual housekeeper. She sometimes cooked, but many of their meals were spooned out of cans. That didn't trouble O'Neill, who never had lived or dined in a well-run home. Trooping from town to town with his actor-father's company for the first seven years of his life, he had learned to swallow third-rate food in third-rate hotels—and those meals had been Lucullan compared with the barely edible sailor's chow of his seafaring days.

Even when his ceaselessly touring parents sheltered him during summer respites in their New London cottage, his mother often was too muddled to cope with household demands and the O'Neills frequently took their meals at a nearby boardinghouse.

Domestic issues aside, the moody, searching twenty-nine-year-old O'Neill and the eager, romantic twenty-five-year-old Agnes were in perfect accord. Sharing their dreams, they swore to live a life dedicated to creativity and mutual devotion—just the two of them, as Agnes pictured it, "in a world of our own." It would be a life that precluded children.

"As for my little girl," recalled Agnes, "so preposterous would have been the idea of my poet-genius with a child around that I don't think the idea even occurred to me." And as for her poet-genius, it did not occur to him until months later to mention that he had a six-year-old son from his brief marriage to Kathleen Jenkins; the boy was being raised on Long Island by Kathleen and her second husband.

O'Neill had never seen his child, he told Agnes, and probably never would. He didn't understand children and couldn't relate to them, he said. Agnes, having impulsively agreed to a childless marriage with O'Neill, flippantly told a friend who asked if they planned to have children that probably all they would have was a book.

WHILE SUPPORTIVE OF O'Neill's talent—here at the dawn of his career—Agnes was not overawed by his growing reputation. Quietly, she regarded her own budding career as equally important. But she was enough in love to put her writing second for the time being and to coddle her lover's capricious artistic temperament, which—even away from his boozing cronies in the Village—included the occasional drinking binge. Agnes endured these binges patiently, always standing by to help him taper off into sobriety when he crashed.

O'Neill, who did his writing in the open upstairs loft of his studio, seemed able to concentrate, even with Agnes moving about below to cook (when she would). She looked forward to their evenings, when O'Neill would read to her from the evolving *Beyond the Horizon*. He invited her comments about the rivalry between the play's two brothers, Robert and Andrew Mayo: Robert the idealistic dreamer, Andrew the realist lured by material gain—both of them in love with Ruth Atkins, the sweet, unambitious girl next door.

O'Neill would query her. Did Agnes "get" what he was after? Did she understand that he was attempting to create "a simon-pure uncompromising American tragedy?" She thought she did. However, with her lack of theater background, she couldn't hope to understand the enormity of the breakthrough O'Neill was striving for, nor did she begin to grasp the huge difference between O'Neill's concept of what a play should be and that of any other contemporary American playwright.

Writing more like a novelist than a playwright, he was fulfilling his long-held ambition to be the embodiment of indigenous American stage tragedy—as Dreiser embodied the tragic American novel. O'Neill summarized *Beyond* as "the tragedy of the man who looks over the horizon, who longs with his whole soul to depart on the quest, but whom destiny confines to a place and a task that are not his."

While there are unmistakable traces in *Beyond* of O'Neill's recent, painful triangular entanglement with the duplicitous Louise Bryant and his brotherly friend John Reed, he chose to describe the play's genesis at a more distant remove. In a lengthy and self-confident letter published in *The New York Times*, he wrote that the idea for the play sprang from the "real life" experience of his voyage on the British tramp steamer *Ikalis*, on which, as an ordinary seaman, he returned to New York from his

perilous adventure in Buenos Aires in March 1911. On board was a Norwegian seaman whom he befriended.

THE NORWEGIAN OFTEN spoke of his regret at trading the security of
the farm where he was raised for the uncertain life of the sea. But, said
O'Neill, the man was "a bred-in-the-bone child of the sea if there ever
was one." With his feet on the plunging deck he was planted like a natural growth in what was "good clean earth" to him. Although he was

> in perfect harmony with his environment . . . he cursed the
> sea and the life it had led him—affectionately. He loved to
> hold forth on what a fool he had been to leave the farm. . . . A
> man on his own farm was his own boss. He didn't have to eat
> rotten grub, [nor did he] have to wait for the end of a long
> voyage for a payday and a good drunk.
>
> But what has this intensely-to-be-envied squarehead got to
> do with *Beyond the Horizon* you will ask? Just this: at exactly
> the right moment, when I was floundering about in the maze
> of the novel-play, he turned up in my memory.
>
> I thought, "What if he had stayed on the farm with his
> instincts? What would have happened?" But I realized at once
> he never would have stayed, not even if he had saddled himself
> with the wife and kids. It amused him to pretend he craved
> the farm. . . . As well expect a seagull to remain in a barnyard—
> for ethical reasons.
>
> And from that point I started to think of a more intellec-
> tual, civilized type . . . a man who would have my Norwe-
> gian's inborn craving for the sea's unrest, only to him it would
> be conscious . . . intellectually diluted into vague, intangible
> wanderlust.
>
> His powers of resistance, both moral and physical, would
> also probably be correspondingly watered. He would throw

away his instinctive dream and accept the thralldom of the
farm for—why, for almost any little poetical craving—the
romance of sex, say.

And so, concluded O'Neill, "Robert Mayo was born, and developed
from that beginning," as was Ruth and the rest of the play's characters,
and "finally the complete play."

Understandably, O'Neill didn't mention his love affair with Louise
Bryant as a significant impetus for the play's love triangle; but, like many
a novelist, he instinctively blended the intimate events of his personal
and fantasy life; his objective, assimilated experiences; and his psychological insights; in order to arrive at the existential plot for *Beyond the
Horizon*.

In the play, Robert is the brother who wins Ruth, sacrificing his
dream of going to sea, trapping himself on his father's farm, segueing
into what is ultimately a loveless marriage, and losing his soul. Andrew,
in his stead—although he loves the farm—sails away beyond the horizon
to achieve material success, but fails to appreciate the beauty and romance
surrounding his adventure. Ruth, realizing she chose the wrong man,
sinks into a numb acceptance of her fate. As is inevitable in O'Neill's
tragic view, all of their dreams, in the end, have been thwarted.

His Robert Mayo is a symbolic version of himself; as for Andrew
Mayo and Ruth Atkins, although they embody few if any of the characteristics of John Reed or Louise Bryant, they symbolically serve to complete the play's tragic triangle.

Agnes must have been aware of the source from which her poet-genius
was drawing inspiration; it was all too obvious he was reliving his recent
passion for his brotherly friend's woman—and for his own "little poetical craving" for "the romance of sex." From the evidence in her memoir,
however, Agnes was convinced she had by now replaced Louise in O'Neill's
heart, and she did not dream it was Louise for whom he might still be
pining.

Agnes soon learned her mistake.

Louise Bryant returned from Russia on February 18, 1918, shortly after Agnes and O'Neill had left Greenwich Village. Louise arrived in New York in a flurry of publicity and without Reed. Reports had reached the United States that Reed had accepted a minor post in the new Bolshevik regime. Louise knew that Reed, momentarily swept up in the Communist vision of revolutionary reform, had acted impulsively, thereby risking indictment for treason upon his return home. She refused to answer reporters' questions about Reed, telling them instead that she was planning to write a book about her own firsthand experiences.

From her friends in Greenwich Village, she soon learned about O'Neill's liaison with Agnes and, although preoccupied with her book and her newfound celebrity, she launched an attempt to reclaim him.

At the end of February, a letter arrived for O'Neill in Provincetown. Louise wrote that she must see him at once—this according to Agnes, to whom O'Neill showed the letter. Louise wrote she'd "crossed three thousand miles of frozen steppes to come back to her lover."

Again according to Agnes, Louise assured O'Neill that her love for him would never change, and she dismissed the rumor that he had "picked up some girl in the Village and become involved." But, Louise argued in her next letter, there was no use writing letters; she had to see him. With glib impudence, she protested it was "all a misunderstanding" and that her going to Russia with Reed did not mean she'd severed her relationship with O'Neill.

Agnes remembered she was trembling when she finished reading the letter. What did Gene intend to do? she demanded. Assuming an air of woe, but relishing the drama of it all, O'Neill replied, "I can't let her suffer like this. I can't do this to her—now!" He'd have to see Louise. "See her!" Agnes retorted in disbelief.

O'Neill took nearly two weeks to consider his situation, apparently not that unwilling, after all, to let Louise suffer—and leaving Agnes in suspense as well. And then he equivocated; perhaps he would go to New York to see Louise: it was the least he could do in view of her own journey of "three thousand miles of frozen steppes" to see him.

"She knew that phrase would get you," Agnes jeered, unnerved by the "surety" expressed in Louise's letter and frightened by what she perceived as Louise's hold over O'Neill. Agnes had begun to suspect that O'Neill liked to suffer.

She was tormented by the image of Louise in a photograph that O'Neill had shown her, a photo depicting "this menacing and determined hussy . . . with legs in tight riding breeches spread apart, hands dug in the pockets of a smart jacket . . . a gamin cap rakishly on her head, a provocative smile on her lips." She was, according to Agnes, O'Neill's vision of the "mythical symbol of the great old and mystic Irish legends."

In the first of four letters O'Neill wrote to Louise after her return from Russia, he nakedly revealed the depth of his painful love for her; they were letters he knew risked the wreckage of his romance with Agnes.

"I don't know whether I shall come to New York or not," he wrote on March 3. His hesitation sprang less from a sense of loyalty to Agnes than from some sort of fuzzy ethical quibble regarding his friendship for Reed. He'd been disturbed by recent rumors that Louise had gone to Russia as Reed's wife. But perhaps he was also toying with her.

"I want to see you as much as you do me," he wrote. "But—I don't want to see you if you are Mrs. John Reed."

Apparently Louise had not told O'Neill she had secretly married Reed on November 9, 1916; about to undergo a life-threatening kidney operation, Reed had told Louise, "I might die . . . and I want you to have everything I've got."

After berating Louise for having hidden her marriage to Reed, O'Neill rambled on, sounding by turns loving and angry, compassionate and impatient, defiant and despondent, self-pitying and self-aggrandizing—but mostly hurt and bewildered and, not infrequently, adolescent and, possibly, drunk.

"How do I think I would act if I should see you?" he began, presumably in answer to Louise's query. "I think I would want to say a lot of things—and find no words; I would want to kiss you—and dare not; would want to weep—and find my eyes had become incapable of tears; would look into your eyes furtively—and be afraid; and I would feel very sad, and very humble, and very dirty!"

O'Neill went on to toss Louise a sulfurous rejoinder to what must have been a self-congratulatory digression about her reportage from Russia, describing the human suffering she had witnessed and, by implication, belittling O'Neill's narrow, self-centered artistic strivings. He declined to applaud the depth of her compassion.

"Perhaps," he wrote, "if I had seen Russia in the throes as you have, I might be aroused to a love for the human race. . . .

"As it is humanity inspires me only with loathing. Everything over here is bombastic cant and cheap sentimentality. I hate it, and my only salvation lies in my ability to sink into myself. . . ." The "reality of this life," he wrote, was "only a pitiful illusion."

After additional caustic comments about life in general, O'Neill returned to his personal dilemma: "If you had only come sooner—a month, two months sooner! But you didn't, or couldn't." They had both "waited too long," he wrote, "and now everything we waited for is here—an impossible possibility!"

O'Neill went on to disparage most of his Greenwich Village friends for having gossiped to him and Louise about each other, and he gave Louise a long-winded explanation-cum-self-exoneration of his drunkenness and his various "disgusting one-night amours" since her departure—and before meeting Agnes.

"If, as you write, it is dangerous for us to see each other," he said, "then we must still be lying to ourselves . . . I would dearly love to see you—no matter how it hurt—for I am convinced that neither your efforts nor mine will ever sever our souls, and that Our Dream of Yesterday is not dead but only stunned into unconsciousness."

Once again, he raises the issue of their triangular relationship, warning that, this time, Agnes must also be considered. "I would not hurt her for the world, she is much too fine for that." If all doubts were definitely cleared up, "the pity of it" would be that "some one or two of us would have to suffer an added pain in order that the other two or one might be free. And there you are!" He ended on a pleading note: "Write me what you think of this matter. Please! The approaching night is long, and—I am afraid!"

Although Louise's reply is not extant as far as is known, her answer may be gleaned from a further, angrier letter in which O'Neill accused her of being blind to the fact that she had "done more to ruin my life than any other person in the world, not even excepting myself." She presented herself as "blameless," he stormed, but it was she who had betrayed their love.

For over a year and a half, he wrote, while he loved her and was faithful, she had lived with "another man"; even though she insisted there was no sexual relationship because of Reed's illness, Louise had been "spiritually untrue" not only to himself but to herself and to Reed "every moment of that time."

Unable to suppress his venom, he taunted: "Does it cause you pain to know I have been living with another woman? Then you know now how I suffered . . . my love for you kept me in Hell. I lived only in that love, in the hope of those fleeting bits of Paradise you tossed me once in a while—only to turn back to the other man the next moment." In his agony, he said, nothing mattered, "my own life least of all." He drank and drank in order to drug himself into "an indifferent apathy."

It was Agnes, wrote O'Neill, who "pulled me together until I realized what I was wasting of myself and felt a longing to be clean and do clean work again." He also praised Agnes for having accepted and understood him, even at his worst; but even though he owed her a lot, he was unsure whether he loved her "in a deep sense."

It was "more than probable," he added, that Louise had "burned" herself too deeply into his soul for the wound ever to heal; "I stand condemned to love you forever—and hate you for what you have done to my life."

O'Neill finally came to a decision. He told Agnes he would meet with Louise in New York. While Agnes did not believe he would actually desert her for Louise, she did fear that once amid the distractions of the city, he would be tempted into a drinking binge. She was bemused as well by his willingness to disrupt his work on *Beyond the Horizon*. Not least, she was loath to give Louise the satisfaction of being able to summarily bring O'Neill to heel.

Quite possibly O'Neill himself recognized the pitfalls inherent in his proposed journey and—whether consciously or not—he might have been testing Agnes's mettle, challenging her to their first major Strindbergian duel.

While he wavered, Agnes accepted the challenge. With uncharacteristic resolve, she took command, proposing a compromise she believed to be fair to him, to herself, and to Louise: O'Neill should meet Louise halfway between New York and Provincetown—in Fall River, Massachusetts. Surprisingly, O'Neill acceded to the plan. But Louise, according to Agnes, haughtily declined his proposal as being beneath her notice.

Letters continued to spin between Louise and O'Neill until March 10. In spite of the "peevish tone" of her last letter, wrote O'Neill, he said he agreed with her verdict of not meeting again. "Your assertion that you belong to no one is quite right: not even to yourself, at any time I have known you." He would always retain his feeling for the Louise "who was and whom I loved so greatly."

In a final scolding, O'Neill sounded more than ever like a suffering Booth Tarkington adolescent: "But you—you who write such letters—I do not know you or care to. You are alien to me in every respect. And so at the crossroads I salute you as we pass: 'Adios, Stranger!'"

There is no evidence that O'Neill and Louise ever met again—although traces of the triangle lingered not only in the plot of *Beyond the Horizon*, but also in other plays to come.

BETWEEN O'NEILL'S PLAYWRITING and letter-writing, and Agnes's hand-wringing over Louise's epistolary intrusions, they found time to befriend a year-round Provincetown resident, Alice Woods Ullman. She was a writer, the recently divorced wife of the Impressionist painter Eugene Ullman, and the mother of two schoolboys whom she'd raised in France, where her circle included Matisse and Gertrude Stein. She had dropped her former husband's name, preferring to be known as Alice Woods. She liked Agnes, but believed her to be "out of place."

"I thought it was shocking for a woman to live under those conditions," she recalled, referring to the ramshackle studios Agnes and O'Neill occupied. In an oblique reference to O'Neill's recent romance with Louise Bryant, Woods concluded that Agnes "wasn't subtle enough to play the game that Gene seemed to be playing."

As an example of Agnes's naïveté, Woods cited an episode that occurred one day in March, when Agnes and O'Neill had been invited to tea. Agnes was in tears when they arrived and told Woods that O'Neill wanted to marry her, but she would not agree.

"Why not?"

Because, said Agnes, O'Neill was still in love with "that girl."

O'Neill looked haggard. Staring out the window at the melting snow in a bare, brown orchard, he made no comment. The younger of Alice Woods's two sons, Allen Ullman, in later years a painter like his father, was eleven that spring. He dreamily recalled Agnes's beauty and the soulful looks she exchanged with O'Neill. Allen worried about the couple's episodic jealous tiffs and about O'Neill's violent drinking bouts. He thought them the most tempestuously romantic couple outside the pages of a book.

DESPITE EMOTIONAL MISGIVINGS on both sides, Agnes and O'Neill rejoiced in a windfall when his one-acter *In the Zone* proved to be a commercial success on the Orpheum vaudeville circuit; it had been touring the circuit since early in the year, earning him thirty-five dollars a week in royalties. Now, at last, he was freed from his near-total dependence on the dollar-a-day dole his father had been supplying, on and off, for most of his adult life.

As a member of the Provincetown Players, O'Neill—along with the group's other writers and actors—earned little more than appreciation, since the expense of operating the Playwrights' Theatre was barely covered by ticket sales.

The Orpheum income, however, though hardly munificent, was enough to support him and Agnes in their modest lifestyle. For the first time in his writing career, O'Neill was on the cusp of financial independence, and this fact was a spur to their marrying. In the event, Alice Woods recalled that by mid-March, she herself was well into plans for the wedding between the saturnine O'Neill and his jittery beloved.

Woods had arranged for a "Mr. Darrell," owner of the town's most prestigious drugstore, to visit O'Neill's studio to help with obtaining the marriage license. She instructed him to arrive after two in the afternoon, when O'Neill customarily stopped writing. But she forgot to alert either O'Neill or Agnes to the visit.

It was an unusually warm spring day and O'Neill was in a particularly affectionate mood. After lunch, he stripped down to his skin. Like the Celtic forebears he often invoked—who preferred to fight naked—he was totally unself-conscious about walking around in the nude. He grabbed Agnes, prepared to make love and then nap.

An hour or so later, Agnes was awakened by a knock on the unlocked door, but was too comfortable and lazy to open it. Darrell, aware that

O'Neill worked in a loft above the main room, and thinking O'Neill hadn't heard his repeated knocking, pushed the door open, stepped inside, and loudly announced, "I've come to see about you getting that marriage license, Mr. O'Neill."

O'Neill, naked, sprang to his feet, as Agnes cowered on the bed. She watched as the two men, frozen, stared at each other.

"Ah!" said Darrell, recovering his poise, "I'm afraid I've come too early." Backing toward the door, he explained that Mrs. Woods had told him O'Neill would be finished working by two, and blandly offered to return at half past four. (Years later, O'Neill bestowed the drugstore owner's name on the character of the psychiatrist who was Nina Leeds's lover in *Strange Interlude*.)

If Agnes had her own doubts about the marriage, O'Neill was having second thoughts as well.

"One part of me is the author of my life—tearing his hair in a piteous frenzy as he watches his 'worser' half playing the lead . . ." he confessed to his close friend Nina Moise, just three days before the date set for his marriage.

Moise, soon to direct *The Rope*, his one-act play (scheduled to open at the end of the month at the Playwrights' Theatre), had frequently been the sympathetic recipient of O'Neill's ruminations about how he wanted to live his life. She knew he felt himself condemned to be forever at war with his bemused alter ego; but he was insightful enough to ridicule himself as a "Jekyll and Hyde."

"Believe me," he wrote to Moise, "from line to line, the poor wretch can never tell whether the play is farce or tragedy—so perverse a spirit is his star." O'Neill knew Moise would understand that Louise Bryant was the reason for his dithering on the verge of commitment to Agnes. But whatever his misgivings, he suddenly made up his mind that Agnes really was the woman with whom he wanted to spend the rest of his life. And Agnes resolved not to let the threat of Louise hinder her happiness.

The marriage took place on April 12, 1918. Agnes and O'Neill would have preferred to be married by a justice of the peace but couldn't find one. Instead, they took their vows, in O'Neill's words, before "the most delightful . . . Godhelpus, mincing Methodist minister that ever prayed through his nose." The minister, wrote O'Neill, conducted the ceremony as though it were "the wedding of two serious children."

"The worthy divine is an utterly loveable old idiot and the ceremony gained a strange, unique simplicity from his sweet, childlike sincerity," continued O'Neill. "I caught myself wishing I could believe in the same gentle God he seemed so sure of."

11

When O'Neill completed *Beyond the Horizon* at the end of April 1918, he sent the script to George Jean Nathan for his appraisal. O'Neill and Nathan had not yet met, but the influential theater critic had recognized the young dramatist's potential ever since publishing several of his one-act sea plays in the iconoclastic magazine *The Smart Set*.

Nathan, much taken with the play, brought it to John D. Williams, one of the rare producers of the day challenging the tawdriness of Broadway. Nathan believed Williams had the courage and imagination to take on *Beyond the Horizon*, even though it was a departure far more radical than anything Broadway had yet dared.

O'Neill could barely contain his glee when Williams sent a check for $500 to option the script for six months. But when the option was about to expire with no word of a Broadway production, a frustrated O'Neill switched his attention back to two one-act plays, *Where the Cross Is Made* and *The Moon of the Caribbees*—the first announced to open on November 22, the second a month later, both under the aegis of the Provincetown Players.

To be on hand for the productions, O'Neill and Agnes had moved in mid-November from Provincetown back to New York City, into the Lafayette Hotel, near the Playwrights' Theatre. The Armistice with Germany had been signed on November 11, and the Village, like the rest of the country, was in a celebratory mood. O'Neill and Agnes were looking forward to the cocktail party arranged by their friends to welcome them back to the Village, and O'Neill gave Agnes his word he'd stay sober.

For once, Agnes let her hair fall alluringly loose and was rewarded with O'Neill's flattering approval. At the party, following the advice of Harold de Polo, a hard-drinking writer, O'Neill diluted his whiskey with plenty of water.

He was in a serene mood at party's end and to Agnes he seemed sober. Joining friends at a nearby restaurant for dinner, they seated themselves casually at a long table, Agnes beside Teddy Ballantine, an actor with the Provincetown Players.

O'Neill sat farther down the table and Agnes noticed him glaring at her, as he seemed to be straining to hear her animated conversation with Ballantine. When she saw O'Neill pour himself a large glass of straight whiskey, she grew concerned. Rising from her seat, she squeezed into a space beside him and whispered that perhaps it was time for them to go back to the Lafayette. Too late, Agnes recognized the signs of his uncontrollable, drunken jealous rage. O'Neill erupted.

"He got to his feet," recalled Agnes, "gave me a push that sent me backward, leaned toward me, swinging as hard as possible with the back of his hand, and hit me across the face. Then he laughed, his mouth distorted with an ironic grin."

Just as Carlotta some years later would feel compelled to record for posterity the day in Shanghai when a drunken O'Neill "knocked" her "flat," Agnes in her memoir described her first encounter with O'Neill's drunken abuse: "I can remember my horrible astonishment and despair at this performance, along with a crazy dazed feeling that it just couldn't be true—it couldn't have happened."

"Get out of here, all of you," O'Neill snarled at the assembled diners, few of whom appeared unduly shocked by his behavior.

Ballantine's wife, Stella, took Agnes firmly by the arm and steered her out of the restaurant. "It means nothing, my dear, nothing," Stella soothed. "Genius must have its outlet!" She sheltered the distraught

Agnes in her own nearby apartment, advising her to give O'Neill time to cool down.

But a few hours later, Agnes returned to the hotel, where she fretted. O'Neill turned up at dawn, haggard and ill; sitting heavily on the edge of the bed, "he reached out and put his arm around me," Agnes recalled, "holding me tightly and quivering." After downing a few restorative swigs of whiskey ordered from the bellboy, O'Neill ceased to shake. But he was in no shape to keep his scheduled business appointments, nor could he keep his promise to introduce Agnes to his parents, who were expecting a midday visit from their new daughter-in-law.

Agnes telephoned O'Neill's mother: Eugene was ill from having eaten bad oysters, she lied, but was recovering. Might they postpone their visit until after dinner?

O'Neill sipped a bowl of soup and soon was almost himself. Lying in bed, with his head in Agnes's lap, he whispered his penitence: "The dream—it's back. I almost shattered it. . . . You and I always. Us always!"

Did Agnes forgive him? Yes, and (as would Carlotta) not for the last time.

That evening, James and Ella O'Neill embraced Agnes. James, who had turned seventy-three a month earlier, had recently retired from the stage. Ella, at sixty-one, had been drug-free for the past four years. In 1914, succored by "out-sisters" from an order of Carmelite nuns in Brooklyn, she'd undergone an epiphany, re-embracing her lapsed Catholic faith and concurrently conquering her morphine habit.

Ella and James now lived a tranquil life, spending winters in New York and summers in their New London cottage. They occupied a comfortable two-room suite on the eighth floor of the Prince George Hotel on Twenty-eighth Street, east of Fifth Avenue. Jamie, whose own tenuous acting career had long since evaporated, lived at the nearby Garden Hotel on his father's dole and was his mother's daily visitor.

The elder O'Neills were bleakly resigned to Jamie's entrenched alcoholism and his inability, at the age of forty, to earn a living. But their disappointment in their older son was ameliorated by the emergence of their scapegrace younger son as a recognized playwright and a dutiful husband.

The old antagonism between Eugene and his father, along with his mistrust of his mother, seemed—at least on the surface—to have been swept away.

Both parents, eager to show their pleasure with Eugene, asked him what he would like as a wedding gift. O'Neill mentioned that the former Coast Guard station on the edge of a rugged stretch of Atlantic beach in Provincetown had recently been put up for sale. It would be the ideal dwelling for him and Agnes, a home where, from early spring until late fall, they could write and swim and walk in the isolation they sought, and yet be within occasional visiting distance of fellow writers and artists.

The renovated structure was owned by the financier Sam Lewisohn, who had shared it as a vacation home with Maurice Sterne, a painter, and his wife, Mabel Dodge, a patron of the arts (and once John Reed's lover); it was she who had transformed the abandoned station into an inviting summer residence.

James, prodded by his wife, agreed to buy it for his son and daughter-in-law. But to raise the purchase price of a thousand dollars he would need to close a real estate deal in New London—and a trip there would have to wait until he was mobile. He'd recently been knocked down by a car as he was crossing Fifth Avenue and one leg was still in a cast; it would be several weeks before he could travel.

He told his son he could commit to the transaction and agreed it should be handled by O'Neill's locally well-connected Provincetown landlord, John Francis. That settled, O'Neill was ready to face rehearsals, in late November 1918, of *Where the Cross Is Made*, while simultaneously fidgeting about his prospects for *Beyond the Horizon*.

John Williams, at the last minute, renewed the play's option, dangling the far-fetched notion of casting John and Lionel Barrymore as the Mayo brothers. Again, O'Neill's hopes soared. But it turned out the Barrymores had other plans. Williams's continuing vagueness drove O'Neill at last to engage both an agent and a lawyer.

The agent was Richard J. Madden, a partner in the American Play Company, founded in 1914. Madden, like a number of O'Neill's male friends, formed an emotional relationship with him. "I saw this gentle, clear-eyed man and I fell in love with him," Madden told his wife after he and O'Neill met. They never signed a formal contract but Madden, who predeceased O'Neill, remained his agent until death.

It was no happenstance that Harry Weinberger, the lawyer engaged by O'Neill, also counted Emma Goldman among his clients. Rebel that he was, O'Neill could not but feel kinship with Weinberger, who was saluted in liberal circles for his unorthodox and widely quoted view that "the greatest right in the world is the right to be wrong."

ALTHOUGH POISED ON the edge of success, O'Neill now began to worry about money. The tour of *In the Zone* was about to end, partly because of flagging interest in the war and partly because the recent flu epidemic was keeping audiences home; and he couldn't afford to stay in his New York hotel with Agnes to await the December 20 production of *The Moon of the Caribbees*.

He and Agnes considered the option of moving into a rambling and somewhat eccentric property in West Point Pleasant, New Jersey. Called the Old House, it had been bought by Agnes's family in the late nineteenth century. Her father loved working in the attached studio, which he himself had built and which was hung with his paintings; but her parents did not normally move into the Old House from their Connecticut farm until early spring, so it was available.

Agnes had spent her childhood in the six-bedroom Old House and regarded it as her own because it was she who had paid off the mortgage with a small inheritance from the great-aunt for whom she was named. Agnes told O'Neill the house was a mere two-hour train ride from New York and would provide a rent-free residence until they could take possession of their new Provincetown home in the spring.

O'Neill, now eager to leave New York, pressed for an immediate move to the Old House, intending to return only briefly to the Village in December for rehearsals of *The Moon of the Caribbees*—long-delayed because of the play's challenging set, which was seemingly beyond the capacity of the tiny stage of the Playwrights' Theatre. This problem had finally been resolved by the theater's guru, George (Jig) Cram Cook.

The Provincetown Players' inspirational leader since its founding in the summer of 1915, Cook had been a professor of English literature at the University of Iowa and was a scholar of ancient Greece; it was his dream to replicate in America the fourth-century Athenian cradle of art and philosophy—what he thought of as a theatrical "threshing ground."

Cook's wife, Susan Glaspell, already a successful novelist, was among the hopeful playwrights he was guiding, along with O'Neill, at the Playwrights' Theatre. For *The Moon of the Caribbees*, Jig Cook had come up with impressionistic scenery conveying O'Neill's stage direction of "a distant strip of coral beach edged with palm trees, as seen from the main deck of an anchored British tramp steamer."

Agnes, having assured O'Neill of the availability of the Old House, wrote of her plan to her mother, Cecil, with whom she'd been out of touch for several weeks, and was quickly confronted with an unforeseen complication.

It seemed that Agnes's grandmother had arrived unexpectedly from London to spend the winter with her family, and since the Connecticut farmhouse was too cramped for the old woman's comfort, the family had been obliged to move prematurely into the more spacious Old House.

In a panic, Agnes replied that she'd promised O'Neill the house for the winter and they had no place else to go. What was she to do?

Evidently a woman of angelic and unflappable accommodation, and likely accustomed to her daughter's flightiness, Cecil now immediately rented a nearby cottage, into which she packed her family of seven (including *Agnes's* baby daughter, her own mother, and Agnes's three unmarried younger sisters).

Cecil left behind in the Old House only their three pets, which Agnes agreed to care for—at the same time shamelessly requesting that her parents not make their presence in the neighborhood known to O'Neill, whom they'd never met.

At least Agnes had the grace to feel embarrassed by the arrangement, which she knew would strike the local shopkeepers and other townspeople as both bizarre and heartless.

O'Neill and Agnes left Manhattan for West Point Pleasant on November 21. Settling uneasily into the Old House, O'Neill, despite his fondness for animals, was not thrilled to find two cats and a small dog named Trixie in residence. He was further daunted by the various coal stoves that not very efficiently heated the house and required constant stoking. And he was annoyed by the noisy windmill that supplied their water.

It was Agnes who tended the stoves, primed the windmill, and looked after the pets. She also set up a room to serve as O'Neill's study. Still keeping it secret from O'Neill that her evicted family was living nearby, she now learned that her father had been having trouble selling his paintings and was obliged to work in the local hardware store to help pay for his family's rented cottage.

In mid-December, O'Neill received the expected summons to return to New York for rehearsals of *The Moon of the Caribbees*. He wanted Agnes to accompany him, but she protested that she couldn't leave the pets, the stoves, or the windmill unattended.

Disgruntled, O'Neill left for New York alone. Agnes, mindful of O'Neill's earlier encouragement to continue her own writing, took advantage of his absence to begin a short story.

ON DECEMBER 20, the day *The Moon of the Caribbees* was to open, O'Neill sent Agnes a telegram demanding she come to New York immediately. Calculating that she could attend the opening and return with O'Neill by the midnight train from Penn Station, Agnes impulsively locked up Trixie and the cats with a supply of food and water, telegraphed O'Neill of her planned arrival, bought a round-trip ticket, and entrained for New York.

She arrived at the Playwrights' Theatre after the curtain had already gone up on *The Moon of the Caribbees*, the first of three one-act plays (the last two by other authors). O'Neill, who had not received Agnes's telegram, was not at the theater, but she found him around the corner, very drunk, sitting with an even drunker Jamie in the Hell Hole. At his feet lay a large white dog.

O'Neill embraced Agnes and introduced her to the dog, who sat up and licked his hand. O'Neill drunkenly explained that he was bringing the hound he'd named "Brooklyn Boy" back with him to New Jersey. Agnes protested that they had more than enough pets to care for. When O'Neill made no response, Agnes hoped he had dropped the idea.

Agnes then reminded O'Neill of the absolute necessity of catching the last train from Penn Station to West Point Pleasant. But O'Neill, who had foresightedly tucked a bottle of whiskey into his coat pocket for the ride home, wanted to have a few more drinks with Jamie in the Hell Hole.

Fearful of missing the train, Agnes somehow managed to marshal O'Neill, Jamie, herself, and the dog into a taxi, suggesting in a whisper to Jamie that they drop him and the dog at the Garden Hotel, while she and O'Neill continued on to the station.

O'Neill guessed what Agnes had in mind, and with a drunkard's slyness, he waited for the traffic light to turn green, then snatched up the dog, let himself out of the taxi, slammed the door behind him, and stepped into the traffic.

Helplessly, Agnes watched as he and Brooklyn Boy headed back downtown. She arrived at the station barely in time to board the Night Owl.

Sometime before dawn at the Old House, she was awakened by loud voices in the kitchen. She found O'Neill, triumphant—and drunker than ever—sitting at the table with the trucker who had given him and Brooklyn Boy a lift home.

Finally sobering up five days later, O'Neill made it plain that he did not care to celebrate the arrival of Christmas; he reminded Agnes that because his parents invariably were on a theater tour during holidays, the family had rarely taken note of Christmas or any other holiday. Agnes understood but, herself nostalgic about Christmas, she managed to slip away for a surreptitious visit to her family in their rented cottage, taking with her a glass angel surrounded by a bouquet of flowers as a gift for her three-year-old daughter, Barbara.

"I could only stay a few minutes for I knew Gene would be restless at home," Agnes wrote in her memoir, making no mention of the quality of her reunion with the child she hadn't seen in months.

RESTLESS AND ANXIOUS though he was about the fate of *Beyond the Horizon*, O'Neill during the early months of 1919, was at work outlining two new full-length plays, *The Straw* and *Chris Christophersen*.

Intended as tragedy but more often emerging as melodrama, *The Straw* (first called "The Cough") was the tale of an ill-fated love affair between a young woman dying of tuberculosis and a male patient on the way to recovery. It harked back once again to O'Neill's own illness and recalled the Connecticut sanatorium where he had a brief (and necessarily perfunctory) love affair with Catherine Mackay, a twenty-three-year-old patient who actually did die after he himself had recovered.

He saw the play as "a tragedy of human hope," fully aware that both subject and setting were alien to anything currently on the American stage. Not even Puccini's *La Bohème* (which had beautiful music to redeem it) was as determinedly graphic in its portrayal of a dying tubercular heroine.

In *Chris Christophersen*, O'Neill, still mesmerized by his own youthful days at sea, portrayed a middle-aged Swedish-born sailor, once a clipper ship's bo'sun, who blames "dat ole davil sea" for having deprived him of a family life. The plot revolves around Chris's efforts to save his well-brought-up young daughter from marrying a sailor and suffering the same fate as her mother, whom Chris abandoned for a life at sea.

———

As the months went by in the Old House, O'Neill and Agnes sensed an increasing hostility from their neighbors and other townspeople. Agnes had noticed a stiffness in the attitude of the jitney drivers she occasionally employed to take her on errands.

But neither she nor O'Neill realized how deep the animosity ran—until one day they found the corpse of Brooklyn Boy on their front lawn, his throat slashed.

Agnes thought that perhaps this hostility was due to the fact that the Boulton family had moved out of their home without explanation, while Agnes, accompanied by a taciturn stranger, had replaced them. And apparently this stranger was truly an enigma; one of their neighbors, an elderly woman, had recently asked Agnes if her husband was a drug addict.

Inevitably, O'Neill learned the truth of how Agnes had dispossessed her family. One day, on one of his rambling walks, accompanied by Trixie, he lost his way and asked a man chopping wood for directions. It was apparent Trixie knew the woodsman, so O'Neill began to chat with him and the truth came out.

Once home, O'Neill chided Agnes for concealing that her family lived nearby. Still, he made it plain he had no wish to meet any of them. Nonetheless, Agnes told her family that secrecy was no longer necessary although failing to communicate O'Neill's sullen wish to avoid them; it wasn't long before two of her sisters paid an unannounced visit. As Agnes greeted them, O'Neill ducked into a closet, and they left without meeting their brother-in-law.

But O'Neill was unable to avoid a formally announced evening visit from Agnes's seventy-year-old grandmother. To his surprise, he was much taken with her. "Granny," as Agnes called her, chatted about everything from the imminence of Prohibition to Woodrow Wilson's presidential style.

Agnes's pleasure at having effected a rapport between O'Neill and a member of her family was displaced by dismay when she learned that March that she was pregnant. She returned home from a visit to her doctor, having been told to expect the baby in early October. She found O'Neill in a jubilant mood. He had written the words *"The Curtain Falls"* on the last page of the manuscript of *The Straw*.

Agnes wasn't eager to convey her own news. She knew O'Neill had not forgotten their oft-reiterated views on the sanctified exclusivity of their union. Indeed, in her memoir, she herself had emphasized her vow that hers and O'Neill's "aloneness" was to be inviolate. She postponed telling him until the following day.

O'Neill's first reaction, Agnes recalled, was that "the doctor had made a mistake." His second reaction was "silence." And that, more or less, was it. According to Agnes, there was no recrimination, no "how could this possibly have happened?" All was resolved; as Agnes would have it, O'Neill—at least for the moment—stoically accepted the shattering of his dream that there would be just the two of them—"Us always!" (Nowhere does she attempt to explain or rationalize this slipup.)

The truth being unknowable, it's tempting to offer an educated guess at what Agnes left unsaid. There must have been a confrontation, given both hers and O'Neill's sworn commitment to a childless marriage (even to the point of ignoring their already existing offspring). Very likely, Agnes's pregnancy was due to an episode of heedless passion fueled by alcohol.

It's easy to conjecture why Agnes chose in her memoir to gloss over the friction that was doubtless engendered by the baby's imminent arrival. She was, after all, writing from the vantage point of 1958, when their son, Shane, was thirty-nine and knew himself to have been irreparably wounded by his father's neglect. Surely, even though she herself had been a sometimes careless mother, Agnes would not have wished to hurt Shane further by suggesting that, from the first, he'd been unwanted by his father.

To his parents and friends, O'Neill in his new role as father appeared solidly committed to his marriage. And yet, however subtly, the accident of Agnes's pregnancy was soon to mark the start of the slow but certain unraveling of the marriage.

Ambivalent as always, O'Neill was destined to grope and stumble his nervous way through the next few years with Agnes, dependent on her, often clinging to her with desperate passion, and at other times eaten by resentment. Although he took refuge in his writing—which flourished even during domestic upheavals—he saw himself year by year growing ever more disillusioned in his marriage.

Not only in his plays (replete with alienated parents and dead children) but in numerous letters, O'Neill reveals his lack of interest and his increasing disappointment (despite moments of forced attentiveness) in both Shane and the daughter, Oona, who followed. His disaffection was a trait that dismayed even the most loyal of his friends, who spoke, after his death, about the ultimate heartlessness of his behavior.

And while Agnes tried in her memoir—which ends with the birth of Shane—to make light of this defect, she couldn't help resenting the self-absorption that turned O'Neill to stone when confronted with the demands of fatherhood; his paternal compassion was reserved for his plays—the children of his imagination.

Four months pregnant by mid-May and still optimistic about persuading O'Neill to accept his fatherhood, Agnes returned with him to Provincetown, where the ever-obliging John Francis handed over James O'Neill's wedding gift—the deed to their summer home, known as Peaked Hill Bars; it was fronted on the north by the Atlantic Ocean and bounded on the east, south, and west by shifting dunes, described in the document as "land unknown."

It was all the isolation O'Neill could have wished for and the closest thing to living on a ship without actually heaving anchor. It was accessible only by foot on a crude trail called Snail Road, over three miles of scrub wood and dune—and by the Coast Guard's horse-drawn wagon, which paid sporadic visits with mail and supplies.

Their closest neighbors were the Coast Guardsmen who had abandoned their former quarters—now the O'Neills' home; fearing the sea's steady encroachment, with its threat to sweep their station into the Atlantic, they had established a new lifesaving station half a mile away. This stretch of coast was so hazardous, particularly in winter, that ships were pounded to kindling within hours of running aground. Agnes and O'Neill knew that corpses had often been laid out in what was now their living room.

By contrast, nothing could equal the serenity of a midsummer evening, with its purity of light and air, the setting sun reddening the sea, and a ceaseless hissing wind that held no sting.

The house, like the French castle O'Neill could never have dreamed he'd inhabit ten years later, had no electricity or central heating. Kerosene provided fuel for cooking and lit the lamps of the two-story structure at night, while a huge fireplace gave a modicum of warmth on chilly days; the house became unlivable in the late fall, when storm-driven sand began to pile up against its outer walls like snowdrifts, soon burying two-thirds of the front door and encrusting the windowpanes, which had to be replaced every spring.

Everything about his new home enchanted O'Neill. Shortly after moving in, he described his delight:

> The stairs are like companionways of a ship. There are lockers everywhere. . . . The big boat room, now our living room, still has the steel fixtures in the ceiling from which one of the boats was slung. The look-out station on the roof is the same as when the coast guards spent their eternal two-hour vigils there. . . .
>
> The place has come to mean a tremendous lot to me. I feel a true kinship and harmony with life out there. Sand and sun and sea and wind—you merge into them, and become as meaningless and as full of meaning as they are. There is always the monotone of the surf on the bar—a background for silence— and you know that you are alone—so alone you wouldn't be

ashamed to do any good action. You can walk or swim along the beach for miles and meet only the dunes—Sphinxes muffled in their yellow robes with paws deep in the sea.

That September 1919, O'Neill wrote a long prose poem, exulting in his newfound surroundings, "O sea, which is myself! How I love to reveal my nakedness to the sun on solitary beaches!"

Once settled in Peaked Hill Bars awaiting the birth of his child in early October, O'Neill regimented himself to a schedule: breakfast at eight, work until one, and then a brief nap. Always intent on keeping physically fit, he swam, took long solitary walks, or exercised with a punching bag. Often, he paddled his kayak far out into the dangerous waters.

He generally spent some time in the afternoon going over his morning's writing. After dinner, he and Agnes read until their bedtime at nearly midnight. They ventured into town once a week or so to hear the latest gossip, and occasionally friends visited. But because their home was hard to reach, O'Neill for the most part led a peaceful, productive life with few interruptions.

Agnes, who did all the cooking and housekeeping, shared that life contentedly. Absent from her account of that first summer at Peaked Hill Bars is any mention that she and O'Neill shared their thoughts about what their life would be like after their child was born—another indication that O'Neill was not looking forward to the disruption of his married life.

He was, however, relieved when his mother-in-law, Cecil Boulton, arrived in August accompanied by Agnes's nineteen-year-old sister, Margery, to spend several weeks helping Agnes shop for baby clothes and equipment, and prepare Happy Home, a small cottage in the town's Commercial Street; the house on Peaked Hill Bars was not only unheated, but also too isolated for Agnes's lying-in. (Even with her mother's supervision, Agnes forgot to buy a crib.)

O'Neill had a nagging concern that superseded his distress about the child to come: October 16 was not far off, and he feared he would turn thirty-one with no sign of a Broadway production for his long-since-completed *Beyond the Horizon*, to say nothing of *The Straw* and *Chris Christophersen*.

OBSESSED AS HE was with his Irish heritage, O'Neill named his newborn son Shane Rudraighe, after "Shane the Proud," the sixteenth-century chief of the O'Neill clan of Ulster. (Among his other achievements, Shane the Proud murdered his half brother.)

Shane Rudraighe arrived late, almost a month later than expected, in the early morning of October 30, 1919, just two weeks after O'Neill's thirty-first birthday. It was nearly ten years since the birth of his first son, who had long since been airbrushed out of O'Neill's life.

James O'Neill had determined to acknowledge neither his first grandson nor his then twenty-year-old son Eugene's irresponsible forced marriage to Kathleen Jenkins. Casting about for a subterfuge that would get Eugene out of the country, he had asked a friend of his, an engineer, to take Eugene along on an impending gold-prospecting expedition to a mine in Honduras in which he'd invested; James hoped that with Eugene's absence the unwelcome birth could somehow be ignored.

Kathleen's mother, Kate, was furious with the O'Neills. Herself divorced from George Jenkins, her alcoholic husband, Kate had encouraged her daughter to accept young Eugene as a suitor. Kathleen was dazzled by his good looks and what she perceived as his aura of "strange romance," and not a little impressed that he was the son of a famous actor.

Kathleen and Eugene took long walks together in Riverside Park, a half block from her home on 113th Street near Columbia University. He wooed her by quoting Wilde, Ibsen, Swinburne—authors unfamiliar to her; he recited tender love poetry of his own. Kathleen fell dizzily in love, believing, as did her mother, that O'Neill wanted to marry her.

O'Neill was in no position to do so. At a loss for a career after being expelled from Princeton toward the end of his freshman year, he'd quit, or refused, the clerical jobs his father found for him. His future was a blank and he knew his father would never consent to support him in a marriage—nor did he himself want to be tied down. Nonetheless, when Kathleen told him she was pregnant, he submitted to her pleas and they were secretly married in Hoboken Trinity Church in New Jersey.

Seeing no other way of extricating himself from the entanglement, he confessed to his father he'd gotten a girl pregnant, and James O'Neill promptly sent him off to Honduras.

When Eugene returned five months later, Kathleen's baby had been born (on September 5, 1910). Kathleen, resigned to having been rejected by Eugene and his family, requested a divorce, asking no alimony. "We could never have made a go of it," she subsequently conceded.

12

Agnes, when writing of her labor during Shane's birth, made no reference to the birth of her daughter, Barbara, nearly four years earlier; in truth, she seemed, like O'Neill, to have all but forgotten the existence of her firstborn.

The doctor who attended Agnes in the small heated cottage rented for the Provincetown winter, was Daniel Hiebert, whose family O'Neill had boarded with five years earlier when Hiebert was a medical student at Boston University and O'Neill was enrolled in his playwriting course at Harvard. Dr. Hiebert remembered handing Shane to O'Neill, who, according to Agnes, regarded the infant with "delighted admiration" before placing him on the bed beside her.

O'Neill grasped her hand and gazed tenderly at his newborn, saying, according to Agnes, "A sort of Holy Trinity, eh Shane?" (Shane's birth marked the end of Agnes's memoir, which was to have been the first in a series of three volumes, never completed. Years later, during a hiatus in the acerbic divorce proceedings, O'Neill wrote to Agnes that he wanted to forget about "the poison and hate" of their marriage, and to preserve memories he never wanted "to shake off"; he said he'd had "a sudden clear vision of the day at the Happy Home when Shane was born, of my holding your hand, remember?")

ELLA O'NEILL RESPONDED with motherly solicitude to O'Neill's telegram announcing Shane's birth: "I am one of the happiest *old ladies* in

New York tonight to know I have such a wonderful grandson—but no more wonderful than you were when you were born and weighed *eleven pounds* and no *nerves* at that time!"

Enclosing a photograph of O'Neill at three months old, Ella said she hoped Shane would be equally good-looking; she cautioned her son not to let Agnes "want for anything, for she is a darling girl." With teasing affection, she ended her letter: "Oceans of love to Agnes, baby, and the biggest baby of the three *You.*"

Although O'Neill seemed ready at this time to welcome his mother's affection, his childhood resentment of her addictive behavior still festered; it would emerge most realistically some twenty years later in his autobiographical *Long Day's Journey Into Night.*

In that play, his mother's stand-in, Mary Tyrone, does not lovingly tell her younger son that he was a nerveless wonder; rather, she reproves him for having been "born afraid" because she "was so afraid to bring [him] into the world." She did not "have a single gray hair" until after his birth, when her beautiful long reddish-brown hair "began to turn white," as she ruefully reminds her husband.

Apparently, no amount of motherly love and attention during the final eight years of Ella's life as a drug-free solicitous wife and mother could ever, in O'Neill's mind, compensate for the terror evoked by her morphine-induced tantrums, accusations, and moody retreats as he was growing up.

Nor could he forget the burden of helping his father and older brother to conceal his mother's shameful addiction.

"Dope fiend," Jamie Tyrone calls his mother in *Long Day's Journey Into Night.*

O'Neill, even at fifty-three, simply could not let go of his resentment. The retrospective fury he felt toward his mother is reflected in an early scenario for the play; in a surprisingly vicious note, he described his mother (as Mary Tyrone), when under the influence of morphine, as changing from "happy chattering girlishness" to the hard, bitter cynicism of an aging woman, "who can taunt with a biting cruelty, as if suddenly poisoned by an alien demon."

But in October 1919, Eugene seemed proud of his fatherhood when he wrote to George Tyler, who had produced several of James O'Neill's triumphant road tours and had become a lifelong family friend. "The Event transpired yesterday, and most successfully," said O'Neill. "A ten-and-a-half-pound boy who looks able to play football right now. His voice already carries further than the Old Man's."

O'Neill's jocular tone was forced; he was actually annoyed with Tyler. The producer had recently optioned *Chris Christophersen*, but was demanding numerous changes. And although Tyler had said he liked *The Straw*, he would not commit to producing it. Meanwhile, John Williams was still being evasive about an opening date for *Beyond the Horizon*.

Added to these concerns was the impending production by the Provincetown Players of O'Neill's recently completed one-act play, *Exorcism* (subtitled "A Play of Anti-Climax"), about which O'Neill had very mixed feelings.

He'd written *Exorcism* in 1919 while in the grip of one of those deeply despondent moods that invariably drew his thoughts back to his attempted suicide seven years earlier. He believed he had temporarily purged himself and he put *Exorcism* aside. But it wasn't long before Jimmy Light, who was operating the Provincetown Players in Jig Cook's absence during the 1919–1920 season, begged O'Neill for a play, citing the dearth of worthwhile new work by American playwrights.

O'Neill felt obligated to Light, who had always been his loyal champion; and so, hesitant as he was about the staging of a play so openly based on his 1912 suicide attempt, O'Neill handed over *Exorcism* for production on March 26, 1920.

By setting the play in "the middle of March some years ago," it's fair to assume O'Neill was thinking of the spring of 1912, the same year as the setting for the two great autobiographical plays, *Long Day's Journey Into Night* and *The Iceman Cometh*—the year he was twenty-three, a down-and-out drunk living in an upstairs cubicle at a Fulton Street saloon, Jimmy the Priest's.

The actual chain of events that led to O'Neill's attempt at self-annihilation had its beginning on December 29, 1911, the day on which he'd agreed to provide Kathleen Jenkins with grounds for the divorce she'd requested. Since adultery was the only grounds for divorce in New York State at that time, O'Neill had to endure a sordid charade of being caught and photographed in bed with a prostitute.

Disgusted with himself, he returned to Jimmy the Priest's, where he'd been subsisting on his daily plate of free soup and his father's weekly dole of seven dollars—enough to keep him in whiskey. A month later, on January 20, he was served with the divorce papers.

Still consumed with self-loathing, and all but insensible with drink, he sought to escape from his tormenting thoughts by a digression uptown to Times Square. On his way, he stumbled on a five-dollar bill on the sidewalk, which prompted him to try his luck at Canfield's, the renowned gambling casino on Forty-fourth Street. Fueled by free champagne, he found himself $200 ahead, but he grew so boisterous he was bounced, albeit with his winnings.

He continued his drinking at a Broadway saloon, and the next thing he knew (as he later liked to tell friends), he was awaking in a train's upper berth as it pulled into the station in New Orleans. To his surprise (so he claimed), he was greeted by a poster announcing the presence of his father in a condensed touring version of *The Count of Monte Cristo*. The production had opened in New Orleans on January 22.

Eugene asked his father for the fare back to New York, but James told his prodigal son he'd have to earn it, and put him to work in a bit part in the bowdlerized melodrama, in which Jamie had a minor role as well. The production was "a horrible hash-up of the play, its general frightfulness reaching a high spot in the formidable lousiness of my acting," O'Neill told a writer researching his father's career many years later.

In fact, during Eugene's two months on the road, he and his brother did their utmost to sabotage the production, staggering onstage drunk during successive performances, goading each other to trip up their fellow actors, humiliating their father, and ultimately wrecking the tour. Hating himself, Eugene slunk back to Jimmy the Priest's. And now, added to his disgust with himself over his shameful role in his divorce from Kathleen, he suffered over his atrocious behavior toward his father. He was, in his own words, "sick in body, brain and soul."

In mid-March, O'Neill determined to put an end to his unbearable burden of guilt. He went from pharmacy to pharmacy collecting veronal tablets, returned to Jimmy's to swallow them, and fell asleep.

His attempted suicide was thwarted when several of his drunken co-derelicts shook him awake and hustled him to Bellevue Hospital. At the admitting office, O'Neill was pronounced fit and dismissed while his rescuers were detained for alcoholic detoxification. O'Neill's own later jocularity in recalling this episode suggests he was making a macabre gesture rather than a sincere attempt to kill himself. When he was in his fifties, he told the psychiatrist Dr. Louis Bisch, his neighbor and friend in Bermuda, that he had changed his mind about wanting to die after swallowing the veronal. One thing seems clear; the attempt was a gesture aimed largely at his father.

Once again, the stalwart James O'Neill came to his son's rescue. Forgiving him for having wrecked his vaudeville tour, he persuaded Eugene to return to New London that summer, where he arranged a job for him as a cub reporter on the New London *Telegraph*.

The suicidal protagonist of *Exorcism*, who has the Irish surname Malloy, has the given name Ned, which is short for Edmund—the name O'Neill gave the character based on himself in *Long Day's Journey* (switching names with his brother Edmund, who died of measles before Eugene was born).

The Ned of *Exorcism* looks like Eugene. He is "a tall slender young fellow" of twenty-four, the same age and build as Eugene in 1912. While his eyes are blue rather than deep brown like O'Neill's, they hold O'Neill's "peculiar possessed expression of the inveterate dreamer" and his face gives the appearance of "conflict" and "inner disharmony."

Ned, like Eugene, swallows an overdose of sleeping pills and is rescued by the seedy fellow boarders who live in the "squalid rooming house" above a "saloon of the lowest type of grog shop." When Ned awakens the following day, they tell him how they sought out his estranged father, who gave them fifty dollars to pay a doctor to come and pump his stomach. His father then visits and father and son are reconciled.

Declaring himself "reborn," his "sins forgiven," Ned drinks with his rescuers, and is raucously singing the opening lyrics of "Alexander's Ragtime Band" as the curtain falls.

O'Neill regretted the play's production—at least in part because he didn't want to hurt his ailing father's Catholic sensibility; but he must also have rued its glib and patently false ending—and despite an enthusiastic review by Alexander Woollcott in the *Times*, he called in all the scripts of the twenty-three-page one-acter and destroyed them. Or so he thought.

For almost sixty years after O'Neill's death, scholars had to base their analysis of *Exorcism* on the scattered recollections of its cast members and on Woollcott's considerably detailed review.

Then, in the early spring of 2011, an intact script magically surfaced. It had been withheld by Agnes—along with other scripts and letters—when O'Neill sent his lawyer to collect the papers he'd left behind in Bermuda in 1928 while planning to leave her for Carlotta.

Many years later, Agnes casually gave the script as a Christmas gift to a friend, the playwright and screenwriter Philip Yordan, whose widow discovered it among his papers after his death and sold it to Yale University's Beinecke Library in May 2011.

BY THE END of November 1919, with three completed full-length plays still lacking producers, O'Neill's nerves were screaming; he found himself helplessly bickering with Agnes, who was almost equally distraught, and she encouraged him to take a break. She suggested he visit his parents in New York and take the time to refurbish his meager wardrobe for his hoped-for future meetings with producers. She was breast-feeding Shane and would not accompany him, but they agreed he would return to Provincetown within a week.

The plan suited O'Neill. Part of his tension was due to Prohibition's anticipated effect on Provincetown. The Volstead Act was expected to take effect in January, only a few weeks away. Liquor stores and legitimate saloons were already shutting down. O'Neill was certain that if anyone had access to good bootleg whiskey, it would be his father, and he believed that once in New York he could look forward to a week of hearty drinking.

He wrote to Agnes the moment he boarded the train carrying him to the Fall River steamship, which would land him in New York on the following day. He begged her to ignore his "bad moods" and "irresponsible tongue," blaming them on his "leopard's spots."

In that letter (and in the dozens he wrote to her on every subsequent separation), he spoke of his anguished dependence on her, deluging her with his pangs of "great emptiness," his loneliness, his insatiable need for her love and companionship, his pledge that she was his heart and soul. Often, he ended with a ritual "Kiss Shane for me"; in this first letter, he insisted, "I do love him—'in my fashion'" (a cynical reference to the Ernest Dowson poem "Cynara," which O'Neill and his brother were fond of quoting).

Impassioned as were these outpourings, they scarcely differed from those showered on previous lovers or, later, on Carlotta. By contrast, Agnes, in her somewhat less feverish replies, emerges as a more substantial and sympathetic woman than the self-portrait she inadvertently draws in her memoir. Replying to O'Neill's affirmations of love, Agnes replied, "I'm glad you do need me—still. The feeling of emptiness you speak of nearly drove me crazy this afternoon—before I got your letter."

O'Neill snuggled into the domestic nest of his parents' suite in the Prince George Hotel on December 3. James and Ella welcomed him with warmth and gentle humor and he gratefully submitted to their nurturing, content to banter with his father, and almost childishly acceptant of his mother's fussing over him.

His visit began with a shopping spree when his mother took him to her favorite Fifth Avenue store, Lord & Taylor, where their purchases included a tweed suit, an overcoat, and some shirts and collars; a few days later "under Mama's guidance," as he reported to Agnes, he bought a hat and shoes.

Less successful than shopping with his mother was O'Neill's first evening at home with his father; it was then he learned that the Volstead Act was taking its toll in New York as well as in Provincetown. His father had only "one-quarter of one bottle left of the treasure when I arrived," he complained to Agnes, "and that is now gone, need I add?" He'd had only three drinks and he feared that was all he was likely to get during the rest of his stay, for James O'Neill was "at a loss where to get more!"

There was nothing for him in a dry New York, he declared—although it did make him "happy to see Paw 'n' Maw again" and he planned to spend the rest of his time in the city "right under their wing."

O'Neill's drinking was becoming increasingly a cause of the friction between him and Agnes. She did not object to his occasional imbibing, but tried to rein him in when she thought it interfered with his writing. Although resentful, O'Neill would try to taper off. But during most of his marriage to Agnes, he found it impossible to control his binge drinking. And yet, during his stay in New York, he assured her he was being "a good, good boy." He had no choice. "Believe me, Prohibition is very much of a fact."

Almost as adept as O'Neill at confessional pillow talk, Agnes now wrote to apologize for previously having misjudged him. In her "meanness," said Agnes, she had charged O'Neill with petty misdeeds that she actually "knew were not true," and asked his forgiveness.

On his third night in New York, O'Neill paid a sentimental visit to the Hell Hole, where he tried but failed to get drunk on sherry with the rest of the barflies; at twenty cents a shot, it was the only alcohol available. "There was just enough kick in the wine to make everyone feel jovial and that's all," he reported to Agnes.

Back in Provincetown by mid-December, O'Neill gingerly reacquainted himself with Shane, and then tried to settle down to writing. Gratified as he was that Tyler, in New York, had told him he was going

ahead with *Chris Christophersen* (although proffering no date for its opening), what he really wanted was a production date for *Beyond the Horizon*;
over and again, he cursed John Williams for dragging his feet.

Williams's most recent excuse was the acute shortage of Broadway
theaters. As O'Neill was petulantly aware, it was Williams himself who
was partly responsible for the shortage; once again bypassing *Beyond the
Horizon*, Williams had launched a new play the week before Christmas
called *For the Defense*, by the rising playwright Elmer Rice.

But in one of those whimsical manifestations of theater magic, it was
Rice's overwrought courtroom drama that enabled *Beyond the Horizon* at
last to reach Broadway.

The popular star of *For the Defense*, Richard Bennett, was the angel
who interceded on O'Neill's behalf. Bennett (the father of Constance
and Joan, who both grew up to be movie stars) had chanced to pull a
dusty script of *Beyond the Horizon* from a cubbyhole during a visit to John
Williams's office and found himself surprisingly moved by the play.
Growing bored at forty-seven with repetitive matinee-idol roles like the
one he was currently playing, Bennett asked Williams to let him star as
the tragic twenty-seven-year-old younger brother, Robert Mayo.

When Williams explained his misgivings about presenting *Beyond* on
Broadway, Bennett offered the producer a solution both for the current
theater shortage and for the financial risk of staging a contemporary
American tragedy.

He suggested the play be presented as a series of "special matinees" at
the Morosco Theatre, where *For the Defense* was now established; and that
Williams recruit cast members from *For the Defense* (along with Bennett
himself) to take on roles in *Beyond*. Williams genuinely did wish to give
O'Neill's play a hearing and since Bennett's plan called for little financial
risk—no more than an investment in some sketchy scenery—he agreed.

Bennett's own enthusiasm was contagious. He persuaded three mem-
bers of *For the Defense* to appear with him in the O'Neill play, along with
Edward Arnold and Helen MacKellar from another Broadway hit, *The
Storm*. Arnold, not yet a movie star, agreed to portray the older brother,

Andrew Mayo, and MacKellar, an upcoming ingenue, accepted the role of Ruth Atkins, the girl both brothers fancy. For these actors it was a commitment of faith and love. They had to rehearse their new roles in addition to performing nightly in their established vehicles, and give twelve performances a week rather than the usual eight.

Williams notified O'Neill that *Beyond* would open in early February, and by now George Tyler had abruptly named a date in early March for the opening of *Chris Christophersen*—with the proviso that O'Neill remain in New York after the premiere of *Beyond* to prepare for the production of *Chris*. Meanwhile, Tyler had finally committed to *The Straw*, although an opening date for that play was still uncertain.

O'Neill headed back to New York on January 11, anticipating the beginning of a new life. Since he would be away from Agnes for much longer this time, he wanted to leave her as comfortable as possible and, although he could barely afford it, he engaged a housekeeper-nursemaid. Fifine D'Orsay Clarke, the French-born widow of a Provincetown ship's captain, was to evolve as a fixture in the O'Neill household as nanny, cook, and general manager.

Emotionally connected as she was to the fate of *Beyond the Horizon*, Agnes was not happy at being left behind, unable to share in the play's progress from script to stage. She and O'Neill would write to each other daily, aware their letters would sometimes cross. Telephoning long-distance was too expensive, but they would telegraph if either grew anxious.

O'Neill again stayed with his parents at the Prince George Hotel while waiting to move into the single room of his own they'd reserved for him three floors below. After all his months of uncertainty, he was both exhilarated and dazed at finding himself caught up in three major productions of his long-orphaned plays.

While O'Neill felt all three plays were being hastily slapped together, he was determined at least to be adequately recompensed. For a start, backed by his new agent, Richard Madden, he confronted John Williams and received a more favorable percentage of the expected profits from

Beyond the Horizon than initially proffered. Reporting his small triumph to Agnes, he also informed her that the opening date for *Beyond* was set for February 3, following a single trial performance somewhere away from Broadway (which turned out to be Yonkers).

The plan called for four introductory matinees, after which there would be several evening performances. The makeshift production, which had no formal director, had already begun rehearsals a week before O'Neill's arrival, under the supervision of Williams and Richard Bennett. At the same time, Tyler was casting *Chris Christophersen* and had offered the eponymous leading role to the eminent British actor Godfrey Tearle; Tyler was also thinking of casting the promising nineteen-year-old Helen Hayes as the doomed heroine in *The Straw*.

Agnes, having long since overcome her indifference to the theater, was now as much caught up in O'Neill's creative life as Carlotta would be eight years later. She thrived on her husband's gossipy letters; *Beyond*, she wrote him, "is nearer to me, somehow, than anything you have done." Wistfully, she told him, "I get a great deal of pleasure and excitement myself out of imagining you at all your interviews and appointments."

O'Neill's own exuberance was diminished by the precarious physical condition in which he found his father, who was still weak and in pain from the shock of the recent car accident. His family doctor, John Aspell, also thought he'd suffered a slight stroke. Ella told her son she'd been so worried she'd thought of summoning a priest, but Dr. Aspell had managed to pull him through.

While concerned about his father, O'Neill took advantage of Dr. Aspell's presence to consult him about symptoms of his own. As was invariable during times of stress, he was suffering from "nerves" due to the demands of readying two plays for production at the same time with a third in the offing. The doctor pronounced him "keyed up tight as a string" and warned him he would "snap" if he didn't slow down; he advised O'Neill to forget his work and to rest.

"Good advice, maybe," wailed O'Neill to Agnes, "but how the hell can I keep it at this stage of the game?" Citing the long hours he was devoting to *Beyond* and *Chris*, he reverted to tongue-in-cheek brogue: "It's a hectic life, divil a lie, and how I'm to keep both the plays separate in my mind and think clearly about each of them is a problem." Immediately contradicting himself, he added, "However, I feel so keyed up I could work 24 hours a day without eating, I think."

He could not, however, go for long without drinking. His father, meanwhile, had found a source of bootleg whiskey, and O'Neill soon grew accustomed to joining him for drinks in the evening—never enough to get drunk, as he assured Agnes.

And now he was about to luck out. He'd made an appointment with Richard Bennett to go over the script of *Beyond*, and after the curtain rang down on *For the Defense* at 11:30 p.m. on January 16, Bennett carried O'Neill off to his elegant town house in Greenwich Village. Before beginning their work, Bennett asked O'Neill if he liked absinthe; he just happened to have fifty cases of Pernod on hand.

"Jack Barrymore and I are the only people in the country who have any," he bragged, reminding O'Neill—unnecessarily—that Pernod, the most popular brand of absinthe, had been banned from the United States in 1915 because it was believed to have toxic effects.

O'Neill suggested he bring it on. "I knew I was going to like you from the first moment we met," he told Bennett.

Pouring the Pernod over ice in tall glasses, Bennett proceeded to read the script aloud, line by line, as he and O'Neill sipped a glass for each of the play's three acts. "If we hadn't had it we couldn't have kept awake," O'Neill confided to Agnes. "Do you know what time the work was finished? 7:30 a.m.! We were both dead." When he returned to his hotel, his brain "was full of subtle fireworks from the queer poison of absinthe," but, relieved that the *Beyond* script was now in satisfactory shape, he went to bed and slept all day.

Drink was again on his mind when he awakened. He was looking forward to what he called a "John Barleycorn party" to be held at the Playwrights' Theatre later that night. O'Neill assured Agnes he was not planning to participate in "any orgy" at the party, and said not to worry about his making a fool of himself. "I'm a wise guy—when I know it's necessary. But it would be silly for me not to drink. Everyone I'm associated with does—Tyler, Williams, Bennett . . . and they'd simply think me a prig if I didn't."

Well, the wise guy, finding himself ill at ease at the party, got drunk, first at the theater, and even drunker later when he went to the Hell Hole. He got so drunk that he ended up sleeping in one of the saloon's unheated upstairs rooms, on a bare mattress, and inadequately covered by his recently purchased expensive overcoat.

O'Neill confessed all this in his next letter to Agnes, along with the news that rehearsals for *Chris Christophersen* were to begin on the following Monday (January 26), for an opening in Atlantic City the first week in March.

Agnes lectured him severely about "the shape you get into after much drinking!" She conceded that a few drinks a day might help him to keep going, "But once you'd had a lot, and your brain is lit up with alcohol, you've got to keep on having a lot, or feel wretched—unless you've changed." She felt "surprised and hurt and depressed" that he should deliberately put himself "in the way of this happening."

O'Neill's response was swift and angry. "No more lecture letters, please! You never used to be a moralist, and I've never in my life stood for that stuff, even from my Mother." His "ethics of life," he said, forbade "even Christ or Buddha" from telling "the lowest slave what he should do," because that slave "has something actuating him that they can never understand."

Although Agnes apologized three days later, O'Neill continued to stew. "Your letter was gall when I prayed for wine," he wrote her. "You always have kicked me when I was down—do you realize that?—you did not mean to, of course, but you always have."

By January 22, O'Neill had a severe cold and had been warned by Dr. Aspell not to go outdoors. The influenza epidemic, intermittently raging since the beginning of 1918, was resurgent. (By the end of 1920, it would have killed somewhere between fifty and one hundred million people globally.) As neither Tyler nor Bennett was ready to work with him, O'Neill was content to stay put at the Prince George. But with too much time to brood, pessimism overwhelmed him.

He was sick of *Beyond the Horizon*, he told Agnes, and was certain it would fail. He wished he didn't have to attend any rehearsals, and he would certainly not attend a performance, for he doubted that any actor could ever fulfill his ideal of the character he'd created. But five days later O'Neill attended his first rehearsal of what he now labeled "the massacre." While the cast all had "the possibilities of being very good," he glumly wrote Agnes, "they all just miss it." The characters didn't "seem to hang together."

"They all appealed to me to dope out for them the real meaning of what they were trying to do. I tried my best, and I'm no director, God knows, and whether my talking will result in any improvement I don't know."

O'Neill's second day of rehearsals restored him to optimism. His report to Agnes, in fact, was buoyant: "For two days now I have occupied that position so unattainable to most playwrights—the only man in the auditorium, director of my own play! And I don't think I've made such a fizzle of it either! They all showed a noticeable improvement today, and also a marked improvement in their respect for me."

At the end of each scene, he went on, "Bennett calls 'Suggestions!' and every member of the cast who has been in that scene lines up at the foot lights while I—a lone figure in a vast auditorium—go from one to one, praising or panning, and not excepting Bennett himself."

Agnes responded with delight, but then grew thoughtful about their future. "Sometimes," she wrote, "I have a dreadful feeling that when the inevitable success does come there will be something to spoil it all for us."

By the time *Beyond* had its tryout in Yonkers on February 2, O'Neill was again disgusted with the production—as well as with the play itself. "It all seemed false and rotten and I wondered why the devil I'd ever written it," he told Agnes. "The sets for the outdoor scenes especially get my goat. To my eye they are the last word in everything they shouldn't be."

O'Neill's parents arrived early at the Morosco for the 2:15 matinee opening—James supporting himself with the cane he'd needed since his automobile accident—and were seated in the box their son had reserved. O'Neill himself was a reluctant member of the audience; Williams had insisted he sit beside him in the orchestra.

The curtain rose on the badly painted, murkily lighted set meant to represent O'Neill's lyrically described section of a country highway, "the horizon hills . . . rimmed by a faint line of flame, and the sky above them glows with the crimson flush of the sunset."

While the grim tale of the two brothers unfolded, O'Neill covertly watched as his father, in his box, "wept his eyes out." However, the rest of the audience—which included a large number of Provincetown Players—seemed to O'Neill unmoved. He squirmed throughout the play's three acts, embarrassed by the long waits between scenes. It was "hell," he reported to Agnes the following day.

When the performance ended a few minutes before six, he was greeted by his departing father, who beamed at him through teary eyes.

"It's all right, if that's what you want to do," said James O'Neill, "but people come to the theater to forget their troubles, not to be reminded of them. What are you trying to do—send them home to commit suicide?"

Recalling the episode years later, O'Neill said he was not surprised by his father's reaction, as *Beyond* was not "the sort of thing he could like. . . . All the same, I think he was pleased." O'Neill himself slouched from the Morosco, convinced that his play was "a flivver" artistically and "every other way."

Most of New York's first-string critics attended the opening despite the early curtain and the fact that they would shortly be reviewing an evening performance of a Georges Feydeau farce, *Breakfast in Bed*. That season, they'd already scribbled their opinions of thirty musicals and revues, sixty comedies and melodramas, and six farces. They had seen little to stir them: some Shakespeare in repertory, a couple of adapted European tragedies, a fantasy or two.

Certainly they had not been challenged to appraise "An American Tragedy," which was how John Williams had decided to bill *Beyond the Horizon*. But several of the more intellectually curious critics, including *The New York Times*'s Alexander Woollcott and the New York *Tribune*'s Heywood Broun, knew O'Neill's work from regularly attending the Provincetown Players' productions, and they expected something out of the ordinary.

To O'Neill's astonishment, all the critics praised his play. "I felt sure when I saw the woebegone faces on opening day that it was a rank failure," he said in an interview two and a half weeks later. "No one was more surprised than was I when I saw the morning papers and came to the conclusion that the sad expressions on the playgoers' faces were caused by their feeling the tragedy I had written."

A number of critics recognized that an event of magnitude had occurred in the American theater. Alexander Woollcott (who, twenty years later, would scorn *Strange Interlude*) described *Beyond the Horizon* as "an absorbing, significant and memorable tragedy, so full of meat that it makes most of the remaining fare seem like the merest meringue."

He characterized O'Neill as "a playwright of real power and imagination," adding, "the play has greatness in it and marks O'Neill as one of our foremost playwrights [and] one of the most spacious men to be gifted and tempted to write for the theater in America."

Broun, slightly more restrained, called *Beyond* a "significant and interesting play by a young author who does not yet know all the tricks." Most of the other critics, while thrilled by the play's originality, were almost apologetic about endorsing it, warning that it could not be a popular success.

They were wrong. When Bennett's vehicle, *For the Defense*, closed, Williams moved *Beyond*—with Bennett—to the Criterion Theatre, where on February 23 it began regular evening performances. The play attracted audiences until June 26, when it closed after 111 performances. O'Neill's share of the $117,017 gross was $6,264—not the highest of royalties, but far more than he'd ever earned before (and which he and Agnes spent as quickly as it was paid). O'Neill had achieved his goal of forcing Broadway to accept him on his own terms.

After reading the extraordinary reviews of the first matinee, he rejoiced, as never before, over his critical success. "It's positively stunning!" he crowed to Agnes on the day following the opening. "Whatever it may or may not do in a financial way, it has done all I ever expected of it already—and more."

13

His joyful rush dissolving, O'Neill gave way to his recurrent longing for Agnes. He wanted her at his side to share his triumph, to coddle him in his exhaustion, to assuage his inevitable sense of post-opening letdown.

Forgotten were their venomous squabbles; Agnes was once again his cherished soul mate. In a letter of frustration and yearning, he fell back on a coy game of sexual wordplay they had devised: He was "Mr. N."— code for the "Nightingale" of Keats's "Ode." Agnes was "Miss P." for pussy (an evolvement of the sixteenth-century "pussie," a lusty euphemism he was to bestow years later on Carlotta Monterey as well).

"Mr. N.," he wrote, "demands that he be put into instant communication with Miss P., or at least, poor lonely bird that he is!, that he send a message by me to her which you are to tell her in the still hour before you fall asleep [that] if you find it HELL to be away from me then I find it triple-plated HELL not to have you beside me in the long, lonely nights!" Then abandoning his cat-and-bird frolic, he cried out, "Oh, My Own, My Darling Agnes, My Own Little Wife, I want you, and need you, and love you so!"

His parents, he said, were being solicitous of him, "but they are not You." Desperate to return home, he reminded Agnes of Robert Mayo's lines in *Beyond*: "'It's hard to stay—and harder to go, sometimes.' You are my life!"

Agnes had earlier declared her own loneliness in what might have been the most candidly lustful letter she ever wrote him: "We have lived together too long to be separated like this! It seems as if I couldn't stand it, I want to love you so! There—do you hate me for being so frank? Gene—your little Miss P. is meowing and howling and behaving like a perfect devil. . . . I'm in such a funny, vibrating physical state, it almost frightens me."

Now, three days after the opening of *Beyond*, she described her regret at not having shared his moment of triumph, of not having witnessed his flash of pride and joy, for she knew it would quickly fade and become, as she put it, "an empty bauble."

Conscience-bound to remain in New York for the production of *Chris Christophersen*, O'Neill was tempted to send for Agnes. But he foresaw the difficulties of her traveling alone with a breast-feeding infant and of finding her an inexpensive place to stay.

George Tyler had promised to release O'Neill after one more week, and while waiting out each endless day, he was buoyed by the prospering of *Beyond* despite a flu resurgence and a heavy snowfall. On February 6, he bragged to Agnes that the day's matinee had had a record attendance and he was being asked for photographs to accompany newspaper and magazine interviews.

"Only a few days more!" he told Agnes, who was stranded in their Provincetown cottage in the midst of a savage blizzard. Fervently, she replied, "I want no other religion, no other belief, it is all there in you—in us."

On the day she mailed her letter, O'Neill came down with the flu, which he believed he caught from his mother, who was confined to bed with severe symptoms. Dr. Aspell diagnosed Eugene's case as mild, but cautioned him to stay indoors for a few days. Agnes was alarmed. She reminded O'Neill of the recent deaths of several young Provincetowners who, weakened after recovering from flu, had died of pneumonia. "*Now you must not do anything to get cold after you are better,*" she pleaded.

In spite of her eagerness to have him back home, she implored him not to take any chances, "for my sake, and poor Shane's, for I swear if anything happens to you I will not live in this world without you—I simply couldn't."

She was resigned, she said, to waiting a little longer. She sounded very much like O'Neill himself in regretting past misbehavior; and she assured him that once they were reunited, she would be "so much nicer—so much more understanding." He was her "perfect husband-lover," and she wanted to make their home "the most beautiful place in this world—in a spiritual sense."

It was now a week and a half since *Beyond the Horizon* had opened—sufficient time for O'Neill to have shrugged himself back into his periodic mantle of gloom. Worn down by illness, unhappy about the coming production of *Chris Christophersen*, concerned about both his parents' health, and missing Agnes, he had lost his elation over the triumph of *Beyond*.

Even a flattering letter from John Williams, telling him, "The Town is Yours," failed to cheer him. He sneered to Agnes, "They can keep it. Success has meant to me the meaningless futility I always knew it would—only more so."

When O'Neill still had not recovered from the flu by February 13, Agnes felt she must go to him; she begged him to take a room for her and Shane in his hotel. But he wrote back that there was a long waiting list at the Prince George, and he didn't have strength to look elsewhere and, besides, he thought it unwise to expose Shane to New York's flu epidemic. Then, unable to suppress his spasmodic resentment of his son's intrusive presence, he sulked, "It would all be so simple, if Shane were not in our midst, or if you only had him weaned."

The following day O'Neill suffered a severe attack of neuralgia. He was, according to his doctor, "worn down to the last notch, without resisting power, open hospitably to all ills." His nearly six-foot frame was skeletal; he weighed one hundred and twenty-five pounds. "I want you—need you—" he wrote Agnes, "and yet, with Shane, what is the use of my heart crying. It's all so impossible."

Three days later, he reported he was having trouble sleeping, had no appetite, and had developed a brutal cough. "Haven't been out of hotel yet. Doc. won't allow me to go to Chris rehearsals. I'm really in awfully bad shape—and can't seem to pick up."

O'Neill and Agnes had been apart for seven and a half weeks and there was worse to come. On February 27, James O'Neill, recovering from his earlier minor stroke, had a second stroke that brought him close to death. His doctor "just managed to keep life in Papa," O'Neill wrote Agnes. "Then he told Mama and me the truth. Papa, it seems, is doomed. He has a growth in the intestines which is bound sooner or later to prove fatal."

The growth was cancer, and it was deemed inoperable. His father's heart was so bad, wrote O'Neill, "he would die at the first sniff of ether." Torn between concern for his father and sympathy for his mother, Eugene most of all was overwhelmed by a childlike confusion and pity for himself. "Mama and I," he told Agnes, "have to go around nursing him," and "pretending to kid him and cheer him up! Can you imagine it?"

James, resilient and optimistic during most of his life, had, even before his accident, been gradually sinking into depression. More than once, Eugene had heard him mutter about "doing as his father did, deserting family, going back to Ireland to die." (This was a reference to Edward O'Neill, the banshee-bedeviled paternal grandfather O'Neill never knew who, in 1856—responding to ethereal Celtic voices—left his immigrant family to fend for themselves in Buffalo, New York, and returned to Ireland, where, soon after, he died of poison under suspicious circumstances.)

O'Neill complained to Agnes that, as he couldn't leave the Prince George to attend *Chris* rehearsals, he was instead obliged to work with the play's director at the hotel every morning. "As if I gave a damn about 'Chris' or any other play now! To have this happen just at the time when the Old Man and I were getting to be such good pals! I'm all broken up and begin to cry every time the meaning of it all dawns on me."

Waiting unhappily to depart for the March 8 opening of the *Chris* tryout in Atlantic City, O'Neill received word that Agnes had fallen ill. Certain that once he'd arrived in Atlantic City, Tyler would press him to stay on for who-knew-how-many days of rewriting, O'Neill seized the excuse of Agnes's illness to duck the out-of-town opening; he hastened instead to Provincetown, where he found Agnes already recovering.

But when he received a summons from Tyler to come at once to Atlantic City, where the play was not going well, he refused. In a wire to Tyler he lied that Agnes was very ill and he could not leave her and the baby. He did, however, send Tyler a lengthy rewrite of a crucial scene.

Chris Christophersen was bound for Philadelphia on March 14 but O'Neill was unwilling to budge, even though Agnes had completely recovered. She was "still very weak and unable to be out of bed yet," he again lied to Tyler. (On the same day, he wrote to a Provincetown Players colleague that Agnes was "quite herself again.")

O'Neill followed up with a message that further jolted Tyler. Ever since rereading the script in Provincetown, he said, he'd realized that *Chris* needed to be completely rewritten; cockily, he advised Tyler to "throw the present play in the ashbarrel." He had "inklings" of how to rework it; he would "keep without change only the character of Chris" and would create "a real daughter and lover, flesh-and-blood people—and the underlying idea of the sea." However, he did not think he would be able to complete such a rewrite until the following fall.

Tyler admitted defeat. He closed *Chris* in Philadelphia and turned his attention to *The Straw*, which O'Neill now averred was the best play he'd ever written—even better than *Beyond the Horizon*. It was not the first or last play he would initially trumpet as his "best," only to acknowledge its faults after it had been produced—and failed.

O'Neill spent much of the next two months squabbling with Tyler over how and where *The Straw* should be presented. They couldn't resolve the problem and the production was indefinitely postponed.

Lifting O'Neill's spirits during the quarrelsome back-and-forth with

Tyler was the March 10 publication of *Beyond the Horizon* by Boni & Liveright; all 1,250 copies of the first printing were wrapped in orange dust jackets containing a blurb from Alexander Woollcott.

Beyond, O'Neill's first full-length play to be published, contained a formal dedication to Agnes, but he saluted her more elaborately on the flyleaf of the copy he gave her: "In memory of the wonderful moment when first in your eyes I saw the promise of a land more beautiful than any I had ever known, a land of which I had dreamed only hopelessly, a land beyond my horizon."

Agnes was having her own bit of publishing luck. She sold two stories to *The Smart Set*, bringing in some welcome cash to add to the modest proceeds from both the production and publication of *Beyond*. In late April, even though their expenses, as always, exceeded their budget, the O'Neills decided it was time for Agnes to take Shane on brief visits to both sets of grandparents—and for Agnes finally to attend a performance of *Beyond the Horizon*.

Agnes would have liked to take Mrs. Clarke with her to help with Shane, but felt she couldn't afford the extra expense. Besides, Mrs. Clarke was needed in Provincetown to look after O'Neill.

Agnes did not have an easy time of it in New York. To save on expenses, she lived in a friend's one-room cold-water flat, where she had to bathe Shane in the kitchen sink (in which she also washed his diapers). When she saw the pleasure that Ella and the ailing James took in meeting their grandson, however, she felt rewarded for the inconvenience. Although reporting to O'Neill that his father did not look well, she wrote that both his parents "were smitten with Shane."

After at last attending a performance of *Beyond*, on April 26, Agnes, as instructed by O'Neill, recorded her impressions; she thought Bennett's performance was "great" but otherwise found much to disapprove of—mostly the bad acting of other cast members. She urged him to sit through a performance and see if he couldn't get director Williams to make some improvements.

While working in Provincetown that June on his new version of *Chris* and monitoring bulletins about his father's sinking health, O'Neill received a telegram from Columbia University, informing him he'd won a prize he hadn't known existed. The Pulitzer Prize, established three years earlier, had been awarded only once (in 1918) in the category of drama, when it went to Jesse Lynch Williams for a play called *Why Marry?* (The prize was withheld in 1917 and 1919.)

The award cited *Beyond the Horizon* as an "original American play" that best represented "the educational value and power of the stage in raising the standard of good morals, good taste and good manners"—not exactly a fit for O'Neill's dark tale of thwarted love and smothered hope. As he himself jested to Nina Moise: "Can you imagine me at the point where Columbia University actually confers one of its biggest blue ribbons on me?"

His first impulse, as he later recorded, "was a disdainful raspberry, 'Oh God, a damned medal! And one of those presentation ceremonies! I won't accept it.' (I have never been fond of medals or ceremonies.) Then a wire from my agent arrived which spoke of a thousand dollars and no medal and no ceremony. Well, I practically went delirious! I was broke or nearly. A thousand dollars was sure a thousand dollars! It was the most astoundingly pleasant surprise I've ever had in my life, I think."

On June 10, O'Neill's joyous mood turned somber when he learned that his terminally ill father had been transferred from his hospital in New York to the Lawrence Memorial Hospital in New London. James, after more than fifty years of ceaseless touring, had come home to die in the only place for which he had any nostalgia.

His doctor shocked Ella when he told her the end might be only days away. Jamie, who accompanied his mother to New London, sent his brother the stark prognosis: "I believe he's going to die—and soon—but that he'll linger some time yet."

After worrying about how much the care was costing and how it would "leave Mama on the rocks," Jamie momentarily put aside his disdain for the father he'd always blamed for his mother's drug addiction, and blurted his sorrow to his brother; he wept, he said, and felt horribly grief-shaken when he "really believed the end was at hand, and Ma was on the verge of a breakdown, staying up purely on her nerve."

O'Neill and Agnes were in the midst of arranging their annual move to Peaked Hill Bars for the summer when, in early July, a telegram warned that James was rapidly failing. Leaving Agnes to cope as best she could, O'Neill sped to New London to take up his bedside vigil with his mother and brother.

Agnes called on friends and hired help to assist in the always cumbersome trek to Peaked Hill Bars. She piled herself, Shane, Mrs. Clarke, and their baggage onto the Coast Guard's horse-drawn wagon for the arduous journey over the great dunes to their ocean-front retreat. She reported her achievement to O'Neill—at the same time chiding him for not sending any news of his father.

As he sat at his dying father's bedside, O'Neill was tormented by memories of his years of youthful rebellion, egged on by Jamie: the times he'd echoed his brother's mockery of their father's high-flown acting style; his father's blind loyalty to all things Irish; his rote obeisance to Catholic ritual; his pleasure in staking his sponging barroom cronies to drinks; his parsimony in wearing his clothes until threadbare; his compulsion to skimp on household necessities while sinking money into often worthless real estate.

Eugene remembered the family lore about his own birth in a Broadway hotel room, when his father summoned the cheap hotel doctor to attend his wife, whose delivery was not easy. He thought about his father's immigrant peasant superstition that called for a spoonful of whiskey as a remedy for an infant's nightmares.

He dwelled sullenly on the summer when he was diagnosed with tuberculosis. His father, presuming in his ignorance that Eugene had been handed a death warrant, sent him to a state farm rather than seek the costly medical help that might cure him. Nor did Eugene forget how he subsequently shamed his father into reversing his decision and sending him to the sanatorium where he recovered. Then there was the time his father withdrew his promise to pay for his second year at the Harvard playwriting course he longed to complete.

As he watched his father's withered face in the hospital, Eugene also remembered all the mean and callous things he'd done to him: how he hurt him by refusing as a teenager to ever again accompany him to Sunday Mass; how, to embarrass his father, he had flaunted an adolescent fondness for whores; how he'd got himself expelled from Princeton for carousing during his freshman year and failing to take his final exams; how he had derided his father's choice of popular and lucrative roles in hackneyed melodramas like *The Count of Monte Cristo* rather than developing his gift as a Shakespearean actor; how he pained his father by his flagrantly irresponsible first marriage.

Thinking back, Eugene remorsefully acknowledged his father's well-intentioned efforts on his behalf. He had sent Eugene to an excellent preparatory school (Betts Academy in Stamford, Connecticut) and to Princeton; he had tried to place him in self-sustaining jobs; he'd given him an allowance, well into his thirties, that kept him from starving; he'd bought him a home in Provincetown; and, in spite of sustained ingratitude, his father had never abandoned him.

Even so, it was only in recent years that O'Neill had come to feel compassion for his father. As he once told a writer who was researching James O'Neill's career, "My father's parents were extremely poor. When he was only ten years old he had to start working in a machine shop for fifty cents a week." O'Neill, at that time, was creating the character of James Tyrone in *Long Day's Journey Into Night*, based, of course, on his father, for whom he wrote a heartbreaking monologue about the travails of his impoverished life as an immigrant child.

Sitting at his father's deathbed, Eugene was engulfed in regrets. Despite everything, he knew his father was a decent and well-meaning man. How few would have had his father's endurance and compassion, or his determination not to withdraw his support from his two dysfunctional sons.

"My father and I hadn't got along so well," he mused in an interview many years after James O'Neill's death. "We had had a running battle for a good many years, and I know there were times when he'd just about given me up. Not that I can blame him. If anything, he was too patient with me. What I wonder now is why he didn't kick me out. I gave him every chance to. And yet, as sometimes happens, we were close to each other—we were a very close family. My father, somehow, managed to believe in me."

O'Neill at last responded to Agnes with a harrowing letter:

> *Am writing this at the hospital. Papa is lying in bed watching me, his strange eyes staring at me with a queer, uncanny wonder as if, in that veiled borderland between Life and Death in which his soul drifts suspended, a real living being of his own flesh and blood were an incongruous and puzzling spectacle.*
>
> *I feel as if my health, the sun tan on my face contrasted with the unearthly pallor of his, were a spiritual intrusion, an impudence. And yet how his eyes lighted up with grateful affection when he first saw me! It made me feel so glad, so happy I had come!*
>
> *The situation is frightful! Papa is alive when he ought to be dead. The disease has eaten through his bowels. Internal decomposition has set in—while he is still living! There is a horrible, nauseating smell in the room, the sickening, overpowering odor of a dead thing. His face, his whole body is that of a corpse. He is unspeakably thin and wasted.*
>
> *Only his eyes are alive—and the light that glimmers through their glaze is remote and alien. He suffers incredible tortures—in spite of all their dope. Just a few moments ago he groaned in anguish and cried pitifully: "Oh God, why don't You take me! Why don't You take me!"*
>
> *And Mama and I silently echoed his prayer.*
>
> *But God seems to be in His Omnipotent mood just now and not in His All Merciful.*

One very pitiful, cruelly ironic thing: He cannot talk plainly any more. Except when he cries out in pain it is impossible to understand him. And all through life his greatest pride has been in his splendid voice and clear articulation!

His lips flutter, he tries so hard to say something, only a mumble comes forth—and then he looks at you so helplessly, so like a dog that has been punished it knows not why.

Death seems to be rubbing it in—to demand that he drink the chalice of gall and vinegar to the last bitter drop before peace is finally his.

And, dear God, why? Surely he is a fine man as men go, and can look back to a long life in which he has kept an honorable faith and labored hard to get from nothing to the best attainment he knew. Surely the finest test of that attainment is the great affection and respect that all bear him who knew him. I don't believe he ever hurt a living thing intentionally.

And he certainly has been a husband to marvel at, and a good father, according to his lights. I know those are the conventional virtues that are inscribed on tombstones—but he is the one person in a million who deserves them. Perhaps these virtues are so common in cemeteries because they are so rare in life.

At any rate, looking at it dispassionately, he seems to me a good man—in the best sense of the word—and about the only one I have ever known. Then why should he suffer so—when murderers are granted the blessing of electric chairs.

James dozed fitfully as O'Neill, in a corner of the hospital room, sat pouring out his anguish to Agnes. Suddenly, James awakened and beckoned his son to his bedside.

Gasping for breath, in hesitant, barely audible words, the old actor delivered the lines of his heart-wrenching confession.

It was, Eugene later told Agnes, "like a dying dialogue in a play I might have written." Indeed, had O'Neill chosen to add a transcription of his father's last words as an epilogue to *Long Day's Journey Into Night* they would have served as a stunning epitaph.

"He made a dreadful effort to speak clearly and I understood a part of what he said," O'Neill wrote.

> *Glad to go, boy—a better sort of life—another sort—*
> *somewhere"—and then he mumbled. He appeared to be trying to*
> *tell me what sort—and although I tried my damndest I couldn't*
> *understand!*
>
> *This sort of life—froth!—rotten!—all of it—no good!" There*
> *was a bitter expression on his poor, sunken face. And there you have*
> *it—the verdict of a good man looking back over seventy-six years:*
> *"Froth! Rotten!"*
>
> *But it's finally consoling to know he believes in a "better*
> *sort—somewhere." I could see he did—implicitly! He will die with*
> *a sigh of relief. What queer things for him to say, eh?*

James sank into a coma; the "weak" heart diagnosed by his doctor, which had precluded an operation, ironically proved strong enough to keep him alive for twelve more days.

Ella and her two sons kept a stoic vigil at James's bedside. Always prone to dwell on the past, Ella might have drifted wistfully to her wedding day on June 14, 1877, when, as a lace-curtain Irish bride of twenty— pretty, educated, sheltered, and still mourning the loss of her own beloved father—she stepped trustfully into the cauldron that was to be her marriage.

Gazing at James's desiccated, pain-wracked face, perhaps Ella saw the exuberant, worldly, self-made thirty-two-year-old matinee idol she'd married—the handsomest and most romantic man she'd ever dreamed of as a husband. She would always remember the ceremony at St. Ann's Church on East Twelfth Street in Manhattan, known as "the beau monde parish," the locale for most of New York City's chic Catholic weddings.

James died on August 10, 1920, three days after Ella turned sixty-three. Agnes joined O'Neill in New London for the funeral. James was buried beside his infant son, Edmund, in St. Mary's Cemetery, where Ella's mother also was buried.

After the funeral, to Agnes's distress, O'Neill and his brother went off to get drunk. But no amount of drinking could banish the valiant old actor's ghost.

"My father died broken, unhappy, intensely bitter, feeling that life was 'a damned hard billet to chew,'" wrote O'Neill to George Tyler. His father's dying words, O'Neill said, were "seared on my brain—a warning from the Beyond to remain true to the best that is in me though the heavens fall."

14

Reunited in late August 1920 with Agnes and Shane in Peaked Hill Bars, O'Neill continued to ponder his father's "warning from the Beyond." He hoped to dispel his grief with disciplined concentration—sometimes devoting as many as eight hours a day to his writing. But it seemed James O'Neill would forever be looking over his son's shoulder.

Inspired by his father's dying words, O'Neill, some months later, forged a credo that would guide him through his life's work. The New York *Tribune* was so impressed with the nobility of O'Neill's uncompromising vision, as well as with his rising eminence, that it published his lofty statement under the two-column headline, "Eugene O'Neill's Credo and His Reasons for His Faith":

> To me, the tragic alone has that significant beauty which is truth. It is the meaning of life—and the hope. The noblest is eternally the most tragic. The people who succeed and do not push on to a greater failure are the spiritual middle classers. Their stopping at success is the proof of their compromising insignificance. How petty their dreams must have been! The man who pursues the mere attainable should be sentenced to get it—and keep it. Let him rest on his laurels and enthrone him in a Morris chair, in which laurels and hero may wither away together.

Only through the unattainable does man achieve a hope
worth living and dying for—and so attain himself. He with
the spiritual guerdon of a hope in hopelessness is nearest to
the stars and the rainbow's foot.

It had taken Eugene some time to understand that his father was hos-
tage to the fearsome deprivation of his childhood, a childhood that cat-
apulted him from Ireland's Great Potato Famine to the terrifying milieu
of the impoverished Irish immigrant community of Buffalo, New York,
where his starving family landed in 1851.

James grew up with a horror of the poorhouse that was ingrained; it
compelled him to acquire as much cash and real estate as he could, as a
hedge against the poverty he always saw lurking.

Eugene knew that when his father, on his deathbed, pronounced his
life as "froth!—rotten!—all of it—no good!" he was deploring his abandonment of a talent that had promised to equal Edwin Booth's as a great
Shakespearean actor; he had done so to accumulate the easy riches from
his endlessly popular vehicle, *The Count of Monte Cristo*.

Touring from coast to coast, season after lucrative season, in the facile
role of Edmond Dantes, James found himself trapped. When from time to
time he tried to shove aside the count for a more substantial role, his audience fell off; in an instant he saw the poorhouse looming, and hastily resurrected *Monte Cristo*, which by then he had come to think of as his albatross.
O'Neill grieved that his father had failed to learn what he himself had
always believed: that the endless pursuit of material gain shriveled the soul.

WHILE SILVER-TIPPED WAVES slapped the sandy beach of the O'Neills'
front yard at Peaked Hill Bars, Agnes, too, resumed her writing; she could
rely on Mrs. Clarke to relieve her of Shane's supervision, as well as of
many household chores. Mrs. Clarke soon would be christened Gaga by
nine-month-old Shane, who adored her, much as O'Neill had treasured
his own nursemaid, Sarah Sandy, as a second mother.

Almost without exception, the O'Neills were viewed by their friends as a romantic, if high-strung couple—Agnes with her sculpted cheekbones and luminous blue-gray eyes, O'Neill with his swimmer's physique and poet's soulful gaze—both slim as saplings and burnished by the sun. None questioned their passionate mutual attachment. It was clear to all, however, that their love was anything but tranquil.

Agnes was often irritated by O'Neill's rigid intolerance of any disruption to his concentration. Like many a writer's wife, she decried his inaccessibility when she craved his advice or solace; and she was always on edge, awaiting the emotional setback, however minor, that might lacerate his precarious nervous system. She tried to balance his needs with her own sporadic writing, her distracted mothering of Shane, and running a household. Invariably, it was his needs that took precedence, for it was he who had become the rapidly rising star.

Wrapped in work and family, O'Neill was disinclined to busy himself with his widowed mother's efforts to resolve her husband's business affairs. His love for her was ever at war with the rancor crouching beneath that love, and he was guiltily relieved that Jamie had assumed responsibility for her. Jamie, jobless and unmarried at forty-two, exulted at the chance to replace his father as Ella's devoted attendant.

Staying with relatives in New London, Ella was attempting, with a surge of newfound energy, to sort out her husband's chaotic local investments; she'd been informed by James's lawyer that his estate, built on invested royalties from his lucrative acting career, might be substantial—worth perhaps more than $100,000. But not much of the estate was available in cash, and gradually it became clear that separating James's good investments from the bad would not be easy.

"The truth is," O'Neill later explained, "he did lose a fortune, and a big one, during his whole career, but 'Monte Cristo' enabled him to afford his losses. He was an easy mark for anyone with a spare gold mine, zinc mine, coal mine, silver mine, pieces of real estate, etc.—and he rarely guessed right. But he never went into anything so heavily it could ruin him."

It fell to Ella to liquidate at least enough property to provide her with an income, and the complex negotiations were a merciful distraction, leaving her little time to mourn her husband. "She is developing into a keenly interested business woman who seems to accept this unfamiliar responsibility with a great sense of relief," O'Neill wrote to Tyler. "Under her hand, I honestly have a hunch that some dividends may finally accrue from the junk buried on the island of M[onte]C[risto]."

Jamie was there to help in any way he could. He had always adored his mother and had long since smothered the pain she'd inflicted on him in his early childhood and adolescence. From infancy, he'd traveled with his parents during his father's acting tours, living with them in closest intimacy on trains and in hotel rooms across the country. Deprived of companions his own age, he was preternaturally attached to and dependent on his mother.

Unsurprisingly, he had been acutely jealous when, at five, he was confronted with the intrusion of a baby brother. Ella found it too difficult to tour with both Jamie and infant Edmund, and mostly stayed behind in The Richfield, a family hotel on Forty-third Street just west of Broadway, that for a time was the O'Neill home in New York.

Jamie was not yet seven and Edmund not yet two when Ella, in January of 1885, succumbed to her husband's plea to join him on his western tour. She was torn about leaving her young children, but she missed James as much as he missed her and, apprehensively, she left the boys in her mother's care and set off by train for Denver.

In mid-February, not long after reuniting with James, Ella received a telegram from her mother; Jamie had come down with measles. Ella wired back, cautioning her mother to keep Jamie away from the baby. But Jamie, disregarding his grandmother's warnings, went into Edmund's room—possibly out of curiosity, possibly out of malice—exposing the baby to his own case of measles.

On February 27, a second telegram informed Ella that Edmund had measles. She immediately entrained for New York. But on March 4, just before her arrival, Edmund died. In her grief, she first blamed herself for having left him; she then blamed her husband for enticing her away; then her mother for her carelessness; and finally she accused Jamie of having deliberately infected Edmund.

Jamie, devastated, was soon banished to boarding school. But typical of the child who helplessly loves the parent who abuses him, Jamie clung to his mother.

Now, WITH HIS father's death, Jamie was so infatuated with his new role as his mother's constant companion that he vowed, for her sake, never again to take a drop of liquor. Jamie and Ella became an inseparable couple, dining together, attending the theater together, and, in tandem, visiting their relatives in New York and New London.

After receiving regular reports from New London of his mother's progress in resolving James's estate, O'Neill felt obliged to invite her and Jamie to spend what O'Neill called "a Thanksgiving rest" with him and Agnes in the rented winterized house in the village of Provincetown to which they retreated when their unheated Peaked Hill Bars home became unlivable.

At sixty-three, Ella, outfitted with a wardrobe of stylish black dresses and accessories, was more self-possessed than her son Eugene had ever seen her. He decided that mourning suited her—spiritually as well as physically. The striking image of Ella O'Neill, blooming as she mourned, would later imbue his portrait of Lavinia Mannon in *Mourning Becomes Electra*.

While he admired his mother's resourcefulness, he seemed not to feel any surge of renewed warmth toward her. His feelings may be surmised from the wording of his inscription in the copy he gave her of the newly published *The Moon of the Caribbees and Six Other Plays of the Sea*. Whereas a typical O'Neill inscription to even a casual friend was apt to pulse with warmth and sentiment, to Ella he wrote with wintry reserve: "To my Mother from Eugene" (adding nothing more than "Provincetown, Mass, Thanksgiving").

THAT NOVEMBER 1920, O'Neill had nearly completed *Gold*, an expansion of *Where the Cross Is Made*, in which a deluded whaling captain, shipwrecked on a coral island and crazed with thirst, discovers a chest of trinkets he takes for gold.

After he and three mates bury the "treasure," they are rescued and return home, where the captain lives in hopes of going back to the island and retrieving the buried treasure. His inability to do so eventually drives him insane; as in *Where the Cross Is Made*, he is hounded to his death by the ghosts of his drowned mates. (In *Where the Cross Is Made*, the ghosts actually confront the captain, causing him to drop dead, whereas in *Gold*, the ghosts are seen only in the captain's mind.)

George Jean Nathan, to whom O'Neill sent the script, said he liked it even better than *Beyond the Horizon*. Nevertheless, in an article praising O'Neill's work in general, the critic chided him for seeing "life too often as drama," pointing out somewhat cryptically, "The great dramatist is the dramatist who sees drama as life."

O'Neill's response was good-humored and respectful, acknowledging that he was "familiar enough with the best modern drama of all countries to realize that, viewed from a true standard, my work is as yet a mere groping." He added that he rated himself "as a beginner—with prospects."

He credited Nathan with hitting "the nail on the head" with his rebuke. "But," he said, "I venture to promise that this will be less true with each succeeding play—that I will not 'stay put' in any comfortable niche and play the leave-well-enough-alone game. God stiffen it, I am young yet and I mean to grow!"

He concluded that if he had "the 'guts' to follow the dream," he would, in time, and after struggle, attain the means to express his "real significant bit of truth" and thereby "merit victory."

Demonstrating beyond a doubt that he was not staying put "in any comfortable niche," after writing *Gold*, O'Neill rapidly crafted three more plays: *Anna Christie*, *Diff'rent*, and *The Emperor Jones*. All three were completed before the end of 1920—each so startlingly unlike the other two they could have been written by three different playwrights of diametrically diverse backgrounds, outlooks, and temperaments.

Anna Christie was the first to be completed. True to his promise to producer Tyler (and himself), it was a total rewrite of the failed *Chris Christophersen*, and he finished it in the summer of 1920. Keeping the basic character of "Chris," he transformed his ladylike daughter into someone far more interesting and original: a remorseful former prostitute who calls herself Anna Christie.

Written in a naturalistic style, the play on its surface is a girl-meets-boy love story, if not quite a conventional one: Anna, who has recently come to live with her father on his coal barge, meets Mat Burke, a virile, naively idealistic seaman, when he is rescued from drowning by Chris; Anna finds redemption in her love for Mat and he returns her love—until she confesses her past—at which point he furiously rejects her. At play's end, he accepts Anna's repentance, acknowledges her transformation, and they marry.

By O'Neill's own account, he wrote both *Diff'rent* and *The Emperor Jones* during the fall of 1920. In *Diff'rent*, drawing once again on his own family dynamic, he reimagined the character of a favorite cousin, Lil Brennan, an unmarried woman in her fifties, with whom he'd become reacquainted in New London during visits to his dying father.

Dwelling on the psychological reasons for his cousin's adamant spinsterhood, he depicted her as the sexually repressed Emma Crosby in *Diff'rent*, set in a New England village of the 1890s; Emma could also have been a sketch for the later, more fully realized, sex-repressed Lavinia Mannon of *Mourning Becomes Electra*. (Lillian Brennan was also the model for the more benign spinster aunt in *Ah, Wilderness!*)

While *Diff'rent* was one of O'Neill's lesser accomplishments, *The Emperor Jones* was the most daringly experimental of the three plays—a tale of primitive terror and devastation and a deliberate distortion of reality. It is one of O'Neill's few major works not emanating from his feelings about the angst-ridden members of his family. He wrote the play in pencil in minute letters, cramming its eight scenes onto three sheets of standard typewriter paper.

Accompanied by throbbing native drumbeats, the play's action centers on a black Pullman porter, Brutus Jones, who has fled to a tropical island after killing a man in the States. The natives, of whom he has made himself the greedy and despotic ruler, stage a revolt, and Jones attempts to escape through the jungle.

The natives, brainwashed into believing that only a silver bullet can kill him, resourcefully melt down coins to make the bullet and then go in pursuit. As he plunges through the nighttime jungle, Jones, facing one ghost after another, loses his way and is caught by the rebels, who kill him with their silver bullet.

The jungle's terrifying effect on the human imagination was drawn by O'Neill from the fear he himself experienced at twenty-one while prospecting for gold in the tropical forests of Spanish Honduras: "a wall of darkness dividing the world," as he described it in his stage directions.

The actual plot came from a circus employee, Jack Croak, who drank with O'Neill in the bar of the Garden Hotel, nearby the old Madison Square Garden on Madison Avenue and Twenty-sixth Street.

Croak, who enjoyed talking about the experiences he'd had while touring the West Indies with the Sells Circus tent show, once told O'Neill a story concerning the five-month dictatorship, in Haiti in 1915, of the late president Vilbrun Guillaume Sam, who was assassinated during a popular uprising.

> This was to the effect that Sam had said they'd never get him with a lead bullet; if necessary, he would get himself first with a silver one. My friend, by the way, gave me a coin with Sam's features on it, and I still keep it as a pocket piece.
>
> A year elapsed. One day I was reading of the religious feasts in the Congo and the uses to which the drum is put there; how it starts at a normal pulse-beat and is slowly intensified

until the heart-beat of everyone present corresponds to the frenzied beat of the drum. There was an idea and an experiment. How would this sort of thing work on an audience in a theater?

Adam Scott, a black bartender O'Neill had known in New London, provided a part model for Brutus Jones's sardonic view of life when, in an early scene, Jones explains he's no longer the religious Baptist he was as a Pullman porter.

"I'se after de coin, an' I lays my Jesus on de shelf for de time bein,'" says Jones, sounding like Scott, who on Sundays acted as an elder of the Shiloh Baptist Church and, when asked how he reconciled his religious belief with his job of tending bar, would reply, "I'm a very religious man, but after Sunday I lay my Jesus on the shelf."

O'NEILL READ *The Emperor Jones* aloud to Jig Cook and his wife, Susan Glaspell, at Peaked Hill Bars, and they sat enthralled, visualizing Brutus Jones, his self-reliance and pride crumbling, his splendid uniform being torn from his body as he stumbled and clawed his way through the tropical jungle.

They listened to O'Neill's evocation of the quickening beat of the voodoo drums, while the emperor's crazed subjects hid and danced in the hills, waiting for their victim to lose his way.

Cook instantly recognized the play's powerful potential; but it was not quite a full-length play, and he agreed with O'Neill that its brevity and boldness dictated its presentation at the Playwrights' Theatre rather than on Broadway. Cook leaped into the task of creating a visually groundbreaking production and, for once, O'Neill did not have to wait long before seeing a play of his come alive. On November 1, 1920, it was the first of his three newly completed plays to be staged.

Climbing new heights of ingenuity, Jig Cook had fashioned a

cyclorama—a cement dome—that could be lighted to magical effect on the small stage of the Playwrights' Theatre. Even viewers seated in the front row had the illusion of distance; an actor could stretch his hand to within inches of the dome's surface and still seem a long way from it. O'Neill, impressed by Cook's passionate dedication as director, left the production entirely in his hands.

Cook puzzled over the casting of Brutus Jones. In 1920, no black actor had ever played the leading role in an American drama, and some of Cook's colleagues argued that the part should go to a white actor who would wear blackface—the conventional solution for its time.

Other colleagues, however, disagreed, thinking back to the year before, when the Players broke new ground with O'Neill's one-acter *The Dreamy Kid* (which opened on October 31, 1919, at the Playwrights' Theatre); for that play, about a young black gangster who risks arrest to visit his dying grandmother, the Players had recruited their four-character cast from a black acting troupe in Harlem—the first time a "white" theater company in New York had taken such a bold step.

Pointing to this example, the Players argued for a black actor to play Jones, and Cook agreed. Interest focused on Charles S. Gilpin, who had recently drawn good reviews in a small role on Broadway in John Drinkwater's *Abraham Lincoln*. Out of acting jobs since then, Gilpin—forty-one, handsome, light-skinned, brawny—was found running an elevator for a living.

He was hustled down to the Playwrights' Theatre, where a script was thrust into his hands. He read the role superbly and was engaged on the spot; as the production's only star, he received the highest salary—fifty dollars a week. The total cost of the production, cyclorama and all, was $502.28.

AFTER MOVING Agnes and Shane into winterized quarters in Provincetown, O'Neill paid an edgy visit to New York in October to check on rehearsals. He expressed his approval and hastened back to Cape Cod, where he stayed, bypassing the play's opening on November 1 and missing the volcanic applause that greeted it. The critics, occupied with openings on Broadway, didn't arrive downtown until two days later, but once there, they reported their stunned reactions.

The Emperor Jones was "just about the most interesting play which has yet come from the most promising playwright in America," said Heywood Broun in the *Tribune*, also lauding Gilpin for "the most thrilling performance we have seen any place this season, a performance of heroic stature." Gladdening the heart of Jig Cook, Broun praised the setting as "fine and imaginative and the lighting effects uncommonly beautiful."

Woollcott in the *Times* called the play "an extraordinarily striking and dramatic study of panic fear," adding that it reinforced "the impression that for strength and originality [O'Neill] has no rival among the American writers for the stage."

Not long after its thunderous opening, *Jones* moved to Broadway, leaving the Playwrights' Theatre free to receive *Diff'rent* on December 27; despite its shortcomings, the play found its audience and ran for a respectable one hundred performances. Meanwhile, *The Emperor Jones* was launched on what would be a hugely successful run of two hundred and four performances; it toured nationally for two years and later became a hit in London.

Gilpin was grateful to O'Neill, but feared his newly acquired stature might be short-lived.

"I am pleased," he movingly told interviewers, "especially with the generous praise of the critics. But I don't fool myself about the stone walls that are in my way. Mr. O'Neill made a breach in those walls by writing a play that had in it a serious role for a Negro."

O'Neill had proved, he said, "that a Negro can act" and that "a play can be written that will give a colored actor a chance." But how many such plays, he asked, would be written? "Where do I go from here?"

It was soon after *The Emperor Jones* moved uptown that Gilpin collided with one of those stone walls. He was invited, along with several other actors, to be an "honored guest" of the Drama League's annual dinner. When several members of the League expressed their offense at being asked to dine with a Negro, the League, in some embarrassment, withdrew the invitation to Gilpin.

O'Neill was irate. In spite of his painful shyness, he paid calls, accompanied by his friend Kenneth Macgowan, on most of the other actors who had been invited to the dinner and asked them to decline their invitations. Virtually all of them did and the League felt obliged to re-invite Gilpin. The dinner was a huge success, with six hundred guests attending, compared with the previous year's three hundred.

While O'Neill fought for Gilpin's rights, he grew irritated with what he regarded as his star's unprofessional behavior as the run continued through 1921. Believing success had gone to Gilpin's head, O'Neill complained that the actor had begun substituting the phrase "black baby" for "nigger"—as called for in the script—along with other terms Gilpin deemed more genteel.

One night—well fortified by drink, unable to control his black-Irish rage, and armed with bravado—O'Neill engaged in a shameful confrontation with Gilpin backstage. "If I ever catch you rewriting my lines again, you black bastard," he hollered, "I'm going to beat you up."

Evidently Gilpin's performance continued to deteriorate, and O'Neill insisted on replacing him for the play's London production. He justified his decision in a letter to his old friend, the Communist writer and editor Michael Gold:

"Yes, Gilpin is all 'ham' and a yard wide! Honestly, I've stood more from him than from all the white actors I've ever known—simply because he was colored! I'm 'off' him and the result is he will get no chance to do it in London. He was drunk all of last season and, outside of the multitude of other reasons, I'd be afraid to risk him in London."

For the role in London, O'Neill continued, he'd chosen a young actor with "wonderful presence & voice, full of ambition and a damn fine man personally with real brains—not a 'ham.'" He was not someone who would "lose his head if he makes a hit—as he surely will." The actor was

Paul Robeson. An outstanding Columbia Law School graduate, he had abandoned a legal career for the stage.

O'Neill eventually forgot his anger at Gilpin, recalling only the actor's brilliant portrayal when he originated the role. At the end of his writing career, O'Neill had only lavish praise for Gilpin. "As I look back on all my work," he said in an interview with *The New York Times*, "I can honestly say there was only one actor who carried out every notion of a character I had in mind. That actor was Charles Gilpin the Pullman porter in *The Emperor Jones*."

The play's move to Broadway's Selwyn Theatre brought the Provincetown Players their first unconditional recognition from uptown audiences and producers. *The Emperor Jones* thrust the Provincetown Players into national prominence, which they found themselves ill-equipped to deal with.

The Players were to last only one more season, undone by internal conflicts and rivalries. Dedicated to experimentation and to the freedom granted by their amateur status, they could not survive the fame and professionalism that had come with *Jones*.

Jig Cook blamed O'Neill for the Players' decline and, in truth, O'Neill deserved his share of the blame. In spite of their splendid production of *The Emperor Jones*, O'Neill had for some time been grumbling to Agnes and others that he'd outgrown the Players.

EARLY IN 1921 and still awaiting the production of *Anna Christie*, O'Neill began work on *The First Man*, a play that was transparently autobiographical. When Agnes read the first draft, she must have wondered if O'Neill was signaling that he'd outgrown not only the Provincetown Players but his marriage as well. Certainly the play could have been interpreted as evidence of an increasing hostility toward her. Their relationship had been insidiously shifting, and *The First Man* gave it another nudge, edging ever closer to the miasma of Strindbergian "love-hatred" that "hailed from the pit"—although Strindberg would have rightly dismissed the play as travesty and disowned O'Neill as a pathetically inept disciple.

Curtis and Martha Jayson of *The First Man* are in their late thirties. Curtis is an anthropologist and romantic idealist, and Martha is a selflessly devoted wife, absorbed in her husband's work.

The play takes its tone from Martha's expository dialogue, a perfunctory and ludicrous story about the death of their two young children ten years earlier (presumably a symbolic, if unsubtle expression of O'Neill and Agnes's wish to permanently eradicate Eugene Jr. and Barbara Burton from their lives).

"It was a Sunday in winter when Curt and I had gone visiting," Martha babbles to a friend. "The nurse girl fell asleep—or something—and the children sneaked out in their underclothes and played in the snow. Pneumonia set in—and a week later they were both dead."

At this point, Curtis and Martha—like O'Neill and Agnes—solemnly swear they will have a childless marriage and devote their lives exclusively to each other.

At the play's beginning, they have returned home after ten years of anthropologic research so that Curtis can write a scientific book. But it seems Martha has betrayed him by becoming pregnant. Curtis greets this news with some dismal dialogue: "How can I pretend gladness? Haven't we been sufficient, you and I together? Can you expect me to be glad when you propose to introduce a stranger who will steal away your love, your interest—who will separate us and divide me from you!"

Martha is conveniently killed off in the third act as, offstage—to the accompaniment of agonizing screams—she gives birth to a son while Curtis prays for the child to be stillborn. No such luck. The child emerges, a strapping eleven-pound boy, and the play ends with Curtis's limp proviso that when his son is old enough, he will "teach him to know and love a big, free life."

The First Man was a jolting reminder that O'Neill was still evolving; nor was this awful play the last of the missteps he would take as he groped his way to becoming Strindberg's worthy disciple. When it was finally produced, in 1922—well after *Gold*, *Anna Christie*, *The Emperor Jones*, and *Diff'rent*—it was a flop.

It would seem O'Neill was motivated to write the play by an urge to publicly express how much he resented being a father—not to mention being the husband of a disobliging wife—and the message, at that, is mixed.

Even after venting the anger and frustration he felt about his own situation in *The First Man*, he continued to cling to Agnes; as for her, the effect of his self-flagellation in the play seemed to be liberating. It was as if she were telling herself, Well, he's finally got that off his chest, now we can move on. (But to what?)

She grew brisker and less submissive in dealing with O'Neill, even at times venturing to taunt him with an ironic tone. Ever more assertively, she was wriggling out from under his thumb. For one thing, she was no longer disconsolate during their separations.

SOON AFTER THEIR third wedding anniversary on April 12, 1921, O'Neill had to leave Agnes for two weeks to have his teeth attended to; he'd always had trouble with his teeth due to neglect during his derelict days. Since money was always a concern, he had gratefully accepted the offer of free dental sessions from his friend Saxe Commins.

O'Neill had befriended Commins in Provincetown, where he was spending his 1916 summer vacation along with his formidable aunt, Emma Goldman, and his sister and brother-in-law, Stella and Teddy Ballantine, members of the Provincetown Players. Recently established as a dentist in Rochester, New York, Commins felt miscast in his profession and was drawn to the literary community.

Learning of O'Neill's difficult teeth, he saw his chance to grow closer to a member of that community, and offered not only to fix the teeth without payment, but also insisted O'Neill lodge with his sister Stella's family during the two weeks it would take to do the job.

O'Neill left Cape Cod for Rochester by train on April 21. After his first session in the dentist's chair (and apparently forgetting his recent disparagement of married love in his still unproduced *The First Man*), he moaned to Agnes, whom he once again addressed as "Own little wife": "I want to lay my head on your breast for comfort, as always when in trouble or pain."

Agnes (who remembered all too well how O'Neill had dispatched the wife in *The First Man*) responded coolly to her husband's effusion. She said she missed him, but her reply was more a merry amalgam of gossip and playful affection than the pining love letter O'Neill expected. He was upset. In his next letter, after graphically describing the "torture session" of a tooth-pulling, he wrote to her self-pityingly:

"I hate to make ill wishes about you, but I sure hope you are feeling as unhappily lost without me as I am without you. I have a poignant pain of emptiness inside."

Agnes felt sorry for her husband after receiving an extravagant ($5.50) telephone call from him two days later—although the line was bad and she had to shout to make herself heard. "Good night my own dearest thing, I love you so—and miss you so," she wrote in her next letter.

After O'Neill's dental torment ended on May 5, he and Agnes went together to New York to attend rehearsals of *Gold* (the four-act expansion of *Where the Cross Is Made*); this time they left one-and-a-half-year-old Shane in Gaga's care.

Producer John Williams, perhaps expecting another success like his hastily thrown-together *Beyond the Horizon*, had agreed to present the play on Broadway after Nathan sent the script to him with his high recommendation. But O'Neill saw from the first rehearsal that Williams was making a mess of it. He got drunk and fled to Provincetown after a week, leaving Agnes behind as his surrogate. Agnes, however, was unable to stand up to Williams, who was himself drinking heavily and seemed indifferent to the shoddiness of his production; it all served only to underline the play's intrinsic shortcomings.

Gold opened on June 1, 1921, at the Frazee Theatre. The reviews were blunt, particularly their headlines: "Shows O'Neill Below His Best"; "O'Neill's Gold Not Glittering"; and "Gold Tells a Weird Tale." In the *Tribune*, Broun, who praised the fourth act (which he remembered having seen as *Where the Cross Is Made*), scolded Williams for a "cheap and tasteless setting."

Gold closed after thirteen performances. Some years later, O'Neill told the critic Ward Morehouse that if he "could go back," he'd "destroy" that play, claiming it had been too hastily written. John Williams would never produce another O'Neill play.

Agnes and O'Neill, reunited in Peaked Hill Bars, anticipated a hectic summer and fall, as both *Anna Christie* and *The Straw* were being readied for November. O'Neill had been unable to persuade George Tyler, to whom both plays were promised, to produce *Anna Christie* first. Himself more interested in *Anna*, O'Neill took it instead to the visionary producer Arthur Hopkins, who agreed to mount it on Broadway.

O'Neill invited Robert Edmond Jones, whom Hopkins engaged to design the sets, to be his guest at Peaked Hill Bars during July. O'Neill knew Jones ("Bobby" to his friends) from his early association with the Provincetown Players in 1916. Since then, Jones had gained a reputation as the most imaginative stage designer in America.

O'Neill thought Jones might like to absorb atmosphere for *Anna Christie*, three of whose four acts were set aboard a battered coal barge. It so happened that just such a barge recently had been cast ashore and abandoned a hundred yards from the O'Neill house. Stuck there, its giant hulk imbedded in the sand, it could not be budged.

No sooner had Jones finished sketching the barge than it mystifyingly burst into flames, and for two days firemen had to drench the O'Neill house to prevent its catching fire. It was an omen for the uneasy weeks to come.

Like the rest of the country, Provincetown was caught up in the postwar frenzy of jazz, the automobile, and bathtub gin. O'Neill, Agnes, and their friends had become smarter about circumventing the restrictions of Prohibition and they were drinking more than ever—in part, just for the illicit excitement of it. Provincetown's parties grew wilder.

The artist Eben Given recalled an evening that began ominously at a pre-party for a costume ball at Town Hall. O'Neill, already half-drunk, grotesquely attired in a sarong and a wild orange wig, arrived separately from Agnes. O'Neill recognized the black lace mantilla she was wearing as a gift to her from his mother, and he tore it from her head. After a boozy reconciliation, they proceeded together to the ball. It was four in the morning when Agnes, Given, and a few others left the ball, but O'Neill had vanished.

"We walked down the street to my car," Given said, "when suddenly, from the depths of the car, something with insane blazing eyes, a mad leer, and an orange wig popped up. It was Gene, of course, very drunk."

O'Neill and Agnes had rented a room in town for the night, but O'Neill suddenly chose to return to Peaked Hill Bars. Agnes protested. "That was when," according to Given, "he grabbed her by the hair and tried to drag her off. She yelled, but no one interfered."

FRIENDS TENDED TO shrug off these public confrontations, which invariably were spurred by O'Neill's drinking and bolstered by Agnes's. It was all too manifest that Miss P. and the Nightingale savored their violent battles with as much zest as they embraced their torrid rapprochements.

And so their marriage lurched along.

15

Agnes, in need of a vacation, was unperturbed at parting from her husband in early August 1921. This time she left Shane behind, along with their two dogs and a recently adopted black female cat that had strayed out to Peaked Hill Bars. O'Neill named the cat Anna Christie, regarding her as an omen of hope for his play.

Agnes's long-planned solo jaunt of two and a half weeks was intended as half holiday, half business; her primary mission was to find an apartment in New York. She and O'Neill had decided they should be together while he was juggling rehearsals in October for both *Anna Christie* and *The Straw*.

After seeing Agnes off on the evening of August 7, O'Neill at once began to suffer from his predictable "pangs of loneliness." The house, he wrote to Agnes, seemed empty without her. Regretting their recent hostilities, he gave her carte blanche to choose any apartment that suited her.

"Your happiness means mine," he assured her. In a subsequent letter he attempted to portray himself as a caring father, writing of a frolic in the ocean with Shane, who "performed no end of antics and extemporized dances in honor of the sun and sea."

After posting three more loving letters and receiving only a postcard in reply, O'Neill tried a provocative ploy, describing a visit to Peaked Hill Bars from "two beautiful young ladies"; one of them, the local bank president's daughter, he wrote, "popped into the studio by mistake this noon and caught me stark naked." He said she shrieked and fled.

"It must have made quite a moment in her 17-year-old life." Her companion, he said, brought him a box of fudge. "They are nice girls and it's rather refreshing—the chatter of youth about the place—when one is lonely."

O'Neill's loneliness was mitigated by his work on *The Fountain*, loosely based on the escapades of Juan Ponce de León, which he'd begun writing in 1921 while still grieving for his father. (O'Neill's sentimental and romanticized attachment to his deceased father was a striking contrast to his continuing lack of affection for his still-living mother.)

Eugene evidently saw parallels between James O'Neill's life and Ponce de León's. Like the Spanish adventurer who left his country for a dream of glory and romance in the New World, James had left Ireland as a child and grown up hungering for glory and romance in his New World.

The Fountain reflects O'Neill's intense and unending need to resurrect his father; it is O'Neill's first symbolic portrait of James O'Neill as a valorous but ultimately defeated man. Like James, the play's protagonist, de León, finds neither glory nor romance (let alone the fountain of youth).

De León, in the play, dies broken, clinging to the religious belief that "death is no more" and that "all things dissolve, flow on eternally!" Here are poignant reverberations of James O'Neill's deathbed avowal that he was journeying to "a better sort of life—another sort—somewhere."

O'Neill would continue to evoke his father as a self-perceived failure in plays to come, portraying him in numerous disguises: as the failed black lawyer, Jim Harris, in *All God's Chillun Got Wings*; the thwarted farmer, Ephraim Cabot, in *Desire Under the Elms*; the betrayed war hero, Ezra Mannon, in *Mourning Becomes Electra*; the tragic poseur, Cornelius Melody, in *A Touch of the Poet*; and—in his thinly veiled final reincarnation—as the actor James Tyrone in *Long Day's Journey Into Night*, a man coping gamely with what life has dealt him.

Agnes at last sent her husband a letter apologizing for her failure to write sooner. She told him of her brief visit with Ella and Jamie in New London, and then bemoaned an abscess in her arm that was causing her severe pain.

"The cricket has left our hearth—honest!" O'Neill responded a day later. "He won't come back until you do. He knows there is no home without you."

"You know," Agnes wrote back, "that beneath it all, we do deeply, and eternally love one another—so let's forget and forgive the silly bickering . . . and start again."

"Come home and bring my life back!" answered O'Neill. "These days crawl sufferingly like futile purgatories."

Agnes, in constant pain from her abscess, told O'Neill she'd finally had to "go and pay $15 to get my arm operated on . . . it nearly killed me—I wept—but I'm glad, as for the first time in two weeks I've been without pain."

In New York, Agnes found a sublease apartment on West Thirty-fifth Street that she thought they could afford if they shared the space with Bobby Jones. He agreed to occupy a bedroom with a separate entrance, paying rent of seventy dollars a month, while the O'Neills would pay one hundred for their larger quarters. In early October, O'Neill, Agnes, and Shane moved in.

George Tyler finally had contrived to put *The Straw* into production for a November 10 opening, and with the premiere of *Anna Christie* scheduled by Arthur Hopkins for November 2, O'Neill would have two plays opening within eight days of each other. He was not happy about having to hop back and forth from the Vanderbilt Theatre on Forty-eighth Street near Broadway, where *Anna Christie* was in rehearsal, to the Greenwich Village Theatre between West Fourth and Christopher Streets for rehearsals of *The Straw*.

He soon lost interest in *The Straw*, as was evident to Tyler as well as to Margalo Gillmore, cast as the lovelorn and moribund Eileen Carmody. Gillmore, who had by now replaced the otherwise-engaged Helen Hayes, remembered O'Neill seated in the front row during rehearsals, looking glum. "I don't think he spoke to any member of the cast," she said, "but I do recall his dramatic brooding face."

O'Neill was far more interested in Pauline Lord, whom Hopkins had engaged to play Anna Christie. She looked nothing like O'Neill's eponymous twenty-year-old heroine—"tall, blonde . . . handsome after a large, Viking daughter fashion." Lord was delicate, almost fragile, with a tiny waist, small hands and feet, a pale oval face, and tragic brown eyes. Her technique was once described by Elizabeth Shepley Sergeant as "betrayal, rather than portrayal." She was on the cusp of stardom and O'Neill was delighted with her.

He also liked Hopkins who, in his own way, was as much of an idealist as O'Neill himself. Unlike Tyler, the old-school pragmatist, Hopkins deplored the Broadway theater's "ceaseless repetition of a familiar and timeworn formula," branding it as "a bag of tricks which anyone with skill can play and assure himself a certain amount of success." There was no longer any excitement in the experience of playgoing, Hopkins asserted. He wanted audiences to leave his productions in heated discussion or even quarreling about the author's intent. He was to have his wish with *Anna Christie*. O'Neill's faith in Hopkins cooled somewhat as opening night approached—much as had been the case with John Williams and *Beyond the Horizon*. By the final run-through, O'Neill—harboring as always misgivings about his play's reception—was convinced Hopkins's staging was off-kilter.

True to form, O'Neill did not attend the opening on November 2, sending Agnes in his place. He had reluctantly agreed to let her host a post-performance party at their apartment. Apprehensive as he awaited word of the audience's reaction, O'Neill was disturbed by a telegram from a friend in Provincetown, reporting that his cat, Anna Christie, was dangerously ill. Superstitiously convinced the fate of his play was wedded to the fate of the cat, he beseeched his friend by return wire to seek immediate medical help for the cat. Growing ever more agitated, he began to drink.

When Agnes showed up with a radiant report of the audience's reaction, O'Neill, already half-drunk, was unconvinced. He panicked as his guests began arriving, among them Pauline Lord and other members of the cast, as well as friends from the Provincetown Players, including Charles O'Brien Kennedy, a Broadway actor much loved by his colleagues, who had known O'Neill's father and, the year before, had helped with the staging of *Diff'rent*.

Kennedy managed to shepherd O'Neill (and a bottle) into an unused bathroom, where they locked themselves in. They sat on the edge of the bathtub drinking while O'Neill told Kennedy the plot of a new play he was calling *The Hairy Ape*.

The next morning's reviews were uniformly favorable, although several critics quibbled about the "talkiness" of the second act and the "contrived" fourth act. Woollcott, who opined that *Anna Christie* did not rank among O'Neill's best, nonetheless labeled it "rich and salty," calling it "a play written with that abundant imagination, that fresh and venturesome mind and that sure instinct for the theater which set this young author apart . . . from a lot of funny little holiday workers in cardboard and tinsel."

On the *Tribune*, Broun had been succeeded by Percy Hammond, soon to become O'Neill's pet hate among the critics, and who would be characterized by him as a bigoted egomaniac eaten by ulcers. Hammond began his cumbersome (if favorable) review, "If the gloomy trademark of Eugene O'Neill's depressing product has kept you hitherto away from his plays, disregard it for an hour or so and go to see *Anna Christie*."

As the play gained popularity, newspapers throughout the country published articles about its controversial ending. The critic John Mason Brown, a consistent O'Neill booster, praised *Anna Christie* but remarked that "the happy ending" worried him.

Not even the ever-supportive Kenneth Macgowan, writing in the *Globe*, got it quite right: "You may call it the happy ending if you like," wrote Macgowan. "It is the acceptance of suffering and happiness lived out into a new life."

Lashing out at the critics, O'Neill growled to friends, "I love every bone in their heads." He denied his ending was happy; rather, he argued, it was equivocal. Mat Burke would probably keep on shipping out to sea, just like Anna's father, and Anna would live a life every bit as frustrating and lonely as her mother's. O'Neill believed he had diluted the happiness of the ending by conveying a sense of foreboding:

"And the sea outside—life—waits," he explained to Nathan. "The happy ending is merely the comma at the end of a gaudy introductory clause, with the body of the sentence still unwritten. (In fact, I once thought of calling the play 'Comma')."

O'Neill continued to rebut those who presumed to accuse him of espousing happiness. To a sympathetic old friend who was interviewing him for an article, he loftily defended his raison d'être. He would write about happiness, he said, if ever he happened "to meet up with that luxury" and found it "sufficiently dramatic and in harmony with any deep rhythm of life."

It was ill-judged, he pronounced, "to think of tragedy as unhappy." The Greeks and Elizabethans, who knew better, "saw their lives ennobled" by tragedy. Then, waxing aphoristic, he explicated his all-consuming dedication to his craft: "A work of art is always happy; all else is unhappy."

O'Neill had learned his lesson. Never again would he equivocate; every play he would write from then on—with the exception of his one unambiguous comedy, the nostalgic *Ah, Wilderness!*—would end in stark, explicit tragedy.

Despite (or perhaps because of) its disputed ending, *Anna Christie* ran for 177 performances and won for O'Neill a second Pulitzer Prize. It was made into a silent movie in 1924 with Blanche Sweet, and a talkie in 1929 with Greta Garbo—(*Garbo Speaks!*)—and while it did not make O'Neill rich, it made his name popularly known—as *Beyond the Horizon* and even *The Emperor Jones* had not.

For a time, O'Neill continued to defend his ending, but eventually he was soured on *Anna Christie*. In one of the sharp—and unapologetic—reversals of which he was capable, he spoke slightingly of the play he'd once considered among his finest.

"In telling the story I deliberately employed all the Broadway tricks I had learned in my stage training," he confessed to the writer Malcolm Cowley. And when the eminent critic Joseph Wood Krutch asked him if he might edit a volume of O'Neill's "representative plays," he said he might, with the proviso that *Anna Christie* not be one of them. (What, one wonders, would O'Neill have made of the continuing fascination with *Anna Christie*, culminating in the 1993 smash hit New York revival starring Liam Neeson and Natasha Richardson?)

Immediately following the play's premiere Broadway production at the Vanderbilt Theatre, O'Neill left for Provincetown with Agnes and Shane, not waiting for *The Straw* to open. He read from afar the respectful, if unenthusiastic reviews, and did not regret its closing after only twenty performances. But he did feel remorse for his cavalier treatment of George Tyler.

With distance, he saw that Tyler's efforts on behalf of both *The Straw* and the earlier *Chris Christophersen*—however misguided—were largely motivated by the elderly producer's sentimental friendship with James O'Neill. Eugene, recalling the times he'd been irritable with Tyler, had the grace to apologize for his behavior. Even so, Tyler, like Williams, never produced another O'Neill play.

DURING THE Christmas holidays of 1921, O'Neill briefly put aside his writing on *The Hairy Ape* to devote himself to his mother and brother, who were soon to leave for a six-month stay in California. Ella hoped to liquidate her husband's West Coast real estate holdings, but she also was counting on the moderate California climate to alleviate the recent recurrence of her severe headaches. Optimistic about her health, she saw no reason to connect her headaches to the breast cancer from which she had suffered two and a half years earlier; at that time (March 28, 1919), she had undergone a mastectomy, after which her doctor told James, "We shall live in hopes that it may not recur."

Still vigorous, Ella not only continued to dress in fashionable mourning black, but also had begun to wear more jewelry, including the large diamond brooch James had given her for an anniversary and that she'd previously considered too gaudy. She and Jamie had dutifully attended the premieres of O'Neill's recent plays and she told Eugene she was sorry she would miss the opening of *The Hairy Ape*. She hoped the play would still be running when she returned; if she waited for a time when Eugene did not have a play opening, she quipped, she'd never be able to leave. It was on this playful note that she parted from her younger son. Neither had a glimmering—why would they?—that it was for the last time.

In early January, O'Neill wrote to Nathan with boyish enthusiasm about *The Hairy Ape*: "I believe you are going to be very much interested in this play, whatever your verdict may be." Nathan was amused, aware that while O'Neill was always eager for his opinion, he never paid the least attention to it—unless it was favorable.

As it happened, Nathan did not like the play. O'Neill later mocked him to Richard Madden for having disliked both *The Hairy Ape* and the subsequent *Desire Under the Elms*; those two plays, said O'Neill, were "certainly two of my finest, while [Nathan] did like *Gold* and *The Fountain* (two of my worst)."

The final manuscript of *The Hairy Ape* was ready by the third week in January 1922. O'Neill had started it "with a mad rush," as he'd written earlier to the critic Oliver Sayler. "Think I have got the swing of what I want to catch and, if I have, I ought to tear through it like a dose of salts." It had taken O'Neill only a little more than six weeks to write it.

Even more daring than *The Emperor Jones*, the play was based on O'Neill's experience in 1911 as an able-bodied seaman aboard the luxury liner S.S. *Philadelphia*. A coal stoker known to his shipmates only by his last name, Driscoll had earlier befriended O'Neill at the Manhattan sailors' saloon, Jimmy the Priest's. At O'Neill's request, Driscoll permitted him a rare look into the fearsome life of the coal stoker.

Driscoll, as O'Neill later told an interviewer for the *Times*, "thought a whole lot of himself, was a determined individualist. He was very proud of his strength, his capacity for grueling work. It seemed to give him mental poise to be able to dominate the stokehole, do more work than any of his mates."

O'Neill lost touch with Driscoll but, in 1915, while still living a derelict life at Jimmy the Priest's, he heard of the coal stoker's death at sea. Driscoll had committed suicide, as O'Neill learned, "by jumping off a liner in mid-ocean to the bewilderment of everyone who knew him, for there never lived a more self-assured, self-contented guy, seemingly."

In an introduction to the play's published version, O'Neill wondered "why Driscoll, proud of his animal superiority and in complete harmony with his limited conception of the universe, should kill himself." That, wrote O'Neill, "provided the germ idea" for *The Hairy Ape*. Continuing to brood about the why of the suicide, O'Neill concluded it was Driscoll's sense of "belonging" (to the human race) that had been shattered; that became the focus of the play: Yank Smith suddenly loses faith in his image of himself as all-powerful and integral to the ship's momentum.

When interviewed by Elizabeth Shepley Sergeant, O'Neill told her the play was "unconscious autobiography," explaining it was his own veiled attack on the hypocrisy of the social system. "He chose to write about the hairy stoker, victim of modern industry, a man far removed from [O'Neill] himself in actual circumstance," reported Sergeant, "in order to voice through Yank that social rebellion and sense of buffeted frustration which was his philosophic message at the time."

What destroys Yank's animal superiority is an encounter with a snobbish first-class passenger, Mildred Douglas, who is taken by a ship's officer on a slumming tour of the stokehold. Mildred is horrified by the appearance of the outsized, sweating, and coal-blackened Yank (a "giant of a man and absurdly strong," as O'Neill described him). Calling him "a filthy beast" (translated by Yank's jeering shipmates as a "hairy ape"), Mildred faints.

The play follows Yank, after his ship docks in New York, in a series of scenes expressing the coal stoker's distorted sense of reality—scenes that track his unraveling as he makes a futile attempt to prove that he "belongs," that he is as good as, if not better than, Mildred Douglas and her kind.

Blindsided by the indifference he encounters, he acts out disruptively and is arrested. Released from jail, he tries to regain his sense of himself by joining the International Workers of the World, but they, too, reject him. Finally forced to accept that he belongs nowhere, he commits suicide—not, like Driscoll, by leaping over the side of an ocean liner, but crushed in the arms of a gorilla in the zoo, whom he greets as "brother." "Even him didn't tink I belonged," says the dying Yank in the gorilla's cage. "Where do I fit in?"

"He slips in a heap on the floor and dies," reads O'Neill's stage direction. "The monkeys [in the adjoining cages] set up a chattering, whimpering wail. And, perhaps, *The Hairy Ape* at last belongs."

The play, like *The Emperor Jones*, was consigned to the Provincetown Players because of its highly experimental nature, but O'Neill was counting on its eventual move to Broadway.

As was the case the year before, when *The Straw* and *Anna Christie* opened within a week of each other, O'Neill, as he wrote to Kenneth Macgowan, was again "about to have the ghastly joy of attending two sets of rehearsals at the same time." The opening night curtains of *The First Man* and *The Hairy Ape* were scheduled to rise within five days of each other.

The First Man had found a producer-cum-leading-man in Augustin Duncan, brother of the storied Isadora, and he was to open the play at the Neighborhood Playhouse on March 4, while *Ape* was set for March 9 at the rechristened Playwrights' Theatre, now the Provincetown Playhouse.

Once again, O'Neill decided to give his full attention to the stronger play. His instinct proved sound. *The First Man* closed after only twenty-seven performances.

The founders of the Provincetown Players, in their sixth year of operation, had lost much of their fervor by the time *The Hairy Ape* was ready to begin rehearsals in early February. Impatient with their amateurism, and bypassing Jig Cook, O'Neill asked Arthur Hopkins (the producer of *Anna Christie*) to help with the staging. Hopkins brought in Bobby Jones to design the sets.

For the crucial role of Yank, O'Neill wanted the Broadway actor Louis Wolheim, a burly ex–college football star whom O'Neill had spotted in a supporting role in the Barrymore brothers' Broadway hit *The Jest*. But O'Neill didn't have the nerve to approach Wolheim, fearing he would be insulted at being asked to play the ugly brute described in *Ape*. Instead, he asked Charles O'Brien Kennedy, who had also appeared in *The Jest*, to feel out Wolheim about the role, and Kennedy complied.

"Wollie," said Kennedy, "would you play the homeliest so-and-so in the world if Gene O'Neill wrote him?" Wolheim, according to Kennedy, "roared his profane affirmative." A triumphant O'Neill felt sure, as he wrote to Nathan, that the production "could be relied on to achieve results," unlike the sort of "amateur affair" that marked too many of his earlier efforts.

Jig Cook was deeply offended. He couldn't believe O'Neill's assertion that he'd outgrown the Provincetown Players, or that he had decided to bypass those who had loyally supported him from the beginning.

Cook did not wait to see *The Hairy Ape*. Leaving the Provincetown Players to reorganize themselves as best they could under a temporary new leader, Jig departed with his wife, Susan, for what was to be a year's sojourn in Greece.

16

Jamie O'Neill had grown ever dearer to his mother since his father's death in the late summer of 1920. True to his vow, he had given up drink, and his mother had come to depend on him for all her small comforts.

Living together, traveling together, confiding daily in each other, the mother and son intimacy mimicked a married life; certainly this was the closest Jamie would ever be to having a wife. Perhaps for the first time in his adult life, Jamie was at peace with himself and the world; his younger brother was both grateful and proud. "He hasn't had a drink in almost a year and a half now!" O'Neill bragged to a friend. "Fact, I swear to you! My mother got him to go on the wagon and stick—and he has stuck."

Jamie and his mother arrived in California at the beginning of February 1922, planning to spend the next six months there. Jamie had never revisited his birthplace, but he had often heard the stories about how his father—then a hopeful leading man in various touring companies—had gone west to join a stock company in San Francisco, whose prospering theater district almost equaled New York's. Audiences welcomed James and, overwhelmed by offers, he had decided to forgo touring for a spell. He stayed on in San Francisco for more than a year, affording Ella, pregnant with Jamie, a sense of stability during her pregnancy and Jamie's infancy.

Now, these four decades later, mother and son settled into a furnished

four-room apartment in a modest two-story house on Oxford Street in
Los Angeles. The flat was not far from Glendale, the locale of one of
James O'Neill's holdings that Ella hoped to sell; she also intended to
inspect a property that James had bought in San Francisco.

As soon as Ella and Jamie were settled, Ella renewed her friendship
with her onetime New York hairdresser, Libbie Drummer, who had previously moved to Los Angeles. A few days later, Drummer noticed Ella's
mouth was somewhat twisted and that she was dragging one leg. Ella
evidently had suffered a slight stroke. She initially refused medical help,
believing the problem would cure itself. But at Drummer's urging, she
submitted to an examination and on February 9 the doctor confirmed
she'd had a stroke.

Jamie was flung off balance. After frantically wiring Eugene, he
turned to Drummer and an old friend, Marion Reed, for sympathy and
support. Reed, who had played minor roles with Jamie during his slip-
shod stage career, was now a small-time movie actress.

From the evidence of Reed's subsequent behavior, she was the sort of
calculating wanton with whom Jamie, in the days when he was befogged
by drink, had felt comfortable. Now, with his resolve to stay sober weak-
ening, he began to lean on Reed. Along with the genuinely well-meaning
Libbie Drummer, Reed opportunistically seized the chance to become
intimately involved with Ella during her illness.

On February 16, less than two weeks after Ella's arrival in California,
she suffered a second stroke. This one immobilized her and left her
barely able to speak. "All of her right side was dead from head to toe,"
Drummer confided in a letter to a Mrs. Phillips, a mutual friend of hers
and Ella O'Neill's who lived on the East Coast.

It was too much for Jamie. His brief happy life as companion to the
one woman he'd ever truly loved had come to an end. Dissolving into
helplessness, he once again sought reassurance in the bottle.

Ella managed to convey to her son that she wished to make her will,
and Jamie, guided by Marion Reed (who found him more manageable

when drunk), engaged a lawyer and enlisted Libbie Drummer as a witness.

Drummer was distressed to find Reed had suddenly taken charge of Ella's care and was "running everything."

"She did not like it one bit that I was there, and let me see it," Drummer later wrote to Mrs. Phillips, "but I stayed for a few hours as Mrs. O'Neill wished me to."

Unable to write and her speech seriously compromised, Ella haltingly dictated the terms of her will to the lawyer. To Jamie, she bequeathed the property in California they'd come to sell. The remainder of her estate she left to her "beloved sons" to "share and share alike." She named Marion Reed as the executor of her will, possibly at Jamie's urging—or perhaps because, aware that Jamie was again drinking, she no longer cared about anything.

Drummer, writing to Mrs. Phillips, confided that Jamie was "very weak" and that "this Mrs. Reed had him over to her home day and night," adding, "I did not like her and could see through her from the first moment I met her."

Jamie, frantic, wired Eugene that their mother was terminally ill and asked him to come at once. Emotionally unable to confront another deathwatch, O'Neill resisted. He telegraphed back, citing his immersion in rehearsals for both *The First Man* and *The Hairy Ape*, stressing his dangerously frayed nerves. He could not leave New York, he insisted.

In response, Jamie berated his brother for invoking artistic temperament to justify his absence. Close to hysteria, Eugene drafted a pleading telegram:

NO QUESTION OF TEMPERAMENT. BE FAIR. SPECIALIST SAYS MEANS COMPLETE NERVOUS COLLAPSE IF UNDERTAKE TRIP PRESENT CONDITION. WOULD NOT HELP MOTHER OR YOU? ALSO YOU WIRE SHE IS UNCONSCIOUS, WILL NOT KNOW ME. O'Neill went on to offer HELP ANY POSSIBLE WAY, promising EVERYTHING I HAVE AT YOUR COMMAND. WIRE ME WHAT AND HOW. He also suggested that Jamie, AS A LAST RESORT, might want to consult a Dr. Ingham, the BEST MAN ON COAST. His own plans, O'Neill said, depended on his health: WOULD LEAVE IMMEDIATELY IF ABLE. YOU MUST ACCEPT TRUTH. I AM IN TERRIBLE SHAPE.

O'Neill had by now persuaded himself that it was unthinkable for him to abandon the production of *The Hairy Ape*, and to rush to Jamie's support; his presence was crucial at the final rehearsals, for which he was doing most of the directing.

Ella died in her Los Angeles apartment on February 28, 1922. Her death certificate listed the cause as "cerebral thrombosis" (a blockage of blood flow through a vessel in the brain). As no autopsy was performed, the diagnosis was speculative. Her New London relatives, the Sheridans and the Brennans, were later told she'd had a brain tumor.

Jamie telegraphed Eugene that he was making arrangements to bring their mother's body east for burial, but his messages became increasingly garbled. Libbie Drummer and her sister went to the O'Neill apartment the day after Ella's death, where they were appalled to find a drunken Jamie being looked after by two of the nurses who had been attending his mother.

"His condition was dreadful," Drummer later wrote indignantly to Mrs. Phillips. Jamie, she said, wanted to ship his mother's casket home unaccompanied, because his friend Marion Reed wanted him to remain in California with her.

But Drummer asserted herself. "You are going back with your mother or I wire Eugene," she told Jamie. She was subsequently informed by the funeral parlor director that Jamie had left it to him to make all the arrangements—not only to engage a New York undertaker to receive his mother's body, but also to purchase a compartment for himself on the train.

On the following day, Drummer learned from one of the nurses that Marion Reed had seen Jamie off at the station, and that he had packed ten bottles of whiskey in his luggage.

"I don't know when I felt so bad for anyone as I did about Mrs.

O'Neill," wrote Drummer. "It was the saddest closing chapter of any story I have ever read."

ON MARCH 4, 1922—the opening night of *The First Man*—O'Neill received the news he'd been dreading: the train carrying Jamie and their mother's casket would arrive at Grand Central Terminal on the evening of March 9. It was the date on which *The Hairy Ape* was to open.

Reading the reviews of *The First Man* on March 6, O'Neill was too numb to react to the pummeling it received. Woollcott derided it as "prolix . . . clumsy of gait . . . at times rubbishy."

Shaken by his mother's death and his brother's relapse into alcohol, O'Neill had three days to pull himself together before confronting—on March 9—both the arrival of his mother's casket and the opening night of *The Hairy Ape*. He couldn't do it.

If, as he'd insisted to Jamie, he'd been in "terrible shape" in late February, he was—by March 9—skidding toward the mental collapse he'd predicted. Agnes, much as she tried, was unable to console him. The news of his mother's death, he later wrote to an old family friend, "came right on top of the strain of rehearsing two plays at once, just as they were about to open, and I was on the verge of a nervous breakdown anyway. Her body arrived the day the play opened."

That evening, O'Neill dispatched Agnes to the Provincetown Playhouse, where she was to join Saxe Commins for the opening of *The Hairy Ape*. O'Neill stayed behind in their suite at the Hotel Netherland (later the Sherry-Netherland), into which he and Agnes had moved temporarily. He had asked William P. Connor, an old friend and theatrical associate of his father's, to accompany him to the station to meet his mother's funeral train and help him with whatever arrangements had to be made. That much is beyond doubt.

There are two versions of what happened next. The first derives from a memorandum Saxe Commins wrote many years later, describing the events of the evening *The Hairy Ape* opened; the memo was found among his papers after his death; segments were included in the book of letters to and from O'Neill edited by Commins's wife, Dorothy Berliner Commins.

In the memorandum, Commins told of how the audience at *The Hairy Ape* stood and cheered when the curtain fell, calling (in vain) for the author. Commins and Agnes, "all too aware," as he put it, "of the pathetic errand" on which they believed O'Neill had been engaged, hurried back to the hotel and called him from the lobby.

O'Neill was so distraught when he joined Commins and Agnes in the hotel lobby that he seemed unable to absorb their effusive report of the play's reception. "It was shocking to see the ashen color of his skin under the usual sunburnt bronze," Commins wrote, adding that O'Neill's words sounded "as if they scraped past a rough lump in his throat."

Commins attributed O'Neill's symptoms to the ordeal of his earlier "gruesome search in the dark cellars of Grand Central Station" for his mother's casket.

Dorothy Commins did not include her husband's graphic description of how O'Neill, after "groping for almost an hour through the subterranean maze," found his mother's casket and arranged for its disposition, after which he roused a semi-comatose Jamie in his train compartment and brought him back to the Hotel Netherland in a taxi, where "he promptly passed out on Gene's bed."

According to the second version of the evening's events, O'Neill never went to the train terminal at all. In this version, which surfaced after Commins's death in 1958, O'Neill, after having asked William Connor to accompany him to Grand Central, changed his mind.

At the last moment—after seeing Agnes off to the theater—O'Neill telephoned Connor to say he could not face going to Grand Central Terminal. This was the recollection of Connor's nephew, Frank W. Wilder, who maintained it was he who accompanied his uncle to Grand Central in O'Neill's stead.

At the terminal, according to Wilder, he and his uncle found Jamie in a drunken stupor, and had to locate Ella's coffin without his help. They arranged to have the coffin sent to a funeral parlor and then took Jamie to an unspecified hotel, after which Connor telephoned O'Neill at the Netherland to give him a terse report and scold him for his dereliction.

Dorothy Commins eventually accepted Frank Wilder's version and, after including her husband's version in her book (in abbreviated form), appended a footnote stating "though Agnes and Saxe never knew it, O'Neill had not gone to the railway station." In other words, Dorothy was saying that O'Neill, doubtless ashamed of his own nonperformance, lied to Saxe and Agnes. (O'Neill could have based his account to Saxe and Agnes on details told to him by Connor during their telephone conversation.)

The question is, where *was* O'Neill and what could he have been thinking during the time between sending Agnes off to meet Commins for the opening of *The Hairy Ape*, and their return together to the hotel two hours later?

It's a good guess that O'Neill had tried and failed to steel himself to confront his mother's casket—let alone a drunken Jamie. Doubtless fortifying himself with drink, he simply waited in his hotel suite for the next thrust of the knife.

WHEN SAXE AND AGNES returned to the Netherland, a barely articulate O'Neill asked Agnes to wait for him in their suite; he needed to walk with Saxe in Central Park, he said.

As the two men circled the reservoir, Commins remembered, he held O'Neill's arm and felt "the tremor that shook through his coat sleeve." O'Neill wished only to speak of his mother.

"Several times I mentioned the damp air and suggested that we return to the hotel. His answer each time was, 'Stay with me.'"

Commins listened in awed silence as O'Neill spoke of the pain that his mother's years as a morphine addict had caused their father, Jamie, and himself, and how their love and guilt had shaped and driven the family. Commins understood that his friend was assailed by pangs of mingled reproach and pity; while O'Neill blamed his mother for his childhood wounds, he couldn't brush aside the times when she was tender and loving.

Commins was all but overcome by O'Neill's tormented memories of his mother's life and their devastating effect on him. As they walked, O'Neill rambled on, a man in a trance evoking his mother's past.

FOR YEARS, young Gene had listened to his mother's tales of personal distress and regret.

Poignant among her oft-repeated recollections was the story of her introduction, as a new bride, to the rigors of a touring actor's life; she was aghast to find herself engulfed in a rough theatrical milieu that took all her courage to counter.

At twenty, Ella Quinlan had been gently raised by an adoring, generous father in a sheltered environment (which, later, she often reproachfully contrasted with her rootless married existence). She fondly remembered her convent-school years at St. Mary's Academy in South Bend, Indiana, close by Notre Dame; there, among the teaching nuns she loved, she had developed her musical gift and become an adept pianist.

Her long-held dream to be a nun was soon superseded by the vision of becoming a concert pianist, encouraged by her doting father. She had lost heart when he died at forty-one in 1874, when Ella was seventeen. She was still mourning her loss three years later when James O'Neill proposed marriage in 1877. Forgetting her aspiration to a musical career and at last releasing herself from mourning, Ella was swept into a romantic dream life as the courted darling of a handsome thirty-one-year-old matinee idol, whose sole object was to please and cosset her.

It took James the better part of a year to win the consent of Ella's widowed mother; Bridget Quinlan had a pretty good understanding of what an actor's life was like, and she feared for her daughter's happiness and comfort. But Ella, though shy and reserved, was also stubborn, and James was persistent. On June 14, 1877, they married.

After a brief honeymoon, James resumed the touring that was to last another forty years, and Ella had her first taste of the seething and alien life she was to endure. Being married to a touring actor in the 1870s and '80s required a willingness to embrace the often rowdy aspects of backstage life, an easy camaraderie with the actor's fellow troupers, and a stoical acceptance of unventilated trains, shabby hotel rooms, unappetizing and hastily swallowed meals, and the prevalence of whiskey.

Ella tried to summon and convey empathy, but the managers, agents, and actors who were James's daily associates sensed the effort it cost her.

The young bride, after three months of unpleasant indoctrination into her husband's world, accompanied him to Chicago, where worse awaited. As Eugene knew from his mother's telling and retelling while he was growing up, she was thunderstruck when a woman she'd never heard of brought a suit for divorce against James; it drew wide notice in the press, not only in Chicago but also in New York, Cleveland, and San Francisco—wherever James was professionally known.

Eugene remembered his mother's disclosure of her hurt so vividly that, decades later, he felt compelled to have Ella's stand-in, Mary Tyrone, refer to it in *Long Day's Journey Into Night*: "Right after we were married, there was the scandal of that woman who had been your mistress suing you," says Mary, in a speech reproaching her husband for his many perceived transgressions.

The scandalous divorce action, as Eugene had learned, was brought by a former actress named Nettie Walsh, who had borne James a son but whom he had not married. James had never mentioned her existence to Ella; she was mortified to read her husband's statement in the newspapers that when (at twenty-six) he took Nettie as his mistress, she was fifteen and "not a chaste and virtuous woman."

Ironically, James's relationship with the fifteen-year-old Nettie had blossomed at the same time and place that Ella herself, as a fifteen-year-old schoolgirl, had fallen in love with him.

It was in 1871, and her father had taken her to one of James's performances. James was acting with a stock company in Cleveland at the time, and he had been introduced to Thomas Quinlan.

The two became friends. But Ella's father had no inkling that James was keeping a teenage mistress, for James had long since learned to conceal the unsavory aspects of his personal life.

Ella shrank from the intrusion of scandal into her private life. In fairness to James, he was to be a scrupulously faithful husband. As Mary Tyrone observes to her maid (in *Long Day's Journey Into Night*), "There has never been a breath of scandal about him. I mean, with any other woman. Never since he met me. That has made me very happy. It has made me forgive so many other things."

Nevertheless, during the first months of her marriage, Ella felt lonely and isolated. She was convinced that her own friends had nothing but scorn and pity for her. She could not immerse herself in James's world, disdaining the well-meant sympathy of his colleagues.

"I've never felt at home in the theater," says Mary Tyrone, speaking for Ella. "Even though Mr. Tyrone has made me go with him on all his tours, I've had little to do with the people in his company, or with anyone on the stage. Their life is not my life."

O'NEILL APPEARED TO be unaware that during the half-dozen years beginning soon after Jamie's birth in 1878, his mother's marriage had been a happy one. When she left San Francisco to once again accompany James on his cross-country touring, Ella took a pleasurable interest in the details that occupied her husband's stage life. This time, traveling with the baby she loved (and a nursemaid), she befriended Elizabeth Robins, a young actress, who had recently joined the *Monte Cristo* company in a small role. Ella recognized Robins as more refined and intelligent than most of the actors she had met thus far and she happily admitted Robins into her life.

Elizabeth, herself inured to the hardships of the road, empathized with Ella's stalwart acceptance of her role as a backstage wife, but she noted in letters to her family and in her diary that Ella took a lively interest in James's daily professional routine and often offered him—and Elizabeth—career advice. Elizabeth recorded no hint of the brooding, unhappy wife portrayed in *Long Day's Journey*.

Ella and Elizabeth became intimate friends during the next two years; Ella, who soon knew all about Elizabeth's ambitions to rise in her profession, took a close interest in her progress. She listened closely to James's appraisal of her acting ability, and, by extension, Ella grew interested in the backstage life of *Monte Cristo* as the company set up and performed in one town after another.

An avid letter-writer and an insightful diarist, Elizabeth Robins left behind a rare portrait of the O'Neills as a compatible (if at times hard-pressed) couple, devoted to each other and to their son, Jim Jr. (as he was then called).

But apparently Ella's memory of those happy, early years of her marriage had been obliterated by the death from measles of her second son, the baby Edmund. She had become a guilty, embittered woman long before her third son, Eugene, was born.

O'Neill, unaware of his mother's happier days, knew her only as a bemused woman who existed in a dark closet of despair, never letting her husband and two surviving sons forget how she suffered over Edmund's death.

O'NEILL SAVED THE most realistic litany of his mother's sorrows for his portrait of her as Mary Tyrone in *Long Day's Journey Into Night*. But in a much earlier play, *The Great God Brown*, composed three years after his mother's death, he did write about her with compassion, if briefly.

In that play, Dion Anthony, the hero O'Neill modeled largely on himself, speaks about the loss of both his parents; after mourning his father's death, he says, "And my mother? I remember a sweet, strange girl, with affectionate, bewildered eyes as if God had locked her in a dark closet without any explanation."

O'Neill's conception of his mother as a girl locked in a dark closet was influenced by Strindberg's *The Ghost Sonata*. In that terrifying drama, a woman referred to as "the Mummy" actually lives in a closet and talks to her family like a parrot. Shortly after Ella O'Neill's death, O'Neill informed Elizabeth Shepley Sergeant that his mother had lived in a room from which she seldom ventured—that, in a way, she was like the Mummy.

ELLA O'NEILL'S BODY was taken to a funeral parlor near St. Leo's on East Twenty-eighth Street, the church she had attended while living with her husband at the Prince George Hotel. Gazing at his mother in her open casket, O'Neill was pained by what he saw. The California undertaker had made her up to look doll-like and artificial; O'Neill could not reconcile that face with his mother's.

He later attributed to James Tyrone Jr. in *A Moon for the Misbegotten* his own reaction: "She looked young and pretty like someone I remembered meeting long ago. Practically a stranger. To whom I was a stranger. Cold and indifferent."

The burial service took place the following day. "The priest who conducted the funeral service turned out to be a Mt. St. Vincent boy," O'Neill wrote to Joseph McCarthy, with whom he'd shared a room at the Catholic boarding school in the northern Bronx, to which he'd been sent after his seventh birthday.

Jamie was too drunk to attend the service, nor did he join Eugene and Agnes in accompanying his mother's body on the train to New London. Ella was buried in St. Mary's Cemetery beside her husband; her infant son, Edmund; and her mother, Bridget.

Among the mourners at Ella's burial service was Mrs. Phillips, the old family friend, who described the burial in a letter to Libbie Drummer. Drummer wrote back: "I am so glad you told me about the funeral. I was so worried. I did not know if Jamie would ever reach New York alive."

Also present at the burial were several of Ella's New London relatives, including O'Neill's favorite cousin, Lil Brennan, who was ten years younger than Ella.

O'Neill's seemingly unalloyed hostility toward his mother appeared to have dissolved, at least temporarily; when his New London cousin, Bessie Sheridan, gave him a photograph of his mother holding him as an infant, he assured her he would treasure it.

Reminiscing about his mother with another cousin, the clearly bereaved Agnes Brennan (Lil's older sister), he murmured, "I was just beginning to enjoy her." As for Lil herself, not given to hypocrisy, she was somewhat more reserved (which was probably why she was O'Neill's favorite cousin).

In fact, Lil nursed a long-standing resentment against Ella. This became apparent many years later when, at eighty-nine, afflicted with senile dementia, she was confined to a nursing home in Norwich, Connecticut, not far from New London.

Visiting her there in 1957, the authors of this biography were lucky enough to catch her just as she lapsed into one of her rare dreamlike states, during which she relived scenes from her youth. Seated in an armchair and watched over by her doctor, Lil was animatedly conversing with someone only she could see. She was obviously reliving a scene from her thirties. With an encouraging nod from Lil's doctor, Barbara Gelb asked Lil a gentle question about her friendship with Ella O'Neill.

We received an unexpectedly uninhibited and comprehensive reply:

"Mama always says, 'Be nice to Ella, she has a difficult life.' Mama never can see any wrong in anyone, but Ella O'Neill keeps to herself; she passes me in the street and doesn't even notice me. She's stuck-up, that's what she is, stuck-up—and she touches up her hair.

"When I go back to New York next week, I'm going to tell Agnes what she said to me." (It was the New York of 1907 to which Lil referred; she and her sister had lived there for a time while Agnes studied the piano, and Lil tried to establish herself as a milliner. It would seem that Lil thought if she could persuade Ella to become her customer, she could use the prestige of the famous actor's wife to attract other fashionable women.)

"Do you know what Ella said when I asked her to buy some hats from me? She said she bought her hats at Bendel, but she'd give me her old ones to make over and sell. I was never so insulted!" (Naive Lil was evidently unaware that Ella's hats, like her dresses, were the last word in expensive good taste.) She rarely went outdoors without a veil as well. The relatives thought she wore veils to protect her smooth white complexion against sun and wind, but more likely she wore them to hide the unnatural, morphine-induced brightness of her eyes.

17

Between the approach of spring 1922 and the fortnight following his thirty-sixth birthday in mid-October, O'Neill underwent one of the most consequential periods of his life.

MARCH 11: Too distracted by his mother's burial rites the previous day, O'Neill finally reads newspaper reviews of *The Hairy Ape*. Woollcott, in the *Times*, assesses the play as "a monstrously uneven piece, now flamingly eloquent, now choked and thwarted and inarticulate"; although he concedes the play has what he oddly calls "a little greatness to it," and adds that O'Neill's imagination towers "conspicuously above the milling, mumbling crowd of playwrights who have no imagination at all;" he nonetheless disparages it as needing "a fierce, un-intimidated blue pencil." And Broun (now writing for the *World*) is even less charitable; he condemns O'Neill for having "found a cause" and "become a propagandist."

O'Neill is both exasperated and imperturbable. "I have had quite a large experience now with the critics," he remarks in a letter, adding that he knows their limitations by heart. "*The Hairy Ape* is a startling dose for them to swallow," he writes. "Considering the demands it makes, I think the reaction from critics & public has been more intelligent and hopeful than that given to any play of mine so far. Most of them are trying in this case. Usually they don't take that much trouble."

It would not be until November—eight months after the downtown opening—that O'Neill took up arms in defense of the play that was to remain one of his all-time favorites: "People think I am giving an exact picture of the reality. They don't understand that the whole play is expressionistic. Yank is really yourself, and myself. He is every human being. But, apparently, very few people seem to get this . . . no one has said: 'I am Yank! Yank is my own self!'"

On another occasion that month, O'Neill further explained that his play was "propaganda in the sense that it was a symbol of man, who has lost his old harmony with nature . . . the struggle used to be with the gods, but is now with himself, his own past, his attempt 'to belong.'"

APRIL 17: As O'Neill had hoped, Arthur Hopkins, unfazed by the adverse criticism, moves *The Hairy Ape* to Broadway (where it will run for 120 performances). Hopkins insists on a new Mildred Douglas, the pampered steamship passenger who faints when confronted by the brutish coal stoker, Yank. The original Mildred, Mary Blair (who earlier won acclaim as the thwarted spinster in *Diff'rent*), does not suit Hopkins, who regards her as "not luxurious enough" for uptown audiences.

He replaces her with Carlotta Monterey (whose recollection thirty-five years later of her first encounter with O'Neill will become legend).

Carlotta: "I thought him the rudest man I'd ever seen, and he had no use for me." (This, after Hopkins has introduced O'Neill to her during a rehearsal break shortly before the Broadway opening.)

"One day," as Carlotta chose to remember it, "I was in the theater talking to someone and a dark young man came over. I'd always heard that O'Neill was dirty, unshaven, messy. This man was clean, neatly dressed. We exchanged a few words and he left.

"'Who's that?' I asked.

"'O'Neill,' I was told.

"'You mean the author of this play?'"

Accustomed to adulation (and unaware that O'Neill is still brooding about his mother's death), Carlotta finds him morose and barely civil.

"He hadn't even had the courtesy to thank me for taking over the part on a moment's notice."

After their meeting, O'Neill concedes (to James Light, an early recruit to the Provincetown Players who has become a close friend and a relied-upon colleague) that Carlotta looks the part, but he doesn't think much of her acting ability.

"'Mildew Douglas' he used to call the girl I played." Carlotta laughs, recalling their next meeting four years later in Maine, the summer they fell in love. "He would tease me by calling me that when he thought I was putting on airs."

EARLY MAY: O'Neill is surprised to receive a letter from his all-but-forgotten first wife, Kathleen Jenkins. She meekly suggests he might care to meet his son Eugene O'Neill Jr. and help with his education.

The boy, nearly twelve, is exceptional in every way, says Kathleen, and should have a chance to attend a first-rate school and college. Kathleen explains she is living modestly in Queens, New York, with her husband, George Pitt-Smith, an office manager, and cannot afford to give Eugene Jr. the education he deserves.

Kathleen had married Pitt-Smith when Eugene Jr. was five years old; Pitt-Smith was divorced and had a son of his own, a few months younger than Eugene Jr., who spent half his time with his mother and half with his father and stepmother. Kathleen once said that her son loved his stepfather and regarded Pitt-Smith's own son as a brother; but she spoke often to Eugene Jr. of his famous real father and taught the boy to think well of him.

Had James O'Neill been alive, it's less likely O'Neill would have acknowledged the grandson his father had so angrily disowned. But as things stand, in deference to the divorced wife who has never importuned him, O'Neill feels it only fair to assume a measure of responsibility for his long-since-abandoned son. Even so, he hesitates, confiding to Agnes that he fears meeting the boy. What if he has been brought up as conventional, a boy with whom he will have nothing in common? But at Agnes's urging, he consents to a meeting.

Eugene Jr., dressed in his best clothes, finds his father shakily await-ing him at his West Thirty-fifth Street apartment. The boy is by far the more at ease and promptly engages his father in a discussion of baseball. He's delighted to learn his father knows the batting averages of many of the players and several times has gone out of his way to meet a player he admired. (O'Neill, in the 1940s, once arranged to be introduced to Ted Williams, who had wound up the season for the Boston Red Sox with a .406 batting average.)

To the relief of father and son, they find they like each other. O'Neill tells friends that Eugene Jr. is bright and has been raised carefully, and that he has decided he will finance his education.

According to Kathleen, her son returns "glowing from the meeting." Soon after, O'Neill writes to thank her for raising a son to make them proud. He feels remorse for the way he treated the sheltered young woman that she was in 1909, carelessly getting her pregnant and, after a pro forma marriage, deserting her. Gratefully, he allows, "The woman I gave the most trouble to has given me the least." So taken is O'Neill with his newfound older son that he invites him to Peaked Hill Bars for a visit during the coming summer.

O'Neill as yet is unaware of Eugene Jr.'s troubled early childhood. The fact is that soon after Kathleen and her husband settled into their home in Douglaston, Long Island, the six-year-old boy was sent away to boarding school in Peekskill, New York—already being pushed along the insecure path that his father had followed as a child. There were episodes of running away from school and being sent back. Eventually, the boy learned that home was a place where he spent vacations—and school was the place where he lived.

MAY 12: O'Neill's better-late-than-never parental obligation fulfilled, he turns his attention to the tedious details of settling his mother's estate, which her lawyers have informed him may be worth as much as $147,000. The lawyers have managed to remove the devious and grasping Marion Reed as Ella O'Neill's executor, and have made it clear to her that Jamie will not return to California to share with her the proceeds from the sale of the Glendale property.

The way is now clear for O'Neill's New London lawyer, Frank Dart, to probate the will, and O'Neill notifies Dart that he and his brother "emphatically do not desire the settling of the estate to drag on one second longer than is absolutely necessary." (He cannot foresee that it will be another two years before the complexities of settling the estate are resolved.)

While O'Neill has spoken for his brother as well as himself, Jamie is oblivious to what's going on. His out-of-control drunken episodes are growing more frequent. O'Neill makes periodic efforts to obtain medical and psychiatric care for him, but to no avail. It is all too evident that Jamie is racing toward self-destruction.

MAY 21: O'Neill's life brightens when *Anna Christie* brings him his second Pulitzer Prize. "Yes, I seem to be becoming the Prize Pup of Playwriting—the Hot Dog of the Drama," he mocks in a letter to the critic Oliver Sayler.

Pleased by the tribute of his Pulitzer, O'Neill is eager to start on a new play. But along with his efforts to curb Jamie's grotesque behavior, he is shrinking from the unwelcome role of paterfamilias, and he is too jittery to concentrate on his work. He almost regrets his impulsive invitation to Eugene Jr. for a summer visit to Peaked Hill Bars; having invited his son, he cannot disregard Agnes's seven-year-old daughter, for whom Agnes recently has discovered a sense of obligation; along with little Shane, O'Neill will have to play Daddy to three children.

LATE JULY: O'Neill's semi-adjustment to the summer's events seems to shift with the dunes. His longtime Provincetown friend, the artist

Eben Given, drives O'Neill and Agnes to the railroad station to meet Eugene Jr. "The boy was reticent, just like his father," Given remembered. "Agnes sat in front with me on the way back and Gene sat in back with his son. They didn't speak to each other all the way home. They just sat there, sizing each other up. Gene would sneak a view of the boy and tug at one end of his mustache, which was a habit of his."

Waiting at Peaked Hill Bars is O'Neill's Provincetown Players colleague James Light, who shares his love of swimming. Light watches as father and son dive into the waves of the Atlantic. "Once they got into the ocean," Light recalled, "the awkwardness between them disappeared."

MID-AUGUST: O'Neill isn't sorry to say good-bye to his older son. Despite his growing affection for Eugene Jr., O'Neill begrudges the time lost from his writing. He is equally chary of the time he spends with Shane, now nearly three. While he takes an occasional interest in his younger son's activities, he rarely is seen to caress or hold him—unless requested to do so by a newspaper or magazine photographer. "I hardly ever saw Gene play with Shane," said Given, reflecting the impression of most of O'Neill's friends. "He seemed detached from the boy."

Not that Agnes spends much time with Shane either. She is still sporadically pursuing her own writing career, and leaves her child's care largely to Mrs. Clarke. But Shane seems a happy child, at least according to his half sister, Barbara, who is six years older. She remembers that Shane called their Peaked Hill Bars home "the house where the wind blows."

Barbara Burton retained happy memories of her visits to Peaked Hill Bars, although she was only rarely in the company of her mother and stepfather, spending most of her time with Shane and Gaga.

"Shane was the most beautiful, golden-haired little boy you can imagine," she recalled. "He was happy and ebullient and I loved him. He had a golden heart as well as a golden head of hair." Barbara and Shane, constant companions, "lived in the ocean."

When she meets Eugene Jr. for the first time that summer, Barbara finds him "fun and full of zest." As for her stepfather, she sees him as "a gentle, shy man, with a soft light flickering in his eyes." Her mother and O'Neill, she said, "would have wonderful evening picnics and invite friends from town."

LATE SEPTEMBER: Grateful to be released from his paternal obligations, O'Neill moves on to his writing—and to the next thorn in his side, his increasingly dicey relationship with Agnes.

OCTOBER 16: By the time of his birthday, O'Neill has begun outlining a play he is calling *Welded*. A transparently personal examination of the fractious state of his marriage, it will be the first of his many merciless scrutinizings of marital strife. The play springs from O'Neill's preoccupation with his parents' ill-suited marriage, which he believes has become an inadvertent model for his own. Even though his parents' final years were sanguine (once his mother recovered from her morphine habit), Eugene still bears the scars of their turmoil as he was growing up.

Although O'Neill has written in his earliest plays (albeit tentatively and symbolically) about aspects of his parents' dysfunctional life together, it isn't until now, at thirty-six, that he at last allows August Strindberg's ghost its uninhibited sway. He has long since learned to empathize with Strindberg's cruelly embattled husbands and wives—couples who, despite their incompatibility, are locked together by their unrelenting need for each other—as dead-on paradigms for his mother and father.

It is Strindberg's *The Dance of Death* that strikes a particularly responsive chord. In that annihilative play, Strindberg put into the mouths of his embattled married couple words that left audiences affronted and even repelled. O'Neill, however, recognized the sense of those words as a motivating force in his parents' relationship (and later in his own marriages). At one point in *Dance of Death*, the husband declares, "We have been trying to depart every single day—but we are chained together and cannot break away." And a little later, the wife, responding to a family friend's "Then he loves you," retorts, "Probably. But that does not prevent him from hating me." In the equally baleful *The Father*, Strindberg declares that "love between a man and a woman is war," and in *The Dream Play*, he offers the thought that "it's terribly hard to be married . . . harder than anything else."

Perhaps most memorable of all Strindberg's misanthropic lines is the way a character in *The Dance of Death* describes the marital relationship: its essence is "love-hatred, and it hails from the pit!"

As Strindberg's ardent apprentice, O'Neill was determined to enrapture and astound his audiences (and, yes, shock them) rather than merely divert and entertain them. He would suffer none of the taboos against dialogue about explicit sexuality or the cruelty of societal exploitation. "It was reading his plays," O'Neill would say in accepting his Nobel Prize in 1936 (in the speech read for him in his absence), "when I first started to write back in the winter of 1913–14, that, above all else, first gave me the vision of what modern drama could be, and first inspired me with the urge to write for the theater myself."

Agnes, who knew nothing of Strindberg when she first met O'Neill, recalled that one night early in their romance, O'Neill read *Miss Julie* aloud to her, "losing himself in the sound of the words and their haunted meaning." O'Neill relished this tale of sexual passion between the aristocratic young woman (who behaves like a whore) and her father's valet (who behaves like an operatic villain). O'Neill, however (judging by his own canon), seems to have been even more mesmerized by the audacious preface Strindberg wrote for the published version of the play:

- Perhaps the time will come when we will be so advanced, so enlightened, that we can witness with indifference what now seem the coarse, cynical, heartless dramas life has to offer.
- If my tragedy depresses many people, it is their own fault.

- I find the joy of life in its cruel and powerful struggles, and my enjoyment comes from being able to know something, being able to learn something.

LATE FALL: O'Neill might well have summoned these words of Strindberg's in support of *Welded*, the play he was now writing, based on his own increasingly conflicted marriage. His and Agnes's misunderstandings were growing more scabrous.

O'Neill, always the protagonist of his own perceived personal tragedy, cast Agnes, in his mind, as the adored enemy, and a worthy antagonist on the matrimonial battlefield—a woman with a masochistic zeal to match his own, a woman who could fight furiously—and who then reciprocates his impassioned lovemaking. He wanted to believe that Agnes answered his insatiable need for a wife-lover-secretary-servant—not to mention whipping boy. (That role, in the end, did not suit Agnes Boulton; it awaited Carlotta Monterey, for whom it was tailor-made.)

In *Welded*, depicting his relationship with Agnes hyperrealistically, O'Neill must have believed he was making a universal statement about the Furies that can drive a marriage. Perhaps, with this work, he hoped to prove himself the American Strindberg. "This play ought to be the very finest, deepest, and the most vital thing that I have done," he wrote to Oliver Sayler, after completing his first draft of *Welded* the following spring.

Welded is about a man and wife, both egoists, welded together in a passionate, jealous, possessive love that renders their lives alternately heaven and hell. They have a soul-shattering fight and the wife sets out to spend an adulterous night with a former admirer while the husband attempts to sleep with a prostitute.

Neither can go through with their plans and both realize their love welds them to each other. There is no solution for them except to stay together, perpetually fighting, reconciling, hating, and loving, in an endless cycle of torment.

Although O'Neill regarded *Welded* as the last word in meaningful truth about love and marriage, it didn't work, for much the same reason that *The First Man* hadn't worked. Not surprisingly, he tended to lose his artistic perspective when he wrote about an intensely personal situation at the same time that he was living it.

George Jean Nathan, after reading the script of *Welded*, issued what must have felt to O'Neill like the ultimate insult. The play, he told O'Neill, was little more than "some very third-rate Strindberg."

This time he was right. But O'Neill, according to Nathan, "sharply observed that I couldn't conceivably understand any such play as I had never been married." The wounded dramatist, Nathan said, "put on his hat, walked out and didn't let me hear from him for two months."

END OF OCTOBER: O'Neill, having celebrated his thirty-sixth birthday, was still the same oft-misunderstood-but-resolute artist, as well as a challenged husband, reluctant father, conflicted brother, and wounded son.

18

O'Neill and Agnes went shopping in October 1922 for a year-round home within easy reach of New York. They had persuaded themselves that with enough space and serene surroundings, they could live together peaceably. They were still strapped for cash, but O'Neill was expecting his mother's estate to be settled soon, and he and Agnes were tempted to buy Stormfield, the Florentine-style villa in Redding, Connecticut, where Mark Twain died in 1910.

When the two were advised that repairs might cost as much as $5,000, they had the good sense to abandon that idea; even so, they overextended themselves when, instead, they put a down payment of $32,000 on a nearby estate in Ridgefield, fifty-five miles from Manhattan. Called Brook Farm, it occupied an area that mingled working farms and mansions.

Their initial payment, plus the cost of furnishings, carved out a substantial chunk of the $44,000 O'Neill earned that year. He was counting, however, on his $73,000 share of his mother's estate. And he and Agnes planned to recoup some of their outlay by renting out Brook Farm during the summer while they retreated to Peaked Hill Bars.

O'Neill hoped that in rural Connecticut he would escape the distractions of city life, and yet be within an easy train or car ride to Manhattan when he needed to attend rehearsals. He was also close enough to New London to keep an eye on the family property, as well as on Jamie, whose behavior was escalating ever more out of control.

To friends aware of his love for the sea, O'Neill explained that a recent medical checkup had showed a "smoky" lung condition. Always fearing a recurrence of TB, he said he was taking his doctor's advice to switch to country air.

Brook Farm had fifteen rooms and was set on thirty-one acres of wide lawns, pasture, and woodland. There was a spring-fed swimming pond, a fish pond, vegetable and flower gardens, a four-car garage, a stable, and a barn. Surrounded by ancient elms, oaks, and pines, the house was a traditional white clapboard New England colonial, with a paneled center hall and a library enhanced by a beamed ceiling. A thirty-foot-square living room with French doors led to a covered patio. Upstairs were four large bedrooms, two with fireplaces, and the servants' quarters.

While O'Neill's penny-pinching father would have disdained such a home as conspicuously wasteful, it was just the sort of house his mother had dreamed of living in (even while knowing herself too incapacitated to manage it).

Brook Farm signaled a radical change of lifestyle for O'Neill, who heretofore had shown no tendency to see himself as a country squire. During his boyhood, when New London was still a fashionable summer resort, he had always sneered—in common with Jamie and his father—at gentrified estates like Brook Farm. But O'Neill appeared to revel in his new persona, going so far as to acquire a pedigreed Irish wolfhound— the breed of Irish kings—which he dubbed Finn, later adding an Irish terrier named for Mat Burke, the sailor in *Anna Christie*. To complete his new image, he splurged on a custom-made, so-called touring car with six seats and a convertible top, designed for family outings.

He seemed to have forgotten his self-righteous pronouncement of two years earlier, while roughing it among the dunes at his oceanfront home on Peaked Hill Bars. It was then that he told a newspaper interviewer he was "a person to whom Rolls-Royces and similar titillations mean less than nothing, and who desires no greater extravagance than food."

He still sincerely believed himself to be scornful of a lifestyle of luxury. But he had, after all, worked hard, and been true to his ideals; his increasing success as a dramatist gave him a sense of entitlement. Why shouldn't he live as well as he could?

Although O'Neill hoped Brook Farm would be a home in which he and Agnes could live companionably, it didn't work out that way. The initial elation of furnishing the house and hiring servants proved to be just an interlude between bouts of hostility. Despite their still-passionate (if inter-mittent) lovemaking, their disagreements about how they should conduct their lives were exacerbated.

Agnes was eager to entertain at her grand new home, and to attend parties both locally and in New York. O'Neill was willing to see a few chosen friends now and then, but, as ever, he craved quiet and seclusion for his writing. Agnes's social propensities got on his nerves.

"Gene was doing a lot of drinking around that time," Kenneth Mac-gowan remembered. "He telephoned me one day in New York from his house in Ridgefield. He asked me to bring him a bottle of whiskey on the way to my home in Brewster. When I got to Ridgefield, Gene met me at the door. All he said was 'I don't like Agnes.'"

Eben Given, who had gone house-hunting with the O'Neills in Con-necticut (and who later bought the Mark Twain estate), believed O'Neill's conflict "stemmed from the fact that [he] was roaring ahead artistically, and he had to be kept free from social demands." Agnes's daughter, Bar-bara, an occasional visitor, recalled that "lots of people were always com-ing for weekends from New York."

Louis Kantor, conceding that Agnes's social yearning was one of the obvious causes of friction between the two, suggested there was an even more fundamental problem. It hinged, Kantor believed, "on the ques-tion of equality." It's true that Agnes felt herself as much entitled to pur-sue her preferred way of life as was O'Neill to pursue his—an attitude that O'Neill, rapidly growing in stature, found unconscionable. He expected Agnes—more so now than ever—to find her raison d'être in him and his work.

He demanded to be pampered, waited upon, obeyed. It angered him when Agnes seemed unable to understand that the importance of his work entitled him to deference. Every time she challenged his supremacy he was shattered anew. And yet, while he didn't "like" her—and longed to change her—he missed her unbearably when they were apart. And Agnes continued to respond in kind—although stopping short of unconditional surrender.

"I have a heartache all the time I am away from you," she wrote soon after the purchase of Brook Farm. "My dear dearest, I want to write my soul out for you, telling the way I feel about you."

Conflict was the air O'Neill breathed. It wasn't only his feelings for Agnes that stifled him. His refractory brother had become an intolerable burden; it was all but impossible for O'Neill any longer to feel charitable toward him. To the lawyer for his mother's estate, who was having difficulty getting Jamie to sign some necessary documents, O'Neill wrote in exasperation from Brook Farm at year's end:

> I don't know what to say to you regarding my brother. The last I heard of him he was in pretty bad shape . . . I have learned by experience that the more I should urge him toward one course of action, the more obstinate and determined he will be to do the opposite. So what can I do?

After a protracted struggle, Jamie consented to enter a drying-out facility in Darien, not far from Ridgefield. But he soon left to embark on a drunken rampage. O'Neill desperately wired the family lawyer:

> HE HAS BROKEN LOOSE AGAIN IS ON HIS WAY TO NEW LONDON AFTER MOST DISGRACEFUL SCENE IN THEATER STAMFORD LAST NIGHT WILL BE ARRESTED THERE IF HE RETURNS ANY MEASURES HOWEVER DRASTIC YOU SEE FIT TO TAKE TO RESTRAIN HIM IN NEW LONDON WILL HAVE MY FULL APPROVAL.

In fuming over his brother's tantrums, Eugene seemed to have forgotten his own years of self-destructive drinking—or, for that matter, his own still-unresolved addiction to alcohol. He was too incensed to feel compassion for the older brother he'd worshipped from early childhood, the brother he'd admired for his worldliness and literary sophistication, and whose cynicism he'd trustingly tried to imitate. For most of their lives they'd been as close as any two brothers of legend. But O'Neill had run out of patience.

On May 20, 1923, Jamie, in an advanced state of delirium tremens, was admitted to the Riverlong Sanatorium in Paterson, New Jersey, an expensive rehabilitation center paid for out of his share of his mother's estate. At forty-five, Jamie's hair was white and he was losing his eyesight.

O'Neill was kept apprised of Jamie's condition by his sanatorium doctor and by a few visiting relatives and friends from New London and New York. Among them was Frances Cadenas, the married sister of the Madison Square Garden circus acrobat Bill Clarke, Eugene and Jamie's drinking crony from bygone days.

Jamie talked to Cadenas of his love for his younger brother. He had been hospitalized for a month when she was informed by his doctor that his condition had grown critical. "The pain is not only in his limbs but in his hands this week," Cadenas wrote to O'Neill. "He does not like the place, the food is wretched, and he cannot sleep during the night."

She went on to describe his treatment for what had been diagnosed as "alcoholic neuritis": gradual withdrawal from alcohol by "giving him ten drinks of whiskey during the day and some other kind of drink before the whiskey, which burns like fire and acts as a purgative." Jamie, she said, "was very skinny, pale, trembles a great deal and of course weak.

"I read him a little part of your letter and he was very happy to hear a message from you. He cannot read or write and he asked me to write for him and to tell you about his condition. He also expressed a great desire to see you."

She promised to continue visiting Jamie and would telegraph O'Neill

if there was any change. "I'm sure a letter from you would be very bracing," she prodded gently.

O'Neill rarely wrote to Jamie and never visited the sanatorium. In a
letter to Saxe Commins, he confided that Jamie was "almost blind from
bad booze. . . . What the hell can be done about him is more than I can
figure. He'll only get drunk, I guess, after he gets out and then he'll be
all blind."

Jamie never did get out. It took him three more months to die. According to a cousin, Phil Sheridan, Jamie was "out of his mind" during his
final days. Death came on November 8, 1923.

O'Neill did not attend the service at St. Stephen's, on Twenty-ninth
Street, a few blocks from the church where his mother's funeral Mass
had been held. Agnes told friends her husband was ill with the flu; other
friends heard he was drunk—as Jamie had been during his mother's
funeral service less than a year earlier. The most cruelly blighted of the
tragic O'Neills, Jamie was buried in New London beside his father,
mother, and baby brother.

Memories of his uncharitable treatment of Jamie festered in Eugene's
mind. Years later, still hugging his grief and guilt, O'Neill answered a
query about his brother from Joseph McCarthy, his former roommate at
their Catholic boarding school. "No, my brother is not alive. . . . Booze
got him in the end. It was a shame. He and I were terribly close to each
other."

Almost two decades after Jamie's death, O'Neill wrote *A Moon for the
Misbegotten*, a play that was, in effect, a requiem for his brother. He
struggled to complete it, fearful that encroaching illness soon would
silence his writing forever.

Begun in 1941, it was O'Neill's final and most brutally tragic work,
completed in 1944 when he was gravely ill. Beneath its splendor as theater, *A Moon for the Misbegotten* was O'Neill's despairing attempt to understand and (at least conditionally) forgive Jamie for the outrageous
conduct that was precipitated by his mother's death.

The play is set on a ramshackle Connecticut farm, recognizable as property owned by James O'Neill near New London. In the play, as in real life, the farm is part of the older son's inheritance. And in the play, it is operated by a disreputable tenant farmer, Phil Hogan, and his daughter, Josie.

While Hogan is based on an actual pig farmer named John Dolan, known as "Dirty Dolan" by old-time New Londoners, Josie, a voluptuous, bigger-than-life Earth Mother, is a character of O'Neill's invention. She is endowed by him with the nurturing qualities possessed by both Dorothy Day and Christine Ell, who had soothed him during his anxious Greenwich Village days.

The time is "early September 1923," two months before the real Jamie's death. As in *Long Day's Journey Into Night*, the character based on O'Neill's brother is called James Tyrone Jr. But while the Tyrones of *Journey* address him by his nickname Jamie, in *Moon* he is called Jim—as the real Jamie was known to many outside the family. The nickname "Jamie" had been given to him in early boyhood by his mother to avoid confusion with his father, whom she had always called Jim.

Unlike O'Neill's harsh early notes (ultimately scuttled) for *Long Day's Journey Into Night*, in which he described Mary Tyrone as an "alien demon," he now made fanciful notes about Jim Tyrone as a mere "alien"; when he was born, wrote O'Neill, the first thing he did was "look around at the round earth and realize" he had been "sent to the wrong planet."

"God had double-crossed him," O'Neill elaborated in his scenario for the play, "and so he began to curse . . . and he reached for a bottle of whiskey and said to himself, By God, I'll show you! Try and catch me now. And so he lived on cursing & drinking, being slapped on the back and no one ever caught him."

O'Neill had, of course, already depicted his brother as a misanthropic second-rate actor—alcoholic but still functional at thirty-three—in his recently completed *Long Day's Journey Into Night*, which was set in 1912. In *Moon*—set eleven years later—O'Neill portrayed his then forty-five-year-old brother as a depressed, guilt-ridden, alcohol-sodden failure who is aware he is at death's edge.

Rather than inhabiting the realistic family setting of *Long Day's Journey*, the James Tyrone Jr. of *Moon* materializes from a twisted fable that is part tragedy, part raucous comedy, and part miracle play.

At the time we meet this older fictional Jim Tyrone on Hogan's farm in *Moon*, the real Jim was actually in the New Jersey sanatorium, nearly blind, recently having suffered a stroke, and in the terminal stage of alcoholism. *A Moon for the Misbegotten*, a wish fulfillment on O'Neill's part, afforded him a second look at his brother's life and death.

In one sense, the play was a belated offering of redemption for his brother as well as expiation for his own guilty lack of compassion during Jamie's terminal suffering. It was as though O'Neill was conjuring a Mass for the long-dead brother who had once been his hero.

It is in the climactic third act scene that Jim Tyrone, seeking atonement, tears from himself an agonizing confession about his own unforgivable behavior. It is based on Jamie O'Neill's drunken confession to his brother of his debauched five-day train trip from California to New York with his mother's casket. O'Neill had listened to the confession with disgust and fury.

Jim's confessor in the play is the earth-motherly Josie Hogan, described as "so oversize for a woman that she is almost a freak—5 feet 11 in her stockings and weighs around 180," but who, beneath a mock-bawdy exterior, possesses a saintly gentleness and compassion.

O'Neill wished Josie to be seen as Jim's savior, the one person to whom he could reveal his betrayal of his mother and be given absolution in his mother's name. *A Moon for the Misbegotten* is essentially a religious play, rooted in the Roman Catholic doctrine that O'Neill never entirely left behind. A startling aspect of the play is how little O'Neill chose to alter the bare facts of Jamie's raw account of his mother's last days and his horrifying five-day train ride bearing his mother's remains from California to New York.

"When Mama died," Jim Tyrone begins, "I'd been on the wagon for nearly two years. Not even a glass of beer. Honestly. And I know I would have stayed on. For her sake. . . . She'd always hated my drinking. So I quit. It made me happy to do it. For her. Because she was all I had, all I cared about. Because I loved her."

He goes on to recall the onslaught of his mother's illness in California. "The docs said, no hope. Might never come out of coma. I went crazy. Couldn't face losing her. The old booze yen got me. I got drunk and stayed drunk. And I began hoping she'd never come out of the coma, and see I was drinking again. That was my excuse, too—that she'd never know. I know damned well just before she died she recognized me. She saw I was drunk. Then she closed her eyes so she couldn't see, and was glad to die!"

He found he "couldn't feel anything," nor could he cry. "All I did was try to explain to myself, 'She's dead, what does she care now if I cry or not.'" She was "happy to be where" he "couldn't hurt her ever again."

Jim describes how, in the train bringing his mother's body east, he'd hidden himself in his drawing room "with a case of booze," but drunk as he was, nothing could make him forget his mother in the baggage car.

"I found I couldn't stay alone in the drawing room," he tells Josie. "It became haunted. I was going crazy. I had to go out and wander up and down the train looking for company."

He grew so boisterous, the conductor threatened to lock him into his compartment. But he had glimpsed a woman passenger "who was used to drunks and could pretend to like them, if there was enough dough in it." He describes her as "a blonde pig who looked more like a whore than twenty-five whores, with . . . a come-on smile as cold as a polar bear's feet."

Jim Tyrone goes on to tell a horrified Josie Hogan that he bribed the porter to give the woman a message, and that night she sneaked into his compartment; he paid the whore "fifty bucks a night," he goes on, and to Josie's shocked response, "Oh, how could you!" he shrugs helplessly.

"I suppose I had some mad idea she could make me forget—what was in the baggage car ahead. . . . It was like some plot I had to carry out. . . . It was as if I wanted revenge—because I'd been left alone—because I knew I was lost, without any hope left—that all I could do would be drink myself to death."

But, he says, he didn't forget "even in that pig's arms!" Exhausted, he ends his story: "Well, that's all—except I was too drunk to go to her funeral." Josie, after her initial dismay, tries to comfort Jim. She realizes he is dying, and—in his mother's name—she pardons and blesses him. As he takes his final leave of Josie, "her face sad, tender and pitying," she gazes after him.

"May you have your wish and die in your sleep soon, Jim, darling," she says, "may you rest forever in forgiveness and peace."

Unlike the fictional Jim Tyrone, Jamie O'Neill had no Josie Hogan to absolve him.

In *A Moon for the Misbegotten*, there is no mention—as there is in *Long Day's Journey Into Night*—of the events of Jamie's early life that led to his final tragedy. At the age of ten and still in exile (at Notre Dame's elementary boarding school in South Bend, Indiana), Jamie seems to have outgrown the jealousy he'd felt three years earlier at the intrusion into his family of an unwanted sibling; he accepted with good grace the arrival of his new brother, Eugene. Perhaps, amid the friends he'd made and his busy academic and extracurricular school life, he had become resigned to living apart from his parents and no longer felt the need to vie for his mother's daily attention—although he did yearn for her school visits.

If O'Neill's early scenario for *A Moon for the Misbegotten* is taken literally, Jamie also drew profound solace from the religious belief in which he was raised. "There was once a boy who loved . . . purity and God with a great quiet passion inside him" reads a line in the scenario describing Jim Tyrone; indeed, wrote O'Neill, Jim had actually contemplated giving up "self & the world to worship of God."

He was popular with his fellow students at Notre Dame's elementary school and something of a teacher's pet. He appeared in dramatic productions and played shortstop on the baseball team. No one who knew this bright, ingratiating, high-achieving boy would have predicted anything but the rosiest of futures for him.

His spiral downward began at fourteen when, during a school vacation, he stumbled on his mother injecting herself with morphine—a discovery duplicated by Eugene a decade later.

When Jamie returned to school, his behavior turned erratic. He still exhibited bursts of exemplary scholarship and literary achievement, but he had lost heart. He left his boarding school just short of his sixteenth birthday and, in quick succession, attended two other schools, performing with sporadic brilliance, but often misbehaving.

He enrolled at St. John's University in New York (later Fordham University), but less than halfway through his senior year he was expelled for what he thought was a grand joke: he brought a prostitute onto campus and tried to pass her off to the Jesuit faculty as his sister—an episode recounted in *A Moon for the Misbegotten.*

It was then that Jamie began the decline from which he would never spring back.

19

have lost my Father, Mother and only brother within the past four years," O'Neill wrote to Mary Clark, the nurse who had cared for him in the Connecticut TB sanatorium in 1912 and on whom he based the character of the nurse, Miss Gilpin, in *The Straw*. "Now I'm the only O'Neill of our branch left."

Since neither of his two sons were "pure Irish," he added with a self-dramatizing flourish, "I must consider myself the real last one. It makes me feel old and weary sometimes."

O'Neill did not mention that his weariness was caused to some degree by the dismal failure of *Welded*. O'Neill had temporarily shrugged off his mantle of mourning—not quite four months after Jamie's death—to immerse himself in this Strindberg-inspired play.

Welded was an almost literal depiction of his fractious marriage to Agnes.

Typical of their perverse and higgledy-piggledy marriage, O'Neill and Agnes were currently reveling in a renewed intimacy. Agnes treasured *Welded* as her play, and they clung to each other as rehearsals got under way in early March 1924. Seated together at rehearsals in the Thirty-ninth Street Theatre west of Broadway, she and O'Neill gloated over the dialogue—by turns vicious and adoring—that the husband, Michael Cape, and his wife, Eleanor, spat or cooed at each other.

The director, Stark Young, was aware that the O'Neills' personal life

was not, as he put it, "all smoothness" between "two such vivid temperaments"; he perceived *Welded* as somewhat of a "confession and a bene-
diction" for both O'Neill and Agnes.

A respected writer and critic, Young had agreed to stage the play even
though he'd cringed at some of the script's excesses; he later sarcastically
described O'Neill and Agnes at rehearsals, "sitting side by side there in
the third row and listening to every speech, good or bad, and taking it all
as bona fide and their own." They believed "every word of the play," he
added, "—those vulgar speeches, God!"

With narcissistic insight, O'Neill had conceived Michael Cape as
a virtual mirror image; he is, like O'Neill, thirty-five and a successful playwright: "His unusual face is a harrowed battlefield of super-
sensitiveness . . . the forehead of a thinker, the eyes of a dreamer, the
nose and mouth of a sensualist. One feels a powerful imagination tinged
with somber sadness—a driving force which can be sympathetic and
cruel at the same time. There is something tortured about him . . . a self-
protecting, arrogant defiance of life . . . a deep need for love as a faith in
which to relax."

Subjective as it is, it's not an inaccurate snapshot of the author himself.

Nor is O'Neill's description of the playwright's wife an erroneous
rendering of Agnes's personality—although Eleanor, an actress rather
than a writer, has made her name as a leading lady in her husband's plays.
"Her face," wrote O'Neill (presumably with Agnes's approval and possibly with her assistance), "with its high, prominent cheekbones, lacks harmony. It is dominated by passionate, blue-gray eyes, restrained by a high
forehead from which the mass of her dark brown hair is combed straight
back. The first impression of her whole personality is one of charm."

Within minutes of the beginning of Act I, Scene I, Cape and Eleanor
are heavy-handedly excoriating each other; their exchange (almost certainly) approximates a typically tedious conversation between their two
married prototypes:

CAPE: You feel the need of what is outside. I'm not enough for you.

ELEANOR: (*pleadingly*) Haven't I a right to myself as you have to yourself?

CAPE: You fight against me as if I were your enemy. . . . At every turn you feel your individuality invaded—while at the same time, you're jealous of any separateness in me. You demand more and more while you give less and less. And I have to acquiesce. Have to? Yes, because I can't live without you! You realize that! You take advantage of it while you despise me for my helplessness!

ELEANOR: You insist that I have no life at all outside you. Even my work must exist only as an echo of yours. You hate my need of easy, casual associations. You think that weakness. You hate my friends. You're jealous of everything and everybody. (*resentfully*) I have to fight. You're too severe. Your ideal is too inhuman. Why can't you understand and be generous—be just!

It befell two respected players, Doris Keane and Jacob Ben-Ami, to deliver these overwrought lines. Before the end of the first week's rehearsals, Keane told Stark Young she could not act the role of Eleanor. Pronouncing the play "a vulgar, stupid dogfight," she pleaded with him to let her withdraw. Although embarrassed on his star's behalf, Young—out of loyalty to O'Neill—appealed to her gallantry and persuaded her to stay. "I'm still ashamed of myself for letting Doris Keane play the role," he later confessed.

Ben-Ami, who also had misgivings, agreed to stay with the play because he realized O'Neill "was in a bad way emotionally" and all concerned "had been breaking their necks to keep him sober."

Welded landed with a thud on March 17. It was unanimously dismissed by the critics as one of O'Neill's misguided high dives. Before even reading what they had to say, O'Neill, in his Work Diary, had pronounced it "A Flop!"

"Two back fence cats in debate" was how Woollcott dismissed it, while other critics found it "repetitious," "prosy," and "dull."

O'Neill complained sarcastically to the critic Oliver Sayler that the play might have "shone through" had it been done without its cast; yet, several years later, in a characteristic about-face, he scorned *Welded* as too painfully bungled to be worth producing at all. It closed after twenty-four performances.

Agnes, cheated of the epiphany she'd envisioned, could only hope that the public airing of her and O'Neill's marital perplexities would in some measure prove cathartic. As for O'Neill, it is ironic that he, in his initial pique, chose to blame the failure of *Welded* on its cast, since he himself, as a part producer, had approved the actors.

WELDED WAS THE initial venture of a recently formed triumvirate consisting of O'Neill, Kenneth Macgowan, and Robert Edmond Jones. They had taken over the Provincetown Players in June 1923, shortly after O'Neill chose Arthur Hopkins as the producer of *The Hairy Ape*, bypassing Jig Cook, who was still living in Greece after having left the foundering Provincetowners to survive as best they could.

O'Neill had seized the chance to solve a dilemma he had in common with most of his peers: how to get his work onto the stage under auspices that would allow him the final say on all aspects of production. He was certain he could count on Macgowan and Jones to accommodate unequivocally his soaring vision for his future work.

As he had predicted at the start of 1922, while flush with the success of *The Emperor Jones* and *Anna Christie*, his work was likely to change in both form and content. At that time, answering questions posed by Malcolm Mollan, his onetime city editor during his ephemeral reporting stint on the New London *Telegraph* in 1912, O'Neill said, "I intend to use whatever I can make my own, to write about anything under the sun, in any manner that fits or can be invented to fit the subject. And I shall never be influenced by any consideration but one: Is it the truth as I know it—or better still, feel it? If so, shoot, and let the splinters fall where they may. If not, not. . . . There is no temptation for me to compromise."

Three months later (in April 1922), O'Neill—albeit with tongue in cheek—expressed his implausible dreams of an Ideal Theater to Oliver Sayler: "The Higher Man of the theater will be a playwright. He will have his own theater for his own plays, as Strindberg had his Intimate Theater in Stockholm." Surrounding the playwright would be imaginative craftsmen who would find their inspiration in interpreting his work. But before that could happen, O'Neill jested, the theater as it existed, must be destroyed.

> Let us then first—oh sweet and lovely thought!—poison all the actors, then guillotine the managers, hang the playwrights—with one omission—feed the critics to the lions (except you, of course), and as a final act of purification, call upon a good God to send a second flood to wipe out the audience, root and branch. Being a just God, and a Great Producer, he will no doubt spare the two of us; and we can then rehearse this dialog on Mount Ararat as a first step toward the Theater of the Future.

Reiterating his conviction that he'd outgrown what he considered Jig Cook's didactic control and zealous amateurism, O'Neill declared himself equally fed up with the foibles and caprices of Broadway potentates like John Williams, George Tyler, and even Arthur Hopkins. In a stroke of luck for O'Neill, part of the solution to his problem came from Cook himself; he unexpectedly decided to prolong his stay in Greece with Susan Glaspell and on June 19, 1923, he cabled his wish that the Provincetown Players be terminated. He bluntly spelled out his reasons in a letter to Edna Kenton, a veteran official of the Players:

"Since we have failed spiritually in the elemental things, and the result is mediocrity, what one who has loved it wishes for it now is euthanasia—a swift and painless death." Cook implied his decision was based on O'Neill's truculence: "Our richest, like our poorest, have desired most not to give life but to have it given them."

With Cook out of the picture at the Provincetown, O'Neill next set about ridding himself of his Broadway producing tyrants. Since there was "no one else," as he wrote to George Jean Nathan, "I'll have to help create a new outlet—or remain gagged."

It was his determination not to remain gagged that had motivated him to invite Macgowan and Jones to join him in the producing triumvirate that would replace the argumentative and haphazard committee system initiated by Cook. The triumvirate would operate with what Macgowan called "a firm, dictating hand." With reference to no one's opinion but their own, the three would choose when, how, and where to produce O'Neill's upcoming plays; in addition, they would fill the Provincetown Playhouse with experimental productions of established classics and modern European dramas, along with fresh new American work.

By the beginning of 1924—two months before the triumvirate's production of *Welded*—Cook was dead. Not yet fifty, he died in Greece on January 14 of glanders, an animal disease rarely transmitted to humans, but mystifyingly contracted by Cook from his pet dog. O'Neill was stunned.

"When I heard of his death, Susan," he wrote to Glaspell in a letter of condolence and appeasement, "I felt suddenly that I had lost one of the best friends I had ever had or ever would have—unselfish, rare, and truly noble! And then when I thought of all the things I hadn't done, the letters I hadn't written, the things I hadn't said, the others I had said and wished unsaid, I felt like a swine, Susan. Whenever I think of him it is with the most self-condemning remorse." Not long after Glaspell's return to America, she resumed her friendship with O'Neill and Agnes.

Not until twenty years later—at the end of his writing career—did O'Neill publicly give Cook his due, saluting him in 1945 as "imaginative in every way," and adding that Cook "was against everything that suggested the worn-out conventions and cheap artificialities of the commercial stage. It's hard to say how much we owe him.'"

AFTER HAVING USED *Welded* to probe, ad nauseam, the reasons for his unflagging battle with Agnes, O'Neill went on—still in Strindbergian mode—to explore the even more convoluted marriage of his parents.

All God's Chillun Got Wings was a play O'Neill would not have dared to write while his parents were living. Indeed, he'd had to wait for the death of his brother as well, for he wouldn't have risked Jamie's condemnation. But once he felt freed to express his true feelings about his family, he became a galactic vacuum sweeper; he began to suck up the painful fragments of his life and redistribute them into one cosmic retelling after another.

Written between October and December 1923, *All God's Chillun* was O'Neill's first attempt to delve into the character of his unstable mother, whom he would continue to portray in one guise or another to the end of his career. In a series of semi-expressionist scenes, the play zeroes in on the stifling marriage between an emotionally unstable woman and her well-intentioned husband, who strives to rise above his humble background, but is ultimately reduced to the role of his wife's caretaker. Like Ella and James O'Neill—and like Strindberg's tormented couples madly dancing to their deaths—the man and wife in *All God's Chillun* are irrevocably locked together.

"I can't leave her. She can't leave me," says the play's husband to his sister, who has asked why he and his clearly incompatible wife don't separate. "And there's a million little reasons combining to make one big reason why we can't. For her sake—if it'd do her any good—I'd go—I'd leave—I'd do anything—because I love her. . . . But that'd only make matters worse for her. I'm all she's got in the world! Yes, that isn't bragging or fooling myself. I know that for a fact!"

Craftily camouflaging *All God's Chillun* as a meditation on miscegenation, O'Neill buried the fact that his parents were his real-life models. So secure was he (now that his brother was gone) that their disguises were impenetrable, he audaciously called the couple by his parents' actual first names—Jim and Ella—(though giving them the fictitious last name of Harris).

He disguised his father (the impoverished Irish immigrant actor avid for stardom) as a slum-born New York black man striving to rise above his background by passing the bar exam and practicing law. And he disguised his mother (the sheltered Irish princess Ella Quinlan) as a raddled white child of the same New York slum, who becomes Jim Harris's unhinged wife.

Not surprisingly, O'Neill was having far more difficulty coming to terms, postmortem, with his once-morphine-addicted mother than with his perplexed if well-intentioned father. His portrayal of Ella Harris was censorious, based on childhood memories of his mother's inexplicable and terrifying switches from maternal warmth to what sometimes appeared to young Eugene as insanity.

At play's end, Jim realizes he will never pass the bar exam and Ella Harris is clinically insane. Cursing her stricken husband as a "nigger," she threatens him with a carving knife—much as Ella O'Neill (although not wielding a knife) sometimes cuttingly derided her husband as an ignorant Irish peasant.

O'Neill's symbolic concept of his mother, when in morphine's grip, was later to be embedded in *Long Day's Journey Into Night*. The notes that O'Neill made about Mary Tyrone applied equally to Ella Harris in *God's Chillun*: a woman who could switch in an instant from loving wife to "a hard cynical sneering bitterness with a bitter biting cruelty and with a coarse vulgarity in it."

O'Neill imbued Ella Harris with an uncontainable fury at her isolation, which she blamed on her marriage to a black man who was socially snubbed for his daring but futile attempt to become a lawyer. This was O'Neill's symbolic substitute for Ella O'Neill's distress at the isolation she suffered as a result of her marriage to an actor, in a day when actors were often snubbed as little better than vagabonds and prostitutes. Moreover, he implied, a contributing cause of Ella Harris's depression stemmed, as did Ella O'Neill's, from the loss of an infant.

As *All God's Chillun* was being readied for production, O'Neill tried to avoid a mistake he believed he'd made with *Welded*; he had come to realize that the heightened dialogue in *Welded* was contravened by the play's realistic setting.

"My notion," he said, "was to have a man and a woman, lovers and married, enact their spiritual struggle to possess one another. I wanted to give the impression of the world shut out, just of two human beings struggling to break through an inner darkness.

"But the sets which I described in my stage directions were so 'natural' that they inevitably conjured up all the unimportant paraphernalia of living, daily existence, to stand between the life of my characters and the lives in the audience."

Whether a more abstract set would have saved *Welded* is doubtful. Nevertheless, O'Neill, avoiding a realistic setting for *All God's Chillun*, called instead for an expressionistic design to represent the Brooklyn apartment in which Jim and Ella gradually smother each other. And so, the Harrises' living room shrinks with each act, its walls closing in, its ceiling descending, its furnishings looming ever larger and more menacing. If anything could have distracted O'Neill and Agnes from the humiliating failure of *Welded*—not to mention the continuing agitation of their faltering marriage—it was the rumble of controversy about the impending production of *All God's Chillun Got Wings*. As he'd often done with previous plays, O'Neill released the script for publication ahead of production (in *The American Mercury*, the newest Nathan/Mencken magazine venture, in February 1924).

Even as printed literature, a play about marriage between an American Negro man and a white woman was remarkably advanced for its time. Presenting it on the stage in 1924 was a challenge only O'Neill would have dared to confront. And his portrayal of Jim Harris's frustrated attempts to become a lawyer predated by a quarter century the putdown endured by Malcolm X when his white teacher told him he could never be a lawyer. ("That's no realistic goal for a nigger!")

But O'Neill—who had sprung to Charles Gilpin's defense when the star of *The Emperor Jones* was snubbed by the Drama League—shrugged off any concern for the incendiary reaction *All God's Chillun* was bound to evoke. Now, with this new play, he was (in his own fashion) scoring a point for what would become his country's most profound social upheaval of the twentieth century.

His choice of title sounded innocent enough, having been drawn from an old Negro spiritual: "I got wings / You got wings / All God's Chillun Got Wings / When I get to Heav'n / Gonna put on my wings / Gonna fly all over God's Heav'n. . . ." The title, obviously ironic, was O'Neill's bold assertion that the wings of a black man in America were shamefully clipped.

As printed literature, *All God's Chillun* caused little stir. There was no public dismay, even over a final scene in which Ella, having lost her mind and reverted to childish babbling, gratefully kisses her black husband's hand. But when the triumvirate of O'Neill, Macgowan, and Jones announced the play's impending production and stated that a black actor would be cast as the male lead opposite a white actress, there arose a thunderous outcry. It was led by Augustus Thomas, the hugely popular writer of what was praised by critics as the "well-made play" (and what was, of course, disdained by O'Neill).

Thomas declared in a newspaper interview that the proposed casting was an "unnecessary concession to realism." The producers, he maintained, should "do what is usually done in such cases, to permit a white man to play the part of the negro [sic]." He elaborated: "The present arrangement, I think, has a tendency to break down social barriers which are better left untouched."

Paul Robeson, whose career had flourished since taking over the role of "Emperor" Brutus Jones, was cast as Jim Harris. Mary Blair, the Provincetown Players stalwart who had been replaced by Carlotta Monterey when *The Hairy Ape* moved to Broadway, agreed to play Jim's troubled wife.

Announced to open at the Provincetown Playhouse at the end of March, *All God's Chillun* was postponed when Blair fell ill with pleurisy. The newspapers thus had several extra weeks to expound on the outrageousness of the coming production; there were stories almost daily.

In place in New York at the time were both a self-constituted "Play Jury," assigned to judge the fitness of a production, and a self-anointed Society for the Suppression of Vice. (The Play Jury was founded in 1922 in response to growing pressure on politicians from ultraconservative groups bent on suppressing "immorality" on Broadway. Formally known as the Joint Committee Opposed to Political Censorship of the Theater, it was formed as a countermeasure against legal censorship. Its members were chosen from the Dramatists Guild and Actors' Equity, among other theater organizations. It proved ineffective and was dissolved in 1927.)

The *American*—a morning paper owned by William Randolph Hearst—published statements from each group on March 12:

"We naturally are opposed to any play that may be construed as immoral in any way," said Brigadier Edward Underwood of the Salvation Army, a member of the "Play Jury," who hadn't bothered to read the play. He was joined by the secretary for the Society for the Suppression of Vice, John S. Sumner, who cautioned: "Such a play might easily lead to racial riots or disorder, and if there is any such possibility, police powers can be exercised."

To the chagrin of these keepers of the public purity, it turned out that police powers could not be exercised to prevent the play's production; nor could the license commissioner's powers be invoked. When the *American* appealed to the commissioner to take a firm stand, he informed the paper that the Provincetown Playhouse was not within the jurisdiction of his department.

"No one may gain admission to a performance of the Provincetown Players unless a subscriber, because theirs is not a licensed house," he said, referring to the fact that Jig Cook and his co-founders had had the foresight to guard against threats of outside intervention in their plan to experiment with complete freedom and had forestalled any such possibility by incorporating themselves as a private club.

Hearst was undeterred. His crusading *American* continued to lead the protests and, on March 14, reported that as a result of "the many complaints received at City Hall," Mayor John Francis Hylan had ordered an investigation of *All God's Chillun Got Wings*. The *American* went on to explain that "the protests against the play are based on the fact that in it a white woman kisses the hand of her negro [sic] husband. . . . The protests come from both whites and negroes in about equal numbers."

While acknowledging that the mayor had no power to close a theater "arbitrarily," the *American* told its readers it "believed" he could prevent the play's opening "if it were shown the presentation might incite riots." Such a danger, the *American* concluded hopefully, "has been pointed out in many protests."

Two days later, the *American* solemnly informed its readers there had been "discussions of the advisability of substituting an octoroon for Miss Blair." (It did not disclose the identities of the discussers.) The paper promised "if the play actually is produced, there will be enough policemen at the theater to prevent any breach of the peace."

On March 18, prompted by his colleagues, O'Neill secluded himself in the Lafayette Hotel near the Provincetown Playhouse and labored over a defense of his play. With many corrections and crossings-out, it covered two and a half sheets of the hotel's stationery. Extracts were published the following day in various newspapers.

O'Neill began by scorning those who hadn't read even a line of the play. He declared:

> Prejudice born of an entire ignorance of the subject is the last word in injustice and absurdity. . . . We are not a public theater. Our playhouse is essentially a laboratory for artistic experiment . . . we make no attempt to cater to the taste of a

general public . . . it is by our subscribers alone we can with any reason be held to account.

Now, have our subscribers protested against the production of *God's Chillun?* Not one. On the contrary, many have written in letters of approval and encouragement, urging us not to "back down" in the slightest. And we shall not.

O'Neill reaffirmed the casting of Paul Robeson: "A fine actor is a fine actor. The question of race prejudice cannot enter here." He reminded readers that Robeson, two years earlier, had played opposite the white actress Margaret Wycherly in a play called *Voodoo* and subsequently had appeared in England with Mrs. Patrick Campbell. "There were no race riots here or there. There was no newspaper rioting, either."

Mary Blair was playing Ella Harris, wrote O'Neill, "because she likes the play and the part. As a true artist, she does not recognize any considerations but these as having any bearing." As to rumors that his objective was to stir up racial feeling, nothing was further from his wish. The play, he declared, was "primarily" a study of its principal characters' "tragic struggle for happiness," and even the "most prejudiced" would be bound to see in the play "a deep, spiritual sense."

He was certain, continued O'Neill, that *God's Chillun* would help encourage "a more sympathetic understanding between the races, through the sense of mutual tragedy involved." He would, he promised, "stand by it to the end."

"I know I am right," he said. "I know that all the irresponsible gabble of the sensation-mongers and notoriety hounds is wrong. They are the ones who are trying to rouse ill feeling and they should be held responsible. . . . They peek at a headline about 'Ella' kissing 'Jim's' hand and their indignation grows stupendous.

"If they would only take the trouble to look up this passage in the printed play, they would see how entirely innocent of all the inferred suggestion this action is. But they don't. Indignation, right or wrong, that's the good old stuff!"

But the controversy raged on. "It seemed for a time there, as if all the feeble-witted both in and out of the K.K.K. were hurling newspaper bricks in my direction," O'Neill later wrote to a Princeton classmate, "—not to speak of the anonymous letters which ranged from those of infuriated Irish Catholics who threatened to pull my ears off as a disgrace to their race and religion, to those of equally infuriated Nordic Kluxers who knew that I had Negro blood, or else was a Jewish pervert masquerading under a Christian name in order to do subversive propaganda for the Pope!"

With Mary Blair's recovery from pleurisy, *All God's Chillun* began rehearsing in April for its May 15 opening. Not only O'Neill, but also Robeson, Blair, and the director, James Light, were now receiving scurrilous letters from the Ku Klux Klan. "We had to intercept Mary's mail, some of the letters were so foul," recalled Light. And one letter to O'Neill, on official Klan stationery, warned him he would never see his two sons again if the play went on.

"We also got a bomb warning stating that if we opened the play we would have a theater full of dead people," Light later recalled. "We didn't let any of this interfere with our plans, but there was a lot of tension all around."

O'Neill almost certainly was unaware that the FBI, under its then acting director J. Edgar Hoover, had him in its sights that April. Alerted to the furor over *All God's Chillun*, an agent of the bureau produced a two-page memorandum for Hoover.

Misspelling his name, the agent described "O'Neil's" authorship of, among other works, *The Emperor Jones*, emphasizing that the play's "central figure is a negro [sic], this seeming to be a favorite theme of O'Neil's." The FBI document implied that O'Neill was a radical who could bear watching.

Four days before the opening on May 15, O'Neill once again attempted to tamp down the public hysteria. "I admit that there is prejudice against the intermarriage of whites and blacks," he allowed in an interview with Louis Kantor for *The New York Times*, "but what has that to do with my play? I don't advocate intermarriage in it. I am never the advocate of anything in any play—except Humanity toward Humanity. . . . I've no desire to play the exhorter in any racial no-man's land.

"I am a dramatist. To me every human being is a special case, with his or her own special set of values. . . . What is the theater for if not to show man's struggle, whether he is black, green, orange or white, to conquer life; his effort to give it meaning?"

By late afternoon of May 15, Macgowan and Jones grew jittery. One aspect of even a non-public theater's activities over which the mayor's office did have jurisdiction was the issuance of licenses to child actors, and there were several in *All God's Chillun*. The play opens on a scene set nine years before the adult Jim and Ella marry, depicting them as children among a group of other children, both black and white.

The triumvirate had applied for licenses in the prescribed manner, but hadn't yet received an answer. They feared Mayor Hylan had at the last moment decided to use this technicality to try to prevent the play's opening. They were right. Shortly before curtain time, the mayor's chief clerk telephoned the theater to say the licenses had been denied; he gave no reason.

In the meantime, the Provincetown's subscribers, who included all the first-string critics, had been seated in the tiny theater, beguiled by the promise of an incendiary evening. Policemen by now were stationed outside the theater to make sure the unlicensed children did not perform their scene—and to intervene if they spotted someone with a bomb.

Momentarily taken aback by the mayor's edict, the company swiftly rallied. Director James Light stepped on stage. He told the audience what had happened and then he himself read the opening scene.

The performance proceeded without incident. "It was a dreadful anti-climax for all concerned," O'Neill later wrote to a Princeton classmate. The critics in particular "seemed to feel cheated that there hadn't been at least one murder that first night." It was, according to O'Neill, "really a most ludicrous episode—not so ludicrous for me, however, since it put the whole theme of the play on a false basis and thereby threw our whole intent in the production into the discard."

Missing O'Neill's intent, many of the critics disliked the play. Some praised Robeson while many dismissed Mary Blair. Heywood Broun found it "a very tiresome play"; Woollcott was "disappointed"; Percy Hammond crudely branded it "a vehement exposition of a marriage between a stupid negro [sic] and a stupid white woman."

Despite the poor reviews, *All God's Chillun Got Wings* had a successful five-month run, having moved to the larger Greenwich Village Theatre, where it played until October 10.

O'Neill, in a subsequent discussion, stressed that Jim Harris represented the "Oneness of Mankind." He went on to say, "We are divided by prejudices. Prejudices racial, social, religious. . . . If Harris of the play had been a Japanese and Ella white, and the play had been produced on the Coast, there would have been as great a storm of protest. Or if Harris had been a German, and the play produced in France. Or an Armenian in Turkey. Or a Jew and a Gentile. And these prejudices will exist until we understand the Oneness of Mankind. Life is hard and bitter enough without, in addition, burdening ourselves with prejudices."

What O'Neill did not say, although surely it was on his mind, was that Jim Harris also could have been a young struggling shanty Irish actor suffering the prejudices of a Protestant bourgeois society.

20

On New Year's Day, 1924—well before the opening of *All God's Chillun Got Wings*—O'Neill awoke at Brook Farm, having dreamed a new play in its entirety. The dream, replete with wrenching personal symbolism, would evolve as one of his most powerful works.

He later boasted it was the first time a plot had come to him so easily. He said that after outlining a brief scenario, he began writing dialogue, "as if I'd pondered over this play for months."

The play was *Desire Under the Elms*. In it, O'Neill, unable to resolve his own persistent emotional dilemma, explored ever more deeply the enigma of helplessly embattled lovers and a son's conflicted relationship with his father and mother. Invoking the Bible as well as Greek tragedy, he folded a batter of sin and scandal, pride and greed, envy and lust into a sulfurous pandowdy of adultery, incest, and infanticide. All this was served up with a brew of cosmic pondering on man's aloneness, God's severity, and the final acceptance of an inescapable fate.

What had ignited these new bursts of tragic insight was the onrushing misery and chaos of his life. That winter at Brook Farm he was still obsessively mourning his parents and brother. Compounding his unease was his sense of being trapped in a household run by a clutch of servants whose salaries were a burden and whom Agnes didn't have the experience to manage efficiently.

He was less than ever reconciled to being the father of a four-year-old (whose presence he barely acknowledged). Most of all, he was troubled by Agnes's insistence on living her own life, which he perceived as a self-ish flouting of his need for her constant attention and reassurance. Thwarted in his domestic dealings with her, O'Neill could count only on their mutual undiminished sexual hunger, as proclaimed in their panting letters during their brief absences from each other.

Within five months, *Desire Under the Elms* was a fully realized script. Unlike *Welded*, which is talky and bloodless, *Desire*, in its richly imag-ined depiction of a sexual tug-of-war, seethes with the anger and mis-trust O'Neill felt for Agnes. Their ameliorating passion is reflected in the play's raw depiction of lust between the volatile lovers, Abbie Put-nam and her stepson Eben Cabot. (O'Neill was never perfunctory about the names he gave his characters and it seems more than coincidental that he chose Eben because it begins with an *E* and Abbie, not only because it begins with an *A*, but because he often called Agnes by her nickname, "Aggie.")

It is the fiery liaison between Abbie and Eben that drives the play, and it's not until Abbie steps onstage in Scene IV of Act I that *Desire* springs to tormented life. That is the point at which Eben's aging father, Ephraim Cabot, arrives back home at his farm with Abbie as his sultry bride; she is thirty-five, half Ephraim's age, and ten years older than Eben, whose recently deceased mother was Ephraim's second wife. Eben, who has sullenly awaited their arrival, is convinced, the moment he sees Abbie, that she will displace him as the heir of the farm he loves, the farm that was originally his mother's.

It's a reasonable fear, for Abbie is "buxom, full of vitality," with a pretty face that is "marred by its rather gross sensuality." She has a strong, obstinate jaw, "a hard determination in her eyes," and there is about her an "unsettled, untamed, desperate quality."

Like the play's other characters, Abbie speaks in a quirky dialect that O'Neill hoped would convey a sense of mid-nineteenth-century New England farm life: "purty" for *pretty*, "har" for *here*, "hev" for *have*, "hum" for *home*, and various odd contractions. As O'Neill later explained, he was "trying to write a synthetic dialogue which should be, in a way, the distilled essence of New England." He never intended the language of the play to be "a record of what the characters actually said." He wanted to "express what they felt subconsciously."

"Har we be t'hum, Abbie," says Ephraim with "a queer strangled emotion in his dry cracking voice."

"Hum!" Abbie responds gloatingly. "It's purty—purty! I can't b'lieve it's r'ally mine."

Cabot reproves her: "Yewr'n? Mine!" Then, relenting: "Our'n—mebbe! It was lonesome too long. I was growin' old in the spring. A hum's got t' hev a woman."

Abbie, possessively: "A woman's got t' hev a hum!"

Eben's fears are confirmed. Attracted to his stepmother against his will, he determines to shun her. At twenty-five—a stand-in for a young Eugene O'Neill—Eben is "tall and sinewy," with "defiant, dark eyes" reminiscent of "a wild animal in captivity." His "fierce repressed vitality" matches Abbie's.

As for Ephraim Cabot, he is seventy-five, hard-bitten, "tall and gaunt, with great, wiry, concentrated power." He is a brutish, self-centered farmer wedded to his land. Although O'Neill dreamt *Desire* whole, he had been shaping an Ephraim-like character for years. He had, in fact, conceived a forerunner for Ephraim in his 1918 one-acter, *The Rope*, the trivial melodrama whose protagonist, Abraham Bentley, shares some of Cabot's crotchets: he is a mean Bible-spouting old farmer who has driven his wife to her death and whose son hates him.

While living with the Ephraim Cabot of 1850 in his mind all through the winter and early spring of 1924, O'Neill, always attuned to nature, was absorbing his rustic environment of the present. His Brook Farm estate still retained enough traces of the working farm it had once been to serve as a model for the old New England farm that forms the setting of *Desire*.

For O'Neill, Brook Farm brought back memories of his father's hardscrabble farm in New London, purchased in the conviction that land was the only financial security. As a young child, James had been traumatized by his family's forced abandonment of their farm in Kilkenny when they were driven from Ireland, along with a million others, during the Great Potato Famine that began in 1845, the year of James's birth. The O'Neills arrived in Buffalo destitute.

It was only after years of deprivation that James, at last prospering as an actor, started to buy land; Eugene well-remembered a derelict farm in Zion, New Jersey, where he and two friends, the then unknown artists George Bellows and Ed Keefe, had camped during part of a freezing January and February in 1909.

His father and the farm. Together they gave birth to craggy old Ephraim Cabot, who in some ways was yet another exaggerated dramatization of James O'Neill. Ephraim is given to quoting from the Bible and he churlishly denounces his son as "soft," as taking after his mother; at times Ephraim is a near caricature of James, who was fond of quoting (and at times adapting) Shakespeare to disparage Eugene ("a poor thing but mine own").

Farms were a motif in O'Neill's plays almost as persistent as the sea; *Anna Christie* and the early one-act sea plays are peopled by inveterate sailors longing for the farms to which they know in their hearts they will never return. And then there are the farm settings of *Beyond the Horizon* (as O'Neill's career was taking off) and *A Moon for the Misbegotten* (at his career's end). If O'Neill was the sea-mother's son, he also was the son of the farmland-father.

O'Neill told a fan who asked for an "explanation" of *Desire* that it was "a tragedy of the possessive—the pitiful longing of man to build his own heaven here on earth by glutting his sense of power with ownership of land, people, money—but principally the land."

One day, nearing the end of his work on *Desire*, O'Neill took his newly employed typist, Bernard Simon (a Provincetown Players recruit), for a walk through the woods of Brook Farm. O'Neill and Simon paused before a wall of stones standing amid weeds. It was the sort of wall he was writing about, O'Neill informed his impressionable young assistant. It had once been part of a fence that marked the boundary of tilled soil.

Walls like this one, which ran for acres through his property and that
of his neighbors', O'Neill told Simon, were representative of the New
England farmer's age-old roots; they were reproachful relics of the farmers who left their fields to go west, where there were no stones and where
farming was less of a struggle.

Falling into the role of Ephraim, O'Neill dramatically began to quote
the old man: "When I come here fifty-odd year ago this place was nothin'
but fields o' stones." O'Neill's audience of one listened in awestruck
silence as the dramatist went on in Ephraim's words to describe how he
had been tempted to abandon the farm after two years of battling the
heavy stones. But after trying his hand at farming in the West, "whar the
soil was black an' rich as gold" with "nary a stone," and where he could
have easily become a rich man, he heard God's voice telling him this life
was not worth living, and commanding him to return home.

"I got afeerd o' that voice an' I lit out back t' hum here, leavin' my
claim an' crops t' whoever'd a mind t' take 'em."

O'Neill paused briefly in his recitation. Then, clearly expressing his
own profound conviction, delivered Ephraim's verdict: "God's hard, not
easy! God's in the stones! . . . I picked 'em up and piled 'em into walls. Ye
kin read the years o' my life in them walls."

In *Desire*, O'Neill was setting off sparks of his most basic and essential
belief. It was his goal, he declared, to illuminate "even the most sordid
and mean blind alleys of life." To that end, he had attempted to "give an
epic tinge to New England's life-lust, to make its inexpressiveness poetically expressive, to release it."

WHILE O'NEILL WORKED on the play, his vacillating moods of antagonism and passion for Agnes pushed him into periodic escapes into alcohol. In one such episode, he disappeared from Brook Farm after a night
of drinking with the writer Malcolm Cowley, who had come on a visit to
gather material for an article about the genesis of *Desire*.

Agnes went to New York in search of him; for a week, she scoured his haunts in the Village. When at last she found him in the Hell Hole, she reported her success to the worried Cowley, telling him, "The proprietor confessed to her that Gene had sat in the back room and drunk himself into a coma."

Bernard Simon also picked up vibrations of domestic turbulence during the ten days he lived at Brook Farm while typing *Desire* (a job made doubly difficult by O'Neill's cramped handwriting and the need to get the synthetic New England dialect right).

"One day," recalled Simon, "O'Neill, Agnes, and I were having lunch. The table was always beautifully set, and the food very good, but the meals tended to lapse into embarrassing silence. Agnes would try to make conversation, for my sake, I guess, and O'Neill didn't always seem to care for the topic she chose." On one such occasion, Agnes ventured a political opinion that elicited O'Neill's ill-concealed contempt. "He muttered something," said Simon, "and they almost came to an open quarrel."

Exasperated beyond discretion, O'Neill later complained to Simon that Agnes was "capitalizing" on his reputation. He griped about her inviting "social people" from New York for weekends at Brook Farm. "What in Christ have I got in common with them?" O'Neill sputtered. "Sometimes I come back from a walk on Friday afternoon and find guests all over the house. Agnes tells them she wants them to meet her husband."

It was at such times, Simon said, that O'Neill would take to the barn with a bottle, staying away from the house overnight—much as Ephraim Cabot, a man uneasy in his home, escapes to his barn to sleep with the animals who are more understanding of him than his contemptuous wife. "I have always loved Ephraim so much," O'Neill once told Kenneth Macgowan. "He's so autobiographical!"

Agnes disputed her husband's plaint. "Sometimes he did drink in the country," she allowed, but usually it was in the company of friends of his—Hart Crane, Louis Wolheim, Jimmy Light, and Harold de Polo—who themselves liked to drink. "And," she added, "this would almost always be when he had come to a stopping point in his work."

DESIRE TRUMPETS O'NEILL'S skill in seizing the dynamics of Greek tragedy to express his own dramatic outlook; themes from Euripides's *Hippolytus* (a woman in love with her stepson) and *Medea* (a mother committing infanticide) are unabashedly on display in *Desire Under the Elms*.

In the swiftly thickening plot of *Desire*, Abbie betrays Eben by seducing him to conceive a child; she plans to present the child to the elderly Ephraim as his own, thereby displacing Eben as the heir to the farm and securing it for herself. But after becoming pregnant, Abbie perversely falls in love with Eben.

When the child is born, Ephraim proudly claims him as his own. Eben doesn't believe Abbie's protest that she abandoned her scheme to acquire the farm when she fell in love with him; he turns on her, blaming the birth of the infant for changing his love for her to hatred, and he vows to leave her and the farm forever. Abbie, desperate to keep Eben, determines to prove her love for him by smothering the baby in his crib.

It's all too tempting to read this plot as a reflection (and almost a parody) of O'Neill's conflicting feelings toward Agnes. At the time he was writing *Desire*, O'Neill, always ready to see himself as a victim of woman's treachery, regarded Agnes's increasingly offhand behavior toward him as one more betrayal.

Still, the play's ending suggests that despite O'Neill's anger and disappointment with Agnes, he still loves her enough to attempt an entente. He does, after all, cause *Desire*'s Eben Cabot to realize that he must share the blame for Abbie's infanticide (just as O'Neill realizes, however reluctantly, that he must share the responsibility for Shane's existence).

Eben, reaffirming his love for Abbie, gives himself up to the sheriff and joins her in whatever fate awaits them. As for old Ephraim Cabot, O'Neill allows him to have the last ironic say:

"Ye make a slick pair o' murderin' turtle doves! Ye'd ought t' be both hung on the same limb an' left thar t' swing in the breeze an' rot—a warnin' t' old fools like me t' bar their lonesomeness alone—an' fur young fools like ye t' hobble their lust."

Eben and Abbie go off with the sheriff and Ephraim resigns himself to his lonely life on the farm. "I'm gittin' old, Lord—ripe on the bough. . . . Waal—what d'ye want? God's lonesome, hain't He? God's hard an' lonesome!"

IN A STAGE DIRECTION THAT—even for O'Neill—is hypernovelistic, he introduces two "characters" who are not flesh and blood. They are the enormous menacing twin elms of the title and they "appear to protect and at the same time subdue. There is a sinister maternity in their aspect," writes O'Neill, "a crushing jealous absorption. . . . They brood oppressively over the house. They are like exhausted women resting their sagging breasts and hands and hair on its roof, and when it rains their tears trickle down monotonously and rot on the shingles."

O'Neill intended the trees to deepen the play's fraught atmosphere; he emphasized that the trees played "an actual part in the drama," along with the farmhouse, and "might almost be given in the list of characters."

His description of these "characters" comes as close as he ever would to an explication of his conflicted feelings about the women in his life. While O'Neill might not have been entirely aware of the revelatory nature of his description, he did know that this sort of elaborate novelistic characterization was impossible to convey to an audience, given the limited Broadway stagecraft of his day. He had an intimate knowledge, from touring with his father, of what would and would not work onstage from a purely mechanical viewpoint.

He often sketched ground plans for his plays—indicating the placement of doors, windows, and furnishings. "I know more about a trap door than any son of a bitch in the theater," he was fond of boasting to his directors. He obviously believed that his stage directions about the elms would instill in the actors and director a heightened sense of the play's portentous mood. And he was right. (A failed Broadway revival in 2009 did away with the elms—a notion as perverse as silencing the drums in *The Emperor Jones* or the fog horn in *Long Day's Journey Into Night*.)

WITH THE SUMMER HEAT oppressing Brook Farm in inland Ridgefield, the O'Neills moved to their ocean-side retreat in Provincetown on July 11. Between restorative swims, O'Neill edited *Welded* and *The Straw* for the published versions of his most recent collected works, which was being readied by Boni & Liveright, the first American firm to publish Sigmund Freud; while its list also included Hemingway, Faulkner, T. S. Eliot, and Robinson Jeffers, O'Neill was the firm's favorite author.

"At Liveright, they liked dead authors, or those who seldom came to the office—and O'Neill rarely came to the office," said his then editor, Manuel Komroff, who acted chiefly as liaison. "No one ever touched a word of his plays while I was there." The firm had published five collections of O'Neill's plays by the end of 1923. He was one of those rare dramatists whose work had a devoted readership, although his royalties from book sales, up to that point, were not princely.

"Most authors would pester us," Komroff said. "They wanted to know why their books weren't selling as well as Dreiser's, or why we didn't advertise them. O'Neill never asked us to advertise or demanded anything special." From time to time, Horace Liveright would ask Komroff, petulantly, "Why doesn't O'Neill ever come in?"

O'Neill knew the new volume would not yield much income; with *Welded* a flop and *Desire* not set to open until late fall, he and Agnes were once again feeling pressed for cash.

"There has been nothing coming in of any account now in over a year and my back is beginning to creak under the strain," O'Neill complained to Kenneth Macgowan. He was still awaiting the settlement of Jamie's estate; he owed an income tax installment and a payment for Eugene Jr.'s schooling. He quipped to Macgowan that he was "homesick for homelessness and irresponsibility," averring that "philosophically at any rate" he'd been "a sucker ever to go in for playwriting, mating and begetting sons, houses and lots, and all similar snares of the property game."

Amid his griping, he worked on *Marco Millions* (all about the snares of the property game) throughout August, September, and the first half of October, taking a week off with Agnes to visit his friend, the writer Wilbur Daniel Steele, in Nantucket.

Even while trying to relax, he was nervously anticipating rehearsals for *Desire Under the Elms*, set to open November 11 at the Greenwich Village Theatre, which the triumvirate was leasing on a seasonal basis (and where *The Straw* had played two years earlier).

Walter Huston, who became one of O'Neill's most fondly regarded actors, was cast as Ephraim Cabot; he had given up a career as an engineer to become a vaudeville performer and had made his Broadway debut only a year earlier in a long-forgotten melodrama, *Mr. Pitt*. Mary Morris, a little-known young actress, was chosen to play Abbie; she had impressed O'Neill when she appeared in a recent hit revival of Anna Cora Mowatt's 1845 satire, *Fashion*. Charles Ellis, one of the original Provincetown Players, was cast as Eben. The play was designed and directed by Bobby Jones.

After celebrating his thirty-sixth birthday on October 16 at Peaked Hill Bars, O'Neill, together with Agnes and Shane, departed for Brook Farm. A day later, leaving his family in Ridgefield, O'Neill went on to New York for the start of *Desire* rehearsals. He checked into the Lafayette Hotel, planning to join Agnes and Shane at Brook Farm when he could find time.

The next day, he also began supervising rehearsals of a long-held dream project—an evening of his four one-act sea plays written between 1914 and 1917 (as combined under the title *S.S. Glencairn*). So bound up in rehearsals was he—*Desire* in the mornings and afternoons, *Glencairn* in the evenings—he could not spare time to be with Shane at Brook Farm on October 30, the boy's fifth birthday. ("Wonderfully received," O'Neill commented in his Work Diary on November 3, the night *S.S. Glencairn* opened at the Provincetown Playhouse.)

On November 11, O'Neill noted in his Work Diary that the

opening-night audience had given *Desire* "a fine reception." But while the play came to be regarded as a landmark American tragedy, at the time it actually received only lukewarm critical praise.

Heywood Broun griped that O'Neill "laid his hand last night upon the shoulder of his finest play and then passed by on the other side . . . as this new tale of vengeance clicked into certain old and well worn grooves." But Stark Young, in *The New Republic*, plainly was relieved by the play's patent superiority to *Welded*; he was particularly impressed with the third-act party scene, in which Ephraim celebrates the birth of the son he believes is his (while his guests snicker behind his back), commenting that it was written "with such poetry and terrible beauty as we rarely see in the theater."

Despite the mixed critical response, *Desire* filled the Greenwich Village Theatre for two months. It was moved to Broadway in February 1925, first to the Earl Carroll Theatre and then to the George M. Cohan, where it flourished until October 26, for a total of 208 New York performances.

Once, when asked if he thought the critics in general knew what he was driving at in his plays, O'Neill parried:

> What do you mean by critics? They can be divided into three classes: Play Reporters, Professional Funny Men and the men with the proper background or real knowledge of the theater of all time to entitle them to be critics.
>
> The play reporters just happen to be people who have the job of reporting what happens during the evening, the story of the play and who played the parts. I have always found that these people reported the stories of my plays fairly accurately.
>
> The Professional Funny Men are beneath contempt. What they say is only of importance to their own strutting vanities. From the real critics I have always had a feeling that they saw what I was trying to do and whether they praised or blamed, they caught the point.

But O'Neill contradicted himself to the theater historian Arthur Hobson Quinn, who was planning a comprehensive article about him as a "poet and mystic."

"Most of my critics don't want to see what I'm trying to do or how I'm trying to do it," O'Neill began. "But where I feel myself most neglected is where I set most store by myself—as a bit of a poet who has labored with the spoken word to evolve original rhythms of beauty where beauty apparently isn't."

Citing as examples *The Emperor Jones*, *The Hairy Ape*, *All God's Chillun Got Wings*, and *Desire Under the Elms*, he went on to explain that he was "always, always trying to interpret Life in terms of lives, never just lives in terms of character." In his mysticism, he added, he was "acutely conscious of the Force behind—(Fate, God, our biological past creating our present, whatever one calls it—Mystery, certainly)—and of the one eternal tragedy of Man in his glorious, self-destructive struggle to make the Force express him instead of being, as an animal is, an infinitesimal incident in its expression."

EVER HOPEFUL OF settling into some sort of domestic tranquillity, Agnes saw, perhaps even more clearly than her husband, that living at Brook Farm was not the solution. For one thing, O'Neill's drinking had worsened since moving there.

Once again, O'Neill grasped at his family doctor's advice to try another climate change—this time back to sea air and to a place more isolated from New York City. He finally acknowledged he must give up drinking to assure his continued artistic growth. With a change of environment—so he believed—he could bury himself in his work.

Agnes had little choice but to accede to yet another move. After Provincetown, West Point Pleasant, and Ridgefield, it would be her fourth shift of residence since her marriage to O'Neill just seven years earlier.

In truth, she was finding it not much fun anymore being married to her "poet." She had recently learned she was pregnant again and she had no reason to believe a second child would be any more welcome to O'Neill than the first. While she wanted a certain amount of independence, she also wanted a sympathetic husband and an attentive father to her children—not just a needy child-husband who now and then spared her a few moments of passion and companionship amid his other preoccupations.

O'Neill had persuaded himself that his own wants were Spartan. He told Macgowan he craved a "neat life with a pattern." He joked that he would like "ten walled acres in Siberia with a flock of Siberian wolfhounds to guard them, and broken glass on the walls."

Instead, however, he chose Bermuda, a two-day sea voyage from New York. It's a puzzle as to why he believed Bermuda was the place where he would find peace of mind—and sobriety. Evidently, he saw no irony in the circumstance that the old Provincetown friend who persuaded him to settle in Bermuda was the short-story writer Harold de Polo, himself an unapologetic drunkard.

The O'Neills planned to rent a house through at least the spring of 1925, after Agnes had given birth. Before leaving for Bermuda, having struggled in vain to conquer his destructive drinking habit, O'Neill had begun seeing Dr. Smith Ely Jelliffe, a prominent psychiatrist of commanding personality and culture. Bobby Jones had introduced O'Neill to Jelliffe, whose patients included, along with Jones himself, Arthur Hopkins, John Barrymore, and Mabel Dodge.

Although wary of being psychoanalyzed, O'Neill was always receptive to sympathetic medical advice. He visited Jelliffe sporadically during 1923 and 1924—not to be "deeply psychoanalyzed," according to Dr. Jelliffe's widow, Belinda, but to receive therapeutic help for "a variety of specific problems."

Belinda Jelliffe retained a blurred memory of the day in late November that O'Neill and his pregnant wife, together with five-year-old Shane and Agnes's ten-year-old daughter, Barbara, used her house as a place to assemble prior to their departure for Bermuda:

There was O'Neill, Agnes, and, I think, two children, all with my husband in his secretary's office, and I had the feeling when I went in that I had stumbled into a suspended tableau. Agnes looked vague and distracted, O'Neill looked worried, and the children were pale and woebegone.

Dr. Jelliffe was speaking of tickets—steamship tickets to Bermuda—which apparently had been lost or misplaced. I offered to go back to their hotel and look for the tickets. I vaguely remember getting into a cab with O'Neill.

At the hotel, we scratched around in bureau drawers and I guess we found the tickets, because I remember later saying good-bye to them all as they left for the pier."

"Off to Bermuda" was O'Neill's terse comment in his Work Diary on November 29, 1924.

21

O'Neill could no longer delude himself. If he continued to disrupt his writing with bouts of destructive drinking, he would never achieve the greatness to which he aspired.

Bound for Bermuda on the steamship *Fort St. George,* he confronted his alternatives. Would he shuffle off into the oblivion that had overtaken his brother? Or would he vanquish his bottled demon and fulfill his grand creative dream?

Struggle as he might, sobriety eluded him during his initial seven months' sojourn in Bermuda. While there were intervals when he managed to stay aboard a wobbly water-wagon, his resolve, all too often, gave way to his unforgiving addiction.

In 1924, O'Neill had begun keeping notebooks he called his Scribbling Diaries, in which he jotted ideas for plays, and commented briefly on the daily events in his life. The 1925 diary minutely records his on-and-off struggle with alcohol, as well as his emotional flip-flops with Agnes; a truly singular document, it is an unsparing and self-revelatory portrait of an alcohol-addicted writer trying to wring himself dry.

The diary begins on January 1, a month after O'Neill rented a small compound in Paget West, Bermuda. Called Campsea, it encompassed two cottages—one for family living, the other for O'Neill's writing.

In his first entry, he speaks of his determination to taper off—always a wretched process, as he well knows. Writing a *d* in the margin to indicate it's a day on which he will drink, he admits to feeling unwell and shaky. "To keep from thinking," he reads old copies of the *Saturday Evening Post* provided by Agnes (who by now has nursed him through numerous such withdrawals); the weather is "clear & warm," but the suffering sea-mother's son has "no ambition to swim."

On January 2 (this entry also preceded by a *d* in the margin), he is no better, and seems "to have acquired bleeding piles"; he goes for a short swim in the late afternoon and spends the rest of the day loafing and reading. Still drinking, he perks up on the next day after some checks arrive in the mail; he swims and exercises with Agnes. They meet a neighbor on the beach, a Mrs. Barbour, "and her beautiful sister," Alice Cuthbert.

On January 4, O'Neill is "cutting down a bit but still too miserably disorganized to really make it . . . no swim today." On the fifth, to soothe his bothersome piles, he takes two swims and exercises, then retires with his *Saturday Evening Post*s, calling them his "favorite narcotic"; he notes that he drank "nothing but ale after dinner."

On January 6, also a *d* day, he begins to "feel a bit more human—out of the woods—but still disorganized." And on the seventh, which finds him "better," he requires two drinks before lunch and three before dinner. By the eighth, he has traded his magazines for Aldous Huxley's *Antic Hay*; he feels "much better," and takes only one drink before lunch and two before dinner.

On the ninth, strolling on the beach, he and Agnes again run into Alice Cuthbert. This time he admires Alice's "athletic swimmer's figure" and describes her as "a peach." Although aware of Agnes's jealousy, he flirts with Alice. On the tenth, he has only "1/2 drink before dinner," and the next day he quits drinking "except ale with meals." Seemingly poised on the brink of victory over his demon, and resolved to be more sensitive to Agnes's feelings, he enters what will be a shaky stretch of sobriety.

But to Agnes's mortification, O'Neill, tentatively sober, begins a ritual of rigorously clocked daily swims in tandem with the athletic and peachy Alice Cuthbert. Agnes, now in her fifth month, resents her husband's attention to the unencumbered and shapely Alice.

"Agnes very sore," O'Neill recorded on January 13, adding that in the fight that ensued, she "stabbed" a screen door. But he didn't give up his morning swims with Alice, insisting they were strictly for exercise. As a gesture of peace, however, he added to his schedule an afternoon swim with Agnes. But Agnes was again "sore!" when, on February 3, O'Neill brought Alice home to lunch, bragging they had achieved a "220 double-crawl" side by side for almost a third of a mile.

Ignoring Agnes's sulk, O'Neill swam with Alice again after lunch. Trapped by her pregnancy, Agnes was helpless against her husband's baiting even though it was almost always followed by repentance of one sort or another; that evening he invited her (with their dog Finn) to a moonlight walk on the beach.

Agnes had no evidence that O'Neill's rapport with Alice went beyond swimming and mild flirtation. (She may or may not have been aware of a poem entitled "For Alice," in which O'Neill wrote, "You, the sun, & sea, Trinity! Sweet spirit, pass on / Keep the dream / Beauty / Into infinity.")

Life in Bermuda was becoming something of a muddle for Agnes. Her husband was faltering, and she doubted he would ever quit drinking.

Once again, she was carrying a child he didn't want. Unsure if the island was to become her permanent home, she was trying to adjust to an ever-grander lifestyle with an uncertain income to support it.

Among other concerns, she was frustrated by how little time she could find for her own writing, and when she did manage occasionally to have a short story published, it was, of course, overshadowed by her celebrated husband's output. Deprived (as she believed) of a career as a writer, she did not fit the role of muse and respected partner; she felt belittled as the wife of an unstable man who at one moment needed her desperately and at the next was barely aware of her presence.

O'Neill, sober in late January, found himself fascinated by an article entitled "Alcohol and the Nervous System," by the preeminent British neurologist Sir James Purvis-Stewart. It had been sent to him (on January 22) by his Bermuda neighbor, Dr. Louis Bisch, with whom O'Neill had discussed his drinking problem. "Very interesting & applicable to me," O'Neill wrote in his diary.

O'Neill had no trouble recognizing himself in Purvis-Stewart's description of the "paroxysmal dipsomaniac" who had a "marked neuropathic heredity" (in O'Neill's case, a functioning-alcoholic father and a drug-addicted mother). Nor could he disavow any of the other symptoms inherent in the "dipsomaniac individual who sometimes drinks himself into a state of acute alcoholic poisoning." The condition, O'Neill read, was well understood by neurologists to be "a recurrent psychosis consisting of attacks during which the patient has an irresistible impulse to take alcohol in excess."

O'Neill knew only too well that (as Purvis-Stewart explained) "antecedent to each outburst of dipsomania, there is a short premonitory or incubation stage of restlessness and mental depression" and that practically all such "alcoholists" (as the doctor termed them) "before they happen to acquire the habit of paroxysmal excessive drinking, have had previous neuropathic symptoms, such as phobias, obsessions, emotional depression, visceral discomfort, etc." Step by step, O'Neill continued to read about his own symptoms:

"Whatever be the special condition which is the starting-point of the dipsomaniac outburst, the patient discovers that he can mask his deficient will-power and 'drown his sorrow' by a dose of alcohol, which comforts him for the time and gets rid of his emotional depression."

Seemingly, there was little that Purvis-Stewart did not know about the condition so piercingly familiar to O'Neill:

> He drinks heavily for a few days until his bout is brought to an end by alcoholic gastritis, with its attendant vomiting, so that he has nausea—for food or drink of any kind, including alcohol.

His attack then subsides and he is free from alcoholic craving, and full of good resolutions, perhaps for weeks or months,
until his next attack. But his psychosis inevitably recurs and
he is irresistibly drawn to it once more. Unlike the chronic
alcoholic soaker [e.g., Jamie O'Neill] the dipsomaniac individual usually realizes his own failing, and feels his degrada-
tion keenly: he is thus more willing than the chronic alcoholist
to accept treatment for his malady.

It was, all in all, a graphic and horrifying depiction of O'Neill's ingrained syndrome.

O'Neill began truly to dread the damage his drinking could wreak on
his creative ability. Far from secure in his present sobriety, he despised
his imprisonment by alcohol. What had become of his long-ago statement that writing was his "vacation from living"? Once again, he questioned himself: Did he really want to trash his dream of greatness? He
decided not. Even so, it would be another year before he was willing to
propel himself into treatment for his malady—and to emerge with a new
weltanschauung.

ONCE O'NEILL HAD paused in his drinking—and it was only a pause—
he went back to work on *Marco Millions*. Aware the elaborate pageant
would be too expensive for the triumvirate to produce, he was hoping to
sell it to David Belasco, his father's old theater colleague and one of the
few Broadway producers who could afford to mount it.

Belasco, as a brash young producer in San Francisco forty-six years
earlier, had presented a clumsily written but extravagantly produced version of the Passion play, in which James O'Neill was cast as Jesus. Believing he would make a dramatic sensation in the role, James was blind to
the production's vulgarity. The pageant caused panic in the theater, followed by street rioting and the jailing of James's entire humiliated company; they were ultimately fined and released. (Eugene might have been

hoping that Belasco would espouse *Marco* as a sort of belated reparation for having led James into fiasco.)

While awaiting word from Belasco, O'Neill, on January 28, embarked on the first scene of a new play, *The Great God Brown*. A daring leap at the moon, the play was also a moan of despair lamenting O'Neill's fear of being measured and misunderstood; it decried a world of conventionality and materialism, a world in which he was forced to wear a figurative mask in order to conceal his own idealistic vision of life. More than anything, Brown mirrored O'Neill's relentless tug-of-war with his own divided self. The play, in fact, was an absurdist rendering of the schizophrenic jig O'Neill was then dancing in his mind.

To say the plot is difficult to follow is a laughable understatement; at times it is all but impenetrable. Despite O'Neill's oft-stated insistence that he never attempted to write when he was drinking, *The Great God Brown* may well be his one exception.

Nevertheless, the play is a touchstone of O'Neill's oeuvre. He himself cherished it, once confiding (in a letter to Carlotta), "There is so much of the secret me in it."

Complexities notwithstanding, it's clear that the play's undercurrent throbs with O'Neill's intense and pervasive mourning for his parents and brother. In a sense, he was writing his family's epitaph (including his own); the play's fictional parents and son are all dead by play's end.

While the nameless parents make no more than a brief appearance (as shadowy, symbolic echoes of James and Ella O'Neill), their only son—as he sprang from O'Neill's tortured imagination—is a split personality whose two personas, Dion Anthony and William Brown, dominate the play; each stands for an aspect of O'Neill's own conflicted personality, and they are portrayed by two separate actors.

Dion is "a stranger, walking alone . . . dark, spiritual, poetic, passionately supersensitive, helplessly unprotected." He is an artist, a creator, with "a childlike, religious faith in life." Set apart from his fellow man, he is unable to make meaningful contact with family or friends. He is locked in a lonely struggle to find God and the meaning of life's mystery and, inevitably, he knuckles under to the callousness of an unheeding and materialistic society.

Dion's alter ego is William (Billy) Brown—"a fine looking, well dressed, capable college-bred American businessman" with a "boyish engaging personality." Billy is Dion's sometime friend, sometime rival, a man whom Dion addresses as "brother." He is both loved and hated by Dion. A potentially fine soul, Billy has grown stunted and envious and destructive.

He and Dion (along with several other of the play's characters) have an unsettling tendency to clap masks over their faces when signaling a wish to conceal their innermost secrets; conversely, they doff the masks when in the company of those they trust.

Dion, for example, feels obliged to wear his mask before his wife, Margaret, knowing she can't comprehend the torment of his naked soul; but he goes unmasked before the prostitute Cybel, who is an understanding earth mother.

Although O'Neill had used masks in *The Hairy Ape* and *The Emperor Jones*, the masks in *The Great God Brown* were more of an integral dramatic device. He once explained his conviction that masks could "be made acceptable to the modern audience—as they were in ancient times—but in a new sense." He believed people "did recognize, from their knowledge of the new psychology, that everyone wears a mask—I don't mean only one, but thousands of them."

That sounds straightforward enough, but even Freud would likely have been stumped by the manner in which O'Neill gleefully masks and unmasks his suffering protagonists in *The Great God Brown*. When Dion Anthony and Billy Brown are swapping personality traits (and masks), it's sometimes hard to know which of them we're listening to. Is it Dion? Or is it Billy wearing Dion's mask? Obviously, that was just what O'Neill intended.

"The audience won't know if it's walking backwards or forwards by the time it's ready to leave," O'Neill once crowed to Dr. Bisch.

Happily, not everything in the play is a riddle. It's clear, for instance, that O'Neill wants his audience to realize that Dion's parents understand neither their son nor each other, nor can Dion summon the means to reach them. In a gripping autobiographical speech, Dion mourns his father: "What aliens we were to each other! When he lay dead, his face looked so familiar that I wondered where I had met that man before. Only at the second of my conception. After that, we grew hostile with concealed shame. What aliens we were to each other!"

The befuddlement begins to mount in the play's later scenes, when Billy Brown—"inwardly empty" and representing (in O'Neill's words) "our new materialistic myth"—permanently steals the identity of Dion, who by now has died (apparently due to an extended alcoholic binge). Billy proceeds to live his life alternating as himself and Dion. This necessitates a maniacal whipping on and off of masks during a series of confrontations with (among others) Dion's wife, who doesn't realize Dion has died and been secretly buried by Brown.

It is Billy to whom O'Neill has given the play's juiciest snippet of dialogue:

"This is Daddy's bedtime secret for today. Man is born broken. He lives by mending. The grace of God is glue!"

On March 25, the day he completed the play, O'Neill jotted in his Work Diary, "I think it really marks my 'ceiling' so far." He would tell Carlotta nearly two years later that *The Great God Brown* was his "pet of all the published plays."

But for now, it was Agnes whose approbation O'Neill sought, and to whom he read excerpts from the newly completed manuscript; she "seemed much moved by them," O'Neill gratefully noted in his Work Diary.

Agnes must have been willing to overlook (or dismiss) O'Neill's unsympathetic portrait of Dion Anthony's wife, who reflected aspects of Agnes's personality that O'Neill most resented: Margaret is not selflessly devoted to nurturing her husband; and she chastises him for venting his jealousy of her love for their three symbolic sons, who are unnamed and identified only as "Eldest," "Second," and "Youngest."

These sons are of little importance to Dion (and just as expendable as all the other children in O'Neill's plays). In their brief appearance in *Brown*, they are mere window dressing: mechanical prigs, confirming that Margaret is a mother who is unhappy that their father ignores them. It's hard to see how Agnes could have empathized with those scenes.

Still, before he dies, Dion begs his wife's forgiveness for having "sinned against her," for his "sick pride and cruelty," and for his "solitude." On all these sentiments Agnes could not help but bestow her approval.

22

At the end of February 1925, with the production of *The Great God Brown* still a long way off and with Agnes in her sixth month of pregnancy, she and O'Neill found themselves tentatively at peace.

They were enjoying the surge of income from the extended run of *Desire Under the Elms* and were awaiting O'Neill's inheritance of $73,593 (in a time when personal income was still only moderately taxed) from the long-delayed liquidation of Jamie's estate.

Enclosing a long-overdue check to his Provincetown landlord, John Francis, O'Neill wrote to explain he'd settled in Bermuda because of the year-round swimming and would return to Peaked Hill Bars in the late spring. His wife, he told Francis, "expects to present me with another heir in April," adding they both had fond memories of the cottage where Shane (nearly five and a half years earlier) was born.

Agnes shared O'Neill's ironic amusement when, two months into the play's run, they heard from Kenneth Macgowan in New York that *Desire* had become a cause célèbre, and together they followed its ludicrous course. This time, the would-be censor was Joab H. Banton, New York's conservative Southern-born district attorney, who was intent on cleansing the Broadway stage.

Banton demanded that *Desire* be shut down, along with three other "immoral" hit plays: David Belasco's productions of *Ladies of the Evening* and *The Harem*, and William A. Brady's *A Good Bad Woman*. Belasco, on Friday, February 20, promised (presumably with a straight face) that he would rewrite both his plays and have them "moral" by the following Tuesday. Brady, not to be outdone, informed the press (with mock gravity) that if Belasco could have his "filthy plays" ready by Tuesday, he would rewrite *his* play by Monday.

Banton did not suggest *Desire* be rewritten. He admitted he'd not seen the play, but even so, he knew it was "too thoroughly bad to be purified by a blue pencil" and if it was not closed by Wednesday, he threatened to put the matter before a grand jury.

"We do not intend to accede to any peremptory demand to take the show off the stage by Wednesday," Macgowan told the press. "If we are indicted, we will defend the play in the courts." He followed up by distributing a pamphlet quoting eminent writers, who argued that "the forced withdrawal of Eugene O'Neill's *Desire Under the Elms* by repressive actions of any kind would be against the best interests not only of artists but of good citizenship."

At Macgowan's request, the Play Jury (that self-appointed committee formed to combat political censorship) attended a performance of *Desire* and voted that it should be neither suppressed nor rewritten. Macgowan cabled the news to O'Neill, who cabled back that he'd been sure of the outcome all along—although he'd earlier acknowledged to friends that he was surprised the play had fought its way to the top in New York. "Fancy that, with infanticide," he quipped to Macgowan.

O'Neill told Macgowan he'd "thought of several wicked cables" he could "send to friend Banton which would make him feel like the cat's arse for a gangrened moment or two." But he thought better of it. "I'm too detached about this," he said, "to get 'my back up' really—it isn't so much being out of touch as the fact that I'm so chuck full of *Brown* that *Desire* seems out of my range of worry."

On March 30, as if determined to contravene his stance regarding visits from children, O'Neill welcomed Eugene Jr., now almost fifteen, for a six-day visit to Campsea. Two days earlier, he had written "Finished!" (thrice underlined) to *The Great God Brown*. At first, all went well. O'Neill and Agnes picnicked and sailed with Eugene and shopped with him for clothes. But four days after Eugene's arrival, the attempt at family togetherness imploded. In his diary, O'Neill again began to place a *d* (for drinking) before the date of each daily entry. The *d* continued after Eugene's departure, appearing daily until nearly the end of April.

While O'Neill was, in a semidetached way, proud of Eugene and willing to help pay for his education, his feelings fell short of devoted fatherly commitment. His detachment was evident when, a year earlier, Eugene fell from his bicycle near his house in Long Island and fractured his skull. Kathleen rushed him to the hospital and then telephoned O'Neill, who, at the time, was in New York and about to leave for Provincetown. O'Neill told her his bank account was at her disposal; he arranged for a specialist and asked Kathleen to keep him informed of Eugene's condition by collect daily telegrams. But he did not postpone his trip to Provincetown. Eugene was in the hospital for five weeks, part of that time in critical condition. O'Neill never visited him.

For all of O'Neill's prolonged dismay over the neglect and pain his parents had inflicted on him, he appeared blind to the fact that he was inflicting a similar hurt on his own child.

He felt no need to be perpetuated by children; he liked to describe his playwriting as "birth pangs." It was clear to his friends that his plays were his children and that he was both father and mother to them. His claim to immortality rested upon his plays; flesh-and-blood children were at best the inevitable appendages of domesticity and at worst irritating hindrances to his work.

On April 11, still drinking, O'Neill nervously moved with Agnes, Shane, and Mrs. Clarke to a larger cottage called Southcote, there to await the birth of Agnes's baby, expected later that month. Agnes and O'Neill celebrated their seventh wedding anniversary on the twelfth. In his diary, O'Neill noted, "Agnes's Chinese shawl for present has not come yet but expected soon."

On May 1, although O'Neill complained to Macgowan that the waiting was getting on his nerves, he managed to stop drinking—perhaps pacified by Agnes's calm; he must be experiencing "couvade," he joked to Macgowan.

O'Neill had to endure the discomforts of couvade for two more weeks. It was not until May 14 that Agnes produced her baby. "It's a goil. Allah be merciful," O'Neill cabled Macgowan. According to indications will be first lady announcer at Polo Grounds. Predict great future grand opera. Agnes and baby all serene.

Both Agnes and O'Neill had been certain it would be a girl, and Agnes had written to the wife of the Irish poet Padraic Colum, asking if she and her husband could suggest a feminine Irish name that would go well with O'Neill. "We suggested Oona, the Irish translation of Agnes," Colum later recalled.

O'Neill and Agnes wished to escape the hot Bermuda summer and, having agreed that Peaked Hill Bars was too rustic and remote for comfort with an infant, they rented a house in Nantucket through September.

But first—still not drinking—O'Neill shepherded his newly expanded family to New York for a week's stay at the Lafayette Hotel. On the day of their arrival, June 29, O'Neill noted in his diary, "To Bisch in the afternoon to start treatment." Evidently, Dr. Bisch, after listening in Bermuda to O'Neill's problem with drinking (among other concerns), had offered to act as O'Neill's therapist.

"O'Neill was very moody," Bisch recalled many years later. "He explained he would become greatly depressed after finishing a play, because it never turned out to be what he really wanted."

That was when O'Neill would go on a bender, Bisch said. "He seemed to be suffering from both overwork and worry—particularly about financial matters. He also worried about the time it took him to answer his fan mail; he said he couldn't afford a secretary. I asked why he didn't just ignore those letters; he said he couldn't, that he just had to answer his mail."

If O'Neill did actually begin therapy with Dr. Bisch, it was short-lived.

After noting his appointment with Bisch, O'Neill made no entries in his Work Diary until a week later when, on July 7, he wrote, "A. left for

Nantucket"; he didn't mention that the children and Mrs. Clarke accompanied Agnes, nor did he give any reason why he stayed behind at the Lafayette.

The next ten days in his diary are blank. On July 17, O'Neill entered a small *d*, before noting he'd been to Harlem with Paul Robeson and some others. "Up all night," he wrote, adding, "Disaster." His curt entries on the four days following—each preceded by the capital letter *D*—spoke of more carousing with friends late into the night followed by hungover bed rest during the day.

At last, on July 22, feeling "punk," he retreated to Kenneth Macgowan's home in Brewster to taper off, spending three days (small *d*'s) "mostly in bed reading."

He also took time to write to Agnes of his loneliness and—surprisingly—of missing Oona: "I really love her! Never thought I could a baby! And I love you, my dear wife and pal, more than I have power to say!"

(He later thanked Macgowan and his wife, Edna, for their comfort. "I must have been a pretty sorry sight to have about the house and by no means a welcome addition to any family retaining their sanity. You were as kind as you could be and I shall never forget it.")

It was on his return to the city from Brewster on July 25 that O'Neill next mentioned Dr. Bisch in a diary entry. "Saw Bisch at hotel. Gave me stuff [veronal]. To bed and to sleep early." (O'Neill did not mention that veronal was the sleeping medicine with which he'd attempted suicide in 1912 at Jimmy the Priest's.)

"Practically no booze," O'Neill wrote in his diary on July 26, the day he left New York to join his family in Nantucket. At month's end (as he wrote to Macgowan), he was "very much on the old cart again, and feel as well now as I ever did, what with swimming, boating and the rest of it." Less than a week later, he confessed: "Off! But not serious."

It was the arrival in Nantucket of O'Neill's old New London friend Ed Keefe that set him off again. Keefe, now a successful architect, had arrived in Nantucket on a schooner with two friends.

"Gene was glad to see me and joined my friends and me for dinner on shore," Keefe remembered. "Then the four of us rowed to the schooner, which was anchored quite a way out in the harbor, and drank and drank and drank. After a while, the two other guys went to sleep. Gene and I kept on drinking. At one point Gene stood up in the hatchway and let his wristwatch fly against the hatch—he was being dramatic about something. Finally we went to our bunks and I fell asleep."

Keefe was awakened by the steward. "I think your friend is overboard," he said. Keefe followed the steward out on deck and, in the bright moonlight, saw O'Neill in the water, fully dressed and still roaring drunk. Keefe and the steward pulled O'Neill back on board, stripped him, and put him into a bunk. The steward woke Keefe again as dawn was breaking. "There's a lady alongside in a rowboat," the steward announced. It was Agnes.

"She had rowed out to collect Gene," Keefe said. "We got him into a raincoat and some slippers and eased him over the side into the rowboat. I watched Gene and Agnes draw away, Gene trying to sit up straight in the boat, Agnes rowing. The sun was coming up as they headed in to shore."

Writing in his diary in September, O'Neill was uncommunicative about both his activities and his state of mind, making abrupt references to his work on scenarios for *Strange Interlude* and a new play, *Lazarus Laughed*, and noting his daily swims. Centered on his own problems, he made no mention of Agnes or his children or of Agnes's daughter, who spent some time with them in Nantucket.

Agnes for her part was occupied (in her habitually haphazard fashion) with preparing Barbara for her return to boarding school. She sent her daughter back to her mother's care, asking her sister Marjorie ("Budgie") to please have Barbara's clothes washed and mended. "I don't want her to go back to school with things in bad shape," Agnes wrote, enclosing a check for her daughter's expenses.

Agnes and O'Neill would shortly be returning to their Connecticut estate for the late fall and early winter, wrote Agnes, and she proposed that Budgie, who was looking for a job, come to live with them and help take care of Shane (soon to turn six) and act as "a governess"—a job neither Gaga nor Agnes had the time for; Agnes suggested "a business arrangement of $50 per month" (in addition to room and board). Budgie would give Shane "an hour's lesson every day, take him for a walk, see to dressing & undressing him (which is not so much, as he does it himself now) and in fact, do what a governess does."

Budgie's additional duties would consist of typing Agnes's business correspondence, paying monthly household bills, and accompanying the family to Bermuda later that winter. "It would mean a lot to me to have you with us," Agnes coaxed. "Gene thinks this would work out very well, too." Budgie agreed to the arrangement.

THROUGHOUT SEPTEMBER, O'NEILL continued to struggle with alcohol and the intermittent shakiness of his marriage. On October 4, he left Nantucket with his family, stopping briefly in New London to check on the state of the remaining unsold O'Neill property.

The capital letter *D* appeared on October 5, the day he visited his vacant family vacation home on Pequot Avenue. "Decay and ruin—sad," he wrote in his Work Diary.

He attended a party that night at the home of a former mentor, Joseph "Doc" Ganey, noting, "Everyone blotto." Although he felt sick the following morning (another *D* day), he drove with his family to New York, checking into the Lafayette Hotel in the evening, and recording, "Fight with Agnes."

The next day, also a *D*, he drove with Agnes, the children, and Mrs. Clarke to Brook Farm, there to await the triumvirate's productions of *The Fountain*, scheduled for December 10, and *The Great God Brown*, finally set for January 23 (1926). He was also hoping for Belasco's half-promised production of *Marco Millions*.

After exercising and walking in the woods during his first few days at Brook Farm, the *D* shrank to lowercase and by October 11, it was gone— although, as he noted, he remained "disorganized mentally."

On his thirty-seventh birthday five days later, there was a startling entry in the Work Diary: "Bisch came out—much talk about divorce." It was as yet no more than talk—an ominous aside in the drama of the O'Neills' up-and-down marriage. He and Agnes were to endure two more years of venomous quarreling, alternating with fervent reconciliations and punctuated by the entrance of "the Other Woman," before O'Neill tore himself from Agnes for good.

After a week of idle reading, letter-writing, and clearing brush in the woods, O'Neill began "to feel fine again." He had been working on the new play, *Lazarus Laughed*, which he had begun to write in Nantucket; but, too fidgety about the upcoming rehearsals for *The Fountain* in early November to concentrate, he invited his older son to spend a few days with him.

Eugene Jr. was infatuated with the small aggressive Irish terrier, Mat Burke, that O'Neill owned along with Finn, his gigantic slobbering Irish wolfhound. Mat Burke had been terrorizing the neighborhood, chasing chickens and challenging any and all local pets and children to combat, from which he invariably emerged victorious. Weighing Eugene's affection for the terrible terrier against the distress of his neighbors, O'Neill conceived a plan to satisfy all parties. A few days after Eugene returned to his mother's home in Long Island, a huge crate arrived for him. Kathleen, to whom her son had said nothing about the impending gift, opened the crate and, with some misgivings, tethered its contents to a tree in the yard.

When Eugene came home from school, Mat Burke was gone. He returned later that evening, bruised and bloody, having established himself as the boss of his new neighborhood. The Pitt-Smiths kept him until his death from old age several years later.

During November 1925, O'Neill frequently commuted between his

Connecticut home and the Lafayette Hotel in New York to attend rehearsals of the long-delayed *The Fountain*. From the start, he thought the play (which he later condemned as one of his worst) looked "wobbly." *The Fountain*—particularly in its portentous final scenes—was O'Neill's initial attempt at a style of pageantry that owed much to the resplendent church services of his boyhood; but these scenes are lackluster, probably because O'Neill, in his never-ending struggle with his Catholic conscience, had lost his enthusiasm for church ritual.

"Disgusted" with the production, he consoled himself with yet another reckless drinking spree, this time with the eminent critic Edmund "Bunny" Wilson and his then wife, the actress Mary Blair.

The next day, he shrank back to Brook Farm, seeking whatever comfort he could coax from Agnes. Gloomily awaiting the play's doomed opening, he worked in the woods, drank, and sulked. "Too bored," he keened. "Ridgefield is no home for me! Dull as Hell."

As O'Neill had expected, the reviews for *The Fountain* were lukewarm. Woollcott (in the *World*) praised the lavish production, but observed that "the spark of life was missing a good half the time." Most of his colleagues agreed, and the play closed after twenty-four performances.

More edgy than ever, O'Neill again sought Dr. Bisch's advice—this time, according to the doctor, to ask if he really thought psychoanalysis helped people.

"Apparently," Bisch recalled, "he had talked to some of his friends about my ideas."

Not long after, O'Neill invited Bisch to join him for lunch with Kenneth Macgowan and Bobby Jones.

Bisch recalled:

> One of them telephoned me and asked if they could consult me about O'Neill, but not to mention this to him. I invited them to my office. They said they thought analysis might be good for O'Neill, but were afraid it could harm him as a

dramatist. They were worried that it might destroy his genius, inhibit his artistic freedom. I told them I didn't think it would, that, on the contrary, it might make him even freer.

But I warned them that O'Neill would be a difficult man to analyze because he had such a strong ego. Most people who are very shy, I told them, have strong egos; they are certain of their own powers but afraid others won't recognize those powers. I felt analysis of this would help him; I said it would probably enhance, rather than repress, his genius.

Macgowan believed it had become a matter of considerable urgency to find someone who could effectively treat O'Neill's drinking problem. Dr. Bisch would have enjoyed psychoanalyzing O'Neill to see whether the theories he held as an observant friend could be supported, but O'Neill ultimately selected someone else.

Dropping in on an early rehearsal of *The Great God Brown*, still set for a January 23 opening, O'Neill commented in his Work Diary (after placing a small *d* in the margin), "Looks fine, must say. Did lot of work in spite of being bit corned up." On Christmas Eve, he attended a "big party" (which earned a capital *D* in his diary). And on Christmas Day he was in bed at Brook Farm, "sick & melancholia."

Agnes's description of how she coped during the final days of December with her husband's bumptious binge is recorded in a sporadically maintained diary of her own; as candid and detailed as O'Neill's portrait of himself as a drunkard, Agnes painted an unwitting self-portrait of the prototypical enabler.

On Christmas Day, she wrote:

> He drank quite a lot and stayed in bed all day . . . finished the Scotch . . . ate very little . . . nausea . . . by nine p.m. he had nothing left to drink . . . began to get very upset that he would be awake suffering, something must be done . . . said he would go to New York . . . finally, I decided to go to town

ten miles away, got two bottles Scotch, concealed one, gave
him couple of drinks . . . Saturday he felt very sick.

Must have drinks. Gave him one. Refused to eat. Insisted
he must have two more and then would promise to eat decent
breakfast. Did this . . . He kept waking me up saying I would
not sleep if he could not, but I did not give in. Finally he took
veronal and went to sleep . . .

Next a.m. [Sunday, Dec. 27] stuck to my plan. Gave him one
drink . . . said he was sick. Couldn't eat . . . finally he shaved,
dressed, ate some breakfast and seemed sober for the first time.
Gave him two drinks before lunch . . . followed by soup . . .
and three before dinner . . . Took veronal . . . very good sleep.

On that same Sunday, Macgowan made what turned out to be a crucial intervention on O'Neill's behalf. He arranged for O'Neill and Agnes
to join him and his wife, Edna, as participants in a research program
headed by the prominent psychiatrist Gilbert V. Hamilton. It was designed to probe the problems of sexual adjustment in the marital relationship.

"In our circle the interviews were the table topic of the day," recalled
Macgowan. (Macgowan became a close friend of Hamilton's, with whom
he later co-authored a book called *What Is Wrong With Marriage?*)

"A ray of hope amid general sick despair," wrote O'Neill in his Work
Diary after learning of the appointment with Hamilton.

The program had been funded in August 1924 by a committee of
unidentified scientists, permitting Dr. Hamilton to select the small sample of one hundred married men and one hundred married women (not
all of them married to each other) to whom he presented more than
three hundred questions designed to elicit information about their pre-
marital, marital, and extramarital sex lives. (This pioneer program
preceded by ten years the research by Alfred C. Kinsey, whose much
wider study corroborated the findings in Dr. Hamilton's book, *A Research in Marriage*, published in 1929.)

None of the subjects in Dr. Hamilton's book are identified by name; all responses to his research questions are anonymous. But it's easy enough to spot O'Neill as the male who responded to card number 15, question 8, about "the chief source of friction" between his parents; the choices were "Mother's nagging," "Mother's sexual inadequacy," "Mother's interest in other men," and "Mother's drug habit." Can there be any doubt it was O'Neill who checked the last?

In his first tabulation, Hamilton posed the question, "What is there in your marriage that is especially unsatisfactory to you?" and then listed sixty-seven possible answers. It's a pretty safe guess that Agnes was one of the three women who checked answer number 47: "Husband's alcoholism."

Most likely Agnes was among the six women who checked number 19: "Husband's inadequacy as a father," along with number 32: "Unsatisfactory social life for which the marriage or the spouse is held responsible," as well as number 40: "Husband is too much the 'clinging vine,' or 'too infantile' in his emotional relationship to his wife." And can there be any doubt that O'Neill was the single male who checked number 22: "Their young children interfere with the spouses' enjoyment of one another."

Of far greater importance to O'Neill than the results of the research was the fact that he could now take advantage of the gratuitous analysis offered to all the participants in the program—an analysis that in O'Neill's case would focus on his problem with alcohol.

Hamilton sought Agnes's help in assessing her husband's drinking patterns, and she showed him some of her notes made during times when he was frighteningly out of control. At a preliminary session, Hamilton advised O'Neill not to quit drinking abruptly and when he returned home, pleased with the doctor's advice, he immediately took a stiff drink and continued drinking until, hours later, he staggered to bed.

On December 28, O'Neill began tapering off with a mere five drinks; he had three the next day and only one on the thirtieth. Two days later he wrote in his diary, "Feel much better but nerves all shot to hell. Have to go down for *Brown* rehearsals soon. *Must* get in shape."

On December 31, he tossed aside the old year, noting, "On wagon. Goodby—without regret—1925 (except for a few months in Bermuda)."

That was not, however, the final entry in his remarkable long-hidden 1925 diary. He found himself skipping ahead to the beginning of the coming year.

In a surge of optimism, he dated his final entry January 1, 1926: "Welcome to a new dawn, I pray!"

23

O'Neill's six therapeutic weeks with Dr. Hamilton, which began in early January 1926, hardly qualified as a classic psychoanalysis even though Hamilton had him lie on a black leather couch in traditional Freudian style.

From the start, O'Neill grasped Hamilton's drift, familiar as he was with the writings of both Freud and Jung. When the sessions ended, he assured Kenneth Macgowan he had no trouble understanding that he both hated and loved his father and mother and was suffering from an Oedipus complex. (As O'Neill later told his friend, the critic Joseph Wood Krutch, "Without ever having gone in for a complete analysis myself . . . I am enormously interested to see what will emerge as science out of all these theories.")

In those early days of psychoanalysis, Dr. Hamilton apparently felt no ethical qualms in explaining to Macgowan that his friend O'Neill harbored "a death wish"—hardly a difficult inference for anyone familiar with O'Neill's work; he'd shouted his preoccupation with death in more than a half-dozen plays so far; in the fifty (or so) plays that would comprise his legacy (depending on who's counting), his characters suffered violent or otherwise unnatural deaths: suicide, poison, disease, mangling, strangling, hanging, suffocation, knifing, drowning, electrocution, incineration, and gunshot.

Presumably with Hamilton's guidance, O'Neill drew a soul-searching, self-analytical diagram of his family history, which suggested the root of his tug toward annihilation and destructive drinking. The handwritten diagram free-floated the stages of his growing up: birth was "Nirvana," followed by "mother love," "weaning," and then "nurse love" (a reference to his nurse, Sarah Sandy, who nurtured him during his preschool years and whom he adored as a second mother); at seven, he viewed his father as "indefinite hero—not dangerous rival"; there followed an indelible memory:

"At early childhood Father would give mild whiskey and water to soothe child's nightmares cause[d] by terror of dark," adding, somewhat obscurely, "This whiskey is connected with protection of Mother—drink of hero father."

In the diagram's second stage, O'Neill blamed his father for causing "break with Mother" by sending him away at seven to boarding school. Still continuing his painful free association, he wrote: "Reality faced and fled from in life of fantasy and religion in school—inability to belong to reality."

By adolescence, the third stage, O'Neill's "resentment against father" became "hatred and defiance of father"; this paralleled "discovery of Mother's inadequacy."

While O'Neill was brooding over his diagram, he also helped Agnes make a list for Dr. Hamilton of dates and durations of various drunken episodes and ensuing periods of sobriety (including his "38 days not drinking [during] rehearsals *Desire*").

O'Neill's first three weeks on the couch coincided with rehearsals for *The Great God Brown*. His immersion in this death-obsessed play obviously fed the analytic process. He told Hamilton (as he'd told Bisch) about the typical letdown following an opening night and the drinking binge that inevitably came after.

With clinical curiosity, patient and shrink awaited the opening of *Brown* on January 23. Would all that therapeutic counseling enable O'Neill, this time, to circumvent the booby trap? To Hamilton's satisfaction and to O'Neill's somewhat awed surprise, it did. He was now convinced that John Barleycorn had been annihilated and—for a long time—it seemed he was right. ("I haven't had a drink in nearly five years! So help me!" O'Neill cheered to an old friend at the end of 1930. "Booze was getting sick of me. After a long huddle with my liver and lights I decided to throw in the sponge—and mean it. Life since then has lacked the uproarious but I must admit I feel better.")

But at least one cynic was laughing up his sleeve. When the Theatre Guild's Lawrence Langner reported to George Bernard Shaw that O'Neill had sworn off drinking, Shaw responded, "He'll probably never write a good play again."

O'NEILL'S NEWLY EARNED equilibrium was boosted by the reviews of *The Great God Brown*, which were more compassionate and intelligent than he had dared expect. Brooks Atkinson and Richard Watts saluted O'Neill's overall achievement despite being discomfited by the play's sporadic incoherence.

Atkinson (now theater critic for the *Times*) wrote that O'Neill "succeeded in placing within the reach of the stage finer shades of beauty, more delicate nuances of truth and more passionate qualities of emotion than we can discover in any other single modern play." In the *Herald Tribune*, Watts, while faulting O'Neill's submission to "the mad ghost of Strindberg," nevertheless declared the play "a fascinating, half-mad enigma . . . as eloquent and stirring and richly imaginative as anything that has come from the pen of this foremost of our dramatists."

Somewhat troubled that these two discerning and supportive critics found his play confusing, O'Neill hoped to clarify its intent for them, as well as for his puzzled fans, and he made several halfhearted attempts to explain what he characterized as the play's "hidden theme."

Three weeks after the play's opening, O'Neill sent a letter to the *New York Evening Post* (also published in the *Times* and other papers):

> I had hoped the names chosen for my people would give
> a strong hint of this. "Dion Anthony"—Dionysius and St.

Anthony—the creative pagan acceptance of life fighting eternal war with the masochistic, life-denying spirit of Christianity as represented by St. Anthony—the whole struggle resulting in this modern day in mutual exhaustion—creative joy in life for life's sake frustrated, rendered abortive, distorted by morality from Pan into Satan, into a Mephistopheles mocking himself in order to feel alive; Christianity, once heroic in martyrs for its intense faith now pleading weakly for its intense belief in anything, even Godhead itself.

Clear so far? What followed was even less so:

I realize that when a playwright takes to explaining he thereby automatically places himself "in the dock." But where an open-faced avowal by the play itself of the abstract theme underlying it is made impossible by the very nature of that hidden theme, then perhaps it is justifiable for the author to confess the mystical pattern which manifests itself as an overtone in *The Great God Brown*, dimly behind and beyond the words and actions of the characters.

O'Neill was a bit more articulate a few months later in a letter to Carlotta Monterey, with whom he had recently fallen in love. Torn between his love for her (the temptress unknown) and his dependence on Agnes (the devil he knew), he voiced his sense of a divided self: "If I could only live at the same time in two worlds! But what a shamefully inadequate gift of half to offer you—or Agnes. And yet each of those halves is really a whole me! See *Brown*. I am two—absolutely!"

The Great God Brown ran for 278 performances—first at the Greenwich Village Theatre, then at the Garrick (on West Thirty-fifth Street), and finally at a Broadway theater, the Klaw (on West Forty-fifth Street); it was the seventh O'Neill play in six seasons to tally more than a hundred performances—a benchmark in those days for a Broadway hit.

Audiences by now had learned to appreciate O'Neill's willingness to bare his innermost fantasies. Even if they couldn't follow all of his concepts all of the time, they could follow some of them much of the time. They had come to understand and respect his fearlessness in trying to stretch beyond his own limits, to reach for what he idiosyncratically defined as "a bigger and better failure."

Although compelling for its time, *The Great God Brown* is seldom revived. Superseded during the more than eighty years since its premiere by a plethora of ever more absurdist, expressionist, and abstract plays, *Brown* has lost its impact. But it remains major in O'Neill's canon as not only an intensely personal revelation, but also as an example of his artistic daring when Broadway was—as he justifiably persisted in castigating it—mere "show shop."

Agnes and O'Neill retreated to Bermuda a month after the opening of *Brown*, this time renting a grand dwelling in Paget East, appropriately named Bellevue. It was "a real peach of a house," O'Neill wrote to Macgowan, "lots of room—beautiful grounds, private beach [and] all at a big bargain price." What most appealed to him and Agnes was the separate quarters for the children and guests, and detached quarters for the help.

For neither the first time nor the last, O'Neill believed he had found the ideal combination of beauty and peace. To Louis Kantor, he confided, "Next to Peaked Hill in the old days, I believe this is the most satisfying habitat I've struck. It really has the feeling of home to me who usually feels in most houses like a Samoan in an igloo."

O'Neill now resumed writing *Lazarus Laughed*, a work that was to share the ill fate of *The Fountain*. A newly imagined saga of the biblical Lazarus's second life on earth following his resurrection, it derived its title (as he once told the journalist Elizabeth Shepley Sergeant) from the "Jesus wept" story of the Gospel.

Boiled down to its essence, *Lazarus*, although filled with the exultant laughter of its hero, was a grim attempt to deny the death wish O'Neill had flaunted in *Brown*. But with all his lip service to the joyousness of life and the fearlessness of death, O'Neill sounded unconvinced by his own argument. His Lazarus simply protests too much. "There is no death," his followers chant over and over and over during four acts (occasionally substituting such minor variants as "Death is dead").

O'Neill, however, was oblivious to the play's pretensions. "Lazarus coming bigger and bigger!" he bragged to Macgowan toward the end of March. "Certainly it contains the highest writing I have done. Certainly it composes for the theater more than anything else I have done." Growing ever more operatic, he suggested that the role of Lazarus be acted (in his native Russian!) by the famed operatic bass Feodor Chaliapin. But he knew the triumvirate didn't have the budget to mount the epic, and was beginning to wonder if it would ever find a producer.

It wasn't long before O'Neill and Agnes once again began to worry about money. "Come on, you *Brown*! Daddy needs a yacht!" O'Neill wrote to Macgowan early in March when he had not yet received his first royalty check.

Bellevue, although cheap to rent, was expensive to maintain, demanding the services of an indoor and outdoor staff. In addition to a household that included the four O'Neills plus Gaga and Budgie, there were occasional visits from Eugene Jr. and Barbara (still mostly in her grandmother's care when not at boarding school) as well as a scattering of the O'Neills' friends from New York.

O'Neill had (for the present) pushed aside his half-formed thoughts of divorce and instead attempted to redesign a more satisfactory lifestyle. With Agnes's approval, he decided to sell Brook Farm and make Bermuda their "home port" for the next two or three years; at the same time, he began casting about for a place to spend the summer months when Bermuda was too hot for comfort. Of one thing he was sure: despite his love for Peaked Hill Bars, he had no wish to return with Agnes to Provincetown.

"I want to avoid all the P'town connotations," he told Macgowan, referring to his hard-drinking friends, protesting that it was not that he was "afraid anymore—but it's no use making it harder for oneself." He was thinking, instead, of renting a camp on a lake in Maine, where he could canoe, fish, and play tennis.

Near April's end, O'Neill complained to Macgowan about his still-unpaid *Brown* royalties, as well as those from a touring company of *Desire Under the Elms* and a revival of *The Emperor Jones*. When Macgowan explained that the triumvirate, financially pressed, was withholding O'Neill's accrued royalties and applying them to general operating expenses, O'Neill exploded:

"I am not Otto Kahn. I have a large family to support . . . I can least afford to play philanthropist just now when I'm making my first determined effort to get my own affairs stabilized so I can work steadily ahead for the next few years in peace." Macgowan, embarrassed, quickly steered the owed royalties to O'Neill.

The Great God Brown was the last play produced by the triumvirate. They acknowledged they were no longer able to muster the funding or enthusiasm to continue. By mutual consent, and while continuing to be good friends, O'Neill, Macgowan, and Jones dissolved the partnership.

The back royalties from *Brown* had reached O'Neill just in time. The owners of Bellevue had declined to give him a long-term lease and now he and Agnes, rebounding from their disappointment, decided they could afford to buy instead of renting. On April 24, they found a property they loved.

This time it was an early-eighteenth-century house called Spithead, large and rambling, unlived in for some years and in need of major repairs. But it was gloriously situated on open water with its own beachfront. On May 1, the O'Neills offered $17,500 and within a week Spithead was theirs.

O'Neill and Agnes shifted residences as casually as nomads. So far, during the eight years of their marriage, they'd folded and unfolded their tent in five places they called home: the Old House in New Jersey, the former Coast Guard station in Provincetown, Brook Farm in Connecticut, the manorial Bellevue—and now, a barely livable "shell," but as O'Neill described it to friends, "a very fine shell." He and Agnes planned to repair and decorate Spithead gradually and occupy it as their permanent winter-through-spring abode.

Agnes's sister Budgie finished typing the first draft of *Lazarus Laughed* on May 11. Although O'Neill was as always overcome with admiration for his newest creation, he was disappointed that no producer to whom he'd outlined the project shared his enthusiasm. It wasn't until 1927 that it was finally presented by the Pasadena Community Players in California—without Chaliapin, but "successfully and imaginatively," according to O'Neill.

On May 16, with *Lazarus* out of the way, O'Neill turned his attention to "scheming out" what he merrily called his "lady play"—the provocative concept that, unlike *Lazarus*, proved to be eminently producible on Broadway.

While *Strange Interlude* was even longer than *Lazarus*, it was neither pageant nor spectacle; its story owed more to Freud (despite O'Neill's later disavowals) than to the Bible. Not too long since, he'd read both Freud's *Beyond the Pleasure Principle* and his *Group Psychology and the Analysis of the Ego*. And Dr. Hamilton, with whom he'd kept up a friendship, served as a sounding board.

Strange Interlude evolved as an even more passionate tale of sexual love and despair than the steamy *Desire Under the Elms*. O'Neill hoped to finish the first scene before escaping Bermuda's summer heat.

On June 15, sailing from Bermuda for the two-day voyage to New York, the O'Neills and their entourage were an exotic presence to their shipmates aboard the *Fort St. George*: the celebrated playwright, handsome, lean, sun-bronzed, his hair edged with silver; his pretty wife, slim, tanned, and chic; the two children—Shane, a beautiful delicate boy of nearly seven, with his golden ringlets, and Oona, a shy, pudgy one-year-old with enormous eyes—together with the sister-secretary, Budgie; Gaga the nanny; and the pony-sized Finn.

Agnes and O'Neill settled their children into the Shelton Hotel on East Forty-ninth Street and, after a weekend visit with Kenneth and Edna Macgowan at their country home, Agnes accompanied her husband to

New Haven. There, on June 23, he received an honorary degree of Doctor of Letters from Yale—the only such degree he ever accepted.

The honor had been proposed by Professor George Pierce Baker, in whose Harvard playwriting workshop O'Neill had studied for one year in 1914. Baker had recognized and encouraged O'Neill's as-yet-undiscovered talent (along with such others as Philip Barry, S. N. Behrman, Sidney Howard, and Edward Sheldon). Baker, in 1924, had moved his renowned "47 Workshop" to Yale when the university agreed to build the theater Harvard had denied him.

"I was his best known pupil," O'Neill later told a friend, "and Yale was really honoring him through me." Elizabeth Shepley Sergeant, who interviewed O'Neill soon after the event, remarked that Agnes "was amused to discover that he became so interested in the spectacle that he did finally enjoy his own part in it, and instead of dying of stage-fright 'took a bow' on the applause."

Most meaningful to O'Neill was Yale's championing of him as "the first American playwright to receive both wide and serious recognition upon the stage of Europe." Yale's salute—together with his recent triumph over alcohol, his success with *Brown*, his completion of *Lazarus*, the start of his beguiling new "lady play," and the beckoning of a lakeside summer vacation in Maine—should have been reason enough for him to count his blessings.

But, somehow, he simply couldn't. He felt encircled by a vague emptiness, an emotional vacuum that he attributed to his withdrawal from alcohol; he feared he could never fill that void.

He had tried to articulate his new malaise to Macgowan during his recent visit to Brewster, but could only hint at it. Macgowan, looking back years later, said O'Neill had spoken to him of his unhappiness over Agnes's social drinking; she thought it unreasonable to expect her—not an alcoholic—to give it up for his sake. Macgowan sensed there was more than that on O'Neill's mind, but O'Neill seemed unable to specify just what else it was that gnawed at him.

Reaching Maine on June 27, his Packard touring car crowded with his family and Finn—and with his endemic devils in tow—O'Neill tried to resume work on *Strange Interlude*. It wasn't easy for Agnes to balance his need for quiet against a houseful of vacationing children, which included both Barbara and Eugene Jr. for part of the summer. (At eleven, Barbara was, in her own words, "madly in love" with sixteen-year-old Eugene.)

"We're a fat family," O'Neill reported to Macgowan, soon after his arrival in Maine. Briefly, he gave himself to the role of benign patriarch, walking with his children in the fragrant woods behind his cabin, gathering with them on the cabin's front porch to admire the sunsets.

Amused that his lakeside compound was called "Loon Lodge," O'Neill wrote to Macgowan, "This, after living in 'Bellevue' all winter, makes me suspect God is becoming a symbolist or something."

What he did not suspect was that the uneasy summer about to unfold would be the springboard for the dissolution of his marriage.

24

It all began with an invitation to come to tea at the home of Elisabeth Marbury, who lived across the lake from the O'Neill campsite. It was Marbury, the business partner of O'Neill's literary agent, Richard Madden, who had recommended Belgrade Lakes as the ideal place for the O'Neills to vacation. When Marbury issued the invitation on July 15, the O'Neills had been in residence for several weeks.

Marbury, with offices in London and Paris as well as New York, had represented and dealt with dozens of globally known writers and publishers, and was herself a glittering member of the international social set, together with her lover, Elsie De Wolfe, a sought-after interior decorator. Now elderly, overweight, infirm, and mostly housebound, Marbury still maintained her love of good food and good conversation. Her houseguest that summer was Carlotta Monterey, who was trying to recover from her recent painful divorce from Ralph Barton. Carlotta knew that Marbury's reputation as a lesbian would inevitably incite talk about her own sexual orientation.

"I suppose you've heard I was a lesbian," Carlotta ruefully remarked to the playwright Russel Crouse years later, explaining she "hadn't a soul to turn to" when she split with Barton, and Marbury had been "so wonderful" to her, taking her in for the summer.

In an interview with the authors thirty years after that Maine summer, Carlotta, as she often did, blended history and histrionics, to say nothing of self-serving hyperbole; in her version of that fateful tea party, she glibly made Marbury sound as though she had thought having the O'Neills to tea was an unwanted obligation, whereas, in truth, Marbury, who had grown attached to both O'Neill and Agnes, was more than pleased to have them as her neighbors.

"I went to Maine as the guest of an old lady who was an invalid," said Carlotta.

> I was living there very quietly. I walked and swam. One day my hostess said, "I have to have the O'Neills to tea and they're very difficult. He never opens his mouth and she never shuts hers. So it makes entertaining rather difficult."
>
> "What O'Neills?" I asked. She told me Eugene O'Neill, the playwright. Well, I didn't see why I had to stay and meet that awful man again, but I was a houseguest, and out of politeness I had to stay. So I put a dress on over my bathing suit. They drove up in a car.
>
> Agnes popped out of the car, and O'Neill followed her. She was very messy. The first thing she said to me was "Oh, Carlotta Monterey, I am so glad to meet you! I want to hear all about your sex life!" Well, I nearly fainted. I thought, *What is this? If it's a joke, it's stupid.* I said, "I have no husband at the moment so I have no sex life." "Oh," Agnes squeaked, "but you must have a lover! Don't you have a lover?" "No," I said, "no lover."
>
> And then O'Neill came up and said, "Do you remember me?" And I said, "Yes, when I went into your play *The Hairy Ape* without any rehearsals and took all the risk—my reputation and everything—you never said thank you."

As she told the story of her hostile encounter at Marbury's home with the man whose world she soon would turn upside down, Carlotta chuckled. Her account of what she described as Agnes's vulgar chatter was patently exaggerated; even three decades after having pried O'Neill away from his wife, Carlotta persisted in vindictively belittling Agnes's role in his life; she never got over the frustration of being unable to obliterate Agnes's existence.

Further embroidering on the tea party, Carlotta frequently bubbled with nervous laughter. She was reminiscing during a three-hour lunch with the authors at Quo Vadis, an elegantly subdued Upper East Side restaurant where she felt at home sipping the Monterey Cocktails (gin and Cointreau) the management had named for her.

"O'Neill tried to be friendly," Carlotta continued, "but I was cold to him. All through tea, Agnes kept chattering about all the writers and theater people she knew. She kept turning to me and saying, 'You know him—or her—don't you, Miss Monterey?' 'No,' I said, 'I'm afraid I don't. I don't know anyone. I live very quietly.' It was an awful tea."

After the stressful tea party, Carlotta said, "my hostess asked me to take O'Neill down to the bathhouse so he could swim. I didn't want to, but I did it—not very graciously.

"'You don't like me, do you?' O'Neill said, as we were walking down to the lake.

"'Why, Mr. O'Neill, I don't know you. How can I like or dislike you?' I answered." But then she again brought up his brusqueness on meeting her backstage at *The Hairy Ape* and, she said, "He apologized, explaining he'd been in mourning for his mother's recent death. He told me they'd painted up the face so—the way they do in San Francisco—that she looked like a painted doll. He couldn't relate that face to his mother, and he'd been terribly upset when he met me."

Neither O'Neill nor Agnes had thought to bring bathing suits, which might explain why Agnes declined to accompany Carlotta for a swim. But according to Carlotta, O'Neill was unconcerned about appearances.

"O'Neill went into the bathhouse and appeared a few minutes later wearing a woman's bathing suit." "It must have belonged to my hostess—it was huge, and hung on him perfectly ridiculously. I guess there just weren't any men's suits in there, but he didn't care. He wanted a swim, and he just paid no attention to how he looked. I decided then that he couldn't be so bad, after all. He dived in and swam—he swam magnificently and the suit kept billowing up. It was most indecent."

"See Carlotta again!" exclaimed O'Neill in his diary the following week. It was mid-August, however, before their next flirtatious encounter.

O'NEILL WAS ONLY vaguely aware of Carlotta's recent divorce from Ralph Barton. Nor could he know that Carlotta at this time was in the midst of an agonizing correspondence with Barton, who, as devastated as she was by their breakup, had fled abroad. From France, Barton had launched an epistolary campaign to win her back.

His most recent letter, received by Carlotta in early June, had told of his despair over their separation, and his inability to concentrate on his work as a caricaturist.

"I think I made a hideous mistake in letting you get away from me," Barton wrote. "I am horribly afraid that the old nonsense about there being one woman in the world for each man is not, after all, nonsense. I am beginning to cringe under the thought that I need desperately what was fine between us and that I can never find it again. This is what you said would happen and I believe you were right. If it turns out that you were, I don't think I want to live any more."

He pleaded with Carlotta to "throw everything in the air, get on the next boat with a free mind, uneaten by memories of what has gone by."

He swore he had learned his lesson. If she did not come, he wrote, "I will shoot myself with a French pistol"—a variation on suicide threats he often made (and that his friends dismissed as posturing). "I am miserable and hopeless and weep."

Carlotta was tempted to forgive Barton, and wrote him so. She received his reply a few days after her encounter with the O'Neills at Marbury's home.

"Your letter just here with your impulse to take the boat. I wish you had obeyed the impulse. . . . I can't see anything else for us but to forget all this damned nonsense and come back together again, really. . . . Be calm. Sleep! All will arrange itself. I love you."

Carlotta appears to have persuaded herself that Barton's faithlessness was a result of her mistreating him, and she wrote as much.

"You didn't fail with me, as you say," Barton wrote back on July 28. "What an imbecile I was—but what a good husband I shall make you after this! It was I who failed with you. We are coming together again— we have never been apart."

Swearing his devotion, Barton informed her he would sail home on September 15. But Carlotta could not have found much comfort in Barton's concluding remarks, in which he described a prospective leisurely tour of Rome, Florence, Rapallo ("to see Max Beerbohm"), Venice, and Salzburg, and concluding with a tour by car in the south of France.

"Then home to you," he wrote blithely. "I somehow feel that we both still need this time between." It sounded as though—believing he'd won her back—Barton no longer felt any urgency to reclaim her.

Carlotta by now must have been beset by second thoughts about the wisdom of her submission. In any event, there was, after all, no reconciliation. After receiving that letter (probably in early August), she considered her relationship with Barton over (although Barton emphatically did not).

Conceivably, she had already begun to think of O'Neill as a romantic replacement. She couldn't help but realize he was more of a prize than Barton—more famous, more handsome, more serious about his work, more needy of a muse. She didn't think it was beyond her power to enchant him.

On August 18, answering a letter from New London friends who inquired about his vacation in Maine, O'Neill casually commented that there were "quite a few theater people" at Belgrade Lakes—"Florence Reed [the actress] just a quarter mile away and Carlotta Monterey, the famous beauty (she played in my *Hairy Ape* in New York at the Plymouth Theatre) visiting not far away."

Florence Reed, who, with her actor husband, Malcolm Williams, owned a showplace with its own sandy beach and picture-perfect garden, inadvertently provided O'Neill and Carlotta with a trysting place. Reed, recently triumphant as Mother Goddam, the whorehouse proprietor in the Broadway production of *The Shanghai Gesture*, had long kept a sisterly eye on O'Neill.

"Gene was extremely shy, dear, sweet, and gentle," she said.

> He would paddle over in his canoe to our beach almost every afternoon about two and I'd take out one of our canoes and paddle across the lake, which was about a mile wide, with Gene swimming alongside. He'd use the sidestroke and talk to me all the while he was swimming. On the other shore he'd rest about twenty minutes and then swim back, using the backstroke.
>
> Once he told me about *Lazarus Laughed* while he was swimming, and another time he described the plot and characters of *Strange Interlude*. When we'd get back to my house, there'd be a tray with drinks waiting; Gene always took tea.
>
> One afternoon when we'd just gotten back from a canoe-swim trip, and Gene was sitting on the porch drying off in his bathing suit, we heard a station wagon drive up. It was Bess Marbury and Carlotta and some other people, come over for a visit. Gene pussyfooted away when I went to receive them, but I saw that Carlotta spotted him as he walked through the garden toward his canoe, and that she talked with him.

When Marbury and her guests left, Reed noticed a scarf on the porch and she asked her husband if he had any idea whose it was. He said he thought it was Carlotta's; he predicted she would be back for the scarf the following afternoon.

"What are you talking about?" asked Reed.

"I suppose you didn't notice what happened this afternoon," replied Williams.

"What happened?"

"Carlotta and Gene," remarked Williams with a knowing smile.

The next afternoon, after O'Neill had arrived as usual, a station wagon drove up. "Carlotta got out," said Reed, "and asked about her scarf. . . . She and Gene went off in his canoe together after they had talked a while."

Reed was not surprised that O'Neill was attracted to Carlotta. "She was miraculously immaculate," said Reed.

> She never wore the same shirtwaist twice; she was a wonderful housekeeper. There was nobody like her. She kept the Marbury house going so beautifully. No staff of butlers could do it.
>
> Agnes's house, on the other hand, always seemed to smell of diapers and lamb stew. There was a lot of noise from the kids. It drove O'Neill almost out of his mind. He finally built himself a one-room plywood-tarpaper shack near the water, about a hundred yards from the house, to get away from the noise and the smells.

Barbara Burton later contradicted Reed's account, recalling that she, Shane, and Eugene Jr. strictly observed the camp rule that demanded "absolute quiet" when O'Neill was writing. They would take themselves away from the cottage to fish at the water's edge. "Shane caught the most," Barbara remembered. "He seemed to have some affinity for the silent sitting and waiting involved in fishing."

Florence Reed said that Agnes seemed to live in "mortal fear" of O'Neill. "She tried very hard to appease him. Once she drove over to my place alone, and when she started to leave, her car wheel got caught in a sapling and it took fifteen minutes to free it. She was in a terrible state because she thought she wouldn't get back in time to fix Gene's supper.

Marbury, by the way, was very fond of Agnes and though she liked Carlotta, too, she was distressed when she realized that Gene seemed to be interested in Carlotta."

Why the O'Neills had not managed to provide themselves with an efficient housekeeping staff and a comfortable place for O'Neill to work was a puzzle. Years later, Barbara Burton recalled that, while the atmosphere in the O'Neill household had seemed, on most of her visits, to be "happy," she supposed that the last years were not.

"Looking back now," she said, "I can realize that summer was probably the beginning of the end so far as my mother's marriage to O'Neill was concerned. I recall a handsome dark-haired woman coming to swim there once and that she wore a boyish white wool-knit bathing suit, with no overskirt, such as bathing suits usually had at the time. I felt there was something very glamorous about this woman, who, in retrospect, I know was Carlotta Monterey. Toward the very end I felt the presence of some sadness which I had never felt in the O'Neill household." As for Shane, he was more than content to fish and romp with his four-legged "buddy Finn." He remembered the summer as "wonderful and happy."

Reed and others were aware that Carlotta had made a friend of Agnes and the children. Carlotta's revisionist tableau of that initial meeting in Maine, in which she sneered at Agnes as an odious yokel, is in stark contrast to the view she expressed in a note written around that time to her former agent and close friend, Lyman Brown.

Chatting about Florence Reed and other theater people at the lake, Carlotta wrote, "See a lot of Eugene O'Neill and family. *Like them*—"

O'Neill was clearly exhilarated by Carlotta's unconcealed interest in him. In his Work Diary, he pointedly noted—without specifying the occasion or location—"Saw Carlotta on August 17, 19 and 21."

It hadn't taken long for O'Neill to grow fretful under the domestic arrangements he'd undertaken. He grumbled to Macgowan that he "could do with less progeny about." He was, after all, not cut out "for a pater familias," he said, "and children in squads, even when indubitably my own, tend to 'get my goat.'"Nor was he unaware that Agnes, too, craved a release from the constant company of their children; they both could "do with more real friends to talk with."

Less than a week later, Eugene Jr. and Barbara were gone. On August 10, Agnes, after presenting Barbara with "a five dollar gold piece and a box of candy," asked Gaga to see her home.

"Gene seems to think it would be much better for his work if there were *no* kids here but Shane and Oona, though he hasn't got a thing started so far this summer," Agnes wrote to her mother and Budgie. "And as we have *no* prospective plays going on in the fall, Laz. and M. Millions both seeming to have a hard time getting any backers, I feel it is most important of all to do all I can to get him started. I hope it will be O.K."

In fact, things were far from okay. The sense of helpless yearning O'Neill had hinted at to Macgowan in Brewster seven weeks earlier had been subtly exacerbated by his dalliance with Carlotta. He was not yet ready to confide in his old friend about his attraction to her, but he did write about his despairing state of mind.

While assuring Macgowan he had no desire to drink, he was feeling "the void" left by what he called "those companionable or (even when most horrible) intensely dramatic phantoms and obsessions which, with caressing claws in my heart and brain, used to lead me for weeks at a time . . . down the ever-changing vistas of that No-Mans-Land lying between the D.T.s and Reality as we suppose it."

Perhaps he did not yet fully understand how much he longed to play solitaire with his scales, to take a headlong chance with his life. As with Poe's "The Imp of the Perverse," O'Neill saw himself standing "upon the brink of a precipice" and peering into it. In that diabolically brilliant story—a favorite of O'Neill's—Poe describes the sinister intoxication of lingering at the brink, contemplating "the idea of what would be our sensations during the sweeping precipitancy of a fall from such a height." Poe goes on to imagine the "rushing annihilation . . . that one most ghastly and loathsome of all the most ghastly and loathsome images of death and suffering," and, he concludes, "for this very cause . . . do we the most impetuously approach it."

Deterred from a plunge into the abyss of alcoholism, O'Neill evidently was seeking an equivalent emotional chasm—one that would shatter his unsatisfactory life pattern. He wasn't long in finding that substitute. In his Work Diary on September 10, he noted, "(Saw Carlotta again.)" She was shortly to end her visit with Elisabeth Marbury and return to New York. Although the diary entry was laconic, with no hint at any future meetings, O'Neill did not intend to let their flirtation end with her departure.

With Carlotta gone, however, there was less to distract him, and he soon found himself contentedly back at work on *Strange Interlude*. On October 3, Agnes, in a letter reporting the summer's events to her ailing father, told him that O'Neill was attempting to put into his *Strange Interlude* script "all the advantages of a novel," which was "most interesting and quite unlike anything I have ever read or seen."

As for the rest of her family, she assured her father that she, Shane, and Oona were "in fine shape"; Oona, at eighteen months, "runs all around now." Agnes herself had done "a little writing this summer, but not much." She said she planned to invite her father and mother to visit in Bermuda as soon as "we get it all fixed the way we want it."

O'Neill and Agnes left Loon Lodge on October 13. Accompanied by Shane, Oona, and Gaga, Agnes headed for a visit to her family's Connecticut farm while O'Neill made his way to New York to pursue backing for *Marco Millions*.

"Hello, old Sweetheart!" O'Neill wrote to Agnes, as soon as he'd settled into the Harvard Club on October 14. After a chatty report of his activities, he ended, "I love you and miss you. There's no one to confide in now."

Three days later, he was earnestly confiding in Carlotta Monterey.

25

On his own in New York, O'Neill was avid to explore his galloping lust for Carlotta. He would have to work fast; it was now mid-October and he and Agnes were planning to move permanently to Bermuda at the end of November. On October 26, after spending two weeks at the Harvard Club, he settled at the Hotel Wentworth near Times Square; for a time it would serve as his theater district headquarters.

After returning from her visit to her family, Agnes was safely out of the way in Connecticut, sorting, packing, and readying Brook Farm for sale.

With Carlotta on his mind, O'Neill told Agnes he had to stay in New York to continue his search for a producer for *Marco Millions*, which David Belasco had finally turned down after months of shilly-shallying. Agnes grudgingly acceded to O'Neill's plan.

While she labored over the shutting down of their home, O'Neill, on October 17, began surreptitiously meeting with Carlotta. He saw her seven times during the next five and a half weeks, punctiliously recording in his Work Diary the dates of their rendezvous—among them three lunches, a concert, and a dinner.

CARLOTTA CHOSE TO put a somewhat different spin on the beginning of her romance with the married O'Neill. Her version, plainly hyperbolic and self-serving, begins, like O'Neill's, when he returned to New York from his summer sojourn in Maine. In this version (recollected three years after O'Neill's death), he invites himself to tea at her apartment.

> He drank four cups of tea. He sat there, looking like Hamlet in distress. He began to talk about his boyhood. He talked and talked as though he'd known me all his life. He began with his birth, with his earliest memories of babyhood.

"And," Carlotta continued, "he talked and he talked, the whole time looking as if he were tortured. He talked about how he'd had no home, no mother in the real sense, no father in the real sense, and how emotionally deprived his childhood had been.

"Then suddenly he looked at the clock, and said, 'Oh, my God, I've got to go,' and off he flew. Then he rang up again, asking if he could come to tea again. I thought, *What is this, that poor man.* So I said, 'Certainly.' He began right where he'd left off the last time."

Carlotta tried to evoke O'Neill's pain as she groped to "recall" his account of his entry into the world, beginning with his mother's labor in a Times Square hotel room.

> There she was, in a hotel room again. She felt pains, and what not, and she rang for the maid and told her to go down to the bar and see if her husband was there, and tell him to come quick. So he came up quick. And she said [to her husband], "Get me a doctor, quick." And this is what angers me, and upsets me.
>
> They had no nurse arranged. They had no layette. They had nothing. And he goes downstairs, asking for the hotel doctor. Now you can imagine what the hotel doctor is like. He comes upstairs smoking a cigar, and he doesn't even wash his hands. Well, she's delivered of Eugene O'Neill. I'm surprised that he lived.

Her imaginative narrative went on:

I sat and listened, and at first I was a little worried and then I
was deeply unhappy. I thought it was terrible that of all people
to be so stricken, it should be this man, who had talent and
had worked hard.

She spoke with a theatrical lilt, often interjecting her comments
with a throaty laugh. She sounded rehearsed. "And his face would
become sadder and sadder, and he would talk and talk, and then would
rush out—and come back the next day and go on."

Carlotta spoke with relish of her life with the man she referred to
variously as "Gene," "O'Neill," and "the Master." She often rambled,
but her memories throbbed with the wonder and exultation of having
captivated—and been held captive by—the extraordinary man who was
her husband.

"Well, that's what got me into trouble with O'Neill," she said with a
husky, self-mocking chuckle. "My maternal instinct came out—*this man
must be looked after*, I thought. He broke my heart. I couldn't bear that
this child I had adopted should have suffered these things."

She paused for effect; there's no mistaking she once was an actress.
"One day when he came to tea he had a bad cold—he always had a cold—
and he looked at me with those tragic eyes and said, 'I need you.' He kept
saying, 'I need you, I need you'—never 'I love you, I think you are wonderful'—just 'I need you, I need you.' Sometimes it was a bit frightening.
Nobody had ever gritted their teeth at me that way and said they needed
me. And he did need me, I discovered. He never was in good health, he
always had a cold, he wasn't properly fed or anything."

Perhaps inadvertently, Carlotta allowed her narrative to drift into
more revealing detail, as she described one of her dates with O'Neill that
November:

I went to this frowzy hotel with rubber plants sitting around,
and I went to the desk and said, "I have an appointment for
lunch with Mr. O'Neill," and they phoned up and said for me

to go upstairs. I said, "Has he a sitting room?" They said, "Yes, he has a sitting room," so I went up.

I wish you'd seen the sitting room. It had a table and a frowzy couch and a couple of chairs. I broke my nail and I said to him, "Have you a nail file, please?" And he went in to his frowzy little bedroom and he was fussing, fussing, fussing, and I said, "Do you want me to look?" I wish you'd seen his suitcase. It had nothing in it but a couple of frowzy, torn pajamas—no dressing gown, no bedroom slippers, no anything. That's what got old, maternal Monterey, you see.

We went downstairs and had a not-too-good luncheon. And I said, "Thank you so much, what size is your neck?" And I went over to Abercrombie & Fitch and I bought him a fitted case, and pajamas and socks and a dressing gown and God knows what else, and sent them to him. Why, he nearly had fits when he got them. He'd never seen such things. [Prolonged throaty laughter.]

Clearly, Carlotta was allowing herself to be carried away. O'Neill was more than adequately clothed during the latter years of his marriage to Agnes. His Work Diary and letters not infrequently noted respectable purchases of both outer- and underwear, and in photographs he is always appropriately attired; Carlotta's disparagement of O'Neill's wardrobe was yet another postmortem jab at Agnes.

"I don't know what his life was like," Carlotta persisted, "but he didn't have anything to wear. And he was working all the time, making money, and I don't know where the money went."

AGNES, STILL EMPTYING the house at Brook Farm in mid-November, began to feel lonely; O'Neill had managed only a three-day visit earlier in the month (continuing to use the excuse of meetings with producers, in addition to rehearsals for a routine off-Broadway revival of *Beyond the Horizon*). Leaving Shane and Oona with Gaga, Agnes joined her husband at the Wentworth for several days.

WHILE O'NEILL FELT GUILTY about his evolving love affair with Carlotta, he had no difficulty summoning his unremitting passion for Agnes. But as soon as Agnes left, he reconnected with Carlotta.

Agnes finally completed packing up Brook Farm and sailed with the children for Bermuda on November 21. Leaning on the excuse of having to await the opening of the *Beyond the Horizon* revival, O'Neill stayed behind at the Wentworth.

Once again unencumbered, he devoted himself for the next seven days to his new love. After the final rehearsal on November 26, he joined Carlotta in her apartment, not parting from her until 2:30 a.m. the following day. Giving himself just enough time to pack—and to send Carlotta roses—he boarded the November 27 steamer to Bermuda. It was not easy to tear himself away from Carlotta, but once *Beyond the Horizon* had opened, he had no further excuse to linger in New York.

Carlotta's involuntary separation from O'Neill, just as he had begun to court her in earnest, was as frustrating to her as it was to him—although she strove, in her interviews with the authors, to give the opposite impression. For example, Carlotta declared that after that "not-too-good" lunch at the Wentworth, she did not hear from O'Neill "for months," which was a blatant obfuscation.

In fact, in a letter he wrote almost the moment he stepped aboard the steamer that was carrying him back to Bermuda, O'Neill cried out to Carlotta of his "hell of lonely longing" for her, and spoke of "the great rare joy your love has given me . . . only just now you seem so far away, so lost to me. If I could only kiss you again, Carlotta." Moreover, continuing his letter the following day, he made it plain that his and Carlotta's intimacy had progressed to the point where he felt compelled to tell Agnes at once about his newfound love. "It will be kinder to all in the end," he wrote, adding that he could not "live a lie." He could hear Carlotta's voice, he said, assuring him "everything will come out as we wish it."

Then, reverting to the ingrained helplessness he often affected with his women, he shifted the burden to her. What did she think he ought to do? "You have a much better head for this than I," he wrote, attempting to soften his effrontery with blandishment. "Try and tell me, Beloved One, whose heart is now my heart. . . . My love, I adore you! Do not forget me!"

O'Neill might not yet have realized it, but in Carlotta he had at long last found the mother substitute he'd been pining for, just as Carlotta was happy to avow, "This Lover of mine is also my child."

IT WOULD TAKE Carlotta a little more than a year to pry O'Neill away from Agnes, his children, and the Bermuda dream home he would never see completed.

As the rites of seduction go, that doesn't seem a long time, especially since, during much of that year, O'Neill was profoundly occupied with his triple-length *Strange Interlude*—another career milestone and one that was to bring him the greatest fame and fortune he'd yet experienced.

Between October 20, 1926, when he'd had his first acknowledged date with Carlotta, and February 10, 1928 (a year and four months later), when he and Carlotta eloped, O'Neill was in an erotic and creative turmoil that was vividly reflected in his "lady play."

He'd actually had the original idea for *Strange Interlude* as early as March 1925, even before completing *The Great God Brown*; but it wasn't until that September that he got around to writing a scenario, and it was not until May 1926 that he hit on the technique of spoken asides; "speech-thought method," he called it.

"I did most of a second scene two separate times and tore them up before I got started on the really right one!" O'Neill wrote to Macgowan three months later, on August 7, 1926. He added that there was going to be more work on *Strange Interlude* "than on any previous one—with no end to the going over & over it, before I'll be willing to call it done."

His work, he explained, was "much deeper and more complicated now" and he was less easily satisfied with what he used to dash off.

This new depth and complexity had coincided with the beginning of his dalliance with Carlotta, when he subtly began to incorporate her essence into the multifaceted character of Nina Leeds (along with the flock of lovers—not excluding Agnes—who'd previously roiled his life).

Macgowan, who was by now in O'Neill's confidence about the love affair, was perplexed upon receiving a letter from O'Neill two days after his return to Bermuda, in which he more or less avowed his hapless intention to hold on to both Agnes and Carlotta. In one breath, O'Neill affirmed his love for Agnes and his children, insisting that nothing could ever take their place; in the next, he spoke of his longing for Carlotta.

"Oh Christ," he agonized to Macgowan, "there are also other things— 'on the other side of the hills'—the curse of being an extremist is that every ideal remains single and alone, demanding all-or-nothing or destruction." Macgowan worried about the game his friend was playing.

In Bermuda, Agnes greeted O'Neill with the news that her father, Teddy, suffering from an advanced case of tuberculosis, was about to be confined to a sanatorium. Obliged to give Agnes some husbandly solace, he postponed the confession of his love for Carlotta. But he couldn't put her out of his mind, any more than he could stop thinking about *Strange Interlude*.

"With all that's inside me now I ought to be able to explode in that play in a regular blood-letting," he wrote to Macgowan on December 7. He enclosed a $25 check with his letter, asking his friend to send Carlotta a bouquet of roses attached to a note he was also enclosing "to get to her on Christmas a.m."

It wasn't long before O'Neill, despite Agnes's growing worry over her father, felt he could no longer keep his new love a secret. Confessing he'd fallen in love with Carlotta, he nevertheless swore he loved Agnes as well and promised he would never leave their marriage.

Metaphorically hopping from one foot to the other, he immediately reported this conversation with Agnes to Carlotta. Sounding a lot like the befuddled Dion Anthony of *The Great God Brown*, he said Agnes was "being very fine about it" and had even offered to set him free. Then, back on the other foot, he solemnly assured Agnes that he and Carlotta had not slept together.

So much for not being able to live a lie. (O'Neill took the precaution, a few months later, of warning Agnes to be on guard against malicious gossip about him and Carlotta from any putative friends; Agnes should, he said, "shut them up" at the first word; "After all, we've got to remember I'm in the 'show business' and a good subject to hang any rag of scandal upon.")

It's difficult to imagine what Agnes did believe. Dr. Hamilton would have recognized that O'Neill was "acting out," as he so often tended to do; he was watching himself play with fire, fascinated by his own daring. He tried to explain his bipolar tendencies to a none-too-pleased Carlotta:

"I have always been either hilariously shooting in on the crest of a wave or else bogged down up to my neck in a swamp. The dry, warm sure-footed ground was the one place where I was never taught to walk. So I finally escaped on to the plane of my work where I can always dance and drown and be reborn to dance and drown again. When work wouldn't come I had to escape via masks of solitude, alcoholic and otherwise, provided only they were excessive."

Agnes, thoroughly aware of O'Neill's weakness, tried to keep her balance. It helped that she could summon the memory of how O'Neill had dithered, years earlier, when faced with the choice of staying with her or resubmitting to the tempting Louise Bryant. As she had done at that time, Agnes evidently decided to wait him out.

Concurrently, a bemused Carlotta was wondering what she'd let herself in for; it looked as if the path to becoming Mrs. Eugene O'Neill was going to be a steep climb, and she communicated her distress to him.

After reading and rereading Carlotta's letters, O'Neill wrote to her at the end of December, expressing his acute distress at learning she was suffering over him. He said she had thrown him into "a terrible state of guilty conscience and self-loathing." He couldn't bear to think it was he who was causing her pain. She ought to put him out of her life—but he couldn't bear to lose her love.

O'Neill realized he was cornered, but he was unwilling to confess that what he really wanted was an extramarital love affair that he could turn on and off at his convenience. With a startling lack of guile, he had thought—after having candidly declared his love for both Carlotta and Agnes—that he had the situation under control. At the time, Carlotta—as fearful of losing O'Neill as he was of losing her—had meekly accepted his determination to stay married to Agnes; but, in fact, she had planned to wheedle him out of that decision.

It distressed O'Neill that Carlotta now appeared to be seeking a deeper commitment. Unwilling to confront the reason for her discontent, O'Neill once again tried to foist on her the responsibility of resolving his dilemma:

"What can I do? What must I do? Haven't you an answer, Dear One?"

Perhaps predictably, he pushed aside his personal quandary and prepared to throw himself back into his writing. To Macgowan, on December 30, he wrote, "I am intending to start work on *Strange Interlude* tomorrow . . . one year on the wagon, my boy! I am going to drink fifty lime squashes watching the new year in."

26

With Agnes waiting him out in Bermuda and Carlotta stewing in New York, it was going to take O'Neill more than lime squashes to sail unscathed through the squalls of 1927.

Launched on his second year of sobriety, he was wrestling with his need for both women while also attempting to portray that need through his Everywoman, Nina Leeds.

As he told Kenneth Macgowan in mid-January, he was "groaning in spirit and sweating blood" over his nine-act *Strange Interlude*. Throughout January and February, he wrote and revised, often working eleven hours at a stretch, taking breaks only for meals, a daily swim, and an occasional inspection of the slow-moving renovation of the house at Spithead.

O'Neill wrote only occasionally to his "Dearest Carlotta," and then it was about his play. When exhilarated by work that was going well, he existed in a world apart.

At such times, no one was real to him but the characters in the play he was writing. He expressed his absolute ruthlessness in a note for an autobiographical work labeled "Modern Faust Play" (never written), in which a terminally ill writer makes a bargain with "the spirit of God" to trade not only his fame and money, but the lives of his wife and children, for time to finish his life's work.

So wrapped up was O'Neill in *Interlude*, he barely registered Carlotta's news from New York that she was planning a trip to Europe from mid-June to early September. She evidently intended the trip to test the strength of O'Neill's attachment to her; perhaps she hoped that the threat of her extended absence would lure him back to New York in time to prevent her departure—and might even bring him around to committing himself to her.

But O'Neill, distanced from the spell of Carlotta's potent sexuality, did not take the bait. "God knows when we will see each other again!" he wrote to her. "Probably not until you return in the fall." He explained he was obliged to stay put in Bermuda for financial reasons. He sounded resigned: "I want you in my life," he wrote, "but I know I am losing you." He has loved her "deeply," he added, "but now Carlotta leaves me and becomes a dream."

O'Neill and Carlotta nonetheless continued to correspond. Still in New York that March, she welcomed the news that O'Neill had completed *Strange Interlude*. All his feelings about it now, he said, were confined to "deep joy that such a 'work' is out of my system. I'm exhausted and pining to rest." His face, he said, was "all caved in as if some vampire had been 'scoffing' my life up!"

What he didn't tell Carlotta was that his exhaustion arose partly from his effort to cope with a sulky, disconcerted Agnes; she had waited long enough for him to decide between her and Carlotta, and was pressuring him to resolve their triangular quandary. Although still vacillating, O'Neill helped Agnes move out of the cramped Spithead gatehouse in which they'd been living and into the main house. While there was as yet considerable renovation work in progress, the house was now livable and even comfortable enough to accommodate visitors.

Among their earliest was Eugene Jr., on his spring vacation. Now nearly seventeen, he was six feet tall and—to his father's delight—had developed an interest in Shakespeare. "I find him a son I can well take a paternal pride in," O'Neill wrote to Carlotta. "He is my sort."

Also visiting were James Light with his new wife, Patty; they had been invited to spend several weeks as a wedding present from O'Neill and Agnes. According to Patty, there was "a good deal of domestic tension" throughout their stay. Agnes was not even on hand to greet them when they arrived. O'Neill explained he and Agnes had quarreled and that Agnes had "gone off somewhere."

Other friends who visited also found the household in disarray. The writer Bessie Breuer recalled that Agnes "didn't seem able to cope with anything. She would have trouble even in finding a shoe." Unlike most of their friends, Breuer regarded O'Neill as a devoted parent. "Gene was in a dream most of the time," she insisted, and "that gave people the impression he may not have been paying attention to his children, but actually he was terribly attached to them."

Elizabeth Shepley Sergeant, who spent six weeks at Spithead during March and April, thought otherwise. "It seemed to me that Shane was neglected by both Gene and Agnes. Once I found Shane walking and shivering by himself near the water in the late afternoon. I took him into the house and asked him if he wanted me to read to him. He was delighted."

The O'Neills had invited Sergeant to Spithead to recuperate from injuries recently suffered in a traffic accident in New York. She had been on her way home from her publisher's office, after picking up an advance copy of her book *Fire Under the Andes* (a collection of profiles, including one about O'Neill called "Man with a Mask") when a truck crashed into her taxi.

Upon her arrival at Spithead, Sergeant was taken aback when Agnes told her O'Neill wouldn't allow liquor in the house because he wasn't drinking, but that Sergeant could have a private bottle of brandy to keep in her closet if she wished. Later in Sergeant's visit, Agnes confided she had fallen in love with O'Neill and married him because he was drunk all the time and needed her help. Agnes thought she was marrying a bohemian, she told Sergeant; she enjoyed going to cocktail parties, but Gene seldom wanted to, and so she sometimes went by herself.

It seemed to Sergeant that Agnes believed O'Neill was helplessly dependent on her. She had the impression, though, that "Gene was getting less dependent on her since he had given up drinking," and that Agnes "was foolishly overconfident of him."

THE THEATRE GUILD'S Lawrence Langner had heard rumors that O'Neill was at work on a highly original new play, and in early March 1927 he decided to combine a vacation in Bermuda with a business visit to the playwright. Their encounter would set O'Neill on a new professional course. Up to now, his relations with Langner had been no more cordial than with any other Broadway producer; the Guild, in fact, had been among the producers who had rejected several of O'Neill's earlier efforts, including *Anna Christie*, a decision Langner deeply regretted.

Most recently, the Guild had been halfheartedly negotiating for *Marco Millions*, but what Langner was really interested in was learning about O'Neill's new play in progress. Pretending an enthusiasm for *Marco*, Langner got in touch with O'Neill. He was not disappointed.

Although O'Neill listened somewhat skeptically to Langner's assurance that the Guild wanted to mount *Marco* in the coming season, he couldn't resist telling the producer all about *Strange Interlude*. Among the play's other innovations, he revealed that its characters would speak their private thoughts aloud. "The idea fascinated me," recalled Langner. O'Neill also mentioned that the play would take six hours to perform. Langner was undaunted, recalling his experience with Shaw's marathon *Back to Methuselah*. Langner asked if he might read the script.

"All night long I read and read," Langner remembered, "and at four o'clock in the morning, my eyes strained and throbbing, I finished the sixth act. I judged it one of the greatest plays of all time."

O'Neill informed Langner he had offered the role of Nina Leeds to the mighty Broadway leading lady Katharine Cornell, who was currently reading the script; if she agreed to play Nina, her husband, Guthrie McClintock, would direct and the choice of producer would be theirs. But if Cornell turned *Interlude* down, the Guild could produce it. (Cornell subsequently did turn it down.)

On the day following Langner's reading of the script, he was "all steamed up about it," as O'Neill reported to Macgowan. Not optimistic about Cornell, O'Neill told Macgowan he was hopeful Langner could communicate his enthusiasm to his Guild colleagues, for he was "in a bad way with no prospects."

Elizabeth Shepley Sergeant recalled that Langner, while assuring O'Neill he very much wanted to do the play, said he was certain it wouldn't run for more than a few weeks. Sergeant, who listened with interest to O'Neill and Langner's shop talk, said that Agnes at one point walked out, later telling Sergeant she "simply couldn't stand any more talk about the theater."

O'Neill originally had thought the nine acts of *Interlude* would have to be presented on two consecutive evenings, but Langner eventually convinced him that it could be performed in one evening if (like the Guild's production of *Back to Methuselah*) it began at 5:15 instead of 8. Including a seventy-five-minute dinner intermission, it would still end only a little past 11.

When Langner left Bermuda, O'Neill promised to send him the finished script as soon as he had edited it. Langner in turn promised O'Neill he would try to obtain a quick decision about a production date for *Marco Millions*.

In the end, though, O'Neill changed his mind about editing *Interlude*. When Sergeant left Bermuda on April 4, he entrusted the unedited script to her for delivery to the Guild. To Langner, he wrote that he was "too close" to the play to do a good job of editing: "I would have liked to let this play rest for a couple of months more at least and then go over it before submitting it to anyone, but as you told me you are now in the midst of plans for next season, I am taking a chance on its present form."

Soon after, Langner reported to O'Neill that the first reaction of the Theatre Guild board was "favorable." He didn't mention that not all board members shared his own enthusiasm; one thought the play would be greatly improved if all the asides were deleted, and others felt it needed serious cutting.

On April 21, Langner wrote his board "a stinging letter," as he put it, pointing out that in *Interlude* the Guild probably had "the bravest and most far-reaching dramatic experiment which has been seen in the theater since the days of Ibsen. If we fail to do this great experiment, if we lack the courage and the vision, then we should forever hang our heads in shame."

WHILE LANGNER WAS extolling O'Neill for his daring and assurance as an artist, O'Neill was berating himself as a man too timid and perplexed to make a choice between wife and mistress.

A week earlier, O'Neill had had a nervous collapse after Agnes hurriedly left Bermuda to be at the bedside of her father, now dying of tuberculosis. (Teddy Boulton was confined at the Laurel Heights Sanatorium in Shelton, Connecticut, on the site of the TB hospital where O'Neill briefly had been a patient in 1912.)

"God how I miss you!" O'Neill wrote to Agnes, immediately after seeing her off on the steamer. "I actually broke down on the bed in our room in a fit of hysterical crying." Admitting the absurdity of his outburst, knowing Agnes was to be gone only a week, he confessed to having lost his "whole control"; his "inner being" was "in pretty shattered shape." He needed her more intensely, he said, than ever before in their married life.

O'Neill had told Agnes, just before she left, that he was no longer in love with Carlotta. Perhaps, as he'd recently told Carlotta, he'd persuaded himself that she truly had become a dream. More likely, he simply hadn't the energy to disrupt his life. Although tempted by Carlotta's overpowering sexual allure, he was unsure if he could meet her deepening demands as a lover, nor could he any longer delude himself that she would agree to be merely his mistress.

Tempestuous as his life was with Agnes, he was used to her, and he did depend on her. And he could always count on her forgiveness when he misbehaved. Going to bed with the bewitching Carlotta was exhilarating, but courting her took an effort he preferred to devote to his writing.

Had Carlotta been privy to the contents of O'Neill's lovesick letter to Agnes, she might well have lost hope of ever capturing O'Neill. As it was, she was growing disillusioned with his dithering. She vented her frustration in a letter to her childhood friend Gene McComas in California.

She was weary of being "crucified again & again," she wrote, and she deplored the injustice of being "game"; peevishly she added that "some natures get their greatest strength & *self confidence* in watching us *wriggle!*" Renouncing marriage, she declared she wanted "no more the responsibility of the home." But did she mean a word of it?

While Carlotta steamed, Agnes rejoiced. In a second letter to her, O'Neill reiterated his devotion. "For over nine years I have loved you and you alone, loved you with my whole being, without reservation given you my life." He wrote of his love for Spithead, "indissolubly intermingled with my love for you," describing it as their "haven," where they would live their "dreams with a sense of permanence and security that here we do belong."

He went so far as to describe his affair with Carlotta as "an outcrop of childish vanity"; he had never been in love with her, he insisted. "One hair of your head is more to me than the whole body and soul, liver and lights, of any other woman. If I lost your love, I'd go mad with grief!"

Abruptly, he mocked himself as "a virginal Casanova," adding with a sudden flash of acute self-knowledge, "It is an awfully adolescent, undeveloped nakedness I am revealing to you!" He wished her now to laugh at his former infatuation with Carlotta and to see it clearly for what it was.

"Was!" he stressed. "'Dead for a Ducat, dead!' as Hamlet says."

He needn't have doubted Agnes's empathy; even before receiving his letter aboard ship en route to New York, she wrote to him tenderly, assuring him "it was awful, seeing you fade out—waving." But although she missed him, she thought perhaps she might benefit from the time their separation would give her for "some amount of introspection." Still, she wished he was there with her, "so I could tell you how much I love you!"

After a two-day visit with her father at the sanatorium, Agnes checked into the Wentworth in New York, where she attended to various errands for O'Neill. She learned there had been no offers to buy Brook Farm; she met with Lawrence Langner, who said the Theatre Guild would soon have a decision about *Strange Interlude*, and suggested that O'Neill come to New York for a face-to-face meeting with the Guild's board; and, carrying out one rather peculiar commission from her husband, she arranged to meet with the astrologist Evangeline Adams, whose clients included J. P. Morgan and Enrico Caruso, and whose specialty was the prediction of financial trends.

"Adams says 'liquidate,'" Agnes solemnly reported back to O'Neill, "get all overhead expenses cut down, predicts bad financial slump for next year for the U.S.A. Your financial status will pick up about October."

Agnes then cabled O'Neill (on April 2) to say she needed to delay her return to Bermuda for another week, to help straighten out a crisis within her family.

O'Neill's response was stony.

He was in bed with "a rotten sore throat," he wrote back. He'd been "counting the days" for Agnes's return to Bermuda; he was dejected about the apparent unsalability of Brook Farm, "and financial worry in general"; he wailed that their "tough luck would never break" and that they were "heading for a most frightful cropper" unless something turned up soon.

And why did she have to involve herself in her family's problems, he scolded, warning her not to commit him to any monetary aid beyond what he was already doing for her father in his illness. If they needed money, they should sell their house in West Point Pleasant, New Jersey: "My foot is down . . . in self-preservation. I'm doing all I can or will do."

Moreover, O'Neill went on, Agnes's absence had completely disrupted his life, he hadn't written a line, and saw no hope of doing so until she came home and life got back to normal.

THE DAY BEFORE Agnes returned to Bermuda, O'Neill received a cable from Langner saying the Guild wanted to option *Strange Interlude*. This longed-for news did little to lighten his gloom. Upon Agnes's arrival on April 26, O'Neill listened impatiently as she reported her conversations with Langner (of considerably more interest to him than her family's problems). Then, peremptorily, he declined the proffered option, insisting on a definite commitment.

As he was pressed for cash, he informed Langner, he would have to offer the play elsewhere if the Guild would not commit to producing it during the coming season. He was concerned that with too long a delay, the play's methodology (its use of asides) would "leak out" and another playwright might copy the technique before *Interlude* opened.

Sympathetic to all of O'Neill's concerns, Langner invited him to come to New York to stay with him and his wife, Armina Marshall (also a member of the Theatre Guild's board), while discussing the details of a production.

When O'Neill sailed from Bermuda on May 14 (which happened to be Oona's second birthday), he was aware that Carlotta had not yet left for Europe. His most recent letter to her, in late March, had been cool and chatty, with scarcely a word of endearment, seeming to underline his intention of dropping the affair. To Agnes, as he was approaching New York on his second day at sea, he wrote, "You can absolutely trust me to keep my word to you. So don't worry, Dearest! I love you and I don't love anyone else and that's all there is to it."

Once again, however, no sooner had O'Neill unpacked his suitcase at the Langners' home in Greenwich Village on May 16 than he sought out

Carlotta. And, day by day, he contrived to meet her for lunch or tea and—when not obliged to dine at the Langners'—for dinner as well.

On May 23, the day before O'Neill was to return to Bermuda, Langner invited Theresa Helburn, one of the Theatre Guild's founders, to meet O'Neill at dinner. It turned out to be the day Lindbergh landed his single-engine monoplane at Le Bourget, and discussion about production plans for O'Neill's plays was swept aside. Instead, the talk, as Helburn recalled, centered on "what lay behind the apparent simplicity of that amazing flight, behind its clean-cut success, its almost poetic precision."

As O'Neill offered his thoughts, Helburn was struck by his empathy for Lindbergh's feat: "I can imagine no one more sensitive to all its implications than O'Neill with his sense of the romantic and the dramatic, with his memories of lonely nights at sea. . . . I have often thought that Gene is a good deal of a lone eagle in his chosen field—daring new and, God knows, long enough flights on his dramatic Pegasus."

Although O'Neill spent at least part of his final three days in New York with Carlotta, her sorcery was not yet potent enough to pin him down. He sailed back to Agnes on May 24, and Carlotta, momentarily thwarted, sailed for Europe.

27

After revising *Strange Interlude* in Bermuda during June and most of July (1927), O'Neill was ready to pronounce it "finally finished." But the play's completion on July 25 did not relieve his malaise.

"I have been in a strange disorganized state," he wrote to Carlotta, who was still abroad, "where it seemed as if it were impossible to concentrate on a single thing outside of my writing." He had labored on *Strange Interlude* "with a sort of feverish intensity," he said, "as if that were the anodyne for all the instability and drab insecurity of the reality of my everyday existence." He had been betrayed "even by the sea," he lamented. "It is such a tepid, lukewarm ocean now, there is no life or sting to it."

Part of his unease might have been attributed to the approach of his thirty-ninth birthday—and the more significant hovering of his fortieth. He tried to keep from weighing his nine-year marriage to Agnes against his adulterous affair with Carlotta. If he had been backed into a corner like this in days gone by, he likely would have escaped into a drinking binge. Now, determined to stay sober, he felt forced to take stock of his life.

Inevitably, O'Neill saw his personal dilemma in terms of stage drama. Among the ideas and outlines for new works noted in his diary before he left Bermuda for New York in late August, two were particularly germane to his present quandary.

The most grandiloquent of these projects, entitled *The Sea-Mother's Son*, aspired to be the odyssey of a man of forty—O'Neill's own looming age—lying on his deathbed and confronting his life's story, beginning with his childhood. It was, in his own words, "based on autobiographical material." O'Neill envisioned it as "the Big Grand Opus" of his career. In form, the "Opus" was neither a novel nor a traditional play; but it would, he believed, have "greater scope than any novel." In fact, it would dwarf *Strange Interlude*, making that novel-play seem "a mere shallow episode!" If he could shape the idea into what he pictured, he told Macgowan, "it will make a work that I flatter myself will be one of those timeless Big Things." His somewhat sententious subtitle was to be *The Story of the Birth of a Soul* and, he said, "it will be just that."

Expanding on the summary of the plot in his Work Diary, O'Neill reemphasizes the play's autobiographical derivation, and describes his protagonist, at play's end, as able to accept the suffering he has endured, to conquer his death wish, to "say yes to his life," and—in O'Neill's own phantasmagorical rhetoric—to "give up the comfort of the return to Mother Death."

It's plain that Ella O'Neill haunts the Opus. (As O'Neill once wrote to Carlotta, "The sea is a woman to me . . . pagan and physically exultant.") As always, that oceanic female entity nibbles at O'Neill's conscious and unconscious mind. She was the seductive, capricious mother who had tried to abort him, who—when poisoned by morphine—blamed him for her drug addiction and told him he should never have been born.

The Sea-Mother's Son was never written as such, but a similar concept eventually would emerge—a soaring, all-encompassing novelistic panorama, inspired by his family history, which, by 1939, would grow into a projected eleven-play cycle with the panoptic title *A Tale of Possessors Self-Dispossessed*.

Partly responsible for stirring up O'Neill's intense introspection during that steamy Bermuda summer were his recent sessions with Dr. Hamilton. During his analysis, O'Neill had written an 858-word fragment detailing his parents' incompatibilities and their attitudes toward him as a child. This document—an expansion of the self-analytical diagram of his psychological history that he drew for Hamilton—may be read as a partial blueprint not only for *The Sea-Mother's Son*, but also for the far-off autobiographical *Long Day's Journey Into Night*.

Crammed onto a single page, the document ruthlessly strips away, layer by layer, all the anguished stages of O'Neill's journey into night.

Describing his mother as "spoiled before marriage," O'Neill takes note of her "lonely life after marriage." He tells of the devastating death of her infant son, Edmund, and her guilty vow never to have another child, which led her—a pious Catholic woman—to submit to a "series of brought-on abortions." And he asks, "Did this mark beginning of [her] break with religion, which was to leave her eventually entirely without solace?"

While her wish to have no more children was thwarted by the unwanted birth of Eugene—and despite her growing dependence on the morphine initially prescribed for her postpartum pain—she focused a "fierce concentration of affection" on him and he was "spoiled from birth." According to O'Neill, this affection "must have been further intensified by the fact that at age of 2 he nearly dies from typhoid."

Startling as is the document's reference to Ella's abortions, its concluding revelation—concerning Ella's relationship with Eugene's nursemaid—is almost equally bizarre; according to O'Neill, the nursemaid became her "companion in beer & stout drinking" and, after Eugene was sent to boarding school, "in whiskey drinking & probably messenger for obtaining drugs(?)"

O'Neill also lists the traits Ella found most upsetting in her husband: his parsimony "due to his childhood experience with grinding poverty"; his refusal to provide her with a proper home, and his "dependence on barroom companionship."

THE SECOND PLAY IDEA that tugged at O'Neill while he sweated out his enforced final August at Spithead was titled *Without Endings of Days*. Plainly spurred by guilt toward Agnes, it symbolically probed the anguish of a religious man's adultery.

The play's unnamed protagonist has been having an extramarital affair, and when his wife dies, "All his sins against her of omission & commission come back on him," writes O'Neill. He feels he has unfairly misunderstood her, that "he must confess, that he has sinned," and he craves absolution from the Church.

WHILE THE PLAY'S THEME is tied to O'Neill's earthbound dilemma, it also reflects the spiritual confusion that has recently reentered his consciousness.

The play's protagonist, like O'Neill, is a man who is constantly fighting against the tug of his early Catholic indoctrination—a man hounded by his half longing to return to his childhood belief in immortality, and his fear of one day being seduced into turning back to the Church for solace.

O'Neill, in the play, vicariously projects the struggle going on in his own mind. His protagonist, guided to a church, kneels before the cross, where "his intellect and emotions fight." Eager to confess, he approaches a priest, who asks if he is a Catholic, and he responds, "I am—was—am—was."

Then, stepping toward the confession box, he whips out a revolver and shoots himself. As he is dying, the priest gives him the last sacrament, asking, "Do you believe?" To which the joyful answer is "Yes, I believe," and the priest gives him absolution. But even then, "with a last sardonic defiance," the nameless protagonist asserts, "All the same, I don't believe." (Six years later, O'Neill would continue his argument with himself when he revised *Without Endings of Days* as *Days Without End*.)

O'NEILL HAD NEVER made a secret of his repudiation of Church doctrine. He could trace his loss of faith to the events of a summer night in New London twenty-five years earlier—the night that sparked the battle with God that led to his apostasy. It was the time when Eugene, not yet fifteen, finally confronted the truth of his mother's withering illness.

TOP LEFT: First among the women who possessed him: Ella Quinlan O'Neill, the mother who wished Eugene unborn

TOP RIGHT: Kathleen Jenkins, the naive twenty-year-old who bore O'Neill an unwanted son

LEFT: Louise Bryant, the free spirit who abandoned O'Neill to join John Reed in Russia while he gathered material for *Ten Days that Shook the World*

BOTTOM: Agnes Boulton, the Bohemian lover O'Neill married on the rebound

Scene from *Strange Interlude*, starring Lynn Fontanne and Glen Anders

O'Neill and Carlotta posed for a portrait before leaving for France. As agreed, the photographer, Ben Pinchot, did not release it to the public until O'Neill informed him the couple were now legally wed.

Carlotta-nee-Hazel, age twenty-one, in London

Hazel with her first husband, the wealthy,
aristocratic Scotsman John Moffat

The former Hazel, soon after she launched
her stage career as Carlotta Monterey

Carlotta with her third husband, Ralph Barton, in the spring of 1925,
inscribed "Ralph, me, the Captain of the 'Paris'"

Carlotta and O'Neill in
Cap d'Ail while awaiting
Agnes's divorce

Le Plessis, the castle rented by O'Neill and Carlotta in Tours, France,
where O'Neill—reveling in his new love—labored over his most
ambitious play to date, *Mourning Becomes Electra*

The abandoned family together for the last time: O'Neill, Agnes, Oona, and Shane in Bermuda

The Provincetown Playhouse
in Greenwich Village

John Reed, the celebrity
journalist who was O'Neill's
friend and rival for the
duplicitous Louise Bryant

O'Neill in a rare moment of
playfulness with Shane—

—and with Oona

Carlotta in Maine
during the fateful
summer of 1926

Bermuda house O'Neill and Agnes bought in 1926, intending to remodel it as their permanent home

LEFT: O'Neill practicing his favorite sport in Bermuda

BELOW: Always at home on the water, O'Neill was never truly at peace away from the ocean

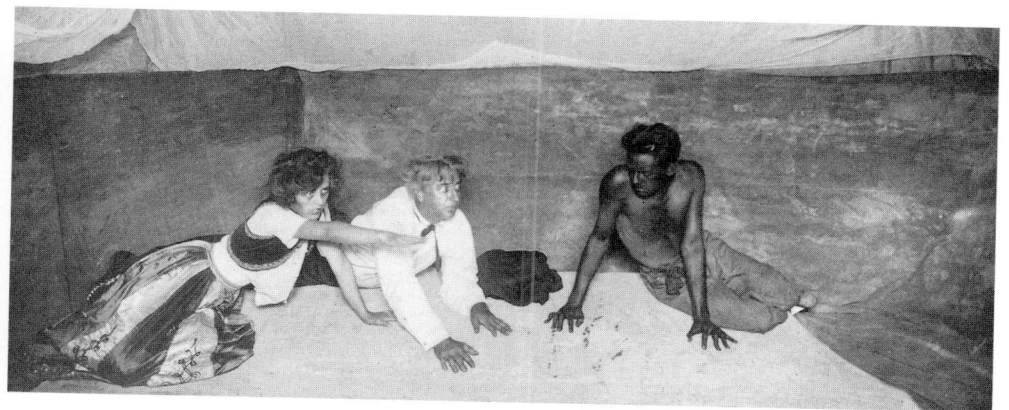

TOP: A production at Provincetown's Wharf Theater of O'Neill's 1916 one-acter, *Thirst*, performed by Louise Bryant, Jig Cook, and O'Neill

ABOVE: A scene from O'Neill's first Broadway production, *Beyond the Horizon*, which won the recently established Pulitzer Prize—his first of four

LEFT: A scene from *Desire Under the Elms*, produced in 1924—a major play written during O'Neill's marriage to Agnes

Charles Gilpin as
The Emperor Jones,
1920

Pauline Lord and
George Marion in
Anna Christie, 1921

LEFT: Eugene, age four, with his first pet

ABOVE: The O'Neills' summer home in New London known as Monte Cristo Cottage, after James O'Neill's most famous role; it became the setting for *Long Day's Journey Into Night*

Eugene, sketching ships and gulls on the grounds of Monte Cristo Cottage, overlooking New London's Thames River, and described by O'Neill as "probably taken in 1893 or '94"

The clipper ship *Charles Racine*, the setting for O'Neill's early sea plays

O'Neill as a proud, salt-of-the-earth sailor

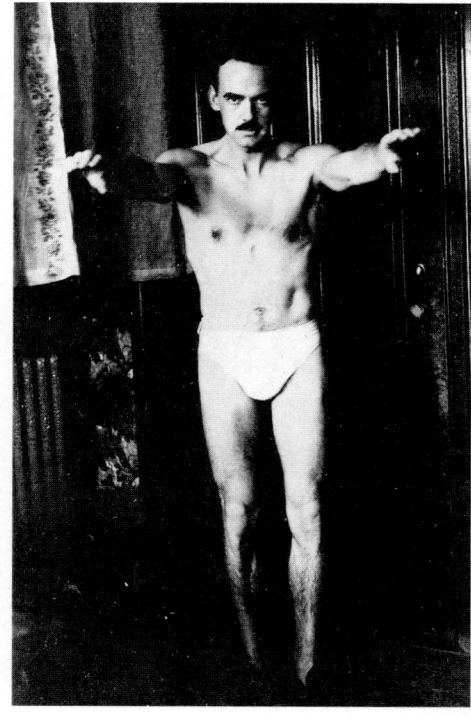

Snapshot taken by a Harvard friend, c. 1914.

James O'Neill as a
successful young actor
and newly married man

Ella Quinlan O'Neill—who
shunned photographers—
posed for this rare photo as
a new wife

An iconic snapshot (from left to right) of Eugene, Jamie, and
James on the front porch of the Monte Cristo Cottage

O'Neill on the terrace
of Tao House with his
beloved Blemie

A.

B.

C.

O'Neill owned numerous other pets over the years:
A. with Ben Lomond at Le Plessis;
B. with Shane and nameless dog in Bermuda;
C. with Carlotta and cat at Le Plessis;
D. with pet Brahma chicken at Le Plessis

D.

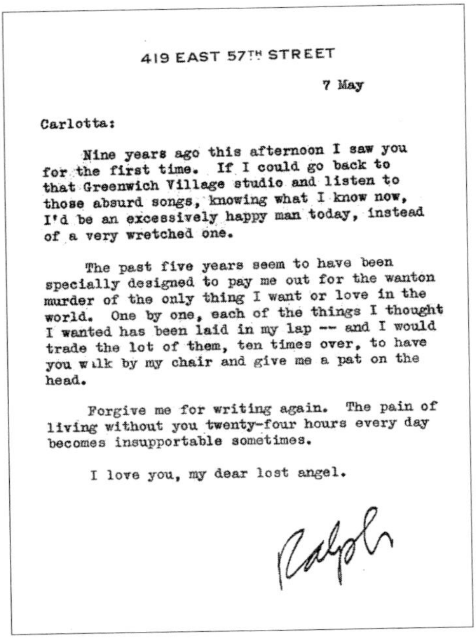

419 EAST 57TH STREET

7 May

Carlotta:

Nine years ago this afternoon I saw you for the first time. If I could go back to that Greenwich Village studio and listen to those absurd songs, knowing what I know now, I'd be an excessively happy man today, instead of a very wretched one.

The past five years seem to have been specially designed to pay me out for the wanton murder of the only thing I want or love in the world. One by one, each of the things I thought I wanted has been laid in my lap -- and I would trade the lot of them, ten times over, to have you walk by my chair and give me a pat on the head.

Forgive me for writing again. The pain of living without you twenty-four hours every day becomes insupportable sometimes.

I love you, my dear lost angel.

Ralph

"I love you, my dear lost angel."
Ralph Barton's suicide note to his
divorced wife, Carlotta

Nazimova and Alice Brady as mother
and daughter rivals-to-the-death in
Mourning Becomes Electra

Scene from *Ah, Wilderness*, O'Neill's only comedy (George M. Cohan in bathrobe)

Exterior view of O'Neill's study at Casa Genotta. The windows faced out to sea, Carlotta said, "suggesting the prow of one of O'Neill's beloved galleons."

Carlotta relaxing in the garden at Casa Genotta

Tao House, where the O'Neills planned to live out their final years—
until World War II disrupted their lives

O'Neill's study in Tao House (and doorway to adjoining bedroom). It was here that he wrote *The Iceman Cometh* and *Long Day's Journey into Night*.

ABOVE: O'Neill and members of the Theater Guild on first day of rehearsals for *The Iceman Cometh*. Seated on the stage of the Martin Beck Theater, from left: Shirlee Lantz, Lawrence Langner, Theresa Helburn, Armina Marshal, O'Neill, Eddie Dowling, and Joe Heidt (standing).

RIGHT: Carlotta and O'Neill at a rehearsal of *Iceman*

BELOW: Scene from the production of *Iceman*

View of the Atlantic from porch of the O'Neills' Marblehead cottage

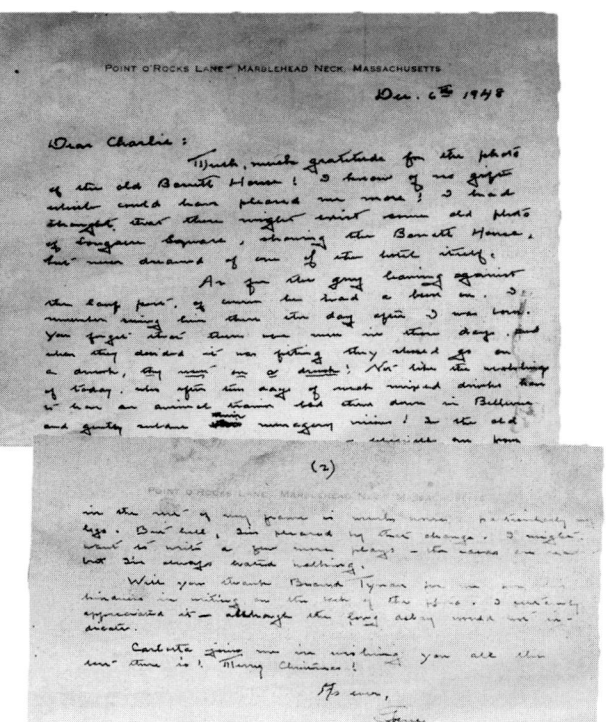

O'Neill's deteriorating
handwriting in a 1948 letter
to an old friend

Eugene O'Neill Jr.,
age twenty-one

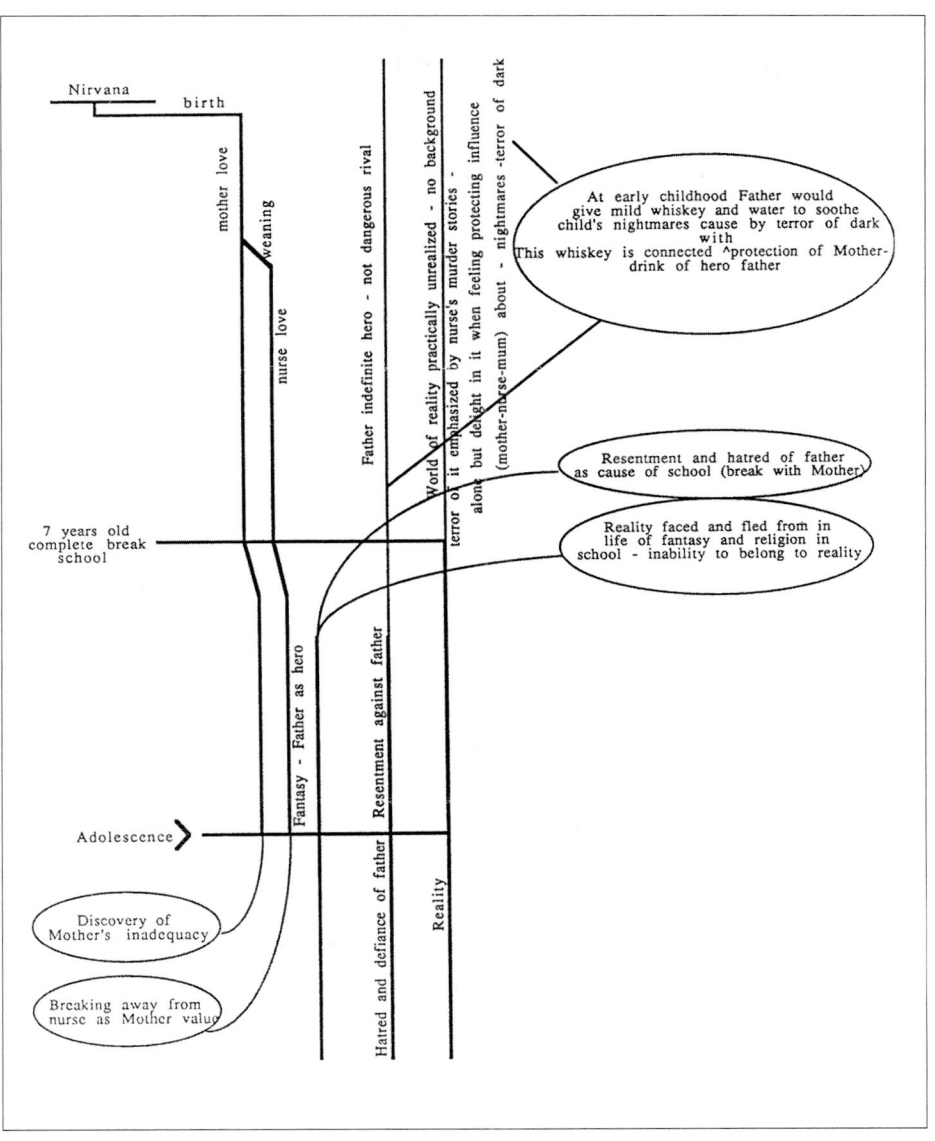

Self-analytical diagram by O'Neill made during psychoanalysis,
summing up his family's dysfunctional history

O'Neill's grave

Ella O'Neill, dressed for bed and craving a fix, discovered she'd let herself run out of morphine. In a panic she rushed from the house in her nightgown, determined to throw herself into the Thames River from the family dock that fronted the O'Neill cottage. It's unclear who stopped her and brought her back to the house; but there was no way that the disturbance could be concealed from Eugene, and it was then that his father and older brother told him the truth.

REFERRING TO THE EPISODE in *Long Day's Journey Into Night*, O'Neill has his alter ego, Edmund Tyrone, say, "It was right after that Papa and Jamie decided they couldn't hide it from me any more."

It was a dreadful shock to Eugene, although, with hindsight, an episode three months earlier might have prepared him; that was when he'd accidentally walked in on his mother in the family's rented apartment off Central Park West in New York, just as she was giving herself an injection. Eugene, bewildered by her fury at being discovered, had questioned his father and brother, but they'd brushed aside his concern, believing him too young to be told the truth.

By the time the full implication of his mother's illness sank in, and his repeated prayers for her recovery went unanswered, Eugene had lost his faith. Determined to stop attending church, he braced himself one Sunday morning for the inevitable confrontation with his father, with whom he ritually attended Mass.

When James saw Eugene descending the stairs from his bedroom in their New London home, he told him to get ready to accompany him. Eugene stopped where he was and told his father of his decision. James started up the stairs, shouting angrily and grabbing his son by the shoulders, and attempted to shake him into submission.

With Eugene trying to twist out of his father's grip, the two lurched to the bottom of the stairs, where they paused, out of breath, glaring at each other. James was rigid with fury but Eugene held his ground and James stomped off to church alone. Ella had long since given up attending church and her plea to her son to reconsider was no more effective than James's. Eugene argued that religion had proved of little service to them, why impose it on him?

DURING THAT STEAMY Bermuda summer of 1927, Agnes somehow managed to take a clinical view of O'Neill's suffering. She was grateful that at least he was showing no sign of backsliding into alcoholic oblivion, and she finally decided, at the end of August, that the best way to cope with his fretfulness was to send him off at once to New York rather than await the expected summons from the Theatre Guild in early fall. He could get himself organized there, she told him, and be on hand whenever the Guild was ready for him. He could also avail himself of the specialized medical checkups he required for the lingering aftereffects of the flu that had recently plagued him.

She vetoed O'Neill's suggestion that they open Brook Farm so that he would have a place near the city to escape to when needed, a space for the whole family once she and the children joined him. Agnes argued that it would be impossible: the house was almost stripped of furniture, she said, and it would be too expensive and impractical to move the family there, especially since a buyer might turn up at any time and wish to occupy the place.

Agnes was aware that Carlotta was due back from Europe in early September, but she had brought herself to accept her husband's repeated assurances that the affair was over; he promised that if he happened to run into Carlotta, it would be as a friend only (and perhaps he'd actually managed to talk himself into believing that).

Almost as if to convince himself (let alone Agnes) that he no longer needed Carlotta, on the night before his departure, O'Neill made ardent love to his wife. Under brilliant starlight, they frolicked passionately in a steamer chair on the stone plaza fronting the house.

Although Agnes was reassured, her trust in her husband was misplaced; his lovemaking under the stars proved to be no more than a ruse to secure her continued devotion. He had never ceased to hunger for the irresistible Carlotta and he fully intended to renew his affair with her upon her arrival home on September 9. As for Carlotta, like a cat watching a mouse hole, she was ready to pounce.

On August 29, O'Neill once again took up residence at the Wentworth. He was now swimming the existential race of his life, with only the most confused notion of where (or indeed if) he would be flung ashore.

His somewhat haphazard jaunt to New York did not begin propitiously. The city in those days virtually emptied during the hot summer months. Langner was on vacation and Theresa Helburn, the only other Guild director still in town, was ill. With eleven days before Carlotta's return from Europe, O'Neill cast about for some sort of diversion. But all his friends were away and those with country houses were entertaining guests and had no room for him.

Very much at loose ends, and overwhelmed by self-pity, O'Neill turned on his usual scapegoat. He wrote to Agnes, berating her for having "acted wrongly" in refusing to move into Brook Farm. "It is not good for me to be lonely and homeless under the most unfortunate conditions when I'm sick in the bargain," he scolded, presumably laying the groundwork for the self-justifying defense he'd need when he resumed his affair with Carlotta.

"You have thought of yourself and the inconvenience that moving the kids would cause you," he insisted, "but you have not considered me or my work—or even my health; and I tell you again it is not fair!"

Not bothering to veil his threat, he warned Agnes that leaving him homeless was "dangerous" for their future. "By the time rehearsals start, I ought to be a fine morbid wreck." He couldn't resist a meanly sneering postscript: "The alcoholic days were much pleasanter!"

All too familiar with her husband's posturing, Agnes allowed his epistolary spite to glide by. She was relieved when O'Neill shifted his fury to the Theatre Guild after Theresa Helburn, on September 2, informed him *Marco Millions* could not be produced until January and that *Strange Interlude* (if indeed the Guild ultimately committed to producing it) would also have to wait for a January opening.

Just as in the bad old days, O'Neill found himself waiting on a producer's whim. Moreover, without the prospect of an imminent production, he would have no excuse to dally in New York with Carlotta. Still, on September 8, with Carlotta expected back the next day, he wrote Agnes without apparent qualm that he was "longing most damnably" for the time when his "Own Little Wife" would be in his arms again and advised her not to "worry about anything!"

It was, however, Carlotta's arms that held him the following day. And it took her only three days to all but persuade him that it was she and not Agnes for whom he had been "longing most damnably" and whom he could not live without.

The ensuing seven-page letter he sent to Agnes was a lordly mélange of guilty dissemblance and self-justifying anger (not to mention literary posturing). His letter veered from wild accusation to professions of tenderness and back again.

He was writing to her, he said, while sitting alone in his stuffy hotel room, "looking out over the dirty, smelly, roofs and streets, feeling low and sick and depressed and lonely." Then—oh so casually—he mentioned he'd had lunch with Carlotta and remarked that Baden-Baden had done her a lot of good "in appearance and nerves."

Shamelessly fishing for sympathy, he told his "Dearest Aggie" that Carlotta had noticed how thin and ill he looked, adding, "She's quite right." Abruptly, he demanded to know why this was all happening to him, and what he had done to Agnes that he should be treated this way.

Then, summoning the trusty device of accusing the injured party of one's own misdeeds, he charged Agnes with having a lover. That, he snapped, would explain why she'd deliberately left him alone in New York. She didn't care what he did.

"Do you want me to love someone else?" he demanded. "What sort of game is this you're playing, Agnes?" Picking up steam, he launched into a madman's soliloquy:

"Either I'm crazy, or you are! Probably I am, anyway." He fervently wished he "could escape from this obscene and snaily creeping tedium of dull days, and empty hours like nervous yawns, into some madness—of love or lust or drink or anything else!"

He said he was "beginning to crack," and then softened his tone: "Oh well, I suppose it isn't as desperate as it feels now"—after which he offered a blatantly false "synopsis of this long story." He said he was not well, he was lonely, he loved her. "That's the whole case in a nutshell," he ended, signing himself "Your Gene."

Letters between New York and Bermuda took their time, for the boat that carried them sailed only twice a week. Before receiving O'Neill's rant, Agnes, in a loving letter, had encouraged him "to try & get some sort of enjoyment out of life that will compensate for drinking," hastily adding, "This does not mean I am trying to force you into a love affair!" (It is to be hoped that O'Neill, on receiving this letter, had the grace to blush.)

When Agnes eventually received that unhinged seven-page missive, she swiftly fought back. He certainly must realize, she said, that the idea of her having a lover was "from any angle absurd." Who could he possibly suspect? "God damn it," she fumed, "if you knew how damned bored and lonely I was here—never mind, I think I'll pack up & arrive in New York, kids & all—then we'll see how that will work."

As for his threat of taking to drink or a love affair, Agnes smugly responded, "Well, do it. (Love not drink)." She seemed unperturbed by Carlotta's reentry into her husband's life; either she chose to believe his relationship with Carlotta actually was platonic—as O'Neill kept insisting—or perhaps she was thinking a fling with Carlotta would once and for all get her out of his system.

She shifted to a subject O'Neill had become expert at dodging—her lack of cash for household expenses and for ongoing repairs to Spithead.

Work had stopped, she said, and she was no longer interested in doing anything about their dream house. She was tired of hearing again "the old mistrust" and almost wished there was "an interesting man around somewhere." Didn't he realize that letters like his were enough to make a woman go out looking for a lover? "Damn you anyhow Gene—something must be all wrong for you to say such things."

She was glad, she concluded, that "Carlotta's nerves are gone. Do you think she would be interested in taking charge of Spithead? If so, tell her I've given up the job." There was pathos in her afterthought: Carlotta, she wrote, "is certainly much more beautiful than I am."

It's conceivable that rumors had reached O'Neill of an affair between Agnes and John Johnston, the head carpenter on the Spithead renovations. He was a married man, six feet two, blond, blue-eyed, the son of a white father and black mother. This putative affair was recorded by a later owner of Spithead, Joy Bluck Waters, who published what she described as a "glimpse of the lives" of the O'Neill family in Bermuda; she recorded the gossip about Agnes's involvement with Johnston—gossip, she said, that had circulated for years among island contemporaries of the O'Neills.

One of the rumors concerning the O'Neills (still according to Joy Bluck Waters) was that their housekeeper, Gaga, had begun to spy on Agnes and had reported to O'Neill (presumably by letter) that Agnes was romantically involved with Johnston.

Agnes was enraged, wrote Waters, when O'Neill passed on Gaga's suspicions, and immediately fired her, putting her on the next boat out of Bermuda. The truth of this rumor is at least partly supported by a letter from O'Neill to Agnes when, six months later, he learned of Gaga's dismissal and of Agnes's refusal, despite Gaga's apologies and pleas, to take her back.

"God damn it, Agnes, whatever her faults, we've both loved her, our children have loved her, and she's loved all of us, and stuck to us since Shane was born." He scolded Agnes for holding against Gaga what he termed her "idiotic" gossiping, thus "wounding an old woman who has been a good friend to us, if there ever was one."

Gossip or not, it would hardly have been surprising if Agnes had indeed succumbed to the handsome Spithead carpenter. During the Bermudian summer, with its thinned population, Agnes had little if any congenial companionship. O'Neill had left her alone in Bermuda with insufficient cash, expecting her to cajole Johnston and his helpers into continuing the major repairs to their too-large, too-expensive home. O'Neill also had burdened her with the sole responsibility for their children and household staff. Agnes surely couldn't help but envy her husband's busy creative life away from her (no matter how bleakly he described his existence).

On September 16, 1927, O'Neill at last received definite word that the Guild would produce *Strange Interlude*—but not until late January, following the opening of *Marco Millions* on January 9. While he had contrived to stretch out his stay in New York, he knew Agnes would now expect him to return to Bermuda and stay there with her until he was needed for rehearsals in mid-November. Hastily forestalling her threat to join him in New York with their children, he promised he would return to Bermuda soon.

It was Agnes herself who inadvertently provided a reprieve when she suggested he pay a second visit to the astrologist Evangeline Adams. He did so, and Adams warned him not to embark for Bermuda before his birthday on October 16, enabling him to celebrate the occasion with Carlotta.

As it happened, Carlotta had just about convinced him to leave his marriage, and he was almost ready to abandon his double game.

28

By early winter of 1927, O'Neill and Carlotta were no longer concealing their love affair from close friends. Lawrence Langner, for one, knew they were seeing each other daily.

"He told me he had fallen in love with her," Langner recalled. "He said one reason he got on so well with her was that she was such a good manager; she arranged for railroad tickets, and so forth. Agnes could seldom plan ahead; she was easygoing and helpless, and needed to be looked after by him. But it wasn't until later that year, in November or December during rehearsals of *Marco Millions* and *Strange Interlude*, that he talked to me about divorcing Agnes."

O'Neill and Carlotta had begun plotting their secret getaway while celebrating O'Neill's thirty-ninth birthday on October 16. Their long-range plan was to sail for Europe on February 10, eleven days after the opening of *Strange Interlude*; they agreed that for their plan to succeed, Agnes had to be kept in the dark. Savoring victory, Carlotta cautioned O'Neill not to "shoot the works" when he returned to Bermuda on October 19.

Within a few days of rejoining his family, O'Neill wrote to Carlotta, assuring her he had said "nothing at all" to Agnes. The next four weeks in the Spithead household throbbed with tension. Agnes, still sharing her husband's bed, was unaware of the depth of his perfidy. She felt oppressed, however, by his emotional distance; ironically, after having helped him to sobriety, she herself now began to seek solace in alcohol.

To her terminally ill father, she divulged two terrifying hallucinatory episodes. "I was wide awake, couldn't sleep," she wrote to him,

> when *something* came into the room. I cannot describe it, as it had no form, was more like a *force*; but I had a terrible feeling of horror, as though it was something evil. It came up close by the bed, and I cannot say that it *touched* me, as it had no hands or form, but it seemed somehow to come in contact with me, and I was unable to move or speak, though I could see everything in the room quite clearly.
>
> Then, two nights later the same thing happened. I seemed to be in a trance, felt this formless thing, when suddenly a little wizened, naked baby appeared and began to nurse! You can imagine how I felt! The poor child seemed to be starving; well I made a final effort and sat up in bed, and it disappeared.

She had never before experienced anything of this sort, she told her father. She had heard that the bones of some murder victims had been discovered in the cellar of Spithead, and she was trying to find out if one of the victims had been a baby. "The queer part of it," continued Agnes, was that she was in a trancelike state, awake and "able to see the room, and Gene all the time."

When O'Neill left Bermuda for New York on November 17, for the casting of *Marco Millions*, he knew he would never go back. He continued to write chattily to Agnes, nonchalantly dropping Carlotta's name from time to time (in case she should hear any rumors); they had attended a concert together to evaluate possible background music for *Marco*, he wrote toward the end of November. His big news was that he'd accepted an offer of $30,000 for Brook Farm, glad finally to get rid of it "even at a loss."

In early December, O'Neill cautioned Agnes not to count on the cash from the Brook Farm sale to pay for additional renovations to Spithead, as he was going to invest the money as a cushion against lean years, should his plays end up as flops. "If you think anything of my peace of mind," he warned, "don't go making plans for Spithead beyond what we've already agreed on."

Uneasy about Agnes's decision to attend the opening nights of *Marco* (on January 9) and *Interlude* (three weeks later), he told her, with feigned sympathy, that he would understand if her chores regarding the final vacating of Brook Farm prevented her presence in New York; he said she could see the plays just as well after their opening nights.

He was now eager to gain possession of his papers and he contrived an excuse for asking Agnes to send him all the original scripts of his plays. He needed them immediately because a prominent dealer in rare books was interested in trying to sell them on his behalf.

"It could be a big 'ace in the hole' for us and the kids," he cajoled, issuing complicated instructions about how to pack the stored manuscripts and how to ship them securely. "Be sure to send everything you find," he said, stressing that the dealer must be convinced the set was complete.

On December 9, O'Neill informed Agnes he'd taken an hour off to buy Christmas toys at F.A.O. Schwarz for Shane and Oona; if he couldn't find "anything good" for her, he said, he would send her a check. The harsh words with which he chose to close his letter signaled that the charade was over. The time had come, he announced, for both of them to reach a new understanding. He now had "a real objective perspective on things," he wrote, and suggested she go out and enjoy herself; she was free to pursue her life "in whatever freedom you desire as I am with mine."

Whatever Agnes's response, it provoked an openly hostile letter from O'Neill a few days before Christmas. Although he began neutrally with progress reports on *Marco* and *Interlude*, he interrupted himself with the caustic apology that it was "tactless" of him to speak so much about his plays when it was "quite evident" she was not interested, since she never mentioned them.

"You can't hurt me any more, thank God!" thundered O'Neill. "You've tortured your last torture as far as I'm concerned. Something in me is so damn utterly dead that I don't care about anything anymore except my work."

More calmly, he rationalized that what had happened to him and Agnes was "simply the curse of the soul's solitude, the grinding, disintegrating pressure of time." He would always be her friend, he assured her, although he feared that as a husband he'd been "a miserable misfit." Thinking better of it, he brazenly attempted to shift onto Agnes the entire blame for their failed marriage: "Look into your own heart and face the truth! You don't love me any more. You haven't for a long time."

It wasn't until a week later that O'Neill stopped jabbing at Agnes and delivered what he must have regarded as a well-considered knockout punch. His announcement was clumsy and insulting; it was expressed in language more appropriate for a *Ladies' Home Journal* romance writer than for America's most distinguished dramatist. It's quite possible that Carlotta had dictated much of it.

He was leaving Agnes, said O'Neill, for "someone else." Withholding the name of that "someone" (as if Agnes could possibly be in any doubt), he dribbled on about how he loved that someone "most deeply," and how that someone "loved him." He felt it would be "impossible" for him to live with Agnes even were she willing.

In short, he wanted a divorce.

It was not quite ten years since O'Neill—on the verge of marrying Agnes—had dismissed her rival Louise Bryant in language not dissimilar. If Agnes, once again at the apex of a love triangle, remembered those letters, she might have allowed herself an ironic grin.

Now, naively, O'Neill invoked the pledge he and Agnes had made at the start of their marriage: if either ever fell in love with someone else, each would understand and readily let the other go. He was certain he could "accept the inevitable in that spirit" if their roles were reversed.

He conceded there had been moments when their "old love flared into life again," but the "moments of a very horrible hate have been more and more apparent, a poisonous bitterness and resentment, a cruel desire to wound, rage and frustration and revenge." In such a climate, he pontificated, "no love, however strong, can continue to endure and live."

For Agnes, O'Neill's patronizing tone did nothing to enhance his argument. He had chosen to present their breakup as a mutually satisfactory solution to their problems; he promised Agnes the use of Spithead for life, and an income sufficient for her "to live in dignity and comfort."

Foreseeing resistance, he reiterated that the only fair thing was for her to divorce him. He dismissed the details as something that could be talked over when next she came to New York.

Agnes was flabbergasted. But she was far from flattened. Over the years, she had survived all too many hateful battles, each inevitably followed by a loving truce. Her husband's virulent invective this time was to her mind just another of his episodic, half-mad eruptions—his adulterous ravings, his indifference to her humiliation, his self-centered assumption that their split was a fait accompli and that she would meekly accede to his idea of largesse.

In point of fact, she still didn't really believe the marriage was over. She accepted O'Neill's infatuation. She acknowledged Carlotta's beauty and sexual allure. But she underestimated the importance to O'Neill of Carlotta's superb managerial skills, coupled with that liberating personal income (from Speyer) and her single-minded, self-sacrificing devotion to all of O'Neill's needs, both artistic and personal.

Agnes, convinced that she herself was the woman O'Neill truly needed for his survival, believed he would soon tire of Carlotta. She failed to recognize Carlotta as a force majeure. For that matter, Agnes sometimes wondered if she really even wanted to stay married to O'Neill. But she could not make up her mind to let him go, if for no other reason than, after all these erratic years, he was about to become more successful—and richer—than ever. Should she just hand him over to Carlotta? Or should she fight to keep him?

Still ambivalent, Agnes notified O'Neill she was coming to New York to talk to him, leaving Shane and Oona in Bermuda in the care of servants (although she'd earlier claimed it "seemed impossible for the kids to be left here alone").

Carlotta, when informed by O'Neill of Agnes's impending visit, sent Kenneth Macgowan a worried note, warning that O'Neill needed all his strength for work on the new productions. She pleaded with Macgowan to help O'Neill keep his balance.

To O'Neill's dismay, Agnes chose to check into the Wentworth. But not wishing to antagonize her, O'Neill suppressed his annoyance and took time off from rehearsals of *Marco* to meet with her for the purpose of negotiating the terms of the divorce. When she caught a cold, he knocked on her door to offer the use of his sunlamp. She was in her dressing gown, preparing for bed, and O'Neill briefly lost himself in one of those moments when their "old love flared into life again," as Agnes had hoped it would. This, too, he confessed to Carlotta, who—with victory assured—found it expedient to forgive him.

Agnes's last-minute attempt to wrest O'Neill from Carlotta came to nothing, although she later used that final coupling in an attempt to blackmail him; she claimed, during their contentious divorce negotiations, to be pregnant with his child—a claim he furiously dismissed as a cheap ploy. (If she was pregnant, he said, it could not possibly be with his child.)

Agnes's daughter (recently turned twelve) was present on the day her mother and stepfather parted. As Barbara recalled, Agnes had summoned her to New York to join her in her final farewell to O'Neill. "I think he kissed me goodbye, too," said Barbara. Presumably, Barbara returned to boarding school when her mother sailed back to Bermuda, well before the opening of *Strange Interlude*. Shortly after her departure, O'Neill wrote to Agnes, chastising her for having spent an extravagant $122 (on items unspecified) during her final two days at the Wentworth.

On her return to Spithead, Agnes found a bewildered three-year-old Oona and a devastated eight-year-old Shane awaiting her. Shane's beloved Finn had been murdered. As Barbara Burton sadly remembered, the "great big wonderful dog who wouldn't harm a fly" had annoyed a neighbor with his barking "and the neighbor had instructed his butler to shoot the dog." Years later, Shane's daughter Sheila recalled, "He was all alone to deal with the death of his dog," attributing this incident to her father's depressive personality.

Agnes saw no choice but to compound her children's misery. As Shane later confided to his daughter, when Agnes had returned from New York, she told him and Oona "that Dad wasn't ever coming back home. He left us all for that woman he met in Maine."

Perhaps Shane derived some consolation from a letter his father had sent him a few months earlier, attempting to assuage his guilt over his neglected son. Never emotionally comfortable with Shane, O'Neill was entirely at ease relating to him on a literary level. The letter was charming, tender, and cannily endearing; it was the prototype for other occasional letters written while Shane was very young.

"Your Daddy—meaning myself—was certainly tickled to death to get your nice letter! It is very lonely for me living in this hotel where I don't know anyone and I often think of you and Oona—and I miss you both like the devil! You mustn't tell Oona this, though—at least when you tell her you must say 'like the deuce' instead of 'like the devil' for it isn't polite to say 'devil' to ladies and Oona, let us hope, is a perfect lady!"

He praised Shane's prowess as "the prize fisherman of the O'Neill family" for having caught eight of "them yaller grunts" and also for his proficiency as a swimmer. "You'll get to be such a good swimmer that one of these days I expect you'll turn into one of 'them yaller grunts' yourself and swim out and leave us, and then we'll have to set the fish pot to catch you and bring you home again!"

Agnes admitted defeat—but only tentatively. She proposed to O'Neill the idea of obtaining a divorce in Connecticut, but was dissuaded by his lawyer, Harry Weinberger, who said that among other complications, it would take much too long; he urged her to go to Reno without delay, a request personally endorsed by O'Neill.

Agnes responded piteously to O'Neill in early February: "Yes, the situation is a rotten one—rotten for you and Carlotta to have to wait a year, & rotten for me to have to go to Reno & get an immediate divorce." She said she was not well enough to travel, and that various other reasons would prevent her from leaving any time that spring.

"As you two are getting all the best of it . . . I think that my wishes— remember, I am giving you the divorce—might be considered." It seemed to her, she chided, that O'Neill was "in a hell of a hurry" to get her "put safely away."

Five months later, Agnes, on a trip to New York, met a hard-drinking former Albany newspaperman, James J. Delaney, in Greenwich Village. They began a love affair. Agnes kept delaying her departure for Reno, hoping to negotiate better terms with O'Neill, but also reluctant to separate from Delaney. He was as devoted to her as she to him, according to a friend of Agnes's from West Point Pleasant, Elizabeth Murray.

"Jimmy told me once that Agnes was the most beautiful woman he had ever seen," said Murray. Another friend, Sarah Ullman, noting that Agnes remained loyal to Delaney for ten years, sympathetically recalled the difficulties inherent in her situation. "She couldn't marry him, although they loved each other," said Ullman. "She had to have the alimony. Her kids loved him. He would pal around with Shane and take him fishing. He was a very charming man."

Agnes had not yet left for Reno in early October, and by then O'Neill had grown so incensed by reports of what he characterized as her irresponsible behavior that he suggested Weinberger hire a detective to tail her—so that she could, in his phrase, be "caught in flagrante."

Four months later, in mid-February 1929, Agnes and O'Neill (by proxy) signed an agreement by which each consented "to live as though unmarried." And on March 11, Agnes entrained for Reno. Shane was in boarding school, and Oona and Barbara Burton were being looked after by Delaney, along with Agnes's sister Cecil, and the long-since-forgiven Gaga, who had returned to help Agnes in the deteriorating New Jersey house.

———

DURING THE THREE MONTHS Agnes was required to spend in Reno, she began to think of her years with O'Neill as "emotional attrition." That, purportedly, was how she expressed it many years later to the writer Max Wylie, who wanted to base a novel on her life with O'Neill.

Agnes had responded with enthusiasm to Wylie's request for an interview. It was three years after O'Neill's death and Agnes, then in her sixties, was drinking excessively; she had not yet begun writing her memoir.

Agnes talked at length with Wylie. Then in his early fifties, he was the ambitious but unheralded younger brother of the prominent author Philip Wylie. Max found Agnes to be "a great gal," who offered to tell him anything he wanted to know. "Lots of fun in her," he recalled. Their friendship lasted for several years, during which Agnes, with Wylie's encouragement, began writing *Part of a Long Story*.

Agnes was more candid with Wylie than she allowed herself to be in her memoir. She told him, for example, that she felt "short-changed about everything" in her marriage, branding O'Neill (as Wylie recorded), "a hell of a bore," as well as "petty, churlish, ungallant, unnoticing, self-immolated, and self-consuming."

One day, Agnes confided, she suddenly "stopped thinking of Eugene as a 'public figure'; of herself as married to such, but instead, as married to a man who was not only unlike all other men, but grossly deficient in every area (except sex) in which a normal woman can find trust, fulfillment, response, or secure companionship."

She said there were times when she almost wished O'Neill would not return home after attending to productions in New York. Too often, she added petulantly, having awaited his return with excitement, she was let down; within a day or two, he would revert to his "joyless moodiness, his habitual peevishness, his verbal abuse."

Agnes also spoke frankly to Wylie about her and O'Neill's undiminished mutual lust, confiding that she was "his lover, but never his wife."

O'Neill, said Agnes, "didn't need or want a wife; didn't know what one was; didn't wish to know nor to think about it."

Agnes permitted Wylie to copy a hoard of letters between herself and O'Neill, letters she later sold to Harvard and Yale. He made notes on his copies, planning to fictionalize her relationship with O'Neill for his novel *Trouble in the Flesh*.

Wylie's portraits of both O'Neill and Agnes turned out to be near-caricatures. Completely spellbound by Agnes, Wylie portrayed her as a patient, forgiving, compliant, and self-sacrificing saint.

While he accurately portrayed O'Neill as self-pitying and demanding, and described how Agnes catered to him on many levels, Wylie glossed over Agnes's own shortcomings—among them her reluctance to concede O'Neill's entitlement to a quiet and orderly environment in which to write—instead, pitting her own self-centered seeking of social status against O'Neill's need for privacy.

PART III

MISTRESS, SECRETARY, WIFE, AND MOTHER

29

It is sixteen months since O'Neill and Carlotta eloped to Europe. They have weathered their Shanghai maelstrom and are settled in their newly rented home at Le Plessis in the Loire Valley a hundred miles from Paris—ensconced as cozily as it is possible to be in a forty-five-room, candle-lit eighteenth-century château with no telephone, no electricity, and no central heating; they have their love (and multiple fireplaces) to keep them warm.

Forgotten is O'Neill's near-fatal backslide into alcohol in Shanghai, as is Carlotta's aborted decision to leave him. Together they have survived the months of nightmare negotiations for the divorce, and O'Neill has all but suppressed the far-off voices of two bewildered young children.

On June 6, 1929, the day they take possession of their château, O'Neill notes his grand new address in his Work Diary: "Le Plessis, Saint Antoine-du-Rocher, Indre-et-Loire." (Carlotta has long since ordered the appropriately engraved stationery.)

In the tower studio Carlotta has created for O'Neill, he gives himself up to the compulsive joy of his writing.

He is now focusing on one of the numerous projects he has been thinking about on and off for the last three years, an updated version of the Greek Oresteia trilogy for which he has not yet found a title. He is contented as never before in his life.

He can take melancholy pleasure in having achieved wealth and acclaim far surpassing his father's quarter century of fame; surely he recalls his youthful boast that James O'Neill one day would be remembered only as the father of Eugene O'Neill.

On June 14, in a surge of creative optimism mingled with his love for Carlotta, he assures her she will soon be Mrs. O'Neill; and Carlotta croons to her diary, "I couldn't be any more his wife than I am— except by law! I have gone through so much that I seem to be *drained!* But I love Gene!"

Not quite three weeks later—on July 3—O'Neill receives the anticipated cable announcing that Agnes's divorce was granted in Reno the previous day. "At last, thank God!" he writes in his Work Diary. Carlotta (who dates the beginning of their ordeal from two months prior to their elopement) is more emotional.

She feels suddenly "weak as after a long illness," she writes. "We can't believe this torture of 18 months is over!" She and O'Neill cling together, weeping with joy. "We can't believe we are free."

Their freedom comes with the price of yet another bout of unwelcome publicity. Two days after the announcement of the divorce, the tabloids begin to speculate about when O'Neill will remarry. They remind their readers that Carlotta's ex-husband, Ralph Barton, is currently seeking a divorce from his fourth wife (the French pianist and composer Germaine Tailleferre, whom he married on the rebound after Carlotta divorced him).

This is particularly galling for Carlotta, though she has had hints that Barton is still attempting to get in touch with her. According to Carlotta's old friend Carl Van Vechten, Barton has been keeping an almost daily watch over news of Carlotta. Her impending marriage to O'Neill has apparently pushed the ever-fragile Barton to the edge. In Van Vechten's view, Barton, despite his own infidelities, had always been possessive of Carlotta, and his egotistical nature "couldn't stand the idea of her marrying someone even more celebrated than himself."

Aware that Van Vechten and his wife, Fania, still see Carlotta, Barton has made a point of often asking them to "give Carlotta my love." Even more brashly, Barton, when he learns Lillian Gish is planning a visit to the O'Neills in France, asks her to hand Carlotta a letter from him. Gish refuses. "I told him I couldn't go to a man's house as a guest and hand his wife a love letter from another man."

The tangled comings and goings of Barton, Carlotta, and O'Neill are a feast of nonstop gossip for the tabloids, which scramble to enumerate the divorces and remarriages among them: Barton's four ex-wives, O'Neill's two, Carlotta's three ex-husbands. "If these people—philosophers, seers, men apart—cannot manage their domestic affairs on a sound and permanent basis," one of the tabloids smirks, "what hope is there for the ordinary bewildered citizen?"

Carlotta is convinced that much of this public backbiting is being whipped up by Agnes and her supporters. And now, indisputably in possession of O'Neill, Carlotta feels empowered to obliterate her nemesis.

To Saxe Commins, she looses her full venom toward Agnes: "Her memory is short—re her 18 mos. of lies—blackmailing—selling scandalous interviews—double crossing etc.—I say she's a liar—G[ene] says she's just a damn fool!" Carlotta wishes that Agnes "and her friends & Gene's would-be friends" would leave them "in peace & ignorance of *her* existence, *her* plans or *her* life!"

But O'Neill can't entirely ignore those who tie him to his life with Agnes—not least among them their two young children, whom he seems determined to keep attached to him. He writes to Shane and Oona affectionately if infrequently, appealing to their imagination and sense of humor, nearly always ending his letters, "Don't forget your Daddy."

A month after eloping with Carlotta, he encloses snapshots of himself in a letter to Oona, "so you can look at them every once in a while and remember your Daddy." He has her picture in his room where he writes plays, he tells her, and often looks at it and wonders "how you are and what you are doing and wish that I could see you." Attaching a check for a present, he ends, "I love you very much. Don't forget me."

He writes at greater length to Shane, also enclosing snapshots of himself and pleading not to be forgotten. Shane, now nearly ten, is treated to a more grown-up account of his father's life: "I am working hard starting a new play," O'Neill tells his son, adding that he hadn't worked during his trip to China "because the tropics took all the pep out of me, it was so darn hot." He urges Shane to write to his half brother, Eugene Jr., who is trying out for the freshman crew at Yale.

Carlotta's eleven-year-old daughter, Cynthia, is tucked away (just like Agnes's daughter) with an accommodating grandmother; Carlotta writes to her and sends her gifts. (Cynthia's father is Carlotta's long-forgotten second husband, Melvin Chapman Jr., whom Carlotta married when she was twenty-seven and Chapman was twenty.)

With no further impediments to their marriage, Carlotta and O'Neill say their I do's (in this case a simple *"Oui!"*) in Paris on July 22. They exchange thin gold bands, both engraved with the same quotation from *Lazarus Laughed*: "Life laughs with love!" (Nine years later, in anticipation of their anniversary, Carlotta and O'Neill changed their wedding bands for new ones inscribed with an alternate quotation from *Lazarus Laughed*: "You are my laughter—and I am yours.")

Carlotta and O'Neill spend the night in their suite at the Hotel du Rhin, then motor back to Le Plessis the following evening during a fearsome thunderstorm. O'Neill, terrified of thunder and lightning, cringes. But Carlotta, unperturbed by the supernal fury, rejoices in her diary: "Mr. and Mrs. Eugene O'Neill at home." Earlier, she had declared that their marriage was "to be for each of us until death! *Thank God!*"

O'Neill authorizes his lawyer, Weinberger, to announce the marriage to the American press (instructing him to include the purposely misleading information that he and Carlotta will travel to the Tyrol for a honeymoon), and the New York newspapers carry the story on July 24. He also cables his friend the portrait photographer Ben Pinchot to release a photograph for which he and Carlotta sat before leaving for Europe; it will appear in the next issue of *Vanity Fair* and subsequently be reprinted in newspapers worldwide.

In the photo, O'Neill is almost surrealistically handsome—a movie star version of himself. He wears a superbly tailored dark suit, white shirt, and wide striped tie. Gazing into the camera's eye, he allows the barest suggestion of a smile to lurk at the corners of his sensual mouth; his eyes are speculative; his hair lies in a thick wave over his right temple, its silver beginning to spread; his mustache, still dark, is immaculately trimmed.

Carlotta ignores the camera. Stunningly beautiful, her gleaming ebony hair brushed sleekly away from her creamy brow, chin tilted upward, swan's neck extended and encircled with jewels, she gazes adoringly, possessively, at O'Neill, with her lovely shadowed (myopic) eyes.

Between them, Carlotta and O'Neill, both nearing their forty-first birthdays, have begun to create a legend about the remote château-dwelling expatriate, secluded in work and in love. For most of the next quarter century, Carlotta will devote herself to perpetuating this fable, while O'Neill perversely—more than once—will attempt to sabotage it. For now, however, all is harmony.

Two months before the wedding, O'Neill, in consultation with Carlotta, had formulated a design for living. To begin with, he would no longer allow anything but his own creative tempo to determine his output. Reflecting that he had written eighteen long plays during the past eleven years, he concluded it was "too much"; he had often forced the plays just to keep himself occupied. Writing would always come first (his "vacation from living"), but he would rest and relax in the periods between creation. "America has had a bellyful of my stuff for a while," he told friends.

What he really wished he could avoid—an oddly contrary wish for a dramatist—was the process of moving his plays off the written page and onto a stage. "My interest in the productions steadily decreases as my interest in plays as written increases," he had explained at that time to Eleanor Fitzgerald, the executive manager of the Playwrights' Theatre, with whom O'Neill had a close friendship.

"I am a bit weary and disillusioned with scenery and actors and the whole uninspired works of the Show Shop," O'Neill told Fitzgerald. He was thinking, he said half-seriously, that he might end up "writing plays to be published with 'no productions allowed' in red letters on the first page," even if it meant holding back plays from production (and even publication) until he was forgotten.

Sick of being a public personage, he was planning life ahead so that he could go back to his old private life of "unpestered artist." Forty, he said, "is the right age to begin to learn and I think my new work is going to show more poise, more patience with itself to reach at perfection, more critical analysis of itself and contemplation, more time given it for gestation and genuine birth, more pains." It was time, said O'Neill, to achieve "a more mature outlook as an artist."

For a man who treasured his privacy, O'Neill was surprisingly open with certain friends, not only about his work but about his personal outlook. To Fitzgerald, he confided it had taken a complete upheaval of his life to attain his new mind-set. He could now look forward to years of undisturbed work, lovingly protected by his Carlotta. "I've everything to back me up now," he concluded, "love of the kind I've always wanted, security and peace."

Only five days after explaining his new vision to Fitzgerald, he made his first significant entry in his Work Diary about the play he'd been contemplating since 1926. "Virtually decide on *Mourning Becomes Electra* as title—trilogy—with separate subtitle each play."

During the next two months, he completed a scenario of *Electra*, and was dreaming of achieving a poetic resonance for his modern-day Greek characters worthy of their tragic fates—a language that would transcend any dialogue he had ever written. But he was far from certain he could ever overcome what he perceived as his own particular inadequacy. For that reason, among others, he was not yet ready to grapple with his new project full-time.

In a singular outpouring to the critic Joseph Wood Krutch, he conveyed his frustration:

"Oh for a language to write drama in! For a speech that is dramatic and isn't just conversation! I'm so strait-jacketed by writing in terms of talk! I'm so fed up with the dodge-question of dialect! But where to find that language?"

His use of dialect to give voice to the inarticulate women and men whose lives he knew so well and for whom he appointed himself spokesman—although arresting in its time—was restrictive (Swedish-American for *Anna Christie*, street-black for *The Emperor Jones*, seaman's vernacular for *The Hairy Ape*, fumbling New England back-country for *Desire Under the Elms*).

There was much he wanted to think about before beginning on the actual dialogue of *Electra*. "It is going to be difficult, this!" he confessed to George Jean Nathan on August 31. "It would be so easy to do well. The story would see to that—and that's the danger I want to avoid. It has got to have an exceptional quality to lift it above its easy possibilities and make it worthy in some sense of its classic antecedents—or it will be a rank flop in my eyes no matter what others may think of it. So I'm going to do a lot more of tentative feeling out and testing before I start."

But he had another reason to delay his return to the trilogy and full-time writing, and that was his sense of obligation to his new marital state. He wished to indulge Carlotta's desire (and also his own) to show off the grandeur of their torturously achieved matrimonial bliss.

Among the series of guests he and Carlotta entertained at Le Plessis were the Carl Van Vechtens, Philip Moeller, and Theresa Helburn, as well as Eugene Jr., on vacation from Yale, who had just been staked by his father to a tour of Germany, and who visited him and Carlotta for two weeks in late August and early September.

O'Neill was proud of his nineteen-year-old son, who had grown to six feet two inches and weighed 180 pounds. To O'Neill's delight, his son and Carlotta hit it off; she took him sightseeing and shopping for clothes. "A fine youth truly!" O'Neill wrote to Nathan. "He fits in very well with us. . . . So all's well."

ZEALOUS IN THE performance of her duties as hostess and secretary, Carlotta appointed herself gatekeeper as well. She began slicing away those of O'Neill's friends she regarded as disloyal because of their ties to Agnes.

HER FUNCTION AS gatekeeper was relentless. It was always she who spoke or wrote the dismissive or severing words, claiming she did so on O'Neill's behalf. She was performing what Strindberg, in his *Spook Sonata*, graphically described as "the labor of keeping the filth of life at a distance"; it was a labor that some of O'Neill's friends believed she pursued with too much relish.

In almost every case, however, the severing was administered because O'Neill desired it, either actively or passively. "Neither God nor the angels could have kept anyone away from O'Neill that he wished to see," Carlotta once protested. If he deferred, in some cases, to Carlotta's dislikes and prejudices, it was the natural deference of a loving husband.

As Carlotta told Saxe Commins, she and O'Neill were looking forward to peace and work in "a new world" of their own making; this, she wrote spitefully to Commins, meant "cutting loose the rotten drift wood" that comprised O'Neill's Greenwich Village coterie.

"We would be delighted if we never heard a word from or about these people again," she said, adding that O'Neill was going through "a new development—new pleasures—new richness." There were "new subjects of study" entering his life; the "old skin [was] being shed!"—and with it, she hoped, "the old parasites!"

And what were these "pleasures," this "richness" of O'Neill's new life? First, according to Carlotta, was his work environment. In his tower studio, Carlotta installed a chair, custom-made in England—a contraption described with amused wonder by the visiting George Jean Nathan as "a cross between a dentist's and a barber's chair with all sorts of pull-in and pull-dash contrivances attached to it, and with a couple of small shelves for reference books."

The chair had an attached board "so arranged that it can be maneuvered in front of him and on it he rests his pad." The pad to which Nathan referred was a blotting tablet held in a leather frame that lay on O'Neill's desk, an accessory that graced all the desks in his subsequent homes.

"It was his writing desk, so to speak," according to Carlotta, who once explained that O'Neill could only write when seated in "a particular chair" with his feet on a footstool and the leather blotting pad on his knees; in that position he could write "for hours at a time," she said, adding that O'Neill had been using "this particular pad" since May 1928 (presumably changing the blotter paper itself from time to time). "He could never write at a table or desk! I bought him various styles of each—but it was wasted money." (He occasionally wrote on the tablet in bed.)

CARLOTTA AND O'NEILL took walks in their woods. They bicycled across acres of the château's private paths. O'Neill sped his recently purchased Bugatti racer up and down the quiet countryside, sometimes at more than a hundred kilometers an hour. He swam twice a day in the pool they'd built, while Carlotta sunbathed.

She shampooed his hair. He exercised with a punching bag. She shopped and had her hair "waved" in the nearby town of Tours. She hired and fired gardeners, chauffeurs, butlers, housemaids, chefs. She concerned herself about food, often describing in her diary meals eaten at restaurants, as well as those prepared at home by her various cooks. (Food was less important to O'Neill than the Coca-Cola he drank all day, and which Carlotta bought for him by the case.)

Carlotta answered mail, paid bills, and even saw to the dozen sharpened pencils neatly arranged on a shelf of O'Neill's writing chair every morning. She looked after a series of pets—two dogs and a collection of parakeets, finches, and canaries, for which O'Neill had developed a liking shared by his wife. When a "darling" canary called Bozo died, they buried it in a Chinese box under a tree in their garden and marked its grave with a headstone. "All this in the pouring rain—we were really quite cut up about it," Carlotta said.

They napped after lunch, took afternoon tea. Carlotta dressed for dinner even when O'Neill couldn't be bothered. When George Jean Nathan was a houseguest, he was amused by his friend's reaction each time Carlotta presented herself at dinner in a new gown: "His face lights up like a county fair. She knows well the effect it has on him and quietly lays in a constantly replenished wardrobe for him."

Carlotta invariably asked O'Neill, "Do you like it?" And O'Neill, just as invariably, mumbled something like "Well, it's pretty, but I like blue better." When Carlotta returned one afternoon from a shopping trip to Tours, O'Neill asked her, "Where've you been?" With a kiss, Carlotta replied, "I've been shopping for dresses, Genie dear. Blue ones."

Lillian Gish, who often accompanied her longtime companion, Nathan, on his visits to Le Plessis, was struck by the ardor of the O'Neills' marriage. Although she herself never married (Nathan married the actress Julie Haydon three years before his death in 1958), she had, she said, been with many married people, but "had never seen a man and woman so passionately in love. They didn't seem to need anything outside of each other.

"Carlotta gave Gene everything she could think of to bring a smile to his face. She wanted everything that touched him to look beautiful, everything around him, including herself. She was his wife, mother, housekeeper, secretary, nurse, mistress, companion—and almost his tailor. If there was a tray to be brought to him, Carlotta brought it. She had a great sense of beauty. We used to dress for dinner at Le Plessis. There was never anything casual."

When there were no guests—which was most of the time—O'Neill and Carlotta sat after dinner before their living room's vast open fireplace, often reading poetry to each other; he at times read her passages from his work in progress; they listened to news reports and

concerts on their wireless radio, music on their windup Victrola—
sometimes classical, sometimes jazz, sometimes popular songs, to which
they danced.

Carlotta, in her diary, noted Cynthia's twelfth birthday on August 8;
O'Neill in his diary noted Oona's fifth on May 14 and Shane's tenth on
October 30. But their children were less real to them than their various
fussed-over pets, especially their dogs. After adopting and rejecting several local dogs, they ordered a pedigreed Dalmatian puppy, Silverdeen
Emblem, from a London breeder. With his name shortened to "Blemie,"
he became their pampered child, fitted with an overcoat, raincoat, and
collar made to order at Hermès in Paris.

They met Carlotta's "Papa" Speyer in Paris for dinner on September
1, during which, anticipating the imminent stock market crash of October 24, 1929, Speyer gave O'Neill sage financial advice. (He continued to
advise both O'Neill and Carlotta by letter and cable after the crash.)

While Carlotta, in her diary, often went on endlessly about humdrum
events in her life with O'Neill, she was less than forthcoming about
manifestations of physical love. Assuming correctly that her diaries
would one day be part of an O'Neill archive, she was not eager to draw
posterity's attention to her fabled qualifications as a courtesan.

She did, however, let slip a coy hint or two about her love life; she
wrote of at least one occasion when O'Neill, feeling lonely during the
night, asked if he might join her in her bedroom (but without revealing
her answer). Another time, when it was she who felt "rather lonely," she
noted, "Ask Gene *may* I sleep in his bed tonight," then girlishly mimicked his response: "'*May*' you? Picks me up & puts me in his bed and
tucks me in! *Angel!*" In yet another (barely whispered) instance: "In our
happiness over his work, we sleep tight—held!"

As it turned out, years later Carlotta edited out the "comments on
their love-making sessions," according to Donald C. Gallup, then in
charge of the O'Neill collection at Yale. She could not, however, censor
a particularly salacious reference about her in the diary of her friend Carl

Van Vechten. His scribbles in the "Daybooks" he bequeathed to the New York Public Library were often so lurid, he stipulated they be sealed until June 17, 1980, his one-hundredth birthday, by which time he expected to be dead. (He died in 1964 at eighty-three.)

In an entry dated September 29, 1925, he ruminated about an evening at the Barton apartment when he and his actress wife, Fania Marinoff, were the only guests—an evening when Carlotta and Ralph, spurred by drink, attempted to put a little extra zest into their faltering marriage.

The entry begins: "6:30—dinner with R. Barton & Carlotta Monterey. Marinoff goes to theater. I stay there & after the Bartons have talked for 3 hours about whether they will live together anymore they take off their clothes & give a remarkable performance. Ralph goes down on Carlotta. She masturbates & expires in ecstasy. They do 69—etc." Laconically, Van Vechten concludes, "I leave about 12:30."

WHILE CARLOTTA DOUBTLESS would have preferred to bury that episode—and while she censored her own sexual commentary in her diary—she was charmed by O'Neill's uninhibited expressions of passion. She welcomed as her due the love notes in which O'Neill extolled—along with her eyebrows, eyes, nose, lips—what he lauded as her "etcetera"; the "etcetera" was illustrated by miniature hand-drawn black ink silhouettes of bewhiskered kittens. (She was, of course, unaware that this symbol was a variation on the Miss Pussy-Nightingale love letters exchanged between O'Neill and Agnes in the discarded past.)

Indeed, Carlotta was so enchanted with those tributes that she published them after O'Neill's death in *Inscriptions: Eugene O'Neill to Carlotta Monterey O'Neill*, privately printed in 1960 by the Yale University Library.

Carlotta was less restrained in her letters and notes to O'Neill than she was in her diary—letters in which she sometimes jocularly addressed O'Neill as "Skinny Bottom—darling." (He called her "Darling Fatbum.") During one brief separation in 1929, she wrote to O'Neill from

Paris, where she was shopping for Christmas presents: "I think of a thousand beautifully mad things concerning you & me,—and get wild with excitement to get back to you."

WHILE BOTH CARLOTTA and O'Neill tried to ignore the world of intrigue in New York, it seemed constantly to intrude. Carlotta, who bore such encroachments less stoically than O'Neill, was greatly upset when she read an item in the September 28 issue of *The New Yorker*'s Talk of the Town column that, to her oversensitive ear, sounded ill-natured. Attributed to "a friend of Eugene O'Neill's just returned from a visit to him," the item declared that "flamboyant descriptions of the chateau he has rented in France have exaggerated its grandeur."

The *New Yorker* item went on to explain that Le Plessis was "not a show-place," that the rent was "about half of what a four room apartment rents for in New York," and that it had no electricity and only one bathroom.

Though it was hardly an attack, Carlotta was deeply upset by the piece and told the magazine so. She "nearly dropped dead," as she put it, when informed by the editor, Harold Ross (whom she knew through Ralph Barton), that the quoted "friend" was none other than Kenneth Mac-gowan. Carlotta knew Macgowan was concerned, on O'Neill's behalf, over increasingly malicious gossip in New York about the O'Neills' highfalutin lifestyle abroad, amid the growing Depression in America, and that his comment was well intended.

She felt compelled to rebuke him, nonetheless. Sputtering like a clueless Marie Antoinette, she shot Macgowan a letter demanding to know why she and O'Neill should apologize to anyone about whether they had "thirty servants or no servants" and scolding him for being so "fussed," just because "a lot of failures, sore heads, drunks, and would-be-artists (in one line or another) thro' envy, disappointment and jealousy criticize a man because he lives in the manner that all middle class people (have they the money!) live?"

Carlotta was impatient to return to the quiet life she'd promised

O'Neill, and after helping him through one of his all-too-frequent marathon dental procedures, necessitating a three-week stay in Paris, she could finally report in her diary that O'Neill had re-embraced his *Electra* trilogy and was once again beginning, in his words, to feel his "bean working."

"I am at last off on the right foot," O'Neill wrote the next day to George Jean Nathan. "It should come with a rush from now on."

30

While O'Neill was engrossed in his *Electra* trilogy, Carlotta redoubled her efforts to rule her castle as a sanctuary for his work; she surrounded him with subservient silence during his creative mornings, with peaceful afternoon walks in their woods, meals impeccably served, and discreet intervals of lovemaking, all set against a background of serene beauty.

He was, after all, writing *her* play, as he'd announced six months earlier when, in bed together on May 11, he'd outlined his blueprint for *Mourning Becomes Electra*. Referring to the play in his mind as, variously, his "Electra idea," his "Greek tragedy plot idea," and his "Life of Aeschylus idea," he saw it as a monumental work that would rattle the ancient bones of the Agamemnon saga.

In words similar to those he'd used to describe the long-since-shoved-aside "Grand Opus" of *The Sea-Mother's Son*, he envisioned *Electra* as grander in its sweep, more advanced in technique, and far deeper in its tragic vision than anything he'd yet written.

"I don't promise by a long shot that after it gets ground down by my inadequacies it will prove any such lofty stature," he wrote to the critic Joseph Wood Krutch, "but at least this time I'll have the satisfaction of knowing I failed at something big, and thus be a success in my own spiritual eyes. If I fail! I have hopes, damn it!"

If, in O'Neill's own view, he was not yet at the top of Mount Olympus, he was nearly there, and Carlotta was more than happy to share his aerie. He felt at home within the heaving currents of the Electra legend; he saw aspects of his own dysfunctional family all too clearly reflected in the Aeschylus tragedy of the fourth century BC. The clash between Agamemnon and Clytemnestra, the rivalry of Orestes and Electra for their parents' approval, the family's disillusionment, their hard deaths and grieving, all resonated for O'Neill.

With his parents and brother often on his mind, he transported the Greek legend from the city of Argos to a small New England coastal town (based on New London, where his family had lived out its own Oresteia). The time was 1865, just as the Civil War was ending. O'Neill reimagined Agamemnon, Clytemnestra, and their children as the Mannon family—oedipal complex and all.

This setting, O'Neill noted, was the "best possible dramatically for Greek plot of crime and retribution chain of fate—Puritan conviction of man born to sin and punishment."

The play would begin on the day of General Lee's surrender, when O'Neill's nineteenth-century Agamemnon, a brigadier general in Grant's army (and formerly the town's leading citizen), was about to return home. O'Neill placed the Mannon family in a "neo-Greek" house of the type popular in the early 1800s—"this fits in well and absolutely justifiable, not forced Greek similarity," he noted.

Drawing on his knowledge of New London's history and architecture, he described the Mannon mansion: its facade was a "white Greek temple portico" fronted by "six tall columns," which he modeled in part on three white Greek Revival houses built in the 1840s by prosperous whaling captains; embellished with imposing Corinthian columns, those houses were landmarks on what was once known as "Whale Oil Row" in the center of New London.

O'Neill wished to retain the flavor of the Greek names for his New England characters without their sounding forced. Agamemnon became Ezra Mannon; his wife, Clytemnestra, was renamed Christine; and their son, Orestes, became Orin. For their daughter, Electra, O'Neill hesitated over Eleanor, Elena, and Elsa, and finally settled on Lavinia, explaining it was a loose approximation of Homer's Laodicea.

While O'Neill deviated from the Oresteia of Aeschylus when it suited his purpose, he retained much of the legend's twisted tragedy, as well as its melodrama. From the expository scenes of *Electra*, we learn that while General Mannon was away fighting in the Union army, his wife, Christine, fell in love with Adam Brant (derived from the Oresteia's Aegisthus), the captain of a clipper ship anchored at a wharf in east Boston. Christine dreads her husband's return; but return he does, and she at once sets about to plot his death.

Knowing that the Mannon family doctor has diagnosed Ezra as having a weak heart, Christine poisons him, confident his death will be diagnosed as a heart attack. O'Neill explains Clytemnestra's hatred of her husband in terms of sexual frustration—"[Agamemnon's] Puritan sense of guilt turning love to lust."

In the rapidly thickening plot, Lavinia/Electra—who worshipped her father and has always been jealous of her mother—suspects her mother's role in her father's sudden death; she has guessed her mother's love affair with Adam Brant (to whom she herself is secretly attracted); when her brother, Orin (who adores his mother and hates his father), returns from the war soon after, she enlists him as an ally in spying out their mother's treachery.

Lavinia and Orin, after confirming their mother's guilt, avenge their father's death by murdering Adam Brant, driving Christine to suicide. After various twists of plot including hints of incestuous love between Lavinia and her brother, Orin takes his own life. The body count is now four (Ezra, Adam, Christine, and Orin). Only Lavinia is left standing.

It is she who is the play's true protagonist (as the title, of course, suggests). To O'Neill, the Greek Electra was "the most interesting of all women in drama." But he believed the legendary Electra had been denied the heroic fate to which she was entitled and he set himself to rectify that failure. In his reinvention of her as the doomed Lavinia Mannon, she became in many ways (never mind the gender) a stand-in for O'Neill himself.

"Give modern Electra figure in play a tragic ending worthy of Greek plot idea," he wrote. "In Greek story she peters out into an undramatic married banality. Such a character contained too much tragic fate within her soul to permit this—why should Furies have let Electra escape unpunished?"

In O'Neill's revisionist telling, Lavinia, overwhelmed by guilt, condemns herself to a life locked away from the world; she is inextricably bound, as she declares, "to the Mannon dead," just as O'Neill felt himself bound to—and haunted by—his own dead.

"I'm the last Mannon," says Lavinia at the trilogy's end, echoing O'Neill's own mournful cry following his brother Jamie's death: "I'm the only O'Neill of our branch left . . . the real last one."

Lavinia's final speech is one of the most soul-baring O'Neill ever wrote; it incorporates both his own consuming preoccupation with the act of suicide and his mordant belief in the inevitability of an even crueler self-punishment.

"I'm not going the way Mother and Orin went," declares Lavinia. "That's escaping punishment. And there's no one left to punish me." It is Lavinia's destiny to punish herself.

> Living alone here with the dead is a worse act of justice than death or prison. I'll never go out or see anyone! I'll have the shutters nailed closed so no sunlight can ever get in. I'll live alone with the dead, and keep their secrets, and let them hound me, until the curse is paid out and the last Mannon is let die! (*With a strange cruel smile of gloating over the years of self-torture*) I know they will see to it I live for a long time! It takes the Mannons to punish themselves for being born!

In his Work Diary, O'Neill explained that in the play's title he was using the word *becomes* in its old sense of the word. "It befits—it becomes Electra to mourn—(it is her fate)—also, in usual sense (made ironical here), mourning (black) is becoming to her—it is the only color that becomes her destiny." (O'Neill did not mention in his diary that this concept was imbued with the memory of his mother as a widow and his notion that, spiritually as well as physically, mourning had "suited" her.)

O'Neill pensively recorded the difficulty he'd undergone (a difficulty presumably not encountered by Aeschylus) in plotting the scenario's crimes so that his criminals could escape detection: "Even history of comparatively recent crimes (where they happen among people supposedly respectable), shows rural authorities easily hoodwinked—poisoning of Mannon . . . would probably never be suspected (under same circumstances) even in New England town of today, let alone 1865."

That degree of violence did not, of course, exist in O'Neill's life, even though both he and his mother had each once attempted suicide; but it is significant that O'Neill causes Lavinia to lose, in rapid succession (and in the same order as O'Neill), first her father, then her mother, then her brother.

O'Neill endowed Christine with the beautiful hair his mother had had as a young woman—"partly a copper brown, partly a bronze gold, each shade distinct and yet blending with the other, beautiful hair that hangs down to her knees." And he gave Christine his mother's snobbish attitude toward the small stuffy town where she spent her summers.

After identifying the town in an early scenario as the New London of his childhood, O'Neill wrote, "Christine has always hated the town of N.L. and felt a superior disdain for its inhabitants"—echoing Ella O'Neill's own disparaging attitude. (In *Long Day's Journey Into Night*, Ella O'Neill's stand-in, Mary Tyrone, declares, "I've always hated this town and everyone in it.")

While Ella O'Neill lent a sprinkling of her essence to Christine Mannon, Carlotta's influence was more pronounced. In O'Neill's description of Christine, she is, like Carlotta, "French and Dutch descended"; strikingly attractive, she is, at forty, Carlotta's age; and, like Carlotta, "she appears younger." O'Neill's bewitchment by Carlotta is reflected in Christine's passionate romance with Adam Brant. It is her love affair (as well as the murder of her husband) that drives the play's narrative.

While refining the first draft of the trilogy in early December 1929, O'Neill had hinted in a letter to Lawrence Langner about his newest project. Considering the phenomenal success of *Strange Interlude* at home and abroad, O'Neill expected the Theatre Guild to snap up his *Electra*. He gave no details about his new work, but said it involved "a lot of hard labor—more than there was in *Interlude*."

As O'Neill envisioned it, the project encompassed three full-length plays: *Homecoming* (four acts); *The Hunted* (five acts); and *The Haunted* (four acts). "It is magnificently done," Carlotta told her diary on December 17, after O'Neill had read aloud Act III of *Homecoming*, and again assured her that *Electra* was *her* play. "I can't hear this without weeping—it is my play! & he loves me!"

To BEGIN THE New Year of 1930, Carlotta and O'Neill treated themselves to the gift of a second dog—a handsome Gordon setter named Ben Lomond (ordered, like Blemie, from a London breeder). As Ben was being let out of his traveling box, a jealous Blemie bit him on the nose. "Not a gentleman's idea of a welcome!" Carlotta quipped. From then on, the two dogs were enemies. "They had to be kept in separate rooms when they were in the house," Carlotta remembered, "but they made a truce out of doors."

She and O'Neill each walked one of them until they reached the woods, where they were released from their leashes. "They'd have a wonderful time stalking rabbits together," Carlotta said, "but the minute they got back to the house, they became hostile and had to be separated again."

The relationship between Ben and Blemie was further complicated when, one day, a small mongrel bitch from a neighboring farm wandered onto the O'Neill property. "The bitch was in heat," recalled Carlotta, "and Blemie kissed her politely and followed her off into the woods.

"Some time later one of our French maids told me she'd heard the bitch had had puppies, and didn't we want to take Blemie over to the farm to see his children. I asked Gene, and he grinned and said yes. So we all trooped over to the farm, Gene, I, Blemie and several of the French servants." O'Neill's grin grew wider when he saw the puppies; they all looked like Irish setters. Poor Blemie walked back home with his head down.

While Ben lived mostly in the servants' quarters when not outdoors, Blemie led a more privileged life. "He acted as host at Le Plessis," Lillian Gish recalled. "He would receive you at the door, follow the servant who brought in your breakfast tray. When a guest left, Blemie would throw himself on the floor with a sigh of relief, as though saying, 'Thank heavens, they're gone'; he behaved exactly as though he were worn out with having performed the duties of a good host." Blemie was trained to respect his master's need for quiet. "Like the servants," according to Carlotta, "he went around on tiptoe when Gene was working."

BLEMIE AND the rest of the household continued to tiptoe throughout the cold and rainy winter of 1931, while O'Neill, in his writer's tower, struggled to come up with an ideal language and style for his masterful trilogy. He had tried out and discarded one stylistic concept after another. Should he butter his dialogue with "rhythm derived from Biblical prose (?)" as he'd asked himself on August 15, 1929; "no go," he'd answered, five days later; August 26 found him "playing around with mask technique notion," but three days after that, he concluded, "not right—give up for present."

He was, as he later wrote to Nathan (in early January 1930), monkeying around "with schemes for dialogue and ideas for production" until his head ached. But, as he assured his friend, the story he had to tell "made all such stuff seem futile.

"I finally settled down to the direct and least noticeable way," said O'Neill. "And I find I can get everything said about these characters' souls, hearts, and loins that can be said."

Nonetheless, O'Neill continued to monkey around. He made three more attempts at embellishment six months later. The first was the insertion of "Strange Interludean" asides; but by July 18, 1930, he realized that they, too, must go.

Unfazed, he decided two days later to replace the asides with "stylized soliloquies." That idea was also soon discarded; he noted (on July 25), "am convinced stylized soliloquies won't do," and he determined then and there to write a third draft of the trilogy "with neither asides nor soliloquies."

He was finally convinced, two months later (September 20), that his use of half masks must also be eliminated. Despite what O'Neill had told George Jean Nathan at the beginning of 1930, it wasn't until he was going over his fifth draft in April 1931, still revising, cutting, reconstructing, that he was finally convinced he'd found the right way to tell his story naturalistically—without recourse to imitation Bible-speak, stage asides, masks, or self-conscious soliloquies.

Carlotta worried about her husband. "Watching Gene's tenseness and fatigue does something ghastly to me," she wrote in her diary on January 17, 1931. And two days later: "His spirit is torn by fatigue of his work. He always has told me he lives through everything he writes—all his strength goes into work—which leaves him physically and emotionally exhausted."

In appreciation of Carlotta's patient understanding, O'Neill had given her an early notebook depicting the characters and story line of the trilogy's first two plays. "These first fruits (very unripe) of my work in Our New Year," he'd written on January 15, 1930, "with all my deepest love and gratitude for all you have meant to me!—and all your help!"

By mid-1931 O'Neill was not only stressed by the challenge of his trilogy, but also worried about where he and Carlotta would live when their lease on Le Plessis expired. They were hoping to find a permanent home where there was sunshine, he told a reporter from the *New York Herald Tribune*; it rained in France month after month, nine days out of ten, he said, and the dreary weather had worn him down. "It's a beautiful country, but a terrible climate."

Typically, it hadn't taken O'Neill long to find fault with the dream home he'd earlier extolled to Saxe Commins. His idyllic castle, the "real home" where he'd found seclusion and inspiration had turned into a gingerbread house.

As Carlotta once noted, "This love of mine is tortured by his search for peace—rest—!"

For the immediate present, O'Neill wished to stay put, for he was now making good progress on *Mourning Becomes Electra*, and intended to complete it before leaving France. A week after marking the second anniversary of their elopement, O'Neill had read to Carlotta the scenario of the trilogy's final play, *The Haunted*. She was "moved beyond words," and made it a point to congratulate herself in her diary on her contribution to the play's progress.

Once Carlotta knew she would soon be vacating Le Plessis, she could admit to the inconvenience of running the vast establishment, which she had come to realize was far too large for them. It was growing more difficult to sustain the role of grande dame, not to mention playing muse and custodian to the Great Dramatist; a merciless role, to be sure, if not (as she sometimes seemed to believe) quite the equivalent of his. "I did everything," she said. "He wrote the plays, I did everything else."

By the end of March, O'Neill was feeling the need "to get a little perspective" on the work he'd done so far on *Electra*; as he wrote Macgowan, he was "all washed up and in need of a change of scene." He also wanted to do some sightseeing in the months before he left the Continent for good.

But before he could go anywhere, he needed more dental work. In Paris, while he had his troublesome teeth attended to, Carlotta shopped— an occupation that continued to consume her almost as totally as writing did O'Neill. But she was appalled when she received her bill for the dresses, suits, shoes, and other accessories she had purchased; it came to $5,841—close to half her annual income from Speyer—equivalent to about $82,000 in today's currency.

It was her "last extravagant plunge," as she later recalled ruefully, for, as she often declared, it was her financial obligation to help her husband with "the burden of the wives and children"; without her help, she insisted, he would not be able to "live decently!" It was, she added, her "duty & happiness to help him."

It is something of an irony that O'Neill was beginning to match his wife's sartorial self-indulgence; between sessions in the dentist's chair, he found time to supplement his already extensive collection of bespoke clothing. "Am so proud of my husband in his beautiful clothes," Carlotta gloated, "—they'll last him forever!"

Further encouraging his dandification, Carlotta supervised O'Neill's purchase of three walking sticks and, at his request, she bought him "an evening watch with platinum and pearl chain!" which, she asserted, was "very correct!" In fact, when he returned to America, Carlotta said, "He never bought a suit, a pair of shoes, or anything. He had a complete wardrobe and he was so pleased."

In spite of all their regal outward trappings, Carlotta and O'Neill could at times behave like a couple of mischievous children in the privacy of their home. One balmy May evening after dinner, they were relaxed enough to engage in one of the playful moments they occasionally shared.

"When we start to go upstairs," Carlotta recalled, "Gene makes a grab at me to carry me—we get to laughing and fall in a heap on the stairs— then we *roar with laughter!* A house maid rushes in and looks very surprised & embarrassed. And we feel perfect fools—but continue to laugh!"

On May 29, still in good humor, O'Neill broke away from *Electra* to attend with Carlotta the Russian Kamerny Theatre's productions of *Desire Under the Elms* and *All God's Chillun Got Wings* in Paris. He was more than flattered, he wrote to a friend, that "one of the world's most famous modern theaters, touring the capitals of Europe, selects for two out of the three straight dramas of its repertoire the works of an uncultured Yank! I feel as if I wasn't a total loss as an American delegate at large of the arts."

In his Work Diary, he noted he was "much impressed" with the Kamerny; by then, O'Neill's plays had already scored a success in Moscow, and the Kamerny's director, Alexander Tairov, was a fan.

"If you were to ask me who is the most brilliant, the most important among contemporary playwrights," Tairov had said, "I would answer without hesitation: O'Neill."

Although Carlotta enjoyed the performances, she was uncomfortable visiting backstage. A self-styled "Tory," she was less willing than O'Neill to mingle with Russian Communists, however gifted.

"I have a strange feeling—as if danger were lurking! If we were in the Tropics I would think it a poisonous snake!" she wrote in her diary.

She grew even more uneasy the following evening. After attending *All God's Chillun Got Wings*, she and O'Neill joined Tairov and his wife, the actress Alice Koonen, together with other cast members, for a festive supper.

The Russians made much of O'Neill, and he—to judge by a rather long-winded note he sent the members of the Kamerny two days later—responded in kind. (He wrote, amid many flourishes, that he felt the "most profound gratitude" for the productions, which "rang true to the spirit" of his work and that they were interpreted by "that rarest of all gifts in actors and actresses—creative imagination.")

In his approbation of "a real renaissance of the theater" in Russia—and perhaps recalling his friend John Reed's heartfelt espousal of the revolution—he chose to ignore what had happened there during the preceding decade. (Even Reed, before his death in Moscow in 1920, had expressed his disillusionment with the new Russia.) O'Neill was concerned only that the Russian theater appeared to be thriving. (When he returned to New York for the production of *Mourning Becomes Electra*, he would tell an interviewer, "It is a new country with new ideas, and tradition does not bind it, nor does commercialism smother it. New men get a chance and new ideas are tried out, and the box office does not play the leading part.") At the supper with the cast, O'Neill heartily entered into the give-and-take with his fellow theater lovers from Moscow. Reticent though O'Neill could be, when in compatible company, he could express himself with passion about the theater, its history, literature in general, and Russian literature in particular (along with his own work). And the Russians couldn't help but respond to his love not only of Chekhov, but also of Dostoyevsky, whose novels, together with Tolstoy's *War and Peace*, had, O'Neill once declared, "become parts of my life." (He'd also been influenced by *The Lower Depths* and he deplored the fact that Gorky had not been awarded the Nobel Prize, calling him, in a letter to Sinclair Lewis, "the top of all living writers.")

At the supper, Carlotta found herself silently writhing under a sense of inadequacy. The ravishing looks, the exquisite clothes and carefully chosen jewels, the unfaltering poise and the practiced small talk that she relied on to carry her through social occasions failed to register among these highly vocal Russian intellectuals.

"Gene *seems* in this atmosphere to be sincere and *free* although he doesn't know one word of Russian!" Carlotta jeered in her diary on June 1. Her own contribution to the animated exchanges did not scintillate. In such company, her beauty was no match for O'Neill's genius and she felt humiliatingly overshadowed.

In his ebullience, it didn't occur to O'Neill that he was not including Carlotta in his dialogue with the Russians. She sat silently listening to the vociferous supper guests, probably expecting that O'Neill would—at the appropriate moment—interpolate into his conversation something about Carlotta's value to him in his work and speak of his absolute need of her. Evidently, no such praise was forthcoming.

That evening was an intimation of what lay ahead. It wasn't a poisonous snake that Carlotta sensed lurking; it was the grinning ghost of Strindberg. In her diary on June 6, after a week of sulking, she sarcastically expressed her distress. "Gene suddenly comes out of his 'fog' & sees a woman here—on close inspection it is Carlotta—good old Carlotta!— Well, Hello, darling!"

The following evening after dinner, a mollified Carlotta told her diary that a penitent O'Neill sat with her on their terrace and discussed "faith—loyalty—love—God!"

31

oth O'Neill and Carlotta fell ill with the flu and were confined to bed during what would be their last Christmas in France.

On January 7, 1931, still enervated from his illness, O'Neill learned that his Peaked Hill Bars home (which he had recently deeded to Eugene Jr.) had been swept into the sea. O'Neill knew the cottage had been teetering for some time at the eroding edge of the Atlantic, but the news dispirited him.

His melancholia deepened when it seemed that neither he nor Carlotta could shake off the flu's aftereffects at Le Plessis.

In Paris, seeking expert medical attention, O'Neill was diagnosed with "anemia, very low blood pressure, kidney and gall bladder upset." But this time it was Carlotta whose illness was the more serious. Her white-blood-cell count was far too high and her doctor ordered a three-week hospital stay.

With Carlotta in the hospital, O'Neill checked into his accustomed suite in the Hotel du Rhin to begin a series of medical treatments as an outpatient. Still in the process of editing *Mourning Becomes Electra*, he engaged a typist to copy his handwritten—and as yet uncompleted—fifth draft. In between his treatments and his editing, he visited Carlotta daily with offerings of flowers and other gifts.

Carlotta was growing concerned about their living expenses, given the still-plummeting American stock market, but she was relieved to find that, due to Papa Speyer's guidance, neither her income nor O'Neill's was seriously threatened.

O'Neill was earning royalties from foreign productions of his plays and domestic revivals, as well as from movie sales, and he had invested carefully. As Carlotta advised Lillian Gish, who had written to her about her own investments with Speyer: "Just hang on. I sit tight." Carlotta assured Gish she was in good hands; although Speyer wasn't "infallible," she said, he was, after all, "a well known international banker."

Toward the end of January, with Carlotta recovered and O'Neill's typescript nearly completed, they returned to Le Plessis and soon after took off for the Canary Islands to recuperate. Believing the islands "would be full of canaries singing in beautiful gardens," Carlotta found it instead "a desolate, ugly place."

She tolerated it for O'Neill's sake, watching her "sun child," as she called him, baking himself in the hot sand after long swims. And when, between swims and sightseeing, he began work on a sixth draft of his trilogy, she rejoiced in going over it with him scene by scene.

O'Neill's adoration of Carlotta at times transcended his own self-absorption. But as uxorious as he was, the proposal he made to Carlotta while relaxing on the beach in the Canary Islands was so much out of character as to be mind-boggling.

"Gene wants me to have a baby!" Carlotta exclaimed to Lillian Gish in a letter from the Canaries on March 2, 1931.

Actually, Carlotta had dropped a cryptic note—"Gene discusses 'baby'!!!?"—in her diary a year earlier. Although she made no further comment at that time, she must have whispered about the discussion to a friend (or two), because seven months later (on September 23), she noted, "Gene receives a telegram from the Associated Press in Paris—asking if it is true I am to have a baby!!!"

It was Walter Winchell who had launched the gossip in his widely syndicated column on September 8, 1930. And on September 25, a note arrived for O'Neill at Le Plessis from a reporter on the Tours newspaper, asking about "the baby." When, a few months later, O'Neill was queried by Kenneth Macgowan, he tossed off the following reply:

"The expectant father rumors were all the bunk. Between us we have four children already and find they are expensive and we are not such gluttons for punishment that we want to take on any more of these responsibilities—in bringing into the world fresh victims for the new poison gases which the lads are preparing for our children."

That sounded more like the old phobic O'Neill, who had felt betrayed when Agnes produced a child; it more accurately reflected the crabby dramatist who couldn't wait to kill off the children in his plays. And yet, after sending that letter to Macgowan, O'Neill changed his mind once again, reiterating his aberrant wish to have Carlotta bear his child.

She, however, felt unsure, as she confided to Gish, cautioning her that this was "entre-nous of course." After voicing her own concern about already having four children between them, she declared, "But he wants *our* baby!" and added, "I told him if we get a home I'll see—but not living as we have all over the place."

Carlotta and O'Neill never did stop living "all over the place"; their precious Blemie was to remain the only child of their marriage.

The O'Neills were still in contented mode on the Canary Islands on March 25, when a cable arrived from Richard Madden informing O'Neill of an offer from Metro-Goldwyn-Mayer to buy *Strange Interlude*, netting O'Neill $35,000. Carlotta was thrilled, noting that the money would be the foundation of their new home in America.

He and Carlotta returned to Paris and, on April 7, he mailed a copy of the completed *Electra* script to the Theatre Guild. He also sent a script to Nathan with an accompanying note, reliving the grueling months of his creative struggle. "Let's hope the result in some measure justifies the labor I put in," he wrote, enumerating his demanding objectives:

"To get enough of Clytemnestra into Christine, of Electra in Lavinia, of Orestes in Orin, etc. and yet keep them American primarily; to conjure a Greek fate out of the Mannons themselves (without calling in the aid of even a Puritan Old Testament God) that would convince a modern audience without religion or moral ethics; to prevent the surface melodrama of the play from overwhelming the real drama; to contrive murders that escape cops and courtroom scenes."

While in Paris, the O'Neills booked passage on the Dutch liner S.S. *Statendam*, departing for New York on May 9. Carlotta, in a sentimental leave-taking, visited the Tuileries: ". . . my beloved Paris that I know I will never see again—when I leave with Gene—a part of me is dying— for I must live *Gene's life* with all my strength and knowledge—it is *him* now. I must always be there to help, to understand, to comfort,—*no matter what!*"

As Carlotta began the process of vacating Le Plessis on April 19, the O'Neills received their final visitor, the editor (since 1922) of O'Neill's previously published plays, Manuel Komroff. It was he who would oversee the published version of *Mourning Becomes Electra* at Horace Liveright.

More than thirty years later, Komroff wrote a reminiscence (never published) about that visit. Komroff was an intense intellectual, without social polish or pretense, and something of a Marxist. Carlotta disdained him as "a weak sort of man, apologizing for living! I don't feel comfortable with this type of man."

Komroff, who had never met Carlotta, soon became aware of her supercilious appraisal. "Here before me was the famous Carlotta," he wrote. "How many times had I seen her picture in the newspapers? It was all true. She was beautiful." He acknowledged her "masterful" management of a large servant-run establishment; and he allowed that "she knew how to write a graceful 'thank you note,' and how to keep sightseers and boring acquaintances away from Gene so that he had free mornings for his work."

But Komroff was disconcerted by the pretentiousness of the lunch served him the following day. Marking his place at the table was "a silver holder with a card neatly lettered in French giving the menu." When the butler poured him white wine, both Carlotta and O'Neill said, "We're not drinking," making him uncomfortable to be drinking alone.

Komroff later pondered O'Neill's complacency in the midst of such display. He found it hard to accept the degree to which Carlotta had transformed the lifestyle of the man who wrote *The Hairy Ape*. He couldn't believe this was the idealistic dramatist who, seven years earlier, had proclaimed himself the theater's spokesman for "the under-dog," the man who wanted to give the public "a chance to see how the other fellow lives . . . his sufferings, his handicaps . . . to see the sort of life which their brothers far down the social scale must face each day."

O'Neill's unapologetic lifestyle was particularly grating to Komroff in view of the spreading Depression. He had just left behind New York's multiplying homeless sleeping in shanties in Central Park and waiting in blocks-long breadlines. He wondered if O'Neill and his Marie Antoinette were aware that there were many thousands of unemployed who could not afford eight cents for a loaf of bread.

Komroff did not count his two-day visit to Le Plessis a success and, soon after, he felt a cooling of O'Neill's friendship.

PROFESSIONAL PACKERS WERE at work in the château on April 23, readying boxes of silverware, linens, and china to be shipped to New York. Carlotta, having ordered several additional Vuitton trunks, was personally packing them with her own and O'Neill's extensive wardrobes, including the seventy-five pairs of shoes he had accumulated under her tutelage.

In the midst of the hubbub, O'Neill sat down to inscribe a manuscript copy of *Mourning Becomes Electra* to Carlotta. The inscription sang with lyrical feeling:

> In memory of the interminable days of rain in which you bravely suffered in silence that this trilogy might be born— days when I had my work but you had nothing but household frets and a blank vista through the salon windows of the gray land of Le Plessis, with the wet black trees still and dripping, and the mist wraiths mourning over the drowned

fields—days when you had the self-forgetting love to greet my lunchtime depressing, sunk preoccupations with a courageous, cheering banter—days which for you were bitterly lonely, when I seemed far away and lost to you in a grim, savage gloomy country of my own—days which were for you like hateful boring inseparable enemies who nag at nerves and spirit until an intolerable ennui and life sickness poisoned your spirit—

In short, days in which you collaborated, as only deep love can, in the writing of this trilogy of the damned! These scripts are rightly yours and my presenting them is a gift of what is half yours already. Let us hope what the trilogy may have in it will repay the travail we've gone through for its sake!

I want these scripts to remind you that I have known your love with my love even when I have seemed not to know; that I have seen it even when I have appeared most blind; that I have felt it warmly around me always (even in my study in the closing pages of an act!), sustaining and comforting, a warm secure sanctuary for the man after the author's despairing solitudes and inevitable defeats, a victory of love-in-life,—mother, and wife and mistress and friend!—

And collaborator!

Collaborator, I love you!

A week before sailing, O'Neill was relieved (if not surprised) to receive a cable from the Theatre Guild accepting *Mourning Becomes Electra* for production.

Carlotta took a tearful leave of Le Plessis's household help. She and O'Neill gave their Gordon setter, Ben Lomond, to the children of one of the staff, since they were taking only Blemie with them to New York.

"Farewell to Le Plessis!" was O'Neill's laconic comment in his diary—and on May 9, boarding the *Statendam* in Boulogne, it was a dismissive

"Good'bye to France!" (Whether knowingly or not, his diary notation mimicked his brisk "Exit—S.S. *Berengaria*" that had recorded his and Carlotta's furtive departure from New York three years earlier.)

It would be surprising if O'Neill, aboard ship, did not glance at his worn copy of *Thus Spake Zarathustra*, which he had kept with him ever since falling under Nietzsche's spell at eighteen. He had remained transfixed by the book all his life and, indeed, it was not long since that O'Neill (then approaching his fortieth birthday) had remarked to Ben De Casseres that *Zarathustra* "has influenced me more than any book I've ever read." At the time, he was recalling his first encounter with Nietzsche in 1906 at the anarchist Benjamin Tucker's Unique Book Store shortly before his expulsion from Princeton.

"I've always possessed a copy since then and every year or so I re-read it and am never disappointed, which is more than I can say of almost any other book. (That is, never disappointed in it as a work of art, aspects of its teaching I no longer concede.)"

Long before uprooting himself from yet another home that had failed him, he had underlined a favorite passage: "I am a wanderer and a mountain climber . . . I like not the plains, and it seemeth I cannot long sit still. And whatever may become my fate and experience—a wandering and a mountain climbing will be part of it. In the end one experiences nothing but one's self."

Five years earlier, after parting from Carlotta in New York to sail back to his Bermuda home, O'Neill had written to her of his own unyielding sense of "seeking flight."

"What a thrill of life it gave me," O'Neill said, recalling his "sailor days" and "that first feel of the great ground swell of ocean heaving under me. It meant a release then, an end of an old episode and the birth of a new. Life then was simply a series of episodes flickering across my soul like the animated drawings one sees in the movies, and I could not then see how the continuity of my own seeking flight ran through them as a sustained pattern."

———

USING ALL HER WILES, Carlotta wangled permission to keep Blemie in her cabin on their six-day voyage. She also arranged for their luggage to be pre-inspected and sent ahead through customs, so that she and O'Neill could disembark quietly, bypassing the reporters who awaited the reclusive dramatist after his long absence from Broadway.

They checked into the Madison Hotel on May 17 and greeted George Jean Nathan and Eugene Jr. at dinner that evening. "Excited, tired and worried," Carlotta told her diary, wondering, "What next?" She had her shocking answer all too soon.

The Theatre Guild's business manager, Warren Munsell, insisting that O'Neill make a statement and answer questions about his forthcoming play, had scheduled a press conference for the afternoon of May 21; O'Neill had five days to steel himself. He and Carlotta secluded themselves in their hotel, resting and taking all their meals in their suite.

On May 20, shortly before 1:00 a.m., Carlotta's ex-husband Ralph Barton sat at his typewriter in his penthouse at 419 East Fifty-seventh Street, just a few blocks from the Madison Hotel, and wrote a long note, which, in red ink, he headed, "OBIT."

He donned his pajamas, got into bed, lit a cigarette, thumbed through a worn copy of *Gray's Anatomy* until he came to a section dealing with the heart, set the book aside—still open to that section—smoked another cigarette, and then shot himself with a .25-caliber revolver—not in the heart, but through the right temple.

Barton's body was discovered at ten o'clock that morning by his maid. The editor of *The New Yorker*, Harold Ross, was one of the first to hear of his death and he called Carlotta at once, hoping to cushion the shock. It was apparent to Ross, as it was to other friends, that Barton's act was an attempt, at once pitiful and tragic, to upstage the triumphant return of the man he considered his rival.

Poor Barton's statement certainly had its shattering impact. The note he left, widely quoted in the press, cited his remorse over his "failure to appreciate my beautiful lost angel, Carlotta, the only woman I ever loved and whom I respect and admire above all the rest of the human race.

"She is the one person who could have saved me had I been saveable. She did her best. No one ever had a more devoted or more understanding wife. I do hope she will understand what my malady was and forgive me a little."

Headlines of the afternoon papers shouted the names of Eugene O'Neill and Carlotta Monterey; *The New York Times*, among other papers, quoted the suicide note in its entirety. In response, O'Neill's lawyer issued a statement to the press saying, in part, that "Mrs. O'Neill, the former Carlotta Monterey, desires to state definitely that she never saw or heard from Mr. Barton since her divorce from him more than five years ago." (Understandably, she neglected to mention the brief and futile correspondence Barton had initiated with her following the divorce.)

By the time Carl Van Vechten arrived at the Madison for a previously scheduled lunch in the O'Neills' suite, he found them fully informed. "Gene was very quiet during the lunch," Van Vechten recalled. "But Carlotta talked about it. She said she couldn't understand this horrible thing—that Barton wasn't in love with her."

The O'Neills had earlier invited Benjamin and Bio De Casseres to dine with them that evening; upon hearing the news, the couple expected to be called off, but they were not.

"Well, Ralph Barton blew his top" was O'Neill's tart comment when they arrived. That was the only reference made to the subject. But Carlotta, stricken, wrote in her diary, "After dinner I almost pass out—Gene is gentle and sweet."

Nearly two weeks before Barton shot himself, he had addressed a letter to Carlotta at Le Plessis; he dated it May 7 and posted it the following day, unaware she would be sailing for New York before the letter could reach her.

Reminding her that it was nine years since he'd first met her, he said he would be a happy man "instead of a very wretched one" if he had known then what he knew now. The past five years, he said, had been his punishment for "the wanton murder of the only thing I want or love in the world." He would trade "ten times over" all the gifts he'd since been given "to have you walk by my chair and give me a pat on the head."

He asked her forgiveness for writing. "The pain of living without you twenty-four hours every day becomes insupportable sometimes. I love you, my dear lost angel."

O'Neill and Carlotta worriedly talked over the impending Theatre Guild press conference, which had been postponed a day, to May 22, because of the Barton suicide. To spare O'Neill the stress of individual interviews, the Guild's Warren Munsell had invited the full contingent of New York's theater reporters. One of the Guild's press agents, Joe Heidt, assured O'Neill that he'd telephoned the drama and city desks of all the New York newspapers, requesting them to instruct their reporters not to ask questions about Barton or Carlotta. "They all promised," Heidt recalled.

O'Neill was not reassured but, as he told Carlotta, he knew he had to go through with the press conference for the sake of *Electra*, no matter how much he dreaded the ordeal. It would be "like walking into hell," Carlotta predicted.

The press conference began at 3:00 p.m. A perspiring O'Neill stood before the reporters, critics, and photographers who packed the Guild's boardroom. It was the largest and most suspenseful theater press conference anyone present could remember. According to the critic for the New York *Daily News,* John Chapman, O'Neill had stipulated that he would take questions from only one of the more than two dozen reporters present, and Chapman was selected by his peers to be that one.

O'Neill was "pallid and shaking and sweating when he faced his lone inquisitor—and so was I," Chapman recalled. During the interview, which lasted an hour and a half, O'Neill declared, among other things, that living abroad had enabled him "to see America more clearly" and "to appreciate it more."

He answered questions about the relative merits of the European and American theater. Europeans, he said, would "soon be coming over here to learn from us," adding that "the American stage has a dynamic quality and freshness theirs lacks."

He discussed his plans for the future. He and Carlotta would go to California soon to visit her relatives, but not to work for the motion pictures; it wasn't that he had "a snooty attitude toward the pictures," he said, but because he had work of his own planned for the next five years. He also announced that rehearsals for *Electra* would begin in mid-August.

As he had feared, one reporter managed to shout a question about Barton, and O'Neill felt obliged to answer. "As far as I know I never met Ralph Barton. He did not call on us. . . . I know that he had made no effort to see Mrs. O'Neill."

According to Heidt, except for that one question, the press "behaved beautifully," although one woman lingered to ask more questions about Barton. O'Neill declined to answer, believing he had more than met his obligation.

After the reporters had left, Heidt and O'Neill congratulated each other on how well things had gone. He was now presumably safe from further inquisition, for his address in Manhattan was a secret and he had safeguarded the privacy of his immediate future by announcing (untruthfully) that he was leaving for California.

O'Neill's tranquillity was shaken when Heidt happened to look out the window and saw taxicabs lining the curb; the reporters were waiting for O'Neill to leave so they could trail him to wherever he was staying.

If the press conference was something of a requiem, its encore was a Harold Lloyd farce. O'Neill was eager to depart, and Heidt knew of a way to smuggle him out of the building. But the escapade would entail some undignified moments and Heidt hesitated to propose it; he would have to guide O'Neill over the roof of an adjacent building and out a side-street exit. Finally, he did suggest it, and O'Neill thankfully agreed.

Heidt telephoned the skating rink that was housed in the building adjoining the Guild, and received permission to cross their roof, "so they won't think we're a couple of burglars and take a shot at us," he told

O'Neill. Then he guided his charge to room 64, the Guild's rehearsal space on the top floor. From there, Heidt and O'Neill clambered up a fire escape ladder leading to the roof, crossed over to the adjoining building, and climbed down its rear fire escape. Heidt put O'Neill into a cab. As he drove off, O'Neill, his dignity intact, wore a mischievous grin. Heidt, also smiling broadly, walked around the block to the front of the Theatre Guild building, where he told the reporters there was no use waiting, because O'Neill had left.

They refused to believe Heidt. They said they knew there was an apartment in the Guild building and that O'Neill obviously intended to spend the night there. They were so preoccupied with tracking O'Neill that it didn't occur to them to question how Heidt himself had managed to get out of the building.

There were still three taxis in front of the Guild when Heidt returned the next morning at ten. "They'd been there all night," he recalled. "They never did find out where O'Neill was staying."

32

"Mother of God, I have another home to create for Genie," Carlotta sputtered to her diary. "I wonder if he will live in it!"

It was the end of June 1931, just over a month since she and O'Neill had returned to New York.

They were barely settled in a rented beachfront house called Beacon Farm on the Sound in Northport, Long Island, about an hour's commute from Manhattan and staffed with Carlotta's accustomed efficiency, when O'Neill underwent one of his Olympian flip-flops.

Abruptly dismissing his long-held conviction that it was impossible for him to get any writing done amid the distractions of the city, he decided he wanted a permanent home in Manhattan. To Carlotta's dismay, he insisted on signing a long-term lease for a duplex apartment in a just-completed eighteen-story building at 1095 Park Avenue and Eighty-ninth Street. "Why I ever left here, damned if I know," he told George Jean Nathan. "There's life and vitality here. It's the place for ideas!"

And now, the man Carlotta had begun to wryly characterize as "the Master," commanded her to have his Park Avenue abode ready by summer's end, when rehearsals were to begin for *Mourning Becomes Electra*. While O'Neill continued to revise *Electra* in their Northport house between swims in the Sound and entertaining an occasional guest, Carlotta shopped relentlessly for their future home on Park Avenue.

First among his guests, on June 16, was Eugene Jr., accompanied by Elizabeth (Betty) Greene, whom he'd introduced to his father and

Carlotta in New York two weeks earlier and who, he now announced, he had just married. O'Neill (in Carlotta's words) was "disappointed" in the choice he'd made.

Recently turned twenty-one, Eugene was distinguishing himself as a Greek scholar at Yale, where he'd just completed his junior year. Tragedy had already touched his life, which in many ways was to mirror that of his father's; Eugene's younger stepbrother (by his mother's second marriage), to whom he'd been close, had recently died in an unexplained fall from the nineteenth floor of an office building in New York.

O'Neill was eager to solidify his relationship with his son and swallowed his qualms about Betty Greene. He saw *Electra* as a project that would bind father and son intellectually, but Eugene Jr. far outshone his father in his knowledge of Greek tragedy. "I can't talk to him. He's too erudite for me," O'Neill told Lillian Gish with a wistful smile after one of his son's visits.

O'Neill had been unable to arrange a visit from his younger son— whom he hadn't seen in more than three and a half years—until later in the summer; they were reunited on August 4, when Shane arrived for a two-week visit. Almost twelve, he was about to enter the Lawrenceville School in New Jersey.

Carlotta and O'Neill were driven to New York by their chauffeur to meet Shane, and Carlotta whisked him off to Abercrombie's to "fit-him-out so to speak." After an early dinner, she and O'Neill drove back with Shane to Beacon Farm.

On the following day, Carlotta tactfully left father and son alone on the beach, so that they could have the whole day to become reacquainted. After that first day, Carlotta took it on herself to entertain Shane while O'Neill wrote. She gave the boy dancing lessons: "He enjoys this and it has become quite a frolic!" she noted. (She had not as yet reunited with her own child, from whom she'd been separated even longer than O'Neill from his children; she was evidently content to wait until Christmas for her mother to bring Cynthia from California for a visit.)

O'Neill swam and conversed with Shane almost every day, but when his son left, he brushed off the visit in his Work Diary with a nonchalant "Au revoir to Shane." He seemed unperturbed at postponing a visit with Oona, the daughter he'd so earnestly beseeched in his letters not to forget her Daddy; at six, she was deemed (probably by Carlotta, if not by Agnes) as too young for an extended visit, and she did not see her father until five months later.

O'NEILL NOW—less than ever—could spare little thought for progeny, his own or his wife's (despite his recent anomalous desire to father a child with Carlotta). He was immersed in casting for the October opening of *Mourning Becomes Electra* and he was about to confront the casting of a Lavinia.

Lillian Gish had asked to read for the role; at thirty-eight, with her spectacular silent-movie career winding down, she was eager to reestablish herself as a stage actress, and in view of O'Neill and Carlotta's close friendship with Gish and George Jean Nathan, he could hardly deny her a reading. But he was certain she was all wrong for Lavinia, and he was uneasy as he took his seat at the Theatre Guild's audition with other members of the production team.

Gish read a scene with Alla Nazimova, the internationally acclaimed Russian actress, soon to be cast as Lavinia's mother, Christine; O'Neill remembered Nazimova reverently from the time he first saw her in *Hedda Gabler* in 1907 during his visits to New York while he was a student at Princeton.

His fears about Gish were confirmed almost at once. Her personality and acting style—as the beautiful, winsome-but-fragile heroine of dozens of silent-screen melodramas—were utterly unsuited to the role of his hard-bitten, ruthless Lavinia.

O'Neill privately and gently informed a crushed Gish that she was not right for the role. "I told her the truth, the whole truth," he reported to Theresa Helburn. "She is a game sport and took it in fine spirit. But it was a tough job for me!"

Gish managed a stiff upper lip until she arrived at the O'Neill's' suite at the Madison Hotel, where Carlotta awaited her. Gish then burst into tears. Carlotta, although she tried to comfort her, was privately unsympathetic, and later observed, "Surely she knows herself better than to ever *want* to play Lavinia. Lavinia was *not* the 'little flower'—the 'tender virgin!'" Both O'Neills were relieved that the episode didn't impair their friendship with Gish and Nathan.

The role of Lavinia was accepted somewhat reluctantly by Alice Brady, the irreverent film and stage actress who (along with Katharine Cornell) had turned down Nina in *Strange Interlude,* and who had her doubts about Lavinia as well.

"Personally I feel that Mr. O'Neill meant Lavinia to be a symbol, rather than a living, breathing human being who buys hats and gloves and eats lamb chops," she said in an interview, shortly after the play opened. "I may be wrong, but I'm quite sure that Lavinia could never eat a lamb chop." O'Neill, she went on, hammered in the fact, at rehearsals, that no sentimentality must creep into the characterization of Lavinia and that "no one should feel sorry for her" at the final moment when she boards herself up in the Mannon house with her memories of the dead.

"The part is not 'me' at all," Brady concluded. "I had to create a character totally foreign to my nature and to anything I had ever done before. . . . But I love the part. It has a tremendous sort of abstract excitement for me."

After approving of Nazimova as Christine, O'Neill also signed off on Earle Larimore (a favorite ever since he'd played Sam Evans in *Strange Interlude*) for the role of Orin. With the selection of Lee Baker (a veteran stage and movie actor) as Brigadier General Ezra Mannon, and Thomas Chalmers (a former Metropolitan Opera baritone) as Adam Brant, the casting of the Mannon family was complete.

Carlotta, as intent as her husband on the impending production, needed no urging from O'Neill to wire Brooks Atkinson an invitation to Beacon Farm.

Shortly after the O'Neills' return from France, Atkinson had asked O'Neill what background reading he should do to help him understand the *Electra* trilogy. O'Neill replied he need not do any research, that the play was self-contained and not at all esoteric. Would Atkinson like to read it? Atkinson, who rarely if ever read a contemporary play in advance of seeing it onstage, made an exception, having long since recognized O'Neill as a giant of the American theater.

He read the trilogy and was somewhat disappointed. He read it a second time before writing to O'Neill to say—after praising the work as a whole—that he thought the public would be overwhelmed by the first play, let down by the second, and would find the third better than the second.

O'Neill, after thanking him for his "favorable reaction to the whole work," disagreed with his appraisal of the individual plays, going into defensive detail about each, and trying to arrange a meeting in New York during which they could "argue a bit."

He followed up with a second letter to the critic two months later: "The more of the inner workings and background of the writing of the trilogy I can set before you . . . the better for me in the sense of my getting more value out of your criticism, for or against."

Most criticism of real value, O'Neill pointed out, did not come until after the opening, when it was too late. "That's one of many reasons," he explained, "why I'm always glad to have any critic (whose opinion I respect, and whose right to criticize the drama I admit) read my scripts before the openings."

It was because O'Neill had failed to connect with Atkinson in New York that he was now suggesting the critic come to stay for a day or more in Northport. Neither O'Neill nor Atkinson seemed to think it at all remarkable that a theater critic of Atkinson's stature should sit down with a practicing dramatist (no matter what his stature) and—in essence—collaborate on the structure of a play that would eventually be reviewed by that critic.

In preparation for their forthcoming discussion, O'Neill reread the trilogy. He found that he liked it. He then added an entry to the *Mourning Becomes Electra* Work Diary he'd been keeping since the spring of 1926. Dating it "August 1931," he wrote that all three plays had "power and drive and the strange quality of unreal reality I wanted."

During Atkinson's two-day stay at Beacon Farm, he and O'Neill discussed *Electra* in detail and the critic bluntly told his host he felt the trilogy was "overwritten." "Gene, of course, disagreed," said Atkinson. He specifically recalled that during his visit, Carlotta was mostly invisible, that Blemie was present "at all meals," and that O'Neill "drank a lot of Moxie" (a then-popular carbonated drink) and swam in the afternoon. "We were both enchanted," he said, "when a Boston steamer, headed for New York, passed by."

WHILE RESOLVING TO keep Beacon Farm open for weekends, Carlotta and O'Neill moved into their Park Avenue duplex in early September. Carlotta had lovingly filled O'Neill's study with mementos of the sea: three paintings of clipper ships including the legendary three-master *Flying Cloud*; a scale model of another clipper ship, the *Thomas F. Oakes*; and a vintage brass ship's lantern.

Rehearsals for *Electra* were now set to begin on September 7, and O'Neill looked forward to working with Bobby Jones, with whom he hadn't collaborated since *The Great God Brown*, nearly six years earlier. He was also pleased to be reunited with Philip Moeller, who had staged *Strange Interlude*. O'Neill attended rehearsals scrupulously, and Carlotta, proudly possessive of "her" play, nearly always accompanied him. "I loved working with Gene behind the scenes," she said. She would sit beside her husband and take notes.

Ann Pinchot, whose husband, Ben, took photographs of O'Neill in connection with the play, remembered Carlotta hurrying along West Fifty-second Street in the September heat, on her way to rehearsals. "Carlotta did all the routine chores," Pinchot recalled, adding that she would bring O'Neill a paper bag with his lunch: a pint bottle of milk, and rye bread–and–butter sandwiches—for when O'Neill was in the midst of rehearsals, he did not leave the theater.

Electra, like *Strange Interlude*, was to forgo an out-of-town tryout and, because of its length, had been allotted seven weeks of rehearsal time instead of the customary four. Carlotta sat through most of them. "I never was bored a minute," she recalled. "It was wonderful."

Ann Pinchot remembered that O'Neill looked to be "in good shape, and not too nervous," although she recalled that his hands sometimes shook badly. She was struck by O'Neill's insistence that none of her husband's photographs of him should be retouched. According to Pinchot, O'Neill was the only man who ever made that request; O'Neill did, literally, want every line, every gray hair, even the faint pouches under his eyes to be visible.

O'Neill pruned extensively during the first two weeks, considerably reducing the trilogy's overall playing length. Schemes for presenting each of the three plays on consecutive nights were abandoned, and it was decided to present the trilogy in one chunk, like *Strange Interlude*. But even with O'Neill's trims, *Electra* was still approximately an hour and a half longer than *Interlude*, and so it would begin a little earlier in the afternoon, end a little later at night, and have a shorter dinner intermission.

The Theatre Guild issued an announcement to this effect, explaining that the first complete rehearsal had disclosed that "the unity and suspensive action of *Mourning Becomes Electra* would be aided if the plays were presented in a single day."

O'Neill was more expansive with his cast than he had been during previous plays, partly because Carlotta, as an actress, felt at home backstage, and eased his way. He was especially affable to Alice Brady, who happened to be an old friend of Carlotta's. One day during rehearsals, Sammy—one of Brady's four dogs—got into a fight outside the theatre with Blemie, and O'Neill had to separate them. He picked up Sammy and carried him into Brady's dressing room.

"Sammy met my dog outside," O'Neill told her. "Sammy sniffed and said, 'My mother's appearing in your father's rotten play,' and my dog naturally leaped on him. Sammy should know better."

As rehearsals progressed, O'Neill, according to Carlotta, became fascinated by the characterizations of Nazimova and Brady. But, although "they were so wonderful," Carlotta said, they were "not what Gene had fancied." O'Neill, she explained, was "disturbed" that Brady's robust Irish-French heritage somehow seeped into the persona of the rigid New Englander she was portraying.

On the other hand, he was amused, rather than annoyed, with the Slavic-born Alla Nazimova's occasional flare-ups of temperament: "A.N. has 'Odessa Vapours,' (as Gene puts it!)," Carlotta once observed. Much later, O'Neill told an interviewer: "Alice Brady and Alla Nazimova gave wonderful performances in *Mourning Becomes Electra*, but they did not carry out my conception at all. I saw a different play from the one I thought I had written."

O'Neill continued to make cuts until the last minute. Alice Brady later recalled her terror on opening night that she would forget her lines. "You see, Mr. O'Neill kept changing and changing the lines at every rehearsal. He even made some minor changes on the day of the opening performance. So that every time I'd think of a line, I'd wonder with horror whether that was the line which had been cut or changed in the script." She calmed down after the first two scenes but even so, she said, she "wouldn't go through it again for anything in the world."

After sitting through the final dress rehearsal on October 25, Carlotta was as exhausted as O'Neill. "My whole body aches," she wrote in her diary. "*He* is silent—& dying by inches!"

In his own diary, O'Neill mourned the end of his frenetic and protracted love affair with the tragic Greek family he'd resurrected and revitalized: "Farewell (for me), to the Mannons!"

To ACCOMMODATE THE CRITICS, the curtain rose at the Guild Theater on October 27, 1931, at 4:00 p.m. and fell shortly before eleven. (Subsequent performances began at five and ended shortly before midnight.) The reviews for the six-hour trilogy were glowing.

Atkinson, delighted with O'Neill's massive cuts and revisions, acclaimed the trilogy "a universal tragedy of tremendous stature—deep, dark, solid, uncompromising and grim . . . heroically thought out and magnificently wrought in style and structure." O'Neill, he said, "has never before ful-filled himself so completely; he has never commanded his theme in all its variety and adumbrations with such superb strength, coolness and coher-ence. To this department, which ordinarily reserves its praise for the dead, *Mourning Becomes Electra* is Mr. O'Neill's masterpiece."

In the *New York Evening Post*, John Mason Brown wrote that *Electra* was "uneven," but so were "the Himalayas." Although he enjoyed the play, *The New Yorker*'s Robert Benchley couldn't resist mocking it. It was less Greek tragedy than "good, old-fashioned, spine-curling melo-drama," he argued, and then asked:

> Are we not forgetting one very important source of O'Neill's inspiration, without which he might perhaps have been just a builder of word-mountains?
>
> Was there not standing in the wings of the Guild Theater, on that momentous opening night, the ghost of an old actor in a white wig, with drawn sword, who looked on proudly as the titanic drama unfolded itself, scene by scene, and who murmured, with perhaps just the suggestion of a chuckle: "That's good, son! Give 'em the old Theater!"
>
> The actor I refer to needs no introduction to the older boys and girls here tonight—Mr. James O'Neill, "The Count of Monte Cristo" and the father of our present hero. It is his precious inheritance from his trouper-father, his father who counted "One," "Two," "Three" as he destroyed his respective victims, one at the curtain to each act; it is his supreme sense of the Theater in its most elementary appeal, which allows Eugene O'Neill to stand us on our heads . . . and keep us there from five in the afternoon until almost midnight.

Electra went on to become more than merely theater news. The *Times* was moved to gently mock its mise-en-scène editorially on October 31:

> Poor New England! She appears to be fated to chronic depression; hush, hark, crash, bang! what is that? It is another cheerful little Eugene O'Neill bulletin about New England. This time it is a couple of murders, a suicide and the regular assortment of repressions, explosions, seductions, lusts and incests.
>
> Critical opinion seems to be unanimous that Mr. O'Neill's restatement of the complicated troubles of the Atreus family has resulted in a dramatic masterpiece. But it does seem a bit hard on New England, coming after the same author's celebrated Elms of a few years ago.
>
> Surely there are enough trunk murders in Los Angeles, enough love-nest slayings in New Jersey, enough axe murders in Seattle, to suggest a respite for the country east of the Hudson. New England has been accused of so many things that there's danger of people coming to regard Horror as peculiarly a New England product.

And an anonymous contributor sent a jingle, parodying an old song, that appeared in the syndicated newspaper column "The Conning Tower" (whose author, Franklin Pierce Adams, famously signed himself "F.P.A."):

> *My sister was Electra,*
> *Like yours, you will allow;*
> *And you may have a mother*
> *That needs a bullet now.*
> *I've come to this great drama,*
> *Destruction for to deal;*
> *And if you dare insult me, sir,*
> *I'll tell Eugene O'Neill.*

Inevitably, the day after the reviews and the outpouring of congratulations, O'Neill's mood plummeted: "Sunk—worn out—depressed," he wrote in his Work Diary. He painfully missed his Mannons, whose breath he'd been breathing, whose thoughts he'd been thinking, for the past five years. "Sad that the Mannons exist no more—for me!"

DESPITE ALL THE ACCLAIM, *Electra* did not capture that year's Pulitzer Prize. The winner was the musical *Of Thee I Sing* by George S. Kaufman, Morrie Ryskind, and George and Ira Gershwin. Perhaps more upsetting for O'Neill, following the play's publication, St. John Ervine, on leave from his job as the highly regarded English theater critic for the *Observer*, viciously tore into it as a guest critic for the *World*.

In his review, Ervine attacked the publisher's claim that O'Neill was "generally regarded as the world's greatest dramatist."

"Generally?" jeered Ervine:

> There happen to be alive simultaneously with Mr. O'Neill the following American dramatists: Marc Connelly, Susan Glaspell, Paul Green, Sidney Howard and Elmer Rice, in addition to two authors of light comedies, Mr. Philip Barry and Mr. S. N. Behrman. . . .
>
> The following British dramatists are also contemporaneous with Mr. O'Neill: Sir J. M. Barrie, John Galsworthy, Harley Granville-Barker, Somerset Maugham, Sean O'Casey, Sir Arthur Wing Pinero and Bernard Shaw. . . . Clearly, if Mr. Eugene O'Neill is superior to all of these authors, he is a most remarkable man, and his plays, therefore, must be tested, not by local and contemporary standards, but by standards that are universal. Mr. O'Neill, in brief, is to be placed in comparison with the great Greeks, with Shakespeare, with Moliere and Racine, with Ibsen and Strindberg and Chekhov. Can he bear to be compared with them?

O'Neill himself had the last word when, five years later, he was awarded the Nobel Prize, becoming his country's only American playwright (as of this writing) to earn that honor, at which time he maintained that *Mourning Becomes Electra* was the play from which he had derived "the most personal satisfaction."

33

With the turmoil of *Mourning Becomes Electra* behind him, O'Neill went in search of that sunny clime he had dreamed of in his rain-bound French château. New York was not, after all, the city he had recently praised for its life and vitality, nor was it "the place for ideas." He hadn't jotted a note for a play in six weeks—not since early October; he knew he must find a more writer-friendly environment.

O'Neill and Carlotta made their leisurely way in mid-November 1931 to the high-end tropical resort of Sea Island, Georgia, recommended by Ilka Chase as the sunny haven in which to build their home. In their chauffeur-driven Cadillac, Carlotta was wrapped against the late-autumn chill in a fur neckpiece fashioned for her by Revillon from the finest Russian sables—a gift from O'Neill for her unflagging support during the ordeal of *Electra*. They were, he said, "Three skins for the Trilogy."

Justifying his possession of a Cadillac in the unrelenting era of the Depression, O'Neill told friends he'd bought it at a bargain. "I snared it second-hand," he somewhat sheepishly informed Brooks Atkinson. "Only used 2,000 miles, ironclad guarantee attached, looking brand new, over one thousand dollars off, who could resist this splendid gift of world depression? Not I, who have always been an A One snob when it came to cars and boats, which must have speed and line and class or 'we are not amused.'"

This "snootiness," explained O'Neill, dated from early boyhood when his father (for once disregarding his penny-pinching Irish-famine roots) "always got me the classiest rowboat to be had, and we sported the first Packard car in our section of Connecticut."

Impressed with the remoteness, natural beauty, and sunshine of Sea Island, O'Neill was eager to price beachfront properties. All too familiar with her husband's impulsive streak, Carlotta ventured that it might be wiser to rent first, to be sure they wanted to live there permanently. But O'Neill insisted—as he had three years earlier when (still married to Agnes) he began rebuilding his "permanent home" in Bermuda; now Sea Island was where he wanted to spend the rest of his life.

"We have just taken an apartment in New York that has cost quite a bit of money to do up," Carlotta reminded him, "and we have it for three years at *over* $7,000 a year."

"Oh, we can sublet that," parried O'Neill.

"In Depression times?" retorted Carlotta.

"Don't you want a home of your own?" demanded O'Neill.

To which Carlotta could only respond, "Of course I do!"

At once they began a hunt for beachfront lots, aware they had to make a quick decision; they would soon have to return to New York to dutifully await their children's Christmas visits. The Sea Island Development Company assigned George Boll, a personable young bachelor who was to become the O'Neills' trusted adviser and friend, to show them what was for sale; they promptly bought oceanfront land and engaged the highly recommended architect Francis Abreu.

Their commitment was not made lightly; their home would be costly and laborious to build. But, as Carlotta averred, they were convinced it was to be their "home until the end!"

The shared design and building of a home from scratch was, for Carlotta, a thrilling adventure replete with symbols of her sustained closeness to O'Neill. He, too, craved the assurance of an endless all-consuming love as symbolized by this commitment—and, with that craving, came a resurgence of longing for the comfort of his childhood Catholic faith that, in turn, revived thoughts of *Without Endings of Days*, in which he had described his protagonist-self as tethered to "the rational world of fact—but always fighting against his deeply religious pull."

Disregarding the fact that that had initially been prompted by his guilt over leaving Agnes, he now thought he saw a way to twist the plot into a new play that would be a paean to the sanctity of his rapturous marriage to Carlotta.

Still struggling with his own perturbing indecision about whether he could re-embrace his early Catholic beliefs, he would retain the original predominating theme of a man's conflicted quest for spiritual reassurance through a return to his abandoned (if never forgotten) Catholic faith.

The newly envisioned play would (as previously planned) depict the deadly yes-and-no battle within the protagonist's mind, as represented by two separately acted selves. It would, in fact, be powered by O'Neill's own yearning for a belief in the eternity of his and Carlotta's sacred love.

O'Neill envisioned it as a "modern miracle play," intended to depict a "modern" man who, in his search for truth, "is forced back to his old God and thereby regains his lost soul."

But he was about to blunder into writing one of the more hapless plays of his career. Falling far short of O'Neill's hyperexalted hopes, it was to turn out as limp and unconvincing as *The First Man*, *Welded*, and *Dynamo*; it was deservedly dismissed by the Broadway critics, and O'Neill himself ultimately acknowledged "it wasn't any good."

If the play is unworthy of O'Neill the dramatist, it does provide a rare insight into the man. At the time of its writing, he was himself in the midst of a profound spiritual crisis; he was again living his protagonist's conflict at the same time that he was trying to make a play about that conflict. The result is a work that in its way (and despite its muddled narrative) is at times more revealing about his spiritual self than even *Long Day's Journey Into Night*, which was written at a great distance from the events it portrays. The action of O'Neill's modern miracle play (ultimately entitled *Days Without End*) is, on the other hand, set in the present and mirrors his own ongoing real-life dilemma; it was almost as though he were keeping a personal diary of his emotional ups and downs.

The back story is readily recognizable as O'Neill's own (with only minor variations). He describes the protagonist of *Days Without End* as a young boy who, like himself, loses the Catholic faith in which he was raised when God fails to respond to his prayers for his mother's salvation; he has spent his life (sporadically pursued by the Hound of Heaven) in a frantic if often unconscious search to regain that faith. (Several lines from the Francis Thompson poem are, in fact, quoted in the play's text.)

Starting in his early teens, the boy, like Eugene himself, has been subject to a spiritual confusion that has driven him by turns to drown himself in alcohol, to thoughts of suicide, to the joyous rebirth of becoming a writer, to plunges into perceived treacherous love affairs and an abandoned marriage—never free of his hungering for the motherly love denied him as a child.

Although in real life O'Neill has convinced himself that in Carlotta he has at last found his lost mother, and has forever shed his wounded self, he believes their love has no meaning unless it can somehow be locked in for eternity. A return to the spirituality of his Catholic roots seems to be the answer (except when it isn't).

This was O'Neill's tormenting dilemma—a dilemma he mistakenly thought he could shape into a play even as he was living it day by day. His overwhelming personal confusion forced him to ponder at length each step of the play's narrative; he worked only in fits and starts, and he allowed other events in his life to tide him over to his next creative step; it would be many months before he completed the play—and even after it was produced, he believed he'd chosen the wrong ending.

THE PLAY'S BEWILDERED protagonist is John Loving, a split personality (as in *The Great God Brown*) personified by two actors: John, the well-intentioned idealist, and his diabolical alter ego, Loving, who is dressed to look like John and wears a mask with John's features—but distorted by a permanent sneer.

This bedeviled creature is married to Elsa, who looks like Carlotta and who has something of her history, notably a recent marriage to a man who betrayed her with other women.

The idealistic John, determined (like the idealistic O'Neill) to imbue his marriage with eternal meaning, believes this can be achieved only by repossessing his lost religious faith. The masked and diabolical Loving (a conflation of O'Neill's detached intellectual self and his cynical brother Jamie) jeers at John and malevolently opposes his intention.

It turns out that John has recently indulged in a thoughtless onetime adulterous fling with a friend of Elsa's, and he is desperately eager not only to conceal this slip from Elsa, but to be absolved for committing it. (O'Neill seems to have been thinking here of his faithlessness to Agnes; there is no evidence that he had been unfaithful to Carlotta.) Loving mocks John's "sacred" love for Elsa and sneers at his "deluded" belief in the concept of expiation.

Elsa learns of the adultery, cannot forgive it, and deliberately causes herself to fall ill with pneumonia by walking about in the freezing rain while still recovering from influenza. As she lies near death, she senses John's suicidal despair and forgives him—upon which he summons the courage to overcome Loving's opposition and rushes out to find a church.

There, in a scene that reads like Theater of the Absurd, John spiritually vanquishes Loving, who dies. These are O'Neill's stage directions: "John Loving—he, who had been only John—remains standing with his arms stretched up to the Cross, an expression of mystic exaltation on his face. The corpse of Loving lies at the foot of the Cross, like a cured cripple's testimonial offering in a shrine."

The curtain falls on the last words of the reassembled John Loving: "Love lives forever! Death is dead! . . . Life laughs with God's love again! Life laughs with love!" Foolish as the plot may be, O'Neill, during its construction, was in torment over whether he himself could, or should, rejoin the Church.

O'Neill worked on a first draft of his modern miracle play in a Sea Island cottage rented by the week from the realtor George Boll while he awaited the completion of his new home. During the next two years, he would, in his own words, "sweat blood" over this play, whose final title derived from the Book of Common Prayer: "Glory be to the Father and to the Son, and to the Holy Ghost; As it was in the beginning, is now, and ever shall be, world without end."

Carlotta encouraged O'Neill in his perfervid religious reflections. Although herself not a Catholic, she was religiously inclined, having basked as a girl in the mystique of her California convent-school milieu. But for now, she was less engaged with his emerging play than in once again meeting the challenge of creating the ideal home for their sacred marriage.

"The trouble with me," noted Carlotta, "is I am good at making homes (if I *do* say it!). It is an awful job—but *worth* it, if you know what you want & get it!" She told her architect precisely what it was she wanted: "an austere Spanish house—thick, brick walls painted white outside and inside. Gothic shaped doors, arched, tiled roof and floors (imported old tiles)."

The day after her return to New York with O'Neill in mid-December, Carlotta excitedly reported their purchase and plans to Ilka Chase. The house would have twenty-two rooms (half that of the number at Le Plessis) and a fraction of the grounds, but it would be an imposing mansion with its own spacious beachfront.

Carlotta kept in almost daily telephone contact with Abreu and, for the third time since her marriage to O'Neill, she shopped for furnishings for a new home. As if desperate to get at least some of her money's worth from her soon-to-be-abandoned Park Avenue duplex, she proceeded to hold an almost manic round of luncheons, teas, and dinners.

It was the sort of ambiance O'Neill had found intolerable while married to Agnes. But he knew it would soon be over and, in fact, it provided him with the proof, once and for all, that it was impossible to work in the city. He resigned himself to intermittent brooding over the slowly evolving miracle play.

Both Carlotta and O'Neill, concerned about a new stock market plunge, spoke earnestly of reducing expenses. Yet soon after their return to New York, they instructed George Boll to buy an adjoining $5,000 oceanfront lot to ensure their privacy in Sea Island; and O'Neill ordered a $2,500 motorboat.

If not for his adoration of Carlotta, for whom the holidays had always held meaningful family obligations, O'Neill would gladly have ignored the holiday season. But he allowed himself to be swept up in Carlotta's fleeting maternal zeal. Along with arranging visits in New York with Shane and (finally) Oona, the time had now come for Carlotta to reunite with her own neglected daughter. Cynthia, accompanied by Carlotta's mother, Nellie Tharsing, arrived in New York from California two days after the new year. As the Park Avenue duplex had no guest room, Carlotta engaged a suite for them at the Mayfair House, two dozen blocks down Park Avenue at Sixty-fifth Street.

Cynthia, not quite fifteen, dined at the duplex on the evening of her arrival, along with her grandmother, who for some time had been urging Carlotta to relieve her of the burden of Cynthia's care. But Cynthia was unresponsive to Carlotta's efforts at regaining her affection and trust. She was unhappy with her mother's plan to take over her care, and resisted her mother's wish that she attend a boarding school on the East Coast.

When Carlotta, hurt by Cynthia's recalcitrance, hesitated over how to deal with her, O'Neill stepped in. It was an astonishing gesture of paternal solicitude in a man who gave so unwillingly of himself to his own children. Carlotta was overcome with amazement and gratitude. So deep was O'Neill's devotion to Carlotta that he took it on himself to decide she "*must* keep Cyn here for at least six months no matter what!"

With O'Neill's approval, Carlotta busied herself with her reluctant daughter. In early January, she outfitted Cynthia for school, and guided her to museums and theaters, including a performance of *Mourning Becomes Electra*. She also introduced Cynthia to thirteen-year-old Shane and seven-year-old Oona at a family luncheon, to which O'Neill lent his presence.

On January 10, O'Neill, still ducking a return to his intractable miracle play, insisted on joining Carlotta and her daughter on the tedious journey to Cynthia's new boarding school in Washington, Connecticut. Continuing in family mode after Cynthia had been bundled off to school, O'Neill, in early February, joined Carlotta at lunch with Shane and Oona, and then accompanied them to the Bronx Zoo on an outing that did not end felicitously. "Coming home," recorded Carlotta, "Oona is 'sick' all over the car, herself & the fur rug! Poor child! Clean her up— give her tea and send them home." (Oona would not see her father again for nearly another two years.)

When Cynthia, five months later, chose to return to California, O'Neill wrote her of his respect and admiration "quite apart from my step-fatherly affection for your mother's daughter"; he invited her to regard his home as hers to come to always "by right of the love I bear you!" She was, he said, "a brave girl and a true one," and he was proud to be her stepfather.

BETWEEN DAILY telephone briefings from Sea Island about the progress on his house, and New York's inescapable social life, O'Neill now and then tinkered with his neglected play. What he seemed to have forgotten was that as a resident of Manhattan he was accessible not only to the friends and acquaintances who lived there but also to the writers, artists, and musicians from abroad who asked to meet him. Although he was flattered to be sought out, after a time it became a burden.

Following an obligatory dinner hosted by the Theatre Guild on March 15 in honor of Gerhart Hauptmann, the German playwright and novelist who had won the Nobel Prize in 1912, O'Neill was on the edge of a cave-in. Unable to sleep, he entered Carlotta's bedroom with what she described as "one of those ghastly nerve attacks." She held his shaking body close, speaking to him soothingly; holding him through the night, she succeeded in calming him.

At April's end, O'Neill once more turned his back on city living.

Leaving much of the final packing up for a later date and not yet having sublet their duplex, he and Carlotta departed for Sea Island in the early morning of April 29. It was none too soon for O'Neill. "Farewell to 1095 Park Ave. (and damn glad of it!)" was his snarling comment to his Work Diary. Now, perhaps, he could get back to his play. Assured their Sea Island home would be ready before the end of June, O'Neill and Carlotta once again rented a cottage. Before returning to New York for the final packing, Carlotta noted, "I am trying to make it a perfect house."

In early May, O'Neill read his first draft of *Without Endings of Days* to Carlotta. But her mind was preoccupied with the horrendous news that the baby of Charles Lindbergh and Anne Morrow Lindbergh had been found murdered, and in her own crowded diary entry she failed even to mention the play.

It's possible her silence was due to bemusement. Not that she didn't appreciate that the play's conflict was prompted by O'Neill's love for her; nor did she fail to understand and sympathize with the concept of that conflict as a duel between the characters representing his two selves. But his abstract method of telling the story was not always easy to follow. O'Neill knew he was falling far short of what he meant to convey about his own ongoing spiritual conflict. He wrote and rewrote, but the appropriate ending continued to elude him.

He was desolate when Carlotta left for New York on May 16. She was to be away for two weeks, during which she would finish packing up the contents of 1095 Park Avenue and also attempt to resolve the disposition of its sublease.

"Longest time we've been separated," he confided to Saxe Commins. "I miss her like hell!" Carlotta missed him equally, but was consoled by being reunited with Blemie, who had been left at the duplex with a housekeeper.

She was relieved at last to find a tenant for the duplex, albeit at a considerable loss; the sublessee would pay only $4,000 a year for the apartment that was costing the O'Neills more than $7,000. "When the lease is over," she complained, "it will mean about $10,000 down the drain!"

In his rented Sea Island cottage, O'Neill poured out his pent-up long-ing to Carlotta, hailing her as his savior; she was a goddess who embod-ied the mythic love denied him by the all-too-mortal women who had come before:

"Mistress, I desire you, you are my passion, and my life-drunkenness, and my ecstasy, and the wine of joy to me! Wife, you are my love, and my happiness, and the word behind my word, and the half of my heart! Mother, you are my lost way refound, my end and my beginning, the hand I reach out for in my lonely night, from my ghost-haunted inner dark, and on your soft breasts there is a peace for me that is beyond death!"

O'Neill's wine of joy was reduced to dregs by the time Carlotta boarded the train for her overnight trip back to Sea Island on May 29. She was staggering from the exhaustion of packing up the duplex. With Blemie on a leash, she oversaw the porter's disposition in her drawing-room compartment of her hand luggage and three cages of birds. Blemie, shaking uncontrollably, looked on. Carlotta was aware that the hyper-sensitive Blemie was bewildered by what was happening to him, and it frightened her to see his eyes popping, his tongue hanging out. As she arrived with him at the baggage car, he collapsed.

Shuddering at the sight of four coffins in the otherwise vacant car, Carlotta—careless of her impeccable travel outfit—plunked herself down on the filthy floor and took Blemie in her arms. After two hours, a porter arrived and helped her to her feet. Together, they contrived a makeshift bed for the prostrate Blemie, and the porter held his paw until he fell asleep. His disheveled mistress dragged herself to her compart-ment for a nap, after which she returned to the baggage car to minister to Blemie.

When O'Neill met her train the following evening, he was startled by her state of disarray. That night, after coaxing Blemie back to a sense of well-being, Carlotta tucked him into his bed. And then she went to her husband's bedroom and "slept in Gene's arms."

Three weeks later, O'Neill and Carlotta moved into their new home. "Wonderful feeling that this is house We have built—never built one before," O'Neill exclaimed in his Work Diary on June 22. On the same day, in her own diary, Carlotta for the first time mentioned the name they had chosen for their new home: "Casa Genotta." This melding of their two first names was a rather fanciful designation to apply to a modern Spanish mansion set in the deep American South and occupied by an Irishman and his Dutch-French-Danish spouse.

The house, which cost $100,000—a lordly sum for the Depression era—and left the O'Neills temporarily broke, was set in an area famous for its cotton crop and for its traditional Southern gentility. The house boasted a courtyard and formal garden in front and a stretch of beach leading to the Atlantic in the back. To its neighbors' discomfiture, however, Casa Genotta announced its un-neighborly aloofness with a surrounding eight-foot-high wall designed to ensure privacy.

O'Neill's study on the second floor jutted out over the ground-floor dining room, and its curved wall, suggesting that of a galleon's prow, had windows facing out to sea. Inside, it was fitted as a ship's cabin, with exposed wooden planking on the ceiling and walls and a built-in bunk-sofa beneath the curved windows, among other nautical touches. A circular iron stairway led from the study to the "crow's-nest" on the roof.

Carlotta once told Ann Pinchot that she'd had a mental image of what she wanted to build, "down to the last towel rack," before one brick of the house was put into place. In notes for a magazine article (which never materialized), Pinchot wrote that Carlotta, after her experiences with the French château, "was very decisive in her admiration of American plumbing, and she made certain that kitchen and bathrooms had the best—including, she told me, a bidet. The house was both comfortable and practical—no waste or extravagance, for display purpose; only a clean and precise and beautiful compactness." The huge living room, rising the full height of the house, was furnished with somewhat starchy comfort; on the walls hung old icons and the masks from *The Great God Brown*.

O'Neill once more put aside *Without Endings of Days* to help Carlotta get settled. He said he had "gone stale on work—thrown off stride by moving and so many distractions." The challenge he'd set himself this time was more than he'd bargained for, but he did not as yet fully comprehend the paralyzing impact of the gauntlet he'd flung at his own feet.

At least he could now conduct his creative combat in surroundings far removed from the clamor of the city. As in his isolated French château, he entertained selectively, inviting occasional houseguests. To test the mettle of their staff, he and Carlotta began with family—Eugene Jr.; his wife, Betty; and Shane—as their first houseguests for a two-week stay in early July 1932. Things ran smoothly enough and the trickle of guests continued. Ilka Chase, when she visited, found the house "quiet and exquisitely clean, with special boxes and bags to keep the mildew out of things and with little colored maids polishing like Dutchmen."

Lawrence Langner, who visited with his wife, Armina, along with Fania Marinoff, was not surprised to find that the household revolved around O'Neill's writing: "He worked in his study until noon. Then, attired in his dressing gown, he came down to the beach. After a while we went swimming in the sandy colored water which is, to me, one of the most unattractive features of Sea Island. Gene was the best swimmer and swam far out to sea."

Sea Island was at its best during the spring. It grew excessively humid and hot in the summer and, according to Langner, was "by no means the paradise the O'Neills expected it would be." It was so damp "that special bronze had to be used for all the window hardware, for ordinary metal would rust away."

The weather was also often stormy. With clear sunny days not to be counted on, Sea Island seemed, after all, not much of an improvement over the Loire Valley. Another unpleasant feature of the island was disclosed to Langner when he asked Carlotta why all the bushes in the patio were clipped up a foot from the ground. "That's so we can see if there are any snakes under them," she told him, explaining that the island abounded in rattlesnakes.

"Gene added smilingly that these were relatively harmless compared to the pretty little pink coral snakes which also disported themselves in this paradise," said Langner, adding that Fania, "who hated snakes even more than I did, trod very gingerly around the countryside after this, and I was never quite at ease either."

The most frequent guest at Casa Genotta was George Boll, who had fled his native New York for the easygoing life of a Sea Islander. A young bachelor with time on his hands, he was invited to join the O'Neills three or four times a week, where he entertained O'Neill and Carlotta with gossip about their well-heeled Sea Island neighbors, and made up a welcome third for the card games and word games the O'Neills liked to play in the evenings.

Once or twice a week Boll accompanied O'Neill on fishing expeditions, and he joined him many afternoons on the beach when O'Neill, after a morning's writing, sought relaxation in exercise. After attacking his punching bag, O'Neill sometimes sparred with Boll, who had particularly endeared himself to O'Neill as a fellow prizefight enthusiast. Boll was an eager listener when O'Neill described the night of September 14, 1923, when he'd sat ringside at the Polo Grounds watching the twenty-eight-year-old Jack Dempsey defend his world championship title against the twenty-nine-year-old challenger Luis Angel Firpo, "The Wild Bull of the Pampas."

O'Neill had stood on his seat, along with everyone else in the stadium, hollering and stamping wildly during the three minutes and fifty-seven seconds that the battle raged. Firpo was knocked down nine times, and Dempsey was belted out of the ring, into the laps of the sportswriters, who promptly threw him back.

Boll listened in awe as O'Neill (at that time already the winner of two Pulitzer Prizes) described his visit to Dempsey's dressing room after he'd knocked out Firpo. Dempsey, nursing a black eye, told O'Neill he had forgotten to duck.

Dempsey was superseded as hero in O'Neill's sports pantheon by Gene Tunney, who, three years later, vanquished Dempsey in Philadelphia. The reason he liked Tunney, O'Neill told Boll with a grin, had less to do with the champion's prowess than with his passion for literature. George

Bernard Shaw, too, had been drawn to Tunney for that reason. But Tunney had disarmed O'Neill when—invited by Professor William Lyon Phelps in 1928 to address his popular class in literature at Yale—Tunney declared that while the Bard was "overwhelmingly great," he "secretly cherished the thought that Eugene O'Neill is greater than even Shakespeare."

When Boll was not available, O'Neill called on Herbert Freeman to be his sparring partner. Freeman, twenty-three, had been highly recommended as a chauffeur by one of the O'Neills' Sea Island neighbors. Born in rural Georgia, Freeman was sketchily educated and spoke with a thick drawl. His German wife, Lisa, was engaged by Carlotta as a parlor maid; but she proved unsatisfactory and was soon fired, prompting Freeman to divorce her.

In addition to driving the O'Neills and their guests, Freeman acted as man Friday and gradually became an indispensable member of the Casa Genotta household. Affectionately called Herb, he was treated almost as an adopted child.

Freeman was devoted to Carlotta. "She was perfect to me," he said, recalling that Carlotta had once invited his mother to spend a week at Casa Genotta. "You couldn't keep from loving anybody like that. But yet, at the same time, we'd battle." Freeman was wary of Carlotta's "awful quick temper," for it led to bursts of fearsome cursing.

"I don't think I heard any Marine drill instructor that could beat her," Freeman once recalled, after returning from a wartime stint with the Marine Corps. "When she'd sometimes raise Cain, I'd say, 'You just told me the other day, Miss, that I was your child. How're you talking to a child like this?' She'd laugh and say, 'Go on, get out of here.'" If O'Neill happened to be nearby, he would side with Freeman, telling him, "That's right. Give it to her!"

O'Neill was completely relaxed in Herb Freeman's company and often joked with him and lightly confided in him. According to Freeman's verbatim report, the following dialogue ensued one day at the beach when O'Neill asked him if he could guess who had just telephoned him.

Herb: "Shane? Eugene Jr.?"

O'Neill: "Oh, no. Katharine Hepburn."

Herb: "What did she want?"

O'Neill: "She wants to be in one of my plays. I don't want her. She's a great actress. But she's just a titless wonder."

One of Freeman's duties was to carry O'Neill's kayak down to the beach. He would watch as O'Neill paddled way out beyond the surf. When he returned, Freeman sometimes joined him for a swim, trying to keep up. "I couldn't do it," Freeman said.

Casa Genotta was staffed with a live-in cook (as well as a housemaid who cooked when necessary), but O'Neill would sometimes ask Herb to prepare a special meal for him. "I'd make cornbread and fried chicken," said Freeman. "I heard him tell the cook one time, 'Why the hell don't you fry chicken like Herb does?' She was a good cook . . . but [after that] she didn't like me no more."

AGAIN TAKING UP *Without Endings of Days* during August 1932, O'Neill blundered into one after another of the traps he'd inadvertently set for himself. "Dull—no go," he scribbled in his Work Diary on August 8. And four days later: "Stuck again—discouraged."

On the following day, Carlotta marveled in her diary: "Gene talks to me at great length of one of his favorite topics 'Mother God'! And then with that most charming smile of his, he says 'I want to go to church'! We went!" That same day he started a "new 1st Scene" and continued working on the play throughout the month, when once more he was stuck. After doing "battle with it again" from midnight to 2:30 a.m. on September 1, he gave in: "no flow—sunk!" He fell into a despondent sleep—and a dream came to his rescue.

HE AWOKE THAT MORNING with the idea for a "Nostalgic Comedy," as he described it. Finding it "fully formed and ready to write," he armed himself with pad and pencil and by 3:30 that afternoon he had sketched an outline for *Ah, Wilderness!* On the following day, noting that the play seemed "crying to be written!" he put aside *Without Endings of Days*. He was only too happy to let himself be distracted from memories of his own tormented Catholic childhood and to deal with the "very simple people" (as he described them to Eugene Jr.) of *Ah, Wilderness!*

"It has very little plot," O'Neill told his son. "It is more the capture of a mood, an evocation [of] the spirit of a time that is dead now with all its ideals and manners & codes—the period in which my middle 'teens were spent.

"Perhaps, if I give you the subtitle you will sense the spirit of what I've tried to recapture in it, 'A Nostalgic Comedy of the Ancient Days when Youth was Young, and Right was Right, and Life was a Wicked Opportunity.'" After cautioning Eugene that it was "not a play one can explain," he nevertheless attempted, haltingly and at considerable length, to explain it:

"Yes, it is a comedy—and not in a satiric vein like 'Marco M'—and not deliberately spoofing at the period (like most modern comedies of other days) to which we now in our hopeless befuddlement and disintegration and stupidity feel so idiotically superior, but laughing at its absurdities while at the same time appreciating and emphasizing its lost spiritual & ethical values."

It was a pleasure, he went on, to switch from his usual preoccupation with the "tragic hidden undertones of life" he ordinarily pursued in his plays. *Ah, Wilderness!*, he said, was surely "the last play they would ever suspect me of writing."

And so O'Neill again put aside his dolorous miracle play in favor of his new comedy. What he now wanted was to capture the spirit of the typical American large small town at the turn of the century, he told his elder son. That past, he said, "possessed a lot which we badly need today to steady us." He was recalling the middle-class families of the New London of 1906 among whom he'd spent the summers of his youth, and which, in retrospect, seemed to have been governed by a homespun ethos that no longer existed.

The play's curtain rises on the morning of the Fourth of July, 1906, and revolves around the Miller family: Father, Nat, the editor of his hometown newspaper; Essie, his maternal, efficient, and sweet-natured wife; their four robust, affectionate children—three boys and a girl ranging from eleven to nineteen; Nat's spinster sister, Lily, in love with Essie's unregenerate bachelor brother, Sid, a reporter for Nat's paper.

The slender plot hinges on the small war between the mildly rebellious second son, Richard—going on seventeen and about to enter Yale—and his morally steadfast but indulgent father, who tolerates Richard's frequent spouting of radical poetry.

The play's modest denouement occurs when Richard, thwarted in his tentative romance with a pretty local girl, fifteen-year-old Muriel McComber, gets drunk in a barroom, where he has a brief and indeterminate encounter with a prostitute.

O'Neill's memory of his own adolescent rebelliousness (and his father's less tolerant attitude) had been jogged by his impulsive visit to New London the previous summer. On July 1 of that year, he noted, "revisit Pequot Ave. old time haunts." Carlotta, years later, recalled that she had thought the visit unwise; but O'Neill insisted, and they stopped in New London during a motor trip up the coast of Long Island and Connecticut.

"Don't do it, darling, don't do it," Carlotta warned him. "Don't ever try to go back; keep your ideas, but don't go back."

O'Neill ignored her. "No, he must go," recalled Carlotta.

As they drove along Pequot Avenue, O'Neill complained, "I can't find it, I can't even see it. This can't be Pequot Avenue." He was aghast at the changed landscape. Carlotta knew that the grounds in front of the O'Neill cottage had stretched to the water, "but in the time that Gene had been away," she noted, "the town had cut a street through and built little houses along here to the water, and everything was so changed. I was thunderstruck when I saw this quaint little birdcage of a house, sitting there." They didn't go in, for somebody had bought it and was living there.

"I shouldn't have come," said O'Neill.

"Well, never mind," said Carlotta, "you have come, now let's get out of here."

"Yes, let's go away," O'Neill agreed. "I don't want to look at it."

It was on September 1, 1932, after a swim off their Sea Island beach, that O'Neill read the first act of *Ah, Wilderness!* to Carlotta. She found it "charming!"—a word she was apt to apply to anything from a new pet canary to a brilliant sunrise, or a love letter. In this instance, she elaborated:

"[The play] is *Gene's dream of how he would have liked his childhood to have been*! Poetic, humorous, & a wee bit pathetic!" The "Gene" she had known in the 1920s, she added, "could not have written this!" She was quite right. But what she didn't specify was that, among other things, it was the only play he had written so far in which all the female characters were motivated by good-heartedness toward the male protagonist (in this instance, O'Neill's youthful fantasy-self).

O'Neill completed *Ah, Wilderness!* on October 3, only six weeks since he had dreamed it. "Great affection for this one," he had noted. On October 28, a week after celebrating his forty-fourth birthday, he reluctantly resumed work on *Without Endings of Days*. After listening to O'Neill read aloud his second draft of Act I, Carlotta privately worried that the play was causing "torment and battle with himself."

Two days later, when he read aloud Act II, Carlotta felt even more convinced that he was heading into an emotional hurricane. But she dared not presume to warn him. "It is all so personal with him," she noted, "and unless he *asks* me to give my *honest* opinion I will remain silent and let him exorcise his own devils—or saints! Poor darling, he *must always* be *tormented!*"

But when he later read aloud Act III, Carlotta described herself as truly moved. "I hope he does not change it." The following day, according to Carlotta, O'Neill was "going through a terrific spiritual experience in writing this play—So am I in watching his reactions!"

So absorbed was O'Neill that he could pay only fleeting attention to the momentous presidential election on November 8. Carlotta, staunch

Tory that she claimed to be, favored the incumbent, Herbert Hoover. "He sounds more honest than Roosevelt—not so much the slick politician," she remarked to her diary.

O'Neill was quite certain Roosevelt would win. "It was a Democratic landslide, as everyone expected," he wrote to Eugene Jr. His own increasing gloom about the future of America was reflected in his cynical comment to his son: "I doubt if the substitution of Democratic crooks and windbags for the Republican brand will put any chicken in anyone's pot." (A few months later, however, he was [briefly] more optimistic: "Roosevelt, whatever mistakes he may make, is a man with guts who is honestly facing the facts and acting upon them—no flabby, spineless Hoover!" he wrote to his son.)

After griping about the state of the nation, he couldn't help boasting of a piece of good news that had come his way. "I was asked to be a member of the Irish Academy being organized by Shaw & Yeats & Robinson, etc.—and accepted."

He regarded it as an honor, he said, whereas other academies meant little to him. "Anything with Yeats, Shaw, A.E. [George William Russell], O'Casey, Flaherty, Robinson in it is good enough for me."

But he continued to feel gloomy about the state of the economy, particularly as it affected his own dwindling bank account. His financial concerns, along with his distress over Sea Island's unexpectedly capricious weather and some new difficulties with his play, caused an outburst that stunned Carlotta.

"He talks to me about *being unhappy here*!?! Mother of God—he has the ocean to swim [in]—the beach to walk on—the ocean to fish in—male companionship." It was, after all, O'Neill himself who had insisted she make a home in Sea Island, she exploded. No place, person, or condition was perfect, nor was any love perfect, "but once in a hundred years it comes damn near it—unless *one is blind*."

It was the first time since their marriage that Carlotta had expressed her open outrage, and O'Neill, realizing he'd overstepped, soon apologized.

The true cause of O'Neill's malaise, as Carlotta realized, was his excruciating frustration not only with his play but with his personal dilemma. Having forced himself into a confrontation with the Catholic God of his childhood, he couldn't make up his mind how to resolve it. Would his protagonist decide yes or no to his return to the Church? And—even more difficult—would he himself re-embrace his lost faith?

"This damn play has a stranglehold on the old bean," O'Neill wrote to Nathan. What he had so far written, he said, seemed to him "a horrid mess." Still working on a third draft, he dropped the word *"Without"* from his title (now calling the play *Endings of Days*); but that did little to help. Momentarily dismissing his dilemma, he permitted himself to spend what he described as a "lovely Christmas with Carlotta."

However, three days later, O'Neill was fretting over "something fundamentally wrong" with the play and he decided to abandon it "until, if ever, the right solution of problem dawns—no good thinking any more—pass buck to unconscious—a little inspiration called for here."

He bade farewell to the year 1932 in his Work Diary with a prayer of gratitude: "What I have to thank God for: *Carlotta!*"

34

O'Neill found he couldn't keep the promise he'd made to himself at the close of 1932; instead of shelving *Days Without End*, he continued to grapple with draft after draft, unable to determine the play's conclusion—let alone its title (in early April 1933, he had renamed it *An End of Days*). Carlotta, worried about O'Neill working too hard, feared another crack-up.

It wasn't until the end of May that O'Neill found the title that stuck: *Days Without End*. The phrase beguiled him for its double meaning: "without end" could be construed as the prayer book's meaning of "eternity," but also as the secular meaning of "without goal."

He'd also found an ending he thought would work: the spiritually inclined John would at last vanquish the skeptical Loving and embrace the Cross. But, as O'Neill hastened to explain to the writer Sophus K. Winther, he himself was still wavering about his own return to Catholicism. Winther, head of the English Department at the University of Washington in Seattle, was completing a critical study of O'Neill's work through the writing of *Days Without End*.

O'Neill had not gone back to the Church, he told Winther, adding, "but I would be a liar if I didn't admit that, for the sake of my soul's peace, I have often wished I could.

"And by Catholicism I don't mean the Catholic church as a politically-meddling, social-reactionary force. That repels me. I mean the mystic faith of Catholicism whose symbols seem to me to approach closer than any other symbols to the apprehension of a hidden spiritual significance in human life."

With the burden of his religious play lifted, O'Neill turned to the more down-to-earth project of finding a new publisher. Horace Liveright was on the verge of bankruptcy, and Saxe Commins, who at O'Neill's insistence had become his editor at Liveright, was attempting to collect his friend's accrued royalties before the firm crashed.

O'Neill was being courted by first-rank publishers, eager for the prestige of his name and aware that his plays in print outsold even those of George Bernard Shaw's. (As of January 1932, *Strange Interlude* had sold 120,000 copies and *Mourning Becomes Electra*, now in its eighth printing, had already sold 60,000; all of O'Neill's plays combined had thus far sold 700,000 copies.)

By the end of May, O'Neill had decided to accept Bennett Cerf's offer at Random House; in addition to meeting all of O'Neill's financial terms, Cerf agreed to give Commins an editor's job. Liveright's bankruptcy was a fait accompli on July 10, 1933.

Both *Ah, Wilderness!* and *Days Without End* were embraced for production in the 1933–34 season by the Theatre Guild. But O'Neill, far from being gratified, was instead driving himself (and Carlotta) frantic with indecision over which play to present first. Ought it to be the nostalgic comedy or the spiritually wrenching tract? He was troubled, as he told Lawrence Langner, that any play following his popular *Electra* was "in a bad spot, no matter how good" it was.

He dragged his dilemma with him on August 4 to a campsite on Big Wolf Lake in the Adirondacks, fleeing from the Georgia heat (and leaving Blemie behind in the care of servants). Arriving in a fit of pique, O'Neill told Carlotta he was seriously considering "the advisability of not producing either of the plays."

He had the good sense to squelch his tantrum, for he was perfectly aware that his only hope of amassing enough cash to support his lifestyle lay in a lucrative Broadway run. Recalling the disastrous reception of the mystical-metaphysical *Dynamo* when it followed the vastly more accessible *Strange Interlude*, he wrote Langner he'd decided that *Ah, Wilderness!* should be produced first. He was, he said, speaking "psychologically" and in the interest of "the best showmanship," explaining that he didn't want *Days Without End* to meet the same fate as *Dynamo*. He added that *Days* was "nothing if not controversial, especially in its Catholic aspect," and he believed *Ah, Wilderness!* would surprise his followers with its light-heartedness, and would provide a breathing spell before confronting audiences with his dark (and often baffling) religious meditation.

A day later, he unabashedly reversed himself, rushing to apologize to Langner for having sounded "a damn sight more definite" than he really was. "I waver and feel one way about it one day and another the next," he said, until he was "quite gaga."

Langner made the decision for him, putting *Ah, Wilderness!* into production at once for an October 2 opening; aware that O'Neill and Carlotta had planned to extend their Adirondacks getaway through September, Langner apologized for having to cut their vacation short. O'Neill would be needed on August 30 for the start of rehearsals. And so, much to his annoyance, he and Carlotta were obliged to take up residence at New York's Madison Hotel on August 29 in the midst of a heat wave.

O'Neill had earlier cautioned Philip Moeller, the director of *Ah, Wilderness!*, that (in spite of the play's setting in Connecticut) he must not think of it as "a New England play!!!" Connecticut, he told Moeller, "never was real New England, as any New Englander will tell you." The play, he explained, could be laid in New York State, or New Jersey, or the Middle West with no change.

"I happened to have my old home town of New London in mind when I wrote—couldn't help it—but New London, even in those days was pretty well divorced from its N.E. heritage" and strongly influenced by New York.

O'Neill always insisted that Nat and Essie Miller and their four children were inventions. He allowed that they might have been very loosely based on those of his own relatives and friends who were present in

New London during his youth; but it was "absurd," he declared, to infer any resemblance between his adolescent protagonist and himself, for they were "exact" opposites.

There is ample evidence, however, that most (if not all) of the play's characters (including himself) are rooted in the real people who surrounded the seventeen-year-old son of James and Ella O'Neill in New London in the summer of 1906, the year of the play's setting.

To begin with, Eugene, like his protagonist, Richard Miller, was readying himself to enter an Ivy League college in the fall (in Richard's case Yale, in Eugene's Princeton). And Richard, like Eugene, is given to sweeping (if often ill-informed) endorsements of Emma Goldman's anarchist philosophy.

The character of Richard, however, was also in a sense an homage to Eugene's New London boyhood friend Hutch Collins, who, not long after accepting Eugene's invitation to join the Provincetown Players as an actor, had died in 1919 during the influenza epidemic. O'Neill admitted that, like Richard Miller, "the boy does spout the poetry I and Hutch Collins used to," including *The Rubáiyát of Omar Khayyám* (the source of the play's title; O'Neill substituted "*Ah*" for "*Oh*" because the former sounded more nostalgic).

But Art McGinley, another frequent companion of Eugene's New London boyhood, was also recognizable as a part model for Richard Miller. Art's father, John McGinley, was a longtime friend of James O'Neill's; it was John who, in 1883, had persuaded James to buy a home in New London. And it was John McGinley's cheerful, closely knit family environment—contrasting so poignantly with O'Neill's own dystopian milieu—that was reflected in the play.

It was McGinley's relationship with his son Art, particularly his amiable tolerance of his son's rebelliousness, that set the mood for *Ah, Wilderness!*—so different from the then smoldering antagonism between James O'Neill and Eugene.

When Art McGinley wrote O'Neill to say he'd recognized his family in the play, O'Neill, fearing he might have offended, wrote back to assure him no character had been taken from life. All his characters were, he said, "general types true for any large-small town." The play, he later said, "was a sort of wishing out loud."

One of O'Neill's concerns about the play was that, if taken as a portrait of his family (rather than of generic Americans), he himself might be viewed as the product of a benign—rather than a tragic—environment. "The truth," he insisted on more than one occasion, "is that I had no youth."

O'Neill, dream-writing *Ah, Wilderness!* at a distance of twenty-six years, had mellowed so much toward his father as to transfer one or two of his benign quirks to Nat Miller, notably James's conviction that "a certain peculiar oil" in bluefish had a poisonous effect on his digestion; it was a family joke that Ella served him bluefish under the guise of weakfish. The other trait was James's tendency to repeat stories of his boyhood and young manhood—illustrated in *Ah, Wilderness!* by what was probably the only nontheatrical reminiscence in his repertory, concerning the way he had once rescued a friend from drowning.

O'Neill also added the traits of another paternal figure present in the New London of 1906—Frederick Palmer Latimore, soon to give up his judgeship in nearby Groton to become the editor of the New London *Telegraph*, where O'Neill, six years later, would briefly work as a reporter.

GEORGE M. COHAN, WHO, five years earlier, had turned down the leading role in *Marco Millions* and had never appeared in a play written by anyone but himself, agreed to portray the father in *Ah, Wilderness!* The self-styled Yankee Doodle Dandy had been lured by the Act I setting of the Fourth of July. Ever the wag, he quipped to the press that O'Neill might decide to appear the following season in a Cohan play. Further explaining his reasons for accepting the role of Nat Miller, he ticked off various points of kinship with O'Neill, among them that their fathers had been friends and were both charter members of the Catholic Actors Guild.

Cohan had picked O'Neill "for a winner," he told the press, when his first Broadway play, *Beyond the Horizon*, opened thirteen years earlier. "I knew right away he had the goods," Cohan quipped. "Jeez, he's written a pile of them, hasn't he? Well, if this play doesn't make a hit, I'll take the kid into vaudeville with me. But I come first. It's got to be Cohan and O'Neill. That's my game."

O'Neill later returned the compliment by inscribing a copy of *Ah, Wilderness!* to Cohan: "With deep gratitude and appreciation for all your grand portrayal of Nat Miller has meant to this play—and with the real friendship of one (I hope) regular guy for another!"

With rehearsals under way in September, O'Neill, in an interview with the *Herald Tribune* critic Richard Watts Jr., waxed nostalgic. "Perhaps it is because I am growing old," he said, "that I begin to look back fondly on my youthful days in a part of the country that was my one real home in those times."

Rehearsals for *Ah, Wilderness!* proceeded according to form—*O'Neill's* form—which was to cut and pare where he saw fit and decline to cut for mere length (which was where the Guild often saw fit). Carlotta's presence at all rehearsals and her obvious influence on O'Neill's decisions were mostly taken in good part by the director, Philip Moeller, and other members of the production, including set designer Robert Edmond Jones.

As the play was a comedy, the actors needed a chance to time their laughs before a paying audience and, over O'Neill's strenuous objections, the Theatre Guild insisted on an out-of-town tryout of at least a week; O'Neill reluctantly agreed to join the company in Pittsburgh, where the play was staged in the last week of September.

He later claimed that his attendance had taught him "nothing whatsoever except to transpose one speech on account of a laugh—which I could just as easily have done from my hotel in N.Y. on information from Phil"; there had been absolutely no need for him to "watch a sticky audience react!"

O'Neill did, however, make one "cut" during the Pittsburgh tryout. The Guild thought the play was running too long and commissioned

Russel Crouse, who was handling publicity, to ask O'Neill to reduce the playing time by ten minutes. Crouse—who eventually quit as a press agent to become a playwright (most notably as co-author with Howard Lindsay of the huge Broadway hit *Life with Father*)—dutifully delivered the message. He anticipated O'Neill's reaction and, in fact, agreed with him.

"Right," said O'Neill. "To hell with them."

The next day Crouse was on his way out of his room at the Hotel Schenley, where O'Neill also was staying, when the telephone rang. It was O'Neill.

"Come down to my room right away," O'Neill commanded. Crouse said he couldn't, he was on his way to the theater to supervise a press interview he had arranged for Cohan.

"I have to see you right now," O'Neill insisted.

Crouse explained he would be back in an hour or so and would see O'Neill then.

"I have that ten-minute cut for you," said O'Neill.

Crouse was in O'Neill's room within seconds.

"Sit down," said O'Neill genially.

"I'm late," answered Crouse. "Just give me the script with the cuts marked."

"There isn't any script. Sit down," repeated O'Neill, with a self-satisfied grin.

Crouse threw O'Neill a trapped look, and O'Neill relented. He explained he had decided simply to collapse the first two acts into one, eliminating a ten-minute intermission.

Amused by O'Neill's tactic, Crouse submitted the "cut" to the Guild, which did not accept it. The play continued to be presented in the original four acts, with its extra ten minutes of running time.

CARLOTTA AROSE AT six o'clock on the morning of October 3 to read the "marvelous notices" for *Ah, Wilderness!* and proceeded to "dance round the room like a fool." As she told her diary, "Gene wakes & thinks I have gone mad! I leap on him in his bed & hug him until he has to fight to protect himself."

Her favorite critic, Brooks Atkinson, led the encomiums: "As a writer of comedy, Mr. O'Neill has a capacity for tenderness that most of us never suspected. *Ah, Wilderness!* may not be his most tremendous play, but it is certainly his most attractive. Mr. O'Neill's point of view is full of compassionate understanding. And in spite of its dreadful title, *Ah, Wilderness!* is a true and congenial comedy."

The other critics, after expressing surprise at O'Neill's shift from dire tragedy to sentimental comedy, lauded the ever-popular Cohan, whose mere presence assured an almost certain hit. The play ran for 289 performances and while Sidney Kingsley's *Men in White* beat *Ah, Wilderness!* for that year's Pulitzer Prize, Metro-Goldwyn-Mayer bought the film rights for $75,000.

At O'Neill's invitation, Brooks Atkinson interviewed him at lunch in his Madison Hotel suite the day after the opening. O'Neill said he wanted to explain the play's background, perhaps wishing to dispel all doubt in Atkinson's (or the public's) mind that the Millers reflected his own family, or that his own youth had been as innocently happy as Richard's. Years later, Atkinson boasted it was the most agreeable interview he'd ever conducted.

> Mr. O'Neill felt like talking about anything. He was even willing to listen; and from the point of view of the interviewer that was bad. Mrs. O'Neill efficiently intercepted the telephone calls, the messengers and the waiters, thus isolating a corner of New York where an amiable dramatist could call his soul his own. And at high noon on the day after the premiere his soul was in excellent condition. Until December, when his next play, *Days Without End*, goes into rehearsal, he was to be scot-free.

His enthusiasm spread the conversation alarmingly. Sea Island Beach, the Adirondacks ... swimming, climates, Cecil Rhodes, George M. Cohan—it hardly mattered what he talked about.

Atkinson went on to report that there were fragments of autobiography in *Ah, Wilderness!* but that O'Neill disclaimed anything but a superficial kinship with Richard Miller or his family. Now that it was on the stage, "and acted very much to his taste," said Atkinson, "Mr. O'Neill is his own best audience. He is ashamed to admit how much the comedy amuses him. Some things have to be confidential.

"At the age of forty-five, Mr. O'Neill is a little grayer around the temples and the lines are a little more firmly drawn on his face, but his eyes have the luster of a man who is in good health and spirits and who is eager to go on vigorously with the job. It is this interviewer's private opinion that the tension has relaxed a good deal."

O'Neill's geniality with respect to at least one aspect of the *Ah, Wilderness!* production did not last very long. As with Charles Gilpin, Cohan's personal triumph went to his head and soon he was embellishing his performance with bits of extra stage business. The curtain was coming down later each night.

Finally, when the play was running twenty-five minutes overtime, the Theatre Guild sent a note to Cohan asking him to please see to it that the curtain came down at eleven. Cohan retaliated by sending his valet to the Guild office with a warning that if any member of the management entered the theater while the play was in progress, he would walk offstage. Then he went right on ad-libbing until 11:25 every night.

O'Neill was less concerned about the late curtain than angered that Cohan was distorting the play's values, and he didn't hesitate—any more than he had with Gilpin—to go backstage and have it out with his star. Evidently Cohan gave in, for their relations continued to be cordial.

Carlotta's gift for O'Neill's forty-fifth birthday arrived belatedly at

Casa Genotta on November 13. It was an ancient player piano that Carlotta had bought for him at the Wurlitzer Electric Piano Company, where it was being outfitted with a new motor; she had taken O'Neill to see it a few days after the opening of *Ah, Wilderness!*

O'Neill christened the piano Rosie. "It was a great moment in my life when she first burst on my sight in Wurlitzer's remotest storeroom in all her gangrenous-green, festooned-with-rosebuds beauty," O'Neill wrote to Robert Sisk, formerly the press agent for the Theatre Guild and now a Hollywood producer. He added, "There sure must have been an artist soul lost to the world in the New Orleans honkey-tonk—or bordello— she came from."

According to Carlotta, the piano resembled the player piano in the barroom scene of *Ah, Wilderness!*

It came complete with rolls of the old songs O'Neill loved, including dance tunes. Late one night, to Carlotta's delight, O'Neill danced her "gaily up and down the long hall of Casa Genotta with a 'bunny hug'—& enjoys himself no end!"

He loved showing Rosie off to visitors. "Gene adored that piano," recalled Carl Van Vechten. To record O'Neill's pleasure, Van Vechten photographed him sitting at it, his hands on the keyboard, his face lit with a rare grin of delight. O'Neill enjoyed posing for Van Vechten. "I could have photographed Gene all day if I'd wanted to," said Van Vechten.

Robert Sisk was amused by O'Neill's habit of keeping a box of nickels on his piano. "He'd drop a nickel in the slot and listen blissfully to the damn thing tinkle." And Lillian Gish recalled that during one of her visits with Nathan to Casa Genotta, O'Neill joined him in a boisterous sing-along. "They were no Ezio Pinzas," she said, "but it was amusing to listen to them."

It was a good thing O'Neill had Rosie to cheer him, for during most of November he was once again driving himself frantic over *Days Without End*. With rehearsals looming, he suddenly felt renewed misgivings about the play's ending, and was actually considering a rewrite of the sixth draft, which he'd submitted to the Theatre Guild on July 3, 1933, as the final version—the one that was now being readied for its January premiere.

"Gene would walk up and down the beach, painfully wrestling with the problem," said Carlotta. "He couldn't make up his mind whether or not to have the man go back to the Church." She worried silently: "He will either reach a big 'Yes'—or go to a much firmer 'NO'!"

O'Neill also sought guidance on aspects of *Days Without End*, as well as on his personal religious quandary, from several Jesuit priests, according to Carlotta. At one point he thought of having his protagonist shoot himself at the church altar.

Despite having toyed with the alternative of a seventh draft, O'Neill returned (albeit only half-convinced) to the affirmative version of his sixth draft, once again calling the play finished.

"It was the Jesuits," said Carlotta, "who finally persuaded him to end the play with the protagonist going back to the Church."

AGAIN OVERRIDING O'NEILL'S PLEA to forgo an out-of-town tryout, the Theatre Guild took *Days Without End* to Boston on January 1 (1934), for a week's run. Once there, O'Neill eliminated three and a half pages of the script. (Earle Larimore, who had played Orin in *Mourning Becomes Electra*, portrayed the "John" half of John Loving, and his wife, Selena Royle, played Elsa, the character modeled on Carlotta; Ilka Chase was cast as Lucy Hillman, the woman with whom John commits adultery, and the English actor Stanley Ridges played Loving.)

Philip Moeller, after dining with O'Neill and Carlotta in their Boston hotel suite on New Year's Eve, was impelled by his sense of the play's significance in O'Neill's life to make notes about that dinner and its postprandial conversation.

"It is obvious from what was said that [*Days Without End*] is more her play than his. They both, definitely, acknowledge this. She says Gene was and is still a Catholic, and that she hopes he will return definitely to the faith and that she will gladly go with him when he is ready. But he must not be forced.

"There were long disquisitions over the mystic beauty of Catholic faith," Moeller wrote, adding that the end of the play was undoubtedly a wish fulfillment on O'Neill's part. "He told me about the simple trusting happiness of some of his Catholic relatives. He wanted to go that way and find a happiness which apparently he hadn't got and which obviously this perfect marriage doesn't seem to bring him."

While Moeller found O'Neill's candor touching, he was less charitable to Carlotta. "Madam was again amply rich in banalities—but her striving to hold it all together is somehow appealing and irritating at the same time." He went on, surprisingly, to theorize that O'Neill, deep down, was not altogether satisfied with Carlotta as a wife, and expressed his misgivings about the ultimate success of their marriage.

Lawrence Langner was blunter than Moeller about the O'Neill marriage. "Because both Carlotta and Gene had been married and divorced," he said, "there was only one subject on their minds: 'Is this marriage going to last?' Gene wrote *Days Without End* because he'd swallowed this guff about love after death."

Both men had accurately intuited the precarious undercurrents of the O'Neills' marriage. O'Neill himself seemed unsure of having truly achieved his ideal union, as witnessed by his inscription to Carlotta in a bound manuscript of the play that he gave her, quoting a speech in which Elsa refers to her husband: "He said no matter if every other marriage on earth were rotten and a lie, our love could make ours into a true sacrament." To which O'Neill appended (pleadingly? doubtfully?), "And ours has, hasn't it, Darling One!"

DURING THE TRYOUT in Boston, O'Neill's mixed feelings about the production intensified. On the one hand, he would have been pleased to have formal Catholic endorsement and, on the other, he wanted his public to judge the play purely on its literary merits. He believed the concessions he'd made to Catholic dogma entitled him to the Church's acceptance, yet he was not happy about those concessions—and he grew furious when he learned some priests regarded them as insufficient.

He was particularly enraged when a priest contacted Russel Crouse with an offer on behalf of the Catholic Writers Guild. He would personally endorse the play, said the priest, if O'Neill would make clear in the script that the heroine's first husband had died rather than leaving a suspicion that there might have been a divorce. After listening to Crouse's report, O'Neill sputtered, "To hell with them! I don't say she's divorced, in so many words—and I won't say the husband died; let them draw their own conclusions."

Evidently there was controversy within the clergy. One prominent Jesuit priest, the Reverend Gerard B. Donnelly, was moved to write a staunch endorsement of the play in the Catholic publication *America*. He called *Days Without End* a "magnificently Catholic play, a play Catholic in its characters, its story and its moral."

Although the play was praised by the critics of the Boston *Transcript* and the *Herald*, it displeased most of the New York critics when it opened in New York on January 8, 1934, at the Henry Miller's Theatre.

Carlotta did no dance when she read Atkinson's review. "One of the most amazing things about Mr. O'Neill is his capacity for seasoning his valiant career with bad plays," said Atkinson. "His *Days Without End* belongs in that doleful category." Citing the play's lack of "size, imagination, vitality, beauty and knowledge of human character," Atkinson could not resist some mild scolding: "Sometimes Mr. O'Neill tells his story as though he had never written a play before. In view of his acknowledged mastery of the theater it is astonishing that his career can be so uneven."

It was soon clear that the play was both critically and artistically a failure. "Critics very prejudiced against play as I foresaw," O'Neill wrote in his Work Diary on January 9. To Sophus Winther, he ridiculed New York's critics for dismissing his play as a "sentimental anachronism" and condemned them as unfit to judge its present-day religious relevance.

Days Without End challenged and insulted their superiority complexes in this respect, he blustered, "and they reacted like bigoted, priest-burning, Puritan atheists!" The clincher to his argument was shockingly naive and blinkered: "Also my play treats adultery seriously—as a sin against love—and how could the first-night intelligentsia of New York countenance that!"

But, as attested to by Carlotta, O'Neill did blame himself for his decision to end the play with the protagonist's return to the Church. "Later he was furious with himself for having done this," she recalled. "He felt he had ruined the play and that he was a traitor to himself as a writer. He always said the last act was a phony and he never forgave himself for it." According to Carlotta, *Days Without End* was his "last flirtation" with Catholicism.

It was not, however, the end of his search for a spiritual faith by which to live. "I do believe absolutely that Faith must come to us if we are ever again to have an End for our days and know that our lives have meaning," he wrote in answer to a fan, taking pains to point out that all of his past plays, "even when most materialistic," were "in their spiritual implications a search and a cry in the Wilderness protesting against the fate of our own faithlessness." O'Neill never abandoned that search; his cry in the "Wilderness," although more obliquely expressed, would be heard in all the works yet to come.

Subduing his rage over the negative reviews, O'Neill sent his somewhat demoralized cast a telegram that would have put a champion cheerleader to shame. He thanked them for their "splendid" work and told them to ignore the bad reviews. "This is a play we can carry over the critics' heads. So carry on with confidence in the final result and make them like it. Are we downhearted? No. We will get them in the end. . . . Again my gratitude to you all."

Days Without End survived for a seven-week run, just long enough to fulfill the Theatre Guild's subscription list. While it failed as the inspiring spiritual drama O'Neill had in mind—and deserves little space in his canon—the writing of it was for him a soul-purging experience. Few of his colleagues sympathized, however, and, in at least one instance, the play cost O'Neill a valued friendship. Benjamin De Casseres, a notorious atheist ("I don't believe in God because I don't believe in Mother Goose"), took the play as a personal insult.

"When Ben saw the play, he blazed," Bio De Casseres reminisced after her husband's death. "He thought O'Neill had betrayed his Demon. He equated O'Neill's 'fall' with the fall of Lucifer."

De Casseres wrote a vicious attempt at parody entitled *Drivel Without End*, which he had privately published as a pamphlet, sending copies to his literary acquaintances, not neglecting to send a copy to O'Neill. The two men never spoke again.

O'Neill's cloud of gloom was somewhat lightened when William Butler Yeats—"no Catholic," as O'Neill pointed out to the Guild's business manager, Warren Munsell—cabled to say that Dublin's Abbey Theatre wanted to produce it immediately. "If a poet like Yeats sees what is in it," said O'Neill, "all my hard work on it is more than justified." (Twelve years later, O'Neill had a total change of heart about the intrinsic splendor of *Days Without End*. Perhaps measuring it against his majestic final works, he succinctly explained to the writer Kyle Crichton why the play had failed: "The critics didn't understand it and it wasn't any good.")

A few days after the play's closing, O'Neill told Russel Crouse he was thankful the production was over and done with. "Hoping against hope is a wearying game," he said, "and the handwriting on the wall was always plainly there to be read—in red ink."

O'Neill said he wouldn't begin work on a new play for some time. He was intent "on doing a little serious loafing and forgetting of 'Ye Olde Show Shoppe,'" as he was "stale as hell on the drama." And he wasn't at all sure what he would take up when he did start writing again.

PART IV

"TIME'S WINGED CHARIOT"

35

Alone with Carlotta in his New York hotel suite, O'Neill was far from contemplating any "loafing and forgetting."

Giving way to his feeling of powerlessness and his dread of the future, he flung himself into the arms of his wife.

"For God's sake, hold me tight," O'Neill gasped, breaking into sobs. "I feel as if I'd burst through my skin."

Holding him, Carlotta told herself she'd "always felt this wretched play would hurt him!" Something hidden was "eating him—at his very heart! He isn't well! I don't know what to do!"

What worried Carlotta most was his new habit of sleeping well into the afternoon; she suspected he might be surreptitiously augmenting his prescribed sedatives. But she hesitated to question him, fearing a quarrel.

She and O'Neill, both haggard with nervous tension, limped back to Sea Island in late January 1934. They were momentarily soothed at being greeted by Blemie, who all but sang with joy on seeing them. While grateful to be home, O'Neill did no writing during all of February; his nerves, liver, and digestion, he complained, were "all shot," and his weight was down to 137 pounds. Carlotta had her own grievance; recently turned forty-five, she brooded about the "torture of being no longer young."

The O'Neills soon were back in New York, where O'Neill's doctor, after prescribing insulin for weight gain, warned he must give up all work for six months if he wished to avoid a nervous collapse. O'Neill obeyed. The daily insulin injections (administered by Carlotta) seemed to have worked; by mid-May, he'd gained fourteen pounds.

He was lucky he had got "due warning," or he would have "cracked up," he wrote to Lee Simonson, the set designer for *Marco Millions*. Even the overwhelming critical acclaim for *Mourning Becomes Electra* had caused him nothing but gloom and a nervous exhaustion so profound he'd been forced to take to his bed for nearly a week.

Success, he told Simonson, was for him "as flat, spiritually speaking, as failure." He no longer derived any "real spiritual satisfaction" from theater productions; he was happy, now, "to forget about work for a time." Indeed, he declared, he might soon confine his future work to "publication only."

On this occasion, his sentiment was heartfelt. Although he would continue, month after month, to write hundreds of thousands of words, the commercial Broadway "show shop" that he derided would hear not a whisper from him for the next dozen years.

He and Carlotta had once again gone to Big Wolf Lake that summer to escape the Georgia heat. On August 10, he glanced through some of his scribbled ideas for future plays, but found "no impulse" to work. Although his weight had gone up to 156, his nerves were still screaming. The end of September found him again in New York being doctored.

Pinned down in the city with his anxious wife during most of October, O'Neill sought distraction in the company of a new friend, Sean O'Casey. This was the Irish playwright's first (and only) visit to New York. He had been living in Devon, England, in what he called "voluntary exile" from Ireland since 1928, the year the Abbey Theatre rejected his play *The Silver Tassie*.

George Jean Nathan brought O'Casey to dinner at the Madison Hotel on October 16 as a forty-sixth birthday gift for O'Neill, and their subsequent sorties gave O'Neill the brief, joyful lift of a love affair.

The feeling was mutual. "He and I fell for each other at once—at least I know I fell for him, and I believe he fell for me," O'Casey later said.

At fifty-four, revered but far from affluent, O'Casey was awaiting the

Broadway production of his play *Within the Gates*. He'd arrived in a brown suit and matching cap, carrying nothing with him but an extra set of underwear, a single shirt, a pair of socks, and a sweater. After registering at the Royalton Hotel on West Forty-fourth Street, where George Jean Nathan lived, he spent his first hours testing all the electrical gadgets in his room and carefully distributing his few items of clothing among the drawers of his bureau.

During their evening at the Madison, Carlotta presented O'Neill with a birthday gift—a pair of slacks—and O'Neill modeled them coquettishly, throwing O'Casey and Nathan into gales of laughter. O'Neill made him laugh often, O'Casey recalled, telling him jokes "only two Irishmen can share."

As for O'Neill, he admired O'Casey enough to brave the crowds of Broadway and attend a performance of *Within the Gates*. For his part, O'Casey had especially admired *The Great God Brown* and *Strange Interlude*, and was impressed by the way that O'Neill had finessed his way "back to the Greeks" in *Mourning Becomes Electra*.

"When O'Casey told my husband, 'You write like an Irishman, you don't write like an American,'" Carlotta said, "Gene was so pleased he didn't know what to do." O'Casey, some years after O'Neill's death, summed up his impressions of his American colleague:

"He was a great and lovable man; deeply thoughtful of the world's woes, but holding fast within him the delightful qualities of a child—reminding me of: 'Except ye become like little children, ye are in no wise fit for the Kingdom of Heaven.' Well, if there be a heaven, certainly Eugene was fit to live there. English critics didn't care for his work; but then they are, I fear, nearsighted, looking at the playfulness of the magpies, but with eyes too weak to watch the soar of an eagle in the upper skies."

AFTER THE BOUNCE of O'Casey's visit, O'Neill slid back into gloom, condemned to struggle with the chokehold of his deteriorating health. He was forced to acknowledge that the damage he'd inflicted on his body during years of drunken dereliction had caught up with him. On top of a genetic nervous disorder, manifested in a recurrent tremor of the hands, he was now, at forty-six, experiencing some of the physical frailties of a much older man, and Carlotta found herself more frequently in the role of nurse; she tamped down her fear that O'Neill, always trembling at the edge of a breaking point, might be propelled back into drink.

O'Neill, in truth, was secretly terrified he might lack the vigor to realize his newest and loftiest dream, a concept far grander than any so far. It was to be an all-embracing fictionalized imagining of the forces that had shaped him; its characters would personify a theme that had long perturbed and preoccupied him: the gradual deterioration of morality in the American soul; he would dramatize the process by which that soul, from generation to generation, had been corrupted by the lust for ever more personal wealth.

Idealist that he was, O'Neill had once held high hopes for his country's cultural and social blossoming. America, he believed, had been given "everything, more than any other country."

Tragically, however, as O'Neill saw it, his countrymen had not acquired any real roots. Instead, the early idealistic immigrant, arriving here with his dream of freedom and his hope for his own bit of land, had all too soon been overtaken by a baser dream—the insatiable lust for more.

"We've followed the same selfish, greedy path as every other country in the world," said O'Neill, pointing out that Americans liked to boast about "the American Dream," but that dream, in most cases, was "the dream of material things."

"I sometimes think," he went on, "that the United States, for this reason, is the greatest failure the world has ever seen. We've been able to get a very good price for our souls in this country—the greatest price perhaps that has ever been paid—but you'd think that after all these years, and all that man has been through, we'd have sense enough—all of us—to understand that the whole secret of human happiness is summed up in a sentence that even a child can understand.

"The sentence? 'For what shall it profit a man if he shall gain the whole world and lose his own soul?'"

The soaring work O'Neill now envisioned was similar in scope to his earlier multi-play concept for *The Sea-Mother's Son* (that autobiographical saga of the middle-aged man, supine on his deathbed, pondering his origin).

But this new project was even more grandiose: a cycle of five or six plays tracing the history of an Irish American family corrupted by greed. The cycle's ultimate title was to be *A Tale of Possessors Self-Dispossessed*.

As much as O'Neill identified with the global scope of the Greek tragedians and Shakespeare, he also felt a kinship with the magisterial reach of Wagnerian opera. (Whereas his jazz recordings gave him an instant high, O'Neill could readily surrender himself to classical music; he was a devoted radio listener—beginning in 1937—to the weekly concerts performed by the orchestra created for Arturo Toscanini by the National Broadcasting Company.)

A Tale of Possessors Self-Dispossessed would be O'Neill's *Ring des Nibelungen*. If Wagner could command a stage for the four double-long evenings required to present his overpowering *Ring* cycle—itself a parable for his disillusionment with a nineteenth-century society corrupted by greed— why should not O'Neill strive for a similar achievement for his own century (albeit without the glorious music)? Thus began O'Neill's years-long struggle to create the opus he was destined never to complete.

After several false starts, O'Neill sketched the idea for the cycle's first play, *The Calms of Capricorn*, which unambiguously set forth his intent: an unsparing scrutiny of power and greed in America, as told through the lives of a plutocratic, avaricious Yankee family named Harford, intermarried with a prideful immigrant Irish family named Melody.

As so often before, O'Neill began by digging deeply into his own family dynamic. The cycle would be haunted by James O'Neill's deathbed howl of remorse, fifteen years earlier, at having exchanged his early artistic idealism for the pursuit of money. Eugene would never forget, when shaping his cycle, how his father's early poverty had driven his thirst for wealth; or how his compulsive parsimony had shattered his wife's dreams of domestic tranquillity.

O'Neill now declared himself ready to devote at least six years to the cycle's creation. At Casa Genotta on New Year's Day, 1935, he congratulated himself in his Work Diary on the "wonderful characters!" he was shaping. He boasted of the cycle's vast outreach to friends, forgetting that eight years earlier he had extolled *The Sea-Mother's Son* in much the same language. "Suffice it that the possibilities are Gigantic, Epic, Colossal, Enormous," he wrote to Lee Simonson.

His various illnesses momentarily forgotten, O'Neill jubilantly attacked his awesome task, spewing notes, outlines, drafts, and scenarios with a feverish scramble of frustrated stoppages and manic mood swings.

In the months and years ahead, the cycle would grow and grow—its chronology drifting backward, its separate plays shifting places in the cycle's sequence, over-length single plays being split into two, their often lurid plots contorting, their flamboyant titles twisting, their characters suffering psychic jumps—until O'Neill himself could barely keep track of who was seducing, betraying, or murdering whom; who would succeed or fail in his or her craftily chosen endeavor; which of his characters would die a natural (if miserable) death; and which character was destined to take his or her own life.

In *The Calms of Capricorn*, he would introduce four Harford brothers—Ethan, Jonathan, Wolfe, and Honey. He depicted them at the beginning of their careers, their lives roughly paralleling those of America's nineteenth-century robber barons—ruthless tycoons like Jay Gould, J. P. Morgan, and Collis Huntington, who made their often illicit billions in banking, railroading, shipping, and politics.

O'Neill planned to trace the careers of each of the Harford brothers in the cycle's sequential plays, building on his overall theme of the soul-destroying lust for money.

The setting for *Capricorn* is the luxurious passenger clipper ship *Dream of the West* (which O'Neill modeled on the fabled *Flying Cloud*).

The play's plot promised to be as savage and over-the-top as anything O'Neill had yet written.

All four Harford brothers, along with their father, Simon, and their mother, Sara (née Melody), are aboard the ship, which is bound from Boston to San Francisco via the treacherous passage around Cape Horn. Also aboard are Nancy, the youthful wife of the ship's aging captain, Enoch Payne, and the ship's owner and his daughter.

Three of the brothers are traveling west in search of lucrative careers. Honey Harford plans to join the California gold rush; Wolfe hopes to find a job in banking; Jonathan will work his way up with a railroad company.

The fourth brother, Ethan, a sailor, is *Dream of the West*'s first mate. He is at spiteful odds with Captain Payne, who opposes his reckless determination to make the coming voyage an historic event and advance his own career. Ethan means for the ship to beat the record run from Boston to San Francisco (a record set in real life seven years earlier by *Flying Cloud*).

Ethan slyly lets out sail while Captain Payne sleeps, straining the graceful clipper beyond her capacity, and when discovered, he is threatened with dismissal. When Captain Payne falls ill, Ethan suffocates him, aided by Nancy, with whom Ethan has fallen in love.

Sanctioned by the unsuspecting ship's owner, Ethan takes over command of the clipper and—almost defeated in his purpose by the calms of Capricorn—in the end picks up enough wind to achieve his goal of beating the *Flying Cloud*'s record. Ethan has seriously damaged *Dream of the West*, however, and the owner fires him—after which he and Nancy commit suicide.

IN HIS SECOND PLAY for the cycle, O'Neill attributed aspects of Jay Gould's persona to Jonathan Harford, who becomes the family's railroad executive, calling that play *Man on Iron Horseback*, a reference to the term "iron horse," coined in the mid-1800s for the steam locomotive.

Similarly, Wolfe Harford was to be the protagonist of a play entitled *The Earth's the Limit,* in which he becomes a prosperous banker partly modeled on J. P. Morgan. As for Honey, the youngest son, he was to represent the family's political ambitions in a play with the ironic title, *Nothing Lost Save Honor.*

Amid all of O'Neill's creative and often anguished thrashing, Carlotta was his steadfast confidante and—when he was under duress—his principal victim. But O'Neill's children also felt the sting of his tension. He had little patience for fifteen-year-old Shane during his visit to Casa Genotta in early January 1935—when the cycle was uppermost in O'Neill's thoughts.

Shane, who was not doing well in school, had exasperated his father a few months earlier by asking for a $400 outboard motor. "I can't afford it and you ought to know I can't," snapped O'Neill. "It's about time you realized I am an author and not a millionaire business man."

He told his son he had "a lot of nerve to ask for such an expensive present"; not until Shane showed he had some brains and dug down and got to work would O'Neill be willing to do things for him—things he could afford beyond the money he allotted Shane's mother for his private-school education.

"But until you do this," warned O'Neill, "don't expect anything from me except the usual birthday and Christmas presents or you will be disappointed."

Shane found an advocate in Herb Freeman, among whose chores it was to look after the boy and his older brother during their visits to Sea Island. Infrequent as these visits were, Oona's were nonexistent. "It is all right for Shane to visit here in the summer, because he is so much more grown than you," O'Neill had written to his eight-year-old daughter in the summer of 1933, "but I am afraid the sudden change to this climate would not be a good thing for you until you are a little older."

O'Neill was content to invite Oona to lunch that September while in New York for rehearsals of *Ah, Wilderness!* She would not see her father again for nearly five more years.

As for O'Neill's older son, Eugene Jr., Freeman sensed an unease between him and his father, which he felt was due to the youth's newly formed antagonism toward Carlotta. Eugene, recalled Freeman, made no attempt to conceal his resentment of Carlotta's autocratic posturing; prompted by loyalty to his employer, Freeman once presumed to caution Eugene to "knock it off," but was rebuffed. "[Eugene] had a hot temper and he let it go," Freeman recalled.

Freeman got on better with Shane. After gently boxing with him one day, Freeman grew concerned about the boy's ebbing strength. "Here you are a young man and you can't even handle an old buck like me," he scolded. "Why don't you straighten up and quit your cigarettes and make something of yourself?"

All in all, Freeman declared himself content with his life at Sea Island. "All I can say is both Mr. and Mrs. O'Neill were good to me, as if they'd been my own parents—even better." But, he added, "I felt so sorry for them kids. They loved their daddy and their daddy loved them. Yet they were held apart. I'd sit there and look at it . . . there was nothin' to do."

Carlotta felt slightly more sympathy for Shane than did O'Neill. She found him "so like Gene—in looks and mannerisms—says so little." Shane, she noted, "never says what he is really thinking about!" She fussed over him, although she, like O'Neill, sought to convince him that his father was not a rich man. By the time Shane left, O'Neill had softened. "Fine kid!" he commented in his Work Diary.

It was no exaggeration when O'Neill (due to his own extravagance) claimed to be far from rich. Even with "Papa" Speyer's guidance, the worth of his investments, in the deepening Depression, had dwindled, as had Carlotta's; that January she learned her principal had shrunk to $200,000, half its original value. Naively, she and O'Neill asked each other, "How (between us) we could have spent $70,000 this past year!"

Despite filial and financial distractions, by February 1935, O'Neill had decided to add a sixth play to the cycle. "He was always working on several of the plays at once," said Carlotta. "He would work on one until he felt he was stuck, get a thought about another one, and work on that."

In addition to propelling the Harford brothers forward in time, O'Neill had decided they needed more back story; accordingly, he outlined two plays to precede the 1850s setting of *The Calms of Capricorn*. The first of these plays, eventually entitled *A Touch of the Poet*, was set in 1828; it dramatized the love affair of the brothers' parents—the Yankee scion Simon Harford and his wife, Sara Melody, whose Irish immigrant father was the delusional Cornelius Melody.

The second play, *More Stately Mansions*, set in the decade between 1832 and 1842, continued Simon and Sara's story as a married couple contending with Simon's fractious mother, Deborah Harford, while resolutely raising their four sons.

After reaching that point in mid-April, O'Neill—always nervous when guests were expected—braced for a visit from old friends, the writer Sherwood Anderson and his wife, Eleanor. The visit was congenial but Anderson sensed a tension beneath O'Neill's habitually courteous manner.

"I know you are always after something not too easily comprehended and that you continually have to go through your own little hells," Anderson wrote to O'Neill a few days after his visit, adding, "You have always been a man I have looked up to as one of the few great figures of the time and I am sorry that I cannot see more of you."

Anderson was more candid in a letter to a friend, in which he deplored O'Neill's marriage to "the actress Monterey—reputed to be one of the really beautiful women of America. I thought her cold, calculating. Certainly she is not one of the women who make a house warm."

Regarding the cycle, Anderson expressed both wonder and doubt about O'Neill's vast design for what he explained would be a series of connected plays to be presented "night after night, the same characters coming and going" throughout. Conceding it was an "ambitious enough scheme," Anderson wondered if O'Neill would ever pull it off.

"He is a very sweet fine man," Anderson concluded, "but I did feel death in his big expensive house. He has drawn himself away, lives in that solitary place, seeing practically no one. He needs his fellow men. I felt him clinging to me rather pitifully." And to Theodore Dreiser, Anderson wrote: "Say, Ted, write a nice note to Gene O'Neill. I've a hunch he is just now a down pin."

O'NEILL CONTINUED WORK on the cycle during the spring of 1935, but Carlotta sensed he was not pleased with his progress. However cold and calculating Anderson might have found her, she repeatedly assured herself in her diary that she loved her "Genie" and could not imagine living without him. She also knew that, regardless of his moods, he needed her with all his being. But it wasn't easy to be married to someone as demanding, as self-involved, as illness-prone as her husband.

That May, Carlotta indulged in one of her frequent threnodies (always expressed in more or less the same words). She privately bewailed her unhappiness and concern: "There is 'something' wrong with Gene— NO doctor has ever been able to name it—They take the easy way & call it *nerves*! . . . I love him so deeply I pray I can be of some help & comfort to him."

She was, and she wasn't.

That sizzling July, sounding not at all like the down pin Anderson had described in May, O'Neill wrote a perky letter to Robert Sisk, sketching the cycle's concept so far. Sisk would have been dismayed had he seen his old friend seated naked at his desk in Casa Genotta on a huge folded bath towel, perspiring into its four thick layers.

With the cycle newly expanded from six plays to seven, O'Neill told Sisk that the work now encompassed a century-long history of the interrelationships among five generations of the family, with the first play beginning in the mid-1800s and the last ending in 1932.

"Two of the plays take place in New England," he elaborated, "one almost entirely on a clipper ship, one on the Coast, one around Washington [D.C.] principally, one in New York, one in the Middle West."

As in *Electra*, he said, there would be an overall title for the cycle and separate titles for the individual plays. "Each play will be, as far as it is possible, complete in itself while at the same time an indispensable link in the whole." O'Neill added that "each play will be concentrated around the final fate of one member of the family but will also carry on the story of the family as a whole."

The cycle, he further confided, would be "less realistic than *Electra* in method," and, he hoped, "more poetic." It would deeply probe the characters' "intermingling relationships" and would contain "symbolical" undertones. He said he had already written scenarios of 25,000 words each for the first three plays, had outlined the fourth, and begun the fifth (not mentioning the status of the sixth and seventh).

"I won't start actual dialogue on the first play," said O'Neill, "until I've completed the scenarios of all—that means, late next fall at the rate so far." He added that he probably would not allow the first play to be produced until he had completed three plays and written first drafts of the rest.

Feeling it imperative to reach further and further back in time, O'Neill was examining the effect of one generation's greediness on the next—"the Harford curse," as one of the cycle characters calls it, mindful of the biblical sins of the father being visited on the sons.

If his time had not run out, O'Neill's search for an answer in the past might well have carried him, as it did Shaw, back to Methuselah. "If you keep on going back," Carlotta chided her husband, "you'll get to Adam and Eve."

Oddly, O'Neill, the father of three children, had little interest in the world his progeny would inhabit, while Shaw, who was childless, had enormous interest in and curiosity about the future. While Shaw went back to Methuselah, he also propelled his vision far forward into a future that no child of his would inhabit, whereas O'Neill was preoccupied only with the world that had shaped his forebears and himself.

O'Neill's personal tragic take on the space-time continuum is memorably expressed by Mary Tyrone in *Long Day's Journey Into Night*: "The past is the present, isn't it? It's the future, too."

36

In early July 1935, routinely opening O'Neill's mail in her capacity as confidential secretary, Carlotta was alarmed by a letter from George Jean Nathan regretting he was unable to send a promised case of imported Pilsner beer.

Carlotta made no comment as she handed her husband the letter, although she could have reminded him of his boast of sobriety, only two years earlier, to his New London cousin, Phil Sheridan, with whom he'd gone on benders in his youth, and with whom he'd stayed in touch by letter.

"I haven't even *sipped* a glass of beer in seven years now," O'Neill had written Sheridan (discounting, as always, his binges in Guéthery and Shanghai). "I hear you tie or better that mark. Well, well, who would have thought it, what?"

Carlotta, thankful there was no Pilsner on its way, was unwilling to confront O'Neill. Yet she feared the worst—"because," as she confided to her diary, "though beginning with simple beer . . . step by step, it will reach *Bourbon* & then, *God help Gene—& me!*"

It was soon evident that God's help would be needed.

On the following day, O'Neill asked Carlotta to see about ordering some imported beer and ale from the nearby Cloisters Hotel, leading her to conclude he'd evidently had "a beer or two" there during Nathan's recent visit. Her heart "turned cold," as she put it, but she didn't dare object, fearing the fury of O'Neill's long-dormant black-Irish temper. "He swears he wants *only that!*" she told herself. "I *want* to believe this."

At dinner ten days later, Carlotta chose to overlook O'Neill's open enjoyment of the imported Scotch ale fetched by George Boll from the Cloisters; and on July 21, she silently noted her husband's consumption of Würzburger beer with his dinner.

Since he showed no sign of tipsy behavior, Carlotta held her breath, hardly daring to hope that the beer and ale would not, after all, lead to anything stronger.

Carlotta worried that if anything was going to step up O'Neill's craving for something stronger than beer, it would be the punishing strain he was under while writing during August's record heat. But O'Neill was determined not to budge from Sea Island before the end of autumn, when he expected to have his entire cycle outlined.

Driving himself to a rigid writing schedule, he spent much of that month zeroing in on his characters' psychological and hereditary traits, and pursuing historical research. But the pounding heat and the ever more complicated details of the cycle's individual plays were making O'Neill edgier than Carlotta had seen him since his alcohol-induced breakdown in Shanghai.

In fact, she was almost certain O'Neill had begun to quench his thirst with something stronger than beer. Although braced for the worst, she was caught off guard when, on August 23, he lashed out at her in a rage that instantly brought back memories of their blowup in Shanghai nearly seven years earlier when, in a drunken fury, he had struck her.

It began when O'Neill stormed into Carlotta's office, where she spent most of her mornings filing, typing answers to her own and O'Neill's letters, and paying household bills. In his trembling hand was a letter from his lawyer, Harry Weinberger (whose correspondence Carlotta never opened), evidently regarding ongoing discussions about O'Neill's will.

He now demanded that Carlotta make a reciprocal will, leaving all her money to him. Although flabbergasted, she kept silent, fearful of arousing his temper. But she could barely wait to express her outrage—to her diary.

"Over a year ago," she wrote on August 23, "I made a Will *leaving him everything* (& *Cyn nothing!*). I feel this is *disgusting* and uncalled for—and showing little thanks or appreciation, or even knowledge of what I have done and am doing for him." Carlotta finally faced her worst fear: "He sounds either *crazy* or drunk."

Crowding her angry thoughts onto a single page of her diary—writing in small cramped letters totally unlike the loopy ones with which she customarily filled the half pages and quarter pages of her entries—she stormed about having always paid "a flat ½" of all their living expenses; in addition to paying for her own clothing and doctors' bills, she had "purchased all linen, silver, glass—& God knows what for our home—always buying things for him."

Beside herself with resentment, she asked, "What, in the name of God, is the matter with the man?" On the following day, O'Neill again brought up the will. Carlotta, although acknowledging she was "frightened," this time blurted out her hurt and disdain:

"One year ago, without being asked, or without even mentioning it to you, I made a Will leaving you anything & all things I own. I left Cyn nothing. I did this because I loved you. Perhaps I shouldn't have done it!"

O'Neill sat silently staring at Carlotta, his face (as she noted) "dark with hate." She stood up, but had to sit down again because she was shaking so. "I began to feel nauseated from fear," she later recollected. "This was the man who was supposed to love me so much? *What was wrong?*" It actually crossed Carlotta's mind that perhaps he was unwilling to wait for her to die. "Did he want what I had NOW?"

The scene was quintessential Strindberg—the "love-hatred" that "hails from the pit." And so was the contradictory scene that followed a day later, when Carlotta assumed the role of martyr ministering to her unapologetic genius when he complained of feeling ill. "I put him to bed, doctor him, & bring him his dinner on a tray," she wrote (unaware of how very much she sounded like the similarly martyred Agnes in the days when she nursed the hungover O'Neill after drinking binges).

Sometime later, O'Neill admitted to Carlotta that Weinberger was trying to bully him into forcing her to accept him as her lawyer; Carlotta interpreted this as Weinberger's attempt to pry into her finances and manipulate her (as she believed he did O'Neill). Expressing her contempt for Weinberger, she told O'Neill she preferred to stay with her own lawyer, and O'Neill acquiesced.

Naturally, she did not tell O'Neill that she feared Weinberger's probing might turn up the fact that it was Speyer—not her aunt—who had set up the fund that gave Carlotta her financial independence.

When a new shipment of beer arrived on the same day that Carlotta was catering to O'Neill's hangover, her heart plummeted anew. It must have been clear to her by now that O'Neill's drinking was unstoppable. "But of course, I can say *nothing*!?!" she noted in her diary, still incapable of confronting him.

Cautiously, the O'Neills passed the next five days in pursuit of their normal routines—he working (or pretending to work) on the cycle and she attending to household and secretarial chores. They gardened, swam, lunched, and dined together—with nary a mention of wills or alcohol.

On the next-to-last day of that doleful August, O'Neill waded into the ocean to where Carlotta was standing after a solo swim, and threw his arms around her. "For God's sake forgive me," he beseeched her. "I must have been crazy—but Weinberger keeps hammering at me!" And then they swam together, returned to the house for tea, listened on the radio to news of increasing unrest in Europe, and ended their day with their accustomed after-dinner reading. Carlotta, the triumphant, forgiving mother, crossed her fingers.

By October, O'Neill had been transported "full force" into one of his "heeby-jeeby" episodes (as he characterized them)—induced, as Carlotta noted, by worry over vanishing income from his European investments, coupled with concern over the ascendancy of Nazism. Nevertheless, he managed to complete the required preliminary work on the cycle—or so he claimed.

He then announced he needed a break from Sea Island, and wanted to consult his doctor in New York about a pain that had been troubling him for the past two months, and which he thought originated in his liver. Carlotta prayed his discomfort was not being caused by hard liquor.

During their two and a half weeks in New York, O'Neill, in addition to visiting his doctors, threw himself, with Carlotta, into an uncharacteristic frenzied social whirl that included dinners with George Jean Nathan, James Speyer, the Van Vechtens, the Comminses, the Skinners, the Langners, Theresa Helburn, Madden, and Sisk.

While Carlotta was unsettled by O'Neill's manic behavior, she voiced no suspicion in her diary that it might be caused by his secretly swigging hard liquor—although she did note that he enjoyed the beer he drank at dinner with Nathan, as well as the Burgundy he ordered during a private dinner with Carlotta to celebrate his forty-seventh birthday.

Toward the end of October, after O'Neill's liver tests indicated no need for treatment, he and Carlotta returned to Sea Island. On October 31, O'Neill wrote in his Work Diary that he was "very depressed—can't concentrate on anything," and Carlotta complained, "he has withdrawn into himself."

When O'Neill voiced regret at being "so far away from his friends," she reacted with a peevish rant to herself, pointing out that after creating a beautiful home for her husband on Park Avenue so he could be with his so-called friends, within a few months he'd come to hate it; and after insisting she create a home in Georgia, he had come to hate that as well.

By November 1, O'Neill had withdrawn to the point of not speaking to Carlotta during meals. She tried to be understanding but she was unnerved. "I become so self-conscious when these silent moods are on!"

O'Neill, without much enthusiasm, took up the scenario for the play he was then calling *The Hair of the Dog*, but noted, three days later, that it needed "to be reconceived." Had he foreseen that this play, in its final version as *A Touch of the Poet*, was destined to be the only cycle play he would complete, he might have had a good chortle over the irony of it all.

ABRUPTLY, ON AN evening in mid-November, O'Neill asked Carlotta to join him for a walk on the beach. As they strolled in the moonlight, he earnestly reiterated what he'd hinted at before: he'd made up his mind that—regardless of the financial sacrifice it would entail—he intended for the time being to keep his future plays to himself and not have them produced or published.

He was convinced, he told Carlotta, that no producer existed who could do justice to his work. He felt demeaned by the Theatre Guild, whose board members knew nothing of "imaginative theater." They had no "pioneer spirit," no "desire to do a beautiful thing," said O'Neill. He asked Carlotta to understand that, after slaving this long to break every tradition in the American theater, he could not bring himself to work for such "an uninteresting, stupid" organization.

Carlotta did understand. "Gene's one dream was never to have to go to New York for production. The only thing he cared about was his writing. He used to say, 'Oh, God, if only some Good Fairy would give me some money, so I'd never have to produce a play, and I could just write, write, write and never go near a theater!"

With that pronouncement off his chest, O'Neill resumed speaking to Carlotta at mealtimes. Grateful for this unexpected benefit, she felt she had to tolerate his beer drinking with meals.

One evening, while she and O'Neill were playing cards with George Boll, Eugene murmured to her, "If I felt any better I couldn't stand it!"

It was the first time in eight years, Carlotta marveled, that she'd heard him utter anything so optimistic—"or be so gay!" Had she heard right? she asked herself. "It sounds too good to be true!" It was.

The next day, Carlotta found her husband sunk in "complete mental lethargy." He did not perk up until December 7, when the O'Neills were hosts to the writer Somerset Maugham and his secretary-lover, Gerald Haxton.

Maugham, himself not a gregarious man, believed O'Neill was carrying things too far in his efforts to safeguard his privacy. To his close friend, the playwright S. N. Behrman, Maugham delivered a memorable description of O'Neill in his splendid isolation: "The house he lived in was by the sea, and far from any other habitation. I didn't see another soul while I was there, but he constantly complained and said he must leave the island because it was so thronged with people."

WHEN GEORGE JEAN NATHAN sent the O'Neills a barrel of Edelbrau beer in mid-December to celebrate the holiday season, Carlotta—lulled into a sense of security and still hopeful that beer was O'Neill's only tipple—joined him in drinking lustily. She joked to Nathan that she and O'Neill had drunk beer with lunch, beer instead of afternoon tea, beer for dinner, and beer for a nightcap, adding, "Rosie plays and the Edelbrau flows."

Carlotta was so intent on denying her husband's true predicament that she was foolishly unworried when, along with Boll, O'Neill toasted Christmas Eve with champagne at dinner. After dinner, however, while O'Neill and Boll played songs on Rosie, Carlotta noticed that O'Neill was periodically slinking upstairs.

Finally she followed him, concerned he might be ill, and to her dismay found him drinking whiskey out of a bottle.

Caught in the act, O'Neill laughed; swinging his bottle, he strode defiantly downstairs to rejoin Boll. In her bedroom, Carlotta suffered late into the night from the sounds of their drunken merriment. She was forced to confess to herself at last that ever since their stay in New York she had known O'Neill was surreptitiously drinking hard liquor.

Actually, it was remarkable O'Neill had stayed sober as long as he had. Like any recovering alcoholic, he was vulnerable to backsliding under conditions of severe stress. He was terrified that encroaching physical disability would render him unequal to the challenge he'd set himself with his cycle and he'd fallen back on alcohol to appease his terror. And now he was trapped in a vicious circle: being drunk gave him the excuse to dodge writing; not writing drove him into a frenzy of frustration—and impelled him to drink even more.

While Carlotta's magical environment and skillful nurturing had enabled O'Neill to leap the hurdles of *Mourning Becomes Electra* at Le Plessis, she had somehow lost her healing touch at Casa Genotta in the face of the cycle's far greater challenge.

Carlotta dreaded to think that O'Neill's drinking augured a secret wish to destroy their marriage (never mind his ability to write). Perhaps even more, she feared posterity would blame her for O'Neill's collapse.

Struggling to keep her balance, Carlotta noted on Christmas Day of 1935 that O'Neill was "feeling very sorry for himself—but we both know he should never touch alcohol in any form." Believing he'd hidden his liquor supply in his study, Carlotta tried to keep him by her side. After giving him a bath, she fed him warm milk and a sedative. She kept watch in his bedroom all night and repeated the routine the following day.

On Carlotta's forty-seventh birthday three days later, O'Neill made an effort to pull himself together. He presented her with his rehearsal copy of the *Electra* trilogy with an inscription dripping in guilt:

> To Carlotta—on this, her eighth birthday since our elopement—with, again, as ever, my amazed wonder at her forbearance with my blunders and weaknesses, my wondering amazement at her patience with my lost preoccupations and forgetfulness—and last and warmest, my heart's and soul's gratitude for her love, which is this Stranger's only home on this earth!

On December 30, however, O'Neill unapologetically drank ale with his dinner and informed an exasperated Carlotta that he had decided to return to a diet of "just wine and beer." And on New Year's Eve, his mood, as Carlotta observed, "turned to elation," a sign she now understood to mean he was sneaking drinks of hard liquor. She silently addressed O'Neill in her diary:

"Whither are we going, darling? . . . Try to remember how deeply I love you—and always will—*no matter what!*" On impulse, three days into the new year, Carlotta wove her long silky hair into two braids and then cut them off. To her surprise, O'Neill asked for them as keepsakes.

DURING THE FIRST WEEK of the new year, O'Neill again began fussing with his cycle, but soon grasped at an excuse to again set it aside; two caps had fallen off his teeth, necessitating a trip to his New York dentist, accompanied, of course, by Mama Carlotta.

Amid the flurry of arranging their departure, O'Neill had fresh cause for distress (and drink). On January 6, he read about the death, in Paris, of Louise Bryant, whose life had ended as bleakly as that of any heroine he himself could have created. She was stricken, at forty-nine, by a cerebral hemorrhage while climbing the stairs of a shabby hotel on the Left Bank.

Following their hostile parting eighteen years earlier, O'Neill had periodically tracked Louise in newspaper accounts. He had read with sorrow of Reed's death from typhus at thirty-three on October 17, 1920, and of the official funeral in Red Square that professed to honor him. It had been a grotesque circus-like ceremony, and O'Neill was appalled to read of Bryant's fainting in the square, overwhelmed by the oppressive crowds and her own emotions.

Three years later, Bryant was again in the news when she married William C. Bullitt, the scion of a Main Line Philadelphia family, who had idolized Reed. Also widely reported was her scandalous divorce from Bullitt in 1930, during which she lost custody of her daughter. Later, O'Neill heard rumors of Bryant's life after the divorce; she had drifted back to Greenwich Village, moving into an apartment she'd once shared with Reed (and briefly with O'Neill), and living a hand-to-mouth existence.

Although Louise had shunned alcohol in their days together and tried to stop O'Neill from drinking, by the time she returned to the Village, she had herself become an alcoholic, and had been drawn into a series of sordid, petty scandals, at least one of which resulted in a court case. Returning to Paris, she drank and took drugs until her death. (Had she stayed married to Bullitt for three more years, she would have found herself back in Russia as the wife of Franklin Roosevelt's ambassador to the Soviet Union.)

Now, briefly, Louise was alive again in O'Neill's mind. Along with his unmotherly mother, the reluctantly motherly Agnes, and the over-mothering Carlotta, Louise (too self-involved to mother anyone) would lend her aura to the conniving women of his cycle.

One of the darkest days of Carlotta's marriage to O'Neill occurred early in January 1936, as he returned from his dentist to their suite at the Madison Hotel. Carlotta spotted him trying to conceal a bottle of bourbon as he removed his overcoat. "Mother of God—now what?" she exclaimed to herself.

During the next three and a half weeks, Carlotta silently suffered as O'Neill continued his visits to the dentist and intermittently locked himself into the bedroom of their hotel suite, pretending to write. Then, on February 20, he approached Carlotta, his hands shaking uncontrollably, pleading for help. About to leave for his dental appointment, he found himself unable to comb his hair or knot his tie.

The next day, even before his morning coffee, O'Neill openly began drinking from the bottle. "I am frantic with fear & heartache," scribbled Carlotta.

O'Neill's binge had already lasted four months, and Carlotta believed the time had come to enlist the help of a doctor. Unfortunately, Dr. Gilbert V. Hamilton, who had pulled O'Neill from his whiskey-soaked doldrums nine years earlier, was no longer accessible; in 1928, he had moved to Santa Barbara, California (where he maintained a private practice until his death in 1943).

Carlotta turned instead to O'Neill's trusted internist, Dr. George Draper. It took some persuasion, but O'Neill finally permitted Dr. Draper to admit him to Doctors Hospital on February 21, "to get all the whiskey out of him," as Carlotta put it. She spent a miserable night alone in the hotel, weeping, and frightened for the future. (Yet—trust Carlotta—the next morning she had herself a haircut, wave, and shampoo.)

During O'Neill's five-day hospital stay, Carlotta, searching their suite at the Madison, found empty and half-empty whiskey bottles in O'Neill's bedroom clothes closet and bathroom.

She asked the hotel manager (not without some embarrassment) to get rid of the bottles. Then, asking herself if "real love is a blessing or a curse!" she collected her dried-out husband from the hospital and, a day later, the ever-forgiving mother and her wayward genius of a child entrained for Georgia.

"Good to be home," O'Neill noted in his Work Diary on February 28. "N.Y. trip was one long siege of troubles & bad luck!" The good luck was that he'd made up his mind one more time—even without the help of Dr. Hamilton—to quit drinking.

Carlotta, thinking back to O'Neill's drunken episodes in France and Shanghai, could congratulate herself on the patient nurturing that had enabled her, once again, to help rehabilitate her blackest of Black Irishmen. O'Neill made it clear he was equally pleased to have been rescued when, some time later, he wrote to Lee Simonson, applauding his friend's recent decision to give up alcohol.

Somewhat softening the facts of his own slip, O'Neill told Simonson that—although he himself had been on the wagon so long he'd "lost count"—he did "at one time for a short period try a temperate light wine and beer schedule," but that "it was no dice" and "no fun," merely inflicting indigestion and "low spirits." Skipping over his brief foray into hard liquor, O'Neill said he found he was "no longer interested, anyway," and "that was finally that."

O'Neill had made scant progress on his cycle three months later despite being back on the wagon. "Getting nowhere," he recorded on May 31. And in June he wrote of his dilemma to Eugene Jr., telling him of his many exhausting "days when I doubt myself and my work, and wonder why in hell something in me drove me on to undertake such a hellish job when I might have coasted along and just written some more plays, as a well-behaved playwright does."

More than pleased that Eugene had recently passed his PhD oral exam and had begun teaching in Yale's classics department, O'Neill found comfort in having him as a confidant. Earlier he'd complained to Eugene that the cycle stretched before him "into a future of seemingly endless hard labor," and it now looked "as if there would have to be still another play—a ninth which will carry me back to 1770."

That play (as O'Neill described it twelve years later to the writer Hamilton Basso for a profile in *The New Yorker*) was actually set in 1775 and dealt with an Irishman who joins the British Army to come to America, where he deserts. Seeking escape from the "slavery of agricultural life in Ireland," he heads for the wilderness determined to live his life "as a truly free man."

His dream is thwarted when, having paused at an isolated farm for food, he finds himself ensnared by the attractive young widow who offers him shelter. It isn't long before he has forgotten his dream of living "as a truly free man" and talked himself into accepting the "slavery of agricultural life" in America.

Writing (as a courtesy) to Lawrence Langner about his progress on the cycle, O'Neill cautioned him not to expect "an American life" in the accepted sense. "I mean," he explained, "I'm not giving a damn whether the dramatic event of each play has any significance in the growth of the country or not, as long as it is significant in the spiritual and psychological history of the American family in the plays."

The cycle, he said, was "primarily just that, the history of a family. What larger significance I can give my people as extraordinary examples and symbols in the drama of American possessiveness and materialism is something else again.

"But I don't want anyone to get the idea that this cycle is much concerned with what is usually understood by American history, for it isn't. As for economic history—which so many seem to mistake for the only history just now—I am not much interested in economic determinism, but only in the self-determinism of which the economic is one phase, and by no means the most revealing—at least, not to me."

Bewailing the difficulties of his task, he added: "Try a Cycle sometime, I advise you—that is, I would advise you to, if I hated you! A lady bearing quintuplets is having a debonair, carefree time of it by comparison."

At the end of August, O'Neill put aside a second draft of the play that would emerge as *A Touch of the Poet*, enjoining himself to let it "rest as is" for the time being. He would tweak it from time to time during the next seven years, but it was already a work of considerable power.

As the only cycle play O'Neill was destined to complete, *A Touch of the Poet* is crucial to an understanding of his tragically unfulfilled vision for the cycle as a whole. It is also significant as the first play O'Neill completed after *Days Without End*, for it continued his search, amid an increasingly materialistic society, for a spiritual faith that would give meaning to his life.

Although the play's title seems to suggest the touch of Irish blood injected into the Yankee Harford family through intermarriage with the Irish Melodys, it is actually the young, idealistic Simon Harford to whom it applies. O'Neill's Irish Melodys turned out to be every bit as susceptible to the lust for money and power as the detestable Yankee Harfords— starting with Sara, Simon's wife-to-be.

Sara is the beautiful, self-willed daughter of the play's protagonist, the Irish immigrant Cornelius Melody, whose own father was a saloon keeper. The father connived and cheated his way up the social scale in his native Ireland, managing to buy himself the castle in which his only son, Cornelius (known as Con), grew up.

Encouraged to assume the airs of a gentleman, the youthful Con Melody was quick to take offense and more than eager to challenge to a duel anyone who scorned him for his origins. Handsome, arrogant, a ladies' man, Melody acquired a commission in the British Army, fighting (and swaggering) his way through the war with the French in Spain, achieving the rank of major, and being commended for bravery.

Melody's career, however, ended in disgrace after a Spanish nobleman caught him making love to his wife and challenged him to a duel during which Melody fatally shot the Spaniard. (All this is expository dialogue.)

When the play jumps to life in 1828, Con Melody is established in a village outside of Boston as the proprietor of a tavern, above which he lives with his wife, Nora, and twenty-year-old Sara.

Despite the trimmings of the backstory, Melody (although he is an ex-soldier turned saloon keeper rather than a touring actor) is readily recognizable as yet another version of James O'Neill. Like James, Con enjoys the limelight, speaks with a studied lyricism, is popular with his barroom cronies, and is a drinker who (with rare exceptions) can carry his liquor.

O'Neill describes Melody's forty-five-year-old body as "heavy-boned" and "bull-like" with an "impervious strength" and "a tough, peasant vitality." Just as James O'Neill felt wounded by his snobbish New London neighbors, Melody smarts under the contempt of the aristocratic Harfords, whose Boston estate is nearby the Melody tavern.

Harford's name and background were suggested by a blend of two of O'Neill's pet villains, both descendants of robber barons: Edward S. Harkness, an heir to the Standard Oil fortune who occupied a forty-two-room mansion on a 235-acre estate in New London known as "Eolia"; and Edward C. Hammond, a railroad mogul, who lived in comparable splendor on a nearby estate called "Walnut Grove." (O'Neill would again draw on both tycoons for the ridiculed character of T. Stedman Harder in *A Moon for the Misbegotten*; Harder is also comically disparaged in *Long Day's Journey Into Night*.)

Melody is given to theatrical posturing and reciting lines from Byron's

Childe Harold's Pilgrimage to his own mirror image ("I have not loved the World, nor the World me.") and he regales his barroom claque with highly colored anecdotes of his past. In moments of extreme emotion, he lapses into the brogue that he, like O'Neill's father, has disciplined himself generally to suppress. Melody's greatest vanity—a beautiful thoroughbred mare he can ill afford to stable—might well have been O'Neill's metaphor for his father's pride in his chauffeur-driven (if secondhand) New London–based Packard touring car.

It's true Melody's wife, Nora, bears no resemblance to Ella O'Neill—except for having won his heart by her fetching looks. Daughter Sara is described by O'Neill as bossy and single-minded and possessing "a curious blending" of "aristocratic and peasant characteristics." While some scholars assume from this description that Sara is "based" on Carlotta, her character can also be seen as a stand-in for the two O'Neill sons; she taunts and belittles her father, much as Jamie and Eugene taunted and belittled James. And their quarrels are just as quickly regretted—with phrases like "it's the poison talking" and "it was the drink talking."

Sara Melody is also recognizable as a blood sister to Abbie Putnam, the covetous, scheming young bride of *Desire Under the Elms*—a character conceived well before O'Neill fell in love with his part-aristocrat, part-peasant Carlotta. Like Abbie, Sara connives to marry a man (Simon Harford) who can raise her status socially and financially. Although Simon is an offstage character throughout the play, we learn that not only is he the heir to the Harford fortune, but also young, attractive, and a dreamer—and much attached to his mother. Not content to be merely a rich man's son, Simon, we are told, has built himself a cabin near a lake in the woods that surround Melody's tavern, where he plans to write a book "denouncing the evil of greed and possessive ambition."

On a recent walk in the woods, Sara has discovered him by the lake suffering from a fever and chills. She persuades him to return with her to the tavern and he gratefully allows her to nurse him. Throughout the play, Simon—constantly spoken of but never seen—is confined to bed in an upstairs room of the tavern.

Further evidence that O'Neill had his father in mind when inventing Con Melody was his comment to George Jean Nathan that there was no contemporary actor who could do justice to the role. What it needed, said O'Neill, was "an actor like Maurice Barrymore or James O'Neill, my old man. One of those big-chested, chiseled-mug, romantic old boys who could walk onto a stage with all the aplomb and regal splendor with which they walked into the old Hoffman House bar, drunk or sober.

"Most actors in these times lack an air. If a playwright doesn't work up entrances fifteen minutes long for them and have all the other characters describe them in advance as something pretty elegant, noble, chivalrous and handsome, the audiences wouldn't be able to accept them for much more than third assistant barkeeps, if that."

O'Neill's imagination, however, soars well beyond the autobiographical in *A Touch of the Poet*—particularly in the way in which Melody finally accepts his loss of illusions. True, there is an undertone of the real-life scene in which James, at last accepting that his life has been "froth" and "rotten," is "glad to go" to a "better sort of life—somewhere." But ever the inspired dramatist, O'Neill invented a more graphically shattering end to Con Melody's delusions.

Melody's disassembling begins when he readies his barroom friends for his annual celebration of the Battle of Talavera. In reliving this triumphant moment of his vanished youth—when the Duke of Wellington publicly commended him for his bravery—it is his custom (derided by his daughter) to dress himself in the resplendent major's uniform he wore during that engagement and which he has preserved in an attic trunk.

Melody's self-esteem gradually diminishes when, while awaiting the evening's revels, he unexpectedly encounters young Simon's mother, Deborah Harford. She has come to pay her son a sickbed visit, but Melody mistakes her for an aristocratic traveler stopping at his inn for refreshment.

Deborah, as O'Neill describes her, resembles both his own mother and Carlotta; like Carlotta, she is middle-aged "but looks to be no more than thirty," and like Ella, she has "thick, wavy red-brown hair"; like both women, "her face is beautiful." But her persona is overwhelmingly Ella's—"remote and otherworldly." Indeed, she is the most enigmatic of all O'Neill's fictional women.

Already buoyed by drink, Melody presumes to flirt with Deborah, but she disdainfully rebuffs him and asks Sara (who has witnessed the rebuff) to take her to Simon's room. Melody, shaken by his gaffe, is further humiliated when, during his celebratory dinner that evening, an emissary from Deborah's rich, autocratic husband arrives at the inn.

Evidently Simon has told his mother he is in love with Sara and Deborah in turn has informed her husband, who has dispatched his lawyer with an insulting offer to Melody of $3,000 to remove himself and his family at once to some distant state.

In a fury, Melody and one of his cronies, Jamie Cregan (who served with him as a sergeant at Talavera), rough up the lawyer and hustle him out to his waiting carriage, instructing him to notify Harford that Melody plans to "call him out" if he does not apologize for his insult. Still fuming, Melody hires a carriage and races off with Cregan to Boston, where they force their way into Harford's mansion and battle his servants—but are, of course, denied access to Harford.

The police are summoned, and after a bloody free-for-all, Melody and Cregan are subdued and thrown in jail. Harford, fearing public embarrassment, soon orders them released, and they return to the tavern, where Melody, in the depth of humiliation, at last crumbles.

Clutching the two dueling pistols he had intended to use on Harford, he staggers to the stable and shoots his treasured mare. He had planned to shoot himself with the second pistol but he is all-too-aware that in shooting the mare—the emblem of his deluded self, he has already committed a symbolic suicide.

With the death of that deluded self, Melody abandons all material aspiration. Castigating himself as "the late lamented auld liar and lunatic, Major Cornelius Melody, av his Majesty's Seventh Dragoons," he gratefully reverts—brogue and all—to his Irish-peasant self; he humbly re-embraces the devout and loyal wife he has disdained during all these years of their marriage. He has regained his soul, and his spirit is finally at rest.

O'NEILL OBVIOUSLY WAS recalling the never-to-be-forgotten scene at his father's deathbed when James, denouncing his own hollow career in pursuit of material gain, deplored the wasting of his great talent as a Shakespearean actor, choosing instead to posture as a matinee idol in the shallow, crowd-pleasing role of the Count of Monte Cristo. Like James, O'Neill's Con Melody threw away a noble career (in his case as a heroic soldier) to pursue superficial self-aggrandizement.

In spiritually redeeming Melody, it would seem that O'Neill, in his mind, was posthumously granting redemption to his father. Moreover, it would appear that this vicarious redemption of his father was one more step in O'Neill's quest for his own spiritual salvation. Having rocketed many moons beyond the clumsiness of *Days Without End*, O'Neill, in *A Touch of the Poet*, had dramatized that quest with skill and subtlety.

WHILE O'NEILL INTENDED each of the cycle's plays to stand alone, *A Touch of the Poet*, despite its emotional power, feels incomplete. The problem is Deborah Harford. Although intrinsically captivating, she is unintegrated into the play's narrative, for she has completely fulfilled her dramatic purpose by the end of the second of the play's four acts, when she precipitates Melody's disassembling.

But O'Neill causes her to linger onstage (after her offstage visit to her son's sickbed) in order to deliver (to Sara Melody) a lengthy, rambling, dreamlike monologue that sounds more like a foretelling of cycle plays yet unwritten than an inherent part of *Poet*. (She does, in fact, reappear in the sequential cycle play, *More Stately Mansions*—as a major and scary presence—to battle Sara, now her daughter-in-law, for dominance over Simon.)

In her monologue Deborah confides to a wary Sara that her son has inherited a tendency to be "an inveterate dreamer" like herself; she then hurtles through the branches of the Harford family tree, reciting the history of its eccentric members, both male and female, as far back as the Battle of Bunker Hill, spilling minute and often horrifying details about how they have been variously corrupted by their lust for wealth and power.

Recounting the details of her honeymoon in the winter of 1804, Deborah reveals that her husband's entire family accompanied them to Paris to witness Napoleon's coronation as emperor, and that she herself, after her marriage, used to dream she was Josephine.

After delivering her outlandish (if hypnotic) monologue, Deborah departs, never to reappear in *A Touch of the Poet*, leaving the audience (and reader) with a sense of the play's incompleteness.

37

After much agonizing, O'Neill and Carlotta made up their minds in July 1936 to sell Casa Genotta.

They confided their decision to their houseguests at the time, the academic Sophus Winther and his wife, Eline. Winther, two year earlier, had published the laudatory work *Eugene O'Neill: A Critical Study* two years earlier, and the two men had become friends. Now the O'Neills told the Winthers of their tentative plan to go west. O'Neill wanted to absorb atmosphere for the cycle's West Coast branch of the Harford family, and Sophus urged him to begin his trek by first renting a place near their own, on the outskirts of Seattle. The plan suited the O'Neills and they asked the Winthers to find them a furnished house.

Carlotta hadn't the courage until nearly two months later to tell George Boll of their decision to sell, after which she fell into a fit of weeping. O'Neill had fewer regrets. In his diary, he grumbled: "Will be glad leave this place—hope we can sell it soon—climate no good for work half of year—and feel am jinxed here."

Debilitated from stress, Carlotta and O'Neill lumbered back again to New York to be doctored. This time they checked into the Lowell Hotel, on East Sixty-third Street (perhaps because they felt embarrassed over their last stay at the Madison). After administering X-rays and blood tests, Dr. Draper told O'Neill the "whole person" was sick, but there was "no definite organ to pin it on." He advised "absolute change—rest—forget work."

Carlotta's own doctor wanted to put her into the hospital, but when she demurred, insisting her husband needed her to take care of him, he compromised by administering a series of injections to bolster her weakened condition.

Both O'Neills were on edge, anticipating their imminent abandonment of Casa Genotta, and could summon little gaiety when Eugene Jr. and various friends dropped in at the Lowell on October 16 to mark O'Neill's forty-eighth birthday.

A LATE AFTERNOON in October found O'Neill and Carlotta boarding the 20th Century Limited bound for Chicago on the first leg of their trip to Puget Sound—once again in search of their Erewhon. For the sixth time in his adult life, O'Neill was turning his back on a home that had failed to live up to his expectations. Provincetown had been too crowded, Ridgefield too close to Manhattan, Bermuda too social, Tours too rainy, Manhattan too distracting, and Sea Island too hot.

After an overnight stay at Chicago's Blackstone Hotel, they entrained for Seattle on the Great Northern Empire Builder. Carlotta was cheered to see that O'Neill was already looking and feeling much better.

They were greeted by the Winthers as they stepped down into the Seattle railroad station at eight in the morning of November 3. Word had somehow leaked of their arrival, for there was a reporter present; he accompanied them to the rented house at 4701 Ruffner Street that was to be the O'Neill home for the next two months, and he interviewed and photographed them there.

O'Neill was pleased with their house and its views of Puget Sound's choppy waters and the snowcapped Olympic Mountains, describing it as "comfortable" with "beautiful grounds." It was staffed with a housekeeper, cook, and maid. That evening, after listening to the election returns on the radio with the Winthers, O'Neill was gratified to learn that President Roosevelt had easily won a second term.

They were barely settled when O'Neill, on November 10, received telegrams from Russel Crouse, Richard Madden, and Harry Weinberger, all telling of rumors that he had won the Nobel Prize. O'Neill refused to credit the hearsay. "This happened before," he remarked in his Work Diary, referring to similar rumors about him when Luigi Pirandello had won the prize in 1934—and even earlier, in 1930, the year Sinclair Lewis became the first American writer to be so honored.

O'Neill had not forgotten Lewis's generosity in telling the Swedish Academy that Theodore Dreiser and Eugene O'Neill deserved the prize as much as he did; he had cited O'Neill as the man who "utterly in ten or twelve years" had "transformed the American drama from a false world of neat and competent trickery to a world of splendor, fear and greatness." O'Neill's reply was equally embracing. Lewis, he said, was the writer who "had seen life as something not to be neatly arranged in a study, but as terrifying, magnificent and often quite horrible, a thing akin to a tornado, an earthquake or a devastating fire."

O'Neill was both grateful for Lewis's praise and amused by his invective. ("I was tickled to death with the whole address," he later told George Jean Nathan.) Disappointed once again when Pirandello won in 1934, O'Neill now shrugged the whole thing off, remarking in his diary that he didn't care either way, as the prize was "a jinx for [the] middle-aged."

On November 12, at 7:30 in the morning, Carlotta answered a phone call from Sophus Winther, informing her that the Associated Press had verified that O'Neill had won the prize. "The morning is a Bedlam!" she recorded. "Associated Press, United Press & International News all call for interviews & photographs—head of the Swedish newspaper etc. It isn't easy to protect Gene from all these people." Because no prize had been given in literature the year before, O'Neill received a very welcome accrued-cash award of more than $40,000.

To reporters, O'Neill said he hadn't thought the award would go to an American so soon after Sinclair Lewis received it in 1930, adding that he'd thought if any American writer merited the honor, it might be Dreiser. Later in the day, after receiving formal notification from the Swedish consul, he expressed his regret that he would be unable to arrange his affairs in time to be in Stockholm for the presentation on December 10.

When a reporter from the *Seattle Daily Times* asked him about the subject of his next play, O'Neill described the Harford family that moves "from the East Coast to the West Coast, back to the East Coast and ends in the Middle West."

"Is that why you're in the West—to get atmosphere?"

"Something like that. I have to live in a place before I can write about it. I have to have the feeling of living there. Of course, the western part of the play takes place in 1870, but I'm going to travel all around the West. Just looking and talking to tradespeople—that's the way I get the feel."

"Is it a very long play?"

"Oh yes. It goes on forever."

Then, ignoring his recently expressed determination to withhold production for years to come, he perversely chose to announce, "I hope it will start next October. With one play a season, people can go on seeing it forever. And when all eight plays are produced I hope they will run them all off on successive nights—that ought to knock the audience cold. They'll never want to see another play."

When the flurry of interviews and congratulatory telegrams at last receded, the O'Neills sat down to dinner with the Winthers, who, at O'Neill's insistence, were to dine with them frequently during what would be their five-and-a-half-week stay in Seattle.

It wasn't until Sophus and Eline departed after dinner that Carlotta and O'Neill were at last left to themselves to absorb the day's momentous event.

For O'Neill—out of the limelight for the past three years, still smarting from the fiasco of *Days Without End*, shakily recovering from his lapse into alcohol, and trying to gain a foothold on his mountain of a cycle—it was a godsend to be recognized by the Swedish Academy as the only American playwright to win the Nobel Prize.

As for Carlotta, by nightfall she was still in a delirium of delight. To her diary, she confided, "Gene takes me in his arms & says, 'Don't forget how much I love you!' I thought that wonderful of him considering all the excitement."

The day after the announcement of the Nobel Prize, *The New York Times*, on its editorial page, applauded, "He deserves it:" The editorial continued, "Although American playgoers have had to bear with him during two or three periods of transition, and have had to suffer two or three disastrous plays from his pen, he has long dominated our theater on the basis of vigorous work performed. His successive days of wrath have yielded a stout library of malevolent tragedies that include several masterpieces."

The *Times* confirmed what it described as "a general respect and admiration" among O'Neill's fellow writers: "For years he has been the boldest influence in our drama, grimly reaching out after big themes and, in his best work, dominating them by the power of his imagination and the depth of his feeling. None of the practical considerations of journeyman playwriting has ever drawn a compromise from him. He has repeatedly cracked the old molds by the largeness of his dramatic vision."

Gratified as he was to be heralded in radio bulletins and newspaper stories as his country's first playwright to win the Nobel Prize for literature, O'Neill, inevitably, was thrown into turmoil. Instead of finding his hoped-for respite in Seattle, he was drained by the need to respond to the congratulatory messages and demands for interviews. He was weary from seven months' work on his "damned cycle," as he wrote on November 15 to Kenneth Macgowan (who, like Robert Sisk, was now producing movies in California):

"So it is not an unmixed blessing. In fact, so far, I'm like an ancient cab horse that has had a blue ribbon pinned on his tail—too physically weary to turn round and find out if it's good to eat, or what." On the same day, in his Work Diary, he muttered about the continuing intrusions on his privacy and, predictably, declared himself close to a breakdown.

He brightened when he read some of the praise from abroad, led by George Bernard Shaw: "An excellent decision. I always thought that this year's prize should go either to Upton Sinclair or O'Neill." O'Neill was even more pleased to read a joint message from William Butler Yeats and Lennox Robinson, expressing their delight with "this European recognition to such a worthy recipient."

In response to a request from the American legation in Stockholm, on November 17, O'Neill pulled himself together long enough to write a brief speech to be read for him at the upcoming presentation ceremony.

After a few obligatory if insincere remarks about "sharing" the honor with all his equally worthy fellow American playwrights, O'Neill got down to his true feelings, expressing his gratitude "to that greatest genius of all modern dramatists, your August Strindberg," whose influence "runs clearly through more than a few of my plays and is plain for everyone to see."

Enclosing a copy of his speech to Russel Crouse, O'Neill wrote Crouse a personal note that was a scathing attack on his fellow dramatists for their lack of honesty and courage.

"You will note," wrote O'Neill, "that the first section [of the speech] is replete with more than a little amiable phonus bolonus about my American colleagues." Then he swung into a petulant tirade:

"Why the hell I should be so amiable I don't know, for few, if any of them, have ever had the decency to admit that my work had ever meant a thing to American drama or to them, or that my pioneering had busted the old dogmas wide open and left them free to do anything they wanted in any way they wanted. (Not that many of them have had the guts to try anything out of the ordinary, but they could have.)"

Complaining he'd been congratulated by only three or four of the "home front playwrights," he vilified them as mostly "cheap shit-heels!"

While excoriating his American colleagues, O'Neill tolerated the disapprobation of a few scattered theater critics both at home and abroad.

One particularly vitriolic attack came from Bernard De Voto, the newly established editor of the *Saturday Review of Literature.*

Smugly acknowledging he was in the minority, De Voto had pronounced O'Neill undeserving of the prize because he fell short "both absolutely and relatively" of being "an artist of the first rank." In fact, he contended, O'Neill had been foisted on the public as a figure of literary importance by the Theatre Guild. He clinched his argument by asserting the award was largely due to O'Neill's "prestige and publicity," which neither the critics nor the public dared to dispute.

O'Neill told George Jean Nathan he was not displeased that there had been at least a few scoffers. "If the praise were unanimous, I should feel very, very Eminent and dead." But, he wondered, "Who in hell is De Voto?"

DURING THE REST of November and the first two weeks of December, O'Neill tried to absorb atmosphere for his cycle, the ostensible reason he'd come to Seattle.

He and Carlotta took long sightseeing walks through different neighborhoods, and he accompanied Winther on several trips, among them a drive around the Mount Olympus Peninsula with an overnight stay at Lake Quinault and an all-day drive encompassing Whidbey Island and Bellingham.

Much as the O'Neills enjoyed the Winthers as neighbors, they concluded that Seattle, with its long spells of fog and rain, wouldn't do as a permanent residence. Northern California, where Carlotta grew up, seemed "best in many ways," Carlotta wrote to Lawrence Langner. "But, we'll just look everywhere and be very sure." Yet less than two years previously, when declining an invitation to visit Kenneth Macgowan in his new West Coast home, she had told him, "We won't go to California. I loathe the place—always have." Her somewhat garbled reason was that she "never drank, played bridge or golf" and "loathed the country clubs."

Presumably, her real reason for avoiding California at that time was that her mother and other relatives lived in the San Francisco Bay area; they knew she had not inherited money from her aunt, and Carlotta feared O'Neill might discover this deception, and probe for the true source of her income. For whatever reason, Carlotta now decided to chance it.

THE O'NEILLS LEFT Seattle on December 14, heading south.

Cynthia had volunteered to drive them the eight hundred miles to the San Francisco Bay area in her Ford. Divorced after a brief marriage at sixteen, Cynthia was now, at eighteen, engaged to marry Roy Stram, a Californian, with whom, much to Carlotta's disapproval, Cynthia was eager to have a baby.

Four days later, they reached San Francisco. Although somewhat uneasy about being back in the city of her "birth and early childhood," Carlotta nonetheless noted that she was "deeply moved" by her return.

O'Neill struggled through the festivities of Christmas Day, exchanging gifts with Nellie, Cynthia, and her fiancé, but on December 26 an attack of increasing abdominal pain drove him to seek medical help. He was examined by Dr. Charles A. Dukes, whom Carlotta called "Dukie" and who had removed her appendix seventeen years earlier. Dr. Dukes diagnosed appendicitis aggravated by a prostate condition, and ordered O'Neill into Merritt Hospital in Oakland.

While chatting with Carlotta, Dr. Dukes discovered that she herself was running a fever and he put her in the hospital as well. It turned out she had the flu. "A fine pair we are!" sighed O'Neill. December 28, Carlotta's forty-eighth birthday, found them confined to beds in adjoining hospital rooms. The following day, Dr. Dukes removed O'Neill's appendix.

O'Neill appeared to be making a normal recovery during the first week of January, but on the twelfth, he took a sharp turn for the worse. He had developed a "prostate-kidney infection" that, in Carlotta's words, "meant fevers (out of his head), chills & pain." She was once again frantic with worry.

In graphic shorthand, O'Neill himself described his near-fatal illness, day by day, in his Work Diary (doubtless reconstructing it with the help of Carlotta and his nurse, Kaye Radovan, on whom both O'Neills had come to depend):

> January 12—temp up to 102—chill—caffeine, adrenalin, codeine, morphine, atropine!—they give me the works!— Carlotta & nurses up all night—Dukes at 4 am—bad sinking spell with everyone worried but I feel too sick and ratty to give a damn whether I croak or not.

> January 13—temp 103.2.
>
> January 14—101.4—feel a little better—Carlotta goes to Fairmont to pack.
>
> January 15—bad again—temp 103—sinking—delirious Carlotta rushes back to hospital.

By January 17, O'Neill's temperature was down to 100 and he felt "better but very weak." Three days later, Carlotta wrote indignantly to Macgowan: "Gene's N.Y. doctors are so full of the 'mental' they couldn't see his abused insides. This prostate has been kicking up for years."

As O'Neill himself later elaborated to Macgowan, the appendix operation had been "the cinch part of it." But it had weakened him and brought on "an interior abscess which burst and flooded my frame with poison so that I was off my nut for a few days and had the medicos worried."

Now, Dr. Dukes has told O'Neill he will have to rest for at least eight months. "It holds up my work on the Cycle," O'Neill told Macgowan, "and I want so much to get back on the job." With an invalid's morbid obsession, seasoned with his own black humor, he was still describing his illness to friends months later; he wrote to the critic Barrett Clark that "an abscess in my inside burst and so poisoned me that they had to inject everything but TNT to keeping me from passing out for good."

O'Neill's condition would temporarily level off but the severity of this illness was a shattering blow; it precipitated the ever-declining health that would prematurely end his career.

GEORGE BOLL FOUND a buyer for Casa Genotta and, on February 2, with O'Neill recuperating in the hospital, Carlotta tore herself away to vacate the Sea Island house for its new owners.

The O'Neills had accepted an offer of $81,000 (with an additional payment of $5,500 for some of their furnishings), a substantial price in the depth of the Depression; but they still owed $15,000 on their mortgage, and calculated they were (as always) taking a substantial loss.

Carlotta estimated she would need to be away several weeks, counting travel time and all the packing and storing, and it was decided that O'Neill—in that more relaxed era of medical care and reasonable fees—would remain in the hospital for the duration of her absence; he would continue to receive treatments for his prostate and also undergo rehabilitative therapy. Carlotta felt reassured that with Dr. Dukes's supervision, and with Kaye Radovan looking after him, O'Neill would be comfortable.

On February 17, the Swedish consul in San Francisco, Carl E. Wallerstedt, visited O'Neill, who was seated in a chair in his hospital room, to present him with the gold medal and embossed diploma that constituted the Nobel Prize. Dr. Dukes and Kaye Radovan were the only witnesses to the ceremony.

Obeying Dr. Dukes's instructions to keep his remarks brief, Wallerstedt said: "It is customary for Nobel Prize winners to go to Sweden to receive their awards, and only on rare occasions is the order reversed. This is one time when custom must give way to emergency, as my nation no longer seeks to defer honor to a man who has won the highest award which can be made in his chosen field of endeavor."

O'Neill was still so weak that his knees shook as he rose from his chair and his hands trembled as he accepted the medal and scroll. While the medal was a replica of all the others awarded for literature, the scroll had been designed especially for him. It stated in Swedish that O'Neill had been chosen from all the playwrights in the world "for his creative drama, for characters marked by virility, honesty and strong emotion as well as for depth of inspiration."

MISSING CARLOTTA DESPERATELY, O'Neill wrote, wired, or telephoned her daily. On February 20, tracking her route back to him (Sea Island to New York to Chicago to San Francisco), he thanked God, in his diary, that she had "finished 1st lap of journey home!—she has done wonderful job getting all settled so quick."

He sent roses to Carlotta's drawing-room compartment when she entrained for Chicago; he sent roses to her hotel room when she arrived there for her layover; and he sent roses and telegrams to her scheduled rest stops—Omaha, Cheyenne, Ogden—on the final leg of her trip to San Francisco. He took pains to book them a hotel room. "Have arranged all for honeymoon at Fairmont including double-bed!" warbled a rejuvenated O'Neill.

Carlotta was thrilled with her husband's newfound tenderness. "*He is amazing to think of doing these things for me. It is so foreign to his past life & upbringing—and therefore doubly sweet.* I pray there will be no more separations for Gene & me! *I am not complete without him!*"

At 7:45 in the morning of March 2, O'Neill, accompanied by Kaye Radovan, met Carlotta at the station in Oakland and proceeded to the Fairmont—where they were shown to a room *without* a double bed. O'Neill barely kept his temper. As he described the scene in his Work Diary: "[Bell]boys stand with bags while we kick & have bed changed!— a scene for farce, but both of us deadly serious & determined! Honeymoon!" Evidently, the effort was worth it. It was "wonderful to wake beside Gene after three lonely nightmare weeks!" Carlotta rejoiced.

O'Neill was obliged, however, to return to Merritt Hospital for further treatment, and Carlotta, on Dukes's advice, checked herself into the same hospital for a week's "rest cure." Although both were eager to quit hotel living, the O'Neills were back at the Fairmont on March 13. "*We must have a home,*" declared Carlotta.

It didn't take them long to find the site on which they wanted to build. It lay atop a 2,500-foot hill situated between the towns of Danville and Walnut Creek, thirty-five miles east of San Francisco. Although it was far larger, and somewhat more expensive than what they had sought, they couldn't resist its beauty and isolation.

The land was cut off from neighbors to the west by high forested hills of pine where deer, bobcats, and coyotes roamed; blue herons nested there, and quail families sometimes emerged from the forest's edge. In the more sparsely wooded acres fronting their house site, an old barn stood amid orchards of almond, walnut, and orange trees. To the east, their site had an unobstructed view of Mount Diablo across the small orchard-filled San Ramon Valley.

Carlotta paid the asking price of $17,000 for the land, and O'Neill assumed the cost of the house, which eventually exceeded something more than $70,000. They took on a sizable mortgage, as they had for Casa Genotta.

Their next step was to lease a house in the vicinity—in Lafayette, Contra Costa County—from which they could supervise the construction. Since that rental was not available until June, they moved temporarily into a house in Berkeley, where they were at last rejoined by Herbert Freeman, who had driven Blemie to California and was looking after him in a San Francisco hotel near the Fairmont.

The unstoppable Carlotta, having decided (with O'Neill's approval) that their new home would be Chinese in style, had already begun to shop for furnishings at Gump's, famous for its Oriental antiques; among her purchases was a "beautiful large (old) opium couch [carved from teak] for Gene's bed!"

After hiring an architect in mid-April, Carlotta and O'Neill made a thorough tour of their 158 wooded acres, seeking the perfect site on which to build. The new house was to be far less grand than Casa Genotta, but just as imaginative in its own way.

"I wanted to build a Chinese house," Carlotta once explained, "but I didn't have the money, so I built a sort of pseudo-Chinese house." Its two stories were constructed partly of solid brick and partly of concrete blocks that resembled adobe and were painted white—Carlotta's concept of elegance, simplicity, and purity of design. Its doors and shutters were lacquered in Chinese red, and the rooms on both floors opened onto porches or balconies. There was a formal garden with seating, as well as a large patio that faced Mount Diablo, whose peak was often wrapped in mist.

"I left the white blocks rough and unpainted on the inside," said Carlotta, "and I put all my beautiful, very delicate and graceful Chinese furniture against these rough stones, which made a very beautiful effect." Part of the effect, she added, was created with mirrors—dark green or blue in the living and dining rooms, and a black one in O'Neill's bedroom.

O'Neill's recovery after the hospital was rocky. Even with regular treatments, the pain from his prostate condition was sometimes incapacitating. And when the pain retreated, nerves attacked. He tried to cheer himself with plans for the new home and with dreams of soon resuming work on his cycle.

O'Neill and Carlotta moved into their second rental, in Lafayette, at the beginning of June, and O'Neill—despite on-and-off medical upsets—tentatively took up his cycle, neglected for the past eight months, as per Dr. Dukes's orders. It seemed, though, that the O'Neills couldn't escape from oppressively hot weather even in the normally moderate climate of Northern California. The temperature rose to a startling 102 degrees on June 27, the day Lawrence Langner and Theresa Helburn brought S. N. (Sam) Behrman to Lafayette for a visit. O'Neill and Behrman, who had never met, quickly hit it off during the course of afternoon tea, a swim, and dinner.

Behrman, whose reputation rested upon urbane comedies, was struck by his host's exquisite deportment. "O'Neill had the kind of manners you find in Europe, but rarely in this country," he remarked. "Carlotta talked a blue streak while we were in the house, and after a while O'Neill took me out into the garden. He said, 'I thought it would be nice to have a word with you.'

"We talked about vaudeville. I told him I used to go to Keith's in Boston every Monday afternoon when I was at Harvard, and later to the Palace in New York. I knew a lot about vaudeville, but he knew more."

O'Neill told Behrman about the infamous road tour with his father in 1910, during which he (at twenty-two) and Jamie "were drunk all the time because their roles in the production of *The Count of Monte Cristo* were so ridiculous."

Behrman described O'Neill as "beautiful—his head in the sun," as he sat looking at the mountains and talking about how his plays had been censored in such countries as Germany, Japan, and Russia. He also spoke with pride, Behrman said, about his son Eugene's achievement as a Greek scholar at Yale.

At Behrman's request, O'Neill showed him his Nobel Prize. They also discussed their common enthusiasm for San Francisco. "We became quick friends that day. He made a great impression on me—I loved him." In his own diary, O'Neill was drier: "Behrman to tea, swim & dinner—like Behrman."

In July, he found himself "stuck" on the cycle "in same old place as in '36." Admitting he was "frightened for a while," he tore up many of his earlier notes; but, he vowed, "I'll get it this time!" And by September, he was making notes for the ninth play, which carried his story back in time to the American Revolution.

Writing to the critic Barrett Clark he said, "The Cycle goes back to my old vein of ironic tragedy—with, I hope, added psychological depth and insight. . . . It will be a unique something, all right, believe me, if I can ever finish it." He explained to Clark how difficult it was to think "in terms of nine plays, and a continuity of family lives over a space of 150 years." He ended his letter with the hope that he would "be ready to drive ahead" on the cycle by the beginning of the new year, when his home would be ready for occupancy. "This is final home and harbor for me," he wrote. "I love California. Moreover, the climate is one I know I can work and keep healthy in."

Healthy climate or not, O'Neill, approaching his forty-ninth birthday, was still making frequent visits to his doctor for the prostate problem, among other ailments, and he was also worrying about Carlotta's health; she was suffering from what she described as attacks of "sphincter pain," and she was also having more than her usual trouble with her eyes. All in all, it didn't sound as though they could be enjoying much of a sex life—yet, on October 6, O'Neill was reciting Baudelaire to Carlotta during a walk with her and Blemie.

"I am deeply moved when he takes me in his arms—and gives me a long, long kiss!" wrote Carlotta. "I go along, hand in hand with Gene—drunk with happiness!"

Her happiness—and O'Neill's as well—was largely due to their anticipated move into their nearly completed home.

They had decided to name it "Tao House"—"tao" meaning in Chinese "the right way of life." Their Chinese friend, the artist and writer
Mai-mai Sze, had listened tolerantly when Carlotta consulted her about
the name. "I didn't think it was particularly apt," she once said, "but I
thought, what does it matter, if it amuses them. The O'Neills had a
naive, romantic idea of China—the wisdom, the pageantry and so forth
were superficially conceived and romanticized by them."

APART FROM O'NEILL's health issues, another disturbance had surfaced the previous fall when Agnes enrolled Shane, for his senior year, in
a preparatory school in Colorado that O'Neill deemed pretentious.
Writing to his lawyer, O'Neill abused Agnes as "that wench [and] tramp
of a Boulton."

His disparagement of Agnes was a matter of course, but his small-
minded irritability toward the beleaguered Shane was something else.
For a man who, as a child, suffered so unforgettably from parental misunderstanding, O'Neill might have been expected to do better for his
own son. But apparently unable ever to forget he had not wanted that son
in the first place, O'Neill seemed incapable of offering Shane any sustained fatherly understanding. His all-too-brief moments of affection
and empathy for Shane could be usurped in an instant by stony anger.

Oddly, O'Neill was consistent in his uncritical affection for Eugene
Jr., who had been an even less wanted child than Shane; one reason was
that O'Neill did not hate Eugene's mother.

Unlike Agnes, Kathleen had made no demands on him during the
boy's first eleven years of life. Then, too, Eugene, unlike his insecure
and waffling younger half brother, had always seemed self-assured,
while Shane was in constant need of propping up. All in all, Eugene was
a more congenial and less burdensome son.

The Colorado prep school was Shane's third in seven years; although he was popular with his fellow students, his grades and his conduct had been erratic at the first of his boarding schools, Lawrenceville, in New Jersey, and he fared no better at his second, the Florida Military Academy in St. Petersburg.

In Colorado, as a senior nearing eighteen, he was thin, handsome, and shy, bewildered about his relationship with his father and confused about his future. O'Neill believed Shane should be attending "a good strict college prep school of the more democratic sort where they expect you to study seriously and fire you if you don't."

O'Neill's tirade had been sparked by a letter from Weinberger, reminding him of a payment of $700 due for Shane's school, plus Agnes's monthly alimony of $500.

"I'll pay for him till he's 21, as long as our agreement states I must. After that, I am through—and when I say through, I mean through," O'Neill blustered to his lawyer.

What was really eating O'Neill was Shane's (and to a lesser extent twelve-year-old Oona's) evident unconcern about their father's well-being. He complained to Weinberger that neither Shane nor Oona had sent a word of commiseration during his entire hospital stay, and Shane "practically never even acknowledges" his Christmas and birthday gifts (although, he conceded, "Oona does—sometimes."). Then, in a petty sulk, O'Neill vowed he was "stopping all presents henceforth"; he would treat Shane with "exactly the treatment he gives," and would neither ask him to visit in California nor "communicate with him in any way."

Even more unforgivable, he said, was "these brats'" unconcern for Carlotta, who always treated them kindly, frequently sending Christmas and birthday gifts of her own, for which she was never thanked by Shane, and only rarely by Oona. In sum, he growled, his "dear little ones—unlike Eugene," were "nothing to be proud of," and unless they changed "drastically," he was "off them for life." O'Neill couldn't resist a final vicious jab at his former wife: "There is too much greedy parasitic Boulton in their blood—I am afraid—not to add Boulton stupidity in their brains!"

O'Neill followed this outburst with a letter in early October to Shane, who had little reason to believe his father had ever had more than a passing interest in his existence. It was an appalling letter—insensitive, egoistic, icy. O'Neill wrote that he hadn't answered an earlier letter from Shane because he was "sore" at him for ignoring his serious months-long illness in the winter of 1936. "During all that time I did not receive one damned line from either you or Oona."

Shane could hardly feign ignorance of his father's condition, O'Neill scolded, as the news of his illness had been in newspapers all over the country, as also had been "the fact that the Nobel Prize medal had to be presented to me at the hospital in Oakland." He had received "letters and wires of sympathy from all over," but from his "own children—except Eugene—nothing." If Shane thought he would tolerate such behavior and still "feel any affection" for him, Shane was "badly mistaken."

He excused Oona—she was "still only a kid"—but from Shane he expected the respect and consideration that he'd received from Eugene at eighteen. "If you give it," he haughtily allowed, "there is no reason why the relationship between you and me should not develop into as fine a one as that between Eugene and me." He and Eugene were friends, he bloviated, "quite outside of being father and son."

He couldn't resist goading his younger son. A friend was what he wanted to be to Shane, and he proceeded to demonstrate his goodwill with a spiteful warning: "If you proved by your actions you are indifferent whether I live or die, except when you want something from me, then you must admit I would be a poor sap and sucker to waste my friendship on you, simply because you happen to be my son."

Oblivious to his increasingly petty, tyrannical tone, O'Neill raged on: "If you take me for granted, and think you can treat me as no friend of mine would dare to treat me without losing my friendship forever, why then I warn you you must be prepared to lose my friendship forever, too." In conclusion, he intoned, "If you are the boy I still hope you are, despite evidence to the contrary, then this letter should make you think, and so much good will come of it for us both. If you are not—well, then it's just too bad."

After flaying his son, O'Neill abruptly pulled himself up short, affably assuring Shane he was "feeling fine again" after his "long stretch of hospital and illness" during the recent winter and spring, and would soon be able to start "hard work" again; he closed with his own and Carlotta's love.

Poor Shane, thoroughly chastened, responded by sending his father a birthday gift, whereupon O'Neill deigned to bestow his pardon. "The carved walrus tusk arrived yesterday. It is a beauty and I don't know of anything I'd rather have had as a present. I've never seen one just like it before. It will look fine on my desk and be very useful as a paper weight. So much gratitude to you! I certainly appreciate your having remembered my birthday with such an unusual gift." He ended with an invitation for Shane to visit during his next spring vacation (almost a year distant).

The O'Neills moved into Tao House on December 30, with plumbers, electricians, and carpenters continuing to swarm in the unfinished wing. "We are so tired at bed time we hardly have the strength to crawl up into our beautiful Chinese beds!" noted Carlotta. They arranged themselves as best they could in the completed wing, which comprised the kitchen, Carlotta's bedroom, and O'Neill's two-room suite. His study—less ostentatious than the ship's prow installed at Casa Genotta—had a blue ceiling, was paneled in oak, and held a wall of bookcases. One large window looked out toward Mount Diablo and a smaller window had a view of wide-open space ending in a thickly wooded hilltop.

As Carlotta summed up, it had been "a year full of illness, worry and upheaval!" But, she was quick to add, "Gene tells me he loves me & couldn't live without me!!"

38

Awakening on New Year's Day, 1938, in their semicompleted mountainside retreat, Carlotta and O'Neill truly believed they were at last embarking on the idyllic life that until now had eluded them.

Carlotta, who had just turned forty-nine, still looked and felt youthful, although she'd lost some of her vivacity and was concerned about her "expanding waistline." She did not want again to uproot herself and prayed in her diary, "Dear God, let this be our real & final home!"

She was infinitely relieved when O'Neill, after a stroll on their vast grounds, assured her that he found Tao House in every way beautiful, and promised that it would be their "happy home" once they were settled and he'd fully regained his health. In his mind, O'Neill was again at work on his cycle—at his own unhurried pace, indifferent to the pressures of production.

As he now reaffirmed to the Theatre Guild's Theresa Helburn (and forgetting his careless ad-lib to the reporter in Seattle), he wanted no Broadway openings until he'd finished at least four or five of the cycle plays (and preferably all nine) if he could manage it "without winding up in the poorhouse."

The problem was his seesawing health. Within a week of moving into Tao House, he suffered an incapacitating seizure of neuritis that rendered his writing arm "practically useless." It was "hell," Carlotta recorded, seeing the man she loved "always so unhappy, depressed, ill or worried." Adept at finding solutions to problems, she confessed that this time she was at a loss for how to help him.

Their first year or so at Tao House, while it held intervals of peace and pleasure, was marred by the endless bouts of ill health that critically impeded O'Neill's writing. He was besieged as well by problems with his children, worries about money, and (not least) his concern—along with the rest of America—about the ever more troubling news from abroad. ("Hitler raising hell in Europe," Carlotta had exclaimed in her diary a few weeks after moving into Tao House.)

Both Carlotta and O'Neill were forced to acknowledge that the prospect of O'Neill's regaining his health completely was a forlorn hope; he would never have more than brief respites of complete wellness, and the underlying cause of his illness was yet to be accurately diagnosed. At least, he was within easy reach of the attentive Dr. Dukes.

"This bad health stuff is a rotten bore," O'Neill had recently complained to Harry Weinberger. "It busts up my working entirely. I only have to tear up the stuff I force myself to do when I'm under the weather. It just won't come right unless I feel reasonably fit. Rotten nerves I don't count. I've always had those. But piling other ills on top of the rotten nerves gets me groggy. I haven't yet learned to take that extra punishment and go on regardless."

For Carlotta, there was the continual worry of finding and keeping experienced servants willing to work in an isolated venue. She also supervised the ongoing work on the grounds, which dragged on with maddening torpor throughout the spring and summer. They were building a pool, grading a patio, planting trees and gardens, creating pathways, and erecting a high wire fence that surrounded the entire property. A private road meandered for three-quarters of a mile to a sturdy locked wooden gate that marked the entrance to their courtyard.

When he felt well enough, O'Neill helped with the planting, as he had on Sea Island; he also indulged himself as the breeder of a flock of pedigreed Brahma chickens—a throwback to his boyhood when his father, in a mellow mood, had granted him a fling at chicken farming and had even gone on to buy eggs from him at inflated prices. Among the Brahmas was a rooster (named by O'Neill for the prizefighter Sugar Ray Robinson) that, according to O'Neill's old friend Charles O'Brien Kennedy, "fought everything, animal or human, that came near him." But O'Neill soon had him eating corn out of his hand, and Carlotta proudly kept track of the Brahmas' daily output and distributed their eggs among her family, friends, and workmen.

Other mitigating pleasures were long walks, accompanied by Blemie; exploring the spacious beauty of their landscape; the carefully spaced dinners and teas with a few selected local friends; and the rare visits of friends from the East Coast who came to occupy their only guest room.

Carlotta bonded with a newly adopted cat, did the marketing, and had herself regularly driven into San Francisco for hair styling and clothes fittings. O'Neill attended an occasional football game and an even more occasional movie; he hungrily bought up new recordings of jazz, show tunes, and classical music to add to his already sizable collection, and often relaxed by treating himself and Carlotta, and sometimes their guests as well, to postprandial recorded "concerts." (He attributed his love of music to his mother's talent as a pianist, recalling how, before arthritis crippled her hands, she had enjoyed playing the old pianoforte in their New London home.)

WHILE SHAPING THE family backgrounds of his cycle's characters, O'Neill's thoughts often drifted to his own heritage as he'd heard it spoken of by his parents. Imagining the lives of his Irish forebears, many uprooted from their homeland by the famine, he strained to understand and empathize with their bewildering struggle to establish new roots in America. He found himself creating a family dynasty that, in his mind, somehow came to replace his own actual family. While reinventing them as the fictional Melodys, they became more alive to him than the factual O'Neills.

And yet, always at war with his own feelings, he couldn't escape the waves of sorrow and guilt that at times enveloped him. He had placed such a vast distance—not only physical but spiritual—between himself and his own roots. He wasn't sorry he'd fled the East Coast and he had no wish ever again to see New London. But his conscience had recently been stabbed when he'd received a notification from St. Mary's Cemetery in New London, where his parents, both his brothers, and his maternal grandmother were buried.

The notice required him to make a decision about repairs at the grave site. O'Neill had little interest in dealing with the remains of his own long-dead family, and this was the sort of decision he always preferred to duck. Compelled to readmit his ghosts into his life, he turned, in something of a panic, to Harry Weinberger.

"I've always had an aversion to visiting graves," he wrote to his lawyer, then explaining that, although he had long ago arranged for perpetual care for the graves, he could not recall what sort of stones had been placed at the site. "In fact," he said, "I know practically nothing about this plot." He asked Weinberger to send someone from his office to the cemetery to assess the situation.

Weinberger responded that the grounds were well kept, but there were no stones marking the graves of his parents or Jamie; there were only two small stones on those of his maternal grandmother, Bridget Quinlan, and his infant brother, Edmund, ordered by O'Neill's father, who had bought the plot in 1882. O'Neill, infuriated and embarrassed, asked Carlotta to respond. She told Weinberger, "Gene was shocked to hear that there were no stones to mark" his parents' or Jamie's graves. She and O'Neill were concerned, however, about the cost of the stones, coming on top of all their house construction expenses; her husband, said Carlotta, feared that if he ordered the stones in his own name he would be "scandalously" overcharged; could Weinberger inquire about prices in someone else's name and get the prices in writing before ordering the stones?

Carlotta further cautioned that O'Neill wanted the cost of the stones and installation to total "within five hundred dollars." That was not to be, but Carlotta (while splurging with her usual abandon on furnishings for their home) continued to bargain, asking Weinberger to price different grades of granite. After months of negotiating, O'Neill told Weinberger he had settled on a design for his family's plots and accepted the negotiated price of $650, although (being the true son of his parsimonious father) he found it exorbitant.

Brusquely, he informed Weinberger that there was to be but a single headstone for the plot that included the graves of his parents, his two brothers, and his grandmother (whom, like Edmund, he had never known). He gave Weinberger explicit instructions for the engraving: he wanted "'O'NEILL' on TOP with list of the five dead underneath," and then issued a warning: "I DON'T want any space left for those to come, because no one else will ever be buried there."

He reiterated what he had often said before: "I am the last of this pure Irish branch of the O'Neills," this time appending the explanation that his children were "a weird mixture, racially speaking." He added vindictively, "I certainly would rather be thrown down the sewer than be planted in New London. I want to be buried wherever my home happens to be when I die."

He had Carlotta type out the words for the marker:

O'NEILL
James O'Neill, actor, Born 1846 Died 1920
Ella Quinlan O'Neill, his wife, Born 1857 Died 1922
James O'Neill, 2nd, their son, Born 1878 Died 1923
Edmund O'Neill, their son, Born 1883 Died 1885
Bridget Quinlan, mother of Ella O'Neill, Born 1829 Died 1887

"This is simple and clear, with no chance of mixing up who's who," he told Weinberger. "It simply follows [the] pattern of [a] cast of characters in a play, which is absolutely appropriate for an actor's family."

WHEN HIS NEURITIS had abated toward the end of March 1938, O'Neill was able to take up work on the scenario of one of the cycle plays he'd been thinking about for the past year and a half—the play that would chronologically follow *A Touch of the Poet* by four years. It was the play he'd titled *More Stately Mansions*, which he had foreshadowed twice in *A Touch of the Poet*: once by Simon Harford's bipolar mother, Deborah, in her interminable monologue about her husband's greedy family, and later by Cornelius Melody when he predicts that his ambitious daughter, Sara, will "live in a Yankee mansion, as big as a castle." The title derived from the first line of the final stanza of the Oliver Wendell Holmes poem, "The Chambered Nautilus": "Build thee more stately mansions, O my soul!"

"Like it," was O'Neill's verdict in his Work Diary, after reading over the scenario's first act on March 26.

O'Neill began writing dialogue for *Mansions* on April 1, with little to distract him beyond routine trips to his doctors and—on April 10—a ten-day visit by Shane; it was his son's first trip to his father's wilderness hideaway. Shane was on spring break from what O'Neill disparaged as his "ranch school in Colorado."

Resigned, if not sanguine, about the course on which Shane seemed set, O'Neill wrote Macgowan that his eighteen-year-old son had "gone heavily horsey, cowboy boots and all—has learned to break horses and is a fine rider. He's getting a job this summer as a wrangler.

"What he will eventually do, God knows, but for once in his life he's genuinely self-confident and enthusiastic—about horses and stock-raising, not scholastic pursuits, I might add."

For her part, Carlotta regretted that Shane (though handsome) no longer resembled her Gene; but she allowed he was "a nice kid" whom she'd always liked. She and O'Neill accompanied Shane to a baseball game in Oakland and O'Neill took him on long walks, discussing his future. Shane returned to school, feeling as much a stranger as his father had at that age; like his father, he was acutely conscious of being overshadowed and belittled by a celebrated parent. Shane, however, lacked the miraculous gift of creativity that had been his father's salvation.

O'Neill, vaguely hoping for the best, soon again lost himself in his writing. On May 5, Carlotta noted, "Gene feels better—his brain full of work—thank God."

Contributing to O'Neill's improved outlook was his first swim in his newly completed pool, which was built into the side of their hill. Missing the sea, Carlotta recalled that "he didn't really think so much of the idea, but it was better than nothing."

On the evening of his debut swim and after a day of satisfying work, O'Neill was in a romantic mood, according to Carlotta. She described herself as "bursting with love" as she sat with her husband on their terrace overlooking the moon-bathed San Ramon Valley; she kept silent "until—he tells me *he loves me!*" With that, she emoted, "I am no longer silent!"

O'Neill continued in a stable (if not always benign) mood throughout the month, writing to George Jean Nathan that he would have a lot to tell him about the cycle when he came to visit. "The old bean is functioning better than it has in years," he wrote, and expressed the hope that, as he approached fifty, "the fatal-forties period of physical bog-down and mental meandering" was coming to an end.

Then, with his usual attempt at jocularity when addressing his wisecracking friend, he spoke about his aging Dalmatian, who would turn eleven on September 9. "We came near losing Blemie last week, and there was much sadness in the Hacienda O'Neill. An intestinal complaint due, I fear, to his lack of will power regarding horse turds, the old rake!" O'Neill explained that teams of horses had been on the estate cutting the hay; "[Blemie] says he can't understand it, that something he drank must have disagreed with him."

At O'Neill's request, Carlotta had been typing the cycle plays so that she could discuss them with him, as had been their habit while he was writing *Mourning Becomes Electra*. She was mesmerized by Deborah and particularly taken with the way O'Neill depicted her battle with her daughter-in-law, once rather simplistically noting, "Deborah fights Sara for her son's love with charm and subtlety, while Sara fights with her body."

But, typing her way through the first three acts of *Mansions*, Carlotta was brought up short when she arrived at Scene I of Act IV. It is in this scene—after many passages of highly surreal and contradictory rantings—that Simon accuses Sara of being afraid of Deborah's influence and of conspiring with her against him, viz:

> SIMON: Are you going to let her come between us forever? Can't you rid our life of that damned greedy evil witch?
> SARA: (*Stares at him with dread, but with a fascinated eagerness too*)— You mean you want me to—
> SIMON: (*Sees that Sara has understood him to mean she should goad the mentally fragile Deborah into the final stage of insanity; he switches to a lover's tone of "playful teasing"*) I want you to do anything in life your heart desires to make me yours.

Carlotta was shocked to realize, as she later recalled, that the play was "full of evil." And by July, O'Neill himself was hearing the drumbeat of defeat; according to Carlotta, he told her that "the devil of Fear" was whispering in his ear, "*You shall not finish this play.*"

Soon, Carlotta had a graver worry. Somehow, over the months, she had evolved as a solicitous mother to her daughter, closely tracking Cynthia's pregnancy.

When, on July 14—a day after Cynthia gave birth to a boy—Roy Stram phoned with the news that their baby had a cleft palate and harelip, Carlotta was crushed. What would this do to her twenty-year-old daughter, she wept to O'Neill, gratefully noting, "Gene, when really needed is calm & helpful. Holds me close in his arms—while I weep my heart out."

She felt somewhat reassured after an eminent plastic surgeon, called in by Dr. Dukes, agreed to perform a series of surgical procedures that would ultimately correct the affliction. "God give Cyn the strength and the courage to face life with this new burden," Carlotta prayed.

Soon her attention was diverted from her suffering daughter back to her suffering husband. Observing that O'Neill was haunted by the "nightmare" of being unable to finish the cycle, she worried he was "either not well, or aging—I notice this in so many ways! His work eats into him—life itself seems to absorb him."

At least part of O'Neill's unease, Carlotta knew, was due to their disordered household. It humiliated her—as a woman who took such inordinate pride in her ability to run things smoothly—that she was unable to lure reliable help out to their isolated residence. She was worn out from her confrontations with recalcitrant servants.

Despite all setbacks, O'Neill, for the moment, was making good progress on *More Stately Mansions*, and he informed Lawrence Langner that he expected to finish a first draft "in another month or two." And now, he prepared to welcome his older son on *his* first visit to Tao House.

In a letter offering to underwrite the visit, O'Neill took concerned note of Eugene Jr.'s recent separation from his second wife after a brief (and childless) marriage; he had expressed his hope that his son's "marital misadventures" would be swiftly resolved and that he wouldn't be "nailed for alimony at the last moment."

On Eugene's arrival, August 18, Carlotta noted he was "much heavier and has a 'black eye' that he got in a barroom brawl." Disturbed by what she saw as a change in his personality, she described her own shock and O'Neill's when Eugene announced he had joined the Communist Party; "The look on Gene's face!" she exclaimed. (A little more than two years later, after Russia declared war on Finland, O'Neill characterized "the Communist Party in this country as a foreign-controlled, traitor organization.")

The visit marked the beginning of Eugene Jr.'s gradual meltdown, and hardened the now-open antagonism between him and Carlotta.

After his son left, O'Neill tried to return his attention to *Mansions*, but the European crisis kept intruding. Carlotta (after her own skewed fashion) spoke for them both when she worried in her diary, "The World waiting for Hitler's Nuremberg speech. Dear God, how Britain has lost face! And to an ex-house painter!" (It's doubtful she spoke for O'Neill when, later that month, she expressed her disapproval of Mrs. Roosevelt's reported disinclination to curtsey to the king and queen of England on a state visit. "Oh, Politesse! Shame!" noted the old Tory.)

On September 8, despite his distress over world events, O'Neill completed his draft of *More Stately Mansions*, noting it was "as long as *Strange Interlude!*—but don't think will be able to cut length much." Permitting himself to slow down, he spent the next four months editing the manuscript, but he couldn't bring himself to pluck more than a line or two of precious dialogue from among its four acts and nine scenes.

The war news was growing ever more ominous. On September 9, listening to radio reports from Prague and Berlin, Carlotta noted that President Roosevelt was "trying to pave the way for negotiations to keep the peace! *It is frightening!*" O'Neill himself rarely mentioned the impending European war in his Work Diary, but had earlier remarked to Nathan that "the Hitler jitters" were affecting him.

Then, on October 12, O'Neill suffered a sudden collapse. Carlotta summoned Dr. Dukes, who brought in O'Neill's urologist; together they concluded—according to O'Neill—that it was a "sinking spell & flare-up of same old infection—pains in back, fever."

After further consultation, Dukes telephoned Carlotta to inform her that "all the leg, arm & back pains are caused from the infection in the prostate." While both O'Neill and Carlotta frequently took note of O'Neill's chronic prostate condition—a not uncommon ailment known as prostatitis—neither ever referred to its effect on their sex life. In fact, according to the prominent New York urologist Dr. Aaron E. Katz, who had access to O'Neill's 1953 autopsy report, as well as to O'Neill's and Carlotta's diary entries, "the painful disease can affect the physiological functioning of the penis, and lead to erectile dysfunction." There can be pain during sex, Dr. Katz noted, and this can increase for several days after sex. Moreover, "the orgasmic sensation normally associated with pleasure can be replaced by pain and discomfort, leading to depression, anxiety, and feelings of despair."

While O'Neill's symptoms could be temporarily relieved by massage, they invariably recurred. (It wasn't until some years after O'Neill's death that doctors began treating prostatitis with antibiotics.)

On his fiftieth birthday, O'Neill, although still weak, rallied sufficiently to work in spurts on *More Stately Mansions*. Responding to the Carl Van Vechtens, who sent him birthday greetings, O'Neill wrote cheerfully: "Blemie remarked to the cat: 'The Old Man doesn't look a day over 183.' And he was right. I didn't feel a bit older than that, either." By the end of December, although suffering from a mild attack of neuritis, O'Neill had managed to devote all or part of thirty-one working days to revising *More Stately Mansions*.

During their first year at Tao House, in their determination to pursue "the right way of life," O'Neill and Carlotta had managed—at least in Carlotta's mind—to strengthen the bond of their nine-year marriage. In an emotional outburst confirming this conviction, she described in her diary how she and O'Neill celebrated the arrival of the new year.

Early on the evening of December 31, they retired together to her bedroom and, ensconced in Carlotta's spacious Chinese bed, they listened on the radio to New Year's Eve celebrations throughout the country. At midnight, she wrote, "Gene takes me in his arms and tells me how much he loves me . . . *we together can take anything!!! I'll stick—no matter what!* Then I weep, like a fool, hanging on to him! God knows why! But I *do* know I love this mad Irishman!"

About to put aside his draft of *Mansions* for later revision, O'Neill wrote to Kenneth Macgowan of the play's tortuous odyssey; it had been the most difficult of the cycle plays so far, he said, because it was "psychologically extremely involved and hard to keep from running wild and boiling over."

What he did not tell Macgowan was that the character of Deborah Harford—only tentatively suggestive of his own mother in *A Touch of the*

Poet—had amassed more and more of Ella O'Neill's characteristics in *More Stately Mansions*; nor did he hint at how grotesquely he had exaggerated some of those peculiarities. Macgowan would have been shocked.

The unrevised and vastly overlong draft begins with a brewing conflict among its three principal characters—Deborah; her son, Simon; and his wife, Sara; but it soon splinters into a schizophrenic nightmare that far exceeds the surrealistic jumpiness of even *The Great God Brown*. O'Neill, in fact, had been quite unable to stop himself from letting his story run wild and boil over.

In no play he'd ever written had he slashed away with such naked fury at the perceived injustices he'd suffered in his early life; never had he sought so mercilessly to avenge what he saw as his mother's betrayal.

Innumerable scenes of *More Stately Mansions* resound to the raw agony of his hatred for the mother whose love he so desperately needed.

The action of the play opens in 1832 (four years after the action of *A Touch of the Poet*) and ends ten years later. It is set in various houses occupied by Simon Harford and Sara Melody after their marriage, as well as in Deborah Harford's garden at her late husband's mansion in Boston. Continuing the story begun in *Poet*, O'Neill depicts the previously offstage Simon Harford as yet another embodiment of the tormented American male. Simon is torn between his idealist's dreams and his lust for material success.

The now-widowed Deborah is teetering on the edge of insanity, gradually morphing into a Sycorax of a mother-in-law. When not daydreaming in her garden's summerhouse about being Napoleon's mistress, she spars with Sara—whom she secretly despises as a greedy Irish peasant slut—for dominance over Simon.

At the play's beginning, Sara is a loving wife to Simon and the mother of their four boys—the future grown-up Ethan, Jonathan, Wolfe, and Honey of *The Calms of Capricorn* (the play O'Neill has now designated to chronologically follow *More Stately Mansions*). Sara sympathizes with Simon's conflict between idealism and greed, but is hopeful he will succumb to the latter. Sure enough, it's not long before Simon does realize his baser dream, and Sara, with equal alacrity, is on her way to becoming a powerful matriarch.

Her only problem is her mother-in-law. At times, Sara allies herself with Deborah against Simon; more often, though, she is at war with Deborah for Simon's love and loyalty (which Deborah doesn't really even want).

The most conflicted of the three is Simon, who swings like an erratic pendulum between mother and wife. At one moment, he is consumed by a need for his distant mother's love—a need that is invariably twinned with mistrust of his wife; the next moment, he is overwhelmed by hatred of his treacherous mother, a hatred accompanied by an irresistible need for his nurturing wife. In O'Neill's fevered brain, the love-hatred among the three antagonists of *More Stately Mansions* grows more and more twisted, as O'Neill seems about to send all three spinning into limbo.

By play's end, however, it is only Deborah who fails to survive. She has willed herself into a state of psychotic oblivion, inevitably evoking an image of Ella O'Neill's escape into a morphine-induced never land. If Deborah sounds deranged, that is what Eugene, as a boy, believed his mother to be (as he'd earlier indicated in *All God's Chillun Got Wings* with his disguised version of his mother as Ella Harris, a defeated wife driven to insanity).

But in Deborah Harford, he drew a more detailed and vengeful portrait of a woman who, O'Neill seems to be saying, was fated for the punishment inflicted on her by both God and man. It is a vicious indictment by a son who could not forgive his mother for wishing him dead at birth.

"I was glad to be rid of him when he was born," Deborah spitefully tells Sara, speaking of Simon. "He had made my beauty grotesquely ugly by his presence." And later, thinking aloud while watching Simon: "How I cursed the night you were conceived, the morning you were born! How I prayed that you would die."

Deborah Harford is (unsurprisingly) one more O'Neill heroine (or antiheroine) consigned to a joyless end. In her case—taunted into madness by Sara—she is metaphorically murdered, even as Christine Mannon in *Mourning Becomes Electra* is *actually* murdered by her son, Orin, and as Evelyn Hickman (in the soon-to-be-written *The Iceman Cometh*) is murdered by her husband, Theodore "Hickey" Hickman. Considered along with the many other characters O'Neill polished off, it's surprising that none of his now-long-gone psychiatric mentors seem to have diagnosed his obsession with death as not only suicidal, but homicidal as well.

Once Deborah has been dismissed into madness, Simon turns to Sara as his new "mother," a role Sara is only too eager to fill. She declares she will be not only his mother, but also his "peace and happiness"; indeed, she promises to be everything he will "ever need in life." It doesn't take a Sigmund Freud to intuit that O'Neill is writing here about the transference of his filial love to Carlotta.

During November and December, O'Neill flailed his way through a second handwritten draft of *More Stately Mansions*, with Carlotta typing each act as he completed it, and on the first day of 1939, he began making revisions on the typed manuscript.

Shortly thereafter, he answered a telegram from *The New York Times* theater reporter Sam Zolotow, requesting an update on the cycle. O'Neill responded he had five plays "still to go, which means five years at present rate." O'Neill liked Zolotow, who had always reported accurately what O'Neill told him, and now gave him a bit of exclusive gossip for his column:

"Possible I may write play outside of Cycle in meantime if I can keep the Elephant opus out of my mind long enough, but no definite idea on this and it isn't probable." Zolotow couldn't know he was being given the first hint of the soon-to-come *Long Day's Journey Into Night*.

IT'S NO EASY TASK trying to interpret the unfinished, structurally chaotic *Mansions*, which O'Neill might (or might not) have resolved. But it's tempting to read the script as a surreal precursor to *Long Day's Journey*

Into Night, with Deborah the garishly distorted model for Mary Tyrone, and Simon as her amorphous son Edmund Tyrone.

In looks, Deborah Harford, at forty-five, is a younger version of Mary Tyrone. Too obvious to be overlooked, the resemblance between Deborah Harford and Mary Tyrone (despite the difference in their ages) begins with O'Neill's stage descriptions: Deborah's face is "framed by a mass of wavy white hair"; she has "a full lipped mouth," a high forehead, beautiful eyes that are "black, deep-set, beneath pronounced brows"; her hands are small, with "thin, strong, tapering fingers"; when first we meet her she is dressed "with extreme care and good taste" and her manner is marked by "a nervous tension and restlessness, an insecurity, a brooding discontent and disdain."

Mary Tyrone, at fifty-four, could be Deborah Harford nine years later. Her "high forehead is framed by thick, pure white hair," and she has the same "full lips" as Deborah; her "dark brown eyes appear black" and are "unusually large and beautiful with black brows"; her hands (now twisted by rheumatism) "were once beautiful . . . with long tapering fingers"; she is dressed "with a sure sense of what becomes her" and, like Deborah in her first appearance, she is unable to control "her extreme nervousness."

Both women exhibit a striking narcissism in their rejection of a baby son at birth; compare Deborah's "He had made my beauty grotesquely ugly by his presence" with Mary's subsequent rueful reminder to her husband that she didn't have "a single gray hair" until her son Edmund's unwanted birth—when her beautiful reddish-brown hair "began to turn white."

And finally, there are the methods by which Deborah Harford and Mary Tyrone escape from their unbearable lives—Deborah into self-induced insanity and Mary into a self-inflicted dreamland of drugs.

By the end of 1938, O'Neill and Carlotta were beginning to wonder if their serene, remote aerie had, after all, been purchased at too great a cost. The difficulty of running a well-staffed home in what most experienced servants regarded as a wilderness was proving to be an insuperable problem. The shrinking of their foreign investments due to the unforeseen threat of war abroad, coupled with the continuing Depression at home, was putting a severe strain on their accustomed lifestyle.

On January 7, with no prospect of income from a new Broadway production and in light of the continuing worldwide recession, Carlotta had actually gone so far as to suggest they trade Tao House for a smaller, more easily managed residence. But O'Neill had vetoed that idea.

Added to their other insecurities, Carlotta was suddenly confronted with a serious medical problem of her own. She was suffering from deteriorating vision and severe headaches, and was scheduled for an exhaustive diagnostic test and possible operation at the end of January. She'd had trouble with her eyes since early childhood ("They began operating when I was 5") and she was terrified. She believed the cause of her deteriorating eyesight was her typing of O'Neill's manuscripts over and over. "He would change a few words and add a few commas and make me type the page over again," she said.

O'Neill was prepared to shoulder the blame for her condition. On January 30, he accompanied Carlotta to a specialist in San Francisco, who advised an operation and made a second appointment for them both to discuss the details.

"How he'll *loathe* that!" Carlotta noted, with what sounded rather like grim satisfaction. "He detests being put in any position where *he* must make a *decision* or shoulder any responsibility—*outside his work!*"

She was hospitalized for twelve days in February, during which she arranged for a distraught O'Neill to dine out with various friends while Freeman looked after him at home. Her recovery was painful, but her chief complaint was that her long lovely eyelashes had been cut off.

O'Neill described Carlotta's recuperation to George Jean Nathan at the end of February: she was "wearing an arrangement of bandages and goggles which only permits her to see straight ahead through a tiny peep hole of dark glass over the sound eye," he wrote, adding she was brave and uncomplaining; but he had been profoundly worried about her.

He then fell into what Carlotta described as "gray, unhappy" spirits, and by mid-March was once again suffering from exhaustion. Carlotta, herself not fully recovered, feared she might not have the strength to cope. "How am I to keep well enough—discipline myself to not let him see how physically exhausted I am—how disturbed mentally—how fearful I am for the future, and to slip into the mood of *that* person he needs, at *that* hour! Wife, mistress, mother, nurse, friend, secretary, his 'buffer' to the world. God help me!"

Her stoicism was rewarded—as she joyfully recorded a week later—when, after finishing a supper she'd prepared on the cook's day off, O'Neill "puts his arms around me & says, 'Pretty good cook, aren't you? Did you ever hear how much I love you & need you & want you?' And he kisses me! I'm struck dumb with surprise and happiness!"

Carlotta didn't mind cooking for O'Neill on the servants' days off, for she and O'Neill were now being well fed and looked after by a dignified and efficient black couple, Will and Naomi. They had replaced a Japanese couple (who left because of the wife's illness) and who, in turn, had replaced a slovenly pair whose service Carlotta and O'Neill had endured for far too long.

O'Neill described that couple in his diary as "the two world's worst servants," characterizing them in a letter to Nathan as "an Irish lady cook married to a Greek—a sour combination!—and believe me, toward the end of their period of strictly faithless service, we never knew what we would get for dinner, if any, or how." He added, "We stood them as long as we could take it, on the theory that bad is better than none, for it isn't so easy to get anyone to work in the country here."

O'Neill wrestled with his cycle while Carlotta, her eyesight sufficiently healed, patiently typed and retyped his revisions and notes. Nothing in his routine hinted at the radical change of creative direction shortly to come.

39

Eight months past his fiftieth birthday, in June 1939, still treading water with no sign of landfall, O'Neill despaired to the writer Richard Dana Skinner, "I work and work and time passes, while, in relation to the whole work, I seem to stand still."

He'd been closeted with his symbolic Irish American family since 1935 and he yearned for a respite. In fact, since telegraphing the *Times*'s Sam Zolotow four months earlier, he'd decided he would like nothing better than to give his "Elephant opus" a rest. Confirming what he'd hinted at to Zolotow, he now told Skinner, "I may try writing a single play which is quite outside [the cycle's] orbit."

On June 5, he tore up his most recent draft of *The Calms of Capricorn* after judging it "no good," and then made a momentous decision.

"Feel fed up and stale on Cycle after 4½ years of not thinking of any other work," he jotted in his Work Diary. "Will do me good lay on shelf and forget it for a while—do a play which has nothing to do with it."

A day later, after reviewing his notes for possible future plays, he outlined not one, but two plays outside the cycle: the first was based on a blend of three saloons where, over several years, he had often drunk himself into a stupor; the second play—to be set in New London—he described in his notes as "N. L. family one."

Whatever constellation had commingled in the heavens over California on that day in late spring, it seemed designed to hoist O'Neill from his doldrums and drop him sure-footedly onto the rainbow bridge that led to the creation of *The Iceman Cometh* and *Long Day's Journey Into Night*. It would take him less than two years (a year and nine months, to be precise) to complete two plays the world eventually came to acknowledge as masterpieces.

As O'Neill later explained, "I felt a sudden necessity to write plays I'd wanted to write for a long time that I knew *could be finished*." His confidant was the critic Clayton Hamilton, a friend of his father's who sometimes vacationed in New London, and one of Eugene's earliest mentors. He told Hamilton that the impending global war had made him feel "there was not enough recognizable future in sight to go on with something that might take four or five more years." He further confided (to Dudley Nichols, who had become a friend after he reviewed *Strange Interlude* for the New York *World* and who was now a Hollywood screenwriter) that the ideas for both plays had been brewing "for years."

What he did not mention to Hamilton was an even greater concern: he feared that the often uncontrollable tremor in his hands might soon curtail his ability to write. The tremor sometimes made it a torment to grasp his pencil, and writing with a pencil was the only way he could express his thoughts, which seemed to him to course from his brain through his arm and onto the page.

There was yet another likely reason for O'Neill's tentative abandonment of the cycle; his mythical Harford family was losing its grip on his imagination and was gradually being replaced by images of his real-life family. He had tried to persuade himself that his father, mother, and older brother were finally at rest after he'd arranged for their tombstones; but it seemed that the months of haggling with cemetery functionaries over a suitable monument for their graves had torn open all the old familial wounds, so that they were still overwhelmingly alive in his mind.

O'Neill suddenly found it more urgent to dramatize the search for his spiritual roots in the immediacy of his actual family history rather than through his cycle's mythical lens.

The Iceman Cometh and *Long Day's Journey Into Night* would encompass his search with far greater impact than anything he'd so far written for the cycle. No one appreciated the drama of his own life as did O'Neill himself.

Both *The Iceman Cometh* and *Long Day's Journey Into Night* were plucked from the depths of his personal experience and, in his mind, were inseparably entwined. Although these two plays are entirely disparate in social content, venue, and characters, they are locked together sequentially. Each play portrays crucial aspects of O'Neill's life when, down and out at twenty-three, he was on the brink of his spiritual awakening.

In *Iceman*, he depicts a world of hopeless castoffs on Manhattan's downtown waterfront, reflecting the derelict life he himself was then living. *Long Day's Journey* pulls him from that world, in which he's drowning, and returns him to his family's summer home in New London, where he is once more ensnared in the stressful family conflict he had tried to escape—but is soon to emerge from as a writer.

So that there could be no mistake about the connection between the two plays, O'Neill set them both in 1912—the year that in his real life transformed him from a lost and aimless youth into a man with a lofty mission. In *Long Day's Journey*, he managed to compress this transformation into one long day beginning at 8:30 a.m. and ending at midnight. For *Iceman*, he needed two long days in which to deliver the prologue for the young O'Neill's spiritual awakening.

A leitmotif of each play is O'Neill's attempted suicide in the winter of 1912 when—broke, depressed, and rotgut-debilitated—he lived in a rented cubicle above Jimmy the Priest's, the sleazy saloon on Fulton Street close by the Hudson River and near the Battery; among his fellow outcasts was a burned-out newspaperman, a former commander in the Boer War, and a onetime captain in the British Infantry.

It was O'Neill's failed suicide at Jimmy the Priest's (an act whose nonconsummation he intermittently regretted) that returned him to the bosom of his estranged family in New London in the spring of 1912. His father helped him land a job as a cub reporter on the New London

Telegraph that summer. It's true that his shaky career ended only a few months later, in October, when he was diagnosed with a mild case of TB. But he speedily recovered after spending six months in a Connecticut sanatorium, where he claimed to have found himself "reborn" as a neophyte playwright.

In the impressionistic *Iceman Cometh*, O'Neill's own unsuccessful suicide at Jimmy the Priest's is symbolized by the successful suicide (at the same saloon) of one of the play's lost souls; in the more realistic *Long Day's Journey*, wherein O'Neill barely disguised his own family, his suicide attempt is briefly mentioned and continues to lurk beneath the surface along with the rest of the family's miserable secrets.

Long Day's Journey depicts a condensed version of the critical events immediately preceding O'Neill's "rebirth." There is, however, no hint in the play that Eugene (thinly disguised as Edmund Tyrone) will survive TB to emerge as the burgeoning dramatist who became Eugene O'Neill. The play, on the contrary, implies that Edmund (Eugene) will likely die of his illness. The play, after all, is a tragedy.

For his 1912 setting of *Iceman*, O'Neill transported some of the clientele of two other saloons of the era, neither of them as disreputable as Jimmy the Priest's. "The dump in the play," he once confided to Kenneth Macgowan, was "no one place, but a combination of three in which I once hung out."

One was the bar at the Garden Hotel, where both his father and brother often did their drinking and where O'Neill's circus friends from the then-nearby Madison Square Garden congregated. The other was the Hell Hole in Greenwich Village, which O'Neill continued to frequent well into the 1920s, along with his fellow Provincetown Players and Jamie, as well as assorted gangsters, gamblers, crooked cops, and prostitutes.

Giving birth to *Iceman* was creatively exhilarating if, at the same time, emotionally shattering. O'Neill was not only revisiting the site (and year) of his suicide attempt; he was also compassionately resurrecting the whiskey-soaked, deluded has-beens who at the time were his chosen compeers and on whom he had depended for survival.

O'Neill had spent hours, sometimes days, sitting in Jimmy's back room listening to the life stories, the maudlin dreams, the ruined hopes of these rootless friends. As one of his characters describes it, "It's the No Chance Saloon. It's Bedrock Bar, The End of the Line Cafe, The Bottom of the Sea Rathskeller! Don't you notice the beautiful calm in the atmosphere? That's because it's the last harbor. No one here has to worry about where they're going next, because there is no farther they can go."

O'Neill once remarked that, compared with Jimmy the Priest's, Gorky's inn in *A Night's Lodging* was "an ice cream parlor." On another occasion—with nostalgic relish—he said the building "was almost coming down, and the principal house-wreckers were vermin."

He had often, since coming to prominence in his thirties, spoken of his fascination with his down-and-out comrades at Jimmy's—and of why he believed it was his mission to portray the lives of such people on the stage rather than writing about "people whose ways are bright and easy," and who "are dramatized frequently and continuously."

"It is life as I see it," he said, dismissing the argument that plays about such people were depressing. "We should feel exalted to think that there is something—some vital unquenchable flame in man which makes him triumph over his miseries—over life itself. Dying, he is still victorious. The realization of this should exalt, not depress."

O'Neill believed himself a spiritual brother to the derelicts among whom he lived in 1912; like them, he had no ambition to change his surroundings. His one preoccupation was getting and staying drunk—especially when his dollar-a-day allowance from his father ran out. One way he and his sailor friends picked up drinking money was to amble down to the waterfront, where they could sometimes earn a few dollars carrying mail sacks on or off the ships. Alternatively, they could "lower the boom on the live ones," which meant putting the touch on sailor friends arriving on incoming ships.

O'Neill raced through his four-act outline for *Iceman*, beginning on June 9 and completing it by June 24. Even while sketching his saga of drunken delusion, he was already afire with twists of the plot for the next play, the one he was basing on his New London family. He shared his onrushing thoughts with Carlotta on June 21.

"Gene talks to me for hours about a play (in his mind) of his Mother, his Father, his brother and himself (in his early 20's) in New London—! (Autobiography) A hot, close, sleepless night—An ache in our hearts for things we can't escape!"

With barely a pause, beginning on June 26, O'Neill completed a four-act outline of *Long Day's Journey Into Night* in just one week. Then, deciding he would first write the full-length scenario of *The Iceman Cometh*, he put the *Journey* outline aside.

"Gene feels *beastly!*" Carlotta observed on July 10, the day before O'Neill began developing his *Iceman* characters. The following day, she reported he had passed another restless night and he "yearns to get away from here." She believed he wished to dodge the coming intrusions of his children's visits. But he could also have been expressing a veiled wish to escape the rush of painful memories he was calling up for his two entwined plays. After dining with friends in San Francisco on July 11, Carlotta found O'Neill in such low spirits that she was moved to remark, "Thank God, Gene *didn't* start *drinking again!*"

On the following day, submerged in his suicidal past, he said to Carlotta, "If you and I could only go to sleep together and *never* wake up." The next day, he began writing the dialogue for Act I of *Iceman*.

O'Neill anticipated an intensive new stretch of work, and was wishing he could avoid all interruptions, particularly his responsibilities as a father.

There was seldom a time, however, when he did not feel put-upon by his responsibility to his children. The insensitive way he treated all three of them was an ongoing vexation for his close friends. They struggled with the cosmic question of whether a great artist is entitled to a pass when it comes to standards of morality; does the value of the artist's creative gift to the world cancel out the damage he inflicts on his offspring?

To argue an unequivocal no—at least in O'Neill's case—is to ignore the relentless expenditure of self that it cost him while shaping a play; any intrusion during this creative process was a torment. It was innately impossible for him to be both an attentive father and a visionary dramatist. (Facetiously speaking, one solution to this cosmic question might be to genetically identify all potential genius-artists at birth and neuter them.)

In any event, O'Neill felt obliged to interact with all three of his children that summer, beginning with Shane. O'Neill had been boiling with anger since February when Harry Weinberger informed him that his younger son, soon to be twenty, had again quit school.

"I am disgusted but not surprised," O'Neill had told his lawyer, once again invoking his despised ex-wife and describing Shane as "just naturally dumb and shiftless like all of [the Boultons], where education and books are concerned." He protested (and doubtless believed) that he had "done all, and a good deal more, for him than he has deserved." Until Shane proved himself "not to be a parasitic slob of a Boulton," he vowed he would do no more. As of now, raged O'Neill, "he simply does not interest me as a human being. Nor as a son."

That July, however, O'Neill was provoked into a confrontation with his wayward son when Shane sought advice about a possible career as a horse breeder. It would have been obvious from that letter to anyone but his father that Shane was pitifully immature and floundering, much like O'Neill himself at that age.

It did not help that O'Neill at this time was actually in the process of recalling (in *Long Day's Journey*) his own deplorable behavior as a jobless twenty-three-year-old college dropout and alcoholic derelict dependent on his father's dole.

"This will get you exactly nowhere," admonished O'Neill. "You will be what you make yourself and you have got to do that job absolutely alone and on your own." (He boasted to Weinberger that he had written to Shane without "the usual fatherly crap.") A month later, Shane gave up horses and decided to pursue a career as a commercial artist.

Next, O'Neill mustered a welcome for his formerly stable scholarly older son, who, a month earlier, had married his third wife, Sally. (On learning of the marriage, Carlotta had snippily observed, "Elizabeth the *first* was a nice girl! I hope Sally the *third* will last!")

O'Neill was not impressed with Sally, whose mother, Marjorie F. Hayward, was curator of the historic American Revolutionary site Pardee House in New Haven, Connecticut. The nine-day visit was uncomfortable, as both Carlotta and O'Neill had anticipated. In a letter to Macgowan, O'Neill described his new daughter-in-law as "rather disappointing," and further disparaged her as "a stalwart stout young woman" of "an all-too-familiar Connecticut small-city type."

On July 16, the day of Eugene and Sally's departure, Carlotta's son-in-law, Roy Stram, was hospitalized with a severe attack of rheumatic fever. "Poor Cyn," Carlotta wrote, "she is to meet Dukie at the hospital—& be told the true facts"—that Roy would "always be an invalid—Cyn at 22! With a baby, no money & no profession!"

A few days later, O'Neill and Carlotta were distracted by the ominous news from abroad.

"Russia & Germany sign a non-aggression pact!! My God!" Carlotta exclaimed in her diary on August 21. And three days later, after more grim news: "We sit at the radio until late at night! Gene is pale & drawn & furious that Man has learned nothing—he can't be taught that in today's world no country can win!"

WITH NO TIME to recover from their recent weeks of stress, the O'Neills now awaited a visit from Oona on August 26. O'Neill had finally (guiltily) invited his daughter—whom he hadn't seen in five years. With effort, Carlotta offered a cheerful welcome to her stepdaughter, whom she and O'Neill met at the airport. O'Neill was in far better spirits than his wife, for he had just finished the scenario of Act II of *Iceman*, happily describing it in his Work Diary as "long but grand!" Thus fortified, he was prepared to be won over by his fourteen-year-old daughter. "Seems darned nice kid," he noted in his Work Diary. Carlotta concurred. "She is nervous of course, but has nice manners & seems very sweet."

O'Neill left Oona to be mostly entertained by Carlotta while he continued to work on *The Iceman Cometh*; but he did join them on a visit to the San Francisco World's Fair, and a sightseeing trip to Chinatown.

As was their custom, O'Neill and Carlotta listened to after-dinner news broadcasts and, on August 28, they stayed up until 3:00 a.m. listening to Hitler's guttural speech declaring war against Poland, after which O'Neill cursed him in disgust as "a ham actor!" On August 31, when English and French civilians were about to evacuate London and Paris, Carlotta noted: "France calm—& ready to fight for personal freedom"; she said she was "moved beyond belief" and had "a queer feeling that all this is really the beginning of the end of all happiness for me!"

Carlotta pronounced herself "a wreck" after listening to another harrowing night of news. She lamented in her diary: "Germans bombing Polish towns—troops have gone over the border! No sleep." Trying to soothe her nerves, she was sitting on her patio darning O'Neill's socks when Oona joined her, looking "very much amused," as Carlotta later reported their conversation.

OONA: I thought the darning-socks wife went out with Queen Victoria.

CARLOTTA (*a bit surprised but trying to appear amused*): Never mind, you'll be darning your husband's socks in a few years!

OONA: Not I. I'm not the sock-darning kind.

Then, noted Carlotta, "We had quite a woman-to-woman talk. She is 14!" Later, Carlotta amended (in her diary) that Oona, "with a curled lip," had said, "You'd never catch me dead doing a thing like that. I'm going to marry a rich man."

On September 3, Oona's father and stepmother saw her off on her flight home with what Carlotta called "a fat cheque" in her handbag. Carlotta and O'Neill had again stayed up late listening to the war news and O'Neill, according to Carlotta, was "in a ghastly state of nerves." With England and France at war with Germany, he noted, "Now hell starts! Spengler was right."

Carlotta attributed O'Neill's jitters as much to exasperation about his children as to concern about the war; Eugene Jr.'s visit with his disdained third wife "upset him terribly," Carlotta observed, and "Oona's visit disturbed him because he felt (as a dramatist!) she had been rehearsed in how she was to act with him—she was not herself!" Carlotta, dreading the onset of a breakdown, herself felt "old—tired—fearful." All they had dreamed of and worked for, she sighed, now seemed useless and inconsequential.

A week later, O'Neill had recovered from his physical and mental weariness and, despite the war news, was again working on *Iceman*. In retrospect, he seemed to have persuaded himself that Oona was, after all, a daughter to be proud of. In the same letter to Macgowan that disparaged his new daughter-in-law, Sally, O'Neill wrote glowingly about Oona, describing her as not only intelligent, but "really a charming girl, both in looks and in manners." He had even softened enough as a father to answer a letter from Shane with a minimum of lecturing, in which he remarked that he and Carlotta had found Shane's sister "loveable."

On September 20, while nearing completion of *The Iceman Cometh*, he and Carlotta celebrated the birthday of Silverdeen Emblem O'Neill, better known as Blemie—the only child they loved unconditionally. Their Dalmatian, O'Neill wrote to Nathan, was "now a patriarch of twelve but still going strong."

In the same letter, O'Neill announced he would shortly forward for Nathan's "valued judgment," the non-cycle play he'd nearly completed. "It looks good to me," he said, adding, "I'm not going to tell you a word about it, not even the title. I want you to read it without any advance information."

He cautioned Nathan not to mention the new play to anyone, as he might want to keep it to himself "for years"—until a "financial pinch" forced his hand. "Every time I think of making that trip East to face casting, rehearsals and all the rest of the game, I feel a great bored weariness and reluctance, as if I'd had quite enough of that for one life."

When he turned fifty-one on October 16, O'Neill was still making revisions and cuts on *Iceman* (with Carlotta obediently retyping the pages he corrected—even those with nothing more than a misplaced comma). He'd felt from the moment he'd begun writing that *Iceman* would be his greatest achievement thus far; it had "flowed right along, page after page," as he later told an interviewer for *The New York Times*. Now he was eager to finish his revisions and move on to *Long Day's Journey Into Night*, for which he had equally high hopes.

Family troubles again disrupted the O'Neills' routine in mid-October; Carlotta's ill-fated daughter, having suffered through her baby's corrective surgery and adjusted to her husband's illness, smashed her knee in an auto accident. Dr. Dukes, who operated on Cynthia, informed Carlotta that her daughter's kneecap had been cut in two; she would be hospitalized for many weeks and would "probably be lame."

Between visits to her daughter, Carlotta continued her conscientious typing of O'Neill's revised pages of *Iceman*, straining over his ever-more-cramped handwriting. Two weeks into November, nearing his finish line, O'Neill was suffused with a surge of gratitude and love. In her diary, for the first time in months, Carlotta coyly hinted at sexual activity. Alongside the words, "I have a siesta," she made a crude but unmistakable sketch of a plump, bewhiskered pussycat—a symbol she continued to draw from time to time during the next several years.

Although she once confided to her intimate friend Mai-mai Sze that O'Neill "didn't function up to par," she never, in her diary, expressed concern about the effect on their sex life of O'Neill's prostate problem; in fact, she took pains to give the impression that O'Neill's sexual desire for her was unflagging.

Herself the possessor of a ravenous sexual appetite and a woman whose physical allure had long been her raison d'être, Carlotta made sure, when she went about the task of modifying her diaries after O'Neill's death, that there was no suggestion he had ever failed to respond to her seductive prowess—prostatitis or not.

To her delight, O'Neill slipped into romantic mode in mid-November. After finishing dinner one evening—as Carlotta coyly recounted—O'Neill "comes to me in my big Chinese bed" where, after a session of pillow talk, he "remains all night!" On a second evening that month, O'Neill forwent his after-dinner period with the war news to serenade Carlotta with a reading of the poetry of Baudelaire and Francis Thompson.

Her response was to sketch another of her diary pussycats—evidently to denote an amorous celebration; O'Neill, she purred, had been "deeply moved" in the midst of writing his final scene for *The Iceman Cometh*. Still euphoric, he completed the play on December 20, declaring it "one of [the] best plays I've ever written!"

O'Neill, however, was determined to keep the play to himself indefinitely. Nearly two years later, he explained to Russel Crouse that he was convinced "a war psychology" was the wrong time to present it, and it would not be produced soon—"not unless the wolves' teeth get set in the seat of my pants." But there was a second reason for delay. "I couldn't let this play be done without being there every minute, and I simply don't feel up to that ordeal now."

With his birthday check to Carlotta on December 28, O'Neill wrote: "Own Beloved: Again and forever, all my love, Darling, and my gratitude for the beauty and peace that your love has given me—and a million poems I am not poet enough to write to your eyebrows and your eyes and your nose and your lips—and your etcetera!" In each of the four corners of the note's envelope he had playfully sketched his own version of a pussycat silhouette—possibly a happy reminder to them both of a brief remission from prostatitis.

———

WITH ITS STARK SURFACE and its even more sinister subsurfaces, *The Iceman Cometh* is as layered as a Roman dig. For decades, it has beguiled and baffled the actors who have portrayed the central role of Hickey.

NATHAN LANE, who starred in a highly praised revival in 2012, aptly likened the play's lunges into the labyrinthine dark to "getting in an elevator and going down to the basement, thinking that's as far as you can go, and then one night you get in and see there are three more buttons leading to sublevels you hadn't seen before."

While Lane saw *Iceman* as an elevator ride to the lower depths, it can also be seen as a merry-go-round from O'Neill's private Hell. It was a ride that began when O'Neill, at twenty-eight, wrote the heartfelt, if callow, short story "Tomorrow," in which the narrator, Art, recalls his derelict days five years earlier; like O'Neill, Art lived near the Battery in a flophouse cum saloon designated as Tommy the Priest's.

Although the time (winter of 1912) and the place are the actual time and place of O'Neill's suicide attempt at Jimmy the Priest's, he was not yet ready to write openly about it. Instead, he chose in "Tomorrow" to examine the successful suicide of a friend, James Byth, whom O'Neill called Jimmy Anderson in the story, and whom he had got to know when he was James O'Neill's valued theatrical press agent.

Hard-drinking and self-aggrandizing, Byth claimed to have been a Boer War correspondent. He was funny and likeable but not strong enough to surmount the long-ago shock of one day finding his wife in bed with a "staff officer." O'Neill, in an early list of characters for *Iceman*, depicted Byth (here in the guise of James Cameron) as one of the drunken derelicts he'd known at Jimmy the Priest's.

In the short story, Anderson vows every day to sober up and reclaim the newspaper reporting job from which he was fired. But there is always

a reason to procrastinate—hence his nickname "Jimmy Tomorrow."
Encouraged by Art, Anderson finally does sober up and manages to
reclaim his job, but he finds he has lost his knack for reporting. Defeated,
realizing at last there is no tomorrow, he jumps to his death from the fire
escape outside his cubicle.

In 1919, two years after the story was published (in *The Seven Arts*
magazine), O'Neill felt emboldened to examine more directly the suicide
attempt ever present in his mind, and he wrote *Exorcism*; he set the one-
act play, like "Tomorrow," in a low dive during a time unspecified, but
obviously 1912. The fact that O'Neill wished he'd never written *Exorcism*—
and that he disavowed it immediately after its brief run in 1920—is
strong evidence that he regretted his candor.

Not until two decades later, at fifty-one and still fascinated by the
subject of his own failed suicide, did O'Neill feel compelled to begin the
four-act play he tentatively called "Tomorrow"—and quickly renamed
The Iceman Cometh, setting it in a low dive circa 1912 modeled (in part)
on Jimmy the Priest's.

The play would, inevitably, be haunted by suicide; but unlike his
youthfully fumbled short story "Tomorrow" and his one-acter *Exorcism*,
this new work would be richly peopled by the ghosts of his drunken past,
and would possess a depth and power undreamed of in those earlier
efforts.

"You will recognize in this play [*Iceman*] a lot of material I have talked
about using ever since you've known me," O'Neill wrote to Nathan in
1940. "But never until a year or so ago, did it take definite line and form
as a play in my mind, its many life histories interwoven around a central
theme." With his conception of *The Iceman Cometh* in 1939, O'Neill
ended his merry-go-round ride back where he'd started two decades earlier with "Tomorrow."

For *Iceman*, however, he had the maturity to reimagine the friendship
of those who shared his days of despondence—along with his flickering
moments of hopefulness—and he fearlessly revisited the life that in 1912
very nearly did him in.

When sending Nathan the script of *Iceman*, he confided that the play had its "basis in reality"; but he added that the play was, of course, his own "imaginative creation." And while none of his characters was "an exact portrait of an actual person," all of them were "drawn from life, more or less."

Stressing this point in a later interview, O'Neill persisted: "I knew 'em all. I've known 'em all for years. All these people I have written about I once knew." He not only knew them intimately, he loved them with a love completely free of judgment, for he believed he owed them his very survival. As a soul adrift, alienated from his family, belonging nowhere, he had found acceptance among them.

The first of these fellow drifters to take him to their hearts and make him one of their own were the sailors with whom he had shipped out to Buenos Aires and back at twenty-two: first as an apprentice seaman on the Norwegian bark *Charles Racine*, then returning to New York as an ordinary seaman on the steam-powered freighter S.S. *Ikala* and, a year later, as a crew member of the luxury liner S.S. *New York* sailing to England; finally, he was befriended by the crew with whom he sailed home—as a proud able-bodied seaman—on the S.S. *New York*'s sister ship, the S.S. *Philadelphia*.

"I look on a sailor man as my particular brother," said O'Neill, shortly after writing *The Hairy Ape*, which was based on the *Philadelphia*'s coal stoker, known only as Driscoll, who was one of his close friends from that period. O'Neill liked sailors better than men of his "own kind," he said, for they were "sincere, loyal, generous."

"You have heard people use the expression: 'He would give away his shirt.' I've known men who actually did give away their shirts. I've seen them give away their own clothes to stowaways."

These men, declared O'Neill, were "direct in action and utterance"; they had "not been steeped in the evasions and superficialities which come with social life and intercourse." They were "crude but honest" and "not handicapped by inhibitions"; they were "free of social hypocrisy."

After leaving the sea, O'Neill felt equally at home spending his days and nights with the similar lost souls of the fleabag saloons who had never worked on a ship; some of them had once had solid occupations on land and now had no other home.

Although these men had already lived their lives, and O'Neill, in his early twenties, had barely begun his own, they heartily welcomed him as one of them; it was here, at what O'Neill called "the bottom of the sea," that he felt at home; with their compassionate understanding, he could drink himself into forgetfulness, down his portion of the daily free soup that kept them all alive, and share with them their hopeless hopes for a better tomorrow.

O'Neill refashioned some of these men for *Iceman*, in most cases lovingly, to suit his dramatic purpose.

They were the true friends whom—despite the patrician aura in which Carlotta had attempted to enfold him—he would never forget.

40

t is 1956, ten years after the heralded but ultimately disappointing Broadway run of *The Iceman Cometh*.

A newly ascending director, José Quintero, has cast an unknown actor, Jason Robards Jr., as Theodore "Hickey" Hickman in an off-Broadway revival of that all-but-forgotten play.

The production—on the small open stage of the Circle in the Square, a remodeled nightclub in Greenwich Village's Sheridan Square—astonished the uptown critics; at last, this most challenging of all O'Neill's plays had received the recognition it deserved. Much of the stage magic was engendered by Robards's stunning performance as the deluded salesman who hadn't a clue how much he hated the wife he loved.

Sanctioned (three years after O'Neill's death) by Carlotta Monterey, the revival was an ironic return for O'Neill. It was here in the Village, forty years earlier, that his genius had first been recognized, when his one-act *Bound East for Cardiff* (playing time twenty-five minutes) had opened at the Provincetown Playhouse on MacDougal Street; and now, only a five-minute stroll west to the Circle in the Square, his four-act *Iceman Cometh* (playing time four and a half hours) was about to resurrect O'Neill's faded reputation.

Hurrying to his cubicle at the *Times* to write his review of the afternoon opening, Brooks Atkinson paused to tell his eager staff, "The actor playing Hickey is pure gold."

The revival became a smash hit, racking up 565 performances; it

launched Robards to stardom and—inevitably—established the character of Hickey as the play's undisputed protagonist. Robards's portrayal of
Hickey (under Quintero's inspired guidance) became the play's iconic
role by which all successive revivals have been judged.

However, there is a caveat. Not to disparage the Hickey character's
grip on an audience's attention, or to understate the way his character
aggressively propels the plot, but *Iceman* also features the equally pivotal
character of Larry Slade; in his own way as deluded as Hickey, Slade,
who believes he is a detached observer of his fellow outcasts, in the end
allows himself to be goaded into an act just as loathsome as Hickey's.

It is Slade who, in *Iceman*, speaks O'Neill's fundamental philosophy,
and on whom O'Neill initially built the play. Indeed, Hickey was an
afterthought—a dramatically brilliant afterthought, to be sure—but
nonetheless a contrivance not conceived by O'Neill until he was well
into the structure of the play.

While Hickey, the frenetic traveling salesman, was largely an invention, Slade, the life-weary former anarchist, was based on Terry Carlin,
who not only had vitally affected O'Neill's spiritual and intellectual
development as a young man, but also had become his sometime mentor
and lifelong friend. It's not surprising that Slade's character, while less
flamboyant than Hickey's, has much the greater poignancy.

Carlin had a gaunt face with a big nose, high cheekbones, a lantern
jaw (always with a stubble), and a mystic's meditative pale blue eyes that
could glint with sardonic humor. O'Neill would never forget his first
meeting with the disillusioned anarchist, then in his mid-fifties, at the
Unique Book Store on Sixth Avenue near Thirtieth Street, owned by
Carlin's fellow philosophical anarchist Benjamin R. Tucker.

It was there, in 1906, that O'Neill, under the guidance of both Tucker
and Carlin, joyfully encountered a treasury of books by advanced political, literary, and philosophical thinkers: Emerson, Shaw, Tolstoy, Zola,
and the German anarchist Max Stirner—not to mention Nietzsche. And
it wasn't long before Eugene had adopted Carlin's nihilistic philosophy
as his own.

AFTER A THRIVING career as an engineer, Carlin, on principle, had dropped out of society to protest the greed of company owners for ever higher profits, even as they ignored the well-being of their employees. He had not worked for years and Eugene couldn't help but admire him for his courage. Here was a man who (while doubtlessly delusional) had the audacity and daring to literally act on the biblical warning about profit, gain, and the loss of one's soul. O'Neill, in developing the character of Larry Slade, surrendered himself to Carlin's still potent spell. *Iceman* contains two parallel plots; the subtler of the two deals with Slade's ultimately futile struggle to hang on to his painstakingly constructed pipe dream; the more spectacular plot revolves around Hickey's shocking evolution from cocky extrovert to maniacal murderer.

While Larry Slade, in the quieter plot, is onstage from the play's beginning and fades in and out of the action, Hickey doesn't make his appearance until nearly the end of Act II; but when he does appear, he seizes center stage. He is an amalgam who may or may not have been inspired by a real-life salesman. O'Neill might have had his brother in mind, for he couldn't help but recall Jamie as typecast in 1910 in the featured role of a traveling salesman named Watts in a touring production of James Forbes's comedy *The Traveling Salesman*; and indeed O'Neill did give Hickey recognizable traces of Jamie O'Neill's cocky mannerisms.

O'Neill described Hickey to George Jean Nathan as "a periodical drunk salesman, who was a damned amusing likeable guy," and who used to "make that typical drummer crack about the iceman, and wept maudlinly over his wife's photograph, and in other moods, boozily harped on the slogan that honesty is the best policy."

Ten months later, however, O'Neill—for whatever reason—gave Kenneth Macgowan a tamer version. "What you wonder about Hickey: No, I never knew him. He's the most imaginary character in the play. Of course, I knew many salesmen in my time who were periodical drunks, but Hickey is not any of them. He is all of them, you might say, and none of them."

O'Neill did not draw the attention of either Nathan or Macgowan to the similarities between the character of Theodore "Hickey" Hickman and Theodore Dreiser. O'Neill had known Dreiser since their Greenwich Village days, when Dreiser's autobiographical novel, *The Genius* (published in 1915), was the subject of a censorship battle.

As has been pointed out by the literary scholar Brenda Murphy, there are striking resemblances between Hickey and Eugene Witla, the protagonist of Dreiser's novel; Witla describes his uncontrollable sexual urges and his guilt toward his wife, Angela, who bore his repeated abuse and constantly forgave him.

Moreover, Hickey's physical appearance and fragments of his personality seem to be modeled on Dreiser himself; with his provincial background and less-than-polished manners, Dreiser was regarded by O'Neill and his Village colleagues as something of a hick—hence the name Hickman—not to mention Hickman's first name, Theodore.

(Although O'Neill, after winning the Nobel Prize, had publicly praised Dreiser as a writer who himself deserved the award, he must have been annoyed that Dreiser had given the name Eugene to his own alter ego in *The Genius*, and perhaps O'Neill was indulging in a bit of revenge.)

Hickey's arrival is eagerly anticipated by the outcasts of Harry Hope's saloon; at play's beginning, on an early summer morning, they are slumped separately or in clusters at each of seven adjacent round tables in the saloon's back room, where liquor can be legally served after the adjoining barroom has closed to the public—which in this case means all night long.

They sometimes doze, heads on tables, intermittently coming up for air and muttering a few words, hoping that Harry, who has joined them from his upstairs flat, will treat them to a drink while they await Hickey's arrival. Hazily, they reminisce about fancied past achievements and exchange pipe dreams of how, one day soon, they will sober up and resurrect their broken lives, regaining long-lost jobs and reconnecting with influential friends.

First, though, they will help Hickey celebrate Harry Hope's birthday, as they do every year. Hickey, they remind one another, is always well-heeled and high-spirited, bursting with a repertory of jokes and wisecracks. He will keep the drinks coming and will himself drink along with gusto. He is the one bright and hopeful diversion in their fog-filled lives.

When Hickey at last arrives, the benumbed, whiskey-soaked regulars are momentarily galvanized. But he is not the Hickey they know. Although still jovial and affectionate, and lavish with his alcoholic treats, he himself is cold sober. The drinks are on him, he says, but he won't be drinking with them; he has found his spiritual salvation by facing his own delusions and no longer needs to seek peace in a bottle.

Thinking Hickey has come up with an elaborate joke to play on them, the barroom regulars uneasily try to go along. But they turn resentful when Hickey begins prodding them (however merrily) to confront their pipe dreams, insisting that is the only way for them to find peace. Hickey is trying to sell them a salvation for which they have no use, and their resentment turns to anger when he urges them to leave Harry Hope's saloon and reclaim their former lives—not tomorrow, but today.

Even as they sullenly question his motive, they are too weak to resist Hickey's slick salesmanship. And Hickey, knowing they will never follow through, nonetheless cajoles and bullies, propelling them, one by one, out the front door—all except for two: the certifiably loony Hugo Kalmar, and Larry Slade who, although rattled, resists Hickey's taunts.

The first to return is Harry Hope. According to O'Neill's early notes for *Iceman*, Hope—like his real-life counterpart, Tom Wallace (the proprietor of the Hell Hole)—had not set foot outside his saloon "since [his] wife's funeral" twenty years earlier; the truth was that she had "nagged him to death and he was relieved when she died."

Transposed to Harry Hope, this stance, putatively a tribute to his undying love for his wife, Bessie, was mocked by Hickey, who told Harry it was time to give it up: "I know better and so do you. . . . She was always on your neck, making you have ambition and go out and do things, when all you wanted was to get drunk in peace." And, after Harry's cringing return and his angry warning to Hickey to "close that big clam" of his, he astounds himself by snapping, "Hickey, Bejeez, you're a worse gabber than that nagging bitch Bessie was."

It isn't long before all the others have slunk back to the saloon, so defeated they can't even get themselves drunk; to their dismay, the kick has gone out of the booze.

Hickey is baffled that their aborted forays haven't liberated them from their pipe dreams. He had expected his barroom pals to feel the exhilaration he feels. But Hickey, believing in his own deluded mind that he has faced the truth about himself, has merely replaced one pipe dream with a more lethal one.

Confronting his barroom cohorts in a long rambling monologue, Hickey attempts to justify his expectations for their redemption, explaining the source of his own salvation.

He has earlier told them of the recent sudden death of his long-suffering wife, Evelyn, to whom he has been consistently unfaithful, and who, he has assured them, is finally at peace.

Now, he confesses that it is he himself who has provided her with that peace. He has shot her, he says, out of his great love and pity for her. He knew she would never stop loving him and forgiving him and pretending to believe his lies that he would change. He also knew that although he loved her dearly, he would never stop betraying and lying to her. The only way to end her suffering was to kill her.

"I'd always known that was the only possible way to give her peace and free her from the misery of loving me," he says. "I saw it meant peace for me, too, knowing she was at peace. I felt as though a ton of guilt had been lifted off my mind."

But then, trancelike, Hickey blurts his true feelings as he recalls the vengeful final words he spat at his dead wife, thereby revealing himself as the most deluded of them all: "I remember I stood by the bed and suddenly I had to laugh. I couldn't help it, and I knew Evelyn would for-give me. I remember I heard myself speaking to her, as if it was something I'd always wanted to say: 'Well, you know what you can do with your pipe dream now, you damned bitch!'"

Horrified, he stammers a denial: How could he possibly have said that? He loved Evelyn. He must have been insane, he cries, pleading with his "old pals" to accept this explanation. Muttering to one another, they are only too happy to do so; at last he has let them off the hook.

Hickey, prepared to take his punishment for the "mercy killing" of his wife, had earlier notified the police where to find him, and two plain-clothes detectives have slipped into the saloon, unnoticed by him, in time to hear his confession. As they arrest him and prepare to take him away, Hickey again begs Harry to believe he is insane.

The detectives attempt to silence him, cautioning Harry Hope and the others that Hickey is trying to establish an insanity plea. But Harry defends him to the detectives, assuring them that Hickey is not bluffing and is entitled to plead insanity; all of Hickey's old pals are only too eager to agree and, as one, they contentedly begin to drink themselves back into their pipe dreams.

THE STORY OF murder and insanity that can keep an audience breathless with suspense now gives way to the denouement of the play's secondary plot, which is centered on Larry Slade and his recently repudiated anarchist connections.

The only back-room dipsomaniac who professes to have no pipe dreams and who has resisted Hickey's relentless prodding, Slade, from early on, has suspected something deviant in Hickey's behavior and he is unsurprised by the manic salesman's confession. Determined, however, to maintain his equilibrium as a disinterested observer of life, he has kept his suspicions mostly to himself.

His more urgent concern is a recently arrived boarder at Harry Hope's named Don Parritt, by whom Slade feels threatened; their private confrontation is dramatized at intervals during the noisier tug-of-war being waged among Hickey and the other barflies.

The eighteen-year-old Parritt has come to the flophouse to seek Slade out, but Slade wants nothing to do with him, and he angrily resists the young man's pull on his emotions. Parritt, however, will not leave Slade alone. Although Parritt (in O'Neill's stage description) is tall and good-looking, he has an "unpleasant" personality; there is "a shifting defiance and ingratiation" in his eyes and "an irritating aggressiveness in his manner." It soon becomes clear he has sought out Slade because he has something to confess.

While Parritt is, like Hickey, an amalgam, there is no mistaking Slade as a stand-in for the man who for so many years was O'Neill's spiritual mentor, and who saturated the young O'Neill with tales of his life in the philosophical anarchist movement. Described by O'Neill in *Iceman* as a "one-time Syndicalist-Anarchist," he is (as was Terry Carlin) "tall, raw-boned, with coarse straight white hair, worn long and raggedly cut."

Slade's connection to Parritt peripherally suggests the long-ago relationship between Terry Carlin and Louis Holladay; O'Neill always remembered his dark suspicion that it was Carlin who knowingly supplied Holladay with the requested dose of heroin that killed him. Parritt, like Hickey, has his "background of fact," as O'Neill once explained in an interview in *The New York Times*.

Parritt's character was largely based on a young man named Donald Vose, whose mother, the anarchist Gertie Vose, was a close friend of Emma Goldman's. Through his mother, Donald Vose had entree to her anarchist cell, and he was the stool pigeon whose information enabled William J. Burns, of the International Burns Detective Agency, to arrest two long-wanted anarchists, Matthew A. Schmidt and David Caplan, who had collaborated with the McNamara brothers in the 1910 bombing of the *Los Angeles Times*.

O'Neill's description of Parritt's betrayal of his mother was partly suggested by Emma Goldman's vilification of Donald Vose in her magazine *Mother Earth* after he testified in the trials of Schmidt and Caplan in 1915 and 1916. Goldman derided Vose as "the Judas Iscariot" whose sellout of the two men had in effect been a betrayal of his mother, whom Goldman pitied for having raised "that cur."

But there is also a whiff of Jamie O'Neill's essence hovering about Parritt, which is hardly coincidental; Jamie was seldom out of O'Neill's mind (as would soon become evident with his horrifying portrait of his brother in *A Moon for the Misbegotten*); like the real Vose and the fictional Parritt, Jamie had arrived in New York after betraying his dying mother in Los Angeles.

In O'Neill's concept for *Iceman*, Larry Slade was once in love with Parritt's mother, Rosa, a leader in the anarchist movement that Slade had then espoused. He has heard that she is now in prison and he suspects it was Parritt who betrayed her. Vehemently resisting Parritt's attempts to draw him into reminiscences of his past love for Rosa, Slade insists he has resigned not only from the movement but from life itself.

Despite Slade's repeated rebuffs, Parritt keeps spilling bits of information about himself—in much the same way that Hickey drops hints about the events leading to the death of his wife. Parritt tells Slade what he has already guessed: that he, Parritt, is the turncoat who was paid to inform against two of his mother's colleagues.

Parritt at first says he did it for the money; he had never intended to betray his mother, believing she would be safely out of the way when the men were apprehended. He loves his mother, he insists; he has always loved her—despite her dedication to the movement, which often caused her to neglect him—and despite the various lovers with whom he had to share her attention. Can't Slade understand he would never have betrayed his mother? And that he grieves over her incarceration?

Then, like Hickey, he spits out the truth—("in a low voice in which there is a strange exhausted relief"): "I may as well confess, Larry. There's no use lying anymore. You know, anyway. I didn't give a damn about the money. It was because I hated her. . . . Her and the old Movement pipe dream!"

Slade finally cannot contain his horror at what Parritt has done.

Abandoning his own pipe dream of passive withdrawal from life, he gives Parritt what he wants: "Go! Get the hell out of life, God damn you, before I choke it out of you!"

Soon after, Slade hears, through the back-room window, "the sound of something hurtling down, followed by a muffled, crunching thud." Parritt has jumped to his death from the fire escape of his upstairs room.

Slade has, in effect, become Parritt's executioner.

SLADE'S PERSONALITY IS based almost literally on Terry Carlin, who had become a second father to the eighteen-year-old Eugene when they'd first met in 1906 at the anarchist Benjamin Tucker's bookstore.

EUGENE WOULD LIVE under Carlin's spell, on and off, for the next twenty years, and *The Iceman Cometh* is in a sense a tribute to Carlin, who died in 1934.

O'Neill, in his days of worst despair, when he had cut himself off from his family and was all but penniless, clung to Carlin. As a perpetually homeless parasite, Carlin had learned innovative survival techniques, which he passed on to O'Neill. The two often stayed up all night, alternately drinking, talking philosophy and radical literature, and napping with their heads on a back-room table, usually at the Hell Hole. One of Terry's skills was exorcising O'Neill's DTs.

The young O'Neill could not help but admire a man who had actually given up all worldly ambition to regain his unsullied soul—a man who, moreover, often relied for his existence on the Irish charm and eloquence he could summon at will. Carlin had managed to acquire a small circle of adherents among the more prosperous writers and artists of Greenwich Village; even practiced storytellers such as Jack London and Theodore Dreiser, enraptured by the lilting, mythic quality of Carlin's yarns, were happy, now and then, to help keep him in liquor and food and, like Eugene, were willing to overlook some of his nastier foibles.

It was Carlin who had accompanied O'Neill to Cape Cod in the summer of 1916, seconding John Reed's earlier invitation to join the recently formed group of tentative playwrights, artists, and amateur actors soon to emerge in Greenwich Village as the Provincetown Players.

CARLIN (WHO HAD shortened his name from O'Carolan) sprang, like O'Neill's father, from Irish peasant stock, and his family, like O'Neill's, immigrated to America when Terry was a boy. The O'Carolan family, including mother, father, and seven children, settled in New York in the mid-1860s and tried to subsist on the father's salary of eight dollars a week. Terry went to work at an early age in a sweatshop—as had James O'Neill.

Terry's thoughts soon turned to the social injustice he saw around him; long before he embraced anarchy as a creed, his thinking was socialistic. In his teens, as a journeyman tanner and currier, while excelling at his trade, he spent his spare time with books, acquiring a radical education.

Like the O'Neill family—often described by Eugene as being "too close"—the O'Carolans were an emotionally interdependent clan.

"We clung desperately to one another long after the necessity was past," Terry informed the journalist Hutchins Hapgood, who traced his life in a 1909 volume called *An Anarchist Woman*, which O'Neill devoured.

Like Eugene, Terry had a dearly loved brother named Jim, whom he described as "my other ego"—but who, unlike the cynical, drunken sometime actor Jamie O'Neill, had a good job with a Pittsburgh tannery and owned $25,000 worth of stock in the company.

It was an episode involving Jim O'Carolan that led to Terry's final disillusionment. Then in his thirties, Terry had already adopted life as a social exile. He'd given up a well-paying job as an expert in leather manufacturing and was living a carefree life in a Chicago slum with a woman named Marie, whom he'd rescued from a career of prostitution; he worked rarely, and only to provide himself and Marie with the bare necessities.

Terry would not have given up his contented life for anyone but his brother. But Jim needed Terry's help in Pittsburgh, where the firm that employed him was losing thousands of dollars a week because of a flaw in the manufacturing process that Jim believed Terry, with his expertise and ingenuity, could pinpoint and correct.

"It was with the utmost repugnance that I quit my happy slum life," Terry later explained in a letter to Hapgood, "but I loved Jim, and it was the call of the ancient clan in my blood. When I arrived in Pittsburgh, without a trunk, and with other marks of the proletarian on me, Mr. Kirkman, the millionaire tanner, showered me with every luxury—every luxury except that of thought and true emotion. Never before did I realize so intensely my indifference to what money can buy. My private office in the shop was stocked with wines and imported cigarettes: but I was not so well off as in my happy slum."

After toiling for a month, Terry found the source of Kirkman's trouble in an obscure process, and advised him how to correct it, thereby saving the firm a fortune. "I had put no price on my services," Terry continued. "For Jim's sake, I had worked like a Trojan, physically and mentally. . . . With unlimited money at my disposal, I had drawn only twenty dollars altogether, and this I sent to Marie, to keep the wolf away."

Kirkman offered Terry the job of running the shop at a large salary and with the option to buy $2,000 worth of stock. But Terry replied he would not exploit the workers, who earned only $7 or $8 a week, and that he would not permit any worker to be discharged for "incompetency"; he had never met a man he could not teach, he told Kirkman.

Not even Jim could persuade Terry to stay, and he departed with nothing but his railroad fare back to Chicago, although Jim assured him that Kirkman would send him between $500 and $1,000 for his services. But within a few days, Jim found that Kirkman, angry that his offer had been spurned, had no intention of sending Terry a cent; he used the excuse that no written or verbal contract had been made for Terry's services.

Jim resigned from the firm in protest, in spite of the fact that he had a wife and children to support. Terry was crushed by the chaos he had brought on Jim and by the lopsidedness of a world in which love of money could play such a vindictive role.

"Mr. Kirkman thought all the world of Jim and could not run the shop without him. Nor could he recover from the blow, for he loved my brother, as everybody did," Terry wrote to Hutchins Hapgood. "Mr. Kirkman died a few weeks afterward, and a year or two later the firm went into the hands of a receiver. All this happened because of a few paltry dollars, which I did not ask for, for which I did not care a damn—and this is business! I heartily rejoice, if not in Mr. Kirkman's death, at least in the dispersion of his family and their being forced into our ranks, where there is some hope for them."

THESE WERE SENTIMENTS the young Eugene O'Neill had readily shared as he harked back to his contempt for the uppity New London neighbors—the despotic millionaire monopolists Edward Stephen Harkness and Edward Crowninshield Hammond—whom he would later parody in *Long Day's Journey Into Night* and *A Moon for the Misbegotten*.

Between Terry and Eugene, there was also an area of sympathetic understanding regarding their vaporized Catholicism; O'Neill was especially struck by Jim O'Carolan's deathbed words, as repeated by Terry in response to the proposal that a priest be summoned: "I hire no spiritual nurse," said Jim.

No one could have been more receptive than O'Neill to Carlin's world-weary lament, as Carlin wrote to the awed Hapgood in 1909: "There must be some meaning for all this ancient agony. Oh, that I might expand my written words into an Epic of the Slums, into an Iliad of the Proletaire! If an oyster can turn its pain into a pearl, then, verily, when we have suffered enough, something must arise out of our torture—else the world has no meaning. . . . It cannot be that I came up out of the depths for nothing. If I could pierce my heart and write red lines, I might perhaps tell the truth. But only a High Silence meets me, and I do not understand."

Terry left it to O'Neill to pierce his heart and write with red lines. And O'Neill, in his writing, did in a way become Terry's missionary, especially in his early portrayals of the inarticulate underdog. Many years before he met O'Neill, Terry had pondered, "How be a mouthpiece for the poor? How can art master the master-problem? They who have nothing much to say, often say it well and in a popular form; they are unhampered by weighty matters. It takes an eagle to soar with a heavy weight in its grasp."

Notable among O'Neill's own half-formed insights, advanced by Terry as he started writing, was Terry's singular compassion for prostitutes, which O'Neill tried to balance against Jamie's sneering condescension for them. Terry believed that marriage for a woman was often a form of prostitution. "Selling your body for a lifetime is perhaps worse than selling it for an hour or for a day," he once told a desperate woman friend who was weighing the choice between domestic drudgery and street walking.

The streetwalker's life, Terry warned, was "very terrible practically," for it could lead to "frightful diseases which will waste your bodies and perhaps injure your minds." The choice between street walking and domestic drudgery, he conceded, was "a choice of evils"; but if forced to choose, he would advise prostitution. "It may be worse for you but, as a protest, it is better for society, in the long run."

Good-hearted prostitutes continued to thrust themselves into O'Neill's plays long after he created *Anna Christie*—and *The Iceman Cometh* was no exception.

41

nto his *Iceman* tapestry of dipsomaniacal outcasts, O'Neill lovingly wove a roster of subsidiary misfits. The rapscallion Hugo Kalmar is one of the most diverting; he is closely modeled on Hippolyte Havel, a friend from O'Neill's old Greenwich Village days who, like Slade, was a onetime anarchist.

While Hugo does little to further the plot, his function is to give an early comic lilt to the play's lower depths; he also serves to emphasize O'Neill's fascination, undimmed all these years later, with the radical politics of the early 1900s, and the absurdist aspects of the anarchist movement.

Hugo is deep in a drunken sleep at the beginning of Act I, when Slade makes some derisive comments about the anarchist movement to Rocky, the skeptical night bartender; he then mischievously rouses Hugo from his drunken slumber to back up his comments. Peering groggily at Rocky and Slade, Hugo blurts, "Capitalist swine! Bourgeois stool pigeons! Have the slaves no right to sleep even?"

With Hugo's anarchist bona fides established, O'Neill then uses him to depict a phase of a drunkard's often infantile behavior, with which O'Neill himself was all too familiar. Hugo's "manner," writes O'Neill, "changes to a giggling, wheedling playfulness, as though he were talking to a child: 'Hello, leedle Rocky! Leedle monkey-face! Vere is your leedle slave girls?'" Reverting to a bullying tone, he barks, "Don't be a fool!

Loan me a dollar! . . . Buy me a trink!" Abruptly overcome by drowsiness, he drops his head into his arms and is instantly asleep again on the table.

O'Neill had long been beguiled by Hippolyte Havel's history and personality; a close colleague of Karl Marx's in Germany and one of Emma Goldman's many lovers, Havel had edited, in Chicago, the anarchist newspaper *Arbeiter-Zeitung*.

At the time O'Neill met him in the Hell Hole, Hippolyte was doubling as lover and cook to Polly Holladay (sister of O'Neill's friend Louis, who died of a drug overdose in 1918). Hippolyte was famous for his drunken temper tantrums during which he was apt to denounce Polly's customers as "bourgeois pigs."

ALSO NOTEWORTHY AMONG the habituées of Harry Hope's saloon was James Cameron, a character based on James O'Neill's theater press agent, James Byth. (Devoted O'Neill fans have met this Byth character before, under the name Jimmy Anderson, in O'Neill's short story "Tomorrow"; but in that story, Byth/Anderson jumped to his death from the fire escape outside the upstairs cubicle of his flophouse; so it's something of a surprise to meet him again as the Byth/Cameron character in *Iceman*.)

O'Neill was evidently so taken with Byth that he couldn't resist resurrecting him for *Iceman* and slipping him (renamed) among the rest of his deluded inebriates. O'Neill gave both Anderson and Cameron (in *Iceman*) the nickname "Jimmy Tomorrow." But unlike Jimmy Anderson in "Tomorrow," James Cameron does not commit suicide, since O'Neill has assigned that fate to someone else in *Iceman*. James Cameron, instead, is consigned the gentler fate of returning, along with the others, to the futility of his pipe dreams.

As for the character O'Neill called Joe Mott, he reflects O'Neill's concern with both the personal and the societal atmosphere of the era. Mott, described as a "one-time proprietor of a Negro gambling house," is significant for being yet another of the well-drawn black characters who populate O'Neill's tragedies—joining Jim Harris (of *All God's*

Chillun Got Wings) and Brutus Jones (the would-be emperor); in this, O'Neill was many years ahead of his time.

Mott prides himself on having been (before his decline) the only Negro accepted in "whites only" Manhattan gambling parlors, and he is the only black man who drinks at Harry Hope's saloon. O'Neill described the Joe Mott character as "hard and tough if it were not for his good nature and lazy humor." It is Mott's pipe dream that he can readily reenter that "whites only" outside world any time he wishes.

Mott was based on Joe Smith, one of O'Neill's black friends in Greenwich Village. In his forties when O'Neill knew him, Smith was light-skinned with Caucasian features. A watchman for an auction company, he was suspected by his friends of supplementing his income with a pair of loaded dice. He was married to a white woman known as Miss Viola, a big blonde who blazed with putatively "hot" diamonds, which she pawned whenever she and Joe were hard up.

On several occasions when O'Neill had drunk himself insensible, Joe took him to his sister's home, where she nursed him back to sobriety; more than once, Joe fed him during a lean period. After his wife died, Joe moved into a second-floor flat in an old frame building on Cornelia Street. "You're as welcome as the flowers in May" was Joe's habitual greeting to whomever climbed the stairs to his rooms.

At the Hell Hole, O'Neill found amusement in Joe's relationship with the pig that the saloon's proprietor, Tom Wallace, kept in his cellar, fattening it on garbage and planning to cook it for Christmas. As the holiday approached, O'Neill and his friends sometimes fetched the pig from the cellar and offered it whiskey. When drunk, it rushed about the back room, upsetting chairs and behaving a bit like O'Neill when he had exceeded his limit; because of the pig's eccentricity, the barflies called it "O'Neill's son." Only Joe Smith could subdue the creature by crooning in its ear; he'd explain, "You got to reason with him." (It is perhaps not surprising that two years after writing *Iceman*, O'Neill, in a notebook, jotted an idea for a one-acter—"Pig of the Hell Hole play.")

———

ANOTHER SUBSIDIARY BUT significant *Iceman* character is Willie Oban, based on the son of Al Adams, a crooked securities dealer of the era, notorious for having served time in Sing Sing; but Oban seems as well to have been designed by O'Neill to represent Jamie, who was a dissipated thirty-four at the time *Iceman* takes place. Oban, a troubled Harvard Law School alumnus, is resentful of his overpowering father, while at the same time dependent on him, as was Jamie on his father.

Oban, when jolted awake from an alcoholic dream, is given to crying out pathetically, "It's a lie! Pappa, Pappa!" Further emphasizing Oban's resemblance to Jamie, O'Neill has him deliver a boozy, self-pitying account of his early history to Parritt, from whom he is trying to cadge a drink; it includes the fact that his father pushed him to attend an Ivy League college.

"He was an ambitious man," Oban whines. "Dictatorial, too. Always knowing what was best for me." But, continues Oban, he outsmarted his father. Although starting out as a brilliant student, Oban "discovered the loophole of whiskey" and escaped his father's jurisdiction. (This characterization would prove to be a jumping-off point for the full-fledged portrait of Jamie O'Neill's downfall in the soon-to-be-written *A Moon for the Misbegotten*.)

Among other minor characters in *Iceman*, Pat McGloin, a "one-time police lieutenant," represents the busted crooked cops from the semi-underworld of Manhattan that O'Neill and his friend Louis Holladay joyfully had explored in their late teens; they rarely missed a Saturday-night visit to the Tenderloin, the site of Manhattan's numerous gambling dens, as well as its red-light district. Its main attraction for the two boys was the three-story Haymarket on Sixth Avenue near Thirtieth Street which, with its racy dance hall and upstairs peep show, was a hunting ground for prostitutes and pickpockets (and where police graft was rampant). Cops like McGloin, after they were rooted out of the force, used to hang out in the Hell Hole, where O'Neill got drunk with them and listened to the stories of their misadventures.

Two other minor characters—Piet Wetjoen (described as "The General," and a "one-time leader of a Boer commando") and Cecil Lewis ("one-time Captain of British infantry") seem to have been dropped by O'Neill into Harry Hope's saloon partly to fill in the inevitable fraught silences and partly (like Hugo Kalmar) for comic relief. They serve their purpose, but O'Neill "knew" them mainly from the bawdy stories told him by his father's press agent, James Byth, who did know them well.

Absent from *Iceman* is a version of O'Neill himself. Although he undeniably drank with the regulars at Jimmy the Priest's and shared their dismal living quarters, he was a vagabond manqué, with options they did not have. Alienated from his family, O'Neill nonetheless knew his father would rescue him if he wanted to be rescued; he was, in fact, leading a double life.

Who among his decrepit barroom pals could have slipped uptown to the theater district from time to time, as O'Neill did, to see the newly arrived members of the Abbey Theatre, imported for the first time from Ireland by James O'Neill's old friend and producer, George Tyler; O'Neill periodically picked up his father's dole at Tyler's office, where he had no trouble obtaining tickets to Broadway performances of plays by Yeats, Synge, Lady Gregory, and Lennox Robinson.

A comment O'Neill later made is an indication that his state of mind at that time was not entirely hopeless: "It was seeing the Irish Players for the first time that gave me a glimpse of my opportunity." He went to see everything in their repertoire. "I thought then and I still think that they demonstrated the possibilities of naturalistic acting better than any other company."

Also unlike his barroom brethren, whose only concern was where the next drink was coming from, O'Neill, between his own drinks, was attuned to the avant-garde world that lay just a few blocks north of Jimmy the Priest's. He was well aware that the streets of Greenwich Village thrummed with young writers and artists fleeing the intellectually stunted lives of their hometowns, swarming into the Village's cheaply rented rooms and welcoming cafés and bars, free at last to pursue careers as writers, painters, poets, actors, musicians—and finally unafraid to speak their minds about everything from radical politics to free love.

O'Neill also was more than fleetingly aware of the strides being made by the socialist movement and the IWW (International Workers of the World) among the searching young Villagers; he himself, along with a million other voters, was rooting for the Socialist Party's presidential candidate, Eugene V. Debs, in an election in which Woodrow Wilson defeated not only Debs but also the incumbent, President William Howard Taft, and the Progressive candidate, Theodore Roosevelt.

THE ONLY WOMEN who appear onstage in *Iceman* are the three streetwalkers who are adjuncts of the play's two bartenders. They are Pearl and Margie, who belong to the night bartender, Rocky Pioggi, and Cora, who belongs to the daytime bartender, Chuck Morello.

All five have pipe dreams of their own. Because Rocky earns a salary and takes his girls' money only as a sideline, he is not a "pimp," and Pearl and Margie, therefore, call themselves "tarts" rather than "whores." Chuck and Cora are engaged to be married; as soon as Chuck gives up his periodic drunken binges (any day now), Cora will stop soliciting and they will settle down together on a farm in New Jersey.

This quintet provides much of the often underrated comedy with which O'Neill peppered *Iceman*. But while the three tarts are the play's only visible females, it is the two offstage women—Evelyn Hickman (the all-forgiving wife) and Rosa Parritt (the negligent mother)—who possess their men and drive the play's action.

In contrast to O'Neill's affectionate portrayal of his drunken barroom friends, there is vitriol in his portraits of Evelyn and Rosa that unavoidably brings to mind his feelings toward his own all-forgiving wife and his own negligent mother (possessive types we have met before in other of O'Neill's women-driven dramas).

Evelyn Hickman, with her over-mothering and her limitless forbearance, literally drives her husband crazy enough to murder her—and he is in turn himself destroyed; and Rosa Parritt, by her self-absorption and egregious neglect of her son, engenders in him such hatred he is goaded into killing her symbolically by his betrayal—leading to his self-destruction.

Granted that the mind of a creative genius is essentially unknowable and that the most well-informed guesswork is still guesswork, it's hard not to leap to certain assumptions in the case of *The Iceman Cometh*.

It would be surprising, for example, if O'Neill, in depicting the mother-son dynamic, wasn't thinking back to Jamie's self-punishment after betraying his mother by getting drunk as she was dying, and then compounding his betrayal by his outrageous behavior on the train that bore his mother's casket back to New York. For that matter, there was O'Neill's own betrayal of his mother—not only in his depiction of her as a madwoman in *More Stately Mansions*, but also in exposing the long-kept secret of her morphine addiction in the family play he had already outlined and was soon to write. Like Hickey, who finally could no longer tolerate his wife Evelyn's self-sacrifice, O'Neill at times found it hard to bear Carlotta's endlessly patient and all-forgiving dedication to his neediness and (often enough) his emotional abuse. Surely there were occasions when he fantasized about getting her off his back. And it's not too far-fetched to speculate that, being O'Neill, his fantasy took him a step further: to thoughts of the revolver he kept in a bureau drawer, and of using it to put Carlotta (and himself) out of her misery. (He'd bought the gun years earlier to protect his Bermuda household after a half-witted native exhibitionist had plagued a friend's nursemaid on the same beach where Shane swam.)

If it's a guess that O'Neill sublimated his fantasy by letting Hickey do the wife-shooting for him, it's a fact that in the not-too-distant future, when his writing had come to a halt, he would brandish that revolver in Carlotta's face with murderous intent.

The Iceman Cometh has been lengthily analyzed in print from psychiatric, religious, and metaphysical viewpoints; it appears to be well on its way to accumulating as large a body of scholarly discourse as *Hamlet*. One of the most illuminating analyses of the play was provided by Dudley Nichols in a letter to Irving Hoffman, a close friend at *The Hollywood Reporter*.

O'Neill had respected Nichols ever since 1928, when his enthusiastic review of *Strange Interlude* ran in the New York *World*. Nichols had gone on to become a well-respected film writer and had recently completed a film adaptation of O'Neill's early one-act sea plays.

As Nichols observed:

> The iceman of the title is, of course, death. I don't think O'Neill ever explained, publicly, what he meant by the use of the archaic word, "cometh," but he told me at the time he was writing the play that he meant a combination of the poetic and biblical "Death Cometh"—that is, cometh to all living— and the old bawdy story, a typical Hickey [and Jamie O'Neill] story, of the man who calls upstairs, "Has the iceman come yet?" and his wife calls back, "No, but he's breathin' hard."
>
> Even the bawdy story is transformed by the poetic intention of the title, for it is really Death which Hickey's wife, Evelyn, has taken to her breast when she marries Hickey, and her insistence on her great love for Hickey and his undying love for her and her deathlike grip on his conscience—her insistence that he can change and not get drunk and sleep with whores—is making Death breathe hard on her breast as he approaches ever nearer—as he is about "to come" in the vernacular sense. It is a strange and poetic intermingling of the exalted and the vulgar, that title.

The truth of the play, as O'Neill explained to Nichols (and, later, to a few other chosen friends), was that Hickey had long ago begun to harbor a murderous hatred for his wife; she represented his own punishing conscience.

"God, how Hickey had begun to hate his wife!" wrote Nichols.

> When he gave her a venereal disease, and she forgave him—
> he wanted to kill her then, deep down in his unconscious. But
> of course the idea couldn't enter his conscious mind—because
> he "loved" her, as she "loved" him. He'd been on that hop for
> years. So, when he finally had to kill her, knowing he had to
> be true to his own nature and go off to Harry's saloon for a
> shot of Hope, a big drunk and a week with the tarts and bums,
> he first had to cook another pill of opium and grab the beau-
> tiful pipe dream that he was killing her for love—so she
> wouldn't suffer any longer from his incurable debauchery.

Hickey's delusion vanishes when he discovers that with Evelyn's death he no longer has the desire to go off on a drunk; he is forced to grasp at a new pipe dream—that his release from a guilt-ridden marriage has cleansed him and removed the need for debauchery.

"How fiendishly clever the human mind is!" said Nichols. "When one dream is punctured, when we are finally brought face to face with ourselves or with 'reality,' the mind jumps to another pipe dream and calls it truth—calls it facing reality!"

But Hickey's new pipe dream also vanishes when he discovers that his friends in Harry Hope's saloon will not buy it; they are appalled when they discover he has murdered his wife and regard it as the act of an insane man. Hickey, forced to seize still another illusion, convinces himself that his friends are right—that he is insane.

"I don't see the play as pessimistic," continued Nichols. "It's surely not a gloomy play. O'Neill himself delighted in its laughter. He'd chuckle over the tarts and the others—he loved them all. He didn't feel that the fact that we live largely by illusion is sad. The important thing is to see that we do. The quality of a man is merely the quality of his illusions. We like illusioned people. No happy person lives on good terms with reality. No one has even penetrated what reality is."

Another of the play's enchantments is its religious symbolism, starting with the seating of the characters in Act II (for Harry Hope's birthday celebration), which is reminiscent of Leonardo da Vinci's *The Last Supper*. In an article written two years after the play's Broadway premiere in 1946, the O'Neill scholar Cyrus Day first called attention to the fact that "Hickey as saviour has twelve disciples," and after they drink wine, "Hickey leaves the party, as Christ does, aware that he is about to be executed." Moreover, as Professor Day notes, "the three whores correspond in number to the three Marys, and sympathize with Hickey as the three Marys sympathize with Christ."

Day goes on to note the many resemblances between Don Parritt and Judas Iscariot:

> He is the twelfth in the list of the dramatis personae; Judas is the twelfth in the New Testament of the Disciples. He has betrayed his anarchist mother for a paltry $200; Judas betrayed Christ for thirty pieces of silver.
>
> He is from the far-away Pacific Coast; Judas was from far-away Judea. Hickey reads his mind and motives; Christ reads Judas's. Parritt compares himself to Iscariot when he says that his mother would regard anyone who quit the "Movement" as a Judas who ought to be boiled in oil. He commits suicide by jumping off a fire escape; Judas fell from a high place (Acts 1:18) or "hanged himself" (Matthew 27:5).

Day argues that these resemblances can hardly be coincidental: "They are no more than an undertone, to be sure—one of many undertones or subordinate layers of meaning—but they are consistent with the main theme of the play, and they account for some of its otherwise unaccountable features; for example, the emphasis on midnight (see Matthew

25:5–6) as the hour appointed for Harry Hope's party, and the unnecessarily large number of derelicts in Hope's saloon."

For the final moments of *Iceman*, O'Neill contrived an audacious and coruscating tableau to capture the deep inner contentment of the saloon's inebriates when they have regained their lost pipe dreams. Hickey's former disciples, writes O'Neill, "are all very drunk now, just a few drinks ahead of the passing-out stage, and hilariously happy about it"; Harry Hope cries out, "Bejeez, let's sing! Let's celebrate! It's my birthday party! Bejeez, I'm oreyeyed! I want to sing!"

Then, writes O'Neill, "he starts the chorus of 'She's the Sunshine of Paradise Alley,' and instantly they all burst into song. But not the same song. Each starts the chorus of his or her choice." And O'Neill, with his vast and loving knowledge of popular and folk ballads of the era, spins out a list ranging from "A Wee Deoch an Doris" through "Waiting at the Church" to "Oh, You Beautiful Doll"—with Hugo Kalmar bellowing the French Revolutionary "Carmagnole." The curtain descends on the singers' pounding their glasses on the table and roaring with laughter.

"AFTER ALL, what I've tried to write, is a play where at the end you feel you know the souls of the seventeen men and women who appear—and the women who don't appear—as well as if you'd read a play about each of them," O'Neill explained to Kenneth Macgowan, who admired the script but found it somewhat repetitious. "I couldn't condense much without taking a lot of life from some of these people and reducing them to lay figures.

"You would find if I did not build up the complete picture of the group as it now is in the first part—the atmosphere of the place, the humor and friendship and human warmth and deep inner contentment of the bottom—you would not be so interested in these people and you would find the impact of what follows a lot less profoundly disturbing."

After intensely studying *The Iceman Cometh*, José Quintero was staunchly in agreement when he directed the play's first revival off-Broadway in 1946. "O'Neill," he said, "knew that life is repetitious, but he did not merely echo this fact; he employed repetition to reveal progressively more of his characters and situations."

A far more empathetic director than O'Neill ever had in his lifetime, Quintero noted about *Iceman*, "There is a different mood with each repetition, giving it a new meaning, orchestrated as music is orchestrated." As an illustration, he cited the thematic line about "the kick" having gone out of "the booze," which, he said, is repeated a half-dozen times and "moves from exposing the reality of a simple drink to the reality of a life lost."

Actually, there are at least seven variations of the line (within fourteen pages of Acts III and IV): "What's wrong with this booze? There's no kick in it"; "What did you do to the booze, Hickey? There's no damned life left in it"; "I've lapped up a gallon, but it don't hit me right"; "I can't get drunk right"; "We all know you did something to take the life out of [the booze] . . . We can't pass out"; "All we want is to pass out and get drunk . . ." ; "What did you do to this booze? . . . There's no life or kick in it now."

In summation, said Quintero, "O'Neill was too dedicated an artist with too great a sense of purity to use anything, including repetition, as a meaningless mechanical device."

42

W ant to do this soon," O'Neill promised himself on January 5, 1940, after rereading his outline for the play he had initially entitled "A Long Day's Journey," was now calling "The Long Day's Journey," and would ultimately call *Long Day's Journey Into Night*. But after the high of completing *Iceman* and its subsequent letdown, he mistrusted his ability to keep his emotional balance.

As he'd confided to Carlotta, he was feeling hounded by his "nervous mental condition." Trying to do anything at all outside his ordinary routine, he told her—even something as trifling as writing a Christmas card to a friend—would hang over his head and fill him with dread.

"The Long Day's Journey" loomed as far more daunting than *The Iceman Cometh*. O'Neill foresaw in his Work Diary it would "have to be written in blood."

Not quite ready to shed that blood, he put off his confrontation with *Journey* and revisited his disjointed and tentatively abandoned cycle. He tinkered with it for a month, but by the beginning of February, overwhelmed by the burden of work it still demanded, he let it go; he was forced to acknowledge that he would never again be the same man he was before his long hospitalization three years earlier. He could hope for periods of remission that would allow him to work, but he knew he could not outrun his unappeasable deterioration. At fifty-two, he often felt like a very old man.

"Even here, in the most healthy environment," he wrote to Nathan, "I get sudden setbacks of complete exhaustion when I have to stay in bed for several days. (I'm enjoying one right now—am writing this in bed)."

Among O'Neill's collection of sometimes misdiagnosed ailments were the periodic seizures that ambushed him, seismically rattling his body. His pencil would sometimes fly from his trembling fingers while he was seated at his desk; at other times, when taking a step forward, his leg might unaccountably tug him backward. It was only his irrepressible need to write that kept him from surrender; he still had something to say to a world that he believed was sliding into a soulless slough.

He felt sturdy enough on February 22 to make a few notes for the play he had finally renamed *Long Day's Journey Into Night*; but, as he told his Work Diary in early March, he was "too low physically now for long stretch work." And when, soon after, his blood pressure plummeted, he had no choice but to succumb to his ailing body.

In mid-March, Dr. Dukes put him on a regimen of unspecified "new shots" that perked him up, enabling him to work "short shifts."

Early April found O'Neill momentarily in high spirits; he'd just read the screenplay that Dudley Nichols had adapted from *S.S. Glencairn*, and that he was calling *The Long Voyage Home*, after the best-known of the four early one-act sea plays that comprised *S.S. Glencairn*.

O'Neill had sold the rights to Fox Films in February (for the welcome if modest fee of $20,000); the movie was to be directed by John Ford, whose outstanding credits included *The Informer* and *Stagecoach*.

After inviting Ford and Nichols to Tao House to talk about the screenplay, O'Neill recorded in his Work Diary, "Like them both a lot." Never a film enthusiast, and always (justifiably) dissatisfied with the movies made from his plays, O'Neill believed Nichols and Ford were on the right track.

"I can see the grand picture it will be," wrote O'Neill on April 27, thanking Nichols for sending the finished script for his approval. Facetiously, he offered "a new love interest angle which would bring box office queues ten miles long." Referring to the sailor Yank, O'Neill suggested he go over the side of the ship down to the anchor.

"And what do you think he finds caught on one of the flukes? A blonde! And by her panties! It seems she has fallen off a yacht—or something. . . . And then—but hell, what's the use of talking to a coupla guys like you what ain't got no practical theater sense. Go on and make a fine picture if you're that nuts!"

The film's artistic, low-key style earned not only O'Neill's warm approval but turned out to be the most successful of all the movie adaptations of his plays (doubtless aided by its provocative billboard, which announced, "The Love of Women in Their Eyes. . . . The Salt of the Sea in Their Blood!"). Its cast was headed by John Wayne (who had finally reached stardom a year earlier with *Stagecoach*), along with Thomas Mitchell, Barry Fitzgerald, Mildred Natwick, and Ward Bond.

After weathering a dislocated sacroiliac and one of his frequent respiratory ailments in early May, O'Neill was again thrown off stride, confessing he had "no ambition for work" on *Long Day's Journey*. And when, on May 10, Hitler launched his attack on Western Europe, O'Neill groaned to his Work Diary, "To hell with trying work—it's too insignificant in this madmen's world."

Dr. Dukes called in a specialist from the Mayo Clinic when O'Neill failed to regain his strength. The two doctors advised a "stronger schedule of shots, one a day for 3 weeks, give it real tryout." The shots (ingredients unspecified by O'Neill) had "a fine effect—feel much better than in years—blood pressure up," noted O'Neill in mid-June; but, unable to take his mind off the war, he grew distraught over the plight of France, which he'd come to sentimentalize as the cradle of his romance with Carlotta.

To Nathan, who had inquired after his health, O'Neill conceded he was feeling "pretty fit again—physically." However, he wrote, "Mentally, spiritually, and creatively I feel like a dead clam—a nerve-ridden, dead clam, if you can imagine such a paradoxical bi-valve."

He said he'd been unable "to write a line for the past couple of months, or take the slightest interest in work," adding he'd become especially demoralized after learning of the fall of Paris: "We may soon hear they are fighting for Tours, which is like an old home town to us, as you know.

Perhaps Le Plessis will be blown to pieces! This war is hitting us where we belong, so to speak."

He went on to ask rhetorically if "an author who tries to remain an artist" should "forget history, forget philosophy, forget the last war and what it did to this country, forget that it was the stupid, double-crossing greed and fear of democratic politicians—(particularly the swinish British Tories whom the O'Neill in me loathes, anyway)—that conspired with Hitler to create Nazi Germany, forget all this and everything else a free intelligence should remember, because one loves France in spite of its politicians?

"And then feel it's one's duty to devote one's work to a hymn of hate? Well, although I hate Nazism as bitterly as anyone, I can never do that in my work."

REGARDING HIS WORK, it was his problematic cycle, rather than *Long Day's Journey*, that was now on his mind. "My main selfish worry is that now the Cycle recedes farther and farther away, until I cannot imagine myself ever going back to it. It isn't that anything that's happening or may happen can affect the main theme of the Cycle. Quite the reverse! It proves it!"

He ended with a despairing cry of self-condemnation:

> It is I who am lacking, who has been affected to the point where I cannot believe the Cycle matters a damn, or could mean anything in any future I can foresee. And if I become convinced it is not in me to go on with it, I shall destroy all I have done so far, the completed plays and everything else down to the last note. If it cannot exist as the unique whole I conceived, then I don't want it to exist at all.

Finally, however, after he and Carlotta had wept over the French government's acceptance, on June 22, of the collaborationist Vichy government, O'Neill recognized the futility of brooding about "the future of individual freedom." Returning at last to *Long Day's Journey Into Night*, he reread his first draft of Act I.

To Nathan, in mid-June, he had already confided a summary of the plot of this most personal of all his works; and now he found himself once again fully engaged. "Convinced I can make it one of my best," he noted in his Work Diary on July 4.

Long Day's Journey, he'd told Nathan, was "the story of one day, 8 a.m. to midnight, in the life of a family of four—father, mother and two sons—back in 1912—a day in which things occur which evoke the whole past of the family and reveal every aspect of its interrelationships.

"A deeply tragic play, but without any violent dramatic action. At the final curtain, there they still are, trapped within each other by the past, each guilty and at the same time innocent, scorning, loving, pitying each other, understanding and yet not understanding at all, forgiving but still doomed never to be able to forget."

Very likely, O'Neill's earlier hesitation in tackling the play had an unconscious cause beyond either his fluctuating health or his preoccupation with the war; after so pointedly leaving himself out of *The Iceman Cometh*, he was now, in his family play, dreading the torment of depicting himself as one of the quartet of principals, and reliving his tragic entanglements with his dead parents and two dead brothers. Nonetheless, once he'd brought himself to begin, he worked on *Long Day's Journey* almost nonstop for the next four months.

He was briefly distracted in mid-July when he received an anxious letter from Lawrence Langner, who had somehow learned about the completed script of *The Iceman Cometh*. An embarrassed O'Neill replied that he'd been planning to let him read the script but had been waiting until they met, so that he could explain in person his reasons for withholding production until after the war.

Carlotta was convinced the leak had come from one of O'Neill's friends who had been sworn to secrecy; she was furious about the aggravation it was causing O'Neill, believing he had misguidedly brought the problem on himself.

"My beloved is a magnificent dramatist but a *child* about the *business* of *living*," she complained in her diary, her motherly forbearance momentarily deserting her. Recalling other instances of O'Neill's perverse behavior, she let loose her long-suppressed resentment, sounding surprisingly like Mary Tyrone when baiting her husband:

"Maybe it is the Irish peasant in him," she scolded. "*He can turn on the charm* as he can turn on the sadistic cruelty—he recognizes no law, no God, and doesn't know what 'playing the game' means—unfortunately he hurts himself more than others!"

On their eleventh wedding anniversary that July, O'Neill wrote Carlotta a placatory note, putting (what for him) was an optimistic spin on their downwardly swirling life: "Time falters, civilization disintegrates, values perish, the old beauty becomes a gutter slut, the world explodes, the income tax rises, the years grow heavy on us and Blemie—But still! There is love that does not die, and there is your [inked silhouette of a pussycat] which is the most beautiful [silhouette of pussycat] in the world—so what the hell!"

All summer long, O'Neill had kept an ear on the war news and, when listening to Hitler's broadcast speech on July 19, 1940, he remarked in his Work Diary, "What could be more squalid than a dictator who is also a fifth-rate ham!"

A month later, he'd abruptly interrupted work on his nearly completed first draft of *Long Day's Journey* to make notes for two plays (outside the cycle) dealing with the "present world collapse & dictatorships," which would be "timely but timeless spiritually." He called one of these plays "Time Grandfather Was Dead"; the second, as yet untitled, he described as a "timeless, timely ventriloquist play."

He had yet another "fascinating new idea" on August 30, describing this one in terms that made sense only to him: a "duality of Man play— Good—Evil, Christ—Devil—begins Temptation on Mount—through to Crucifixion—Devil a modern power realist—symbolical spiritual conflict today and in all times." He first called it "The Thirteenth Apostle," later changing it to "The Last Conquest."

And then it was back to *Long Day's Journey Into Night*; nearing the completion of his first draft, O'Neill spoke in depth to Carlotta about his real family, tracing, as she recalled, "their true relationships one to the other," scrutinizing "their idiosyncrasies & disloyalties!" And a month later, on the day he wrote "finished" to the first draft of *Journey*, he pondered what it had cost him "in strength & emotion to write it!"

After spending the next month making revisions, he put the play aside on October 16—his fifty-second birthday. (He would not take it up again until March of the following year.)

To Carlotta's amazement, O'Neill put aside not only *Long Day's Journey Into Night* but also the three new play ideas that had excited him in August. Instead, unpredictably, he chose to ensnare himself ever more intensely in his cycle, which he now had definitely decided to expand to eleven plays. He had, however, lost all interest in ever producing the cycle on Broadway. There was no longer a theater to which he belonged, he wrote to Macgowan, "a theater of guts and idealism." He dreaded to have a play of his produced "in an atmosphere to which neither I nor my work belongs in spirit, nor want to belong."

Production, he insisted, was "a long, irritating, wearing, nervous, health-destroying ordeal"; it was backed by "no creative enthusiasm"; it was "just another Broadway opening." Reminiscing about the old Playwrights' Theatre, he added, "there is no longer a theater of true integrity and courage and high purpose and enthusiasm. . . . The idea of an Art Theater is more remote now, I think, than it was way back in the first decade of this century." So long as he shunned production and lived quietly with Carlotta, "doing my job of writing plays," he concluded, "I rate myself the most fortunate of men."

Resigning himself to writing for an ideal theater of the future, O'Neill grimly chiseled away at his cycle during November, making notes for rewriting *A Touch of the Poet* and *More Stately Mansions*. He also began plotting a series of short "monologue plays" with the overall title *By Way of Obit*.

As he explained to Nathan, enclosing a copy of the first of those monologues, *Hughie*, "There will be seven or eight of them if I ever manage to get them all done." Like *Iceman*, *Hughie* illustrated O'Neill's thesis that survival depends on clinging to one's illusions, even knowing they are pipe dreams.

In each playlet, O'Neill told Nathan, the main character was to talk about a person who has died to a person who does little but listen: "You get a complete picture of the person who has died—his or her whole life story—but just as complete a picture of the life and character of the narrator."

O'Neill said, "These plays are written more to be read than staged," adding, "some of them will be based on actual characters I've known—some not. *Hughie* isn't. The Night Clerk character is an essence of all the night clerks I've known in bum hotels—quite a few!" The narrator of *Hughie*, continued O'Neill, "is a type of Broadway sport I and my brother used to know by the dozen in far-off days." He is Erie Smith, a small-time gambler and horseplayer down on his luck. Although set in 1928 in a cheap hotel just off Broadway, its narrator and his near-silent foil, the hotel's night clerk, would be at home in Harry Hope's waterfront saloon of 1912. Erie is a less astringent Hickey, a Hickey not burdened with O'Neill's symbolic message of despair, a coarser, more elementary type—but a blood brother nonetheless.

O'Neill describes Erie and Hickey in almost the same words. Both are short, stout, balding, with boyish faces, blue eyes, button noses, and pursed mouths. Both have the shrewd glance and breezy familiar manner of the wised-up salesman confident he can always find a sucker. Underneath the facade, both are on the verge of crumbling.

"Gene started writing these plays as a diversion," Carlotta later recalled. "He had been writing so many serious things at the time, this was something to play with—required no responsibility. It amused him."

She said one of the playlets dealt with an old Irish chambermaid O'Neill knew when he and Jamie lived at the Garden Hotel.

"They would wake up in the morning with hangovers," said Carlotta, "and the chambermaid would be scrubbing the bathroom. She would tell Gene stories and gossip, and Gene would encourage her to talk."

After a lifetime of writing double- and triple-length plays, and struggling to complete an eleven-play cycle, it's something of an irony that *Hughie*, the next-to-last play O'Neill completed, was one of his shortest. It was published in 1959, six years after his death, and did not receive its American premiere until December 22, 1964, when Jason Robards Jr., directed by José Quintero, brought it to Broadway. Robards performed the play (in his words) "on and off everywhere for thirty-two years."

While O'Neill busied himself with writing *Hughie* that November, Carlotta was typing *Long Day's Journey Into Night*, squinting her way with a magnifying glass through handwriting ever more difficult to decipher. "Am so moved," she wrote, after finishing Act III, "so torn to bits by it—that I feel *ill*. . . . No wonder he is as he is now! Poor Darling— no proper upbringing, no love, no tenderness, no discipline, no real care of any kind—oh, I can understand so many things now!"

The typing of Act IV nearly undid her. "This is now a torture to me!" she wrote, adding, "I have *never* been so disturbed by any piece of writing before! . . . I feel '*possessed!*' *Long Day's Journey Into Night* absorbing all of my thought—& what an insight into the very soul of Gene!"

Absorbed as she was with her suffering husband's soul, she was almost as wrapped up in concern for their aging adopted canine child. She had returned home from a shopping trip on November 19 to find that Blemie had fallen backward down the kitchen steps, tearing ligaments in his leg. "Blemie in great pain trying to walk 3 legs," she recorded. She and Blemie spent an unhappy restless night together. "I take blankets & lie on the floor with him—Give him aspirin—."

Blemie's condition had seriously worsened by November 25, and Carlotta found herself nursing him with the same tender devotion she'd so often lavished on O'Neill. "Blemie has the jitters—he is getting so blind—I pull his bed up close to mine so I can hold his paw—that gives him a feeling of security. He sleeps—which allows me to."

Carlotta might have been describing an experience with one of O'Neill's worst seizures when she wrote, on December 4, "Have a God awful night with Blemie. Poor darling is either in pain or his nerves are bedeviling him! He paces the floor dragging his bad leg! It is heartbreaking to watch him. I have tried all my known remedies."

By now, Carlotta herself was feeling shaky: "Hope to goodness I don't get flu—then things *will* be in a mess! 'Mama' must never fall down on her job! The *very few* times I have *had* to rest in bed for a day or so— Gene always does some not-so-good thing! I think it is thro' terror that *'Mama' isn't there to give him care* & protection!"

"Blemie seems to be fading out," Carlotta noted on December 10, "—his face looks so thin &—he is quieter!" Dr. Dukes advised her, a few days later, that Blemie had either stomach ulcers or cancer, and should be put to sleep. After the veterinarian examined Blemie and confirmed this diagnosis, Carlotta asked him to give Blemie something to make him comfortable and to return the following morning.

O'Neill, she told her diary, "is not good at a time like this—he says it upsets him!" Snappishly she added, "it more than 'upsets' me!"

In truth, as O'Neill recorded in his Work Diary, he was plagued during the period of Blemie's illness with "bad night pain," "terrible nerves," and "exhaustion," and gave up all work on his cycle from December 12 till month's end.

Carlotta, after sitting up with Blemie most of the night on December 16, found him, in the early morning, sunk into a coma. The vet arrived at 10:30. "I take Blemie in my arms & hold him tight—he looks up at me *once*—[the vet] gives him a huge 'shot' & Blemie *sighs* & he's gone!"

The dog is tenderly placed in a coffin that has been fashioned by the O'Neills' devoted factotum, Freeman; it is lined with Blemie's mattress and pillow, and Carlotta covers him with his blanket. With O'Neill, Carlotta, Freeman, the groundsman Roberts, and his two helpers in attendance, Blemie is buried on the side of the hill under the pines.

"Carlotta & I completely knocked out," wrote O'Neill, "—loved him for 11 years—a finer friend than most friends!" The following day, after visiting Blemie's gravesite, Carlotta and O'Neill planned a headstone.

Amid their dispirited Christmas preparations, O'Neill once again came down with flu, followed by bronchitis, and was confined to bed from Christmas Eve until January 6, 1941. But, knowing how hard Carlotta was taking Blemie's death and hoping to alleviate her pain, he rallied long enough on December 26 to write for her a lengthy touching essay. Heading it "The Last Will and Testament of Silverdeen Emblem O'Neill," it was an expression of O'Neill's philosophy that might almost have served for his own epitaph:

> I, Silverdeen Emblem O'Neill (familiarly known to my family, friends, and acquaintances as Blemie) . . . do hereby bury my last will and testament in the mind of my Master . . . I have little in the way of material things to leave. Dogs are wiser than men. They do not set great store upon things. They do not waste their days hoarding property. They do not ruin their sleep worrying about how to keep the objects they have, and to obtain objects they have not.
>
> I ask my Master and Mistress to remember me always, but not to grieve for me too long. . . . It is painful for me to think that even in death I should cause them pain. Let them remember that while no dog has ever had a happier life (and this I owe to their love and care for me), now that I have grown blind and deaf and lame, and even my sense of smell fails me so that a rabbit could be right under my nose and I might not know, my pride has sunk to a sick, bewildered humiliation. I feel life is taunting me with having overlingered my welcome. It is time I said good-by, before I become too sick a burden on myself and on those who love me. It will be a sorrow to leave them, but not a sorrow to die. Dogs do not fear death as men do. We accept it as part of life, not as something alien

and terrible which destroys life. What may come after death, who knows?

I would like to believe with those of my fellow Dalmatians who are devout Mohammedans, that there is a Paradise where one is always young and full-bladdered; where all the day one dillies and dallies with an amorous multitude of houris, beautifully spotted.

I am afraid this is too much for even such a dog as I am to expect. But peace, at least, is certain. Peace and long rest for weary old heart and head and limbs, and eternal sleep in the earth I have loved so well. Perhaps, after all, this is best. . . .

Carlotta and O'Neill never owned another dog. "It was *Blemie* we loved, not the *dog*!" Carlotta once pronounced.

WHILE IT WAS CLEAR to O'Neill at the beginning of 1942 that his physical strength was waning, his intellectual prowess was as piercing as ever. Even sunk as he was in physical and emotional doldrums between January and mid-March—he erupted with ideas for two new plays.

In "Blind Alley Guy," he depicted a contemptible political extremist modeled on Hitler and his equally contemptible wife; in the second play, a "comedy idea" entitled "The Visit of Malatesta," he portrayed the legendary Italian insurrectionist of that name.

"Never have written about Italian-Americans although in past have known many of them as close friends." The never-completed play seems to have been a kind of postscript to *The Iceman Cometh*; some of its characters are reminiscent of those in *Iceman* and it is set in the same year (1912).

O'Neill also summoned the energy to work on his two earlier concepts, "Time Grandfather Was Dead," along with "The Thirteenth Apostle."

This astonishing surge of creativity equaled (if not surpassed) the torrent of ideas that filled the notebooks of his earliest writing days. But his was not an easy mind to follow. He switched tracks on March 17, returning to his nearly completed job of cutting and revising his second draft of *Long Day's Journey Into Night* and, within two weeks, he pronounced it finished.

"Like this play better than any I have written—does most with the least—a quiet play—and a great one, I believe," he noted in his Work Diary.

O'Neill's close friends Sophus and Eline Winther were among the chosen few to whom O'Neill showed the manuscript, describing it as "autobiography." To them, he confided, "I think the greatest lines I ever wrote were the final words of the play when Mary [Tyrone], holding her wedding gown in her hands says, 'That was in the winter of senior year. Then in the spring something happened to me. Yes, I remember. I fell in love with James Tyrone and was so happy for a time.'"

That May, Carlotta noted that O'Neill had recently told her about the "many things that he did not put" into *Long Day's Journey*. "He is glad I know the play so well," she wrote, "I can now understand why he has done and does do things that he is not proud of doing! He tells me why he hated his brother in his later years!"

Two months later, O'Neill dedicated the original script of *Long Day's Journey* to his wife (the dedication was signed "Gene" and dated "Tao House, July 22, 1941"):

> For Carlotta, on our 12th Wedding Anniversary
>
> Dearest: I give you the original script of this play of old sorrow written in tears and blood. A sadly inappropriate gift, it would seem, for a day celebrating happiness. But you will understand. I mean it as a tribute to your love and tenderness which gave me the faith in love that enabled me to face my dead at last and write this play—write it with deep pity and understanding and forgiveness for all the four haunted Tyrones.

These twelve years, Beloved One, have been a Journey into
Light—into love. You know my gratitude. And my love!

(In 1955, shortly after she authorized the publication of *Long Day's
Journey Into Night*, Carlotta wrote to Dudley Nichols, telling him O'Neill
had insisted that his dedication to her must be included in the published
version of his play "and no other 'forward' or 'introduction' be used in
place of it or with it." O'Neill's reason for this command, claimed Carlotta, was that "the 'inscription' showed what his mood was when writing
it—and what hell he went through!")

LONG DAY'S JOURNEY INTO NIGHT, as O'Neill noted, is indeed "a
quiet play"; to make his point, he did not require the pileup of poisoned,
stabbed, or drowned bodies that signified so many of his earlier savage
forays. There is plenty of bloodletting in the Tyrones' vacation home
(a faithful reproduction, in the author's stage description, of the O'Neills'
summer cottage in 1912 New London). But it is symbolic—inflicted via
the cruel and cutting taunts exchanged among the four Tyrones: about
buried misdeeds; shocking betrayals of trust; deeply wounding bursts of
repressed jealousy; scathing accusations of turpitude, parsimony, hypocrisy, gross ingratitude, and other excruciating misbehavior, both past
and present.

And all the while, in a dissonant descant, the four Tyrones profess
their great love and forgiveness for one another.

While it's true that all four members of the emotionally roiled Tyrone
family are still standing at the final curtain, each has been brutally
wounded.

Mary Tyrone has relapsed into her drug habit, pleading her inability
to cope with her ailing younger son's shocking diagnosis of consumption; the implication that she is forever lost is voiced by her older son,
who sneers that addicts "never come back."

James Tyrone, the onetime matinee idol, has become a crushed and hopeless old man; devastated by his wife's relapse, he is almost equally concerned about his younger son's illness—and the expense of treating it.

James Jr., once a bright and promising student and now, at thirty-three, a misogynic, washed-up actor, has—by play's end—sunk into the alcoholic depths that his doctors have warned will soon kill him; his imminent death is plainly signaled in *Long Day's Journey* (and O'Neill will shortly administer the coup de grâce in *A Moon for the Misbegotten*). The direst fate of all has been reserved for the younger son, Edmund, who represents O'Neill himself. Edmund is not unduly surprised, at play's end, to receive a diagnosis of what is probably a lethal case of tuberculosis. He is destined to die young, O'Neill strongly implies, transparently dramatizing the death wish long attributed to him by a swarm of psychiatrists.

O'Neill acknowledged *Long Day's Journey Into Night* as autobiographical to Elizabeth Shepley Sergeant, as well as to the Winthers. "This is the real story," he said, giving Sergeant the manuscript to read. And yet, even though O'Neill invited his friends to do so, it's a mistake to take *Long Day's Journey Into Night* as literal autobiography. It is, rather, a dramatically heightened, drastically condensed, and factually manipulated version of the events that took place during the New London summer of 1912.

Buried within O'Neill's extensive notes and early drafts are some startling instances that demonstrate the masterful way in which he manipulated aspects of his real life, molding them into inspired dramatic invention.

Although O'Neill undeniably wished the world to understand his life's true torment, his first priority was to the crafting of a work of art; the dedicated artist in him understood that he could use the true facts of his life only as a figurative road map.

In willful opposition to the family that in life had tightly held the secret of Ella's addiction, denied James's terror of the poorhouse, and somewhat tempered the profligate behavior of the two sons, O'Neill deliberately left a paper trail that revealed the truth—his truth—about them. While he placed restrictions on the availability of this material during his lifetime, he plainly wanted the world, one day, to understand the full extent of his suffering; had he wished otherwise, he would have destroyed those notes and early drafts rather than leave them to be probed and analyzed by scholars.

It's clear from these notes that most of O'Neill's fictional deviations in *Long Day's Journey* were dictated by his sure sense of theater, and that he withheld various pieces of autobiographical information that did not conform to the play's tragic contour. And deviations there are aplenty.

For example: Mary Tyrone bewails her husband's neglectful behavior on their honeymoon, implying that her only happy time with James was during the months of their courtship. And although she does speak often of the lifelong love she has shared with her husband, she implies that since the beginning of their marriage he has always preferred spending time with barroom friends rather than her.

But O'Neill left out the real-life fact of James and Ella's exhilarating early years together, her pleasure in mothering her firstborn son, Jamie, and her ongoing warm friendship (recorded in letters and diaries) with the young actress Elizabeth Robins. (If O'Neill had ever heard his mother speak of those happy early years, he chose to ignore them.)

To make the character of the younger son (himself) more sympathetic, O'Neill left unmentioned his own reckless first marriage (to Kathleen Jenkins), his abandoned son from that marriage, and his ugly divorce; but he did drop an inside reference to those events by giving the Tyrone maid his first wife's name, slightly altering the spelling from Kathleen to Cathleen. (He also gave the offstage cook the name of his maternal grandmother, Bridget, long dead in 1912.)

In a more complicated twist, O'Neill even softened the evidence of his father's appalling penury. In the play, James Tyrone first plans to send Edmund to be treated for consumption at the Connecticut State "poor farm"; but, yielding to the taunts of Edmund and his older brother, Jamie, he agrees instead to send him to a privately endowed sanatorium. In real life, James did send his son to the free state institution; it was only after Eugene had fled that place and begged his father to send him elsewhere that James arranged for his treatment at the exemplary Gaylord Farm Sanatorium.

In another instance of soft-pedaling, O'Neill reconsidered an early note for the play in which Jamie tells Edmund he "hated" his baby brother and went into the baby's room on purpose, "hoping he'd get my measles. I was glad when he died."

In the final version, Jamie makes no such confession; a reference to Jamie's involvement in the baby's death is voiced by Mary Tyrone, who is reliving Ella O'Neill's mistake in leaving her children with her mother in a New York hotel so she could join James on his theatrical tour in the West. If she hadn't left them with her mother, she says, "Jamie would never have been allowed, when he still had measles, to go in the baby's room. I've always believed Jamie did it on purpose. He was jealous of the baby. He hated him. Oh, I know Jamie was only seven, but he was never stupid. He'd been warned it might kill the baby. He knew. I've never been able to forgive him for that."

Still beset by love-hate for his mother eighteen years after her death, O'Neill struggled hardest to soften the character of Mary Tyrone. This is evident (as previously noted) from that vicious note in an early scenario in which he described her, when under the influence of morphine, as changing into "an alien demon." Although he deleted those words in the play's final version, he did retain a later note describing Mary confronting her younger son "with a hard, accusing antagonism—almost a vengeful enmity"; but that's about as nasty as it gets. And unlike the venomous and unremitting slings and arrows with which O'Neill riddled Deborah Harford in *More Stately Mansions*, he gave

Mary Tyrone enough redeeming qualities to render her in the end an object of pity.

Similarly, in subtly altering the characteristics and interactions of his real-life family, O'Neill achieved the exquisite, tragic balance and universality of *Long Day's Journey Into Night*.

43

Soon after completing *Long Day's Journey*, O'Neill sank into a morbid funk. Although Carlotta, after all those years, should have been braced for his inevitable letdown, she was appalled this time at his near-pathological reaction.

"He talks & talks—about him being finished as a dramatist—& as a man!" she wrote in her diary. "He kills me when he talks like this. My heart aches so I can hardly breathe!"

With O'Neill laboring to cheat his sliding health and keep writing amid increasing wartime deprivations, he and Carlotta faced a besieged existence. Carlotta was gradually being stripped of the help she counted on to run Tao House and its vast grounds; sturdy as she was, she began to buckle under the demands of her increased responsibilities.

Both O'Neills made heroic stabs at hanging on to the legend of their idyllic love and for a time they succeeded. Month by month, however, their relationship was fraying; not surprisingly, the martyred Carlotta found it ever more difficult to suppress her resentment at being undervalued by her husband.

A persistent cause of distress for O'Neill (shared, of course, by Carlotta) was his perceived betrayal by the children of his marriage to Agnes. The deterioration of his relations with both Shane and Oona did not abate and in April 1941, he was affronted yet again by Shane, with whom he'd believed he was finally on good terms. "The last time he visited I thought we were closer than ever before," O'Neill had written to Eugene Jr., recalling Shane's visit in 1940.

That was when Shane had got himself engaged, and O'Neill, remembering his own precipitous entanglement with Eugene Jr.'s mother, for once responded sympathetically; he rescued his younger son by writing to the father of Shane's fiancée and explaining that Shane, at twenty, hadn't yet passed his prep school exams and couldn't even support himself, let alone a wife.

A grateful Shane had promised to heed his father's advice about his future behavior. But O'Neill, reverting to his scolding mode, sent Shane a peremptory follow-up letter: "You've got to find the guts in yourself to take hold of your own life. . . . You have got to go it alone, without help, or it won't mean anything to you."

As usual, O'Neill had amnesia about his own inability to go it alone without his father's help until he was well into his twenties. Shane continued to dabble in this and that. Then, in April 1941, with typical naïveté he asked his father to help start him on a movie career.

"Your letter is comprehensible to me only if I assume that you have decided to forget every word I said to you when you were here a year ago," O'Neill wrote back, adding it was evident Shane didn't think any of his advice worth taking.

"I am not questioning your right to decide for yourself, but on the other hand you have no license to ask my help as long as you continue to live as you are living. . . . You seem to have no realization of what is going on in the world. You write as if these were normal times, in which a young man of twenty-one could decide exactly what job he should choose as offering him the pleasantest prospect for a normal peacetime career."

Did Shane not realize that the country would probably soon be at war and that he was likely to be drafted? Or that "no one can possibly predict what conditions will be like even a year from now?" Unless Shane could demonstrate he was "making some decision which faces realistically the crisis we are all in," continued O'Neill, he didn't know what to say to him.

But O'Neill did have a great deal more to say to his bewildered son: "I am absolutely certain that planning to start a career in the movies at this time is no answer to anything. In fact, at any time, I would not regard it as an answer for you. The farther you stay away from any job that has to do with the theater, the better off you will be." He then flatly refused Shane's request for a letter of introduction to Kenneth Macgowan (whose Hollywood career as a producer was not flourishing), admonishing his son it would do him not "the slightest good, anyway, as Macgowan is not in position to hire anyone."

O'Neill's final jab was to express his "big disappointment" that after all their talk a year ago, Shane had done so little to make himself independent.

OONA ARRIVED FOR her second visit to Tao House on July 11, 1941, and it wasn't long before O'Neill found her even more daunting than her brother. Oona had turned sixteen in May, but with her well-developed figure she looked far more mature. Combining the best features of father and mother, she had dark silky hair, deep-set eyes, and a sensual mouth.

Unlike Shane, she was self-confident; despite growing up in an irregular and unpredictable ménage, she seemed to know what she wanted and where she was going. Her early haphazard education was topped off when Agnes transferred her to Brearley, the private Manhattan girls' school chosen by her mother for its social cachet; Agnes had moved herself and Oona from their New Jersey home to a small family hotel in New York to have easier access to Brearley.

Somehow O'Neill had always expected Oona would turn out to be a daughter he could be proud of. But Oona's ideas of glamour and fun were not much different from those of other girls similarly situated. Her two closest friends at Brearley were Gloria Vanderbilt and Carol Marcus—both bright, pretty girls who, like Oona, had grown up in hyper-dysfunctional families. Gloria Vanderbilt was impressed by "Oona's wonderful quality of Oriental objectivity about life," while Carol Marcus cited her "enormous understanding." The three had made a pact to seek out and marry rich and/or famous older men.

Oona's second visit to Tao House was less successful than the one she'd paid two years earlier. This time, when she left (on July 18), O'Neill grumbled that she had "changed not for better"; he blamed her "damned N.Y. school—or maybe she's just at silly age."

His misgivings materialized some nine months later when, in his Work Diary on April 12, 1942, he said, "News comes that Oona has become Stork Club publicity racket Glamour Girl—at this of all times!—I am not amused."

It seemed that the trendy nightclub had named Oona "New York's Number One Debutante." Not yet seventeen and in her final semester at Brearley, she was a girl-about-town, currently dating (among others) J. D. Salinger, the twenty-three-year-old aspiring writer, and Orson Welles, who, at twenty-seven, had already established a successful theater and movie career.

Interviewed at the Stork Club by Earl Wilson, the New York Post's gossip columnist, Oona pertly described herself as "shanty Irish"; asked how her father would feel about her "triumph" as the "Number One Debutante," she replied, "I don't think he's going to be wild about it. I won't write; I'll just let him find out about it himself." She also confided that, although her college board entrance exams had gained her admission to Vassar, she planned to study art in New York the following year rather than attend college, and was "also going to find out whether I'm any good at acting."

O'Neill exploded when he received this clipping sent him by Harry Weinberger. Oona's "adventure into stupid exhibitionism," he stormed, was "unpardonable," and the interview she gave "was tops in empty-headed, nitwit bad taste and vulgarity." He was further incensed that she chose to "trade on her father's name" to seek newspaper publicity at a time "when everyone is worried to death about serious matters. I'm afraid the young lady is mentally and spiritually a Boulton. Could one say worse?"

Oona had "not dared" to write to him, O'Neill told Weinberger; and he had no wish to see or hear from her "until she has proved she has come out of this silly, brainless stage."

A FEW MONTHS before receiving the aggravating news about his daughter, O'Neill had returned to what he had by now outlined as definitely an eleven-play cycle. "Have not told anyone yet of expansion," he noted in his Work Diary on May 21, 1941. "Seems too ridiculous—idea was first 5 plays, then 7, then 8, then 9, now 11—will never live to do it—but what price anything but a dream these days!"

His return to the cycle had been prompted by his determination to rewrite *A Touch of the Poet*; on February 16, 1942, he had written that he wanted "to get at least one play of Cycle definitely & finally finished." The play's reshaping was to take nine months of on-and-off work.

When he began his revision, Oona had been far from his mind; and, of course, she had been a child of ten when he originally conceived the idea for this play that revolved around a fateful father-daughter relationship.

But as it happened, during most of the same nine months when he was rewriting *A Touch of the Poet*, with its focus on the antagonistic relationship between Con Melody and his headstrong young daughter, O'Neill found himself assailed again and again by news of his own headstrong young daughter. Oona O'Neill—like the character of Sara Melody, whom O'Neill was developing—had suddenly become a willful, strong-minded young woman to be reckoned with.

It's a fair guess that to some degree O'Neill's consuming anger over Oona's evident disregard for her father's sensibility influenced his reshaping of Sara Melody's character.

It was in late September 1942, while in the midst of rewriting Acts III and IV of *A Touch of the Poet*, that O'Neill was infuriated all over again by Oona's behavior. He'd received a second letter from Weinberger, asking (on Agnes's behalf) to approve Oona's plan to attend the Neighborhood Playhouse dramatic school. Emphatically disapproving, he told

Weinberger that Oona should realize the way to become an actress was to prove her ability by getting a job in the theater "however small"—not by going to an acting school.

Egged on by Carlotta (although she herself had attended an acting school in London at eighteen), O'Neill persisted. Why didn't Oona train to be a Red Cross nurse if she wanted training that meant something? He then proceeded to attribute to the adolescent daughter he'd been neglecting since she was two every vile quality he could summon: in addition to being "a spoiled, lazy, vain little brat" and "a much sillier and bad-mannered fool than most girls her age," she was sly, parasitical, prideless, "begging and grafting," and too weak "to face the world and the war—or, for that matter, to face oneself in any world of decent values—in short, pure Boultonism."

Con Melody's contemptuous treatment of Sara might well be a reflection of O'Neill's anger toward Oona; in the revised Act III of *A Touch of the Poet*, Melody castigates his daughter for taking "satisfaction in letting even the scum see that she hates and despises her father!" Surely Melody's words convey O'Neill's own sense (after reading his daughter's flippant interview with Earl Wilson) that Oona was "letting the scum" see her hostility toward her father.

O'Neill made no reference to if or how he had altered the relationship between Melody and Sara. But that November, O'Neill declared himself convinced that "considering sickness & war strain," he had made *A Touch of the Poet* a "much better play . . . a triumph."

Poet ends with Melody crushed and his daughter triumphant. O'Neill, however, had no intention of allowing his own daughter to better him. His animosity toward her, soon to explode into a Lear-like frenzy, was a decided overreaction. Clearly it had slipped his mind how he had traded on his father's name (to get his plays read by theater associates of James O'Neill's) and how his father had paid to privately publish a volume of his early one-act plays (under the collective title *Thirst*) despite his disapproval of its contents.

Also forgotten was that the woman to whom O'Neill was now married was a non-college-educated former glamour-girl-about-town who'd gone on the stage with scant training and little talent. True, Carlotta had been a great beauty; but Oona, alluring and vivacious, was beautiful enough, and just as qualified to attempt an acting career as Carlotta had been.

O'Neill's outrage over Oona's behavior sprang largely from his festering hatred of Agnes, and probably also from the suppressed guilt he must have harbored for failing to give her any emotional support, letting her grow up virtually fatherless.

On October 28, 1941, well before he began to revise *A Touch of the Poet*, O'Neill imagined a sequel to *Long Day's Journey Into Night*. He'd suddenly felt a tug to finish the story of his benighted brother, a story in which Jamie would be the central character, in a situation that would be "entirely imaginary, except for Jamie's revelation of self." It could, wrote O'Neill, "be strange combination comic-tragic—am enthused about it."

Mulling over the play idea while also suffering another attack of prostatitis, he took no note in his diary of the death on October 31 of James ("Papa") Speyer. Carlotta, however, felt the passing of her onetime lover and longtime benefactor as a wrenching loss.

"A really good man," she mourned in her diary, "—unselfish, kind, understanding, generous, always helping those in need or unhappy. The best and most loyal friend Gene & I ever had. He can never be replaced!"

Carlotta's love for and gratitude to the Jewish-born Speyer were unquestionably genuine; it was one of her more bizarre quirks of character that at the same time she harbored a lifelong anti-Semitism, evidently unsuspected by Speyer. But neither was it suspected by one of Carlotta's closest friends, Van Vechten's wife, Fania Marinoff. Fania, who was born in Odessa and made her stage debut in New York at twelve, passionately embraced her Jewish faith and (with her Gentile husband's understanding) regularly attended synagogue services.

Carlotta's willingness to overlook both Speyer's and Marinoff's despised heritage is hard to comprehend; her bigotry was not the sort of casual (if deplorable) knee-jerk anti-Semitism that was, at the time, ubiquitous and unabashed.

In Carlotta's case, the hatred—from wherever it stemmed—was deeply internalized. During the year following her marriage to O'Neill, when she was trying to rid their life of those of O'Neill's friends who sympathized with Agnes, she wrote to Kenneth Macgowan, "The jews [sic] in N.Y.—that man [Norman] Winston (or whatever he calls himself), even G's attorney—I never in my long and varied experience, have come across such tactless, thick skinned people."

She was unable to banish O'Neill's "little Jew-lawyer," as she labeled Weinberger; but two of O'Neill's friends before his elopement with Carlotta, Norman Winston and Robert Rockmore, were among those who became persona non grata. "Carlotta didn't want O'Neill to have any contact with us, because she knew we all knew too much about her," Rockmore said angrily many years later, insisting she was "a woman of no morals."

In a letter to her Seattle friend Eline Winther, Carlotta attempted to analyze and justify her long-held contempt for the world's Jews. As she told Eline, she was reading *The Brothers Ashkenazi* by I. J. Singer who, "being himself a Polish Jew," as she put it, "shows us Gentiles . . . how *different* we are" in terms of "opinion, of upbringing, viewpoint, of emotional reactions. . . . It is the old oil-and-water thing. They just don't mix." If Eline had read Singer, Carlotta opined, she, too, would doubtless feel "no kinship with these people."

It wasn't a question, she said, "of feeling one is above or beneath—it is a question of not belonging to that particular civilization. One just doesn't speak the same language. One doesn't fight with their weapons—one doesn't stand a chance to exist with *their* emotional reactions towards each other."

Not that she believed Gentiles were "angels, and honest, and fine," she said, concluding with an incoherent pronouncement: "But, we do know what is going on in their heads even when we are the defeated one. Or am I just an idiot??????"

She reserved her most vicious spates of Jew-hating for Saxe Commins, who (at the time) she did not dare disparage to O'Neill, but who she ran down openly and often to Sophus and Eline Winther. With close friends she sometimes slyly used the word *Eskimo* as code for *Jew*.

O'Neill tolerated Carlotta's bigotry, as he did her reactionary politics and her social snobbery. But he himself, sad to say—despite his warm friendships with Weinberger and Commins, among others—failed to rise above the sort of thoughtless, almost Pavlovian bigotry then practiced by most of his Gentile friends.

An early example: during negotiations in 1919 over James O'Neill's purchase for his son of the abandoned Coast Guard station in Cape Cod, O'Neill wrote to John Francis, his Provincetown landlord, of his concern regarding the transaction. He said he feared the owner of record, the philanthropist Samuel Lewisohn, might remove some of the cottage's furnishings. "This may sound mean, Mr. Francis," wrote O'Neill, "but I have had too many dealings with Jews, and millionaire Jews, too, in the theatrical business not to trust one of them any farther than I could throw your store with my little finger."

In another instance, O'Neill wrote to his agent, Richard Madden, complaining of his then publisher Horace Liveright's response to a request for an advance on royalties: "All he sent was a lousy $200—which is no way to treat me even if he is a Jew."

To Kenneth Macgowan, he dispatched a similar disparagement of the prominent investment banker Otto Kahn, who had made Macgowan a business proposal: "Kahn, I think, is a two-faced tin-horn Kike whom you can trust not to double cross you about as far as a worm can walk on its hands."

Also to Agnes, when he thought he had lined up a buyer for their Ridgefield home, he wrote that an agent "has a rich Jew in tow who seems to mean business." And, when the deal fell flat: "the damned Jew changed his mind."

Even in his published writing O'Neill (on at least one occasion) couldn't resist an anti-Semitic slur; Waldo Frank, co-editor of *The Seven Arts* magazine in 1917, felt obliged to delete the characterization "a fat little Jew" from the short story "Tomorrow." All this despite O'Neill's steadfast moral stand on the subject of prejudice in general.

O'Neill's casual bigotry, while unworthy of him, has, of course, been prevalent among many of the world's most revered writers, from Shakespeare to Dostoyevsky. It was only slightly less reprehensible than other of his lamentable traits, like his blind insensitivity to his children's emotional needs or his nasty tendency, when in a drunken rage, to knock his women about. (One scholar, a literary purist, has suggested facetiously that O'Neill's callous disparagement of Jews was no more unworthy of him than the bad poetry he persisted in writing.)

It took Hitler's persecution of the Jews to awaken O'Neill to the lethal consequences of casual anti-Semitism. In a version of his unfinished play "Blind Alley Guy," he equated his gangster antihero Walter White with Hitler, imbuing White with Hitler's anti-Semitism, along with his "inability to feel" and his "hatred for Christ."

"My work is one of the few things I don't feel depressed over," O'Neill wrote to Eugene Jr. shortly before embarking on his sequel to *Long Day's Journey*. Confronting a recurrence of bad health, he said he lacked "the vitality for the grind" of hard work. "When you live through the play you write, you have to have a lot of reserve life on tap." He persuaded himself that somehow he would summon the strength to write a final masterwork.

O'Neill first entitled his sequel "Moon of the Misbegotten," but changed it five days later to *A Moon for the Misbegotten*, noting that the addition of "A" and "for" rendered the title "much more to [the] point." Thus began his wracking trudge through the last play he would ever complete.

O'Neill launched himself into the writing of *Moon*, periodically battling the attacks that at times made walking an unbalanced hazard and other times deprived him of the use of his hands. He worked on his misbegotten moon until December 7 when, with the rest of the free world, he was stunned by the Japanese attack on Pearl Harbor. "Now the whole world goes into the tunnel!" he wrote in his diary. "We should have beaten the bastards to the punch!"

But war or not, he was determined to complete at least a first draft of *Moon*. It was, he admonished himself, the "artist's responsibility to stick to his job" and he forced himself to work at least part of almost every day. "It was terrible to see him come out of his study, shaken and miserable," Carlotta later recalled.

A Moon for the Misbegotten, like *Long Day's Journey Into Night*, was a play of "old sorrow," carrying the story of Jamie O'Neill to its tragic conclusion. Carlotta believed, as she once said, that O'Neill was writing it to give Jamie "his final due." She did not like the play, convinced it was "unnecessary to rub it in." Indeed, the demonic intensity with which O'Neill relived the last chapter of Jamie's life was, in itself, enough to give both Carlotta and him a retrospective hatred of the play.

One night Carlotta was lying on her Chinese bed, listening to a Hitler speech on the radio. "Gene came in and asked if he could lie down beside me and listen," she recalled. "It was horrible, guttural—and Gene was terribly distressed by it." After quietly talking about the speech, they began to make love; but O'Neill suddenly pushed her from him and sprang from the bed. "Goddamn whore!" he shouted, and ran from the room.

A few seconds later, Carlotta heard him weeping in his own room. Controlling her mortification, she went to comfort him, and found him lying, facedown, on the floor. "He implored me to forgive him," Carlotta said. "He told me he hadn't known what he was saying, and explained that he had been reliving his days with Jamie—the days they had spent in whorehouses together. He was completely shattered. We talked and talked for the rest of the night."

Doubtless, he was also reliving the episode of Jamie's despicable behavior—both at his mother's deathbed and while locked in his state-room with a whore when accompanying his mother's body home from California.

"Gene was such a peculiar mixture," said Carlotta. "Sometimes he was so soft-spoken, and he had the smile of a child of five; you would forgive him anything. But then he could turn around and—like that—I don't think the word 'savage' exaggerates when he was in those moods. He was very much a sadist at times, terribly so; but if he did anything, when the mood changed and he realized it, he suffered terribly from guilt. And his guilt—to watch his guilt hurt me much more than when he was a sadist. I couldn't stand to see my child so miserable."

Although exhausted, O'Neill was close to completing *A Moon for the Misbegotten* in late December when, one evening after dinner, he abruptly told Carlotta, "Darling, this is the end of us. I won't be able to work any more, and when I can't work I'll die. Maybe not physically—but all the best of me that loves you—and that you love." It was an ominous echo of the last time he'd declared himself "finished," and this time there was no rapid recovery. He had been given a diagnosis of Parkinson's disease, which was, in effect, a death sentence. There were medications to alleviate the symptoms and prolong life, but there was no cure.

O'Neill accepted the diagnosis; but it was, in fact, erroneous, and the various medicines he was given often worsened his symptoms. Not until after his death was it revealed that O'Neill had, in the words of his autopsy report, suffered from "a rare disease that only superficially resembles Parkinson's, in which the cells of the cerebellum are subject to a slow, degenerative process." Whether O'Neill could have been more successfully treated if that particular "rare disease" had been correctly identified is anyone's guess.

O'Neill, stunned by his recent diagnosis of Parkinson's, and believing himself unfit to work, nonetheless struggled through the end of December to write the final scene of *A Moon for the Misbegotten*.

"Parkinson's very bad," he wrote in his Work Diary. "Can't control pencil this a.m.—also [tremor] in upper arm & shoulder—not so good, this progress!"

On the last day of 1941, he spoke to Carlotta of his "damnable disease," which made it "impossible for him to write 85% of the time." As they sat pressed close together, she grew "conscious of the tightening of his muscles & of the tremor—which becomes worse & worse as he talks. His whole body shaking, his solar plexus, his arms & hands—then he stops—& begins to weep—as I do! What in the name of God is going to happen to us? This man beside me, my husband & my child!"

In spite of all, O'Neill did manage to finish the first draft on January 20, 1942. He noted, however, that the play needed "much revision—wanders all over place."

When Lawrence Langner wrote to O'Neill about a recent illness he'd undergone, O'Neill countered with a burlesque of his own monstrous ailments. "Next time we meet, you can tell me all about your intestines, and I'll tell you all about my gall bladder and liver and low blood pressure and pyloric spasms." Hour after pleasant hour would pass unheeded, he said, and then, if anyone asked them about the war, he and Langner would reply, "What war?" There was, quipped O'Neill, "nothing like having a real good ailment."

Relishing his own wit, O'Neill went on to spin a mocking scenario of the French Revolution, in which "one of the Knitting Women" called out to Louis XVI as he ascended the scaffold to the guillotine, "Well, Capet, how are the old kidneys lately?" and he would have "waved the headsman aside and begun a serious conversation" about having "to get up and urinate no less than eleven times," at which point the executioner would have offered "a little anecdote about his arthritis, and all the Knitting Women would have told of their hot flashes, irregular menstrual periods, varicose veins, flatulence, flat feet and what not."

Danton would have "muscled in" with a harangue about his "horrible hangover," Robespierre "would have addressed the mob for two hours on the new pills he was taking to get rid of his pimples, and the Revolution would have been forgotten."

O'Neill went on to suggest that "the quickest way to stop Hitler" would be for "some Allied agent" to ask, "Well, Adolph, how are the old hysterics lately?" Hitler, opined O'Neill, "would promptly ask for an armistice in which to start the tale properly, and then sue for peace at any price" so he would have time to detail all his symptoms.

"Fantastic?" O'Neill challenged Langner. "Not a bit of it. Nerves are the most absorbing ailment of all. There is practically no limit to their symptoms. Why, listen, Lawrence, only last night I woke up in a cold sweat. Everything was shaking. I thought, my God, an earthquake! But it wasn't. It was me. And then—But I better stop or I'll be writing you a brand new farce."

AFTER COMPLETING HIS first draft of *A Moon for the Misbegotten*, O'Neill filed it away at year's end (1941), unsure of its final fate. He rallied sufficiently to complete his revision of *A Touch of the Poet* during 1942.

That was a particularly perplexing year. With inefficient (if not disastrous) household help and the prospect of gas rationing that would limit access to medical treatment, O'Neill and Carlotta had concluded early in the year that they would have to leave Tao House.

To compound their misery, on March 13, two days after they'd made their decision to move, Dr. Dukes died. "Gene and I have lost our best and dearest friend," Carlotta mourned. *"We are now alone!"*

O'Neill worked halfheartedly on one or two of his earlier play ideas until mid-December, when he was stopped by a serious tooth infection, followed by one of his old sinking spells:

"Lower than low—mind dead," he complained in his Work Diary on December 13; three days later, he appended, "Complete exhaustion—can hardly crawl—melancholia & Parkinson's very bad."

The O'Neills ended 1942 with Carlotta suffering from back pains and a severe sore throat, while O'Neill declared himself ready to "hop right out of my skin."

44

The last thing O'Neill needed was to deal with the public antics of his daughter. To him, Oona's behavior was incomprehensible.

At least one of Oona's suitors—the young writer, Jerry Salinger—would have agreed with her father about her pursuit of frivolity. Oona had met Salinger in the early fall of 1941, soon after returning home from her second visit to Tao House. She was still living with her mother in West Point Pleasant, together with her mother's lover, Morris ("Mack") Kaufman, a married man ten years Agnes's junior who—like her previous lover James Delaney, enjoyed drinking along with her; he affected a black eye patch and called himself a writer, but he earned his living, such as it was, as a casual fisherman.

It was in this freewheeling environment that Oona was casually introduced to Salinger by Agnes's neighbor and close friend, Elizabeth Murray. When mother and daughter moved to New York in anticipation of Oona's transfer to Brearley, Salinger began dating her. He confided to Mrs. Murray that he was "crazy about Oona"; but the romance did not run smoothly. "Little Oona's hopelessly in love with little Oona," Salinger told Mrs. Murray. He continued to see Oona, however, and they wrote to each other after he was drafted into the army in 1942.

They were still corresponding when, after graduating from Brearley in June 1942, Oona accompanied Carol Marcus on a cross-country motor trip that ended in California, where Carol's fiancé, the thirty-five-year-old playwright William Saroyan, lived. Awaiting induction into the army, Saroyan had asked Carol to come west to meet his family.

Saroyan was sent to Sacramento for his basic training and Carol, accompanied by Oona, followed him there. After checking into a motel, Oona telephoned Tao House, asking if she could visit, but was put off with an excuse by Carlotta.

Then, in the late fall, Oona wrote to her father, saying she'd like to see him, and infuriating him—as he indignantly reported to Weinberger— by offering "no word of excuse or apology for all her cheapness in the eight months she had not written me." Self-righteously, O'Neill bragged to Weinberger that he'd answered his daughter with a letter designed "to knock her ears down."

"You appear to have developed into a vain, seventeen-year-old nitwit, without manners, good taste, self-respect, or pride," wrote O'Neill. He told her he had no way of judging what she had become, except from newspaper clippings of her interviews; but from reading them, he concluded she was unaware of "living in a gigantic world upheaval, which affects the lives and work and ambitions and future of everyone, including you—and me.

"Your present joyride to the Coast, at a friend's expense, when no one is supposed to travel except on absolutely necessary business, hardly convinces me you have gained any pride, or a realization of responsibility toward anyone but yourself."

He went on to berate her for "the cheap publicity" she'd engendered in New York. With unrestrained sarcasm, he told her that one thing he happened "to know a little about" was that "newspaper men never tie you down and pry open your mouth and force you to give interviews"; she'd invited the "wrong kind" of publicity—unless it was her ambition "to be a second-rate movie actress of the floozie variety—the sort who have their pictures in the papers for a couple of years and then sink back into the obscurity of their naturally silly, talentless lives.

"No one but a fool, especially in these times, likes reading interviews with young girls who have accomplished nothing themselves but whose fathers happen to possess the dubious asset called 'news value.'"

What he really found unforgivable was that she had never written him to take advantage of his experience and ask his opinion "while all the time you were riding on my name!" In a calculated slap at Agnes, he told Oona that her advisers were "surely the Goddamnedest morons extant!" and compounded the insult by suggesting there was always a possibility that Oona had been manipulated out of "deliberate malice" toward himself.

"Cut out the kidding," he snapped, unable to stem his venom. "You don't want to see me. Your conduct proves that. And I don't want to see the kind of daughter you have been in this past year." In any event, he and Carlotta could not receive her at Tao House; the guest room was "definitely closed" as they no longer had servants or anyone to drive a car for them.

Not yet satisfied with the cruelty of his caning, O'Neill flung one final insult at the daughter he barely knew: "I had hoped there was the making of a fine intelligent woman in you, who would remain fine in whatever she did. I still hope so." And in closing, he wrote, "If I am wrong, goodbye. If I am right, you will sometime see the point in this letter and be grateful—in which case, au revoir."

As with his letters to Shane, O'Neill doubtlessly believed he had delivered a discourse that, although stern, was both fatherly and salutary. But to his spanked daughter, his undisguised hostility was perfectly clear; Oona confided to her friend Carol that she was deeply wounded. There was to be no au revoir.

After giving Weinberger a self-satisfied synopsis of his letter to Oona, O'Neill explained he was telling him "all this" so that he would be armed with the facts "in case her idiot mother tries some tale on you. Please don't see Oona. I meant all I said in my letter to her, and I want it left at that. It was a kick in the pants she richly deserved. If she's an all-Boulton fool it will have no effect. If she has any latent guts or pride, it may have a good effect in the long run when she eventually realizes what a nitwit public nuisance she has been."

Although momentarily knocked off balance, Oona was resilient enough to shake off her father's evisceration and lose herself in the romantic turmoil of her teenage world. Marking time in Sacramento, her own plans still unformed, she agreed to collaborate in a plot to advance Carol's tempestuous love affair. Saroyan had made Carol promise she would send him a letter every day during his boot camp training, but Carol feared she couldn't meet his literary standards.

"Oona was receiving a letter almost every day from a boy named Jerry," recalled Carol. "Some of the letters were fifteen pages long, and they were very witty, with comments about all kinds of things. I told her I was afraid that if I wrote to Bill he'd find out what an idiot I was and decide not to marry me, so [Oona] marked the clever passages in her letters from Jerry and let me copy them as my own in my letters to Bill."

When Carol next visited Saroyan at his camp, his greeting was surly.

"I asked him what was the matter, and he told me he'd changed his mind about marrying me. He said he had thought I was a sweet girl, but that 'those lousy, glib letters' I'd been sending him had made him wonder." When Carol reported this to Oona, she said they would have to tell Bill the truth about the letters. "But I knew that Bill hated liars more than anything else," recalled Carol, "so I didn't tell him."

The two girls left Sacramento for Hollywood, where Oona was met by her mother; and Carol, feeling defeated, soon after returned to New York. Somewhat later, Saroyan got back in touch with Carol and they were married.

AGNES BOULTON WAS in Hollywood with Mack Kaufman, who had recently been hired to work on a screenplay by Charlie Chaplin. Agnes was trying to peddle a screenplay of her own, as well as writing a novel (not about O'Neill) called *The Road Is Before Us*. (Although it received favorable reviews when published in September 1944, Agnes never wrote another.)

Eager to launch Oona on a film career, Agnes laid plans to introduce her to Charlie Chaplin, whom she had known casually during her Greenwich Village days. (An admirer of the Provincetown Players, Chaplin had offered to appear as one of the ghost-convicts in *The Emperor Jones*—under an assumed name. He was thanked but turned down when O'Neill cautioned that if it ever leaked out that Chaplin was in the cast, audiences would flock to see him and disregard the play. Chaplin understood.)

But he had never forgiven O'Neill for stealing Carlotta from his dearest friend, Ralph Barton, and (as he believed) precipitating Barton's suicide. When Agnes, at the end of 1942, introduced O'Neill's daughter as a potential movie actress, Chaplin was at first wary. But he was taken with Oona's beauty and spirit and offered to coach her for a screen career; with Agnes's blessing, he was soon escorting Oona about town.

Once again, Oona became the subject of gossip columns, provoking the expected reaction from her father. Learning that Agnes and Oona were living in Hollywood, O'Neill agreed with Carlotta, who remarked, "They must be up to no good!"

Oona, by now eighteen, and Chaplin, fifty-two, had fallen in love, and the whole world, it seemed, was shocked at their coupling. It wasn't just the disparity in their ages.

For one thing, Chaplin was facing a scandalous paternity suit; he was accused of taking a neophyte actress named Joan Berry across state lines "for immoral purposes" and she claimed he was the father of her unborn child. (Blood tests ultimately proved he was not the father and the charges were dropped.)

Then, too, he had been married three times—most recently to the film star Paulette Goddard—and had two grown sons close to Oona's age.

The scandal evidently did not trouble Agnes, nor did she seem concerned that Chaplin was only a few months younger than Oona's father. But those facts did trouble O'Neill.

"You've read about my charming young daughter, I expect," he wrote to Saxe Commins. "Nice! Especially the bit about her mother being there to aid and abet. Two of a kind." He added that a Hollywood friend "told us stuff he knew from a friend who had an apartment right under the one A. had rented in her name where Chaplin hid out—drunken parties, etc. . . . a nice thoroughly Hollywood affair!"

But were Oona and Chaplin indeed the grotesquely mismatched couple as they were being painted by the press and being gossiped about from coast to coast?

Perhaps not, if one listened to the exhaustive explanations of Chaplin's and Oona's backstories proffered by the pseudo-psychiatrists. These often simplistic depictions could have come straight out of O'Neill's own Freudian-inspired *Strange Interlude*.

To wit: Chaplin, like many men who grew up unfathered, had a need to feel fatherly; this need (never mind his somewhat less praiseworthy penchant for teenage girls) was what evidently drew him to Oona.

As for Oona (still according to the psychobabblers), how could she not feel the loss of a father, and be only too ready to be fathered, protected, and adored; she doubtless saw (and savored) the irony of her situation: Here she was—the rejected daughter of a world-famous, fifty-three-year-old stage icon of tragedy—in the embracing, fatherly arms of an even-more-famous fifty-two-year-old film icon of comedy.

As the newspapers gleefully followed the Chaplin-Oona romance (along with developments in Chaplin's paternity scandal), Carlotta asked herself grimly (if cluelessly), how Oona could be such a fool as "to give up her father's love and friendship—for the cheapness & vulgarity she looks upon as glamour & worldliness!"

Nothing could have disabused the humiliated and anguished O'Neill of his conviction that he was the injured party. Oona, in his mind, had betrayed him—just like all the women in his life except (so far) Carlotta. Doubtless his pent-up anger over all those past betrayals was in some part responsible for his overreaction to Oona's behavior.

CARLOTTA RECEIVED A phone call at 8:30 a.m. on June 16, 1943, from Herbert Freeman, warning her that word was being broadcast that Oona and Chaplin were to be married that day. (Freeman, who had reluctantly left his job as majordomo at Tao House to join the Marines, was now stationed in San Diego but had stayed in close touch with the O'Neills.)

"She is doing what she told me she *would* do, marry a rich man (old!) to insure a good alimony if things didn't work out!" Carlotta noted. "Gene is very quiet—numb—doesn't listen to the radio or read papers! I have to answer all queries—Am like an automaton. . . . God—what a life!" When the local doctor, Clifford Feller, who made regular house calls, arrived at Tao House that day, he felt he was walking into a funeral parlor. "You could have cut the gloom with a knife," he recalled. The next day's papers (as noted by Carlotta) were "filled with usual filth & nonsense."

In a self-pitying and spiteful outburst to his New London cousin Agnes Brennan, O'Neill unburdened himself about the daughter he now regarded as disowned.

> When she last was here with us—two years ago—she appeared to be developing into an intelligent, charming girl. But in New York with her mother to advise her, she suddenly changed into a silly, cheap publicity grabber. . . . She couldn't see that all they wanted was to use her news value as my daughter.
>
> That has been her line ever since . . . to get any kind of display no matter how vulgar and stupid—and finally ending up in this typical Hollywood scandal and marriage with a man as old as I am (probably older, for what actor gives out his real age?). Of course he's rich, and that is the answer, or one of the answers. I need not tell you, I know, that you are never

going to hear of our entertaining Mr. and Mrs. Chaplin, or of their entertaining us. Enough is enough!

Carlotta had her hands full protecting O'Neill from the onslaught of outraged anonymous letters that began arriving, some of them asking how O'Neill could have allowed his daughter "to marry that—pervert!" "Gene," she noted, was "silent—& does not mention her name! Nor do I—of course."

One night, some days after the wedding, O'Neill asked Carlotta to come to his bed and hold him in her arms. "He talks & talks as I hold him close. About his health—his state of mind—the *blow* Oona's behavior has been . . . We hold tight and weep—like two sick and frightened children!"

A year and a half later, writing to Eugene Jr., O'Neill predicted an "Oona Chaplin divorce." But the marriage was long-lasting. Oona spent the early years of her married life in childbearing. In 1951 (by then the mother of four of her eight children), Oona invited Carol Marcus and her husband, William Saroyan, to spend a weekend at the Chaplin home in Vevey, Switzerland.

During the weekend, Saroyan raved about a book he was reading— J. D. Salinger's just-published first novel, *The Catcher in the Rye*. "This kid is great," he told Oona and Chaplin. "He's got it!" Oona threw Saroyan a wicked glance. "You didn't think much of his style eight years ago," she said. And Saroyan was nonplussed to learn that Carol had cribbed those disdained phrases from Jerry Salinger's letters.

BEGINNING IN THE spring of 1941 when, due to the war's inroads, Carlotta and O'Neill had begun losing their employees one by one, they had striven to manage with makeshift help. Still loath at that time to surrender Tao House, they oversaw a parade of household servants as they came and went. Exasperating as it was, they soon taught themselves to view the experience as a black comedy, its multiple scenes being enacted, week by week, until the end of June 1943:

CARLOTTA (addressing her diary, May 7 and 8, 1941): "Naomi & Willie asking for more advance money . . . Leonard & Hazel [new couple] come out to look at house! They might be all right—but I wonder! . . . All servants now realize how owners of large houses *need* help—so are asking for ridiculous wages. Of course this will end with me cooking, washing dishes & taking care of this huge house with no help!"

O'NEILL (addressing his Work Diary, May 22): "Willy & Naomi give notice—the damned servant problem—poor Carlotta!"

CARLOTTA (May 25): "Leonard & Hazel are good so far!" [They would turn out to be slovenly.]

CARLOTTA (August 8, 23, 27): "Exit Leonard & Hazel. . . . A Florence Oliver is en route . . . quiet, neat & a widow! . . . This changing of cooks etc. seems to upset Gene & me no end—his work & mine is completely thrown out of gear!"

CARLOTTA (May 5, 1942): "Florence is acting 'queerly.' I am afraid there is something in the wind!"

O'NEILL (to his Work Diary, July 30): "Freeman leaves for his Marine training base, San Diego. Carlotta & I up at 5:30 to see him off—hell of a blow to lose him."

CARLOTTA (July 30, 31): "A dreadful night—I feel as if were entering an era of trouble & tragedy—& don't know which way to turn! Our whole program for living must be changed!"

O'NEILL (August 4, 5): "More servant problem—Florence to go . . . Exit Florence."

CARLOTTA (August 6): "Lucille Edmundson to come & cook for us—our first dinner not bad at all!"

O'NEILL (January 11, 1943): "More servant problem—Lucille sick."

CARLOTTA (January 12): "[Lucille] *wants to leave—is afraid to say so because I have been so kind to her*!!!"

O'NEILL (January 14): "Exit Lucille, enter Hulda."

CARLOTTA (January 14, 15, 18): "Hulda looks like a man in her uniform—and is rough, noisy & a very plain cook. . . . I am staying away from the kitchen—Hulda is a strange being! . . . Gene up in his study 'away from that damn savage downstairs' (I agree with him)."

CARLOTTA (January 28, 29): "While Gene and I are in the dining room trying to eat what Hulda calls 'dinner'—Hulda comes prancing into the room and starts shouting about Hitler . . . screams at us, 'Hitler is just a *nice* poor young man, whom the world hates because he wanted to be something & have power & not do dirty things with women!!!!? (God help us through War and what it brings.) . . . Hulda [the following day] is sheepishly coy! I am sure she is not normal. Must get rid of her!"

CARLOTTA (January 31, February 2): "After dinner Hulda runs berserk! Dear God, what one has to endure—but, an insane woman is easier to face than a bomb! . . . After much unpleasantness & trouble [get] Hulda in the car." [She is driven to the railroad station.]

O'NEILL (February 2, 3): "Hulda eliminated . . . enter Mrs. Green—temporary—nice woman."

CARLOTTA (February 3): "[Mrs. Green] comes to work after luncheon. A sweet, motherly soul who is not used to 'working out'!"

O'NEILL (March 4, 5): "Exit Mrs. Green . . . [Enter] Mrs. Holladay—nice woman—hope she will do the job & stay with us."

CARLOTTA (March 5): "Mrs. Holladay *seems* efficient, intelligent & willing to do her work & not expect me to! Dear God, I hope so."

O'NEILL (April 20): "Exit Mrs. Holladay . . . Carlotta wishes [to] cook—has to teach them anyway and more trouble with them than do work herself."

CARLOTTA (April 21): "Get Gene's breakfast, lunch, tea and dinner. Quite a performance at 54! So *begin* cooking! And keep 22 rooms in order! And—type for the Master!"

O'NEILL (writing to Saxe Commins, June 30, 1943): "Now Roberts [the groundskeeper] is leaving us. Tough to keep Tao House above water. May have to close up or sell out."

Carlotta, who never did anything by halves, had long since assembled a collection of menus for use by the stream of unreliable cooks who dribbled through her kitchen. She patiently typed daily recommendations for luncheon, tea, and dinner, imaginatively varied from month to month, and based on recipes culled from a collection of cookbooks; there were eighty-two loose-leaf pages, held in a ring binder and labeled "Mrs. O'Neill's Book.

Her collection contained a recipe by Escoffier; partial to rich desserts based on eggs, butter, and cream, she often served *pots de chocolate* and crème brûlée, and she also emphasized O'Neill's favorite foods, among them popovers and sour cream hot cakes. Included in her menus were three recipes sent her by Carl Van Vechten in 1940: for an Armenian eggplant dish, a frozen salad dressing to be served over avocado, and an elaborate *cassoulet à la Languedocienne* (with instructions to "follow recipe exactly" and a reassurance that if well made "it gets better every time it is warmed up").

"Carlotta taking job in fine spirit, getting [to] be excellent cook— works hard at it," noted O'Neill in his Work Diary, sounding genuinely appreciative; she "does the cooking, and I wipe the dishes."

Eight months later, both cook and dish wiper had had it. In his study, awaiting the new year of 1943, O'Neill once again confided in Carlotta about his horror of a complete breakdown and once again she tried to soothe him. "We lie in each other's arms and weep until we are exhausted! We are both *terrified* of the future!"

On a foggy, chilly day a week and a half into the new year, they discussed how they would live after leaving Tao House. Carlotta wrote, "There'll be no more houses & all they mean! We'll live in an apartment! Dear God, if I am ever able to get all the responsibilities & hard labor of this place off my shoulders—I'll be a new human being."

At the end of January, still in Tao House and still able to summon patches of energy, O'Neill told Robert Sisk that the rewriting of *A Moon for the Misbegotten* was "going well"—on those days when his "hands behaved." But in his Work Diary, he complained that as eager as he was to finish the play—for which he had developed a "real affection"—he could not produce more than one page during three hours of writing before "fading out."

When he tried to work on March 1, it was "no go . . . would ask any Jap to kill me, and many thanks for the favor." And on March 10: "Eager but little done because nerves jumping out of hands, arms, can't control." And so it went.

By month's end, Carlotta and O'Neill, sounding like a couple of pipe-dreaming escapees from *The Iceman Cometh*, were imagining their ideal future home: "Five rooms—none for servants—just Freeman—no ground other than a pool for Gene, easy to keep up—small expense—!"

There were days when, by steeling himself for the effort and forming minute letters with his pencil, O'Neill could still cover page after page. But on other days, his fingers could not grip a pencil, and no effort of will could produce anything but a tremulous, illegible scrawl. Carlotta confided to the Theatre Guild's Theresa Helburn that the situation was becoming more difficult every day.

"There is nothing to do for Parkinson's, it just gets worse and worse," she explained. "And now that I have fallen apart I am not so brave in facing it! There are days when my heart aches so I can hardly face him—which, of course, is the worst possible thing for him. . . . I am really stuck, for the first time in my life, as to what is the best thing to do regarding a future home for Gene. He should have warmth, ocean and sand (!), doctors and good nourishment."

Finding her job as typist too stressful, Carlotta paid her daughter to type O'Neill's revisions for *A Moon for the Misbegotten*, but since Cynthia often could not decipher O'Neill's minuscule writing, Carlotta had to dictate to her. "Even *he* can't re-read it!" Carlotta exclaimed.

It wasn't until July that the O'Neills actually put Tao House on the market; for Carlotta it was more of a relief than a sorrow, but O'Neill truly hated having to give the place up and his unhappiness further exacerbated his nervous condition.

One afternoon in early August, Carlotta found her husband "in his study doubled up in his work chair—his tremor ghastly & he is weeping!"

Two weeks later he broke down again, weeping and shaking. They were rescued the following day by Kaye Radovan (now using her married name of Albertoni), the nurse who had remained a friend since caring for O'Neill during his appendectomy at Oakland's Merritt Hospital in 1936. "Now she can take over," noted Carlotta gratefully, herself close to collapse.

"I have not written a line lately, not even a note," O'Neill told Nathan in late September, describing his recent series of illnesses. He had little hope of his Parkinson's getting better, he said; he'd had to quit taking the standard drugs like atropine and stramonium because he reacted badly to them. (He also reacted badly, according to Carlotta, to a sleeping medicine called hyoscine.)

"The Docs have also discovered I have an adrenal deficiency and I have to drink large tumblers of a mixture of sodium citrate, plain table salt and water with a bit of lemon juice to take the curse off. You can have no idea what a loathsome beverage this is . . . you may get a grin from the picture of me absorbing salt water highballs."

After dinner one evening, O'Neill, according to Carlotta, told her that he would kill himself if he didn't love her so much. "I tell him we both love each other—so we must work *together* to *protect that love* and keep it."

Somewhat later, Carlotta professed herself amazed by what O'Neill had said to her: "Can he really love me that much?!" she asked her diary. "*No!*" she answered herself. "One day he loves me better than life itself!— the next he hates me! Oh—if he could only make up his mind—& be loyal! So that I could feel *he was there*, behind me—as I have always been with him."

The diary entry sounded like the aftermath of an episode Carlotta had omitted to record: she had locked her bedroom door for privacy while having a massage, and when O'Neill tried to enter and couldn't, he flew into a rage, accusing Carlotta—quite possibly with justification—of having sex with the masseuse. O'Neill hadn't been seized by such a fit of jealousy since Shanghai, and a terrified Carlotta telephoned her friend Myrtle Caldwell. "Please come quickly, something terrible has happened," she said.

Myrtle Caldwell and the O'Neills had grown close during the past two years, according to Myrtle's daughter Jane. Myrtle and Carlotta had renewed their childhood friendship in April 1941, when they attended a reunion party in San Francisco for alumni of St. Gertrude's Convent Academy, the Bay Area boarding school both women had attended.

At Tao House, Myrtle calmed O'Neill down. "Gene loved my mother," recalled Jane, "she could always jolly him in various ways."

At the end of October, a somber Carlotta noted, "We must get *back* . . . into a living life . . . here, with no help—so many worries—ill health—everything wrong—it is like waiting for death!" Nonetheless, while waiting—if not for death, at least for someone to buy Tao House—O'Neill continued revising *A Moon for the Misbegotten*, and Carlotta—between nursing O'Neill, cooking, and housekeeping—continued to dictate his revisions to Cynthia, who obediently typed them.

With the decision to leave Tao House by year's end, buyer or not, O'Neill and Carlotta hobbled through the holidays. On her fifty-fifth birthday, Carlotta began the arduous dismantling of Tao House, the third of their "final" homes. "All the chickens have gone!" she wrote. "The beautiful Brahmas . . . it seems impossible for Gene & me to keep pets, homes, or anything!" A drawing at the page's bottom, of four pussy cats enclosed in a heart, was an indication of a celebratory coupling.

When a local attorney, Arthur Carlson, made them an offer of $80,000 in early February 1944, they didn't know whether to be glad or sorry; "We had luck—found a buyer quickly—got out at a good price—what we put into it," O'Neill reported to Nathan.

After arranging to sell her major pieces of Chinese furniture back to Gump's, Carlotta busied herself with packing their personal belongings and sorting items for storage: linens, china, and other household items that required twelve large trunks and crates crammed with gramophone records and more than seven thousand books. When the movers from Gump's left with their booty six days later, Carlotta locked herself into her bathroom and burst into tears over "all the thought, knowledge, labor, love & money I put in this house for our old age!" She and O'Neill were obliged to move into the downstairs guest room "because our Chinese beds are gone!"

Carlotta's strength was waning and, on February 19, she began to suffer from what she was sure was a serious problem. She noted in her diary, "Every time I void I pass blood—the pain is *horrible*." Still suffering on February 24, she had herself driven to San Francisco's Nob Hill to supervise the unpacking at the suite she'd rented in the Huntington Apartment Hotel; she was determined to have everything in order and welcoming for her husband's arrival. She returned to Tao House in such pain she could eat no dinner.

The O'Neills left Tao House two days later. "I know it has been *our last real home*," she lamented.

45

Still suffering silently, Carlotta moves with O'Neill into the Huntington on the bleak Saturday afternoon of February 26, 1944. Her pain isn't lessened by O'Neill's instant reaction to his new home. He hates the suite she has meticulously prepared for him.

The Huntington is among San Francisco's most elegant hotels, and the O'Neills' spacious suite includes a good-sized living room, two bedrooms with adjoining baths, a dining alcove, and a kitchenette (to supplement room service meals). But O'Neill can't help resenting it for not being Tao House, and Carlotta, trying not to add to his misery, continues to ignore her own worsening physical condition.

Soon, however, she is forced to see a doctor, who diagnoses an infected bladder, places her on sulfadiazine, and orders her to bed, where she collapses with a high temperature and has to be nursed by the faithful Kaye Albertoni.

O'Neill, as anxious as he is about Carlotta, is further distressed to learn of the death of Harry Weinberger on the following day. "Twenty-eight years of friendship," he writes to Nathan. "I only hope he knew the depth of my affection for him—and I feel sure he did." He also confesses to Nathan he has dosed himself with bromide and chloral to get his hand steady enough to write this letter legibly, explaining that Carlotta is too ill to type it for him.

When O'Neill comes to sit by Carlotta's bed, she notes that he is "in a shocking state." Far more distressing than either Weinberger's death or Carlotta's collapse is O'Neill's pounding conviction that he will never write another play. As Carlotta is all too aware, he has been trying to deny this by tinkering with *A Moon for the Misbegotten*, and tweaking *A Touch of the Poet* and *Hughie* (sulkily working in his bedroom because he no longer has a study).

O'Neill recently has told Lawrence Langner he fears there will be no more plays because he is rapidly losing all ability to use a pencil. As Carlotta's health improves, he attempts to dictate bits of dialogue and stage directions to her, but finds it impossible. Langner thinks the stumbling block might be the presence of another person in the room, even someone as close to him as his wife; he sends O'Neill a newly invented recording machine called a SoundScriber.

O'Neill writes Langner that he has started experimenting by reading "a favorite bit" from *The Iceman Cometh* into the machine's microphone.

It is the passage, O'Neill tells Langner, wherein Hickey forces Larry Slade "to admit, while refusing to admit, that his saving dream—that he is finished with life and sick of it and will welcome the long sleep of death—is just a pipe dream."

O'Neill read the harrowing bit while stricken with "the inner shakes," which he said, you feel "all over your body until even your brain seems to do the shimmy."

When he played the record back, he heard the voice that was his and yet not his: "I'm afraid to live, am I?—and even more afraid to die . . . and praying, 'Oh, Blessed Christ, let me live a little longer at any price! . . . let me still clutch greedily to my yellow heart this sweet treasure, this jewel beyond price, the dirty, stinking bit of flesh which is my beautiful little life!'—well, it sure did something to me. It wasn't Larry, it was my ghost talking to me, or I to my ghost. . . . It really was quite a moment of strange drama."

But when O'Neill tries, with Carlotta's encouragement, to dictate dialogue, or any sort of creative amendment to the three plays with which he is still puttering, he finds it impossible. Carlotta, although disappointed, is hardly surprised; she has heard him explain more than once that his thoughts flow from his brain, through his arm, and into his pencil; there is no other process by which he can write.

O'NEILL KNOWS (and refuses to know) that he will never write another play. Perhaps without conscious thought he has already devised a sly way to compensate for his inability to write a new tragedy; he will, instead, spin one in his mind and then perform it on the stage of his life.

He had cast his leading lady long ago when he eloped with Carlotta, and he has seen signs of her readiness to take on a new role; after years of playing the protective mother of a querulous semi-invalid who is trying to outrun time, she is, O'Neill surmises, ready to adopt the new role in which he plans to cast her (with Strindberg's collegial approbation)— that of fiery antagonist.

He's right. Carlotta is feeling mentally and physically bruised. "Even a mule has a breaking point!" she acidly notes, when she has failed to regain her strength by the end of March. And when she is finally back on her feet in mid-April, she complains she is "just weary unto death from being worked beyond my endurance."

Among his other offenses, O'Neill peremptorily asks her to assume payment of all their living expenses in San Francisco because he's temporarily broke; grudgingly, she agrees.

Sounding like Mary Tyrone, Carlotta complains of the Huntington suite that O'Neill hates, "Keeping up the ridiculous fantasy that this is a home!" She can hardly be blamed if she mourns the enchanted world she created fifteen years ago as the chatelaine of a French castle, not to mention as the wife of America's most acclaimed dramatist. Now, having presided over two more grand residences, she is adrift.

The man to whom Carlotta has bound herself is all but forgotten by the public, stubbornly keeping his new plays to himself and depriving himself and his wife of income. She feels cheated out of her onetime role as the glamorous consort of the adulated international wunderkind of the American drama.

Her grand isolation in the hills of Northern California had, in recent months, felt like a sentence to house arrest. No matter how fervently she has always echoed O'Neill's own genuine horror of public mingling, and no matter how she has (with him) disparaged the superficiality of the Broadway scene and the social bustle of life in New York, she privately misses both. (It would be a wonder if she didn't.)

Locked inside the martyred mother-nurse-secretary she voluntarily became is the once-fabled beauty who preened in her fashionable gowns and jewels as she attended select social gatherings at the side of the Great Dramatist, or presided over discreet dinner parties for notable men and women who acknowledged her role as O'Neill's muse.

Much as she always professed to share O'Neill's frustration over the production of his plays, she felt at home in the theater among the actors, directors, and producers who were her own former peers. It has been a long, long time since she has had that sort of gratification.

Although an aura of romance still hovers over the marriage, Carlotta, like O'Neill, has suffered wounds that will never heal. Time and again, she has warned herself that O'Neill, without the release of his writing, would implode.

Now, as O'Neill embarks on the tragicomic improvisation written only in his mind, Carlotta is about to see her prophecy fulfilled.

It is to be a Grand Guignol that she will later sardonically describe as "a little drama in the home."

The Huntington family hotel is where O'Neill's unwritten but intensely lived "little drama" begins, and the young woman he will cast as his ingenue is conveniently close at hand. The plot is motivated by O'Neill's overwhelming urge to relive a passionate episode of his youth:

his romance (at twenty-six) with Beatrice Ashe, the teasing, pretty nineteen-year-old New London girl he wooed with passionate poetry and letters, but couldn't win.

THIS TIME (at fifty-five) his object is the twenty-three-year-old Jane Caldwell, who reminds him of the flirtatious Beatrice.

The O'Neills anticipate a longish stay in San Francisco—at least until the German part of the war is over (as O'Neill writes to Nathan in March, three months before the Allied invasion of Normandy). Eager to secure a confidante for the duration of her stay, Carlotta has redoubled her hospitality toward Myrtle Caldwell, to whom she still feels grateful for her intervention in the recent incident with the masseuse at Tao House.

Carlotta also welcomes Myrtle's daughter Jane, pleased to have her do some desultory typing for O'Neill; soon both mother and daughter are frequent visitors to the Huntington, and Carlotta is relieved that O'Neill finds them an enjoyable distraction. Able to concentrate on work for an hour or so every day, he gives Jane minor corrections to type for his manuscripts of *A Moon for the Misbegotten*, *A Touch of the Poet*, and *Hughie*. Thus begins O'Neill's misbegotten courtship of the young woman he calls "Janie," and his declaration of war on his already hostile wife.

Carlotta at first sees no threat from Janie, who had occasionally typed for O'Neill at Tao House (during his writing of *Long Day's Journey* and *The Iceman Cometh*) and with whom O'Neill had formed a casual friendship. Carlotta appears not to have noticed that their pretty, girlish guest has been evolving and is now a sensual woman, nor does she seem to notice that O'Neill's behavior toward her has changed.

Kaye Albertoni, during her own extended visits to the O'Neills' Huntington suite, is startled to observe that O'Neill kisses Janie on her mouth in greeting. Kaye, who marvels at Carlotta's forbearance, refrains from commenting on this perceived unseemliness, thinking, "It's up to her"; but, as Kaye later remarks, she does not have "a good feeling, watching them."

According to Janie, Kaye has assumed the role of nurse-companion to O'Neill, mainly to take the burden off Carlotta. "O'Neill doesn't really need a nurse," says Janie. "He can shave himself and his tremor isn't that noticeable." Janie believes that Carlotta exaggerates his illness to keep people away from him.

Carlotta had heretofore never doubted that O'Neill's relationship with Janie was avuncular. In fact, Carlotta was herself much taken with the vivacious young woman. At dinner one evening in Tao House, Carlotta had been extolling O'Neill's lovable qualities to the Caldwells, and had fondly declared she could live in a tent with him. Carlotta was amused when Janie blurted, "Well, who couldn't?"

Janie recalls that those were "almost the first words I said to him." As a consequence, O'Neill gave her a book of his collected plays inscribed, "From one about to order a tent" and signed "Uncle Gene." Janie suggests that might have been "a forerunner of what was going to come."

Carlotta had sent Janie notes and gifts, including (on January 1, 1942) a snapshot of O'Neill sitting on the end of a diving board in his bathing trunks (taken at Big Wolf Lake in the Adirondacks). Addressing her as "Janie Sweet," she wrote, "I thought this would make you smile. You are a good child—and I love you!"

At the Huntington, Janie and O'Neill sit at separate desks in O'Neill's bedroom with the door closed. On most days, O'Neill declares his work day over at eleven, and he and Janie and Carlotta—sometimes joined by Myrtle and/or Kaye—have coffee. In the living room, O'Neill puts on a record and invites Janie to dance with him.

She is impressed with his record collection, to which he continues to add; he has employed a Mr. Hollis to flesh out his music library, explaining he is "especially weak in 1910–30." When Mr. Hollis sends him a list of available recordings, O'Neill requests all those made by Al Jolson, Frank Tinney, and Nora Bayes, plus "The Song Is Ended," "Wistful and Blue," and "Sam, the Old Accordion Man."

"I have quite a few of [Ruth] Etting already," writes O'Neill. "Re the Hoosier Ha-chas, if you could send them all to me, I would imagine there would be a lot I would want because they revive so much of popular forgotten stuff. The same applies to Frank Novak and his Rootin-Tootin Boys, about as terrible an aggregation of orchestra and chorus as ever drenched the air. But somehow I love them because I remember the tunes played by just such orchestras, 5th rate Ted Lewis, and joining in choruses myself which contain just as many flats."

To give Mr. Hollis a more rounded sense of his eclectic taste, O'Neill mentions his affection for Irving Berlin's "I Love a Piano," "That Mysterious Rag," and "At the Devil's Ball," as well as Al Jolson's "Don't Blame It All on Broadway," which he describes as "a beautiful lament and apology" for that world-famous thoroughfare. When sung "with upturned eyes by a well-stewed waiter endowed with the proper adenoids, it positively wrung you to pieces!"

O'Neill's doctor has told Carlotta it's good for him to dance. "That is the fun part," Janie recalls. "That's when he begins whispering sweet nothings in my ear; and Carlotta is sitting there, sometimes my mother is sitting there, and I am dying—right in my ear! And it is sweet. And I laugh and laugh—I bend over with laughter."

Janie's mother warns her about Carlotta's jealousy, saying she can "see it coming." Janie cannot fathom Carlotta's apparent blindness to what's going on. "If my mother senses it, Carlotta should; but she doesn't."

One explanation might be that Carlotta, feeling remorse for her own little sexual jaunt with the masseuse, thinks O'Neill is entitled to a retaliatory fling, and is prepared to wait it out. But not indefinitely.

Janie, whose long hair was blonde when she first met O'Neill, has let it grow back to its natural light brown, which she believes O'Neill prefers. "He'd save my hair and use it as bookmarks," she recalls. "I thought that was pretty cool; I know that was pretty romantic." She is touched when, after failing to turn up at the Huntington on a weekend when she has a date, O'Neill tells her it was a "black weekend." But she doesn't take him nearly as seriously as he does her.

Janie is dating several young men, including the man she hopes to marry, and she is accustomed to being flattered and courted. Although she concedes, after a time, that O'Neill has her heart—"not my body, my heart"—she feels she can keep the romance within bounds.

When O'Neill, one day in late May, complains to Carlotta that he has no privacy, Carlotta indignantly scribbles, "He hasn't a special 'study,' but he has an extra large bedroom" that she never enters "unless asked." She is even more outraged when, the next day, he asks her to find a better apartment, one that overlooks the Bay—fully aware that in the crowded wartime city he is asking the impossible. (She nonetheless goes through the motions of seeking another apartment, knowing her search is futile.)

In her diary, Carlotta initially attributes O'Neill's insensitivity toward her to his absorption with his work. "It is like the *slavery* of a man *wooing a woman he adores!*" she writes. His work "is his *love*, his *passion*, his *integrity*, his *joy*, his *achievement!*"

But she is at last unable to ignore the signs that O'Neill has begun to woo an actual woman he adores. Carlotta, in many ways narrow-minded and a bigot, is nonetheless shrewd and intuitive; less of a self-pitier than O'Neill, she can read him more clearly than he reads (or wants to read) her.

On August 6, Carlotta records that when Myrtle and Janie come to take her and O'Neill to their home for dinner, she notices "a queer smile on Genie's face"; she offers no explanation, but complains about the uncomfortably long drive to their house and back, and the fact that at dinner "they drink and we don't." After sitting together in glum silence in their suite, O'Neill mutters, "God, I wish I could drink a bottle of 'Old Taylor.'"

He resists the temptation, but he is casting about for a reason to quarrel with Carlotta, and, a few weeks later, he accuses her of "not being interested in his work." That was the charge O'Neill brought against Agnes (with Carlotta's encouragement) as a justification for his leaving her. Carlotta is deeply offended. Although she frequently protests (in her diary and to one or two intimates) that she suffers O'Neill's "sadistic" stabs silently, she knows how to be cruel to him in her turn.

Janie recalls a time when Carlotta is angry at O'Neill and spitefully serves him his luncheon soup in a shallow bowl rather than his accustomed cup; instead of drinking the soup, he is obliged to use a spoon that he can barely hold in his trembling hand. He doesn't blink an eye, said Janie. "He just goes ahead and has his soup that way."

Although Janie recalled that O'Neill's tremor often is not noticeable, Kenneth Macgowan, on a visit to the Huntington, is shocked at how bad it is; when O'Neill attempts to inscribe a couple of sheets of his early poetry, "his hands are so unsteady that he writes the inscriptions with one hand helping the other to hold the pen."

Carlotta evidently believes she has persuaded O'Neill they will be more comfortable waiting out the war in New York, for at the end of July (1944), she begins negotiating to reserve a drawing room on the so-called streamliner train going east in October and books a suite at the Gotham Hotel on Fifth Avenue in Manhattan for November 14. But O'Neill doesn't really want to leave San Francisco.

On September 21, after wangling to reserve the train tickets, Carlotta notes her worry about O'Neill's fluctuating mind-set. "Gene changes every day as to *where* we should go & *what* do! Has even mentioned South Africa—& Mexico!"

O'Neill receives a reprieve when, on October 10, his doctor cautions him against leaving California so late in the year. "We can't go East until spring," a resigned Carlotta tells her diary, "winter too dangerous for us."

A week later O'Neill celebrates his fifty-sixth birthday by visiting what he calls "a really swell columbarium." Describing the trip to Carl Van Vechten, he writes, "California, as is well known, leads the world in the swellness of its columbariums designed, apparently, to keep the dead lively, cheerful and constantly amused." He had intended "to price a few snappy urns," just by way of safeguarding his future, but neither the "curator of the dump" nor he could make themselves heard above "the roaring of ten thousand savage canary birds and horrid gush of fancy fountains," so it all came to nothing. He had left the place swearing he would live forever "to spite those damned canaries" and vowing that his next pet bird would be a buzzard.

O'Neill was still in a macabre mood when Sophus and Eline Winther visited the Huntington a week later. "He stood there," recalls Winther, "tall and slender, his arms folded in the way he could best control the shaking of his hands, and said, 'Remember that this is what I want on my tombstone:'"

EUGENE O'NEILL
There is something to be said
For being dead.

He shows the Winthers some of his early efforts at poetry and gives them *Hughie* to read. When they leave, he falls into a state of melancholy.

"Poor darling," records Carlotta, "life hasn't ever given him happiness—& never will—I now understand that I am useful (more so than he realizes) but am in no way a fulfillment to him . . . Nor would any woman be—"

In late November, O'Neill and Carlotta make the incomprehensible decision (which they will shortly rescind) to return to Sea Island and build a house there; they speak of being reunited with Freeman, who has agreed to accompany them to Georgia after his discharge from the Marines.

In a letter to Elizabeth Shepley Sergeant, whom O'Neill has come to address affectionately as "Essie," he explains this seemingly perverse decision: he and Carlotta left Sea Island, he says, "because we had been too blind to its virtues and too impatient of its minor defects." And Casa Genotta (like Tao House) had been too large for two people.

"We will not make that mistake again." (Eight years earlier, as they were about to abandon Sea Island, Carlotta had listed those "minor defects" in a letter to Eline Winther: "decay, heat, storms, snakes, insects, uninteresting people." She and O'Neill had been "idiots" to have settled in "a resort," she said. "Only fools with more money than brains ever live in resorts.)"

O'Neill goes on to bare his soul to Sergeant, who has never failed to respond with empathy; but not even to her does he mention his forlorn obsession with the twenty-three-year-old Janie Caldwell (although an intuitive reading between the lines might have alerted Sergeant to something troubling being suppressed).

"I haven't done a line of work in a long while," wrote O'Neill. "It came to a point where sickness, worry, and uncertainty kept piling one on top of another month after month." His "creative urge just balked." The worst of his Parkinson's, he continues, are the spells of melancholia. "God knows I have had enough of Celtic Twilight in my make-up without needing anymore of the same. And this isn't the same. It isn't sadness. It's an exhausted, horrible apathy."

After spending Christmas day with the Caldwells, Carlotta sourly notes (conspicuously not referring to her husband as "Gene"), "Janie and Eugene dance before and after dinner—& have much fun." On Carlotta's birthday four days later, Kaye Albertoni gives her a "surprise" party. "Quite a fuss for an old woman of 56!" she observes in her diary, mentioning the presence of her friend Myrtle, but not her daughter Janie.

O'Neill presents Carlotta with a check, together with what she listlessly describes as "a charming edition" of *Grimm's Fairy Tales*; in his inscription, he declares he has tried but failed to think of something "new" to say; he writes that he must fall back on "the one thing which retains its old deep meaning: My love and your love and my gratitude for your love," adding, somewhat lamely, "With that love we can grow old together without fear, even in this kind of world."

In view of O'Neill's hurtful behavior with Janie, Carlotta surely reads these words with considerable skepticism. She nonetheless sees fit to draw an emphatically plump pussycat at the bottom of her diary entry.

WHEN GERMANY SURRENDERS that May, Carlotta doesn't see how O'Neill can any longer postpone their departure from California. But, still atremble on the cloud of his romance with Janie, he clutches at new reasons for delay.

On a sunny day in June, Janie drives O'Neill and Carlotta to the beach so that he can glimpse his beloved ocean. Carlotta stays in the car; she is having trouble with her eyes again and, even with dark glasses, she can't tolerate the bright sunlight. She later mis-dates their drive to the beach as October 1944; it is one of numerous misleading notes and omissions in her sanitized diary regarding both Janie and Myrtle.

JANIE AND O'NEILL stroll at water's edge. After remarking how charming she looks in her purple coat with its high collar buttoned under her chin, he at last tells her she reminds him of Beatrice Ashe, his early love who proved to be unavailable despite the amorous poetry with which he wooed her. Thinking back to those poems, including one called "On the Beach," he murmurs a few lines of a new poem he is writing to Janie in his mind:

> We walked to the sea's edge,
> You and I,
> Driven in hopeless pilgrimage
> To beseech the sea
> For a moment's dream
> Of life's forgotten mystery.

Aware of Janie's fluttering responsiveness, O'Neill tells her he has fallen in love with her; he wants to marry her!

Janie, in a trance, feels she could stand there on the beach listening to

O'Neill forever. At the moment, she believes she truly returns his love. "If the ocean washes us away right now, it would be okay," she remembers thinking.

She soon realizes, though, that she has misread her own feelings and also misjudged the depth of O'Neill's. Years later, she acknowledged she was too inexperienced to cope with the situation: "If I'd known how to handle it, I might've—I don't know what I would've done—I didn't want—he was older, he was older, he was older—"

One day soon after the scene on the beach, Janie—after typing some minor revisions for *A Moon for the Misbegotten*—comes from O'Neill's bedroom into the living room, closely followed by O'Neill. She announces to Carlotta, "Oh, we finished the play." This is too much for Carlotta; she finally decides to notice what is happening. As Janie recalled, "The 'we' sets her off, and she lays into me. Who do I think I am? I'm not that important; she mentions about my 'flirty flirty eyes.'"

O'Neill intervenes: "Don't pay any attention to her," he tells Janie. "It doesn't mean anything."

But Janie is dismayed. Suddenly she feels the full impact of a situation well beyond what she can handle. "I don't know where that would have gone," she later mused. "I couldn't take care of him; I mean, I wasn't about to."

In any event, Carlotta has had it with her sweet Janie. She tells her to leave and not come back. As Janie is about to walk out, O'Neill pulls her aside and asks her to meet him at a neighborhood coffee shop on the following day, when he returns from a doctor's appointment; they need to iron things out, he pleads. Janie believes Carlotta's reaction "made O'Neill more intense about wanting to marry me." Fully aware now that she is in way over her head, Janie decides not to show up at the coffee shop.

"So that was it," she later recalled. "But I've never forgotten him. His eyes, and the beauty of speech he had—his laughter, his dancing, I loved to dance with him." Janie Caldwell married not long after and lived on, unaware of the disaster she was leaving in her wake.

O'NEILL, FOILED IN his pitiable attempt to relive his youth, is now at
Carlotta's mercy. Carlotta, in turn, can now openly exploit her role as
the betrayed wife of a philandering husband. The mutual resentment
they've barely managed to hold at bay erupts into a furious weeks-long
confrontation; it requires the frequent intervention not only of Nurse
Albertoni, but also of Carlotta's and O'Neill's doctors.

On the advice of those doctors, Albertoni gives both Carlotta and
O'Neill daily injections of potent sedatives. Carlotta stays in touch with
Myrtle by phone, but only to run down Janie. Kaye Albertoni is now
Carlotta's closest confidante. She becomes a sort of buffer, or mediator,
between Carlotta and O'Neill, Kaye recalled (mentioning that she her-
self never called O'Neill by his first name).

According to Kaye, "Carlotta would have such tantrums." She and
O'Neill hurl insults. She calls him "a nasty, dirty senile old man"; he
counters with accusations of her sexual betrayal with her masseuse. She
tells Kaye one morning that the only reason she has decided not to commit suicide is to spare Kaye from having to cope with the mess. But, she
tells Kaye, she would happily kill O'Neill.

After one argument, Carlotta asks Kaye to help her pack, as she is
leaving immediately for New York (which she knows is impossible, as the
war with Japan is still imposing restrictions on train travel). When Kaye
returns the following day, Carlotta tells her to keep O'Neill away from
her or she will kill him. A few days later, she describes to Kaye how
O'Neill, brandishing the pistol he has kept by him since purchasing it in
Bermuda, threatened to shoot her, and that she armed herself with a
butcher's knife in self-defense.

Then, says Carlotta, they both dropped their weapons and O'Neill
began choking her, after which he knocked her out. Kaye believes her
after she examines Carlotta's slightly swollen jaw, and later notices
O'Neill's slightly puffy right hand.

Despite all, within a few weeks Carlotta and O'Neill have negotiated a fragile truce. She has too much invested in him; she can't walk out before at least sharing the excitement of the upcoming Broadway production of *The Iceman Cometh*; if nothing else, a successful run could bring in enough cash to refresh her dwindling income. And can she really bring herself to abandon this ailing man who depends on her for every aspect of his well-being?

For his part, O'Neill is forced to acknowledge he has been deluding himself about the possibility of an independent existence; he knows full well his survival depends on Carlotta. And on whom would he vent his fury and frustration if they were to separate?

According to Kaye, Carlotta is more than ever eager to return to the East Coast, but O'Neill, blaming his ill health, is still reluctant to leave; perhaps he has not quite shed his illusory hope of somehow reuniting with Janie. But he knows he can't dangle indefinitely in the limbo in which he now finds himself.

When the atom bomb is dropped on Japan, ending the war shortly thereafter, Carlotta renews her pressure on O'Neill to return east; although he continues to procrastinate, citing his ill health, Carlotta begins pulling strings, chopping through red tape, and, for the second time, she secures train accommodations.

"I had everything packed and on the train," she recalls, "and just at the last moment Gene said, 'No, I don't think I want to go.' So I had to return to the public relations man at the railroad, thank him for his courtesy, and tell him I was very sorry, but Mr. O'Neill had changed his mind. He told me I needn't be sorry, he had a hundred people waiting for the canceled space."

In mid-September, O'Neill writes to George Jean Nathan: "Carlotta and I continue to suffer from ill health spells, and I'm so sick of this apartment I wish they'd give me a short stretch at Alcatraz just to enjoy the sea breezes, a change of view, and the interesting company." They are longing to return to New York, he tells Nathan, and "will surely make it by the end of March." But, he adds—thinking of his promise to the Theatre Guild to produce *The Iceman Cometh* after the war ends—"I have become so apathetic about the theater that I really don't give a damn whether any play of mine is produced again or not. I have to fake an interest."

Carlotta begins anew to pursue passage on a train east, but is unable to book space until almost the end of 1945.

While O'Neill confronts his return to New York (and the Broadway theater) with profound misgivings, Carlotta can't wait to get back.

PART V

UNRAVELING

46

O'Neill dreads his return to Broadway after his voluntary nine-year absence. Still unable to write and with the mock love affair behind him, he is about to recast himself on his fantasy stage—this time in the role of the returning exile, the ultimate hero of his own tragic fate.

Ostensibly, he has returned to prepare for the long-delayed production of *The Iceman Cometh*, as yet eleven months away, and he allows his spirits to momentarily soar. But he and Carlotta have carried with them that "little drama being practiced in the home." The thwarted dramatist and his complicit leading lady—henceforward poised to meet him halfway in battle—will soon find themselves mired in Strindbergian darkness.

All of O'Neill's philosophy of the tragic, for all these years channeled into his plays, is viscerally taking over his life and, by extension, Carlotta's. But why not? It is O'Neill himself who has pronounced it ill-judged "to think of tragedy as unhappy," citing the (more enlightened) Greeks and Elizabethans, who "saw their lives ennobled" by the tragic.

And isn't it O'Neill himself who sees life as "a gorgeously-ironical, beautifully-indifferent, splendidly-suffering bit of chaos the tragedy of which gives Man a tremendous significance, while without his losing fight with fate he would be a tepid, silly animal"?

Then elaborating on the credo formulated years earlier:

"I say 'losing fight' only symbolically for the brave individual always wins. Fate can never conquer his—or her—spirit. So you see I'm no pessimist. On the contrary, in spite of my scars, I'm tickled to death with life!"

Has not O'Neill suggested, as well, that "The tragedy of life is what makes it worthwhile," adding that "any life which merits living lies in the effort to realize some dream, and the higher that dream is the harder it is to realize. Most decidedly we must all have our dreams. If one hasn't them, one might as well be dead—one is dead. The only success is in failure. Any man who has a big enough dream must be a failure and must accept that as one of the conditions of being alive. If he ever thinks for a moment that he is a success then he is finished."

Moreover, O'Neill has long since provided himself with what some might consider a casuistic alibi: "If a person is to get the meaning of life, he must learn to like the facts about himself—ugly as they may seem to his sentimental vanity—before he can lay hold on the truth behind the facts; and that truth is never ugly!" If that is what O'Neill still believes, it lets him off the hook about his sometimes outrageous behavior, including his recent folly with Janie Caldwell.

Lawrence Langner finds O'Neill, upon his arrival in New York in late November 1945, looking aged and gaunt; but he is soon pleased to see the moody dramatist's spirits rising. Langner believes it is O'Neill's return to the theater that is "doing wonders in bringing him back" to physical and spiritual health.

O'Neill has been readying his manuscript of *Iceman* for production but he is in no hurry, for it will be many months before rehearsals begin. The active life he now chooses to embrace with friends he hasn't seen in many months—for him the equivalent of a wild social whirl—appears to soothe his nerves.

He and Carlotta have moved into a two-room suite in the Barclay Hotel at 111 East Forty-eighth Street, while Carlotta searches the crowded postwar city for an apartment to rent.

"I never want to build again," she writes to the Winthers in Seattle. What she does want is to live in a small New York apartment for six or seven months a year and also "*rent* a *small* place in Sea Island or wherever Gene wants to go."

She evidently has chosen to forget that O'Neill has always claimed to hate living in New York. Perhaps she reasons that, as he is no longer writing, he will now adjust to city living. The subject, which launches an ongoing battle, is held in abeyance pending the production of *Iceman*.

Soon after arriving in New York, O'Neill dictates to Carlotta a letter for Kenneth Macgowan, updating his plans. *Iceman* will begin rehearsals in September 1946, he says, to be followed at the beginning of 1947 by either *A Moon for the Misbegotten* or *A Touch of the Poet*. Macgowan has asked if he might "grab" for himself the SoundScriber that O'Neill has rejected as useless in writing creatively. He receives a startling refusal: "I have simply got to learn how to use it when I start being creative again, which probably means when we go to Sea Island . . . on May first." (The O'Neills were planning a four-month stay in Georgia prior to the beginning of rehearsals for *Iceman*. As it turned out, they did not go, nor did O'Neill ever learn to use the SoundScriber.)

One of O'Neill's first forays in New York is to Random House, where he ceremoniously consigns to his publisher, Bennett Cerf, the final version of *Long Day's Journey Into Night*, to be placed in a safe with instructions that it not be published until twenty-five years after his death.

Another early stop is the northeast corner of Broadway and Forty-third Street, the site of his birthplace. Here is where once stood the family hotel called the Barrett House. Built to the imposing height of eight stories in 1883, five years before he was born, the hotel's gabled tower with its embedded clock was a landmark for uptown residents and visitors who traversed the cobblestone streets in horse-drawn carriages.

O'Neill had been saddened to learn, in 1940, while still living at Tao House, that the hotel—renamed the Cadillac—had been torn down; he thought back to the many times over the years when he'd pointed out to friends the third-floor room in which he was born. "Every time I go past, I look up," he once said. "Third window from Broadway on the Forty-third Street side. I can remember my father pointing it out to me."

In at least one instance, he impetuously hustled a friend to room 236, knocked on the door, explained his mission to the startled occupants, and was granted permission to look around. Now, he complained, he hardly recognized the area. "There is only empty air now where I came into this world," he quipped.

Joe Heidt, the Theatre Guild's press agent, is O'Neill's designated escort. He takes him, sometimes with Carlotta, to hockey games and bicycle races. O'Neill also goes out on the town with Winfield Aronberg, the attorney who has succeeded Harry Weinberger. They go to ball games, prizefights, and the race track (where O'Neill is a ten-dollar bettor), and they delight in hitting the jazz clubs that line Fifty-second Street. "Once in a while," Aronberg recalls, "Gene will take a sip of a drink just for appearances."

O'Neill seems to be enjoying a remission of his "sinking feelings," as well as his difficulty in walking. Carlotta has no faith in the bursts of energy her husband has been displaying since his return to New York; she fears that his near-manic behavior portends an imminent collapse, but she feels helpless to rein him in.

Aronberg earlier endeared himself to O'Neill by negotiating a financial settlement with Agnes that relieved him of annual alimony payments (and enabled Agnes to marry Mack Kaufman). The settlement does not endear Aronberg to Carlotta, who thinks it's overly generous; she is no more enamored of him than she was of Weinberger. When Aronberg, who finds her "too much of the grande dame," tells O'Neill, "She hates my guts," O'Neill does not contradict him.

Aronberg is also of service to O'Neill in dealing with Shane, with whom he has been out of touch for some time; in a letter to Eugene Jr. a few months before leaving California, O'Neill speculated about the chasm that had been steadily widening between himself and his younger son.

Shane, wrote O'Neill, "is like me but also very different from me, as far as a relationship with a father goes." He was referring to Agnes's role in "pulling" Shane from him, ignoring his own virtual abandonment of his son.

Leading up to that difference, O'Neill told Eugene Jr., who had by then read the script of *Long Day's Journey*, "My family's quarrels and tragedy were within. To the outer world we maintained an indomitably united front and lied and lied for each other. A typical pure Irish family.

"The same loyalty occurs, of course, in all kinds of families, but there is, I think, among Irish still close to, or born in Ireland, a strange mixture of fight and hate and forgive, a clannish pride before the world, that is peculiarly its own. Well, there is nothing like that in Shane's past. He has a background all torn apart, without inner or outer decency."

Nevertheless, Shane's biography up to this point has not differed all that much from his father's youthful searching. After quitting school, Shane tried (and failed) at various attempts to support himself. In 1941, instead of shipping out on a clipper ship like his father, he joined the Merchant Marine, and two years later he was hospitalized with battle fatigue.

When O'Neill and Carlotta arrive in New York, Shane is working at an electrical-fixture factory and living in a cold-water flat on King Street in Greenwich Village with Catherine Givens, to whom he has been married since the summer of 1944. Eugene Jr. has moved into the same building to keep a brotherly eye on Shane, as he reports to his father. O'Neill responds, "Tell Shane to call me, I'd like to see him."

Cathy Givens is eight months pregnant and feels shy about meeting her in-laws for the first time in this condition, so Shane goes alone to dine with his father and Carlotta at the Barclay Hotel. "We got along well together," he reports to Cathy. Carlotta is interested to learn about the expected baby, and O'Neill says he is eager to meet Cathy. On November 19, Shane telephones his father to announce the birth of a boy, who has been named Eugene in his grandfather's honor.

O'Neill, pleased, says he would like to see the baby. Carlotta visits Cathy at French Hospital in downtown Manhattan, bringing a plant and candy; Cathy is impressed with Carlotta's stylish appearance and with her nonstop chatter. O'Neill did not come with her, Carlotta apologizes, because he isn't feeling well; but the next moment she explains that the real reason is his fear he might run into Agnes. For the same reason, O'Neill doesn't accompany Carlotta when she visits the King Street flat, bringing a complete layette for the baby.

Cathy sees that Carlotta is "uncomfortable about our cold-water flat and its meager furnishings." She preaches to Cathy about the importance of a young couple's standing on their own feet, and tells her she will soon invite her and Shane to dinner so she can finally meet her father-in-law. A few weeks later, the invitation is issued.

Cathy, who has been "sort of" expecting "the old sailor, the saloon guy" she has read about, instead finds herself in the company of "a very elegant man." She is impressed by the dinner, served in the O'Neill suite by a hotel waiter; it is accompanied by wine, which O'Neill barely sips, explaining he is "in temperance." They converse pleasantly, O'Neill asking first about the baby, then switching to literature and discovering that Cathy is quite well-read. Shane pleases his father by talking with animation about jazz, which Carlotta chooses to disparage as "savage" music, "the music of Negroes" who "go by their instincts." As Cathy drily notes, "None of us commented much on her views of jazz."

The older O'Neills continue to see both Shane and Catherine at intervals until early the following year, when their cordial relationship ends abruptly.

On February 10, 1946, at 2:03 p.m., Eugene O'Neill III, aged two months and twenty-four days, is rushed to St. Vincent's Hospital. The examining doctor pronounces him dead on arrival. An autopsy is performed the next day by Dr. Peter Castiglia, of the Chief Medical Examiner's Office at Bellevue.

For his report, Dr. Castiglia interviews Shane, who tells him Catherine last saw the infant Eugene alive and well at 4:00 a.m. on February 10. At noon, she awoke and found him in his crib, not breathing.

"The infant showed evidence of neglect," Castiglia states in his report, "with maceration of scrotal tissue and abdomen, probably the result of unchanged diapers." The death certificate lists the probable cause of death as "postural asphyxia from bed-clothes, accidental."

The infant's death would have been a stunning blow for any grandfather; for O'Neill, still emotionally bruised from having relived his mother's anguish over losing her infant son, Edmund, it was more than enough to unhinge him. Melancholy Irish visionary that he was—disciple of Shakespeare and Aeschylus, a man who was living a Strindbergian tragedy—the death of Eugene O'Neill III must have seemed like the fulfillment of an evil prophecy. Shane and Catherine had several more children, but O'Neill (according to Carlotta) never saw them again—although on several occasions, as Shane's mental and physical health deteriorated, O'Neill sent Aronberg to assist him with cash and legal help.

IN A MOVE that strikes some of their friends as ghoulish, Carlotta and O'Neill, in late April 1946, leave the Barclay Hotel and take over the penthouse apartment at 35 East Eighty-fourth Street, vacated after the death of Edward Sheldon, the once-celebrated playwright. Sheldon, who had been blind and partially paralyzed for twenty years, had succumbed to a coronary thrombosis that April 1. O'Neill, always at home with his own ghosts, is spiritually attuned to that of his tragic fellow dramatist.

Years earlier, he had sent Sheldon a warm response to his congratulatory wire about *The Great God Brown*:

> You are one of the rare ones who really understand and have
> a spiritual right to speak, and be listened to whether of
> praise or blame. And I have always felt that we should be,
> and would be friends—(not that you haven't proved very
> much of a friend already as far as my work is concerned!)—if
> my good fortune should ever be to meet you.

Possibly Carlotta finds the atmosphere of her new home less congenial, although she labors, as always, to refurbish the space with O'Neill's comfort in mind; she decorates the six large rooms in bright colors, moves in some of their stored furniture, and buys a canary (not, as

O'Neill had threatened, a buzzard), which she names Jeremiah, and which helps compensate just a bit for their still painful loss of Blemie.

O'Neill buys his first television set so he can watch prizefights, but he mistrusts it, and when the picture fades during a particularly suspenseful bout, he feels insulted and demands that the set be removed the next day.

For the most part, however, he continues in his newly adopted role as a normal social animal; he encourages Carlotta to give small dinners, they dine out with friends, they occasionally attend movies and the theater. But this time, it is Carlotta who feels the stress of an extended urban existence and whose nerves are beginning to fray.

A conciliatory note written by O'Neill to Carlotta on their seventeenth wedding anniversary indicates, despite its warm salutation, that all has not been well between them.

> With the same old love deep in my heart I felt for you on
> that day in Paris, 1929! I wish you could say the same,
> forgiving as I forgive, all the mistakes and injuries done one
> to another through thoughtlessness or lack of understanding.
> In justice, as everyone but ourselves seems to know, our
> marriage has been the most successful and happy of any we
> know—until late years. Here's for a new beginning!

O'NEILL IS NOW devoting his full attention to the production of *The Iceman Cometh*. It has been nearly six years since he last had a play on Broadway, the doomed *Days Without End*, his valentine to the wife he loved with such passionate abandon that it had blinded him to the play's defects. Perhaps, in one of his mind's smoky tunnels, he blames the play's ill-conceived concept on his hyperbolic adoration of Carlotta at that time.

THE PROMINENT ACTOR and director Eddie Dowling has long since agreed to play Hickey, as well as direct *The Iceman Cometh*. George Jean Nathan had introduced O'Neill to Dowling in 1939 in San Francisco, where he was starring in Saroyan's *The Time of Your Life*, which he'd also directed (and which won the 1940 Pulitzer Prize for drama).

O'Neill had given Dowling *Iceman* to read during one of his several visits to Tao House. As Dowling recalled, O'Neill told him, "This is the wrong time for this play. Tragic as the characters are in my play, after all, what are they? Just a roomful of broken men. But there's a bastard in Germany breaking a world. We'll have to wait until they bury this fellow and the world gets more back on keel before I'll allow this play to be done."

Now it was a question of waiting for Dowling to end his run in the play he'd taken on after *The Time of Your Life*—Tennessee Williams's first Broadway success, *The Glass Menagerie*, which Dowling directed and starred in as Tom Wingfield, the play's narrator. When at last faced with readying *Iceman* for production, Dowling realized he couldn't both perform and direct, and he chose to direct, casting the veteran character actor James Barton as Hickey. "I became not only O'Neill's director, I practically became his nurse," recalls Dowling. For a time, he accepts Carlotta's apparently spiteful caution that O'Neill is "completely helpless, can't go to the gents' room without somebody assisting."

Dowling tries to follow her instructions to light O'Neill's cork-tipped cigarettes and lift his coffee cup for him. "She said I couldn't leave him for a minute."

Soon, however, Dowling is convinced Carlotta was exaggerating, and it isn't long before O'Neill expresses his resentment.

"Eddie, I can take care of myself," said O'Neill.

"Well," replied Dowling, "Carlotta told me all the things that I should do for you, Gene. I don't want you to think that I mind. It's a great honor to help you, I'm happy to do it. But I'd be twice as happy if I thought you could do them yourself. So I won't offer to do anything unless you ask me."

"I'll tell you, Eddie, when I need you."

The Broadway opening for *The Iceman Cometh* is set for October 9, but because O'Neill once again has declined to submit to a pre-Broadway tryout, the Theatre Guild has allotted an extended rehearsal period. The Guild has assigned a young production assistant, Sherlee Weingarten, to provide O'Neill with secretarial assistance. Sherlee is a slender, pretty, dark-haired woman with large blue eyes; in her early twenties, she is gifted with a rare sense of tact and empathy and quickly endears herself to O'Neill.

"At our first meeting I was scared," she later recalled. "O'Neill had been an institution to me. The day after we were introduced, he was given a little office at the Guild, where he arranged to come every afternoon at two o'clock. He was in his office ahead of me the first day he came in to work, and when I arrived he stood up."

"Please don't stand up, you don't have to do that sort of thing in an office," Sherlee murmurs.

"But offices would be so much more pleasant if men would observe the rules," O'Neill replies.

Unlike Dowling, Sherlee finds O'Neill to be somewhat incapacitated. She recalls his accepting a proffered cup of tea, but because of his trembling hands he cannot bring it to his lips.

Embarrassed for his sake, Sherlee remarks that the day is too warm for tea and suggests O'Neill might prefer Coca-Cola. O'Neill, embarrassed by Sherlee's embarrassment, agrees, and she fetches him a bottle and two straws, which he accepts with relief.

Sherlee works with O'Neill almost daily, typing not only the final edited script of *Iceman* but also his revised versions of *A Moon for the Misbegotten* and *A Touch of the Poet*. O'Neill grows so dependent on Sherlee's assistance that he asks her to be present at all rehearsals.

O'Neill smokes "a lot," recalled Sherlee, and it's a struggle for him to light a cigarette because of his tremor. Thinking it will discomfort him if she lights his cigarette every time he reaches for one, she takes one too; that way, she says, she can light his without making a production of it. The price is that she becomes "a cigarette fiend." (In an inscription to her copy of *Iceman*, O'Neill thanks her for "all the kindnesses in the many small things that only the sensitive do, or the sensitive appreciate.")

Carlotta accepts Sherlee with the same warmth she initially offered Janie Caldwell, apparently believing O'Neill has learned his lesson; she is also reassured by Sherlee's impending marriage to Steve Alexander, the production assistant on *Iceman*. Sherlee responds happily to Carlotta's affection and is invited to dinner at the O'Neill penthouse on several occasions.

Carlotta is less sanguine about O'Neill's mild flirtations with the three young actresses who have been cast as the status-conscious prostitutes who insist they are "tarts" rather than whores. O'Neill has personally chosen Marcella Markham to play Cora (the chattel of the saloon's daytime bartender, Chuck Morello). Marcella, who has vivid red hair and is a student of the Stanislavski method, asks O'Neill at a rehearsal one day, "Have you ever really known a Cora?"

"Now, Marcella," O'Neill chides, "do you want to know, did I know a Cora, or how well did I know a Cora?" Marcella blushes, and O'Neill smiles at her confusion. "He loved to tease the girls in the play," recalled Marcella, "not only me, but Ruth Gilbert whom he knew from *Ah, Wilderness!*" (Gilbert had played the adolescent Muriel McComber.)

Once during a rehearsal, Marcella recalled, O'Neill happened to overhear a kidding conversation she was having with one of the actors, who was propositioning her; she tells him he is "marvelous, but doesn't have the right smell." O'Neill teases the actor, "Too bad, boy."

When the actor walks away, O'Neill asks Marcella, "Do I have the right smell?"

"Positively," responds Marcella.

Later, she recalled, he is "the most gentlemanly man I've ever known." Even though he is ailing, Marcella said, he has a remarkable vitality.

She is unaware that this newfound vitality springs from his long-unaccustomed and joyful interaction with the many colleagues and friends who have welcomed him with warmth and obvious adulation into their own stimulating environments.

Only Carlotta (and her domestic staff) know that he returns home exhausted and collapses into unmasked physical and emotional fatigue, from which he doesn't recover without steely effort.

IN EARLY FALL, during the period allotted for dress rehearsals, Dowling arranges for the entire *Iceman* cast of nineteen, together with O'Neill and himself, to lunch at Gilhuly's, a respectable, old-fashioned Irish saloon, out of place in the seedy area of raunchy bars, pawnshops, and porn movie houses of Eighth Avenue.

As they walk the short distance uptown from the Martin Beck Theatre on Forty-fifth Street (later renamed the Al Hirschfeld)—the actors in costume and makeup, looking like bums and streetwalkers—they notice that half a dozen real bums have fallen in with them, apparently thinking they are joining some fellow derelicts.

When the group arrives at Gilhuly's, the owner, who recognizes O'Neill and Dowling but not all the actors, starts throwing out some of the *Iceman* cast along with the genuine bums. O'Neill asks Gilhuly to let them all stay, and the real bums lunch along with the actors as O'Neill's guests.

Another time, when just O'Neill and Dowling are about to enter Gilhuly's for lunch, a tall heavyset man with a black Vandyke beard approaches them and, to Dowling's surprise, addresses O'Neill as "Dad." It is Eugene Jr. He asks if he can look in on a dress rehearsal, and Dowling invites him to come to the theater that afternoon. Eugene tells his father the production is wonderful.

After rehearsal that evening, although a light rain is falling, O'Neill decides to walk all the way home from the Martin Beck to his East Eighty-fourth Street apartment. Dowling, fearing the walk might be too much for O'Neill, decides to accompany him. As they walk, O'Neill talks about Eugene with warmth and admiration for his accomplishments as a scholar.

Eugene attends several more rehearsals, and his father is always glad to see him at the theater, for it has become uncomfortable for father and son to meet in O'Neill's apartment.

Carlotta's disapproval of Eugene's leftist political affiliations has grown into open hostility. "He changed suddenly; he grew a beard, a fat belly from drinking and became a Communist," she later recalled. Eugene enjoys taunting her. "How's the old Tory?" becomes his habitual greeting whenever he and Carlotta happen to meet.

The beard was grown as payment for an election bet and was considered rather attractive by Eugene's friends. The fat belly was barely noticeable, for Eugene's large frame could carry considerable weight. It's true he was a heavy drinker, but none of his friends considered him an alcoholic; at his worst, he never matched his father's youthful excesses. Eugene had been antiwar (as his father, with better reason, had been in 1914). Nonetheless, Eugene had made a contribution to the war effort, working in two factories that supplied military weaponry; when called up by his draft board, he was turned down because of his childhood injury (the result of his bicycle accident). He then tried to get into the OSS (predecessor of the CIA) but was rejected.

Now thirty-six, Eugene is teaching the classics at Yale, and has co-edited a two-volume edition of Greek drama, which is acknowledged as a major scholarly accomplishment. But his personal life has grown increasingly unstable. He is divorced from his third wife, Sally, and is living with a woman named Ruth Lander, who is separated from her husband. His radical politics, heavy drinking, and messy love life are beginning to draw censure from his colleagues.

Yale is beginning to have misgivings about him. According to his close friend Frank Meyer, Eugene is "running away from his real gifts and diverting his real talent." In May 1944, while still teaching at Yale, he became a radio announcer at WTIC in Hartford, Connecticut. This led to a fifteen-minute Sunday-morning program during which he discussed such erudite subjects as *Marius the Epicurean* and Cicero's *Orations.*

Eugene's father may have been among the few who understood what he was talking about and he enjoyed engaging Eugene in intellectual discourse by mail. Acknowledging that the brief time span of the program precluded analysis in depth, O'Neill wrote:

"What would have interested me would have been to show the importance of Oratory in Cicero's time and the period in our history when the orations, not speeches, of our Senators had a comparable importance—the pre–Civil War period of Webster, Hayne, Calhoun, etc."

After the program had run its brief course, Eugene also had a fling as a panelist on a television program, but he began arriving at the studio in various degrees of intoxication and was soon disinvited.

O'Neill professes to be far less perturbed by Eugene's increasingly aimless lifestyle than Carlotta, and refuses to intervene when she and Eugene argue. "Gene just sits there and never interferes," says Carlotta. After Eugene leaves, Carlotta tells her husband, "I make a home for you; how can you sit there and let him talk to me that way? And Gene says, 'Why don't you leave the room when he comes? Why don't you go into the bedroom?'"

THE IMPENDING BROADWAY OPENING of the first new O'Neill play in more than twelve years, coupled with O'Neill's personal reemergence from isolation, does not go unheralded by the press. He gives multiple interviews to reporters and patiently answers questions posed by magazine writers who are preparing extended profiles. Most of the reporters find him genial and expansive, if physically frail.

In early August, two months before the premiere, O'Neill sits on the terrace of his penthouse with the *New York Post* columnist Earl Wilson (presumably having forgiven him for his interview with Oona), and tells him his wife can't join them because she's "terribly busy killing cockroaches in the kitchen." When O'Neill later tells Carlotta of his quip, she is not amused. Humorlessly, she phones Wilson, who solemnly reports in his column that Carlotta "didn't like the joke at all" and that she told him "pretty severely" that she'd been busy cataloguing O'Neill's books and that "they DO NOT have cockroaches."

A few weeks later, O'Neill grants George Jean Nathan an exclusive interview, in which he discusses not only his current work, but also a jocular scheme to join Nathan in opening a saloon. He informs his old friend that he has been unable to cut *The Iceman Cometh* by more than fifteen minutes. "If there are repetitions, they'll have to remain in, because I feel they are absolutely necessary to what I am trying to get over."

He also tells Nathan that *A Moon for the Misbegotten* will go into rehearsal immediately after *Iceman* has opened; it requires no cutting, he says, which will give him "just that much extra time" to worry about the third play, *A Touch of the Poet.*

As for the saloon, it is to be the realization of a boyhood ambition. Nathan quotes O'Neill (with his typical freewheeling inventiveness): "When these three plays of mine are on, why don't we open up one together? Not in town, but somewhere out on Long Island near the ocean because I still don't want to miss my swimming. You once said you had a good name for such a dump, 'High Dive.' It wouldn't cost us much to start it, and I'll throw in my old barroom piano that you drop nickels into. . . . It's in storage now and I'm getting lonesome for it. We might not make any money, considering that most of our friends would open charge accounts and lovably forget them, but it would be a great sensation again to eat up the free lunch."

During a later interview with an out-of-town reporter, Herbert Stoeckel, who asks about the saloon, O'Neill assures him he hasn't forgotten about it. "Nathan can handle the bar, but I want to be at the cash register."

AMONG HIS LONGER interviews are three with Elizabeth Sergeant, who is planning—with his blessing—to go far beyond the intuitive "Man with a Mask," which she wrote in 1927; she will undertake a full-length biography. Although she jots voluminous notes and sketches dozens of random assessments, she never manages to put it all together. But in her many meandering and sometimes illegible pages there are nuggets of a kind only she could elicit, insights into the state of mind of this celebrated fifty-eight-year-old dramatist whom she has known through the production of five plays and two marriages.

She is now confronted by a man who—anticipating his eleventh Broadway production—is helplessly ailing (but denying his illness); a writer no longer capable of shaping words with his pencil (but determined to continue writing); a still-handsome and charismatic man who is fed up with his marriage of seventeen years and yearning for romance (but unable to function without the care of his disillusioned, aging wife).

Sergeant notes that despite his incapacities, "Gene looks wonderful, entirely different." He is relaxed and garrulous, as she leads him to reminisce about his early life and all aspects of his career. He goes into intimate detail about his unfinished cycle (which he still hopes to finish) and, of course, he dwells on the forthcoming production of *The Iceman Cometh*.

At one point, Sergeant remarks, O'Neill appears to be reassessing "his intuitive insight, the hopelessness of the mind that produced a world war. Look below the mean repellent surface (he seems to say) and complex, terrible and unadmitted aspects of the human ego come to light: a man may really hate his mother enough to destroy her. Another may despise his wife to the point of murder because in her mothering she tolerates his vices and yields to his charm, instead of lambasting him and throwing him out of her life."

Sergeant quotes O'Neill: "I was a bum myself, with my head on a barroom table, and shared a room with a suicide. With my head swimming in alcohol and bright-dark dreams, I wondered if I'd ever get out of that door myself." She adds, "He did, for the obvious reason that he was a genius of enormous will power, a worker of workers, a man of great purity, no real choice but to contribute to the art of his time." Commenting that many of his fellow idealists had succumbed to the hostile political and social atmosphere of the time, she says that O'Neill was "the lucky guy who could always work, always write"—until now.

"God, if you only knew how I long to get back to the sea," O'Neill tells Essie, pointing out that *Iceman* was written at his inland estate in California, unlike some of his successful midcareer plays that were written while he lived near the sea.

One thing his ranch in the San Ramon Valley taught him, he continues, was that although he could objectively admire the beauty of the hills, woods, and meadows, "in a deep spiritual sense" he did not "belong."

"I am not it and it is not me. Beach grass is the only verdure I really understand. Dunes are my hills, the beach sun is my only sun, and the sea is the symbol of life to which I belong and has been that for me since I was a small boy. Sometimes, in a moment of sun-beach-sea, or on the sea, I have lost myself, all identity, and am at one with the rhythm of life itself."

Sergeant comments, "His big attentive ears probably never cease to hear the sound of the sea, no matter how far he feels from it." Sergeant ends by describing him as "still a silent, tender man; he dresses like a dandy, but the forehead dome, from which very well-brushed gray hair recedes, is still wrinkled with thought and concern for the underdog."

She suspects he continues to identify with the loser despite his "great good fortune to earn over two million dollars by dramas greater or lesser."

ON SEPTEMBER 2, a month before the opening of *The Iceman Cometh*, the Theatre Guild sponsors a press conference with O'Neill as it did fifteen years earlier, pegged to the opening of *Mourning Becomes Electra*. O'Neill is outspoken, disregarding the conformist postwar optimism of the day, indifferent to the surge of elation over his country's victorious emergence as the leading world power. With resolute calm, he expresses his view that the victory is a hollow one and that America "is a flop."

"I had a French friend, one of the delegates at the San Francisco Conference, who came to see me," says O'Neill. "I asked him, 'If it's not betraying any great secrets, what's really happening at the Conference?' He shrugged his shoulders and said, 'It's the League of Nations, only not so good.' And I believe it. Of course, I may be wrong. I nearly always am."

He then offers the dumbfounded reporters the philosophy that underlies his cyclical eleven-play *Tale of Possessors Self-Dispossessed*, which he still hopes against hope to finish:

"I'm going on the theory that the United States, instead of being the most successful country in the world, is the greatest failure. It's the greatest failure because it was given everything, more than any other country. Through moving as rapidly as it has, it hasn't acquired any real roots."

O'Neill plows ahead: "Its main idea is that everlasting game of trying to possess your own soul by the possession of something outside it, thereby losing your own soul and the thing outside of it, too. America is the prime example of this because it happened so quickly and with such immense resources." And lest anyone doubt the sterling source of his doctrine, O'Neill once again invokes a favorite maxim: "This was really said in the Bible much better. We are the greatest example of 'For what shall it profit a man, if he shall gain the whole world and lose his own soul?' We had so much and could have gone either way."

In his summing up, O'Neill rises to his most majestic: "If the human race is so damned stupid that in two thousand years it hasn't had brains enough to appreciate that the secret of happiness is contained in that one simple sentence, which you'd think any grammar school kid could understand and apply, then it's time we dumped it down the nearest drain and let the ants take over."

Allowing this pronouncement to sink in, O'Neill shifts to a lighter vein, griping that during his absence from New York "they tore down the old Cadillac Hotel where I was born," and adding, "That was a dirty trick."

He then answers questions about *The Iceman Cometh* and—making no mention of illness past or present—he says he hopes to resume writing soon. "But," he explains, "the war has thrown me completely off base, and I have to get back to a sense of writing being worthwhile."

In a separate interview for *The New York Times Magazine* a few days later, O'Neill once again sits for the writer-artist S. J. Woolf, who draws him with sunken cheeks and fiercely burning eyes. "Like Poe," writes Woolf, "he looks as if he were surrounded by an aura of mysterious sorrow." O'Neill talks to Woolf about his father's oft-repeated prediction that the theater was dying.

"Those words," says O'Neill, "seem to me as true today as when he said them. But the theater must be a hardy wench, for although she is still ailing, she'll never die as long as she offers an escape."

Analyzing his father's era, he adds, "It was a prudish age which has left its impress in the form of present-day censorship. This to me is one of the biggest obstacles to the artistic development of the theater. Now, before a play can be safely produced, somebody has to say it will not corrupt the morals of six-year-olds."

Three days before the opening, O'Neill, recovering from a bad cold, is interviewed for the *Times* Sunday drama section by Karl Schriftgiesser. O'Neill says he is confident that *Iceman* will hold the audience's attention throughout its four-hour running time.

"I do not think that you can write anything of value or understanding about the present," he tells Schriftgiesser. "You can only write about life if it is enough in the past. The present is too much mixed up with superficial values; you can't know which thing is important and which is not. The past which I have chosen is one I knew.

"You ask, what is the significance, what do these people [of *Iceman*] mean to us today? Well, all I can say is that it is a play about pipe dreams. And the philosophy is that there is always one dream left, one final dream, no matter how low you have fallen, down there at the bottom of the bottle. I know, because I saw it."

47

The last O'Neill play produced on Broadway during his lifetime opens at 4:30 in the afternoon of October 9, 1946. O'Neill has given his opening-night tickets to his lawyer and spends the evening at home with Carlotta.

It was nearly eighteen years ago that Carlotta, as O'Neill's exultant mistress, was his emissary at the opening of *Strange Interlude*; since then, she has trembled with him through the Broadway openings of *Mourning Becomes Electra*; *Ah, Wilderness!*; and *Days Without End*. She can't help but speculate that this is the final opening night they will ever share.

For the theater world, the premiere of *The Iceman Cometh* is a momentous event. Committed theatergoers and the usual celebrities along with the critics all press into the Martin Beck Theatre; at intermission, they gobble dinner at Sardi's and other theater-friendly hangouts, then hurry back to their seats.

Although many in the audience are fascinated, a good number are puzzled, and a few are bored—a fact that must be blamed largely on the muddled production.

Lawrence Langner is unwilling to shoulder the blame for the inadequacies of the Guild presentation; justifiably, he points out that O'Neill himself had considerable supervisory power over the production. But he later concedes that James Barton's performance as Hickey is a disappointment; he recalled that during the dinner intermission Barton "unfortunately for us all," entertained a crowd of friends in his dressing room instead of resting.

"By the time he came to make the famous speech which lasted nearly twenty minutes in the fourth act," Langner recounted, "he had little or no voice left with which to deliver it. As a result, the last act, which should have been the strongest of all, fell apart in the center."

Even so, *The Iceman Cometh* has a respectable run. Langner insisted it would have been even longer, but Barton soon developed laryngitis, and later audiences could barely hear him during his big scene.

"I could not help remarking to Gene," said Langner, "that, in my opinion, *The Iceman Cometh*, like [Shaw's] *Saint Joan*, would never be properly presented until after the expiration of the copyright, when it might be possible to cut it." Langner remembered that "Gene smiled at me in his usual disarming way and said it would have to wait for just that." Later, O'Neill gives Langner a copy of the manuscript, on whose first page he has written: "To Lawrence Langner, The hell with your cuts!"

In fact, most of the critics are respectful of the Theatre Guild production and say nothing of Barton's sorry performance (unaware of what it could have been in the hands of an actor with more depth of understanding). As for the play itself, the critics are divided among those who praise it (with reservations) and those who find it disappointing. But most of the critics, even those favorably disposed, complain it is unnecessarily long and repetitious.

Brooks Atkinson in the *Times* salutes O'Neill for having written "one of his best plays," calling him "a man who writes with the wonder and heart of a poet." Murmuring gently about its great length, he allows, "But if that is the way Mr. O'Neill wants to afflict harmless playgoers, let us accept our fate with nothing more than a polite demurrer. For the only thing that matters is that he has plunged again into the black quagmire of man's illusions and composed a rigadoon of death as strange and elemental as his first works."

Richard Watts Jr., in the *New York Post*, calls the play "a superb drama of splendid and imposing stature, which is at once powerful, moving, beautiful, eloquent and compassionate."

Among the influential critics who find the play wanting are Howard Barnes of the *Herald Tribune*, Louis Kronenberger of *PM*, and John Mason Brown of the *Saturday Review of Literature*—who scolded O'Neill for "having said at least twice everything that could have been better stated by being suggested."

O'Neill is disappointed by the overall critical reception, but unshaken in his own high opinion of his play; and—if he really means what he says to an interviewer for *Time* two weeks after the opening—he is far from despondent:

"I'm happier now than I've ever been. I couldn't ever be negative about life. On that score, you've got to decide Yes or No. And I'll always say Yes. Yes, I'm happy." It's a statement that must have jolted Carlotta—which might have been his intention.

The magazine follows up on this uncharacteristically ebullient comment by disparaging O'Neill as "a master craftsman of the theater," but not "a great dramatist." It smugly concludes that although O'Neill "does not seem to be a man of great, searching or original intelligence," he "remains the greatest master of theater the U.S. has ever produced."

Many other publications, both in the United States and abroad, choose the production of *Iceman* as a jumping-off point to review the body of O'Neill's work; a surprising number have an even testier viewpoint than *Time*. As a result, O'Neill's stature during the next few years will undergo a steady decline, and the consistent sniping of small but shrill voices—the voices of "the megaphone men," as O'Neill derides them—will help to undermine his already ragged spiritual and mental health.

Dudley Nichols commiserates with his friend about the mixed reviews. And ten years later, when the play is posthumously revived as a smash hit off-Broadway, Nichols speaks for O'Neill, suggesting the reasons for those earlier, disparaging notices.

Writing to a friend, Nichols points out that even though all the reviewers complained of the play's length, they were held by it to its end. "What is really at fault is ourselves," says Nichols:

> I use the phrase which Gene used in telling me, years ago, why he was reluctant to have the play produced.
>
> He said we have been conditioned by radio, TV, the movies, advertising, capsule news and a nervous brevity in everything we do, to a point where we have lost the power of sustained attention, which full-bodied works of art demand.
>
> Unless something moves and jerks, we soon turn away from it. If it doesn't chatter or talk like a machine gun, we don't listen for long. [Walter] Winchell knows this perfectly— he adopted a style which can hold anyone's attention for fifteen minutes and make what he says sound important no matter how trivial it may be. Winchell is a master of the modern style. He is its arch-creator.

Nichols cites Joshua Logan as an example of a Broadway writer-director who adopts this style for the theater; he and his imitators "make things happen for the eye all the time, no matter whether the play is saying anything or not. Now, a trivial play can be all movement, but a great play cannot. . . ."

"The truth is, about *The Iceman Cometh*, all kinds of things are happening all the time, but you have to listen and watch, and you hear repetition because that is the way O'Neill planned it, so that you cannot miss his meaning, and the emotions generated by his drama."

Soon after the opening, O'Neill answers a letter from Tennessee Williams, who has written in praise of the play. O'Neill, blatantly contradicting his claim in *Time* that he is "happier now" than he's ever been, tells Williams his letter has come just when he needs it, as he always feels a sense of "let-down" after an opening.

Three years after O'Neill's death, recalling the exchange of correspondence, Williams maintained he'd been troubled at first by the exorbitant length of *The Iceman Cometh*, but soon "became aware that its length was indispensable to its power, its fullness of passion."

In an interview for the *Times*, Williams said O'Neill was his "hero," and held forth about how O'Neill had fought the Broadway critics years earlier to accept him on his own terms as a writer of tragedy, pronouncing, "O'Neill gave birth to the American theater and died for it."

If O'Neill, despite good ticket sales for *Iceman*, is truly feeling a "letdown," he conceals it from most of his friends. Indeed, during the next few months, his geniality and social expansiveness will reach a high unprecedented since his marriage.

O'Neill's attitude toward Carlotta, however, has grown alarmingly cavalier; very much troubled, she anticipates new disasters.

SOPHUS AND ELINE WINTHER haven't seen the O'Neills for two years when they eagerly pick up their friendship in New York in November 1946. They are pleased to accept Carlotta's invitation to the penthouse for an intimate Thanksgiving dinner.

Eline, who has never seen Carlotta less than stylishly dressed and groomed, is shocked by the change in her friend's appearance. Carlotta has gained a good deal of weight and is wearing a shapeless slate-gray dress "much like that of a very proper housemaid," noted Eline; and because Carlotta is cooking and serving the meal herself, she has tied an apron around her waist.

Eline is also startled by the change in O'Neill since their last meeting in San Francisco. Although he manages "a smile of friendship" (as she later wrote), his face is haggard and his eyes are "like the eyes of a man who has been looking at death"; when she takes his hand, "his fingers are cold and lifeless."

While Sophus accompanies O'Neill into his bedroom to leave his hat and coat, Eline follows Carlotta into her own beautifully appointed bedroom.

"Sit down," Carlotta commands, pointing Eline to a sofa and seating herself opposite on a small Chinese stool in the center of the room. Politely if insincerely, Eline tells Carlotta she is looking well. This prompts an outburst from Carlotta.

Eline doesn't know, says her hostess, that illness had reduced her to "nothing but skin and bones" by the time she left San Francisco; but since arriving in New York she has steadily been gaining weight.

"Now look at me! Why, do you know, I weigh a hundred and sixty pounds! In San Francisco I was under a hundred and twenty. I can't wear any of my clothes. I'm enormous. I just don't care anymore. One of the few pleasures I have left is eating, so I eat what I want and when I want it." Taken aback, Eline concedes that Carlotta has gained "a good deal," but insists she looks well and is "as beautiful as ever."

Eline knows Carlotta well enough to realize she is now onstage and playing a role; it's plain she has prearranged not only her drab costume, but the setting, as well as Eline's front-row seat, for her performance— and what a performance it is.

If she looks well, inveighs Carlotta, "it's a miracle, considering the life I lead. You have no idea how terrible things are." And, after obtaining Eline's promise not to tell Sophus, she proceeds to disgorge a horrifying tale.

"Not long ago," Carlotta begins, "I attempted suicide." She felt such "utter fatigue" that she swallowed the contents of a tube of Amytal (a barbiturate prescribed as a sedative) that she had brought back with her from Europe and stashed away.

"I remember pouring it into a glass, adding water, and holding it up to the light, admiring the color of the liquid, and then I drank it down. I lay down on my bed, and that would have been the end." But, she tells Eline, she "didn't time it right." O'Neill, who had been out, came home for dinner and found her unconscious; he phoned a doctor, who gave her an emetic. "Gradually I began to come back. I was terribly sick. I opened my eyes, saw a blurred image of a nurse. 'What happened?' I asked."

After reassuring Carlotta, the nurse called in O'Neill and left the room. "He came in and he was furious with me," Carlotta continues. "Would you believe it? I was just barely regaining my consciousness and he began to berate me, saying I had planned this so it would look as though he had murdered me." Eline, shocked, doesn't know what to think or how to react; although she knows this is a performance, it's a pretty gripping one, and it has brought Eline to tears. Finally she asks, "But how could Gene have such an idea about you?"

"How could he?" Carlotta jeers. "Do you know he even suspects me with Freeman? Yes, he thinks I go to Freeman and that we are together in that house out there." She points out the window to a servant's annex at the end of the apartment's terrace, next to the kitchen. "And when I go out on some errand, he thinks I'm meeting men." Just the other day, says Carlotta, he gave her a "terrible look" as she was about to step into the elevator and—in front of the operator—said, "Well I hope you enjoy yourself."

She should never have married O'Neill, she rails; she didn't know "what kind of man he was." She then tells Eline about the "typist" [Jane Caldwell] in San Francisco whom she'd discovered locked in O'Neill's bedroom with him. Eline, who has been wondering if she can believe Carlotta's story of her suicide attempt, does believe her about the typist; Carlotta apparently has forgotten that she mentioned a problem with Caldwell (although not using her name) when Eline and Sophus visited in San Francisco.

Carlotta goes on about the "typist" in greater detail: she hated having "this woman in the house in the first place," and finally "got so furious," she confronted her, calling her "a damned whore" and ordering her to get out and never come back. And now, says Carlotta, "he accuses *me* with Freeman, a servant."

As Eline recalled, "To hear that Gene was accusing Carlotta of carrying on an affair with this stupid, childlike, good tempered servant of years and years! Fantastic, if true. What was I to think of all this?"

Carlotta then tells Eline that O'Neill, not long since—angry over some imaginary grievance—took her by the shoulders, shook her, and then flung her away from him. Lying in a heap against the wall, Carlotta says, she admonished him, "Next time do that in front of the radiator so that when I fall my head will strike the radiator and I'll be killed."

O'Neill responded, says Carlotta, that he could hit her with the belaying pin he kept as a souvenir of his sailing days.

Eline listens spellbound as Carlotta goes on and on—about how O'Neill sometimes comes to her after she has gone to bed and lies down fully dressed beside her on top of the covers and talks of the terrible things he has done in the past, things she doesn't want to hear—like how he once hit Agnes so hard her teeth came out. But, she says, he won't stop talking and she thinks she will go mad.

Engrossed in her monologue, Carlotta seems not to notice it has grown dark in the bedroom as she voices a new complaint. She is worn out by O'Neill's dependence on her. "Gene doesn't concern himself with the details of living," she says.

She has brushed aside the fact that it was precisely by offering to relieve him of those details that she won him away from Agnes; and she has chosen to forget how, for all these years, she has prided herself on having assumed the joyful burden of being his "mother."

Eline is further dismayed by Carlotta's depiction of O'Neill as a near-invalid who—with the help of herself, a part-time nurse, and Freeman—requires three hours to ready himself for his day. But when Eline asks if O'Neill's illness has worsened since he left San Francisco, Carlotta retorts, "He has the constitution of an orangutan," and adds that "anyone but Gene" who was afflicted this long with Parkinson's would have been in a wheelchair ages ago. "His doctors all say so. This can go on for years and years."

If she were to leave him, Carlotta says (which evidently is something she has seriously considered as an alternative to suicide), everyone would think her "a criminal for deserting him in his illness." Finally, Carlotta confesses that the optimistic plan she voiced on her arrival a year ago, for

living at least half of every year in New York, has been angrily vetoed by
O'Neill. "He hates it here. He complains all the time that he feels caged
up like an animal. I could be contented in New York. But he wants to go
away from here, and we quarrel over this constantly."

Eline is thinking that Sophus and O'Neill, who have been chatting in
the living room, must wonder how much longer she and Carlotta will be
closeted. But she senses the monologue is drawing to an end.

With a last melodramatic flourish, Carlotta says that she wants Eline
to know "all this" in case "anything happens" to her—"For instance if I
should die what seems to be an accidental death." But she warns Eline
never to mention any of this in letters to her, "because Gene reads every
scrap of mail that comes in"—a statement that would have amused those
of her detractors who believed it was she who scrutinized the mail and
kept things from him.

As Eline has come to know, Carlotta frequently modifies the actual
facts of her life, sometimes heightening, but more often hedging. Although she lacked the essential talent required for a successful stage
career, she has many of the attributes of a splendid actress and is in her
element assuming a variety of personae in her own offstage drama; her
life—at least in the opinion of her detractors—is an endlessly spun-out
impersonation. And in truth, her Thanksgiving Day monologue is as
operatic as the endless aria of a dying Brunhilde.

It's not unreasonable to assume that if she could, for years, sustain her
lie to O'Neill about her relationship with Speyer, she could lie to him
about a brief encounter or two with Freeman. (It should be noted that
Sophus Winther, who is well aware of Carlotta's intense sexuality, and
who must have guessed that O'Neill is no longer functioning vigorously,
if at all, suspects that Carlotta did sleep with Freeman.)

O'Neill, himself hardly a model of sexual probity, has no claim to a
wife with an unsullied past or a chaste present. Despite the sanctimo-
nious posturing of *Days Without End*, the match they made was essentially cynical: her beauty, her private income, her housekeeping skills—in

exchange for his artistic prestige and undoubted personal charm (which he could switch on and off).

There is, however, no doubt that Carlotta is miserable, that she blames her misery on O'Neill, and that the two regard each other with enmity.

Nor is there any doubt that O'Neill is tormenting himself over his inability to write; his new role as boulevardier is a flimsy cover-up for his suffering. Carlotta has acknowledged from the beginning that writing is O'Neill's life, and she has always dreaded what might happen if he couldn't write.

What they are actually fighting about can only be surmised: clearly she resents the enthusiasm with which he is responding to the attention of flirtatious young actresses; but it's obvious she also is terrified by the way he is shutting her out of his daily life.

Perhaps, as she has told Eline Winther, she genuinely believes O'Neill wishes her dead (although it's hard to believe he's actually plotting to murder her). And if O'Neill truly demands all that time and effort to get him on his feet every day, who can blame Carlotta for resenting his then going off to disport himself without her?

There is also the difficulty of gauging how much the behavior of either O'Neill or Carlotta is influenced by the variety of sedating and/or stimulating medications they are each taking. (All of their doctors appear to have been oblivious to any such side effects.)

All the while that Carlotta is performing "The Imperiled Wife" for Eline, O'Neill and Sophus have been engaged in their own conversation. Carlotta, now slipping without apparent effort into the character of hostess, guides Eline into the living room to join their husbands.

She serves hors d'oeuvres and produces a bottle of sherry, filling four glasses. It seems O'Neill is drinking wine again, and that Carlotta—doubtless bullied by him—is making no effort to discourage him; perhaps she is even encouraging him, for she takes no notice when he also drinks the champagne she serves with dessert, and the crème de menthe she pours after dinner.

The dinner conversation has been bland. O'Neill has thrown off his earlier gloom, and he and Sophus recite poetry. O'Neill tells Sophus he has been unable to write and that he hates living in New York. Significant looks are exchanged from time to time between Carlotta and O'Neill, but there is no sign of the turmoil Carlotta has earlier depicted.

O'Neill gives Sophus the scripts of *A Moon for the Misbegotten* and *A Touch of the Poet* and, well into late evening, the Winthers take their leave. Eline can't wait to convey to her husband every word of the confidential story Carlotta has confided.

Some time later, O'Neill and Carlotta accept an invitation to dine with Russel Crouse and his wife, Anna, at their home, and to meet the Irving Berlins. Carlotta calls Crouse before the evening of their date to say she and O'Neill have decided to come after dinner; she explains O'Neill is uncomfortable dining with strangers, as he is having difficulty with his tremor and she has to cut his food for him. Crouse says no, please come, he will ask the Berlins to come after dinner.

The Berlins arrive at nine, themselves wary of the meeting. "I found out later they'd told their chauffeur to wait, thinking they'd stay for a short time," Crouse remembered. Berlin starts to play some of his songs on the piano, and before long, O'Neill is standing next to him, croaking along with the tunes. Berlin goes on to other popular songs after he's exhausted his own. At 11:30, the Howard Lindsays and the Bennett Cerfs arrive, having been summoned by Crouse when he sees how well things are going. The O'Neills stay until two o'clock.

"Carlotta, who had been a little stiff at first, had fun too, after a while," Crouse recalled. "And Gene had the time of his life. Carlotta told me later that Gene had been so stimulated he had not been able to sleep for hours after he got home." She writes Crouse a note thanking him for "making Gene so happy." Like many an embattled couple before them, they have their moments of peaceful remission; but they are moments only.

Inspired by the success of Crouse's Irving Berlin evening, Cerf invites the O'Neills to his home for a Burl Ives evening. Ives sings after dinner and O'Neill joins him in some sea chanteys.

"The songs got dirtier and dirtier," recalls Cerf, "and Carlotta finally went home by herself. I took Gene home at 3 a.m." Cerf does not receive a "thank-you" note from Carlotta, who has always been cool to him.

"Burl Ives is all right for five or six songs," Carlotta—assuming her pose as the grande dame—later writes to Sophus Winther, who has heard about the evening. "But, as he drank straight brandy along with his singing—& *would* continue singing—it got to be blurry & a bore after a bit! His 'off the record' songs are all right for *old* gentlemen—but for a mixed party of so-called respectable folk—a bit misplaced & embarrassing! . . . personally, I am not old enough, nor young enough, to be excited by ribald songs."

Long buried is the mischievous, ribald Carlotta who, in her early thirties, performed in *The Hairy Ape*. "We used to play jokes backstage on Wolheim and the other men in the cast," recalls James Light who, as stage manager, had moved with the production when it transferred from the Provincetown Playhouse to Broadway. One day, before a matinee, Carlotta and Light concocted a scheme to "get the boys riled up," in Light's phrase. According to Light, Carlotta volunteered, "Let's pretend we're having sexual intercourse."

As Light tells it: "We left the door of her dressing room ajar and Carlotta, who was dressed for her entrance in her white gown, sat down in one corner and I sat in another and we began improvising some impassioned and largely inarticulate dialogue—mostly 'Ahs' and grunts—and it wasn't long before heads began popping in at the door. "There we were, at opposite ends of the room, Carlotta sedately reading a book, and my face buried in a newspaper."

Small wonder Light was among the earliest of O'Neill's old cronies to be shut out of their lives by Carlotta. She would have liked to banish Bennett Cerf as well; like Light, he had known Carlotta from the days of her uninhibited love affair with Ralph Barton.

But the best she could manage, when Cerf came to Sea Island, hoping to add O'Neill to his Random House roster, was to pretend not to know him; eager as Cerf was to land O'Neill, he didn't make an issue of Carlotta's assumed amnesia. (On the other hand, Carl Van Vechten, who knew Carlotta's ribald side better than anyone, remained a trusted confidant to the end of her life—and she would never have believed he would ultimately betray her in his diary.)

On December 5, Crouse invites the O'Neills to accompany him to a performance of Irving Berlin's musical *Annie Get Your Gun*. After some hesitation, they accept. Carlotta tells Crouse she is afraid O'Neill will be swamped by acquaintances and autograph hunters and makes him promise not to let anyone know they are going.

They both enjoy the show and afterward, Crouse takes them backstage to meet the star, Ethel Merman. They spend about an hour in her dressing room.

According to Crouse, Merman and O'Neill get on very well. "Chorus kids keep coming in for autographs and Gene has a wonderful time," says Crouse.

Carlotta, however, is not enjoying her husband's social blossoming. She clearly resents that O'Neill, during his recent months in New York, has dispelled the aura of reclusiveness Carlotta has helped him nurture over the years; while she claims to be tired of taking care of him, she is also increasingly jealous of his ability to roam free of her care.

O'Neill seems equally conflicted. Attempting to make amends at year's end, he inscribes a hard cover copy of *The Iceman Cometh* to Carlotta:

> Though I have seemed ungrateful and unaware and lost at times, that was only the surface irritation. But deep in my heart I have never forgotten all you have meant to me and been to me, have loved you as much and needed you.
>
> I am sorry for the unhappiness I have caused you. How unhappy it has made me, you have seen and know.

Let us forget and forgive, Darling, as now for a time we have forgotten and forgiven. We have love still, Sweetheart. We [have] the chance of a new life! I love you!

Forgetting and forgiving, forgiving and forgetting. It was the tragi-comic theme for the final act of the O'Neills' self-propelled drama; helplessly, they would forget and forgive and forget again, spinning in their deadly dance toward the destruction of their marriage.

48

A *Moon for the Misbegotten*, which the Theatre Guild put into rehearsal early in 1947, becomes a playwright's and producer's nightmare.

The major casting headache is the outsized twenty-eight-year-old Josie Hogan. It isn't easy to find an experienced and charismatic young actress who can convey (while looking uncharismatically overfed) the supernatural earth-motherliness that O'Neill demands. And he insists that the actress who plays Josie must be of Irish descent, as must also be the male lead, Jamie Tyrone, and the actor who plays Josie's father, Phil Hogan. "We just killed ourselves trying to find Irish actors," Langner later recalled.

Mary Welch, who has recently returned to New York from a road tour and who is, in her words, "one hundred per cent Irish from County Cork," reads for the role but is told she looks "too normal"; O'Neill wants someone who is at least fifty pounds heavier.

After weeks of stuffing herself with potatoes, bananas, and rich desserts, the twenty-four-year-old actress auditions again. This time O'Neill pronounces her "emotional quality" just right and says he's confident she'll continue to gain weight.

"I signed the contract to play Josie," remembered Mary Welch, "with the added, unusual clause, 'The artist agrees to gain the necessary weight required for the role.'" After Barry Fitzgerald turns down the role of Josie's father, J. M. Kerrigan is selected; James Dunn, an established film star, is cast as Jamie Tyrone, and Arthur Shields, with long experience playing Irish roles onstage and in film, is engaged to direct.

At the first rehearsal, O'Neill uncharacteristically chooses to tell the cast of his agony when writing the play and, one by one, actors and director dissolve into tears of empathy, O'Neill weeping along with them. But it isn't long before O'Neill finds fault with the way his play is shaping up. He voices his displeasure to Lawrence Langner.

"Gene was worried about James Dunn," said Langner, who had taken O'Neill to see the actor in the movie *A Tree Grows in Brooklyn*. O'Neill had approved Dunn as being "just right for James Tyrone."

But during rehearsals, according to Langner, O'Neill "kept complaining that Dunn wasn't playing the role with enough gentlemanliness." O'Neill insisted that his brother, Jamie, had been "a gentleman."

Langner's response was that the real Jamie "may very well have been a gentleman," but the way O'Neill had written the character of James Tyrone, "that quality didn't exactly come across." Dunn, Langner asserted, was "playing the role as written."

O'Neill couldn't accept this, said Langner, adding, "I felt that [Gene] had idealized his brother and would never be able to accept any actor in the part."

Dunn's performance is not O'Neill's only problem. During one rehearsal, he tells his cast they are playing the tragedy of the play too soon; they should be playing almost for farce in the first act, he says, and develop into tragic stature in the fourth.

WITH BAD GRACE, O'Neill agrees to the Guild's ill-considered plan for a pre-Broadway tour of several Midwestern cities, to begin on February 20, 1947, at the Hartman Theatre in Columbus, Ohio; but after attending the final dress rehearsal in New York, he refuses to accompany the cast on its tour.

Predictably, *A Moon for the Misbegotten* meets with the same sort of puerile reaction once drawn by *All God's Chillun Got Wings* and *Desire Under the Elms*. When, after receiving mixed notices in its earlier stops, the play opens in Detroit on March 10, it is scorned by the local press and greeted with indignation by the chamber of commerce, whose secretary declares himself shocked by reports of "the smut in it." On the second night, it is ordered closed by the police.

"It isn't just a matter of profanity," declares Police Censor Charles Snyder. "The whole theme is obscene. It is a slander on American motherhood. The play will have to be rewritten before I will let it go on."

Theresa Helburn and Armina Marshall, who are overseeing the play's tour, are summoned to meet with a member of the censor's staff. "One of the objections he made," recalled Marshall, "was that the word 'mother' was used in the same sentence with the word 'prostitute.' He mentioned other words which, he said, should not be used on the stage."

"Now, mind you," the censor warns, "the actor can go ahead and say the sentence right up to the obscene word, and then he can make a gesture. But he cannot use the word."

Marshall retorts, "You've allowed *The Maid of the Ozarks* to play here in Detroit and yet you will not allow a play written by Eugene O'Neill, the greatest playwright in America, who won the Nobel Prize?"

"Lady," says the censor, "I don't care what kind of prize he's won, he can't put on a dirty show in my town."

"This is not a dirty show," protests Marshall. "This is a great play—which *The Maid of the Ozarks* is not."

"Lady," he scolds, "when *The Maid of the Ozarks* came here, it was a very different play. I helped rewrite that play, and we finally let it stay here." (The play was on tour after having been greeted in New York by the critic for *Time* as "very likely the most needlessly disgusting play" on Broadway—a play whose "publicity stresses sex, but [whose] long suit is actually scatology—lice, bedbugs, outhouses, and bare, dirty feet planted on the breakfast table . . .")

"Well," responds Marshall, "I'm afraid you'd have your problems cut out for you to rewrite a play by Mr. O'Neill."

This visibly disconcerts the censor. "Listen, lady," he shouts, "I don't have to sit here and take that from a woman." At this point, James Dunn intervenes, and eventually the censor agrees to talk things over with him, stipulating he does not want a woman present. After a tedious conference, an agreement is reached: the producers will delete eight words.

Joe Heidt, who still handles publicity for the Theatre Guild, telephones O'Neill about the deletions. O'Neill laughingly agrees to them.

SAINT LOUIS IS the last stop on the tryout tour for *A Moon for the Misbegotten*. The Guild wants to recast the play and have another try at it but, according to Langner, "Gene asked us to defer this until he was feeling better and he also asked us to postpone the production of *A Touch of the Poet* for the same reason." Shortly before *A Moon for the Misbegotten* had left for its out-of-town tryout, O'Neill confronted censorship problems with *The Iceman Cometh*, which had concluded its Broadway run of 136 performances and was being readied for a road tour.

In this instance, it was the Boston censor who took umbrage at some of the "unclean" O'Neill dialogue. O'Neill flatly refused to make any of the requested changes, characterizing them as "idiotic."

"Boston audiences, I am sure, want plays as written by their authors and produced originally in New York," O'Neill declared to the press. "They do not want plays weakened and made silly by an ignorant and stupid censorship which knows and cares nothing about drama. This is the sort of censorship I experienced years ago with *Strange Interlude*, which was barred from Boston and forced to play in Quincy so Bostonians could see it." In support of O'Neill's blast, the Guild rerouted the play to Baltimore.

WHILE O'NEILL'S HEALTH continues shaky during the winter and early spring of 1947, his thirst for social contacts remains unslaked. He even manages to have several brief clandestine (if platonic) meetings with Patricia Neal, a young actress who had read for the role of Josie (and whom O'Neill was considering for Sara Melody if and when *A Touch of the Poet* was to be produced). She has written O'Neill to tell him she liked *The Iceman Cometh*, and O'Neill has replied, congratulating her on her recent success in Lillian Hellman's *Another Part of the Forest*.

It is soon after receiving Neal's letter that he decides to pursue the relationship, and she and O'Neill meet several times during the next few months.

> The Theater Guild would call me and ask me to come to their offices to see O'Neill. We would sit and talk in Miss Marshall's office, usually for about two hours. He'd insist on lighting my cigarettes, even though it might take as much as two minutes.
>
> We talked about everything. Once we talked about my name. I had some Irish blood, and my grandmother's name was Fitzgerald. He said he was sure that the name, Neal, was actually O'Neill, gone north.
>
> After one of our meetings, he decided to take me to Hick's for a soda. He held his glass in both hands, close to his chin, and kept it there, drinking his soda through a straw. He was pleased he did so well. He had the kind of face I loved— craggy. That day at Hick's I told him, "I'm twenty-one today." He said, "I wish I'd known someone like you when I was twenty-one." He told me that I could do any of his plays I wanted to.

But she never saw O'Neill again after she left for Hollywood.

Carlotta learned of those meetings and was reminded of a humiliating episode six years earlier while living in Tao House, involving her husband's brief encounter with the even more alluring Ingrid Bergman. He had learned that the twenty-six-year-old Bergman, recently launched on her movie career, was making a lauded stage appearance in a revival of

Anna Christie in San Francisco; he sent Carlotta to see it, thinking Bergman might be right for *More Stately Mansions* and some of the other cycle plays when and if they were completed and produced.

Carlotta thought Bergman promising and invited her to lunch at Tao House. Explaining that O'Neill was not well, and tired easily, Carlotta told Bergman she would signal the beautiful young actress with an emphatic nod of her head when it was time for her to make her excuses and leave.

Bergman was struck by O'Neill's "stillness" and entranced by his eyes, which she thought were "the most beautiful eyes I have seen in my whole life. They were like wells; you fell into them, and you had a feeling that he looked straight through you."

Soon after lunch, Carlotta gave Bergman the agreed-upon signal, but Bergman ignored it and accepted O'Neill's invitation to visit his study, where he showed her his manuscript for *More Stately Mansions*. He told her about his plans for a repertory company that would produce all the cycle plays over a four-year period and asked Bergman to join it. Bergman couldn't see herself committing to a four-year stage project when a promising movie career was looming, and declined his offer. He said, "You're abandoning me," and she replied, "Maybe later," and finally, to the relief of a jealously stewing Carlotta, Bergman took her departure.

If Carlotta couldn't revenge herself on Bergman, she did manage to spite Patricia Neal. In 1952, a year before O'Neill's death, when a revival of *Desire Under the Elms* was being planned, Neal was asked by the producer Robert Whitehead to play the role of Abbie Putnam.

"I began arranging my Hollywood schedule so I could come east to do the play," recalled Neal. "Suddenly I got word from Whitehead that I couldn't have the role, after all. He told me he had received a wire instructing him to stop negotiations with me. He said that the O'Neills felt I hadn't developed enough as an actress to play Abbie." (Carlotta made no objection when José Quintero cast Ingrid Bergman in *More Stately Mansions* in 1967, fourteen years after O'Neill's death.)

IN THE SPRING OF 1947 (after *A Moon for the Misbegotten* has closed out of town), Carlotta is growing frantic about O'Neill's overextending himself. In a distraught letter to Sophus Winther, she blames it on their environment. "This town (that I always loved)—I *loathe*," she writes.

"God knows where the real New Yorkers are," she complains, citing the lack of gentility among the people with whom she comes in contact. "Gene is exhausted—his tremor much worse" and "more depressed than usual."

Abruptly, she confides that she is "trying to get a parcel of land in a very select part of East Hampton," asserting that "the village is very charming and quiet," and approvingly describing "all the people" there as "'bloody reactionaries!'" It will be "quiet, dignified and restful" and will, she hopes, allow them "to die in the manner *we* prefer—not in the manner of 'Uncle Joe' [Stalin]!" She is busy designing what will be their "*last* home"—a "wee house—but I hope unusual and attractive"; they probably won't be able to build it for at least a year, she says, as they are having to budget their money.

Carlotta has all but given up her attempts to restrain what she regards as her husband's unseemly social prancing. Answering a letter from Charles O'Brien Kennedy, the old actor friend of O'Neill's father, she complains (in a restrained way) of the "over fatigue" that has led to a recent spell of "temperature & tummy upset."

Evidently, O'Neill has been consulting doctors (doubtless at Carlotta's urging), all of whom, she tells Kennedy, have warned her against allowing him to do too much; she tries "to guard him against this evil." But "who can keep an Irishman from stepping over a cliff?"

O'Neill, however, is still riding a wave of youthful optimism. He has never stopped hoping a cure for his illness will be found that will allow him to write again.

"It's very hard right now, not being able to work," he tells the writer

Hamilton Basso, who is interviewing him during this period for the three-part profile that will be published in *The New Yorker* the following winter. "I want to get going again. Once I get over this thing—these shakes I have—I feel I can keep rolling right along."

O'Neill takes time to express his optimism to Carlotta's daughter when he sends her his wishes for a happy birthday that August; he tells Cynthia he will write soon to her husband, Roy, now that his "ability to write in long hand has improved."

Still trying to curtail her husband's social activities, Carlotta takes it upon herself to decline Sherlee Weingarten's invitation to her wedding to Steve Alexander on November 7; she says she and O'Neill never go to parties, but to soften the refusal she amends that she would like to arrange a wedding dinner for Sherlee at their apartment.

To Sherlee's surprise, O'Neill does attend her wedding party— without Carlotta. "He was gracious to everyone, and wonderfully alive," Sherlee recalled. He drinks two glasses of champagne. He listens happily to a pretty actress who (according to Sherlee) lectures him for being too reserved and for not having a political conscience. "She shook a finger at him; he adored it," says Sherlee. As O'Neill is being dropped off at his apartment house by the newlyweds after the party, he remarks, "I'm going to catch hell for this." (The marriage lasted fewer than three years; after divorcing Alexander, Sherlee married Robert Lantz, a prominent literary agent, in 1950.)

O'Neill apparently relishes his little fling and is rather pleased to have piqued Carlotta, for soon after the party, he gleefully tells his old Princeton classmate Richard Weeks of his escapade and of Carlotta's disapproval.

Carlotta gives the promised wedding dinner for Sherlee and her husband a week later, presenting them with their wedding present, a check for $170—the royalties for the Czechoslovakian production of *The Iceman Cometh*. But Sherlee notices a coolness in Carlotta's treatment of her. Sherlee later attributes Carlotta's attitude in part to her having given

O'Neill a copy of Djuna Barnes's sexually provocative novel *Nightwood* after learning of his friendship with Barnes during his Greenwich Village days. Carlotta, the next time she sees Sherlee, expresses her disapproval of the book and of Sherlee's interest in it.

To such transgressions as his meetings with Patricia Neal and his having gone alone to Sherlee's wedding party, O'Neill now adds another solo social engagement. On December 18, he attends a stag dinner at a West Forty-fifth Street restaurant to celebrate the sixtieth birthday of Robert Edmond Jones. He makes the effort to speak in tribute to Jones, painstakingly signs the souvenir programs of the other twenty-two guests (among them Arthur Hopkins, Jo Mielziner, Lee Simonson, Walter Huston, and John Mason Brown), and sits for a group photograph for which he produces a cheerful grin.

Soon after, however, he grows remorseful about upsetting his wife. His birthday message to her on December 28 is abject. Asking her please not to "sneer," he assures her, once again, of his love for and need of her—a truth, he says, which can support them in their old age against "the sneers of the world."

"I do not offer you anything but my love, my heartbreak, my need of your love—and my apology that I should have forgotten your card at Christmas," he writes. "I paid for that in tears. I love you, Carlotta, as I have loved you, as I always will!" Carlotta chooses to disbelieve him.

AT THE END OF 1947, Carlotta has resumed keeping a diary, but it is a haphazard one; some of its pages are blank, the writing at times is incoherent and at other times illegible. On December 29, she writes: "No Christmas or birthday presents for me—but he gets all the suggests [sic] I get for him. It is like living in a mad house!"

She describes New Year's Eve as "ghastly!" and on January 2, she notes O'Neill is "in a fog—and *loathes* me"; he is drinking too much Dubonnet, she writes, and she is terrified it will lead once again to rampant drunkenness.

ON THE EVENING of January 16, O'Neill, Carlotta, and Saxe Commins are having after-dinner coffee in the penthouse when Carlotta answers the phone, hears the name of the caller, and angrily thrusts the instrument at O'Neill.

The caller is Eleanor Fitzgerald, known as "Fitzi" by her colleagues from the long-ago days when she was the nurturing executive manager of the struggling Playwrights' Theatre. O'Neill has lost touch with his old friend, as he has with most of the Provincetown Players. Fitzi tells O'Neill she is in the emergency room at Mount Sinai Hospital with severe abdominal pains; her doctor wants to admit her to the hospital for tests, but she doesn't have the hundred dollars required as a deposit on a room. She is calling O'Neill in desperation to ask for a loan.

Carlotta grows more and more enraged as she listens to O'Neill's assurances to Fitzi that he will send her a check immediately for the hundred dollars, and asks if she is sure that will be enough. Hanging up and trying to ignore Carlotta's rage, O'Neill begins to reminisce with Commins about Fitzi and the Greenwich Village days. But Carlotta will not be ignored.

"All of Gene's former friends were roundly cursed [by Carlotta], blamed for his illness and branded as parasites and hangers on," said Commins, recalling that "Fitzi, particularly, was singled out as the worst miscreant, as a bum and scrounger who was interested only in preying on Gene." O'Neill's efforts to placate his wife have no effect, said Commins, and, embarrassed to be a witness to their quarrel, he excuses himself and goes home.

In her diary, Carlotta confirms that she and O'Neill had a quarrel on January 16; but, without mentioning its cause, she blames it on O'Neill. "It is obvious," writes Carlotta, "he is working up one of those black rages." The quarrel continues the next day; its "sadistic climax" is that he hurts her "badly."

The following day, O'Neill calls Commins to tell him, "My frau has flown the coop," and asks him to come to the penthouse. It is spookily reminiscent of the episode twenty years earlier in the Shanghai Hotel when Carlotta packed her things to escape a drunken O'Neill after he knocked her down. However, in Commins's version of the actual events leading to Carlotta's current departure, she is cast less as victim than as co-instigator. (It was not until years after Carlotta's death that Commins dared to set down his version.)

When he arrives at the penthouse, said Commins, O'Neill gives him an account of what happened after he left the previous evening. Carlotta, says O'Neill, renewed her harangue against his friends and accused him of "weakness and cowardice" in tolerating them.

O'Neill, determined not to reply to any of Carlotta's accusations, maintained a stoical silence that further infuriated her; she rushed into the bedroom and "lifted the glass that covered his dressing table over her head and crashed it to the floor where it broke into hundreds of splinters."

"Underneath this glass," Commins continued, "Gene had kept the only picture he had of his mother and himself as a baby. Carlotta, now at the summit of her frenzy, snatched the picture and tore it into bits, crying, 'Your mother was a whore!'

"This was the last straw," said Commins. With obvious reluctance, Commins went on to reveal that his gentle-mannered friend slapped Carlotta's face. She responded by screaming "maniacally" and, after hurriedly packing a bag, "made a melodramatic exit, swearing she would never return."

For the moment, at least, Carlotta means it. After checking into a hotel, she consults her lawyer, Melville Cane, and then sets about removing her clothes and some of her other possessions from the penthouse.

O'Neill somehow discovers where Carlotta is staying and, on January 19, writes her an anguished note. "Darling: For the love of God, forgive and come back. You are all I have in life. I am sick and I will surely die without you. You do not want to murder me, I know, and a curse will be on you for your remaining days. I love you and I will! Please, Darling!"

Carlotta does not respond to O'Neill's plea. But on January 22, she telephones O'Neill's doctor, George Draper (who had helped O'Neill dry out twelve years earlier), telling him her husband has begun to drink again, and asking his help in "getting Gene into a sanatorium."

Commins, concerned about O'Neill living alone in the penthouse, urges him to invite a friend to stay during Carlotta's absence, and O'Neill calls on Walter Casey. A boyhood friend, Casey had worked on the New London *Telegraph* with O'Neill and hero-worshipped him; now living in New York as a freelance writer, he is only too happy to move in with O'Neill.

What Commins doesn't know is that Casey is an alcoholic; nor is Commins aware of O'Neill's several dives back into drink since his boastful "conquest" of his own alcoholism in 1926—invariably in conjunction with a hard-drinking male companion; Walter Casey is following in the footsteps of Louis Kantor (in France), Alfred Batson (in Shanghai), and George Boll (in Georgia).

O'Neill conceals his drinking from Commins, who checks regularly on his welfare. Commins spends the evening of January 27 at the penthouse drinking coffee with O'Neill and Casey until 1:00 a.m.; as soon as Commins leaves, they switch to whiskey and stay up drinking until 3:00, when Casey takes several sleeping pills and they both retire.

An hour later, O'Neill trips on his way to the bathroom. He feels a sharp pain in his arm, but isn't aware how badly he is injured until he tries to lift himself up.

"You don't realize," he later tells Sherlee Weingarten, "that when you lose the use of an arm, you lose your equilibrium. I couldn't coordinate—couldn't get to my feet."

He shouts for Casey, but Casey, in a deep sleep, doesn't hear him. He kicks his feet against the floor, hoping to arouse the tenants below, but that brings no response. "It was a terrifying experience," as he later tells Sherlee. "I lost all track of time. I felt as though I was alone, in a nightmare."

Casey, waking at about five in the morning on January 28, finds O'Neill lying on the floor in a semi-stupor. Casey is appalled and remorseful over the drinking and the sleeping pills. He immediately notifies Commins and then telephones Dr. Draper, who sends a younger associate, Dr. Shirley Fisk, to the penthouse; Dr. Fisk orders O'Neill into Doctors Hospital.

In his thirties, Dr. Fisk is lanky and blond and his blue eyes are good-naturedly appraising behind horn-rimmed glasses. Like every doctor who treats O'Neill, he is immediately charmed by him, as is Dr. Robert Lee Patterson, the orthopedist Fisk calls in. "O'Neill was a damn good patient," recalls Dr. Patterson. A congenial man, with more than a trace of Southern drawl, Patterson (who had once been Franklin Roosevelt's doctor) is some years older than Fisk. "O'Neill would always greet me with a little smile, and say, 'Nice to see you, Doctor,'" Patterson recalled.

O'Neill's X-rays show that the fracture is severe, and Patterson realizes he must be in considerable pain, but O'Neill never complains and it is difficult for the doctor to estimate what sedatives to prescribe.

"We didn't have his arm in a cast. It was in a sling with a circular bandage around the chest wall. I always saw him when he was propped up in a semi-sitting position—we kept him cranked up like that because it made it easier for the fracture to heal. He always managed a smile at the end of our meeting, even when he was uncomfortable."

Evidently, O'Neill's primary doctor, George Draper, knew where to reach Carlotta, for she hurries to the hospital on the day O'Neill is admitted. She finds him ensconced in a corner room on the tenth floor, gazing from his bedside window at the passing boats on the East River. "He seems touched & glad 'mama' has come back," Carlotta writes in her diary on January 28.

His hospitalization, which will last until late April, will subsequently be testified to by his doctors and his friends, often minutely and sometimes conflictingly. Carlotta herself left an episodic, frequently muddled, and at times deliberately distorted account of those twelve weeks.

According to her diary, Carlotta enjoys amicable visits with O'Neill on each of the first five days of his hospitalization; but on February 2, she finds him depressed: "We go over same old thing & tells me 'if you can't come here with a smile, forgiving all, & thinking only of our future, I don't want to see you at all.' Naturally, I go!" No longer amicably inclined, she sobs in her diary that she has "wasted twenty years" on O'Neill, asking herself, "Where can I take up life at 60?"

Meanwhile, she writes, she has a visit with Dr. Fisk, who has asked to see her.

According to Fisk, it was Carlotta who approached *him*. "As soon as Carlotta found out I was taking care of Gene she got in touch with me. She'd call me and tell me how he used to beat her up; my own private feeling is that she was the more powerful, and if anyone did the beating, she was the one who did it.

"I was a young doctor then and got all emotionally involved in the life of the great playwright. I felt he was married to a virago; he looked so benign, he was a warm, understanding human being, he never was temperamental or complained; the nurses all loved him."

On one of Carlotta's visits to Fisk's office, she makes a derogatory comment about O'Neill, which Fisk counters by insisting O'Neill is a gentleman. "My remark set off a volley of ranting," said Fisk, "and there were patients waiting outside who heard every word." He finally quiets her but he knows she will always regard him as a villain. He's right; she describes him in her diary as "stupid, insensitive, trouble-making."

Dr. Fisk is among the many who have seen only O'Neill's gentle, thoughtful side and who have sympathized with his sorrowful stories of ill treatment by Carlotta. But then, O'Neill has always been a more adept dissembler than his wife; she can be warm and gracious to those she trusts and can simulate charm and generosity to those she needs. But she doesn't trouble to ingratiate herself with those she regards as nobodies, nor does she check her outspoken antagonism toward those she suspects of bearing her even the slightest ill will.

Carlotta impulsively resumes her visits to O'Neill's bedside on February 10, the twentieth anniversary of their elopement. When she arrives with a token gift for him, a nurse hands her roses he has ordered for her, together with a sealed note addressing her as "Darling" and begging her to "let this anniversary of our setting out together not make you think of a flop!"

Assuring her she has been his "life," protesting that without her he is "nothing," he pleads, "Please, Sweetheart, I have been through hell and you have. I could never act again as I have acted. I love you, Darling, Darling! I love you! I love you. I am yours! Don't leave me!" Carlotta exits the hospital, her head in "a whirl."

During a long visit two days later, she and O'Neill agree they will never return to the penthouse, nor will they rent or buy a house; they will live in hotels where they can get prepared meals; they will let Freeman go, for they will need no servants.

On February 16, Carlotta finds O'Neill feeling sorry for himself. He must always dramatize himself, she storms in her diary, "—weep— miserable—but never remembers *fact*, *truth*, or what he has done to me—my loneliness—humiliation, hurt—just because he 'hated me!!'"

Ten days later, after speaking on the phone to Walter Casey, as well as to the man she describes in her diary as "that disgusting Palestinian"— her latest euphemistic denigration of Saxe Commins—Carlotta angrily notes, "It is no go—Gene would be all right—but not his horrible friends—I am so weary of all this." She stays away from the hospital for the next ten days, presumably to make O'Neill long for her; when she does visit on March 1, O'Neill exasperates her by failing to give her a promised check. "I can't make him out," she writes.

The following day, O'Neill sends the check "with a very offhand note." He acts, she says, "as if he were in a fog like the old days." A day later, she telephones Dr. Fisk to inquire about O'Neill's condition; he asks her (so she says) why she doesn't get a divorce. "The impudence!" she fumes in her diary. "Have had enough of this." She hastens to instruct Melville Cane to sue for a separation.

Two days later she has another inexplicable change of heart; she records that she has tried to discuss with O'Neill the possibility of their renting a suite at the Lowell Hotel on Sixty-third Street off Park Avenue when he leaves the hospital.

"Gene does not seem to know what I am talking about," complains Carlotta. "Does not hear well or misconstrues. And insists the past must not be mentioned."

As a conciliatory gesture, she presents him with an expensive tie; it's no easier to gauge cause and effect in the unwritten drama unreeling in O'Neill's mind than it is to track Carlotta's twists and turns. From March 8 onward, Carlotta visits O'Neill almost daily, sends him flowers, and brings him cakes—at least that is what she sets down in her diary.

O'Neill's room at Doctors Hospital has begun to hum with the intrigue of a sixteenth-century royal palace. The courtiers are divided between those who want O'Neill to separate from Carlotta, and those who realize he needs her and will never leave her (if only she will take him back).

Saxe Commins, in Carlotta's view, is a crafty Cromwell who wishes to control her husband's literary legacy, although poor Commins wants only to save his friend's life; he sincerely believes Carlotta is a witch who has placed a spell on O'Neill and is waiting for him to wither away.

Long after Carlotta's death, Saxe described an event that for him substantiates his opinion of her "cruelty and vindictiveness." He explained, "It was not the first time that I had been made privy to domestic scenes of spite and violence on one side and a tormented meekness on the part of the other." Evidently, Commins has never witnessed any of O'Neill's equally cruel and vindictive onslaughts against Carlotta.

In the episode he described, Commins is a dinner guest at the O'Neills' suite in the Barclay (before they moved into the Fifth Avenue penthouse). He is aware that Carlotta is angry at O'Neill and that O'Neill is apprehensive. It seems that a large bundle of manuscript material, including finished and unfinished playscripts, has gone missing; it is a bundle that, earlier in the day, O'Neill ascertained was safely stored in the trunk where he kept it.

He and Carlotta have fruitlessly searched everywhere in the suite and O'Neill is devastated. Carlotta, said Commins, was taunting O'Neill with having lost his memory, growing senile, and not knowing "what he was doing most of the time." Commins suggests a second search and, after opening every closet and drawer in the suite, Saxe concedes the bundle has "disappeared without a trace."

Two days later, says Commins, when he and O'Neill are alone for a moment, O'Neill tells him the manuscripts have been found, and begs him to "forget the entire unhappy episode." Carlotta, he explains, had taken them out of the apartment and hidden them, to "punish him for reasons totally obscure to him."

O'NEILL PUTS ON different faces for different visitors to his hospital bedside. To some, he seems in good spirits. He dictates upbeat notes to friends that are transcribed by Sherlee Weingarten, who has offered her services as secretary. "I'd love to see you anytime in the evening beginning next week," he writes to Russel Crouse on February 3. "By then I ought to be able to cook up a smile of welcome or sing to you faintly, 'Oh, Come and Be Sweet to Me, Kid.'" He also writes to Carl Van Vechten and his wife, Fania Marinoff, thanking them for their flowers and asking them to visit.

He is amused and cheered by a visit from George Jean Nathan and Eddie Dowling, who (in Dowling's words) round up "three lovely little girls," and "burst in on him." The "girls" are young actresses who are flattered to be at the bedside of the great dramatist. "O'Neill beamed," recalled Dowling. "We had a lovely visit."

Some of O'Neill's friends interpret his cheerful frame of mind as evidence that he is resigned to a permanent break with Carlotta; those who believe she has been holding him on too tight a rein are ready to congratulate themselves on his timely escape. Among them, according to Carlotta herself, is Eugene Jr.; it's unclear how she knows this, but she later maintains that Eugene called his father at the hospital "and told him to leave the old Tory and come and live with him."

Others are convinced the separation is temporary. "It was Tristan and Isolde all the time," Crouse said, adding that whenever Carlotta got angry with O'Neill, she would go out and buy a hat; sometime during this period she shows off her impressive millinery collection to Anna Crouse.

(The director José Quintero once fondly recalled a mystical encounter with Carlotta's hats, to which he attributed her granting him permission to revive *The Iceman Cometh*. When he visited her hotel suite, she astonished him by taking his hand and guiding him to her bedroom, where she had laid out several boxes.

"I am going to show you four hats," she said, taking the first one from its box and settling it on her head. Quintero, intuiting this was some sort of test and too terrified to dissemble, said a soft but brief "No." Carlotta replaced the hat and modeled a second and a third, to both of which Quintero whispered, "No." Finally, according to Quintero, "she brought out, like a bird from its nest, the last hat and quickly and expertly placed it on her head, then turned to look at me. 'That one,' I said." Carlotta's response was to grant him, on the spot, the rights he sought, explaining the hat he chose was the one she wore to bury her husband.)

The Crouses were amused by Carlotta's hat fetish, but Saxe Commins might have argued that no hat could conceal the serpentine locks of a Medusa. Carlotta, during the prolonged period of O'Neill's hospitalization, mentions fittings at Mainbocher, in addition to shopping for shoes as well as hats, nor does she deprive herself of regular visits to her hairdresser and manicurist.

"We knew Gene couldn't live without Carlotta," Fania Marinoff said. "A great many people thought he could, but Carl and I knew they needed each other, and would always go back together."

Carlotta, who has begun packing up the penthouse prior to subletting, makes a routine visit to O'Neill's hospital room on March 15, and is thrown off balance when O'Neill switches from his "quiet mood" to a burst of anger. He shouts at her for her refusal to "forget the past," and makes a rush at her. In a panic, Carlotta rings for the nurse. "She lets me out of room—Gene runs down the hall after me! It is *ghastly*."

While she doesn't explain what actually provoked O'Neill's outburst, there is a likely reason for his rancor: he has recently learned (as he has told Sherlee Weingarten and several others) that Carlotta was Speyer's mistress and that it is Speyer's money she's been living on (and helping O'Neill to live on). The matter surfaced when Carlotta's lawyer, apprised her that Speyer's heirs were contemplating a suit to void Carlotta's trust fund. To her huge relief, the relatives decided for the sake of Speyer's reputation not to sue; but O'Neill's lawyer has probably got wind of the proceedings and reported to O'Neill.

In the days following, Carlotta grows more and more incoherent. In her diary on March 26, she scribbles that her doctor has given her "heavier sedative & other remedies." On March 27, the day before Easter, she writes, "My mind goes round and round. *How will it all end?*"

According to Carlotta, she becomes Dr. Patterson's patient on March 27, for treatment of an arthritic toe, but according to Patterson's records, she comes to him for treatment of "an acute back pain"—no mention of a toe. Back pain is one among Carlotta's many ailments; she is seeing other doctors at this time and she could have been confused by drugs and stress. Patterson, for his part, appears to have simply misremembered certain details when interviewed some years later. Between the two, it's possible to reconstruct only a fuzzy picture of the next several weeks.

Carlotta seems to have been admitted to Doctors Hospital on April 2. Patterson's recollection is that O'Neill, on the tenth floor, is unaware of Carlotta's presence on the floor below, and that he does not enlighten him. "I'd listen to her side of the story, and then take the stairs up to the tenth floor and listen to O'Neill's side. I talked to both of them about being understanding." Carlotta leaves the hospital on April 5.

On that same day, she records that her lawyer and O'Neill's are to meet "tomorrow." She also mentions for the first time that "Master has detectives watching me" and claims that they follow her when she goes out. "Nervous, detectives still there," she writes on April 8, adding that the meeting between Cane and Aronberg has been postponed.

On April 9, O'Neill writes a jittery note to Melville Cane, explaining that Carlotta "has forbidden any direct communication with her" and "would only tear up" any note from him. "Nevertheless," he writes, "will you tell her from me that I love her and always will." He continues: "It is disgraceful, that a marriage rightly estimated for fifteen years to be a model of mutual respect, and help, and love, should end up in bitter recrimination over nothing, suspicion over less, and loss of temper by two sick people."

After excusing himself for being "emotional," he ends, "In a case like this, I don't see how anyone ever understands any of the true issues."

On the same day, Freeman phones Carlotta to say good-bye. The relationship that she and O'Neill have shared with the man they once regarded as a son has finally shattered.

"Poor soul, he is as baffled as I am," writes Carlotta, "his faithfulness to the Master is thrown into gutter [together] with my 20 yrs service & love & loyalty." In fact, Freeman has found that he hates New York and is only too happy to return to California.

None of their friends can pinpoint precisely when or how Carlotta and O'Neill become reconciled—and surely none would venture a bet on how long that reconciliation will endure. But by mid-April, even though O'Neill's arm is not completely healed, he is deemed sufficiently fit to continue treatment as an outpatient.

He and Carlotta have agreed to move to Boston. They have decided that they must, after all, have a real home, and they will live in a hotel only temporarily while they search for a small house in the near suburbs. There they can reside in semi-seclusion away from New York and yet be close to what Dr. Patterson considers "the tops in orthopedic circles."

A week before leaving New York with O'Neill for Boston, Carlotta telephones Walter Casey, foolishly hoping to placate as well as mislead him. She offers Casey her hypocritical thanks for his loyalty to O'Neill and tells him (falsely) that together they are going to enter the Silver Hill psychiatric and rehabilitation center in New Canaan, Connecticut. Instead of voicing his approval, Casey (as she notes in her diary) "says the most horrible things to me—that I'm trying to *kill* or *drive Gene mad!* He and Gene's friends are watching me to turn me in! The shock to my already sick body and nerves almost ends me."

ON THE EVE of O'Neill's departure on April 19, Dr. Patterson admonishes him jocularly: "I want to receive a letter from you in your own hand after you arrive in Boston."

"I can't do it" is O'Neill's rueful response.

"You go to your desk and sit down," instructs Patterson, "and you'll hear a voice." The voice would be Patterson's and it would say, "Quit shaking and write me."

A few weeks later, Patterson receives a letter from Boston on Ritz-Carlton stationery; it is written shakily in O'Neill's own hand. "Just a few inadequate words of gratitude: that my arm was saved, that I had for a while the privilege of knowing as fine a man as you—and lastly that through your influence Mrs. O'Neill and I are together again with hope and love and a future!"

49

The sentiments of love and hope that O'Neill relayed to Dr. Patterson in May have a somewhat delusional ring. It's hard to believe he foresees any such rosy future. True, he is desperately trying to convince himself that his tremor has actually begun to abate and that he will miraculously recover the manual strength to transpose his ideas to paper.

Even if that happens, though, both he and Carlotta know (much as they may deny it) that this time they have wounded each other too poisonously to ever again be trustful lovers. Now, as hero and heroine of their own self-willed tragedy, they see no choice but to ad-lib their way through the baleful final scenes of their epic marriage. O'Neill writes to Melville Cane, thanking him for his painstaking efforts to get him and Carlotta back together without undue publicity, thus sparing them from becoming what O'Neill calls "a gutter tabloid sensation." (At least for the moment.)

Carlotta is surprisingly clear-eyed in her retrospective judgment of their climactic last act: "O'Neill died when his violent shaking hands made it impossible for him to write," she told José Quintero in 1956, three years after her husband's death.

"I, too, began to die then. His work was what [had] held us together. It was what made it possible for me to bear the insults, the humiliations, the betrayals. When that was gone there was nothing but disappointment and despair between us."

O'Neill doesn't succumb without a last desperate effort. "I feel I shall be able to write again," he tells Saxe Commins in August 1948 shortly after he and Carlotta have reconciled in Boston. "The tremor is better, too, but I'm just cursed with it for life, I guess, and the best to hope for is to circumvent it. This letter, for example, is written during a good spell and it's not so bad, eh? And why complain when the world itself is one vast tremor."

Four months later, he confides in two other trusted friends about his renewed hope to circumvent his tremor. He plans to return to his "old occupation of playwriting before too long," he writes to Nathan, adding, "God knows I have plenty of ideas." His legs have gotten shakier, he admits, but "the tremor which had me stopped for so long—along with war, critics, hotels, and apartments—seems now to affect my hands less." The "proof," as he pathetically points out, is that "this letter is being written legibly, without medication."

The following day, he sounds the same theme to Dudley Nichols, again citing his letter as an example, but hastily adding, "I better knock wood! The damned thing has nothing predictable." He goes on to tell Nichols he derives some hope from the new medical research under way into the cause of Parkinsonian tremors. But even with continuous medical treatment from the best specialists in Boston, O'Neill's tremor steadily worsens. As the months go by, he is forced to acknowledge he will never finish his cycle, nor will he take on any of the many lesser plays he has outlined. He is now convinced he has forever lost the strength for the sustained physical effort needed to write.

"I will never write another play and there is no use kidding myself that I will," he writes soon after to Aronberg.

ACTUALLY, THE CURTAIN went up on Act III of the O'Neills' "Little Drama in the Home" a few months earlier—in late April—with a deceptively benign hiatus during which Carlotta and O'Neill—living on cautiously good terms—went shopping for the "permanent" home that must be secluded, yet within convenient reach of medical attention in Boston.

It takes them only a month to find a "little gray house on tip of Marblehead Neck," reads Carlotta's diary entry on May 13. The notation is accompanied by one of her pussycat silhouettes.

"Gene and I feel happy about having house," she writes two days later. "New era!" This entry also is emblazoned with a pussycat; she and O'Neill appear to have convinced themselves they are blissfully at one. At month's end they are discussing the rewriting of their wills to reaffirm that each is the other's sole beneficiary. And on June 1, another pussycat blossoms in Carlotta's diary.

In spite of the overwhelming evidence to the contrary, both the O'Neills are still unwilling to confront the brutal fact that O'Neill's writing days are at an end. They appear to be heedless of the fault line on which they teeter: If he can't write, O'Neill will have no escape from Carlotta's suffocating watchfulness; and without the escape into his insulated realm of creativity—a realm where Carlotta dares not intrude—surely he will not survive. And it follows that Carlotta—if no longer needed as muse and guardian of O'Neill's creativity—will grow resentful and snappish in her constricted role of mere nurse and housekeeper.

The O'Neills have given their new home no fancy designation, just plain Number Four, Point O'Rocks Lane—a two-story, six-room house perched on a cliff overlooking the Atlantic, about twenty-five miles from Boston. Separated from Marblehead proper by a long causeway, the neck is an exclusive, affluent summer resort and a haven for yachtsmen, but mostly deserted during the winter. The O'Neill house is on the outermost curve of the neck.

With workmen putting in overtime, the little gray house is expected to be livable by the first of August and, on June 30, in happy anticipation, O'Neill and Carlotta sit on their terrace overlooking the water. Entranced by the passing sailboats and circling gulls, they have decided to convert the terrace into a thirty-five-foot glass-enclosed porch. Europe lies in a straight line over the horizon. Cape Cod is to the south, Cape Ann to the north, and the treacherous waters of Marblehead harbor are guarded by a bit of O'Neill's favorite scenery, an offshore lighthouse.

"The house was so much on the water," Carlotta once recalled, "that it was tied to rocks by steel cables and when the storms came up they came right up over our heads—we expected to go out to sea at any moment."

Between visits to supervise the work on their new home, O'Neill receives treatment for his mending arm; and Carlotta, who complains often of feeling ill—her eyes, her back, her arthritis, her nerves—visits various doctors. Both are routinely dosed (if not overdosed) with multiple drugs for their various chronic ailments, including some dubious sedatives to which they react badly.

They both complain often of the hot, humid weather; but throughout June and July the pussycats continue their parade through the pages of Carlotta's diary. On July 11, O'Neill presents Carlotta with the published version of *The Iceman Cometh*, lovingly inscribed:

"To Carlotta, my love and my life—out of great sorrow, and pain, and misunderstanding, comes a new vision of deeper love and security and above all, serenity, to bind us ever closer in our old age. Sweetheart, all my love and all of me."

The handwriting is cramped but has barely a trace of tremor. It has shrunk a week later when, on their wedding anniversary, he writes Carlotta a note accompanying his gift of a volume of Christina Rossetti's poetry.

"Nineteen years ago in Paris," his note begins, "each with knees knocking together, you said 'Oui' and I said 'Oui,' not boldly but with frightened happiness." Now, he goes on, with "chaos looming over the world, I want to say to you—'You are my love—forever my love, Sweetheart!'"

The one thing Carlotta hopes she can count on is that O'Neill has sworn off drinking forever. The consequence, however, is an overdependence on his prescriptive "nerve" medications.

In addition to not drinking, he promises to do his "utmost" to banish all "selfishness or thoughtlessness" that could possibly hurt her; he wishes only to make her happy, "for your happiness is my happiness!" His handwriting is now so minuscule as to be barely legible and this time there is a noticeable tremor in the date and in the signatory "Gene."

Writing (presumably behind Carlotta's back) to Saxe Commins in late July, O'Neill describes their "good luck" in finding the Marblehead house "right on the ocean." It is "a tiny house," he writes, "with little rooms, the upstairs ones with sloping eaves—built in 1880." It reminds him, he says, of the first home his father bought in New London when he was "a kid." Carlotta, he confides, has paid for the house "out of her reserve fund." (The total cost of the house, which he does not reveal to Commins, is Carlotta's initial $48,000, supplemented by an additional $25,000 of O'Neill's.)

The house requires considerable modernizing and insulating to make it a livable year-round home. "Our last," continues O'Neill in his letter to Commins. "Everything to cut down overhead and make it a cinch to run with just a cook." The aim, he emphasizes, is to "simplify living and gain as much security for our old age as is possible." In his optimism (his hopeless hope, his pipe dream), O'Neill has decreed that one of the four small upstairs rooms adjoining his bedroom be furnished as a study.

He rejoices in again having "some roots—of seaweed—with my feet in a New London sea. It is like coming home, in a way, and I feel happier than in many years." He adds that both his and Carlotta's health has improved (since New York), although his arm is not expected to be fully mended for another six months.

O'NEILL AND CARLOTTA are amid preparations for their move to Marblehead when, on August 13, they are rattled by a phone call from Winfield Aronberg; Shane has been arrested for drug possession.

Aronberg arranges for him to plead guilty and he receives a two-year suspended sentence on condition he enter the federal hospital at Lexington, Kentucky, for treatment. The fact that Shane will avoid jail does not mollify Carlotta. "Gene does *not* in any way deserve this last heartache," she deplores to her diary.

The news is enough to put a crack in the thin veneer of O'Neill and Carlotta's tentative compatibility; indeed, a few days later it sends O'Neill into a paranoiac spin and he accuses her of "concealing" or "destroying" a letter to him from Aronberg. Although the letter turns up in the afternoon, Carlotta keens, "A day of nerves, tears & collapse—All my joy & hope flies out the window. I don't fancy 'accusations' beginning again—an unhealthy sign."

A week later, O'Neill, sunk in gloom, suffers (in Carlotta's words) "the worst attack of Parkinson's I have ever seen. His whole body needs extra sedatives . . . watch him all night."

On September 12, O'Neill instructs Aronberg to make it clear to Shane "that he cannot ever expect money from me." Shane has "his interest in Spithead," writes O'Neill, and should appeal to his mother for financial help. Then, crying poor (like his father), O'Neill says that after paying for his new home he is so broke that "we can't even afford a car!" O'Neill never saw Shane again.

Carlotta's diary for the troubled year of 1948 breaks off with a final entry on September 14; on that date, she and a temporary housekeeper move into the "little house" for a final inspection and to unpack. O'Neill arrives to occupy his new home on the following day.

O'NEILL ANSWERS A LETTER from Dudley Nichols in early December, two months after settling in: "This is our home—our last since we can never afford to have another, or stand the strain of moving—the terrible sheer strain of it." The "old Western Ocean" is crashing on the rocks beneath his study window, he writes. "There is peace here for me, and for Carlotta too."

When Sophus and Eline Winther visit early in 1949, O'Neill shows them the second-floor study adjoining his bedroom; it is neatly set up with notebooks, paper, and pencils. "It's a hell of a thing," O'Neill confides, "to want to write, to have everything but control of the hands."

It was "the saddest moment of all the years I had known O'Neill," recalled Winther.

The Winthers, at O'Neill's urging, check into a nearby hotel so as to prolong their visit to several days. Winther described an evening in Marblehead, sitting on the porch "with the full moon hanging in a faint mist," when O'Neill tells him his life "has come full circle." Suddenly, O'Neill looks up and says, "Goodbye Old Moon. Fall out of the sky. I don't need you anymore."

As always, both Winther and O'Neill have a lot to say; every now and then, after deploring a bygone or recent event, one or the other facetiously quotes Ephraim Cabot from *Desire Under the Elms*: "God's hard, not easy"; it's a catch phrase they adopted five years earlier in San Francisco. On the night of Sophus and Eline's last visit, when O'Neill once again quotes that line, Winther thinks it has "an ominous ring."

As they sit on the porch, O'Neill points: "Straight across the Atlantic, right over there, is Ireland," he says, adding, "My critics have never recognized how much my work is indebted to the Irish in me." O'Neill, observed Winther, "seemed to be filled with a longing for his ancestors."

AT THE END OF 1949, O'Neill gives Eugene Jr. a full report of his deteriorating condition. His legs are now so badly affected, it takes all his willpower to walk without weaving about. "I've been a guinea pig for several of the new concoctions which are alleged to help some people [with Parkinson's] but all they do is make me much sicker."

He tells Eugene that on his second day of the most recent medication, he passed into "a strange state of benumbed sickliness" he can't describe; on the third day, his "eyes looked like a maniac's, bright as polished ebony encased in reddish eyeballs"; he could hardly see and was "so sick and feeble" he had to abandon the "cure," and swore his "guinea pig days were over for good!"

His one hope, he says, is that a lot of research is being done to determine whether all tremors are in fact Parkinsonian and, ipso facto, incurable.

O'Neill's tremor has continued to plague him, he informs George Jean Nathan some months later. "As for writing, that is out of the question. It is not only a matter of hand, but of mind—I just feel there is nothing more I want to say."

O'Neill sits in his study or on his glassed-in porch and broods, staring for hours out to sea through a pair of powerful binoculars. He reads desultorily, dipping most often into Spengler's *The Decline of the West*.

With work no longer filling his life, and love no longer a reliable palliative (much as he tries to persuade himself to the contrary), O'Neill is pathetically happy to see such friends as are still persona grata to Carlotta; in addition to the Winthers, they include the Crouses, Charles O'Brien Kennedy, Bobby Jones, Dudley Nichols, Macgowan, and Mai-mai Sze.

Charles Kennedy recalls O'Neill's tremulous welcome when he visits, bringing tomatoes picked from his sister's garden in the nearby Massachusetts town of Waltham. The two men sit on the porch in companionable silence, as O'Neill, with trembling hands, removes each tomato from its individual paper bag, then peels away its cellophane wrapping, studying it in silent appreciation. Kennedy can't help but be touched by his friend's pleasure and saddened by his isolation.

On another visit, he and O'Neill sit looking out at the boats in the harbor. "It was a beautiful scene, and I knew, in his heart, Gene would have liked to be on one of those boats. He said very little, but once in a while he'd drop a word, and the longing was evident. I would never want to repeat those heartbreaking visits."

Also warmly welcomed by O'Neill, and distressed by his barren existence, is a local doctor, Frederic B. Mayo, who is called in frequently to treat his patient for colds and other minor ailments.

Mayo is a tall, crisp-mannered New Englander, with a long-legged stride and a hesitant, boyish smile. His initial reaction to O'Neill's situation is shock at the famous writer's lack of contact with the outside world. Mayo knows little of O'Neill's personal background, but falls quickly under the spell of his charm.

Like Dr. Shirley Fisk in New York, Mayo responds to O'Neill's seeming need to be rescued from his isolated life, and from Carlotta's overprotectiveness. He makes several efforts to rouse O'Neill from the apparent apathy in which he is immersed; he can't bring himself to accept O'Neill's sedentary resignation to his illness. But his well-meant attempts to get his patient out of the house for a change of scene are aborted.

At one point, he invites O'Neill for an outing on his family's yacht, which O'Neill accepts with delight; Carlotta dissuades her husband, however, probably after learning that Mayo's in-laws will be aboard and worrying O'Neill will find that stressful.

Dr. Mayo resigns himself to personally supplying O'Neill with the companionship he seems to crave. At O'Neill's invitation, he often extends his professional visits to include an hour or more of talk, or a session of listening to jazz, of which Mayo himself is fond.

Once, he brings his patient a newly issued Louis Armstrong record and O'Neill, after listening appreciatively but not uncritically, says, "Louis can't hit that high C any more." Mayo notes that Carlotta has looked on sullenly and is clearly irritated by the loud music that reverberates throughout the small house, and from which she cannot escape, as she could in Tao House.

Mayo, of course, is unaware that O'Neill initially had agreed with Carlotta that the Marblehead house was too confined to accommodate either the player piano, Rosie, or his vast record collection; in June 1948, when listing the items they wished to have with them in Marblehead, Carlotta had noted, "Gene doesn't want gramophone or records sent for a year or so, if ever" and, a week later, "Gene's gramophone & records to be stored."

To Carlotta's displeasure, O'Neill changed his mind. Annoyed with him though she might be, she seldom leaves O'Neill's side, for his food has to be cut, his cigarettes lit, and many other homely chores managed for him.

She doesn't even let him sleep unsupervised. Her bedroom is directly across a narrow hall from his; at night, she always keeps her door open and makes sure his bedroom door is open too, so she can keep an eye on him from her bed.

Carlotta nurses O'Neill tenaciously and, although she sometimes complains of the grueling job in letters to friends, she refuses to engage anyone to help. They have in their employ a discreet Japanese houseman Carlotta calls "Saki," who lives in, and a cook, Doris Manning, who comes in daily from the nearby town of Salem to prepare and serve their meals.

There are occasional rumors in the press about O'Neill's having recovered from Parkinson's and being at work on a new play, and, as a result, he has been receiving mail from dozens of afflicted persons asking him to share the secret of his successful recovery. Distressed at being the unwitting source of false hope, he instructs Carlotta to make a formal statement about his health to the press at the end of 1949.

"He hasn't worked for three years—and God only knows if he ever will be able to," she tells *The New York Times*. "It's terrible. It gets worse. The hands tremble and then the feet." Explaining that O'Neill is obliged to live in seclusion, rarely seeing anyone but herself and a servant, she adds, "It makes him nervous to have someone in the house."

Added to O'Neill's woes are the nasty attacks on his reputation being launched by literary detractors both at home and abroad.

"Among the untragic tragedians the most spectacular is Eugene O'Neill," jeers the prominent American critic Eric Bentley in his book on modern drama published in 1946. "At everything in the theatre except being tragic and being comic he is a success . . . the good clean fun of a Hitchcock movie is better."

In 1962, Bentley, after reading his quoted comment in the just-published biography *O'Neill*, wrote to the authors, protesting that he was "anti-O'Neill" only "in part" and only "sometimes"; he pointed out that his preproduction review of *The Iceman Cometh* in *The Atlantic Monthly* in 1946 "was not anti, nor (on the whole)" was his "brief survey of O'Neill's career" in a recently published book, *Major Writers of America*, which, Bentley regretted, "came out too late to be of any use to you."

The prolific and acerbic Mary McCarthy, after seeing *The Iceman Cometh*, has scorned O'Neill's body of work as "maudlin," "crude," and, of course, "repetitious."

She criticizes him for knowing nothing about how real drunkards behave—he who is a walking encyclopedia of firsthand knowledge of drunks; she labels him a playwright who cannot write. (Like most of the critics, she did not discern that the production was clumsily directed and badly acted. And, like Bentley, she later somewhat softened her overall view of O'Neill's work.)

From London's *The Times Literary Supplement* in April 1948 comes an attack so scathing the New York newspapers feel obliged to report on it.

"Mr. O'Neill is as puritanical as Mr. [G. B.] Shaw, but his puritanism, unlike Mr. Shaw's, unlike Milton's, unlike Andrew Marvell's, has no grace or geniality," writes the anonymous critic for the most important of Britain's literary publications. O'Neill's characters, he goes on, are "ineffectual egoists" and his stage tricks are "the sort of stuff that might be written by an earnest sophomore."

And there is more, much more.

O'Neill takes what consolation he can from Brooks Atkinson's lengthy response in *The New York Times* on April 25, 1948. Atkinson, while vigorously defending O'Neill and mocking the anonymous English critic, does not hesitate to point out O'Neill's weaknesses, along with his great strengths.

"The Literary Supplement . . . has gone to some scholarly pains to prove that Eugene O'Neill is humbug," Atkinson begins, citing the critic's disparagement of O'Neill as "not equal to Shakespeare or Aeschylus" and inferior to Somerset Maugham.

"Even for a critic [these] animadversions are excessively obtuse and prejudiced," writes Atkinson. Himself believing that *The Hairy Ape* is "one of the most powerful plays in the language," Atkinson scorns the English critic's disparagement of it as "the sort of stuff that might be written by an earnest sophomore who has listened too long to professors of dramatic literature at chautauquas in the Rocky Mountains.

"Yes, that's what he says," chaffs Atkinson. "It's there in plain print on fairly good paper."

Conceding the futility of trying to convince "the Cato of the Literary Supplement" to like O'Neill, Atkinson backs into what will ultimately be a resounding tribute, but first he concedes, "As a prose stylist he has always been curiously inadequate. He cannot wrap his singing robes about him, like Milton." Atkinson allows that "many Americans do not like him at all" and that "even his best friends do not conceive of him as perfect."

Soon, though, Atkinson can't help but submit to the power of O'Neill's genius, which, he writes, lies in "the raw boldness and the elemental strength of his attack upon outworn concepts of destiny." He is "a moral writer," who "thinks the spiritual glories of America have been sold out for materialistic gains. . . .

"He came into our theater at a time when most plays were aimless, post-prandial charades. A pioneer in method, he broke a number of the old molds, shook up the drama as well as audiences and helped to transform the theater into an art seriously related to life. . . .

"The peevish article in *The Times Literary Supplement* overlooks the one thing in O'Neill that is inescapable: the passionate depth and vitality of his convictions. Nothing said about him is worth the paper it is printed on unless it recognizes the vitality he has brought into the theater. Nobody is so impervious to vitality as a writer who has none."

Like Atkinson, other critics at home and abroad believe they are evaluating the final and complete O'Neill. They know he is too ill to write another play and they think they have a handle on his body of work. But, of course, they are all, including Atkinson, as yet unaware of the global reach of this unpredictable genius.

The fact is that in 1948, only *The Iceman Cometh*, among O'Neill's four final plays, has even had a Broadway production—and *Iceman* will not be recognized as a masterwork until it is brilliantly revived off-Broadway nearly a decade after O'Neill's death.

As for the other three plays, the initial production of *A Moon for the Misbegotten* was aborted (at O'Neill's own request) before any but a minuscule provincial audience had a glimpse of it; and *A Touch of the Poet* was withheld from production, due to O'Neill's failing health. (*Moon* will not receive its iconic production until 1974, when Quintero directs it with Robards playing the dying Jamie Tyrone opposite Colleen Dewhurst as the earth mother Josie Hogan. And *A Touch of the Poet*, first staged on Broadway in 1958, as of this writing has still not received its definitive production.)

But most important, virtually no one at this time knows of the existence of *Long Day's Journey Into Night*.

Even without being able to refer to these defining works, Atkinson, in his 1946 tribute, helps somewhat to reaffirm O'Neill's stature, as does a revival of the *S.S. Glencairn* plays at New York's City Center on June 12, 1948. Lawrence Langner suggests to O'Neill that a production of *A Touch of the Poet* or a new attempt to present *A Moon for the Misbegotten* would be a healthy thing both for the theater and for O'Neill's reputation. But O'Neill cannot make the effort. "I don't believe I could live through a production," he tells Langner.

By the winter of 1949, the O'Neills' snug home on Point O'Rocks Lane has become a virtual prison. Marblehead Neck, bustling during late spring and summer, is something less than cheerful during late fall and winter, when most of the homes are closed and the neck is a desolate landscape of shuttered windows and wind-torn naked trees. The O'Neills rarely venture beyond their own property. When they do, it is to Boston to consult specialists and, once in a very great while, to attend a movie in Salem; on those occasions, they are driven by Saki (in his own car).

There is not the slightest chance that O'Neill will accept Arthur Miller's cordial and respectful invitation (in a letter on February 22, 1949) to attend a performance of his new play, *Death of a Salesman*, which opened to great acclaim on February 10. Miller has recently learned from

Kenneth Macgowan that O'Neill has questioned him about the structure of *Salesman*. Macgowan has also told Miller of O'Neill's crippling physical condition.

As Miller recalled, he issued his invitation as "probably more a salute than anything else," and also "as a sort of refusal to recognize the reality."

In his letter, Miller wrote, "I have long wished to speak with you and I take this occasion to ask whether we might get together for an afternoon or an evening. Will you let me know if and when you could see the play and whether a meeting is possible at this time." Miller had been "deeply affected" by *The Iceman Cometh* despite, as he later wrote, "that first awful production."

"I can't say that O'Neill's work was a direct influence on me," Miller reflected some years after O'Neill's death.

> It was his personality and relation to theater that always moved me. His personality and his uncompromised dedication to his art. Dimly as I understood everything in those days, I did realize that to him the theater was a life's dedication despite all its silliness and trivialities.
>
> O'Neill ennobled theater; in his hands playwriting was a vocation almost in the religious connotation of the word—an engagement in the holy search for some ultimate order in the chaos of existence. O'Neill, the most troubled of men, did triumph in one sense at least—he transformed his most personal spiritual dilemmas into roles for actors in plays that an audience bound by the illusions of materialism could take to heart.
>
> He opened the door to the invisible dimensions of life. He made it seem possible for others as well to fight the Broadway mountain and survive with an armful of works that told the tale. In that particular his example was inspiring.

O'Neill's reply to Miller (delayed because it had been forwarded from two addresses in New York) was equally cordial; but, as Miller expected, his invitation was declined. O'Neill expressed himself as "deeply grateful" for Miller's "expression of esteem" for his work in the theater.

"There is nothing I would like better than to have a long talk with you," O'Neill went on, "or to accept your kind invitation to see *Death of a Salesman*. But I am afraid both are impossible now. I am really too sick to go anywhere. My tremor is now so bad it makes me unfit for practically everything. I tell you this because I want you to understand.

"But I don't mean that the chance of the talk is entirely off. I hope sometime you will have to come to Boston, and then we can arrange for you to come out here." He added that he had an order in for *Death of a Salesman* "as soon as the book appears," and he would surely be able to add his "cheers to all the others." The two never did meet.

WITH HIS CHRISTMAS GIFT to Carlotta in 1949, O'Neill writes, in a shaky hand: "To 'Mama'—and still as over all the years, 'Sweetheart' and 'Darling' and 'Beloved Wife' and 'Friend,' too!—in these days of sickness and despair."

Carlotta's own health is consistently poor. The constant strain of caring for her husband is sapping her strength. She and O'Neill are both "in very low spirits," she writes to his boyhood friend Joseph McCarthy in the spring of 1950.

She doesn't mention that O'Neill speaks of being once again tempted to take that long swim into the moon's wake, nor does she tell McCarthy that he has recently joined the Euthanasia Society of America. A pamphlet issued in 1949 bears O'Neill's name as a member of the society's American Advisory Council (along with, among others, Max Eastman, Robert Frost, Somerset Maugham, and Robert Sherwood).

The pamphlet lists some "Typical Tragedies," in which a wife or husband gave or attempted to give the gift of annihilation to a suffering spouse. (Ironically, mercy killing is one of the few methods of death-dealing O'Neill has never got around to in a play.)

ONE OF CARLOTTA's self-imposed duties is shielding her husband from telephone calls; rarely if ever has he answered the phone in any of their homes, and never in Marblehead.

And so, late in the afternoon of September 25, 1950 (two years since moving into the little house at Point O'Rocks Lane), he sits by silently when Carlotta picks up the ringing phone in their living room.

It is Aronberg on the line; he says (according to an account by Saxe Commins published many years later), "Hello, Carlotta. This is Bill Aronberg. I have terrible news for you. Try to be brave and break this gently to Gene. Young Gene has just committed suicide."

Carlotta answers, according to Commins's account, "How dare you invade our privacy?" and slams the receiver down. "That," writes Commins, "was the entire conversation," as Aronberg reported it to him in a voice "blazing with anger."

Carlotta gives a very different account:

"Gene was sitting in a chair right across from me. The lawyer told me, 'Eugene has killed himself.' I said, 'Are you sure?' and he said, 'Yes,' and I said, 'I don't believe it,' but he repeated, 'Well, I'm sure,' and this and that. Well, I hung up the phone and you can imagine what I felt like, and I sat down, Gene watching me with those black eyes of his."

"Well, come out with it, what is it?" O'Neill demanded.

"Eugene is ill, very ill," Carlotta replied.

"When did he die?" asks O'Neill.

"I don't know, the lawyer didn't give me the exact time," said Carlotta.

"Come on, let's talk sense," said O'Neill. "Is he dead? He surely wouldn't ring you up if he wasn't."

Then, said Carlotta, O'Neill "lapsed into silence and he never mentioned Eugene again."

Whatever the truth of how the message was delivered and received,

O'Neill must have known that he had wounded his son when he allowed Carlotta to keep him at a distance. O'Neill's last words to Eugene, written seven months earlier, in answer to a letter from him, had been all but a total rejection.

"No, I don't think the idea of dropping in here this summer is good. In fact, it's bad." O'Neill suggested instead that they meet in the adjoining town of Salem, where he made periodic visits for medical treatment—"arranging a meeting beforehand," presumably at a time when he would be unaccompanied by Carlotta. (The letter was typewritten, doubtless by Carlotta; no such meeting took place.)

EUGENE JR. HAD bought a small house on acreage adjoining the property of his friend Frank Meyer, in the bohemian colony of Woodstock in upstate New York. "He loved the outdoors and enjoyed chopping wood," recalled Meyer. "He told me his father had co-signed a bank loan for the payment on the property. He also told me soon after his father left New York for Boston, that he didn't think he'd be seeing him any more. His relationship with Carlotta had deteriorated, he said."

Eugene told Meyer that during a bedside visit at Doctors Hospital in New York, his father had told him, "I have to go back to her; I can't live without her." Eugene had interpreted this as a farewell. He inferred his father was telling him Carlotta had given him a choice between his son and herself, and his choosing Carlotta meant Eugene's exclusion in the future.

It had been Eugene's routine to spend several days a week in New York City in scattered teaching jobs, earning barely enough to support himself. He and his lover, Ruth Lander, lived together frugally, and not in tranquillity; Eugene was unfaithful to her and occasionally struck her.

"His hands often trembled, especially when he was shaving the side of his face and trimming his beard and mustache," Ruth recalled. "His tremor was worst in the morning. He thought he was getting Parkinson's like his father. He told me that he knew he needed a psychiatrist, but that, as he put it, the daddy of them all—the only one who could have understood him—was dead.

"One morning, he said to me, 'As of today, I can commit suicide any time.' He explained he had just gotten a special clause written into his life insurance policy. He told me he had tried to kill himself once, in New Haven."

Ruth walked out on Eugene in the summer of 1949. According to Meyer, the incident set Eugene off on a year-long orgy. "He had eighteen girls during that period," Meyer recalled. "He also started drinking heavily, more than I realized at first—although I never saw him really drunk."

By the summer of 1950, Eugene, who was now forty, persuaded himself he truly loved Ruth. He asked her to marry him, and that September she agreed. "He told me we'd have a baby, and I could leave my hair blond, although he preferred me as a brunette," Ruth said.

Eugene conveyed the good news to Meyer. "I told Gene to stop worrying about women and get back to serious work," Meyer recalled. "Gene said he had to have someone to work for. I told him he had himself to work for and asked him if he couldn't make the effort to get back on the right track." Eugene answered, "I've slipped too far. I can't get back."

The reconciliation with Ruth did not last long.

"I had told Gene I'd marry him, after he'd pounded me about it for three hours," Ruth said. "I was slightly hysterical by the time I said yes. But when I went back to his house with him, later, I told him I couldn't go through with it. I felt sorry for him. He had been rejected by everyone—first by his father, then Yale, then his father again, then me—but I couldn't stay with him. There was insanity in his eyes."

Late on Saturday night, September 23, a common friend of Eugene and Meyer's telephoned Meyer to tell him that Eugene had been seen in various bars around town talking of Ruth's desertion and declaring he was going to commit suicide.

"I didn't think Gene would kill himself over Ruth," Meyer said, "but I knew he was capable of suicide. We'd discussed the subject many times and we were thoroughly agreed that in a case where things became intolerable for a person he should kill himself. Both of us were against the Christian viewpoint of suicide being sinful."

Meyer and his wife, Elsie, went in search of Eugene, but failed to find him in any of the bars or in his home. "I even searched his land, to see if he'd tried to hang himself from a tree," Meyer said. Finally, early on Sunday morning, the Meyers gave up their search and went to sleep.

Eugene telephoned them late Sunday morning. Meyer and his wife drove down the road a quarter of a mile to visit him at his house.

"He looked beat," Meyer said. "I didn't want him to be alone and asked him to come to us for dinner. He didn't want to, at first, but he finally said he'd drive over in a little while.

"At dinner we talked about our worry of the night before. Elsie told Gene he shouldn't speak of suicide, and added, 'Of course, you'll never kill yourself.' I said I realized now I had been foolish to worry, that I should have known he would never commit suicide impulsively, but would take time to plan it properly."

Then Eugene, in perfect seriousness, told the Meyers that he had been thinking, the night before, of using the chain that hung across a private lane adjoining his and the Meyers' property to hang himself. "I thought you'd plan something more thorough than that," said Meyer uneasily.

Eugene left the Meyers' house at eleven. He'd had a few drinks before dinner and some beer after. He seemed relaxed, but he was unusually quiet and his face was gray.

"I went to bed at three but couldn't sleep," said Meyer.

Around 3:30, Gene came back. He said he'd slept, but was wide awake now and wanted a drink; he had no liquor in his house. I had half a bottle of bourbon, and each of us had two stiff drinks. We sat talking for about two hours, mostly reminiscing.

He mentioned at one point that perhaps he had been wrong about suicide, that maybe the Christian viewpoint was the right one, after all. Elsie was in bed in the adjoining room and she didn't get up, but she and Gene exchanged a few words through the door. He told her, "I'm a man of iron if I come through this."

He had a teaching engagement in New York later that day—it was now 5 a.m. Monday—so he decided to get a few hours of sleep on my couch. He asked me to leave the bottle where he could find it, and I did. There wasn't enough left in it to make him drunk.

I went to sleep, and when I got up at eleven, Gene was gone and so was the bottle. I guessed he had followed his usual routine of driving to Poughkeepsie, from where he would take the train to New York.

An hour later, Ruth telephoned Elsie Meyer.

"She said Gene had given her permission, before she left, to go back to his house and pick up her clothes," Elsie recalled, "but she claimed she was afraid to go alone, because she couldn't be certain Gene had gone to New York, and if he was home he might hit her. I was positive Gene was in New York, but I said I'd pick her up and go with her to the house."

Elsie put her five-year-old son, John, into the car, and started out. She had to pass Eugene's house to fetch Ruth and was startled to see his jeep parked in the driveway. He must have felt ill and canceled his teaching appointment, she thought. She parked, told her child to wait in the car, and knocked at the front door.

There was no answer but the door was unlocked and Elsie, fearing Eugene might be really ill, walked into the living room. She saw Eugene lying at the foot of the stairs.

"Intellectually I knew he was dead," Elsie said. "But emotionally I couldn't accept it."

Eugene's telephone had been disconnected because he'd neglected to pay the bill, so Elsie ran to the nearest neighbor's house and phoned for a doctor. Then she called her husband and told him, "He's done it."

"When I got back to my house," Elsie said, "Ruth telephoned, wanting to know what had happened to me. I'd forgotten about meeting her. I told her Gene had killed himself."

Eugene had apparently left the Meyers' house around seven or eight that morning, possibly intending to bathe, shave, and change for his trip to New York—for Monday, according to Ruth, was the day he always went through the ritual of trimming his beard and mustache. But sometime during his preparations, he decided to put his razor to a different use.

He drank off the last of Frank Meyer's bourbon, sat down at the driftwood desk on which his father had written plays in Provincetown, and scribbled on a scrap of paper: "Never let it be said of O'Neill that he failed to finish a bottle. Ave atque vale."

Then he climbed the stairs, filled the bathtub, stepped into it, and slashed his wrists and left ankle. According to the coroner's report, he had apparently stumbled downstairs about twenty minutes later, in a kind of animal-panic attempt to save himself.

Neither the Meyers nor Ruth attributed Eugene's death (as gossip subsequently did) to straitened finances; he had back salary coming to him and was due to earn a minimum of $10,000 during the next year from lectures and various other freelance activities to which he was committed.

Nor did the Meyers consider the possibility that Ruth's rejection caused the suicide, although Ruth herself tended, at first, to assume the blame.

"I went to pieces after Gene died," she said. "I went to a psychiatrist for help, and he finally convinced me that the most I could have done was postpone his suicide, but that I couldn't have prevented it."

It devolved on Elsie Meyer to break the news of Eugene's death to his mother. Kathleen Pitt-Smith, now widowed and still living in Douglaston, Long Island, had a standing dinner date with her son in New York for either Monday or Tuesday of each week.

If Kathleen did not hear from Eugene on a Monday, she knew he would call her Tuesday to confirm the time and place of their meeting.

At 5:50 p.m. that Monday, the twenty-fifth, a newspaper reporter telephoned her and asked if she expected to hear from her son that day.

"I thought Gene had gotten married suddenly," Kathleen later said. "He had told me he was planning to marry Ruth. I told the reporter I didn't expect to hear from Gene any more that day, but that I'd be seeing him the next day."

The reporter, with a tact Kathleen later acknowledged gratefully, informed Kathleen her son had been involved in an accident in Woodstock that morning, and urged her to telephone the Meyers at once. Not until then did she learn, from Elsie, that Eugene had killed himself. (Kathleen not only rallied after her son's death but—perhaps because she'd escaped living with his father—managed to survive O'Neill himself by twenty-nine years, longer than either Agnes or Carlotta; she died in 1982 at the age of ninety-four.)

O'Neill did not attend his son's funeral, but he paid all the expenses. According to Pitt-Smith, he and Carlotta each sent separate flower arrangements for the coffin.

Two and a half weeks after the suicide, Frank Meyer wrote to O'Neill that Eugene had always wanted his father to have his PhD diploma in case of his death, and asked if he could forward it to him in Marblehead.

"I should have written you much sooner had there been anything I could presume to say," Meyer went on. "You are probably the only person to whom I can say nothing of significance about him which you do not already know. But if you would like me to write—or care at any time to talk to me—please say so."

O'Neill answered from Point O'Rocks Lane a week later, saying that Meyer's letter had been a great pleasure to him. "To learn that Eugene had wanted me to have his Ph.D. diploma warmed my heart," he said, asking that it be sent to him.

O'NEILL WAS SPARED the knowledge of his younger son's suicide on June 22, 1977. Shane was fifty-seven when he leaped to his death from the fourth floor of an apartment in Brooklyn.

"The suicide of Shane O'Neill, whose life in so many ways reflected the problems of despair raised in the plays of Eugene O'Neill, was made known recently," wrote Richard Shepard, one of the *Times*'s most gifted reporters. Shane had reportedly jumped "just before midnight" after an argument "with a woman friend." He had by then separated from his wife, Cathy, and his four children were all grown. In his two-column-long obituary, Shepard vividly summed up Shane's troubled life, pointing out that his drug addiction had "caused more than normal distress in the father, whose own mother had been addicted to drugs and whose tragedy had inspired what many believe to be O'Neill's greatest drama, *Long Day's Journey Into Night*."

50

I t is four months since Eugene Jr.'s death—time enough to heighten O'Neill's guilt at having kept his son at a distance and to inflame O'Neill's anger at Carlotta for persuading him to do so. O'Neill has been tormenting himself over the loss of not only a beloved and admired son but also a trusted friend and confidant.

Indeed, O'Neill's already frayed mental balance has been rapidly slipping and the idea of his own suicide is much on his mind; he deplores the vestiges of Catholic indoctrination that deter him from taking that step.

He tells one of his rare visitors, Lawrence Langner, with whom he has earlier shared his thoughts about suicide, that he wishes he could kill himself by jumping off his rock into the Atlantic; but, he adds with bleak humor, he's too good a swimmer and would instinctively try to save himself.

Among the few who have an occasional glimpse of O'Neill during the grim months following Eugene Jr.'s death is a local patrolman, John Snow. A fair-haired man of medium height in his early forties, Snow is a familiar figure to residents of the area. He has been assigned during five consecutive winters to the beat that includes Point O'Rocks Lane, and he makes it a part of his routine to drop in now and then on the scattering of winter residents in the area as a gesture of reassurance.

On several occasions he has been invited into the O'Neill home by Carlotta, who brings him into the dining room for a five- or ten-minute chat with O'Neill. Seated at the long dining table, O'Neill exchanges brief pleasantries with the patrolman. Although Snow, during his first visit, finds it difficult to follow O'Neill's halting speech, he gradually grows accustomed to it. He listens attentively when O'Neill explains he came to Marblehead both for seclusion and for the pleasure of listening to the pounding surf, especially during stormy weather.

Snow finds Carlotta gracious, and he commiserates with her about her arthritis. The last time Snow visits the house, O'Neill does not speak at all; Snow assumes that speech has become too much of an effort. He's right. Brooding about past failures, present futility, and a future in which he will grow increasingly helpless and dependent upon Carlotta— O'Neill wishes he was dead.

Wrapped in her own gloom, Carlotta can't bear the thought of another bleak, icy winter on Point O'Rocks Lane. The little gray house has become a prison of smoldering emotions. She wants to sell it, but O'Neill says they have nowhere else to go.

Carlotta's growing anxiety dates from Eugene Jr.'s death and O'Neill's frightening withdrawal. It was then she began taking several teaspoons of a prescribed sleeping medicine nightly, according to doctors who later recorded her medical history. She believes it is chloral hydrate and safe to take regularly, but, in fact, the medicine contains bromide, to which (unsuspected by her doctor) she happens to be violently allergic and— although she doesn't realize it—it is having a toxic effect.

Carlotta is beginning to hallucinate, and, as she later tells a psychiatrist who takes her medical history, she has episodes of thinking "there is someone around the corner, listening at the door." She has periods of confusion, during which (in the words of her psychiatric history) "she cannot carry through certain trains of thought."

By December, she is unable to write a check legibly.

That Christmas, there is no written greeting of love from O'Neill to Carlotta, no birthday gift, and no message of hope for the new year.

Now, both past their sixty-second birthdays, they manage—but only just—to get through the first month of 1951 with no outward sign of the violence seething within. But by the beginning of February, Carlotta (again according to her psychiatric history) has become "a completely disoriented woman, at times calm and at others excited, who speaks of people driving her insane, trying to blind her and hallucinations of rats or bugs in the room," a woman "lacking insight and judgment."

The scene is now set for the horrific episode of February 5, 1951, that will become one of the legendary and often-retold events of O'Neill's life.

It is an occurrence of such operatic thunder that, sixty years later, it will inspire an actual opera with a libretto by the playwright Tony Kushner (who was not yet born in 1951) called *A Blizzard on Marblehead Neck*.

The real-life setting is nightfall on the Neck. The front door of the little house opens and O'Neill rushes out. Although the temperature is in the low thirties, he is dressed only in slacks and a wool shirt. He has forgotten his cane and, after only a few wobbly steps in his front yard, he stumbles on a rock that is hidden under eight inches of crusted snow, and falls to the ground. His right leg is broken at the knee and he loses consciousness from the pain. For some time, perhaps as long as an hour, he lies in the snow.

Where he was going—whether it was just as far as his legs would carry him, or if he was heading for that final swim in the ocean—is uncertain. But, only too aware that even with the aid of a cane his legs are unreliable, he surely was not out for a stroll in his garden.

There will be many conflicting accounts of the night's maelstrom and its aftermath—from O'Neill himself, from Carlotta, from Dr. Mayo, and from a number of other (more or less) biased witnesses, as well as from secondhand confidants.

Carlotta's version—that of a woman suffering from severe drug-induced psychotic hallucinations—is obviously the least reliable (and will be several times revised by Carlotta herself).

"O'Neill and I were sitting in the living room one afternoon and he said he was going out for a walk. When he didn't come back, I became very much worried. And I heard a noise, like an animal caught in something. Walking to the balcony, I saw it was O'Neill, who had fallen on the rocks and could not get up. I went to him and tried to lift him.

"At that moment, Dr. Mayo arrived. I thought it was very strange he should arrive, when neither of us had telephoned for him to come."

Dr. Mayo's account is cautious (if inadvertently biased). He recalls that he received a message at about nine o'clock that night summoning him to Point O'Rocks Lane. Since the message had not stipulated an emergency, he completed his round of calls before heading for the O'Neill house; it's about 10:00 p.m. when he turns his car into their driveway.

He climbs the front step and rings the doorbell. As he waits in the dark, he hears a faint cry from somewhere in the yard but is not sure of its source. The door opens, spilling light from the house, when he hears the cry again. This time he recognizes it as a call for help. He leaps down the step and starts across the yard, almost tripping over O'Neill, who is lying in the snow, wet and shivering. Mayo helps him up and, concerned about his injured leg, half-drags him into the house. He has no recollection of Carlotta assisting him.

Carlotta, however (in her drug-dazed condition), believes she helped carry O'Neill into the house. "The doctor took O'Neill's arms and shoulders, and I took his legs very carefully, and we carried him inside."

According to Mayo, O'Neill lies silently in the living room while Carlotta, wringing her hands, utters phrases of dismay. Preoccupied as he is with O'Neill's broken leg, and worried about shock and hypothermia, it seems not to occur to Mayo that Carlotta, too, is in need of medical attention.

Dr. Mayo is focused on getting O'Neill quickly into a hospital and he telephones for an ambulance—a private one, so that the call will not be registered in the local police office, thus avoiding publicity in the local newspapers. He can't help but wonder what has led up to O'Neill's fall, but he doesn't ask for an explanation and neither Carlotta nor O'Neill offers one.

"I asked the doctor what should be done about O'Neill's injured leg and he said O'Neill had better go to the hospital," Carlotta recalled years later. "The next thing I knew, an ambulance drove up. The Japanese boy [Saki] went to the door and said, 'Madam, ambulance for the Master.' I thought the ambulance arriving was very strange, because, as far as I knew, nobody had rung for one.

"I didn't say anything, because I didn't think it was my place to say it. But I realized it was necessary for Gene to get proper medical care. I helped the doctor put him into the ambulance, and off he went to the hospital."

Dr. Mayo is convinced Carlotta has been keeping the all-but-helpless O'Neill a virtual prisoner and, like Dr. Fiske before him, has come to detest her. Evidently feeling no qualm about leaving her to fend for herself, he follows the ambulance in his car to the modern red-brick hospital in the nearby town of Salem. It's 11:30 p.m. by the time he has seen O'Neill comfortably installed in a private room and has arranged for a bone surgeon to attend to his broken leg.

Driving home, Mayo is haunted by the look of despair that distorted O'Neill's ashen face.

"After they left," recalled Carlotta, "I became terribly nervous and worried. I had been instructed by [Dr. Mayo] to take my medicine whenever I felt very nervous and really on the edge of things, and I took a large dose to calm my nerves. After a bit, I began to feel very dizzy."

In fact, Carlotta has fallen into a drugged sleep, and doesn't wake until late afternoon of the following day, February 6. Unaware she has lost a day, she continued her account:

"I began to get more worried. I put on my street clothes and told Saki, 'I'm going over to the hospital to see Mr. O'Neill.' He said, 'Shall I take you in my car?' and I said, 'No, you better stay here and take messages if anything happens.'

"I walked out to the main road and stood there, thinking maybe a taxi would come along and I could take it, and if not, I'd start to walk. Well, I was walking along quietly, and an automobile stopped; it was an automobile the Marblehead Neck police officers used for going over all the roads in the area once or twice a day."

Patrolman John Snow, in his own car, is making a desultory check of the neighborhood on the evening of February 6 and recognizes Carlotta, inadequately dressed against the biting cold, walking down the street not far from her home. In a later, very discreet interview with the authors, he describes how he stopped his car beside her and tried to persuade her to return to her house, but she refused. (According to her later psychiatric evaluation, "She stated there were many friends in the house having a party and she wanted to get the friends out of the house.")

After vainly trying to induce Carlotta to take shelter in a neighboring house, he himself enters that house and telephones the police station to request a police car—all the while keeping an eye on the forlorn figure standing in the street.

The police car arrives with two patrolmen, John Tucker and Norman Powers, and, together with Snow, they coax Carlotta into the car. In a suddenly self-possessed voice, she asks them to drive her to Salem Hospital. Tucker and Powers start off, with Snow following, when, seconds later, Carlotta becomes hysterical. Unsure how to proceed, the cops return Carlotta to her own house, and from there Snow telephones Dr. Mayo. He arrives, calms Carlotta, helps bundle her into the patrol car, and follows it to Salem Hospital.

In Carlotta's version, she gets into the police car and asks the officer to take her to see her husband at Salem Hospital. "While we drove," she recalled, "things began to get a bit fuzzy. The last I remembered, I was taken to the patients' entrance of Salem Hospital. Then I went out like a light."

Mayo, unaware Carlotta is being poisoned by bromide, believes her behavior requires psychiatric care and he arranges for a staff psychiatrist to examine her early the following morning.

This is the third time in their marriage that O'Neill and Carlotta are patients under the same hospital roof.

Earlier, on that same Tuesday, Lawrence Langner and his wife, Armina Marshall, return from a trip abroad to their home in Westport, Connecticut, and are told by their caretaker that Mrs. O'Neill has called from Marblehead to say that Mr. O'Neill broke his leg and that Mrs. Langner had better come up and look after him; the caretaker says Mrs. O'Neill was barely coherent and "sounded drunk."

Armina Marshall immediately puts through a call to the house at Point O'Rocks Lane, but is told by the person who answers the phone that Mrs. O'Neill has gone out. Puzzled, Armina tries several times again to reach Carlotta and then makes a series of calls that eventually elicit the information that O'Neill is a patient at Salem Hospital.

When she reaches him there by phone that evening, he says, "Armina, it's just like before when I broke my arm"; she assumes he is referring to his previous fall, in the New York penthouse. In response to her concerned inquiries, O'Neill tells Armina he had to lie a long time on the snow-covered ground before help came. According to Armina (and later repeated to other friends), O'Neill said that Carlotta, standing in the doorway of their home, called out, "Lie there, little man!"

Armina, although knowing nothing of the bromide poisoning, assumes Carlotta was hallucinating. She promises O'Neill to visit him soon, and makes plans to visit Carlotta.

On Wednesday morning, Dr. Mayo finds O'Neill despondent. His leg has been put into a cast and everything that can be done for his physical comfort has been attended to. Mayo tells him as gently as he can that Carlotta was brought to the hospital the night before, that a psychiatrist has examined her this morning and found her, in the official words of the "Temporary Care" request issued by the Commonwealth of Massachusetts, to be "in need of immediate care and treatment."

Dr. Mayo tells O'Neill that the Salem Hospital medical staff thinks it best Carlotta be transferred to McLean Hospital, the renowned psychiatric facility in the nearby town of Belmont. O'Neill listens, but does not respond. At noon, Carlotta is taken away.

Carlotta remembers nothing about the hours she spent at Salem

Hospital, but she is later told she kept repeating, "My husband is sick, my husband is sick, please take me to my husband, I want to see how he is." Carlotta does remember waking up "just a little bit" in the ambulance that took her to McLean; her feet hurt her, she recalled, "because they were tied." She lost consciousness again as she was wheeled into McLean.

Waking the next day in a strange bed, she is "scared to death" upon seeing bars on the windows. "I didn't know whether I was in jail, or where I was—or what O'Neill had done to me," she remembered. At last, a nurse arrives and quietly assures her that "everything will be alright." Soon she is moved to a building in which the patients can come and go as they please, and she gradually recovers her poise. The doctors tell her, "You shouldn't be here, you should never have been sent here."

In the diary Carlotta resumed keeping in March 1951, after the bromide has been flushed from her system and she has been pronounced sane, she pens a cursory summation: "Gene falls on rocks in garden—Friday, Feb. 7 [the wrong date] and Dr. Mayo of Swampscott takes him to Salem Hospital to have leg set—I am sent to McLean Hospital for bromide poisoning—my temperature is outlandishly high & I am delirious! In 48 hours, all is well. During next 4 days receive 2 charming letters from Gene!"

Inexplicable as it seems, O'Neill does indeed dictate a letter to Carlotta almost as soon as he arrives at Salem Hospital: "My dearest, I had my leg put in a cast last night," he writes. "I should be able to get around on a crutch within a few days, and I know you will progress rapidly under treatment. Write me as soon as you can. I feel dreadfully lonely for some word from you. With all my love, [signed in a hand indisputably his own] Gene."

Soon thereafter, he dictates another letter to Carlotta (received by her, as she carefully notes, "about 4 days after my husband was in hospital"). He is overjoyed, he says, to hear from Dr. Mayo, as well as from Dr. Howard Horwitz at McLean, that she has made steady progress and will soon be well again. He himself has made progress, he says, and can walk a few steps on crutches with the help of "one man on each side of me."

O'Neill has been visited by Bobby Jones, Langner, and Aronberg, he informs Carlotta, as well as by their Marblehead cook, Doris, who has also visited Carlotta at McLean.

"Doris tells me you are worrying about money and what you are going to do." He assures her that there will be plenty of money. "If you will write to me we can make advance plans about that," says O'Neill. "There never was a situation that love and money couldn't conquer."

The letter is signed, "All my love, sweetheart," followed by a painfully shaky "Gene."

O'Neill is attended by private nurses in his third-floor hospital room. His day nurse, Clare Bird, is tall and pretty with blond hair, light brown eyes, and an unfailingly gentle manner. Like Patrolman Snow, Bird finds O'Neill difficult to understand at first because his speech is thick; his hands also shake pitifully, and his mind is often cloudy, particularly during the night when he has occasional drug-induced hallucinations.

Evidently, it doesn't occur to Dr. Mayo to take O'Neill off the chloral hydrate and bromide sedative he has prescribed for him, but O'Neill happens to have less of a reaction than Carlotta to the drug's toxic effect.

An experienced and intuitive woman, Clare Bird tactfully offers O'Neill such help and sympathy as she senses he will accept. She sees it embarrasses him to be fed, and that it upsets him even more to be watched while he feeds himself, so she serves him food that is cut up and then leaves the room. Responding to her thoughtfulness, O'Neill talks to her about Carlotta—one minute calmly, the next weeping and asking to see her.

"He seemed to want to be alone most of the time," Nurse Bird recalled, "but every once in a while he wanted to talk, and then he would ramble on about what a mess everything was." Surprisingly, O'Neill sometimes talked to Bird about his older son's suicide. "He never mentioned his daughter directly," says Bird, "but he gave the impression, in his ramblings, that his entire family had gone wrong."

Nurse Bird recalls that O'Neill felt guilty when she had to spend Easter Sunday tending to his needs. "You should have been in the Easter

Parade," he tells her, giving her a check for thirty-five dollars with which to "buy an Easter bonnet."

A small group of friends, informed of O'Neill's condition by the Langners, have begun flying from New York to visit him, among them Saxe Commins and Sherlee Weingarten, who had not been welcome at Marblehead. To some of them, O'Neill seems bewildered and helpless, in need of their assistance in reassembling his life. But, according to Clare Bird, "He never got excited when they came to see him, and when they left he would sometimes shrug, as though to say he was glad they were gone. He just let anyone do what they wanted with him."

O'Neill does tell Langner that on the night of his fall in the snow, he and Carlotta had "a filthy fight"; he doesn't elaborate but says he rushed from the house simply to get away from her.

He gave a more detailed account to Commins, who set it down in an essay that was later included in the book, *Love and Admiration and Respect*, edited by his wife, Dorothy Commins. It's an emotional recap, colored by Commins's virulent hatred of Carlotta and his adoration of O'Neill; it is further embroidered and distorted by the passage of time.

"What I know," Commins begins with a melodramatic flourish, "came to me from Eugene's own lips as he lay immobilized in a bed in the Salem Hospital."

His summary of O'Neill's fall in the snow is similar to Dr. Mayo's and Armina Marshall's, except that Carlotta, in Commins's version, glared from the doorway at her husband lying helplessly on the snowy ground, and said, "How the mighty have fallen! The master is lying low. Now, where is all your greatness?" (Not as Armina remembered O'Neill telling her, "Lie there, little man.")

Commins writes that O'Neill "pieced out the story" for him "haltingly and with desperate sadness." O'Neill told Commins, as he had told Langner, about quarreling with Carlotta, but not saying what the quarrel was about, only that "to escape her wrath" he left the house "coatless."

Some weeks into O'Neill's hospital stay, Dr. Mayo receives a call from one of Carlotta's doctors at McLean saying Carlotta is eager to visit her husband, and McLean will sanction the visit if O'Neill wishes to see her. When Mayo relays this message, O'Neill cringes. Evidently he has forgotten his recent longing love letters to Carlotta; according to Mayo, he pleads, "Keep her away from me." He then tells Mayo of a visit by Carlotta to his bedside at Doctors Hospital in New York, when she grabbed his broken arm and shook it, saying, "There's nothing wrong with you, you're putting on an act."

Nonetheless, and unbeknown to his friends, O'Neill does receive a visit from Carlotta, who is accompanied by a nurse from McLean. Clare Bird, who leaves the room during the O'Neills' half-hour reunion, later finds her patient just as joyless as he was before Carlotta's visit.

To BOTH DR. MAYO and Nurse Bird, O'Neill seems reluctant to face a decision regarding his future. He knows he can't stay hospitalized in Salem indefinitely and he also knows he must decide soon about his future, with or without Carlotta, who is still being cared for at McLean. Whatever their views of O'Neill's relationship with his wife, both Mayo and Bird are concerned about his pliability in the hands of friends who are pushing him to break with Carlotta and go to New York to complete his recovery.

Langner, believing O'Neill requires professional therapeutic support, takes it upon himself to call in the Boston psychiatrist Merrill Moore. He has been vouched for by the prominent Broadway writer and director Joshua Logan, who is among Moore's celebrity patients. A somewhat controversial figure, the psychiatrist is also a prolific writer of pornographic poetry. More's entrance into the precarious situation complicates rather than ameliorates it.

After meeting with O'Neill, Moore presents Mayo and Langner with his bleak diagnosis: O'Neill is mentally ill and is unable to take care of himself. The dramatist's mental condition, Moore adds, is due to his son's recent death, plus worry over his wife's illness; O'Neill needs protection from his "difficult domestic situation."

In Moore's opinion, O'Neill "has depression and slowness of timing"; he is "unable to plan" and "cannot make decisions." Since he cannot stay indefinitely at Salem Hospital and, as it is "unsuitable" for him to return to his home in Marblehead, Moore smugly recommends he be separated from Carlotta and either be confined to a mental hospital or be placed under the care of a legal guardian.

While Langner et al. are chewing this over, Dr. Moore arranges to meet with Carlotta, whose originally mandated ten-day stay at McLean has been extended, with her consent, for her own protection.

"I have never felt so frightened of a human being in my life," Carlotta later recalled, adding she had not wanted to see Moore, and that her doctors at McLean had not been happy about his visit; in fact, one of them remained in the room while Moore interviewed her.

"He wishes to tell me *I must give up Gene!?!*" Carlotta scribbles furiously in her diary on March 22. "*I must forget him! I must make a new life!* (at *62*—& having been married to Gene for 23 years!).

"He is a fool," Carlotta continues. "He gives himself away as to the real reason for his visit," she writes, when he tells her, "You must remain here where you will be looked after and guarded." The word *guarded*, says Carlotta, "hit me between the eyes. I couldn't imagine how a stranger *dare* tell me I must give up my husband."

In a later interview, Carlotta elaborated: Merrill Moore "took my hand and kissed it and said, 'Beautiful Carlotta Monterey. Oh, this is such a pleasure.'" Shrinking from his unctuousness, she tells him that the only reason she has agreed to see him is that she wants to know about her husband. Moore tells her O'Neill is ill and needs quiet.

"I noticed there was a sort of accentuation on the word 'quiet,'" Carlotta remembers, "and I said, 'Well, I've lived with him a good many years and we've never had anything but quiet.' I said if there was ever any noise or disturbance, it was through him not through me."

Carlotta reports that Moore cautions her, "I think it would be better if you made up your mind to live in one place and take up writing, or whatever you like, and allow your husband to have quiet in some sanitarium we can find for him. You know, dear Carlotta Monterey, you wouldn't want to see the leaf wither on the vine."

Carlotta's doctor at McLean advises her not to worry, as Dr. Moore has "no standing" or influence on McLean's procedures. But she is so shattered after Moore leaves she is unable to sleep. "I walked the floor all night," she says.

Dr. Moore reports back to Langner that Carlotta's condition necessitates prolonged treatment—a diagnosis that meets with considerably more enthusiasm than Moore's appraisal of O'Neill's problems (which is ignored, and is later modified by Moore himself).

O'Neill and Carlotta by now have spent six and a half weeks in their respective hospitals and it is at this point of confusion that lawyers are called in. On March 23, a day after Moore's visit with Carlotta, O'Neill allows himself to be persuaded to take a vindictive step that he regrets almost at once. He files a petition in the Probate Court of County Essex, in Salem, stating that Carlotta is "an insane person and incapable of taking care of herself."

Urged on by Aronberg and Langner, O'Neill has requested that a local attorney, James E. Farley, "be appointed guardian of said Carlotta Monterey O'Neill." The petition, signed in O'Neill's shaky and barely legible hand (and signed also by Merrill Moore), is returnable in one month's time—on April 23.

Farley, a portly self-styled country lawyer, pays O'Neill several visits at the hospital "to assess his mental condition from a legal point of view." He comes away convinced O'Neill is under no mental confusion whatever; he talks clearly, if haltingly, and appears "perfectly aware of what he is doing."

O'Neill, however, later tells several friends he hadn't known what he was doing when he signed the petition. Conceivably, he signed it in the delusional hope that it might serve as a thunderous curtain for Act III, Scene III of his real-life tragedy. Perhaps he was slyly invoking Carlotta to prove her mettle as his leading lady.

CARLOTTA, TRAUMATIZED BY Merrill Moore's visit and O'Neill's petition, makes no diary entries for several days. On March 28, she notes she has been told by her McLean doctor she is free to go home.

The McLean discharge report states that she received "general supportive care and psychotherapy." She was given no medication except sodium chloride for a few days to aid in the elimination of bromides from her system.

Her "delirium and hallucinations persisted unabated for approximately ten days, then gradually decreased over the next ten days," the report continues. "Following this period she seemed somewhat unstable emotionally, but was not psychotic. It was possible for her to be moved to the open ward, where she had friendly relations with many of the other patients, and was able to go to the library, to the coffee shop, and out of the hospital for walks or drives."

Carlotta's prognosis, as described in the "Discharge Summary," signed by William H. Horwitz, MD, is "good."

51

On March 29, 1951, Carlotta telephones Saki to fetch her home from McLean. Her doctors wish to see her rights protected regarding the pending guardianship petition filed by her husband. To that end, they have called in Dr. Harry L. Kozol, a dynamic forty-two-year-old Boston psychiatrist on the Harvard medical staff; his expertise is legal medicine (and his pioneering research will later help establish the emerging fields of forensic psychiatry and neuropsychiatry).

Fascinated by the case, Kozol suggests Carlotta countersue her husband and he offers to engage a local law firm to initiate the proceeding. In her diary, Carlotta crows, "The clearing of my name begins."

Her petition, filed by Robert Meserve of the eminent Boston law firm Nutter, McClennen and Fish, accuses O'Neill of cruelty, and asks for separate maintenance; it states that O'Neill has failed "without just cause, to furnish suitable support" for his wife, and that she is living apart from him "for justifiable cause"; the petition further states that on or about the first day of February 1951, and "at divers other times prior thereto," O'Neill has been guilty of "cruel and abusive treatment" of her. The date of return—April 23—is the same as that of O'Neill's lawsuit.

When O'Neill learns of Carlotta's petition, he agitatedly confides to Lawrence Langner that he's worried about the possibility of "political pressure" being exerted to have him institutionalized; Boston's power structure has always been hostile to his plays, O'Neill reminds Langner, and if the question of his own sanity arises, he might have a hard time eliciting sympathy.

Langner seizes on O'Neill's concern to coax him to New York, believing that—away from Carlotta and surrounded by caring friends—he will recuperate faster than he ever can in Salem Hospital.

"I loved and respected Gene," Langner said, in justifying the manipulations going on behind O'Neill's back. "I felt the transfer would be in his best interests."

Nurse Clare Bird recalls O'Neill's ambivalence about leaving Salem. "He finally agreed to go, with a reluctant 'Yes.' But, even on the day he was supposed to leave, I thought he might change his mind."

It is no coincidence that Langner and his allies choose March 30, the day after Carlotta's release from McLean, as the day to spirit O'Neill away. His leg is healing nicely but it is still in a cast, and they have arranged for an ambulance to take him to Boston's South Station. Accompanied by Nurse Bird, he is carried by stretcher from the ambulance to a compartment on the New York–bound train.

That same day, Carlotta worriedly reads the *Boston Herald*'s article about the two O'Neill lawsuits. Newspapers all over the country pick up the story and to many it appears that the O'Neill marriage, whatever traumas it has withstood in the past, can't possibly survive this dizzying new round of hostilities.

It is drizzling when O'Neill's train pulls into Grand Central Terminal, where an ambulance waits to take him to a small private facility in the East Seventies, more convalescent home than hospital. Tucked into his bed by Clare Bird, an exhausted O'Neill takes in the dreary hotel-like atmosphere of the room and mutters, "Get me out of this place."

Bird reaches Aronberg by phone and he promises to have O'Neill transferred in the morning. With Bird seated nearby, O'Neill sinks into fretful sleep.

On Saturday, March 31, O'Neill is grateful to find himself once again in a cheerful room with a river view at Doctors Hospital. He laments the departure on Sunday of Clare Bird, who must return to Boston, but he is reassured to be under the warmly welcoming care of Doctors Fisk and Patterson.

Fisk, who has received a report from Dr. Mayo, expects to find O'Neill's nervous disorder worse than it was three years earlier and is surprised that he is "fairly well oriented" although "generally frail and unsteady"; he weighs only ninety pounds.

Mayo has briefed Patterson about O'Neill's tendency to intermittently hallucinate, and one of the first things Patterson does is substitute straight chloral for the chloral-bromide mixture O'Neill has been taking. With the new medicine (as in Carlotta's case), the hallucinations gradually disappear.

Patterson is most concerned about O'Neill's palsy; he refuses to believe that O'Neill has to tremble. "I would give him heck for shaking," Patterson recalled. "I'd get furious. I'd see he'd be ready for a cigarette and start to shake. I'd scold him for it—with a smile, of course. And when he thought about it, he could control it." Patterson arranges his schedule of rounds so that O'Neill will be his final call in the evening and he can take the time to sit and chat with him.

DURING THE two and a half months O'Neill is a patient in Doctors Hospital, he appears to take a savage, if concealed, delight in putting on a multifaceted theatrical performance. Releasing all the pent-up dramatics he would much prefer to put into a play, he tells his visitors conflicting stories about his past and present relationship with Carlotta.

To some, he woefully declares he can't face returning to her; to others, he signals that a reconciliation is the one thing he longs for. He seems to be testing the psychological effect on the unwitting friends he has cast as minor characters in the play he can't resist writing in his mind. He is seeking the appropriate denouement for the inchoate scene (or scenes) of his tragedy's final act.

He alone understands that Carlotta's response is the only one that will ultimately matter. He knows (hopes) he hasn't much longer to resolve his situation. "I'm done for," he tells Russel Crouse early in his hospital stay. And yet, ineluctably the dramatist, O'Neill is determined to wring the last ounce of drama out of his weeks at Doctors Hospital.

Possibly, he has recalled, and decided to abide by, some Nietzschean advice that has always been an underpinning of his philosophy: "To many men life is a failure; a poison-worm gnawing at their heart. Then let them see to it that their dying is all the more a success."

The pattern of O'Neill's life has often mirrored Nietzsche's, and their last years in particular present a striking parallel. Like O'Neill's collapse in Marblehead, Nietzsche's final breakdown was brought on, in part, by prolonged physical suffering, heightened by his mental isolation and exacerbated by excessive dependence on the very same hallucinatory drug that O'Neill was taking. And as with Nietzsche, whose friends believed he had gone mad, O'Neill's sanity is questioned not only by Dr. Moore but also by a number of his acquaintances.

Not long after his arrival in New York, and unknown to most of the friends who swoop to his bedside, O'Neill is making overtures to Carlotta for a reconciliation.

Carlotta, still advised by Dr. Kozol, is temporarily living at the residential Shelton Hotel overlooking the Charles River in Boston. Kaye Albertoni, her faithful nurse from California, has flown to her side, with Dr. Kozol's approval. He tells Kaye that Carlotta has suffered "a nervous breakdown." It will be Kaye's job to help Carlotta readjust to the outside world and to make sure "she would behave and not do anything irrational." As Nurse Albertoni has recalled, "I stayed a long time."

On April 4, Carlotta, accompanied by Albertoni and her Boston lawyer, Robert Meserve, drives to the Marblehead Neck house to begin preparations for its sale. Two days later, she agrees to talk to the sympathetic

Boston correspondent for *Time* magazine, Francis Wylie, about her separation from O'Neill, and invites him and his wife to Marblehead. When they arrive in the late afternoon, they find cardboard cartons all over the place with *Eugene O'Neill* written on them.

"She served us sherry," said Wylie, "and she told my wife and me that O'Neill has been writing her love letters and sending her red roses. She told us how much she loved O'Neill and how dependent he was on her and how cruel he had been to her."

She also informs Wylie that O'Neill's action in trying to have a guardian appointed for her "was partly in response to his instinct for drama." Still quoting Carlotta, Wylie reports that O'Neill "could no longer arouse her romantic interest in him, so he had to do something else to get some sort of a passionate response."

Carlotta does not say so, but the reverse is probably just as true: she can no longer arouse his romantic interest; she has lost the authority of her great beauty, and her diminished allure is something she finds hard to live with—as hard as O'Neill finds living without writing. Absent her beauty, Carlotta is no longer secure in her skin.

Wylie reports the gist of the interview to *Time*'s home office in New York on April 6, trying to interest his magazine in a thoroughly researched story about the O'Neills' difficulties. In his summation, Wylie notes that Dr. Kozol, who is seeing Carlotta regularly, is "confident there will be a reconciliation in three weeks." *Time*'s home office considers the story "too sad" to publish. (Wylie ultimately agrees, but continues to keep his editors posted, so they will have the background if and when the O'Neills reconcile.)

On April 17, three weeks after her release from McLean Hospital, Carlotta responds to an elliptically worded letter from Sophus Winther, who has recently learned of her situation; he believes O'Neill is the injured party, but wishes to stay on good terms with Carlotta, at least for the time being.

Carlotta's letter is a dire sequel to her Thanksgiving Day rant to Eline Winther five years earlier; it exemplifies how, over time, O'Neill has driven her berserk—and how he himself is just as unbalanced (if better able to disguise it) as she.

To "Dear Sophus," Carlotta writes:

"You carefully omit the crime (*literally*) committed by my esteemed husband of paying an unscrupulous doctor [Merrill Moore] to swear I was insane so that a guardian could be appointed for me—& if it could be arranged, to keep me in McLean's. Thank God, McLean's is of the honest brand—(there are few these days)."

She should never have been sent to McLean Hospital in the first place, she affirms, but O'Neill was "delighted" to sign her into a mental hospital and to petition to have a guardian appointed for her. Unable to control her bitterness, she goes on, "Poor Gene! As a writer he is *superb*, & it has been for the writer I have worked all these years."

Carlotta then proceeds to condemn O'Neill's "failure [as] a man." Unable to acknowledge her own Iago-like role in prodding O'Neill's abandonment of Shane and Oona—and perhaps worst of all, her successful attempt to keep Eugene Jr. at bay—she accuses her husband of having "failed his children & his wives"; he loathes women "except when he needs them," and when he no longer needs them, "out they go!" Carlotta is perceptive enough to observe that "with Nietzsche & Strindberg as his gods one can understand this."

She goes on to tell Winther that in the "final play" O'Neill is writing "in his imagination," in which she figures as the leading lady, she is destined either to commit suicide or be killed by him—"by hiring someone to do it, of course." Carlotta describes to Winther her humiliation when O'Neill "was sneaked out of Salem," leaving her with no money to pay their numerous bills, and no instruction about what he wished done with their home. Clearly, she writes, O'Neill is either "a despicable cad, or mentally unsound. Or both!"

Being penniless, she continues, her rage unabated, she cannot afford even a cheap hotel room but has had to return to Marblehead Neck "to this ghastly tomb." She needs to "be able to live," she tells Winther, and now she is afraid of her "esteemed husband," against whom, she says, she has been warned "since '45" (during the production of *The Iceman Cometh*) to be on her guard. (She does not say who warned her.)

CARLOTTA IS LIVING in Marblehead at the end of April, completing the dismantling of the little gray house. Although no longer clinically psychotic, she is still (not without cause) a nervous wreck, unsure of O'Neill's next move, burdened with the responsibility of disposing of all their joint possessions, and—because the legal proceedings against her have blocked her access to her bank account—in temporary financial difficulty.

In her diary, she mixes up dates, repeats herself, improvises, and sometimes dissembles to mask her forgetfulness. She writes to Mai-mai Sze, asking her to come to Marblehead and to bring some cash. When she arrives in Marblehead, Mai-mai Sze is shocked by Carlotta's appearance. "She was fat, pale and puffy and had let her hair go gray. She was a proud woman, and had always touched up her hair and kept her weight under control.

"She talked for three days without a stop, didn't leave me alone for a second. She even followed me into the bathroom. She made me sleep with my door open, as she'd always made Gene. She talked about how Gene always had to dramatize everything; she said, 'He'll be back, he'll come crawling to me on his knees.'"

When Mai-mai leaves on April 22, Carlotta reflects in her diary, "Her visit has helped me a great deal. She is intelligent, clear-headed, & objective."

On the following day, Carlotta learns O'Neill has withdrawn his petition for guardianship over her. On Dr. Kozol's advice, Carlotta withdraws her countersuit for separate maintenance. Nevertheless, the end of April finds her still in financial limbo, with the lawyers on both sides still negotiating about money.

"It is so easy," she sneers on April 28, "to be in a hospital, in a distant city, refuse to return to your home to face the result of an act of utter stupidity, dishonesty & cruelty—& have the one you've hurt face the music, clean up & pack for you—. Wicked, wicked man—always choosing unscrupulous persons as your friends and advisers!"

And on the thirtieth, referring to one of those unscrupulous persons (probably Aronberg) as "the Worm," she notes that said Worm has left her a message via Dr. Kozol saying that *"Gene wanted me to come to New York & talk with him personally!!!??"*

By May 2, according to Carlotta, not only does O'Neill's lawyer telephone Carlotta's New York lawyer, suggesting a reconciliation, but Russel Crouse also phones Carlotta herself, at O'Neill's behest, to say, "Gene sends his love—and *wants you back!"*

Carlotta's petulant comment: "'Back' to *what?"*

According to Aronberg, O'Neill has told him, "I can't make a new life for myself. I know that I'm going to die."

At Carlotta's request, Dr. Kozol agrees to visit O'Neill in New York on her behalf in early May.

Among O'Neill's visitors at Doctors Hospital who, like Crouse, are in touch with Carlotta as well, are Charles O'Brien Kennedy and George Jean Nathan, both of whom have been sure from the start that the O'Neills will patch up their differences.

Armina Marshall also is in contact with Carlotta, who, having learned of Langner's role in separating her from O'Neill, will no longer speak to him. Carlotta tells Marshall that O'Neill has asked her to take him back, and Marshall replies that she knows O'Neill loves and needs her, and, of course, Carlotta must take him back.

While the long-distance battle of wills between O'Neill and Carlotta is being waged under the eyes of one faction of friends, there are those friends who are unaware O'Neill and Carlotta are in touch. This faction consists mainly of people who have been cut off by Carlotta and who, O'Neill knows, will not be pleased to see him return to her.

One exception is Kenneth Macgowan, heretofore a staunch supporter of the O'Neill-Carlotta alliance. He has somehow got the impression that O'Neill is now through with Carlotta.

"When I came to New York and saw Gene in the hospital, he took my hand in both of his and said, 'It's nice to see you this way,'" Macgowan recalled. "I thought he meant without Carlotta around. I felt very strongly that he was not going back to her."

The most misled—and ultimately the most grievously wounded—is Saxe Commins. He rejoices at being reunited with his beloved friend following the dreadful accident in Marblehead Neck, but is overwrought (and sometimes egregiously misinformed) in his later published narrative of their reunion.

Every day for four weeks after O'Neill's installation in Doctors Hospital, writes Commins, "We visited together for at least one hour, usually in the evening after work." O'Neill, says Commins, has "hideous" and "delusional terrors, asleep or awake"; he recounts an instance when O'Neill "sprang from the bed" and "cowered in a far corner of the room." He quotes O'Neill: "She's on the window sill. She's coming toward me. Please keep her away." Clearly, Commins wants his readers to believe the menacing woman on the windowsill represents Carlotta.

After citing this bizarre incident, he notes incorrectly that Carlotta "had been committed by Dr. Moore" to a "sanitarium" and, when released, had come to New York and "engaged a room in Doctors Hospital underneath Gene's." It was then, writes Commins, that O'Neill begins receiving phones calls from his wife, and although Commins tactfully waits in the hall during their conversations, he feels it is "all too manifest" that Carlotta is "regaining control."

By his further account, Commins tries to convince O'Neill that a future without Carlotta is not unthinkable; he goes so far as to beseech O'Neill to allow him and his wife, Dorothy, to become his caregivers. His obsessive devotion has clouded his thinking; he fails to see that no amount of sacrifice or loyalty will signify when and if Carlotta chooses to reenter the picture.

Toward the end of his account, however, Commins himself is forced to come to this conclusion. He finally acknowledges that "after all, Carlotta had lived with him for almost a quarter of a century, and when she was not in an acute state of disturbance, she could be competent and devoted and even sacrificial in her imperious and managerial way. . . . Together they might help each other; apart there could only be even greater torture and then dissolution."

Apart from Commins, the person who spends the most time with O'Neill is Sherlee Lantz (formerly Weingarten). Early in his hospital stay, O'Neill asks Sherlee for a favor: he doesn't want to deal with his mail—won't read it and doesn't even want to be told who it's from. Sherlee finds the responsibility scary, but can't refuse him. Uninformed about the relationships between O'Neill and some of his correspondents, she improvises answers as best she can.

O'Neill is interested in hardly anything. "He was barely articulate most of the time," according to Sherlee. The one thing that seemed to give him momentary pleasure was listening to classical music over radio station WQXR.

Within the first week or two of O'Neill's arrival at Doctors Hospital, Sherlee—knowing little about the background of his estrangement from Oona—asks him if he will consider writing to his daughter; Sherlee innocently thinks a renewal of his relationship with Oona will give him something to live for.

He is firm in his refusal, and Sherlee—unlike Commins—soon intuits that O'Neill, in spite of having charged his wife with insanity (and despite her countercharge of desertion), is "never anything but en route to Carlotta—even while he appears to be traveling away from her." In Sherlee's opinion, the return to Carlotta "was never weighed against any other possibility."

"Where can I go?" O'Neill asks her. "You can't take care of me." And Sherlee weeps silently over his predicament. "I held him in my arms once, and he cried," Sherlee recalled some years after his death.

"He didn't seem to have any flesh left. The neurologist at the hospital told me one day that in the type of disease O'Neill suffered from, the heart goes on but little else. The doctor said, too, that shortly he would become a vegetable. I was so upset I felt like slapping him."

O'Neill explains to Sherlee what she has already realized—that he is terribly sensitive about the loss of dignity imposed by his illness. He can't bear the thought of letting his friends take care of him, nor can he face the dreary prospect of spending his last days alone in an apartment with a male nurse. That, however, is one of the plans that has been advanced for his consideration.

For some reason, Merrill Moore is still active in the case and is summoned to New York by his co-conspirator Langner to help O'Neill get straightened out. It is Moore who recommends the apartment-with-male-nurse in New York. Having dropped the idea of a guardian for Carlotta, he further proposes that she take an apartment in Boston; the two are to agree to live separately, but they are to be on friendly terms.

Moore has some misgivings about the reception of his plan and he asks Russel Crouse to present it to O'Neill as "The Crouse Plan."

"You present it to him as 'The Moore Plan,'" snaps Crouse.

On April 26, Crouse drily notes in his diary: "Gene wants none of the Moore Separation Plan." A conscientious diarist, Crouse also records that O'Neill was suicidal during the early part of his hospital stay and that the windows of his room are kept locked.

At the end of April, O'Neill is recuperating from a severe case of pneumonia, which has lasted six days. He is conscious during his illness, but runs a high fever. "We had a bad scare," Dr. Fisk recalled. "But after the pneumonia he improved quickly. He was up and about most of the day. His tremor improved too."

His visitors, during the period of his recovery, find O'Neill often standing to greet them, for the cast has been removed from his leg. One of his visitors is Eugene Jr.'s Ruth Lander. It is Aronberg's idea, and it is a strange and poignant meeting for both. Trembling with anxiety, Ruth allows Aronberg to present her to O'Neill, whom he has briefed. "He embraced me," Ruth recalled, "and buried his head on my shoulder."

In early May, Dr. Fisk finds O'Neill so much improved, he recommends an outing. Illustrative of the esteem in which he holds O'Neill, Fisk proffers his own services as chauffeur and, at O'Neill's request, they head downtown.

"We drove along the waterfront and O'Neill pointed out to me many of the places where he had spent his early days—here had stood Jimmy the Priest's, there a brothel."

O'Neill talks about the dockworkers and the men of the sea. They led a rough life, he tells Fisk, and they were his friends. Driving through Greenwich Village, "O'Neill talks about whores, comparing them with Mother Earth, endowing them with what he calls 'real souls' and the capacity to 'solace man and give him comfort.'"

This leads O'Neill into a discourse on the mythological giant Antaeus, whose mother was Earth and whose strength was indestructible as long as he stood on the earth.

Surely O'Neill is thinking of the strength he has long derived from Carlotta, and his helpless weakness when separated from her, as he goes on about how Antaeus loses his power when Hercules wrenches him away from his strength-giving source.

However Fisk interprets this, and as much as Fisk hates and distrusts Carlotta, he is among those most firmly convinced that O'Neill will go back to her.

On May 7, with her packing up of the Marblehead house completed, a weary Carlotta talks to Dr. Kozol about his imminent visit with O'Neill in New York. She wonders, in her diary, what O'Neill will tell Kozol— and what it is that she wants from the man who, after twenty-three years of marriage, threw her "out to the dogs?"

For one thing, she wants to know "*why* & *how* that dreadful Salem incident occurred. The cruelty of it—& the *stupidity*." She asks herself whether O'Neill wants her because he loves her, or to save the money it would cost him to pay for her to live separately.

She wonders if O'Neill feels at all guilty, and whether he is willing, for her sake, to "give up" Langner, Moore, and Aronberg. Never, she tells herself, will she be able to "trust or love him again."

Invariably, she's quick to console herself. The next day, she has her hair done and the day after that she has a fitting for a new black suit.

Kozol spends three hours with O'Neill in the hospital on May 9. He appears to have been a somewhat tactless intermediary, for his report (as Carlotta records it) propels her on a fresh rant of fury and resentment.

He confirms that Merrill Moore is "the real villain" of her breakup with O'Neill. Moore, it seems, is a cousin of Ralph Barton's and (like Charlie Chaplin) blames Barton's suicide on Carlotta's marriage to O'Neill. Moore claimed that the staff at McLean informed him Carlotta would have to be confined to the hospital for eight months; he reported this to O'Neill, who (Kozol tells Carlotta) believed it.

"How *could* he," storms Carlotta, "when he knew I had left the hospital and was in Boston the day he left? Gene lies as beautifully as Moore!" What O'Neill said to Kozol, Carlotta notes, is "proof to me his memory & thinking is through a haze—anything to give himself an alibi. To live with him would be dangerous—because he has no moral sense and always hides behind someone else when he, Gene, is at fault.

"There is nothing else for him to do but kill me! And, as he has often boasted, Aronberg could easily find someone to do that '*for a consideration*.'"

Carlotta then phones her former McLean doctor, William Horwitz, who, she maintains, informs her that "Moore is a liar" and says he himself told Moore that Carlotta for weeks had been ready to go home, but was waiting for her husband to make up his mind what he wanted to do. But Moore kept repeating that McLean must keep her there.

In response to this dismaying information, Carlotta undergoes a "ghastly attack of 'terrors'—is Gene up to some trick—or can he really want me?" After speaking on the telephone with her husband at the hospital on May 10, however, she notes that she feels better.

Dr. Kozol meets with Russel Crouse at New York's Waldorf Astoria and informs him of his conversation with O'Neill, after which Crouse writes in his diary: "Gene very gay and reports he and Carlotta will live in a hotel opposite Dr. Kozol's office which is good." The hotel is the

Shelton, where Carlotta currently has a room, and the reconciliation is scheduled for May 17.

On May 15, two days before O'Neill is to leave for Boston, Carlotta rises early for an appointment with her dressmaker. In a flutter of nervous anticipation she is having her dresses altered to accommodate her newer, thirty-pounds-lighter figure.

Robert Meserve phones from New York to confirm that O'Neill, as agreed, has altered his will to once again make Carlotta his executor. "This 'agreement' thing breaks my heart," she notes. "That I should need *legal protection* from my own husband whom I love so dearly."

She asks God for "the strength to nurse Gene & make him feel secure." Not even Strindberg himself could have conjured so potent an embodiment of the marital love-hate trap (or *hatkärlek* in his native Swedish).

For the past week, Carlotta has been speaking with her husband by phone twice daily. She has also been in touch with his primary nurse at Doctors Hospital, a middle-aged woman named Sally Coughlin, who will accompany O'Neill to Boston.

Nurse Coughlin, along with Sherlee, has been opening the letters O'Neill refuses to read. There are two from the Winthers, both informing O'Neill they have heard from an irate Carlotta, who decried her husband's actions against her during the past two months. Carlotta, writes Sophus, was offended by his skeptical response and he and Carlotta are now on "unfriendly" terms. Sophus wants to assure O'Neill that his loyalty "makes it impossible [for him] to accept her story at its face value." He is sorry for Carlotta but, he pronounces, "she is trapped by her own nature and from that there is no escape."

Eline, hedging her bets, informs O'Neill that she wishes to avoid taking sides, as she loves him and Carlotta equally.

Nurse Coughlin takes it upon herself to write to the Winthers on April 18, informing them she will give O'Neill their letters "when his nerves are in better shape." She is "dreadfully sorry" for O'Neill, she says, but there is little she or anyone can do to help him, as "his one desire now seems to be to return to Carlotta even though he regards her as a mental case."

Not quite a month later, on May 11, Nurse Coughlin writes again to Sophus Winther, informing him that O'Neill will be leaving Doctors Hospital within two weeks, that he is joyful at the prospect of being reunited with Carlotta, and that she (Coughlin) still believes it unwise to give O'Neill the letter Sophus wrote to him and therefore is returning the letter to Sophus. Rather sourly, she comments, "He only seems interested in being with her again." (She doesn't mention Eline's letter, but presumably she returns that one as well.)

A TWO-ROOM SUITE at the Shelton is being readied for O'Neill's arrival. The little gray house on Marblehead Neck is a mansion by comparison, and as for Le Plessis, Casa Genotta, and Tao House, they are dream palaces from a distant past. But the irony of Carlotta's reduced lifestyle isn't something she dwells upon. She doesn't comment in her diary on the fact that she and O'Neill will now, of necessity, share a bedroom (albeit furnished with two beds); she describes the suite that is to be their final destination as "charming," with its sun-filled living room whose windows overlook the Charles River.

"Phone Gene—he says he has jitters! So have I!" she notes on May 16. Dr. Kozol phones to tell Carlotta he plans to see O'Neill "every day for a bit & then three times a week." The "beginning," he says, is *most important.*"

Although O'Neill has known for several weeks that he is going back to Carlotta in Boston (on her terms), he has once again deliberately misled a number of his friends. To Joe Heidt, for one, he has confided he doesn't want most of his friends to know he is going back to his wife; he is particularly reluctant to mention his imminent departure from the hospital to those who, he is certain, will never be allowed by Carlotta to come near him again. But to Heidt, he confesses his eagerness "to get home." As

Heidt recalled, "He was all smiles." He had just talked to Carlotta on the telephone, he said, and "was only waiting to get a little stronger."

Bennett Cerf is among the unenlightened. Visiting O'Neill on May 16, the day before his planned departure, Cerf presses his own offer of moving O'Neill into a suite at Manhattan's Carlyle Hotel with a male nurse (already tentatively engaged), to which O'Neill makes a vague answer that Cerf evidently misinterprets. "The nurse was supposed to call for him the next day," Cerf remembered. "O'Neill was all set to go to the Carlyle. The next day, he left for Carlotta, instead."

Another visitor, Brooks Atkinson, observes that O'Neill is in good spirits. "He said he was happy about going back," recalled Atkinson, "but I was shocked at how thin he was; and his hands shook so. He was in a humorous mood. I told him I had just seen the movie version of *The Long Voyage Home* and he said he had had the opportunity of taking a flat sum or a royalty on the deal; he'd chosen the flat sum and lost a lot of money. He said he always made the wrong decision when it came to money." (The surprising fact is that O'Neill's enormous output during his lifetime brought him a net profit of under a million dollars.)

The most emotional leave-taking occurs between O'Neill and Commins. Among the last to be told that O'Neill is going back to Carlotta, Commins goes with Dorothy to say good-bye; he is certain he will never see O'Neill again.

"Saxe brought a letter he had gotten from Oona," Dorothy Commins later recalled. "Oona had asked Saxe to give the letter to her father. Gene said he'd like to have it, and he put it under his pillow." (The gesture was probably to avoid offending the Comminses, who, being devoted parents themselves, were distressed about O'Neill's estrangement from his children. It is highly unlikely that O'Neill answered the letter, nor did he ever see his daughter again. Oona, with a happy marriage and eight grown children, seemed to be O'Neill's one stalwart offspring. But as Chaplin— by then Sir Charles—began to ail, she herself gradually fell apart; after he died, at eighty-eight, on Christmas Day 1977, Oona, now Lady Chaplin, set about drinking herself to death. (She died fourteen years later of pancreatic cancer, on September 28, 1991. She was sixty-six.)

"SAXE AND I had offered Gene a home with us in Princeton," Dorothy recalled. "I would have nursed him. But Gene said, 'I'm absolutely helpless. I can't even hold a cup of water. I can't burden you with this.'

"Gene put his arms around Saxe; his whole frame shook. He said, 'Goodbye, my brother! God knows when I'll see you again.'" Dorothy left the room weeping.

Commins was shattered; try as he might, he could not understand O'Neill's motives in preferring to return to Carlotta rather than live with him and Dorothy.

Taking his leave of Armina Marshall, O'Neill tells her: "I know you and Lawrence and Saxe would do everything to help me, but I just can't live on your doorstep—or on anyone else's." According to Armina, O'Neill fears he and Carlotta might be short of cash, and he asks for a loan of $5,000.

"Of course, I wrote him a check at once," Armina recalled, "and I asked him to sign a slip of paper with 'I.O.U. $5,000' written on it—no date, no strings or anything—just a note for the Theater Guild's records." (A few days after O'Neill's departure, Armina receives a check for the $5,000 and a request from Carlotta to return the I.O.U; Armina puts the I.O.U. in the mail. She never hears from either of the O'Neills again.)

Aronberg, although he has loaned O'Neill no money and has not offered him a home, knows that because of his part in the legal proceedings against Carlotta he is slated for amputation. With cynical foresight, he tells O'Neill, on the day he leaves the hospital, "Goodbye, Gene. I'll be fired in a week or so." O'Neill protests. (But it isn't long after O'Neill rejoins Carlotta in Boston that Aronberg receives notice of his dismissal.)

Sherlee comes to say good-bye on the morning of May 17. She is touched when O'Neill, forming the words with painful hesitance, comments on the new hat she is wearing. "That is very natty!" he says. Sherlee herself is all but speechless with grief.

"You can't look at someone you love and just say good-bye, when you know it's the last time you'll see him," she later said. She finally thinks of a way to save both herself and O'Neill the pain of an emotional farewell.

"I'd like to take you to your train," she tells him, knowing that arrangements have already been made for a nurse to accompany him, and that neither she nor O'Neill would wish to say good-bye at the station. O'Neill, understanding, answers gratefully, "I'd like you to do that." Sherlee throws him a kiss. "I'll phone you later," she lies, and hurries from the room, fighting back her tears.

Later, knowing O'Neill has left, she calls the hospital, asking to speak to him. As she expected, he has left her a message saying good-bye and asking her not to come to the train, because he doesn't want a dramatic farewell scene; he has already played too many.

It is shortly before noon on May 17 when O'Neill leaves Doctors Hospital with Nurse Coughlin. She settles him in a roomette on the Yankee Clipper for the four-hour ride to Boston's Back Bay Station.

O'Neill sits huddled in an overcoat that emphasizes his fragility, and Sally Coughlin sits opposite him. As they await the train's departure, Dr. Patterson hurries into O'Neill's roomette to say his good-byes.

"I don't think I would have done this for any other patient," Dr. Patterson later said. "I wanted to make his trip easier for him. I felt that he loved Carlotta and wanted to go back to her. But he was suffering from hospitalitis. Everything had been secure for him at the hospital. We took care of all his thinking, and he hated to make a break."

Accustomed to seeing O'Neill in his bathrobe, Patterson observes that he "looks small, for all the clothes he is in." But Dr. Patterson is pleased to see O'Neill is not shaking.

Patting O'Neill's shoulder, the doctor reassures his patient, "You're going to a good place. Everything is going to be all right."

O'Neill at first cannot bring out his words, but finally manages a broken "Thank you."

Doctor and patient shake hands and Patterson leaves the cramped roomette with a cheery wave.

52

Dr. Kozol meets O'Neill's train with a wheelchair in the late afternoon of May 17 and drives him and Nurse Coughlin to the Shelton, where Carlotta nervously awaits them.

"Seeing Gene again is a ghastly shock," she notes. "He looks so thin and ill." Her mind instantly goes to her three arch-nemeses. "What a curse Langner, Moore and Aronberg have been!" she deplores. O'Neill is exhausted and Carlotta and Coughlin put him to bed. After the nurse and Kozol leave, Carlotta sighs, "Finally we are left alone. I can't believe Gene has finally come home."

In a later, rehearsed version of O'Neill's homecoming, she recalled the occasion with more brio: "When O'Neill came back to me in Boston, I didn't go to the train to meet him. I couldn't do it. He had done something to me that never could be erased. I didn't know how he would act.

"The nurse brought him to the Shelton Hotel, and when he came in, he looked like a dead man. And as he walked by me, he said, 'I'm sorry, forgive me, I love you.' He didn't even stop to say it. He walked right on and into his room. And that was that."

Carlotta and O'Neill have raised the curtain on the last scene of their final act. It will stretch painfully over the next two and a half years and the single confined setting—their small suite at the Shelton—will resound to the histrionics that both will savor to their last breath.

While there's no question O'Neill is now a fragile invalid and needs Carlotta's constant nursing, he needs her even more to stir his soul. His

mind is still robust; he has somehow summoned the ferocity of a thrashing five-hundred-pound tuna determined not to be landed without a
fierce fight.

As for Carlotta, she more than adequately fulfills his expectations; she
is prepared to assume the heroic double role of tender nurse-protectress
and vengeful widow-in-waiting. They both go through the motions of
pretending (at times, no doubt, even believing) they are lovingly reunited.
Within less than two weeks of his return, O'Neill formally signs the
revised will he agreed to as part of Carlotta's condition for taking him
back. After bequeathing all his worldly goods to his wife in Article III,
and excluding Shane and Oona and "their issue now or hereafter born"
from "any interest" in his estate in Article IV, he gets down to the nitty-
gritty.

In Articles V and VI, he appoints Carlotta as his executrix and states
that she "shall have power to sell at public or private sale, without the
necessity of obtaining license or authority of any court, the whole or any
part of my real or personal property . . . to which I may be entitled at the
time of my decease."

In other words, Carlotta, after her husband's death, will have absolute
control of the disposition of O'Neill's entire oeuvre, including *Long
Day's Journey Into Night*, which O'Neill has heretofore consigned to a
twenty-five-year postmortem slumber in the vault of Random House.
Dr. Harry Kozol is one of the three witnesses to the will, a copy of which
is filed in the Suffolk County Probate Court.

O'Neill's role is to humor Carlotta from time to time by playing the
converted miscreant, ostensibly chastened and contrite. Hers is to propi-
tiate the goose that laid the golden egg and make certain that egg will be
ultimately her own.

Two weeks after O'Neill's return to Carlotta, he inscribes a set of
uncorrected proofs of *A Moon for the Misbegotten*, which Random House
is preparing for publication:

"To Carlotta, my beloved wife, whose love I could not possibly live without, in a spirit of the humblest gratitude for her love which has forgiven my recent shameful conduct toward her."

But he will never convince Carlotta he is sincerely penitent, nor can she refrain from periodically confronting him with his horrendous betrayal; how, she persists, can he have been so beastly to her? Didn't he realize that Langner was interested only in retaining control of Gene's plays? Didn't he see that Langner—still hoping to revive *A Moon for the Misbegotten* and produce *A Touch of the Poet*—perceived Carlotta as a huge stumbling block in her role as O'Neill's executor, and wanted her out of the way?

And couldn't he see that Aronberg was a "crook" who had abetted Langner in persuading Gene to change his will? As for his willingness to accept the monster Merrill Moore's judgment of her "insanity"—how could Carlotta ever forgive O'Neill for that?

O'Neill has already agreed with Carlotta's assessment of Aronberg and she is pleased, on May 27, to take her husband's dictation for a letter notifying Bennett Cerf that Aronberg is no longer O'Neill's attorney, and enjoining Cerf to give Aronberg no data as to his "business plans or money involved," nor any data "as formerly" about his income for tax returns.

When Aronberg is requested by Carlotta's lawyer (now also acting for O'Neill) to give up his files of O'Neill's papers, he demands he first be paid a back fee of $3,000—but finally settles for $2,500. Although she and O'Neill are "very hard up," Carlotta concedes it "is better psychologically to get rid of Aronberg and get Gene's papers! Farewell to crooks!"

A more anxiety-provoking problem, which Carlotta has been dealing with since early June, is O'Neill's craving for narcotic medication. Dr. Kozol has prescribed a variety of drugs, among them Luminal, to subdue his tremor; Nembutal, to relieve his anxiety; and an additional sedative, hydrocodone bitartrate—"Elixir"—which he takes in a liquid form. Dr. Kozol doubtless is aware of O'Neill's past addiction to alcohol, and it's probable he has been informed that O'Neill's mother became addicted to morphine while she was breast-feeding him. (In fact, O'Neill later gives Kozol *Long Day's Journey Into Night* to read, and he and O'Neill discuss the play.) In any event, Kozol has taken the precaution of putting Carlotta in charge of her husband's medications, with strict instructions about administering them.

It's not always clear from Carlotta's diary entries which drug O'Neill is taking or when, but it is clear he craves (and sometimes sneaks) more than he is allowed.

On June 14, for example, Carlotta notes: "Gene deeply disturbed he can't have another dose of Nembutal after his six grain allowance for 12 hours. Has to wait for his bedtime dose. It makes my heart ache for him—but must follow doctor's orders." A week later, Dr. Kozol has a long talk with O'Neill about the danger of overdosing (as if the son of an addicted mother and a brother who drank himself to death needed any such instruction).

Along with all their other difficulties, O'Neill's prostate condition flares up again in late June. A urologist assures them the condition is "tied up with tremor" and is not, as they first feared, cancerous.

There is, however, another medical and/or emotional problem connected to O'Neill's condition, to which Carlotta refers on the following day; she notes that both she and O'Neill are "very nervous" when Dr. Kozol comes to them "to discuss a situation that has caused [her] no end of worry and unhappiness." The three "talk it over from all points of view and understand what must be done for health's sake & any chance of happiness." That's all Carlotta chooses to tell the future readers of her diary, leaving us to wonder why she mentions the "situation" at all. (It's notable, however, that there have been no pussycat drawings since July 1948, nor will there be any in the future.)

July is not a good month for the O'Neills. On July 3, the day after they move across the hall to a quieter suite, they are readying themselves for sleep when O'Neill asks Carlotta (in her words) to "help him regain his self-respect!" Carlotta tells him he alone can do that, and solemnly lists the attributes he must acquire: conquer bad habits and learn the meaning of "honesty, decency and loyalty"; she will help him do so, she says, in every way possible.

After giving him his bedtime medicines, she locks them up, as Dr. Kozol has ordered. "Loathe doing this," she notes, "but must for Gene's sake."

Somehow, on July 6, O'Neill finds a way to break into the drug supply and Carlotta notes, "Find Gene taking Elixir—again—it is hopeless!" O'Neill's wish to regain his self-respect appears to have evaporated. "Catch him after lunch trying to steal sedative!" laments Carlotta on July 21, adding, "He now tells me with pride that he has been an addict for years!"

That evening, Kozol again lectures O'Neill about the danger of overdosing. O'Neill feigns penitence and persuades Kozol to put him on his honor, but before long, he is again sneaking Elixir (and childishly watering down the medicine bottle's contents).

O'Neill is still overdosing three months later. "Admits he took Elixir out of new bottle in my bag," notes Carlotta on October 12, at a time when O'Neill is undergoing a "ghastly" all-day tremor; Kozol prescribes Mesantoin (an anticonvulsant commonly given for epileptic seizures) and O'Neill's tremor temporarily abates.

The day before O'Neill's sixty-third birthday, Carlotta notes that she fears he has become "more neurotic than ever & can induce the tremor so well—that he, himself, cannot separate the self-induced from the disease."

During O'Neill's bouts of physical and emotional pain, accompanied by Carlotta's arthritis-ridden and often dispirited nursing, the two are confronted with a string of problems concerning the rights to O'Neill's plays. For one thing, it appears that Aronberg earlier misinterpreted O'Neill's contractual instructions. "This may be serious," worries Carlotta, noting that a contract to televise *Anna Christie* might have to be canceled because the play is "so tied up, we can't let it go" and "will lose the money which we need."

For another, there is now open hostility between both the O'Neills and Lawrence Langner, who evidently is unwilling to give up his rights to *A Moon for the Misbegotten*; according to Carlotta, he has sent a "rude reply" to O'Neill's literary agent, Jane Rubin (Richard Madden's successor), in response to a request to return the script of that play: "Langner who spoiled my marriage to Gene," storms Carlotta, "Langner, Aronberg & Commins—but now Gene has learned (very unpleasantly) what they really are & what they always were to him!"

O'NEILL FALLS SERIOUSLY ILL in late November 1951, and W. Richard Ohler, a Boston internist, orders him into Faulkner Hospital. Dr. Ohler has been paying house calls at the Shelton since July 12, 1951, at the behest of Dr. Kozol. "There was nothing specifically wrong," recalled Ohler, "but Dr. Kozol thought O'Neill should have on call a doctor who was familiar with his condition." Like all his medical predecessors, Dr. Ohler is much taken with O'Neill.

"He was a pliable, lovable patient," said Ohler:

> But he struck me as a man in whom the flame had died. His wife would complain to me about him, and I had the feeling that they argued a lot.
>
> When I visited, I would usually find him sitting by the window, watching the sailboats on the river or the cars on the road along the riverbank. He was usually fully dressed—when he couldn't dress himself, his wife dressed him.
>
> One of my big problems was trying to get him to eat. I thought if I could interest him in something, his appetite might improve. I was a detective story fan, and I urged him to read some. He did, and we used to discuss them. O'Neill spoke slowly and was slow in his movements, but his mind was alert. What he lacked was spirit.
>
> We kept him on barbiturates to ease his tremor, but none of the drugs we had could help him fundamentally. He was

unsteady on his feet. He had one or two falls getting out of bed, and joked about them to me.

Dr. Ohler is unaware that O'Neill has always enjoyed detective stories, along with his other vast reading, and innocently attributes O'Neill's improved appetite to his advice. In fact, O'Neill has never ceased to read avidly and eclectically; during his final years at the Shelton, according to Carlotta, he rereads Kipling's poetry, Mark Twain's collected works, and *Alice's Adventures in Wonderland*. With most of his books in storage, he asks Carlotta to buy him James Whitcomb Riley's collected poetry "to be able to read 'An Old Sweetheart of Mine.'"

He also asks Carlotta to buy him the Wolfville stories, a series written by Alfred Henry Lewis that he had adored as a boy. According to Carlotta, "Whenever he was fed up with writing plays, the business of living, or was not well," he would reread those books "over and over and over again"—much as he had retreated into old copies of the *Saturday Evening Post* when recovering from a drinking binge during his marriage to Agnes.

"Of course I had to advertise for them and pay collector's prices!" said Carlotta. "But he had what he wanted." Most of all, O'Neill enjoyed Lindbergh's *The Spirit of St. Louis*. "It was, to him, so well written—& had the poet's insight. He was reading it for the second time—when he died."

When O'Neill arrives at Faulkner Hospital on November 24, he is treated for gastroenteritis. He is released after three days, only to return almost at once, after an attack of gallstones, followed by fluctuating fever and chills, a seizure of unstoppable hiccups, and "ghastly night sweats"— all of which aggravate his tremor.

Carlotta is at O'Neill's hospital bedside for hours every day. On his return home on December 11, he agrees to accept the service of a home nurse, at last conceding that Carlotta can no longer care for him twenty-four hours a day. The nurse she engages is Jean Welton, who cared for O'Neill at Faulkner. Both O'Neill and Carlotta grow to love and trust her, as they did Kaye Albertoni; she will help Carlotta care for O'Neill until his death and will remain close to Carlotta in her widowhood.

Two and a half weeks after O'Neill's return to the Shelton, on Carlotta's sixty-third birthday, O'Neill gives her the typescript of the third version of *Long Day's Journey Into Night*. He inscribes it in shaky but legible handwriting: "To Carlotta, my beloved wife, this play, written in blood and tears, is dedicated."

He acknowledges that she "did the slavery on it," typing it and encouraging him, giving him "faith and love" and making it possible for him "to go on with work which daily broke [his] heart with poignant memory!"

He addresses her as "again wife, friend, helper and lover [in the] hope this work is worthy of her help! I have loved you for 23 years now, Darling, and now that I am old and can work no more, I love you more than ever!"

THE NEW YEAR of 1952 sees two revivals of O'Neill plays in New York— *Anna Christie* at the City Center and *Desire Under the Elms* at the ANTA Playhouse. Far from signaling that O'Neill is at last being recognized as a treasured staple of the theater, this double revival simply serves to emphasize how neglected he is in his own country.

"*Desire* has been played all over the world and it makes ninety-five per cent of the plays written sound like pretty weak sisters," says Harold Clurman, who has directed the revival. "If O'Neill had written in Germany or France, his plays would be done in the national theatre. Here we neglect them."

O'NEILL IS OBLIGED to return to Faulkner Hospital on January 12, 1952. "We had to have him somewhere for proper care," Carlotta said. Her arthritic back is so painful, and she is so exhausted, that, even with the help of Nurse Welton, she believes she can no longer properly care for her husband at home; she anticipates it would require three nurses daily, which they cannot afford.

"We must see what is best to do," Carlotta said. "If we go to a sanitarium (*where?*) could we go together?" Neither she nor O'Neill "have much to look forward to," she conceded, "but we should stick together. We are both alone in the world."

It is decided, after all, that O'Neill should return to the Shelton, with only Jean Welton as Carlotta's part-time surrogate nurse. O'Neill makes Carlotta promise never again to have him hospitalized.

O'Neill spends most of his waking hours seated in an armchair in the living room, reading or gazing out the window at the river traffic on the Charles. He has few visitors apart from his doctors and lawyers and the hotel manager, Philip McBride, who is a notary public and is occasionally summoned to put his official seal on legal documents.

One such document—a further token of O'Neill's love (or a payment for his need)—is a literary trust fund, presented to Carlotta on March 3, 1952, on which she can draw funds for their immediate needs.

The fund goes so far as to stipulate that if Carlotta should predecease her husband, ownership and control should pass, on his death, to "her estate or to such persons as she may have designated by will or otherwise by instrument executed during her lifetime."

He makes these provisions, explains O'Neill, "in recognition of the loyalty and care afforded me by my said wife as well as the expenditure by her of her own substantial funds as well as funds I provided her with and which were prematurely disbursed because of compelling needs." He points out that he is making no provision for his children, since he has "otherwise provided for them heretofore" (a reference to his having turned over the Bermuda estate to them).

That summer, attention is again briefly focused on O'Neill, when *A Moon for the Misbegotten* is published by Random House. In a brief foreword to the published text (dated April 1952), O'Neill writes that the play "has never been presented on the New York stage, nor are there any plans for its production," and since he "cannot presently give it the attention required for appropriate presentation," he has "decided to make it available in book form."

Francis Wylie has been assigned by *Time* to ask O'Neill a few specific questions, as a sidebar to the magazine's review of the book, scheduled for the week of July 20, 1952. When Wylie reaches Carlotta by phone, she scolds him for trying to bother her husband, but takes it upon herself to tell him (in answer to one of the stipulated questions) that there is no particular reason for the decision to publish the play at this time.

Wylie, however, advises his editors, off the record, that he has it "on authority" the play is being published because the O'Neills are pressed for cash, and Carlotta later confirmed this, recalling, "In 1952 we were terribly hard up. My income was getting low, Gene's was getting low, and I was very worried."

The published play doesn't make much of a splash, and Carlotta expresses her concern to O'Neill. It is at this point (according to Carlotta) that O'Neill informs her the publication restrictions on *Long Day's Journey Into Night* no longer apply.

In Carlotta's verbatim account (to the authors) of her conversation with her husband, O'Neill says: "What are you worried about?"

Carlotta replies: "Money."

O'Neill: "But you don't have to worry, we've got a nest egg."

Carlotta: "Where is it?"

O'Neill: "Why, *Long Day's Journey.*"

Continuing her account, Carlotta said, "Well, I thought he had completely gone out of his mind." It is then, she went on, that O'Neill discloses "for the first time" that it was Eugene Jr. who asked his father to withhold the play for twenty-five years because of its personal nature, and that Eugene's death makes it possible to release the play.

O'Neill now tells Carlotta (according to her account), "If things get worse, we will publish it." (It must be noted that this version of Carlotta's conversation with her husband is highly suspect; it later evolves that she has other, contradictory versions up her sleeve, and after O'Neill's death she will whip them out, offering them, ad-lib, to various publishers, directors, and producers as needed to serve her own agenda.)

Evidently, however, sufficient cash trickles in to alleviate the O'Neills' financial straits (from sources such as foreign royalties and investments) so that the nest egg does not have to be tapped just yet.

That July (1952), on their wedding anniversary, O'Neill gives Carlotta a copy of the newly published *A Moon for the Misbegotten*:

> *To darling Carlotta, my wife, who for twenty-three years*
> *has endured with love and understanding my rotten nerves,*
> *my lack of stability, my cussedness in general—*
>
> *I am old and would be sick of life, were it not that you,*
> *Sweetheart, are here, as deep and understanding in your*
> *love as ever—and I as deep in my love for you as when we*
> *stood in Paris, Premier Arrondissement on July 22, 1929,*
> *and both said faintly "Oui!"*

These lines of the inscription are probably the final words O'Neill ever wrote.

ON A GRAY late-autumn afternoon in 1953, O'Neill and Carlotta sit quietly together in their living room. O'Neill, as on most days now, is pondering his impending death. In spite of what he wrote to Carlotta the previous summer, he is sick of life. Although he still speaks wistfully of suicide and/or death by euthanasia, he is waiting for death by atrophy.

Suddenly, he exclaims, "Nobody must be allowed to finish my plays." Carlotta knows he means the cycle plays that still exist in scenario or rough draft. He asks her to fetch all the manuscripts so that he may destroy them. "It isn't that I don't trust you, Carlotta," he says, "but you might get run over and I don't want anybody else working on these plays."

Carlotta then experienced what she described as "one of the most ghastly half-hours of my life," during which she helped the man she called "the Master" to "destroy" four of his cycle plays. "I thought I would die—& he looked as if he had!"

Three years after O'Neill's death, Carlotta (as is her wont) gives a more histrionic rendering of the event: O'Neill, she said, began tearing the manuscript pages into pieces, but he could "only tear a few pages at a time, because of his tremor"—so she helped him. "We tore up all the manuscripts together, bit by bit. It took hours. It was awful. It was like tearing up children."

"Didn't you try to dissuade him?" Carlotta was asked by an interviewer some years later. "Certainly not," she replied. "I'd not be so presumptuous. No one could get very far trying to persuade him to do anything."

With the destruction of the cycle, O'Neill gave up his last feeble pretense of a grip on life. Nietzsche's "poison-worm" gnawed more fiercely at his heart every day. Often he wept with despair that death would not come.

"There was nothing Gene wanted to do, no one he wanted to see," Carlotta said. "I'd ask him if there were any of his old friends he wanted me to write to for him, or ask to come for a visit, and he always said 'No.'" Carlotta herself seldom left the hotel or had any visitors, but in letters to a few chosen friends, she whispered poignant scraps of what she knew were her final days with O'Neill.

In one such letter, she confided the pathos of listening to O'Neill while she prepared him for sleep one night in early October, as he spontaneously (with his flawless memory) recited a poem by the mid-nineteenth-century English poet Austin Dobson, "In After Days":

> In after days when grasses high
> O'er-top the stone where I shall lie,
> Though ill or well the world adjust
> My slender claim to honour'd dust,
> I shall not question nor reply.

I shall not see the morning sky;
I shall not hear the night-wind sigh;
I shall be mute, as all men must
In after days!

But yet, now living, fain would I
That someone then should testify,
Saying—"He held his pen in trust
To Art, not serving shame or lust."
Will none?—Then let my memory die
In after days!

On October 16, 1953, O'Neill reached his sixty-fifth birthday. He hoped it would be his last. One day, Carlotta tried to feel him out about his wishes regarding a funeral. She decided to approach the subject obliquely. "If I should die," she began, "I want a simple burial and no man of God."

O'Neill "saw through" what she was driving at, wryly recalled Carlotta.

"I'll go long before you," he retorts.

"Well, what do you want if you do?" asks Carlotta.

"Get me quietly and simply buried," he says. "And don't bring a priest. If there is a God and I meet Him, we'll talk things over personally, man to man."

Carlotta later declared, "I admire Gene more for this than anything I can think of. There are so many Catholics who have lost faith and, the last minute, they have doubts and ask for a priest. Gene stuck to his ideas to the end."

Carlotta had been present when O'Neill, some years earlier, had expressed to Sophus Winther his deep disappointment in the Church; O'Neill's words eloquently echoed his disillusionment with religious orthodoxy after the disastrous failure of *Days Without End*.

"Man has been told the truth," said O'Neill (according to Winther's meticulous notes). "He has been shown the way to the good life in simple language. Jesus, Confucius, Lao Tzu—a little more complex—Socrates; but it has been futile. Great and simple truth has been perverted into worldly power by organized institutions. The Church in our world has no relationship to Christianity. The Church is a fraud."

In her diary, Carlotta had earlier noted, "Gene wants to die with no one near him but Dr. Kozol, Mrs. Welton & myself. He knew we were loyal and loved him—he trusted no one else. He wanted no one but us to see him when he was dead."

It is Carlotta's words on which we must rely for O'Neill's state of mind during his final months, for he has long since given up dictating letters to friends; those very few friends who still visit do so under Carlotta's watchful eye, and their recollections are of a strangely altered man—vague, placid, almost vacuous. Now, manifestly close to death, it's likely he is permitted all the sedation he craves. The only person to whom Carlotta allows her husband to speak privately is Dr. Kozol (who declined to be interviewed by the authors after O'Neill's death).

Among O'Neill's own last recorded words are a letter to Bennett Cerf, signed by him (as dictated to Carlotta) on June 13, 1951, in which he thanks Cerf for sending him back some miscellaneous writings deposited with Random House in 1948, and assuring Cerf he does not want back *Long Day's Journey Into Night*, reminding his publisher, "That, as you know, is to be published twenty-five years after my death—but never produced as a play." (This, of course, contravenes Carlotta's statement about her husband's designation of *Journey* as a nest egg to provide funds whenever needed.)

TOWARD THE END of October 1953, according to Carlotta, O'Neill finds he can no longer smoke a cigarette without burning himself. He loses his appetite and barely eats at all. On October 25, Carlotta describes a heartbreaking episode that takes place after a quiet evening of reading and talk in their living room:

"At about 9:30 [Gene] said he was tired and would go to bed. I got him his stick—he was slow in getting out of his chair and had shakily taken 2 or 3 steps—then, suddenly, he fell over on his back!" Carlotta, with her arthritic spine, could no longer lift him, and asked O'Neill to let her call for help from the hotel staff.

"No, I'll do it myself if it kills me!" was O'Neill's response. "He struggled with all his strength & could not lift himself—then fell on his face and wept like a child!"

Carlotta phones the hotel manager for help and he sends two men to the suite. They carry O'Neill to his bed. Later, he tells Carlotta he had tried to walk to see "if this was the end." He says it is.

O'Neill had night sweats, and Carlotta had to change his clothes, struggling to lift and turn him. "He tried to help, but he just couldn't. He had great trouble moving, and even talking," she recalled.

Nearly a month later, on November 24, O'Neill stopped eating entirely.

"An infection had set in," Dr. Ohler recalled. "What he had was the rapidly fulminating type of pneumonia.

"It spread quickly because he was at a low level. He had shortness of breath, a cough, and a high fever. He was given antibiotics, but the heart was too weak to rally, and there seemed to be no will to live."

Ohler's words were echoed by Carlotta: "He wanted so much to die. He gradually lost all coordination of his muscles. At last he was like a stone man—his nurse and I had such difficulty in moving him. . . . Together we kept him as comfortable as possible—and loved him, each in her way, which meant much to him. He felt protected, secure."

In an interview with the authors shortly after the 1956 premiere of *Long Day's Journey Into Night*, Carlotta repeated what she said were O'Neill's last words, uttered on November 24, three days before his death:

"He clenched his fists, raised himself slightly in his bed and gasped, 'Born in a hotel room—and God damn it—died in a hotel room!'"

O'Neill, she said, "was in a coma for thirty-six hours. He never opened his eyes or moved all that time. There was no suffering. I don't know whether I could have stood it if I'd had to watch him suffer. I never left him during the whole time. I held his hand and stayed at his side. He had beautiful hands."

This account by Carlotta was published seminally in the authors' 1962 biography, *O'Neill*, at a time when some of her diaries were still unavailable to scholars; in her 1953 diary (later released by the Beinecke Library), she gives a different account:

> On the night of the 25th of November [O'Neill] tried to say something to me—I couldn't understand—his speech was muffled—I got up on the bed, held him in my arms & said, "Darling, say it again, slowly—please—so I can understand." He tried once more—his eyes were troubled—he was afraid— I could not understand him—he closed his eyes, I began to cry—he never spoke again!

Evidently, in her original, highly dramatic version, Carlotta got carried away, as she so often did. O'Neill very probably did utter those "last" words at some point during his final days, if not on his actual deathbed; a more befitting curtain line is hard to imagine, and one can hardly blame Carlotta for making use of it. (But it behooves the conscientious biographer to correct this widely disseminated misapprehension.)

O'Neill died at 4:39 on Friday afternoon, November 27, 1953.

"Gene wanted no religious service," noted Carlotta, and "a private burial with only Dr. Kozol, Mrs. Welton & I [sic] at his grave. I carried out his wishes to the letter—but it was most difficult—&, at times, heartbreaking—the scavenger Press after me—& criticism on many sides. But, thank God, he is at rest, no one can harm him now."

EPILOGUE

I: BOSTON

Before Carlotta allows O'Neill's body to be placed in the J. S. Waterman Funeral Parlor, she insists on an autopsy.

"I wanted to know what in the name of God was the matter with this man I had nursed so long," she recalled. In an interview with the authors nearly three years after O'Neill's death, Carlotta looked back in anger: "He never had Parkinson's disease. Never."

As arranged by Dr. Kozol, "Necropsy No. 16,697" was performed on November 28 "at 9 a.m., 16 hours post mortem." The nine-page report reveals that O'Neill suffered from a rare disease that only superficially resembles Parkinson's, one in which the cells of the cerebellum are subject to a slow degenerative process.

Drawing no conclusions about whether, in O'Neill's case, the disease was inherited, "Necropsy No. 16,697" does point out that one of the initial symptoms, trembling hands, was shared by O'Neill with both his mother and his brother. The report concludes with Dr. Kozol's "clinical impression" that O'Neill's "cerebellar degeneration" was "perhaps familial, although the family history was never clear as to details."

Carlotta asks Dr. Karl Ragnar Gierow, the director of the Royal Dramatic Theatre in Stockholm, to write her an interpretation of the pathologist's findings; she and her husband, during O'Neill's final years, had grown close to Gierow, who has proudly presented many of O'Neill's plays in Swedish translation.

Gierow is fascinated. "The sickness," he writes, "destroys only the motor system of the organism. Thus the horror of it is that the cerebrum remains unharmed. O'Neill's mind was completely clear the entire time, able to comprehend his misery." As a result of the affliction, Gierow points out, "from top to toe the body loses all control; a helpless wreck, a foundering ship, a hull without a helm."

CARLOTTA EMBRACES THE ROLE of grieving widow; her diary and letters to friends during the weeks and months after O'Neill's death are awash in tears.

"He wanted so much to die," she writes to Brooks Atkinson on December 11. If he hadn't left her so much to do, she adds, she herself would have no reason to go on. "The being without him is at times almost more than I can bear."

On her first Christmas without her husband, Carlotta exclaims, "Oh, God—what a price one pays for love such as we had—and it was worth it a hundred times—no matter how deep the pain!"

LOCAL AND WIRE-SERVICE REPORTERS had tried for four days to find out when and where O'Neill would be buried. His friends in New York, where a newspaper strike was in progress, also attempted to discover when the funeral would take place. But Carlotta, determined to keep the plans for the burial a secret, secluded herself and issued no comment.

"I carried out every wish of [O'Neill's] to the letter," she later protested in an interview with *The New York Times* that appeared on November 4, 1956, "and it was very difficult; he wished to keep everything from the papers; he wished no publicity; he wished nobody to be at his funeral; he wished no religious representative of any creed or kind.

"Well, what I went through! But the employees of the hotel, and particularly two men who were strong of arm, and determined, good Bostonians, were throwing people downstairs and I don't know what."

She added that she and Nurse Welton were forced to go out of their way, changing taxis, to get to the undertaker's, which was only two blocks from the Shelton.

"We'd ride miles to keep the place a secret. And then my lawyer and I went out and bought the burial site." (In his will, O'Neill had written: "I desire to be buried in a burial lot with my wife and I authorize my Executrix to purchase such a lot and erect a simple stone thereon.")

A little before ten o'clock on the morning of December 2, the hearse bearing O'Neill's body moved quietly away from the Waterman undertaking parlor and slipped unobtrusively into the stream of Boston traffic. It was followed by a car bearing Carlotta, Nurse Welton, and Dr. Kozol. No one would have guessed—not even the waiting and watching reporters—that this inconspicuous procession was Eugene O'Neill's funeral cortege.

The two vehicles pulled up at a remote corner of Forest Hills Cemetery, on Boston's outskirts. There, under a pale sun that yielded no warmth, Carlotta, Welton, and Kozol stood in silence as O'Neill's coffin was lowered into its grave.

Only one story describing the burial appeared in a local newspaper; it was written by Warren Carberg, of the Boston *Post*, who did not reveal the source of his information.

"There were no formal prayers," wrote Carberg. "A funeral director's assistant stepped forward and placed a single spray of white chrysanthemums on the casket, and then the three mourners turned and walked to the automobile.

"Not a word was spoken. No hymns were sung. Mrs. O'Neill wore simple black clothing, with no mourning veil. She was pale and appeared without make-up. There seemed to be tiny lines of grief about her eyes and mouth. No tears showed in her eyes."

Carlotta eventually provided the stone—cut from Italian marble, rough around the edges but highly polished in front where the lettering was engraved. It is four feet high and six feet wide, and is inscribed as O'Neill wished.

"It's a very lovely cemetery," Carlotta once reminisced. "It's got beautiful trees, enormous rhododendrons, and in the spring and summer, with the dogwood, it's quite, quite lovely. I planted laurel around the headstone, like the laurel wreaths of the Greek heroes."

FOR A TIME, Carlotta secludes herself in Boston, dredging up memories both good and bad of her life with O'Neill, and "working over" her personal diaries. She decides that the two contentious years she and her husband spent in New York during the production of *The Iceman Cometh* and the tryout of *A Moon for the Misbegotten* "were tragic and senseless!" and she destroys the diaries she kept for 1946 and 1947.

Uncannily, Carlotta has begun to think of herself as O'Neill's alter ego, in much the same way that Lavinia Mannon in *Mourning Becomes Electra* assumes the character of her dead mother, Christine.

Carlotta plays a dual role: that of the dramatically mourning widow who dresses exclusively in black (down to her judiciously chosen brooches and rings of onyx, opal, and obsidian, and strings of black pearls), and that of O'Neill's alter ego; she manages his literary property in a manner she sometimes chooses to believe is mystically dictated to her by O'Neill's spirit.

Carlotta can imagine O'Neill's acknowledgment that mourning becomes her. "I will never wear anything but black, now that Gene is dead," she vows in her diary on April 8, 1954, four months after O'Neill's death.

Two months later, still absorbed in editing her diaries, Carlotta writes again to Brooks Atkinson from the Shelton:

"Have been working hours a day—up to eleven or twelve at night— Good, in a way. I sleep at least four solid hours a night! A heart-breaking job—beginning February 10, 1928 [the date they eloped to Europe]—

until Gene's death. But, this must be done—I found the diaries were fading! And it must be done right and honestly."

After Carlotta confides to other friends that she has deleted certain of her diary entries "to avoid scandal," a rumor surfaces that she is rewriting O'Neill's diaries. This is patently untrue; she did ask her husband to delete, or slightly alter, some of his Work Diary entries when he transcribed them into the new set of leather-bound diaries she bought him soon after their marriage. O'Neill obliged his new bride in her wish to erase traces of Agnes and strengthen her own importance in his life. But she would have to have been a master forger to simulate his distinctive crabbed penmanship.

"I must stick to [rewriting my] diaries—which will take me all summer!" she tells Atkinson. "All I do is work and talk to Mr. Meserve—my lawyer here."

Three more months go by before she again writes to Atkinson, this time complaining, with mixed anger and humor, that the Random House set of O'Neill's plays has been allowed to go out of print. If the books are not to be had in the stores, she argues, "the would-be purchaser gives up his effort of owning O'Neill's works—and Mrs. O'Neill eats less—so to speak! . . . Gene isn't dead nine months and this is how they behave! It sickens me!"

WITH THE FREEDOM O'Neill has legally bestowed on her, Carlotta has slipped into the heady role of O'Neill surrogate, and she can be as imperious (and as contradictory) as O'Neill ever was.

She has by now wrested *Long Day's Journey Into Night* from Bennett Cerf's stubbornly protective custody in its Random House vault. When Cerf insists on honoring O'Neill's injunction that the play not be published until twenty-five years after his death, Carlotta tells him that O'Neill only wanted to restrict the stage production of the play, not its publication. She puts *Long Day's Journey* into the willing hands of the Yale University Press.

II: NEW YORK

Toward the end of 1955, having completed the sly refining of her diaries, Carlotta emerges from seclusion in Boston and establishes herself in New York at the Lowell Hotel, where she and O'Neill stayed briefly years earlier; O'Neill's ghost moves in with her.

"Two years ago today—at this hour—Gene was dying!" she writes to Atkinson. "Will I ever be able to free myself from this man—and the love I felt for him!"

Carlotta, at the start of 1956, awaits the publication of *Long Day's Journey Into Night*. Having forgotten (or not caring) what she recently told Cerf at Random House about O'Neill's wish to restrict the stage production of the play, Carlotta has agreed to allow Karl Gierow and the Swedish Royal Dramatic Theatre to present the premiere of *Long Day's Journey* in Stockholm on February 2.

In view of O'Neill's long silence, both the book and the Swedish production create something of a stir, and Carlotta is courted by a number of American producers and directors eager to mount the play on Broadway. She bides her time, turning them down one by one, offering different and often contradictory reasons.

To one prominent Broadway entrepreneur, Alexander H. Cohen, she writes (in April 1956): "I regret to have to tell you *Long Day's Journey Into Night* is not available for production in this country. I am carrying out O'Neill's wishes to the letter. He wished me to publish this play but not to allow it to be produced by anyone under any conditions! I hope you understand."

Carlotta knows perfectly well she is not carrying out O'Neill's wishes; on the other hand, he did leave his entire estate to her to handle as she saw fit and, knowing her as he did, O'Neill surely expected her to disregard his instructions if she was so inclined.

Eventually, Carlotta permits herself a remission from active grieving, and adopts a life of moderate socializing. While carefully maintaining an air of semi-seclusion and noblesse oblige, she deigns, from time to time, to invite select acquaintances to lunch or dinner. The meals—sometimes served in her hotel suite at the Lowell, other times in the adjoining Quo Vadis restaurant—are always lavish, prolonged, and festive.

Despite Carlotta's volatile temper, her guests find her often funny, loquacious, and entertaining.

José Quintero has by now become a vital presence in Carlotta's life. Although presumably she knows he is gay, she has fallen in love with the young director who magically breathed new life into *The Iceman Cometh* when he recently revived it off-Broadway.

Quintero is mercurial, sensitive, and often passionately theatrical. In his early thirties, he is handsome, slim, and dark, with O'Neill's piercing eyes, and he has long identified with O'Neill in a way he himself finds spooky.

Evidently, in Carlotta's mind, he is a Latin incarnation of the black-Irish O'Neill. (He was, in fact, born into a Catholic family in Panama, and he attached a mystical meaning to the fact that his birthday—October 15—and O'Neill's were only one day apart.)

Smitten as she is, Carlotta suddenly "remembers" that O'Neill actually told her she could allow *Long Day's Journey* to be produced on Broadway if she found the right director. And it's doubtful that anyone but Quintero, with his psychic connection to O'Neill, could have brought off that delicately perceptive and thrilling American premiere, a premiere that forced the critics to reevaluate and reacknowledge O'Neill's incalculable contribution to the way the world experiences theater.

ONCE THE PRODUCTION of *Long Day's Journey* is launched on its successful run, Carlotta has ample reason to congratulate herself. With O'Neill's ironically grinning ghost looking over her shoulder, she has triumphantly won the battle to restore his luster.

She sees no reason why she should stop there. Some of the producers who had vied to mount *Long Day's Journey* are now petitioning her for the rights to the as yet unproduced *A Touch of the Poet*, as well as the long-since-abandoned *A Moon for the Misbegotten*. She rejoices that those plays are now hers to exploit.

Carlotta, by this time, can afford to move into more lavish quarters, and she settles into the Madison Hotel on East Sixty-third Street (where she and O'Neill had so often stayed twenty years earlier). It is there that she entertains two of her many courtiers, Carmen Capalbo and Stanley Chase. Their off-Broadway revival of Kurt Weill's *The Threepenny Opera*, directed by Capalbo and produced by Chase, opened in the fall of 1954 and is a sensational long-running hit. Both young men are captivated by Carlotta.

One day, in the fall of 1956 (shortly before the Broadway opening of *Long Day's Journey*), Capalbo and Chase are invited to the Madison for dinner. They send ahead a huge bouquet of yellow chrysanthemums and bring with them a bottle of choice Burgundy.

"Mrs. O'Neill was appreciative, but acted very coy," Capalbo recalled. "She said, 'So charming, so European.'"

Capalbo is surprised by the lack of sentimental clutter on display in her suite. There are, of course, bookcases filled with volumes of O'Neill's plays, but the walls are sparsely hung; there are a few framed inscriptions to Carlotta from O'Neill, and several photographs of her and O'Neill together, including a charming one taken shortly after their wedding in Paris, in which they lean against a majestic ivy-covered tree trunk, gazing into their future idyllic life.

Capalbo ventures to ask where all of O'Neill's scrapbooks and other effects are kept.

"I sent everything to Yale," Carlotta says. "When I need something, they send it here for me."

A small ceramic Dalmatian, symbolizing the O'Neills' beloved Blemie, stands on the mantelpiece of the living room. And then there is the stuffed monkey, Esteban (O'Neill's first gift to Carlotta), seated in a corner of the couch.

"That monkey had the silliest grin you ever saw," recalled Capalbo. "Mrs. O'Neill would jokingly address wisecracks to it, every so often."

Carlotta asks Capalbo and Chase what they want to drink. They hesitate, worrying she might disapprove of drinking, but take a chance and ask for cocktails.

"Good, I like people who take a drink," says Carlotta, freed from tiptoeing around O'Neill's alcoholism. "There are three important things in this world: Eating, drinking, and making love."

The meal, sent up from the hotel's haute cuisine restaurant, Passy, is "sumptuous," Capalbo recalled. "Steak, broccoli Hollandaise, French peas, wine. The waiter who served us was an elderly man whom Mrs. O'Neill had known for years. They reminisced a little about the old days at the restaurant. She treated him in the manner of a great lady to an old retainer—warmly, but aware of the distinction."

After dinner, Carlotta insists on serving brandy. The suite is uncomfortably warm, and Capalbo, slightly stupefied from the meal, the liquor, and the heat, suggests opening a window. Carlotta says she keeps the windows closed because the cold affects her arthritic hands, but she allows him to open a window for a few minutes.

"We'd open it and close it every so often till around 12:30 a.m., when we finally left," Capalbo remembered. "Stanley and I were reeling." The two went to Reuben's, an all-night restaurant, where they sat until dawn talking about their dazzling experience.

"There had been no sequence to her conversation—it was as though she were on a psychiatrist's couch. Within a half-hour after we arrived, she started telling us the most intimate things about her relationship with O'Neill.

"We were stunned, not so much by the information she gave us, but because she talked so freely. She would say things like 'Gene was such a horror, crazy.' Then she'd cast her eyes heavenward and say, 'Oh, Gene, he was my darling baby. I was his mother. He never had a mother. She was a dope fiend.'"

Carlotta told the two rapt young men, "O'Neill was a tough mick, and never loved a woman who walked. He was an impatient lover—not like a Latin, who is content to simply sit at the edge of a bathtub and watch a woman bathe. With O'Neill everything had to be quick, quick. He loved only his work. But he had respect for me. I had an independent income, and I told him I'd marry him if he would let me pay one half of all the household expenses. 'I want a home properly run,' he told me. And that is what I did for him. I saw to it that he was able to work."

Carlotta's fondness for Capalbo and Chase culminates in May 1957, with their production on Broadway of *A Moon for the Misbegotten*. It's a disappointment despite the presence of Franchot Tone as James Tyrone Jr. and Wendy Hiller as Josie Hogan.

A Touch of the Poet was presented a year later (October 2, 1958) by one of Broadway's most distinguished producers, Robert Whitehead. Like *Moon*, it curdled despite its starry (but fractious and embattled) cast: Eric Portman as Con Melody; Helen Hayes as his wife, Nora; Kim Stanley as his daughter Sarah; and Betty Field as Deborah Harford.

THE MONEY FROM the healthy sixteen-month run of *Long Day's Journey* (it closed in New York in March 1958), plus royalties earned from the published book (it sold better than any of O'Neill's previous plays), have provided Carlotta with the means to move into the even more posh Carlton House, a residential hotel at 21 East Sixty-first Street.

Theodore (Ted) Mann begins visiting her there regularly in 1963. Mann is Quintero's producing partner at Circle in the Square, where they are planning a revival of *Desire Under the Elms*, and he discusses with Carlotta their ideas for casting and other details. By the time the well-received production opens, Mann has fallen into the habit of calling on Carlotta once or twice a week.

"I got to feel very responsible for her," Mann said. "To spend lunch with her was to practically spend the day."

While Carlotta's appetite is undiminished, she is, at seventy-four, feeling her age.

"She used to walk very, very slowly" during their strolls together, Ted Mann recalled. "She was afraid of falling. But she enjoyed the exercise. Sometimes we'd walk to the Central Park Zoo. She always went to the monkey house. She loved the monkey house."

Mann is amused but not surprised by Carlotta's evident affinity for monkeys. He had early on been introduced to Esteban and he knew that she had met O'Neill for the first time during the Broadway production of *The Hairy Ape*. But Mann is startled to see that the zoo's monkeys seem to return Carlotta's affection.

"Even when there was a whole crowd of people looking at the monkeys, they would pick her out," he remembered. "They would look right at her. She really had a very close thing with them."

In a gust of irony, Carlotta, like other of O'Neill's abandoned lovers (most notably Agnes Boulton and Louise Bryant), has taken to drink. But she is also beginning to have periods of pronounced mental instability that are due to more than heavy drinking. She begins impulsively to give things away—jewelry, clothing, bric-a-brac, even the rights to plays. Mann recalled that once, during the summer, her behavior becomes so erratic that her doctor, Gilbert R. Cherrick, puts her into Regent Hospital, a small private facility on East Sixty-first Street.

Carlotta "just clicked out," according to Mann. "She was there about four weeks. I visited her, but I'm not sure she knew who I was." She made what Mann termed "a remarkable recovery," during which she would have periods of "tremendous lucidity." But there were also "times when she would kind of drift off."

Mann said that Carlotta, centered on recalling her life with O'Neill, "would interweave episodes and characters from the plays into her conversation, without making any distinction between them and the actual episodes and people in her and O'Neill's lives.

"She would also say, often, that she wanted to die. She wasn't bitter about it, she said she was just tired."

QUINTERO, TOO, is aware that Carlotta is drifting away from reality. Spellbound by her from the day they met, on intimate terms ever since, Quintero acknowledges that their friendship has had its inevitable ups and downs. How could it not, given the volatile nature of each? The qualities that have enabled Quintero to interpret O'Neill brilliantly and intuitively—the very qualities that recommend him to Carlotta—are also the cause of their quarrels.

"She would drive me, sometimes, to the point where I wanted to choke her," Quintero once recalled. "She had a tongue that could cut."

III: LIMBO

Those few people to whom Carlotta draws close during the ensuing years are aware she is a haunted soul; in her mind, she is still embattled with O'Neill, endlessly reliving their marriage, unable to shake off the weight of her guilt, locked into daily conflict with O'Neill's truculent ghost.

On October 23, 1964, Carlotta writes a new will bequeathing to Yale's Beinecke Library all of O'Neill's papers not yet formally assigned, and naming Yale as the beneficiary of all royalties from the O'Neill plays. (Under a complicated copyright arrangement, Yale shares the interest in some of these royalties with the estates of Oona Chaplin and Shane O'Neill.)

Carlotta stipulates that a portion of the royalties be assigned to the establishment of "Eugene O'Neill Scholarships," to be awarded to "worthy students of playwriting."

She bequeaths her jewelry, apparel, and personal household effects to Cynthia (who has never fully recovered her health and who will survive Carlotta by only eight months). And in a codicil to the will drawn on

March 3, 1967, Carlotta leaves $25,000 each to Cynthia and to her grandson, Gerald Eugene Stram.

Carlotta's signature on the 1964 will, while not as flamboyant as it once was, still flaunted the large capital *C* and confident *M* of her (assumed) middle name; by contrast, the codicil, signed two and a half years later, bears the signature of a feeble old woman—not cramped like O'Neill's, but every bit as shaky. That signature is a sorrowful symbol of Carlotta's decline from the self-assured, assertive woman she was at seventy-five, to the distraught wraith she has become only four years later.

According to her latest lawyer, Richard Crockett (of the law firm Cadwalader, Wickersham & Taft), Carlotta, nearing eighty, had been in poor health for some time. Almost blind, recalled Crockett, she could barely see to sign the codicil even when seated under the brightest lamp in her Carlton House suite and peering through the magnifying glass she'd used to decipher O'Neill's handwriting.

THE THREE PEOPLE who are in almost daily touch with Carlotta throughout the time she lives in New York are the play agent Jane Rubin, the Beinecke's Donald Gallup, and Crockett. Of the three, Jane Rubin is probably the most long-suffering.

After O'Neill's death, Rubin found herself assuming a number of duties for Carlotta, more out of an old friendship than as the representative for O'Neill's plays. When Carlotta is in failing health, physically or mentally, Rubin helps to look after her.

More and more often, there are times when Carlotta is completely helpless. Cynthia is herself unwell and cannot come to her. Most of Carlotta's former friends are dead or live far away, or have, by now, been dropped.

Jane Rubin seems to be Carlotta's only woman friend within calling distance; it is Rubin who, in consultation with Carlotta's doctor, oversees her stays in the hospital, visits her regularly, pays her bills, and acts as a buffer between Carlotta and her dwindling social and business obligations.

Carlotta feels closest, however, to Donald Gallup because of his guardianship of, and intimacy with, the O'Neill papers at Yale. In a sense, he and Carlotta now share O'Neill's life.

While she lives with her memories of O'Neill, Gallup lives with the tangible evidence of O'Neill's body of work. He spends the major part of almost every day at Yale's Beinecke Rare Book and Manuscript Library collating the material in the vast O'Neill collection.

Dr. Gallup's involvement with both O'Neill and Carlotta has led him, in 1962, to abet a project that is both quixotic and questionable. With Carlotta's befogged blessing, he becomes a partner in the reconstruction of the triple-length, very rough, manifestly unfinished manuscript of *More Stately Mansions* that somehow was overlooked at the time Carlotta helped her husband tear up his cycle notes and unfinished scripts, and then found its way into the O'Neill collection at Yale.

Describing this misbegotten project, Gallup writes: "In the spring of 1957, Mrs. O'Neill informed Karl Ragnar Gierow, the director of the Swedish Royal Dramatic Theatre, of the existence of *More Stately Mansions* and eventually gave him permission to attempt to shorten the script for possible production in Swedish translation. There was at that time no question of its publication, either in Swedish or in English."

After five years, Gierow believes he has succeeded in making an acting version, guided "in part" (so he claims) by the author's own extensive notes, but following Mrs. O'Neill's stipulation that only O'Neill's words may be used.

Carlotta herself has once again either forgotten or shrugged off one of her husband's injunctions: "*Nobody must be allowed to finish my* [cycle] *plays*" (authors' italics). But these are the years during which she is often in a state of confusion.

When the authors of this biography query her (on April 21, 1961) about the details of the Swedish production (and the coming publication) of *More Stately Mansions*, Carlotta delivers a tart tirade:

"Dr. Gierow didn't change one comma, one dash, one period. He followed instructions left by O'Neill on how it should be cut." She adds that the working notes by O'Neill on how he intended to cut the play "were contained in the typewritten copy." And she complains: "I can't stand it when people question what I'm doing with O'Neill's plays. I am carrying out his wishes. He gave me the plays and said I could do anything I wanted with them—burn them, destroy them."

Giving *More Stately Mansions* to Sweden's national theater, she insisted, is a tribute from O'Neill; compounding her lie, she concluded, "The play is not to be produced by any other theater and not to be published ever."

In 1964, in a "Prefatory Note" to the published version of *More Stately Mansions*, Gierow writes:

"Mrs. O'Neill now feels that this play should be produced in future only in the repertory of the `Swedish Royal Dramatic Theater, but she has agreed that its text may be made available for students of O'Neill's work."

Gierow concedes that O'Neill, "had he lived, would certainly have revised and rewritten extensively, as he always did." He then brazenly asserts that the text he himself has presumed to shorten "is one which O'Neill himself might well have authorized for publication," because he, Gierow, was a man "in whose judgment [O'Neill] had confidence."

Gierow, as a writer, might have deluded himself that this was so; but surely Donald Gallup, in his heart, cannot believe that. Nor is Gallup embarrassed to mention in his own preface to the published play that, on a flyleaf laid into the unfinished manuscript of *More Stately Mansions*, O'Neill had written: "Unfinished work. This script to be destroyed in case of my death!"

That Gallup ignored O'Neill's written instructions is bizarre, as is his clumsy and misleading claim, in the published version of *More Stately Mansions*, that it is "a new play by Eugene O'Neill."

In fairness, the record should show that *More Stately Mansions*, as published and promoted, is the Gierow/Gallup version of an unfinished and disowned manuscript. It is simply and unequivocally not "an O'Neill play."

From publication, it's a short, greedy hop for Carlotta to a Broadway production that opens on October 31, 1967, at the Broadhurst—again in the misleading guise of "a new play by Eugene O'Neill." It is directed by Quintero, who at the time is undergoing treatment for a life-threatening throat cancer.

The play is not well received by the critics but it ekes out a four-month run, largely because it stars Ingrid Bergman making a Broadway comeback as the more-than-half-mad Deborah Harford (the role O'Neill once jokingly suggested should be played by Carlotta).

QUITE EARLY IN their friendship, Carlotta had presented Quintero with O'Neill's wedding ring, insisting he wear it. Now, during mental lapses when she relives frightening moments with O'Neill, she sometimes addresses Quintero as "Gene." She shouts at "Gene" to stop tormenting her, to stop accusing her. At other times, she tells Quintero, "He comes and stares at me in the night."

On these occasions, Quintero does his best to defend Carlotta to her husband's ghost. Quintero is well aware that Carlotta feels persecuted not only by O'Neill's ghost but also by those of O'Neill's friends who believed him a prisoner and who accuse her (behind her back) of faking the ardent inscriptions that she claims O'Neill wrote to her in his frail final years. (It is primarily to dispel this myth that Carlotta, in 1960, has had O'Neill's handwritten inscriptions photographed, and has shared the cost with the Yale University Library for privately printing five hundred copies of the volume she has entitled *Inscriptions: Eugene O'Neill to Carlotta Monterey O'Neill*.)

While Quintero's conversations with Carlotta were certainly authentic (he took notes), his report should probably be read as a blend of his own vivid vocal timbre and Carlotta's actressy declamation—as when, for example, he quotes her thus:

"When I accepted O'Neill's terms, I committed myself to a monastic existence surrounded by silence. Like a deaf mute I stood by his side, watchful of anything or anybody that could penetrate the enclosure we had built so his work could go on undisturbed.

"I became the feared dragon by the gate. That is why I am hated so. Not that Gene, in spite of all his dedications and little notes swearing love and begging for forgiveness, didn't also hate me."

SHORTLY BEFORE THE breakdown that sent Carlotta to Regent Hospital, Quintero became aware that Carlotta was (as he put it) "falling into a certain kind of pattern."

"She gave away a ruby bracelet to the [hotel] elevator operator," he recalled. "She would give me jewelry for my sister and my mother. I'd leave it on the table when I went. One time she began talking to an empty chair, as though O'Neill were sitting on it.

"But when she was at her best, she was the most charming conversationalist. She had a very broad, all-encompassing kind of humor. She was enormously pleasant to look at. She hadn't just shared a life with O'Neill. She had embraced his life and lived it with him. She really had a right to be Mrs. Eugene O'Neill. And she was tremendously loyal to him as an artist."

Early in 1968, Quintero leaves for Mexico. (He has not planned a long stay, but for various reasons his visit there is extended to a year.)

By October 1968, Carlotta is nearing her eightieth birthday, and her behavior has become increasingly irrational; she seems again to be verging on a breakdown. Some members of the Carlton House staff attribute her behavior to drinking, but as it turns out, she is in the early stages of senile dementia.

Donald Gallup, who sees Carlotta in October, recalls it is he who persuades her to enter a nursing home. "It was very plain that she needed care," he explained.

But it is Jane Rubin who, toward the end of October, accompanies her, once again, to Regent Hospital. The stuffed monkey Esteban is among those personal effects of Carlotta's that Rubin takes along for her comfort.

Carlotta's doctor tells Rubin that Carlotta will never again be able to live on her own, and Rubin realizes it is "clearly hopeless" for Carlotta to return to the Carlton House.

As Dr. Cherrick recalled, "The management was becoming exercised about Mrs. O'Neill's behavior. She would wander in the halls, and go down to the desk and complain that people were spying on her."

Carlotta had become Dr. Cherrick's patient in 1967 when the older doctor who had attended her for many years during her stays in New York retired and left Cherrick his practice; although quite young, Dr. Cherrick has excellent credentials. He becomes quickly convinced that Regent Hospital cannot give Carlotta the care she needs, and in November 1968, he arranges for her admission to the psychiatric ward at St. Luke's Hospital on Amsterdam Avenue at 114th Street.

It's highly unlikely that Carlotta, given her mental state, is aware of the death in that same month—November 1968—of her nemesis, Agnes Boulton Kaufman. There is no evidence that either Carlotta or O'Neill had known or cared about the mess Agnes made of her final years. By then a confirmed alcoholic with little means, she had retreated to the Old House in New Jersey where, from afar in Vevey, Switzerland, she was looked after and partly supported by daughter Oona.

Agnes's health rapidly deteriorated. When she was hospitalized in 1967, Oona flew to the United States to be briefly at her mother's side (to the distress of the aging Charlie Chaplin, who hated being separated from his wife). And on November 25 of the following year, Agnes died; she had outlived O'Neill by fifteen years.

THE SUITE AT the Carlton House is given up, and Rubin packs Carlotta's possessions and sends them to storage. In an interview with the authors, Rubin listed those possessions: "Several wardrobe trunks of clothes, her jewelry, books, papers and a few items of furniture." The one item that Rubin, while packing, was unable to account for was Esteban; she couldn't recall ever seeing the stuffed monkey again after she deposited it with Carlotta at Regent Hospital. Of no intrinsic value, its loss was keenly felt for its sentimental value by several of Carlotta's old friends; they believed that, rightfully, it should have taken its place among other memorabilia in the O'Neill collection at Yale.

Rubin's explanation of why Carlotta, with her ample financial means, was transferred to St. Luke's, and not to one of the better-known local psychiatric facilities such as Payne Whitney, was that "we wanted to avoid publicity, we wanted Carlotta somewhere she would not be known."

Dr. Gallup's recollection, however, was that St. Luke's was chosen because Dr. Cherrick was an attending physician there; Cherrick himself believed the psychiatric facilities were much the same as those of any other reputable hospital.

"The only thing better would have been round-the-clock nursing care in her own home," he said, "and that kind of arrangement for Mrs. O'Neill, or for almost anyone, would have been prohibitively expensive. [Plus the Carlton House did not want her and she had no other home to go to.]

"At St. Luke's," concluded Cherrick, "Mrs. O'Neill was very attentively looked after by the staff, and she could not have had better treatment in any other hospital."

Carlotta, according to Dr. Cherrick, is now suffering from a severely aggravated form of senile psychosis. "Her behavior was, at times, violent," he recalled. "She was somewhat paranoid and believed that certain people were out to molest her. She had delusions." At St. Luke's, she is given custodial care and treated with Thorazine, a strong tranquilizer.

Gallup visits Carlotta for the first time at St. Luke's in late December 1968. "She was on the violent ward, and a visitor had to be passed through locked doors," he recalled. "Off the corridor there were four rooms, and Mrs. O'Neill was in one of them. It was a large, bare room, with a barred window." To Gallup, she seemed "quite rational."

On Gallup's second visit, about a month later, he observes that Carlotta's condition has worsened, and he attributes this to her grim surroundings.

"At one point," he recalled, "a woman wandered into Mrs. O'Neill's room and began talking to me about something that was obviously very important to her, but didn't make much sense. Mrs. O'Neill said, 'Pay no attention, she's a loony.'"

JOSÉ QUINTERO RETURNS to New York at the end of January 1969. He has brought back a few small gifts for Carlotta, with whom he has been completely out of touch. When he telephones the Carlton House, he meets with what he regards as "very mysterious" resistance.

The manager tells him Mrs. O'Neill has left, but won't say when or where she has gone. "He was very courteous," Quintero says, "but told me he was under strict orders not to let anyone know where Mrs. O'Neill was." When Quintero called Jane Rubin and told her of the Carlton's refusal to inform him of Carlotta's whereabouts, he ran into another stone wall. "I could tell by her voice that she was sorry she had answered the phone," Quintero recalled. "But I told her that the hotel would not tell me anything about Mrs. O'Neill, and that I wanted to know where she was. She said she was very sorry, but she couldn't tell me that. I said I had to find her, I was going to find her some way, even if I had to put an ad in the newspapers. Finally she said that the best she could do was to give me the name of Mrs. O'Neill's doctor."

According to Quintero's account, he telephones Cherrick, who, after some hesitation, concedes that Carlotta is "very ill" and confined at St. Luke's. Dr. Cherrick suggests Quintero meet him in the hospital lobby at seven that evening. The visiting hour is seven to eight, he tells Quintero; they will have coffee in the cafeteria, and he will "explain certain things."

"I went," said Quintero, "and it got to be 7:15—no doctor; 7:30—no doctor." At 7:40, fearful of missing the visiting hour entirely, Quintero, armed with the doctor's name, talks his way onto the floor where Carlotta is confined. There, he tells the nurse he is a relative of Carlotta's "on the Spanish side, the Monterey side, we're first cousins," and he is let into the ward.

"It was not a private room. It was not even a room for two," Quintero said, recalling his initial shock. "Three women were in this room. There was a small window with bars in it. Part of the room was in gloom. Mrs. O'Neill's lamp was off and she was sitting at the very edge of the bed, looking out through the barred window. I didn't recognize her from the back at first, because her hair was down to her shoulders.

"I said, 'Mrs. O'Neill.' No response. I said, 'Carlotta.' No response. Finally, she looked at me and said, 'There you are—bothering me again, Gene. Haven't I expiated enough? Not even Lavinia had to go through what I've gone through.'

"Finally," according to Quintero, "she recognized me, and we had a chat." He is horrified at how Carlotta looks. "She was wearing a once-elegant black street dress, now soiled.

"Her hair was a mess, and her nails, which she always wore very short and polished, were so long and ragged. . . . I couldn't believe that the widow of America's greatest playwright was in this kind of situation.

"And she told me she had only that one dress she was wearing, and a white hospital gown that she could change into while the black dress was being cleaned. She said she didn't need much."

During the course of the conversation, according to Quintero, Carlotta switches back and forth between addressing him as "José," and accusing him of being "Gene, who has come to upset her." At one point, she begins talking about "those beautiful kimonos we bought in Shanghai."

"Don't you remember, Gene?" she asks. "Or were you too drunk to remember?"

Quintero is able to follow Carlotta's rambling, for she has previously told him about the trip to Shanghai. "The conversation did not seem mad at all to me," he recalled.

Carlotta has moments in which she is oriented enough to ask Quintero quite rational questions about his mother and sister. She tells him that she wants to leave the hospital, and asks if he will come back.

At one point, Quintero asks her why she has let her hair grow so long. She replies that she won't let "that butcher" (the hospital barber) touch her hair.

Quintero, like Gallup, feels that Carlotta's surroundings might be a contributing factor to her mental condition.

"I could understand how she felt," he said. "You couldn't ask Carlotta Monterey O'Neill to submit to that. She had grown accustomed to a certain way of being handled. It was impossible for her, really impossible. She was a vain woman—with cause.

"When I left, I promised her I would come back."

To mitigate somewhat the squalor of Carlotta's existence, Quintero does the one thing in his power; he persuades her former hairdresser from the Carlton House to accompany him to St. Luke's and give her a proper trim.

"He cut her hair, and she was perfectly willing to let him trim her nails, too," recalled Quintero. "People came to the door to watch. I chatted with her, and she was quite lucid. We talked about the theater, and about O'Neill. She was wearing a clean dress. Jane Rubin had brought it."

Shortly after this visit, Quintero's father dies, and he is obliged to return to his native Panama for a long stay. He never sees Carlotta again.

Donald Gallup speaks to Dr. Cherrick about the possibility of moving

Carlotta into a more felicitous atmosphere. Cherrick agrees that Carlotta is deteriorating but believes, as he puts it, that "she would not have reacted well to any institutional setting," and her disorder is such that an institutional setting is mandatory. But he professes his concern.

"At one time, I really feared for her life," Cherrick recalled. "She stopped eating, and lost a shocking amount of weight."

Surprisingly, however, Carlotta makes a sudden recovery. "In a sense, you could say it was a complete recovery," recalled Dr. Cherrick. Although Carlotta still has senile trends, "she got back to the state she had been in before coming to St. Luke's."

On his final visit to St. Luke's, shortly before Carlotta is discharged, Donald Gallup finds she has been moved out of the psychiatric ward into a private room in the general medical section.

IN MARCH 1969, Carlotta is transferred to the DeWitt Nursing Home on East Seventy-ninth Street, where she spends the next fifteen months—until July 1970. There she is visited regularly by Richard Crockett, as well as by Gallup and Rubin. Dr. Cherrick continues to attend her.

"She was no longer on Thorazine," he recalled. "That had gradually been tapered off before she left St. Luke's." With Cherrick, Carlotta would "ruminate about O'Neill, and often about her own early life."

In the winter of 1970, Jane Rubin is seriously injured in a car accident and confined for a lengthy hospital stay. When she recovers, she decides to retire and move with her husband to Sarasota, Florida.

"Carlotta didn't know me," said Rubin, recalling her last visits before she leaves New York. "There was really nothing I could do for her anymore."

To fill the gap left by Rubin, Crockett engages a part-time aide, Marjorie Miller. "She looked after her clothes, bought her underwear, did the kind of things Carlotta needed a woman for," Crockett recalled. "She visited Carlotta twice a week."

———

CARLOTTA GROWS UNHAPPY with the DeWitt Nursing Home.

"It was as good a nursing home as any," said Crockett, "but it was a big institution, with all the drawbacks of that sort of place.

"One of the things Carlotta complained about was that an attendant was always at her side. Carlotta still had a tendency to wander; she would wander into other patients' rooms and disturb them. DeWitt insisted on keeping someone with her to prevent this. She didn't like the way she was handled."

It is decided in consultation between Crockett and Gallup that Carlotta will be happier in the country, and in June 1970, the lawyer and his appointed aide, Miller, drive Carlotta to Westwood, New Jersey, to look at the Valley Nursing Home, which is situated in restful country surroundings.

The place appears to please Carlotta and, accordingly, she is transferred there in July.

"It was not a place you'd choose to give a party," said Crockett, somewhat defensively, "but for a nursing home, it was pleasant."

Both Crockett and Gallup, who visit her there, feel that Carlotta is reasonably contented.

Crockett, who sees her in October 1970, says she is alert and appears to relate to the staff and other patients. Gallup visits her at the beginning of November and both men speak with her attending physician, Dr. H. Richard Hoff, who assures them that for a woman of her age—she is now nearly eighty-two—she is in good health and might live to be one hundred.

Carlotta's death a month later, on November 18, 1970, takes both men by surprise. Evidently it is sudden, for neither man has had any word from the nursing home that she is failing.

"Arteriosclerotic coronary thrombosis" is given as the cause of death. More simply, her heart has worn out.

CARLOTTA HAS INSTRUCTED in her will that her remains be cremated, and her ashes interred in the plot she bought for O'Neill and herself. She has left no other instructions in her will regarding the disposition of her remains, but Crockett recalls she wrote him a memorandum asking that there be no religious rites at her burial.

Crockett sends a paid announcement of Carlotta's death to *The New York Times*, and it appears in the agate-type alphabetical listing on the obituary page. He reasons that someone on *The Times* will recognize Carlotta's name, read that his law firm represents her, and call him for details.

That is what happens. The obituary editor spots the paid obit and orders a full-length obituary, which appears in *The Times* on November 21. The date of the burial is not given.

On November 28, within four days of the date that O'Neill, seventeen years earlier, was secretly buried in Boston's Forest Hills Cemetery, Carlotta's ashes are interred beside her husband's grave. The interment, like O'Neill's, is accompanied by no ceremony.

Dr. Kozol is present, as is O'Neill's nurse, Jean Welton. Also present are Crockett, Gallup, and Robert Meserve.

There is no one to grieve for Carlotta as she has grieved for O'Neill, no one to offer the loving symbol of valor that she laid at her husband's grave—no one to plant laurel for Carlotta.

ACKNOWLEDGMENTS

Foremost, we thank Yale University, which houses the world's premier O'Neill archive. Without Yale's generous permission to draw on this vast treasury, we could not have gleaned the intimate detail we sought for *By Women Possessed*—let alone for our two earlier biographies, *O'Neill* and *Life with Monte Cristo*. Our heartfelt thanks, as well, to Yale's librarian Susan Gibbons, and to Nancy Kuhl, the curator for American Literature, Beinecke Rare Book and Manuscript Library, and also to Frederick Iseman and Ellen Iseman, Yale alumnae and board members.

Of parallel importance is the generosity of Gerald Stram, who granted us permission to quote from the revelatory and often stunning diaries of his grandmother Carlotta Monterey O'Neill. And to the children of Shane O'Neill and Oona O'Neill Chaplin we offer thanks for their permission to quote from the plays of the grandfather they never knew with particular thanks for her help to Shane's daughter, Sheila O'Neill.

We are grateful, as well, for permission to draw on the archives of numerous institutions that hold letters and other material related to O'Neill's life and plays:

Boston Public Library, Boston University, Columbia Rare Book & Manuscript Library, Columbia University, Connecticut College, Cornell, Dartmouth, *The Eugene O'Neill Review*, The Eugene O'Neill Society, The Fan Fox and Leslie R. Samuels Foundation (and Robert Marx), New York University's Fales Collection, Harvard University, Huntington Library, The Library of Congress, Museum of the City of New York, New London Public Library, New York Public Library and its Library of the Performing Arts (and Jackie Davis), Princeton University, Southern Connecticut State University, Syracuse University, Tao House Library, University of Notre Dame, University of Oregon, University of

Pennsylvania, University of Texas, University of Virginia, University of Washington Library.

The hundreds of individuals who generously shared with us their recollections of O'Neill's life and times—and who otherwise supported us during the writing of our two previous biographies—march across eighteen pages of *O'Neill* and seven pages of *Life with Monte Cristo*; we trust our readers have long since committed all their names to memory (and therefore we will not retabulate them here).

As for those individuals whose assessments of O'Neill's tangled life apply specifically to *By Women Possessed*—they all appear by name in our text, since they are, of course, part of our story. We are deeply indebted to them all.

We do wish, here and now, to thank an awesome coterie whose members contributed to *By Women Possessed*, all of whom, one way or another, tirelessly assisted, guided, and/or lavished moral support during our years of research and writing:

Marian Wood is the most punctilious, imaginative, demanding editor we have ever been lucky enough to work with. A merciless perfectionist who, fortunately, is also an empathetic mentor, she vastly improved our text, draft by draft. Our private pet name for Marian is "Madame Le Mot Juste"; there is scarcely a paragraph in *By Women Possessed* that didn't profit from one of her felicitous tweaks, however subtle.

Anne Ryan, an old and dear friend, impulsively volunteered to take on the intricate, time-consuming task of categorizing the hundreds of sources on which we drew for *By Women Possessed*. A retired assistant U.S. attorney, Anne was laughably overqualified for the task. But out of pity for our plight, along with selfless, loyal friendship, she brought to it all her fastidious intellectual expertise—a gift for which we can never thank her enough.

Dr. Harley J. Hammerman, a prominent diagnostic radiologist in St. Louis, Missouri, is a lifelong collector of O'Neilliana, and owns the comprehensive website An Electronic Eugene O'Neill Archive. Ever eager to share with O'Neill scholars and fans the information he amasses month by month, he has been an invaluable source of arcane data and family lore for our current biography.

Jeffery Kennedy happened to be researching his book about the history of the Provincetown Theater during the same time we were working on *By Women Possessed*. The millieux of our two books often overlapped, and since Jeff also happened to be the incumbent president of the Eugene O'Neill Society, our paths often crossed. With his impressive professional theater background, and as the current head of the Division of Humanities, Arts and Cultural Studies at Arizona State University, Jeff is an evolving Renaissance man, and it was always rewarding to exchange insights with him.

The Eugene O'Neill Society also brought us into serendipitous contact with Sheila Hickey Garvey. A past president of the O'Neill Society (and still active on its board), she is a professor of theater at Southern Connecticut State University, and a one-woman cultural whirlwind who finds time to write, direct, and act in regional theater. Although steeped in the intricacies of academia, she is also joyously at home in the real world. She never failed us when we sought a way to cut through red tape, pin down an elusive contact—or guide us to the perfect place for a relaxed dinner during an out-of-town O'Neill conference.

Jo Morello—yet another member of the Eugene O'Neill Society—has a successful day job as a public relations counselor, and is also a freelance writer and playwright. She somehow makes time to turn out the society's edifying, and meticulously written bimonthly newsletter. In all her capacities, Jo, since the beginning, has been one of our sturdiest friends and supporters. She has our enduring appreciation and gratitude.

Our special thanks to Howard Fishman, who (as he is accurately described on his website) "has quietly carved a niche as one of the most diverse and multi-faceted composer/performers working today." We first encountered Howard as a very young man when we attended the off-Broadway opening of his revival of Elmer Rice's *Street Scene*. Howard had cast himself as a charming entr'acte; seemingly oblivious of the wandering audience, he sat on the stage apron before the closed curtain, strumming his guitar and casually singing ballads appropriate to the play's 1920s setting. He turned out to be a knowledgeable O'Neill fan, and, living in New Haven in the shadow of Yale University's fabled O'Neill collection, he soon appointed himself as our occasional informal researcher—an honorary undertaking that he graciously has found time to perform throughout his own ever more demanding career.

We were lucky as well to meet another young man, Stephen Kennedy Murphy, who has devoted his life to O'Neill. He is the founder of two academically supported theatrical enterprises (at Yale and Columbia) and, as artistic director of the Playwrights' Theatre of New York, has undertaken to produce O'Neill's entire canon chronologically— sometimes with student casts, sometimes with seasoned actors like Zoe Caldwell and Marian Seldes—in various venues. (He has announced a "completion date" of December 10, 2036, the one hundredth anniversary of O'Neill's winning the Nobel Prize for Literature.) Like Howard Fishman, Stephen volunteered as a researcher and, over these many years, has allowed us to take advantage of his connections within the world of O'Neill.

We particularly wish to acknowledge the colleagues without whose professional competence and support this book could not have been published: Rose Schwartz, Neil Rosini, Jeff Roth, and Greg Collins. And also our good friend and oracle of the stage, Paul Libin, who has lived and breathed the theater for almost as long as we have.

Our very special thanks to our dear friend and former *New York Times* colleague Frank Rich (now a brilliantly successful HBO mogul). As we groped for a title, it was he who came up with what we have hopefully embraced as a label that has legs.

And, for adding luster to our title, we are grateful not only to the preeminent artist Alex Katz for his unexceptional gift of a jacket portrait, but also to our mutual friend, Dodie Kazanjian, the arts and specialist writer, who smoothed the way between his studio and our publisher.

It would be remiss not to acknowledge here our highest praise and heartfelt appreciation to the actors who—in the decades following

O'Neill's death and up to the present day—have brilliantly reinterpreted O'Neill's characters in revivals of his plays. Even though the demanding dramatist, during his lifetime, rarely approved of an actor's interpretation of a role in any of his plays (and sometimes put his characters into masks in anticipation of their shortcomings), he would have been hard-pressed not to appreciate the performances of the clan of unmatchable actors who, since his death, have kept his plays alive and flourishing.

To name only the most prominent among them: Gabriel Byrne, Zoe Caldwell, Brian Dennehy, Colleen Dewhurst, Cherry Jones, Nathan Lane, Helen Mirren, Liam Neeson, Al Pacino, Vanessa Redgrave, Natasha Richardson, Jason Robards, George C. Scott, Kevin Spacey, and John Douglas Thompson.

We will never forget their stunning performances in notable revivals of *Long Day's Journey Into Night*, *The Iceman Cometh*, *A Moon for the Misbegotten*, *A Touch of the Poet*, *Desire Under the Elms*, *Anna Christie*, *The Emperor Jones*, and *Hughie*. We especially thank those of them who shared with us their insights into O'Neill's wrenching global vision.

SELECT BIBLIOGRAPHY

Alexander, Doris. *O'Neill's Creative Struggle*. University Park: Pennsylvania State University Press, 1992.

———. *The Tempering of Eugene O'Neill*. New York: Harcourt, Brace & World, 1962.

Atkinson, Brooks. *Broadway*. New York: Macmillan, 1970.

Barlow, Judith E. *Final Acts*. Athens: University of Georgia Press, 1985; New York: Scribner & Sons, 1956.

Basso, Hamilton. "The Tragic Sense," *The New Yorker*, February 28, 1948; March 6, 1948; March 13, 1948.

Bogard, Travis. *Contour in Time: The Plays of Eugene O'Neill*. New York: Oxford University Press, 1972.

———, editor. *Eugene O'Neill: Complete Plays* (3 Volumes: 1913–1920; 1920–1931; 1932–1943). New York: The Library of America, 1988.

———, editor. *The Unknown O'Neill*. New Haven, CT: Yale University Press, 1988.

Bogard, Travis, and Jackson R. Bryer, editors. *Selected Letters of Eugene O'Neill*. New Haven, CT, and London: Yale University Press, 1988.

Boulton, Agnes. *Part of a Long Story*. Garden City, NY: Doubleday, 1958.

Bowen, Croswell (with Shane O'Neill). *The Curse of the Misbegotten*. New York, Toronto, and London: McGraw-Hill, 1959.

Brustein, Robert. *The Theater of Revolt*. Boston: Little, Brown, 1964.

Bryant, Louise. *Christmas in Petrograd*. Unpublished memoir (circa 1936), Granville Hicks collection, Syracuse University Library, Department of Special Collections.

Bryer, Jackson, editor. *The Theater We Worked For: Letters of Eugene O'Neill to Kenneth Macgowan*. New Haven, CT: Yale University Press, 1982.

Cargill, Oscar, N. Bryllion Fagion, and William J. Fisher, editors. *O'Neill and His Plays*. New York: New York University Press, 1961.

Clark, Barrett H. *Eugene O'Neill: The Man and His Plays*. New York: Robert McBride, 1929; New York: Dover Publications, 1947 (revised).

Commins, Dorothy, editor. *"Love and Admiration and Respect": The O'Neill-Commins Correspondence*. Durham, NC: Duke University Press, 1986.

Crichton, Kyle. *Total Recoil*. Garden City, NY: Doubleday, 1960.

Deutsch, Helen, and Stella Hanau. *The Provincetown: A Story of the Theater.* New York: Farrar & Rinehart, 1931.

Dowling, Robert M. *Eugene O'Neill: A Life in Four Acts.* New Haven, CT, and London: Yale University Press, 2014.

Engel, Edwin. *The Haunted Heroes of Eugene O'Neill.* Cambridge, MA: Harvard University Press, 1953.

Estrin, Mark W., editor. *Conversations with Eugene O'Neill.* Jackson and London: University Press of Mississippi, 1990.

Falk, Doris. *Eugene O'Neill and the Tragic Tension.* New Brunswick, NJ: Rutgers University Press, 1958.

Floyd, Virginia. *Eugene O'Neill: A World View.* New York: Frederick Ungar Publishing, 1979.

———. *Eugene O'Neill at Work*, annotated & edited. New York: Frederick Ungar Publishing, 1981.

Gallup, Donald, editor. *Eugene O'Neill Poems, 1912–1944.* New Haven, CT/New York: Ticknor & Fields, 1980.

———, editor. *Eugene O'Neill Work Diary 1924–1943.* New Haven, CT: Yale University Library, 1981.

———. *What Mad Pursuits!* Beinecke Rare Book & Manuscript Library, Yale University, New Haven, CT, 1998.

Gelb, Arthur and Barbara. *Life with Monte Cristo.* New York/London: Applause, 2000.

———. *O'Neill.* New York: Harper & Bros., 1962; New York: Harper & Row, 1973 (revised).

Gelb, Barbara. *So Short a Time.* New York: W. W. Norton, 1973.

Glaspell, Susan. *The Road to the Temple.* New York/Toronto: Frederick A. Stokes, 1927.

Goldman, Emma. *Living My Life.* New York: Garden City Publishing, 1931.

Goodwin, Donald W. *Alcohol and the Writer.* New York: Penguin Books, 1990.

Hamilton, Clayton. *Conversations on Contemporary Drama.* New York: Macmillan, 1925.

Hamilton, G. V. *A Research in Marriage.* New York: Albert & Charles Boni, 1929.

Hapgood, Hutchins. *An Anarchist Woman.* New York: Duffield, 1909.

———. *A Victorian in the Modern World.* New York: Harcourt, Brace, 1937.

Harrington, John P. *The Irish Play on the New York Stage, 1874–1996.* Lexington: University Press of Kentucky, 1997.

Heller, Adele, and Lois Rudnick, editors. *The Cultural Moment.* New Brunswick, NJ: Rutgers University Press, 1991.

Hicks, Granville. *John Reed.* New York: Macmillan, 1936.

Kenton, Edna. *The Provincetown Players and the Playwrights' Theatre, 1915–1922.* Edited by Travis Bogard and Jackson Bryer. In *The Eugene O'Neill Review,* Vol. 21, Nos. 1 & 2, 1997.

———. Unpublished manuscript. Fales Library, New York University, and revised unpublished manuscript. Gelb collection.

King, William Davis, editor. *"A Wind Is Rising": The Correspondence of Agnes Boulton and Eugene O'Neill.* Madison, NJ: Fairleigh Dickinson University Press, 2000.

Kinne, Wisner Payne. *George Pierce Baker and the American Theater.* Cambridge, MA: Harvard University Press, 1954.

Krutch, Joseph Wood. *The American Stage Since 1918.* New York: George Braziller, 1957.

———. Introduction, *Nine Plays by Eugene O'Neill.* New York: Modern Library, 1954.

Langner, Lawrence. *The Magic Curtain.* New York: E. P. Dutton, 1951.

Lockridge, Richard. *Darling of Misfortune: Edwin Booth 1833–1893.* New York/ London: Century, 1932.

Luhan, Mabel Dodge. *Movers and Shakers.* New York: Harcourt, Brace, 1936.

Maddux, Percy. *City on the Willamette.* Portland, OR: Metropolitan Press, 1952.

McCandless, Marion. *Family Portraits.* Notre Dame, IN: Saint Mary's College, 1952.

Moody, Richard. *Edwin Forrest, First Star of the American Stage.* New York: Knopf, 1960.

Nathan, George Jean. *As Ever, Gene: The Letters of Eugene O'Neill to George Jean Nathan.* Edited by Nancy L. Roberts and Arthur W. Roberts. London/ Toronto: Fairleigh Dickinson University Press, 1987.

———. *The Intimate Notebooks of George Jean Nathan.* New York: Alfred A. Knopf, 1932.

Nietzsche, Friedrich. *The Philosophy of Nietzsche.* New York: Modern Library, 1954.

O'Faolain, Sean. *The Great O'Neill.* Cork/Dublin: Mercier Press, 1986.

O'Neill, Eugene. *Inscriptions: Eugene O'Neill to Carlotta Monterey O'Neill.* Edited by Donald Gallup. Yale University Library, New Haven, CT, 500 copies. Privately printed 1960.

O'Neill, Patrick. *History of the San Francisco Theater,* Vol. 20: *James O'Neill.* San Francisco Writers' Program of the WPA in Northern California, 1942.

Quinn, Arthur Hobson. *A History of the American Drama from the Civil War to the Present Day.* New York/London: Harper & Brothers, 1927.

Ranald, Margaret Loftus. *The Eugene O'Neill Companion.* Westport, CT/London: Greenwood Press, 1984.

Reed, John. *Insurgent Mexico*. New York: D. Appleton, 1914.

Ruggles, Eleanor. *Prince of Players*. New York: W. W. Norton, 1953.

Sergeant, Elizabeth Shepley. *Fire Under the Andes*. London, New York: Alfred A. Knopf, 1927.

Shaughnessy, Edward L. *Down the Nights and Down the Days*. Notre Dame, IN: University of Notre Dame Press, 1996.

Sheaffer, Louis. *O'Neill, Son and Artist*. Boston/Toronto: Little, Brown, 1973.

———. *O'Neill, Son and Playwright*. Boston/Toronto: Little, Brown, 1968.

Skinner, Richard Dana. *A Poet's Quest*. New York: Russell & Russell Inc., 1964.

Vorse, Mary Heaton. *Time and the Town*. New Brunswick, NJ: Rutgers University Press, 1991.

Weissman, Phillip. *Creativity in the Theater*. New York: Basic Books, 1965.

Winter, William. *The Life of David Belasco*. New York: Moffat, Yard, 1913.

KEY TO ABBREVIATIONS IN ENDNOTES

A/BG	Arthur (AG) and Barbara (BG) Gelb
AB	Agnes Boulton O'Neill
AMcG	Arthur McGinley
BA	Brooks Atkinson
BB	Barbara Burton
BC	Bennett Cerf
BDC	Ben De Casseres
Beinecke	Beinecke Rare Book and Manuscript Library, Collection of American Literature, Yale University
CM	Carlotta Monterey O'Neill
CVV	Carl Van Vechten
DD	Dorothy Day
DG	Dr. Donald C. Gallup
EG	Eben Given
EK	Edward Keefe
EO	Eugene O'Neill
ESS	Elizabeth Shepley Sergeant
Fales	Fales Library, New York University
FBM	Frederic B. Mayo
FM	Fania Marinoff
GCC	George Cram ("Jig") Cook
GJN	George Jean Nathan
GRC	Dr. Gilbert R. Cherrick
HH	Hutchins Hapgood
HW	Harry Weinberger
IC	Ilka Chase
JC	Jane Caldwell
JJM	James Joseph (Slim) Martin
JL	James Light
JMcC	Joseph McCarthy
JQ	José Quintero
JR	Jane Rubin
JWK	Joseph Wood Krutch

KA	Kaye Albertoni
KJP	Kathleen Jenkins Pitt-Smith
KM	Kenneth Macgowan
LB	Louise Bryant
LDJIN	*Long Day's Journey Into Night*
LG	Lillian Gish
LK	Louis Kantor
LL	Lawrence Langner
LS	Louis Sheaffer
LWMC	*Life with Monte Cristo*
MBE	*Mourning Becomes Electra*
MHV	Mary Heaton Vorse
NM	Nickolas Muray
NW	Norman Winston
NYT	*The New York Times*
PM	Philip Moeller
PS	Philip Sheridan
RB	Ralph Barton
RC	Russel Crouse
RL	Ruth Lander
RR	Robert Rockmore
SB	Stella Ballantine
SC	Saxe Commins
SD	O'Neill's Scribbling Diary
SG	Susan Glaspell
SL	*Selected Letters of Eugene O'Neill*, Yale University Press, 1988
SNB	S. N. Behrman
SO	Sheila O'Neill
SP	Seymour ("Sy") Peck
SW	Sophus Winther
SWL	Sherlee Weingarten Lantz
TC	Terry Carlin
"TTWWF"	*The Theater We Worked For*
WD	O'Neill's Work Diary
"Wind"	*"A Wind Is Rising"*: *The Correspondence of Agnes Boulton and Eugene O'Neill*, Fairleigh Dickinson University Press, 2006

ENDNOTES

PART I: UPHEAVAL

CHAPTER ONE

4 **"Oh very much so!"** EO to KM, Thursday (Dec. 1926), Yale, SL.

4 **warmly greeted by friends and stared at by strangers.** A/BG interviews with JL, KM, LL, & Theresa Helburn.

4 **a bequest from a childless aunt who raised her.** Following her divorce from Barton, the *American Magazine* (4/14/27) published a gossipy item about Carlotta's "imminent marriage" to Speyer, and Carlotta has written to an intimate friend, dismissing the report: "He is a darling—the kindest—most unselfish, most charitable man I have ever met—and clever—and has a keen sense of humor—and above all—gentle—I adore him—but no marriage! Ours is a beautiful & most thoroughly satisfying friendship." Carlotta adds that "of course," the fact that he is a millionaire and she is an "ex-actress" has fueled the gossip about them "by damned fool society reporters." (Carlotta in later life told friends Speyer did propose marriage, but that she had already determined to marry O'Neill.)

5 **Her accessories, Chase notes, are "of the finest material, her shoes made to order of special leathers at great cost" and sometimes sewn with jewels.** IC, *Past Imperfect* by IC (Doubleday, Doran & Co., New York, 1942); & A/BG interview with IC.

5 **"there is a lot of you in the woman, I think . . . and yet, wholly unlike you."** letter, from EO to CM, 3/4/27, Yale, SL.

8 **"I am interested only in the relation between man and God."** EO in conversation with JWK, *Nine Plays by Eugene O'Neill* (Modern Library, New York, 1932).

9 **at the Wentworth Hotel on Forty-sixth Street near Broadway.** The Wentworth was renamed Hotel at Times Square in 2008.

10 **sworn to withhold the photos until after their marriage.** A/BG interviews with CM.

10 **wishing it were over, missing her, fighting his anxiety and guilt.** Ibid.

10 **"a blow-by-blow account" of how the play is being received.** A/BG interviews with LL & his autobiography, *The Magic Curtain* (E. P. Dutton & Company Inc., New York, 1951).

10 **"I've never forgotten it."** A/BG interview and correspondence with Clarke's sister, Frances Cardenas.

11 **"O'Neill never knew about this sly business of mine."** A/BG interviews with Fontanne, Langner, SNB & *The Magic Curtain*.

12 **"The mechanics of acting stop me from seeing the play."** Flora Merrill, 7/19/25.

12 **"They'd be able to express the meaning without them."** *The Magic Curtain*.

12 "From what I hear they are both pretty dull in the old bean—but that hardly astonishes me." letter, EO to AB, 12/2/1927, Harvard, SL.

13 hardly a statement to placate the Shuberts. New York *American Magazine*, 2/25/28.

13 "It was a funny scene." EO to KM, 9/21/28, *The Theatre We Worked For* (Yale University Press, New Haven, CT, 1982).

CHAPTER TWO

16 two fabled courtesans, one mythological, the other seventeenth-century French. "Five O'Clock Friday Morning," 5/19/22, Yale.

16 Among the guests—always formally attired— A/BG interview with NM.

16 "Ralph was not the first man who had made her unhappy." *Past Imperfect.*

17 debate, for three hours, whether they will "live together any more." Entry in CVV "Daybook," 9/29/25, NY Public Library.

17 not happy at the way her life is turning out. A/BG interviews with CVV & FM.

17 describe him rather grandly as a "horticulturist." letter, 6/5/36, to SW, Tao House Library.

17 high-spirited woman of Dutch and French-Alsatian descent. According to DG, Beinecke, CM—in her later years—told him her mother spelled her name "Gottcheet."

18 difficulty focusing her eyes, causing severe headaches. A/BG interviews with CM; letter, EO to GJN, 2/27/39, *As Ever, Gene* (Fairleigh Dickinson University Press, Madison, NJ, 1987); CM's grandson Gerald Stramm, interviewed by A/BG, said he believed she suffered from glaucoma.

18 scold her for spending so much time in chapel genuflecting. A/BG interviews with CM & Gerald Stramm (CM's grandson) & *Pigeons on the Granite* by DG (Yale University Library, 1988).

18 think it over for a year before making a decision. told to JQ, who repeated it to the authors.

19 aided by her beauty, might attract an upper-crust husband. *Pigeons on the Granite* & A/BG interviews with JQ & CM.

19 "I had never seen anyone so radiantly beautiful." San Francisco *Sunday Call*, 5/7/07; added details, *Sunday Call*, 6/2/07.

19 "They will be pleased." Ibid.

20 "In 18 months she leaves & if we are then both of the same mind we will be allowed to announce our engagement." The finishing school was known as Mme. Yeatman's.

20 "I don't wish to be laughed at if it falls through." Moffat letters, Tao House Collection.

20 as long as it remained a secret, she would have no objection. *Pigeons on the Granite* & A/BG interviews with CM.

21 the marriage was platonic. Ibid.

21 schooled, as she once recalled, in "how to be a conversationalist." A/BG interviews with CM.

21 gave back the Rolls-Royce and the jewelry, and returned to America. Ibid.

21 "I'll always love Carlotta." A/BG interview with John E. S. Moffat, John Moffat's son.

21 Hazel Tharsing became Carlotta Monterey. A/BG interviews with CM.

22 star Lou Tellegen in a farce called *Taking Chances*. "Placing the Newcomer," NYT, 8/26/23.

22 he'd earned a reputation as a Casanova. NYT, 3/13/28.

22 decided to marry the internationally renowned opera diva, Geraldine Farrar. Never a model of stability, Tellegen committed suicide at fifty-three by stabbing himself in the chest seven times with a pair of scissors.

22 eugenically suited to father her child. A/BG interview with Mai-mai Sze, a writer and artist, close friend of Carlotta.

23 magazines pressed her to pose for photo layouts. To her closest woman friend, Gene McComas, who lived in Monterey, CM wrote (12/30/18), "So you saw the picture in *Vanity Fair*?—there is one in Jan. Harper's *Bazaar*—also a three-year-old-one in this month's 'Theater'—I don't know why, but they are always asking me to sit for them & I try always to find time—because it is free advertisement!!!"

23 soon to be associated with the as-yet-little-known O'Neill. The play, by Clare Kummer—in which CM portrayed a siren who drives the character played by the leading lady to near suicide—was well reviewed and ran for eighty-four performances at the Booth Theater.

24 realized he had been—in his own words—a "blithering idiot." letter, RB to CM, 7/28/26, Yale.

24 his insensitivity that finally wrecked the marriage. Ibid., & A/BG interviews with CVV.

24 "What do you think of my pussy?" she asked the nonplussed photographer. A/BG interview with Pinchot.

25 sternly watched her diet, determined to maintain a lissome figure *Past Imperfect*.

CHAPTER THREE

27 recognized a veiled Carlotta as she passed him in the hotel lobby on her way out. A/BG interview with RR.

28 volunteers cuts of his own that exceed Moeller's concept A/BG interviews with PM.

29 Moeller once remarked to Langner, "for if he does, out it'll go." *The Magic Curtain*.

29 "That should do it." GJN in *Cosmopolitan*, Aug. 1957, by GJN.

29 that his marriage to Agnes has collapsed. A/BG interviews with ESS.

30 "he gives the impression of being still at the very beginning of a career which is incalculable, except that it will be precipitate, fertile, concentrated, and solitary." *The New Republic*, 3/16/27. Also published as "Man with a Mask" in ESS's *Fire Under the Andes* (Alfred A. Knopf, New York, 1927).

30 what gives her "standing in Gene's eyes." A/BG interviews with ESS.

31 continue providing her with financial guidance, along with a lifetime income. A/BG interviews with Richard Ernst, partner in law firm handling Speyer's affairs & Charles B. Stackelberg, a Speyer business partner.

32 off by one year as to the date of O'Neill's death—he died in 1953— A/BG interview & correspondence with BDC; also letter, EO to BDC, 5/10/27, Dartmouth, SL.

32 book separate cabins under false names on the ocean liner they have selected. A/BG interviews with NW.

32 "And when you fall in love—as I am sure you soon will—you better bear that in mind, too." letter, 2/7/28, Harvard, SL.

33 "always remember that I love you and Oona an awful lot—and please don't ever forget your Daddy." letter (early Feb. 1928), Harvard, SL.

33 James Speyer sees them off, bringing flowers for Carlotta. CM diary, 2/10/28.

34 "God help us both!" Ibid., 2/15/28.

34 waterfronts of Southampton and Liverpool with his brother sailors, not venturing farther afield. interviews with O'Neill's friend, former seaman James Joseph ("Slim") Martin.

35 "I got him the case—& he was flabbergasted!" CM to DG, former director of Beinecke, *What Mad Pursuits!* (The Beinecke Rare Book & Manuscript Library, Yale University, New Haven, CT, 1998).

35 when they were briefly apart soon after the birth of their first child. letter, 11/30?/19, Harvard, SL.

35 "In a few days I'll be back in your arms, My Own, and be your other—and firstborn!—baby again!" letter, undated (12/27/19?), Harvard, SL.

35 "Be my Mother!" letter, 2/5/15, Berg Collection, NY Public Library.

36 actually as conventional-minded as her father, and the affair was never consummated. BG interviews with BA.

CHAPTER FOUR

37 "I wander about foolish and goggle-eyed with joy in a honeymoon that is a thousand times more poignant and sweet and ecstatic because it comes at an age when one's past—particularly a past such as mine—gives one the power to appreciate what happiness means and how rare it is and how humbly grateful one should be for it." EO to KM, 2/22/28, Yale, SL.

38 "He is letting go." 2/24/28, Beinecke.

38 "I will go Carlotta one better and say that I am so happy I can live!" addendum to letter from CM to ESS, 2/24/28, Beinecke.

38 he dropped it on the floor in a mock repudiation of its grandeur. A/BG interview with Mielziner.

39 "But, as his wardrobe grew & he could pick & choose—he was like a happy child—all smiles and pleasure." CM diary, 2/20/28.

40 "Lots of other men—though few who were such drunkards as you, I admit—have cut out drinking without selfishly insisting that their wives, to whom it did no harm, cut it out absolutely too." AB to EO (probably 2/11/28), Boston University.

40 she expresses the hope that he will learn to respond in kind. CM diary, 2/24/28.

41 "And altho' our address must *not* be told now—when all this mess is over I will be proud & happy to scream it from the housetops." 5/5/27, Francis McComas collection, Huntington Library, San Marino, CA.

41 "All deepest friendship always, dear!" EO to AB, 3/10/28, Harvard, SL.

41 "Outside of the fact that I should hate you for dragging such a nasty mess of notoriety around our children's ears, when, if you weren't so eager to get all you can, everything could be arranged quietly on a decent human basis." late March, Harvard, SL.

42 until it was too late to disentangle from Carlotta. Ibid.

43 "I will be the one to take the *beating* for all this!!" CM diary, 3/19/28.

43 "I have my little Puritan prejudices!" 4/22/28, Yale, SL.

43 nine-page letter in which he declares all-out war on Agnes. beginning of a nine-page letter from EO to AB.

44 actually envious of his work "as compared to what she could do," and even, at times, "did her best to hamper it." Ibid.

44 "I'll gladly blow up the works no matter who it crushes so long as it crushes her." Ibid.

45 Agnes, he winds up in a frenzy of frustration, is "a skunk!" Ibid.

45 specter of a tabloid scandal hanging over his head "like an unexploded bomb." 4/23/28, Yale, SL.

46 "there is no question of any correspondent, that we simply cannot hit it off together anymore, etc." Ibid.

46 "they'll lay off of us for good." late April 1928, University of Virginia, "Wind."

46 "But the wife explained that this was a business visit purely, in connection with a mortgage on a house or something of that kind." New York *World*, 4/27/28.

47 when he departed for London in 1928 ultimately "were either destroyed or stolen." letter to Julian P. Boyd, 1/28/43, Princeton, SL.

47 "He has gained, at last, a real mother—combined with mistress!" CM diary, 4/30/28.

47 He urges her once again to accept his terms and to leave for Reno. early May 1928.

47 He is "too old to start in being a sucker," he adds. letter, EO to KM, 4/27/28, "TTWWF."

47 more generous than Sinclair Lewis's wife got from him, "considering he must have been making three times my income!" Ibid.

48 "they will find out I have been a good father . . . when they are old enough to understand all that has happened and when they really come to know me and about me." letter, c. 4/8/28, Harvard, SL.

48 for the damage he believes Agnes (never he himself) has done to them. 4/22/28, Yale, SL.

48 even though it is "hell on the nerves" and "it's raining boxing gloves!" 4/29/28, Dartmouth.

49 "I am your lover!" *Inscriptions: Eugene O'Neill to Carlotta Monterey O'Neill* (Yale University Library, New Haven, CT, 1960), 5/8/28.

CHAPTER FIVE

50 by writing adulatory articles about the then rising young playwright. A sample article, "O'Neill Lifts the Curtain on His Early Plays" appeared in NYT, 12/21/24.

51 "Though I started drinking because of Gene, I became a better drinker than he, because I had a stronger stomach." A/BG interviews with LK.

51 the proprietor caught Kantor, who had climbed up the fire escape, handing O'Neill a bottle through the window. Ibid., & unsigned article in NY *Tribune* after opening of *Beyond the Horizon*.

51 "I don't know *where I am or what to do*!" Carlotta scribbles in her diary on her return. 5/14/28.

51 **Carlotta later discovers them collapsed on beds in one of the villa's guest rooms.** A/BG interviews with LK.

51 **"I nearly died!"** CM diary, 5/15/28.

52 **"He** *mustn't* **drink—He should realize this is just what A. wants him to do."** CM diary.

52 **"I am** *frightened***!"** Ibid.

52 **his brain would turn into "the white of an egg" and sabotage his ability to write.** A/BG interviews with KM & ESS, in whom EO confided that it was the psychiatrist Dr. Gilbert V. Hamilton who warned him about the grave consequences of continued heavy drinking; also LL in *The Magic Curtain.*

52 **"So, this is genius—this is love! God help us!" she explodes.** CM diary, 5/19/28.

53 **even sanctions a "loan" to Kantor of $500 when at last, on May 21, he leaves the villa.** A/BG interviews with LK.

53 **she was "taught to respect others—& to have self respect" and to be "honest, loyal, unselfish & decent"; and finally, irrelevantly: "to remember I was a woman!"** CM diary, 5/23/28; during interviews with A/BG thirty years later, CM frequently recited her pedigree.

54 **"But how A. & Co. would love to get hold of it!"** copy of letter, 8/2/28, given to A/BG by LK.

54 **the intention being to mislead those friends as well as the press as to O'Neill's whereabouts.** Ibid.

54 *Dynamo*, **which he expects the Guild to produce—although he will not venture to predict when it will be completed.** EO to Theresa Helburn, 6/10/28, Yale, SL.

55 **the play is "a good symbolical and factual biography of what is happening in a large section of [the] American (and not only American) soul right now."** 8/26/28, Cornell, *As Ever, Gene.*

55 **his conviction that "anyone trying to do big work nowadays must have this big subject behind all the little subjects of his plays or novels, or he is simply scribbling around on the surface of things and has no more real status than a parlor entertainer."** Ibid.

55 **"He is too worried to do his best—but so anxious to prove to A. he can work in spite of her & the worry she is causing him! Of course that is all wrong—but I dare** *not* **offer any suggestions."** CM diary, 6/28/28.

56 **the detective tail Agnes, so that she can be "caught in flagrante," which would give him "a weapon" that would enable him "to dictate terms."** 7/2/28, Yale, SL.

56 **Young ceded the farm to "Agnes B. Burton" on December 30, 1915, soon after Agnes's daughter Barbara was born.** Research by William Davies King for *A Wind Is Rising*, and confirmed by additional research by A/BG in the Sharon, CT, Town Hall land records: Vol. 46, pp. 325–326. This is further confirmed by the 2014 publication, by Harley Hammerman, on his comprehensive and invaluable website, eOneill.com, of *A Formidable Shadow, The O'Neill Connection*, by D. C. (Dallas Cline) Thomas, Agnes Boulton's niece. Cline writes that when Barbara was nearly two, Agnes confided to her mother, Cecil, that there was no marriage in England to a man named Burton, and that Barbara's father was in fact the unhappily married Courtland Young, who published Agnes's fiction, and with whom Agnes had a long-term affair; it was he who had paid for

the farm, Agnes told her mother; Barbara herself knew who her father was, writes Cline, and kept the secret of her birth.

56 **so fascinated a scholar of Oriental wisdom that he had learned both Chinese and Japanese.** "Alchemy and the Orient in Strindberg's Dream Play" by Leta Jane Lewis, as noted in *Eugene and Oriental Thought, a Divided Vision* by James A. Robinson (Southern Illinois University Press, Carbondale & Edwardsville, 1982).

57 **By 1925, he was describing himself as "a most confirmed mystic."** letter to KM, Friday (Summer 1923), Yale, "TTWWF."

57 **"It's going to be infinitely valuable to me in its bearing upon my future work."** letter, 9/14/28.

57 **"I am, for some idiotic reason, fearful of going to China under present conditions— six weeks is a very long time for Gene to be caged up—worrying about so many things—& I am in a humiliating position."** CM diary, 7/21/28.

58 **"Honestly, to me it is a sort of miracle."** 8/26/28, SL.

58 **"And then, what about me, his mistress?"** CM diary, 8/29/28.

58 **"My honeymoon is over!"** CM diary, 8/30/28.

58 **"Poor Barbara!"** Ibid.

59 **"Gene is sunk in depression all day."** CM diary, 9/14/28.

59 **the monkey has long arms, "like Gene," as Carlotta recalled years later.** A/BG interviews with CM.

59 **the Marquis Esteban de Gonzales, Grandee of Spain, ruined himself with drugs.** Ibid.

59 **informing him he'll be gone for a year and asking him to have copies made for several friends, including Nathan and De Casseres.** letter, 9/14/28, Tao House Library.

60 **"We are off on our pilgrimage—dear God—guide us."** CM diary, 9/25/28.

60 **"All men make mistakes in their youth . . . why must he be tormented and made ill?"** CM diary, 10/1/28.

61 **He signs his letter, "With love as ever, James."** 9/25/28, Yale.

61 **"*Whores* are paid for their bodies,—*not wives*!"** CM diary, 10/1/28.

61 **"Much deep love to you, my son, from Your Daddy."** late Sept. 1928, Harvard, SL.

61 **"All night we hang on to each other—as though we were in deadly danger!"** CM diary.

CHAPTER SIX

62 **"Germ idea use Greek Tragedy plot in modern setting," he had noted two and a half years earlier.** WD, 4/26/26.

62 **he makes another note for his Greek tragedy,** WD, 11/4/28.

62 **He also tinkers with another inspiration, "It Cannot Be Mad,"** WD, 10/7/28, 10/8/28.

63 **"*His work is him* & he is it."** 10/11/28.

63 **and other one-act plays of the sea.** letter to Patrick O'Neill, 9/18/40.

63 **O'Neill replied he didn't need vacations. "Writing is my vacation from living."** Gaylord Farm Sanatorium questionnaire, 1924.

63 **proclaimed his recovery from tuberculosis and his newfound mission as his "re-birth."** letter to Dr. David Russell Lyman (Summer 1914), Yale, SL.

63 **jolted awake by a nightmare: she's had a baby and O'Neill has left her.** CM diary.

64 unnerves Carlotta by impetuously diving into water she regards as dubious. CM diary, 10/22/28.

64 she manages a detour to purchase several yards of the black satin-silk she knows is unique to Saigon. CM diary, 10/31 & 11/1/28.

64 both he and Carlotta are once again "in awful state of nerves." CM, 11/9/28.

64 grumbles that O'Neill's swims in the foul tropical waters "didn't do him any good." CM diary, 11/13/28.

65 "He particularly loved the Police Museum," Batson recalled years later, "where they had an exotic display of torture items confiscated from the Chinese." A/BG interviews with Batson.

65 Suspicious of Batson, she thinks she recognizes the signs. CM diary, 11/19/28.

65 Agnes's lawyers are "trying to hold me up for an agreement that would make me her financial slave for life." Feb. 1928, Beinecke.

66 the director to whom, after O'Neill's death, she consigned the Broadway premiere of *Long Day's Journey Into Night*. A/BG interviews with JQ.

66 She says she "wept like a fool." CM diary, 11/22/28.

66 has been ordered by Dr. Renner to stay in bed. CM diary.

67 he'll arrange for O'Neill to be admitted to the British hospital, and will notify Carlotta. A/BG interviews and correspondence with Batson.

67 she plans to return to France—alone. CM diary.

67 "I do not trust him!" she cries. CM diary, 11/25/28.

67 "A million kisses, Blessed!" note (c. 11/25/30), Yale, SL.

67 he simply growls, "The climate is enervating—bad for work," and adds, "Tropics wore me out." letter (11/28), Columbia Rare Book and Manuscript. Library & *"Love, and Admiration and Respect": The O'Neill-Commins Correspondence*, ed. Dorothy Commins (Duke University Press, 1986).

68 "Had a touch of sun at Singapore because did what Englishmen and mad dogs did— bathed at noon." letter, 8/3/46, Yale.

68 she despairs, "Why drink when you know you are not sane with alcohol in you—literally not sane!" CM diary, 12/5/29.

68 Carlotta suspects that this is "just the beginning!" CM diary, 12/10/28.

69 "Let us be such *good friends* now dearest . . . I love you." Beinecke.

69 she writes: "My illusion that *all will* be *well* smashed—things seem blacker—his brain befogged!" CM diary, & A/BG interview with CM.

69 locking her into her cabin and keeping the key until the reporters have left. CM diary, 12/18 to 12/19/28.

70 "Gene is off again and it won't be pretty this time because he has found a drunk to drink with him," Carlotta notes. CM diary, 12/28/28.

71 "What would be *best for him*?" CM diary, 1/5/29.

71 "HOW ARE YOU I FEEL SO TERRIBLY WORRIED ABOUT YOU." Yale, SL.

72 She answers herself: "I'm afraid I do!" CM diary, 1/8/29.

72 "Oh, God—oh, God." CM diary.

72 O'Neill's recorded reaction is no less rapturous: "Carlotta again!—and happiness!" WD, 1/15/29.

72 "Genie has come home!" she marvels "My dreams have come true." CM diary, 1/16/29.

CHAPTER SEVEN

74 records that he spent zero "creative work days" in January. WD.

74 as always, he asks them not to forget their "Daddy." late Jan. 1929, University of Virginia.

74 he confides that "the whole trip, in spite of sickness and the lousy publicity I ran into, was a wonderful, stimulating experience that I wouldn't have missed for a million." 2/5/29, Yale, SL.

75 regrets there isn't sufficient time to rewrite the entire play. WD, 2/4/29.

75 his "brains were woolly with hatred" for Agnes. letter to M. Eleanor Fitzgerald, 5/13/29, University of Texas, SL.

75 George Jean Nathan, who tells him that *Dynamo* is "far, far below you." letter, 3/19/29, *As Ever, Gene.*

75 marked the start of his long-lasting friendship with Nathan. *The Long Voyage Home* was published Oct. 1917; *Ile*, May 1918; *The Moon of the Caribbees*, Aug. 1918.

75 "Henceforth," he tells Nathan, "I cast not only actresses but legs." GJN quoted this to Atkinson, as per A/BG interviews with Atkinson.

76 "No one knows what I see in my stuff during rehearsals, or the changes I suggest or veto." letter, 3/12/29, Dartmouth, SL.

76 thoughtful and tender and, as she remarks in her diary, "all self-consciousness is gone!" CM diary, 2/9/29.

76 "Believe me," he vows, "I can do with it!" letter to BDC, 3/12/29, Dartmouth, SL.

76 he's convinced it will be then that his "inner self" will be "freed from the dead" and he will be "liberated and reborn." letter to Bio De Casseres, 5/10/29, Dartmouth, SL.

77 some, in Carlotta's view, "too grand," others "too run down for decent housekeeping." CM diary, 4/17/29.

77 warm, comfortable environment where O'Neill will feel "loved—so he can *work*." Ibid.

77 "I'll sit in the car." *Pigeons on the Granite.*

77 Amused, she calls his attention to the bidet. Ibid.

77 "*I loved this place!*" she enthuses, relieved that "strangely enough, so did Gene!" CM diary, 4/17/29.

77 asks if she may install a swimming pool, having found a suitable site on the grounds. CM diary, 4/19 & 4/20/29.

78 all part of what it pleases her to call her "dot" (dowry). CM diary, 4/22/29.

78 She thanks him, but says no. CM diary, 5/1/29.

78 "I made him very comfortable." A/BG interviews with CM.

78 he'd always dreamed of, but could never have afforded in the United States. letter, 6/14/29, "TTWWF."

78 "Altogether the grandest bargain—this Le Plessis—that I've ever heard of!" Ibid.

79 removed from her diaries "an occasional comment on their love-making sessions." In *Pigeons on the Granite*, DG noted that CM retrieved the diaries she deposited at Yale in order to edit them.

79   doesn't want the Mercedes after all and buys a red Bugatti. CM diary, 4/26/29.

80   She is so moved, she can't speak. CM diary, 5/11/29.

80   "Are we cursed?" CM diary, 5/28/29.

80   "It's a grand law that permits such stunts to get by!" EO letter to his publisher Horace
     Liveright, 6/14/29.

81   would give her and O'Neill "more time for those we love—& who really love us!"
     letter, 5/15/29, *Love and Admiration and Respect.*

81   anyone says she is "ruining" O'Neill and "spending all his money—say 'yes'—and
     that I'm planning to *eat* his children & my own!" CM to SC, 5/15/29, *Love and Admi-
     ration and Respect.*

81   she "cannot distinguish a lie from the truth." CM to SC, 6/19/29, *Love and Admiration
     and Respect.*

PART II: ABOUT AGNES

CHAPTER EIGHT

87   published nearly thirty years after their divorce and five years after O'Neill's death.
     Part of a Long Story by AB (Doubleday & Co. Inc., New York, 1958).

87   "But I did not return—not until many years later." Ibid.

88   Christine introduced him: "This is Gene O'Neill." Ibid.

88   drawn to her earthy warmth, once referred to her as "a female Christ." A/BG inter-
     views with MHV.

88   society's wrongful neglect of such people as herself, and she pulled herself together. *A
     Victorian in the Modern World* by HH (Harcourt, Brace & Co., New York, 1939).

89   "'Nothin' happened. See?'" O'Neill saw. NY *Daily News* series, 1/24 to 1/30/32.

90   he'd been deferred because of his earlier bout with tuberculosis. see LWMC.

90   She said she "must go upstairs"; but she lingered. *Part of a Long Story.*

90   "I thought him the strangest man I had ever met." Ibid.

90   "But she pours on the romance and remembers too much and too little." undated
     letter to A/BG headed "Macgowan, 833 Stradella Road, Los Angeles 24 California."

91   brief exchange of empty pleasantries, and then he was gone. *Part of a Long Story.*

91   His performance was greeted with embarrassed laughter. A/BG interviews with
     Romany Marie Marchand, Nina Moise, Holger Cahill, DD, JL.

93   It was then that she abruptly dropped O'Neill. LB & JR left for Russia 8/17/17.

94   "Please Louise!" letter, 9/19/17, Louise Bryant papers, a collection broken out from the
     William C. Bullitt papers in Manuscripts & Archives, at Sterling Memorial Library, Yale.

94   nor did she promise a timely return. Ibid.

94   O'Neill confided to an indiscreet friend, who couldn't resist broadcasting the remark.
     EO to TC as reported to A/BG by JL & JJM.

95   fifty dollars, the first respectable money he'd earned for creative writing. In Oct.
     1916, *The Seven Arts* published O'Neill's one-act play, *The Long Voyage Home.* A/BG
     interview with Waldo Frank.

95 he doubted the magazine's editors "were as overwhelmed by its hideous beauty as I was." letter to Mark Van Doren, 5/12/44, Princeton, SL.

CHAPTER NINE

96 "But by then . . . my cross had become too heavy to bear." letter (early March 1918), William Christian Bullitt & Anne Moen Bullitt papers, Manuscripts and Archives Section, Sterling Memorial Library, Yale.

97 agreed to meet there with Hutch Collins, an actor with the Provincetown Players. *Part of a Long Story.*

97 which bound them "hilariously together." letter, EO to SG, 1/29/19.

98 at first dumbstruck and then, outraged, left the apartment. *Part of a Long Story* & interviews with SB, DD, Eleanor Fitzgerald, & Mary Pyne, to whom AB later related parts of the above incident.

98 completed his cycle of four early one-act sea plays later collectively produced as *S.S. Glencairn.* The other three are *Bound East for Cardiff, The Long Voyage Home,* and *In the Zone.*

98 strange songs of the natives coming over the waters mingled with the sounds aboard ship. Olin Downes, Boston *Sunday Post,* 8/29/20.

98 It was plotless, as he once noted Brentano's Book Chat, Malcolm Cowley, July/Aug. 1926.

98 *The Moon of the Caribbees,* he later added, was his "favorite short play." *New York Sun,* Ward Morehouse, 5/14/30.

99 featuring an appealing photo of Agnes. 10/7/16.

99 she instinctively disbelieved it, and, of course, she was right. *Part of a Long Story.*

99 he cheerfully confessed to casual affairs in letters to Louise during his work-driven absences. John Reed collection, Houghton Library, Harvard.

99 he was not "absolutely sure" whether he was still in love with Louise. *Part of a Long Story.*

99 "Agnes knew this feeling of mine and accepted it." letter, EO to LB (early March 1918), William Christian Bullitt & Anne Moen Bullitt papers, Manuscripts and Archives Section, Sterling Memorial Library, Yale.

99 declared he had no intention of ever again going through anything like his turmoil with Louise. *Part of a Long Story.*

100 an idea for a full-length play that was nagging at him, along with several possible one-acters. Ibid.

100 the Provincetown Players were holding their collective breath. A/BG interviews with GCC, SG, JL, etc.

100 O'Neill asked Agnes if she would come with him to Provincetown. She said yes. *Part of a Long Story.*

101 several friends among O'Neill's classmates, whom he often visited. A/BG interviews with Princeton classmates, Warren H. Hastings, Richard Weeks, & Ralph Horton.

101 O'Neill was dismissed from Princeton by the Committee on Examinations and Standings "for poor scholastic standing." Secretary of Princeton University files.

101 Holladay was "the most loved man friend Gene ever had," as he told Carlotta years later. CM diary, 2/19/32.

102 establish himself as a fruit farmer while curing himself of his drinking habit. A/BG interviews with DD, & *Part of a Long Story.*

102 telling her he wanted to return to the Hell Hole to be with Holladay. *Part of a Long Story.*

102 soon became evident to those gathered at the Hell Hole that there was something amiss. A/BG interviews with DD & Romany Marie.

103 he had no qualms about obtaining drugs for a friend. Ibid.

103 unoccupied Village flat, sleeping on the floor on cast-off mattresses. A/BG interviews with CM & various Village friends including JL & JJM.

104 he'd fled the restaurant, hurrying back to Agnes's flat for solace. A/BG interviews with DD & Romany Marie, & *Part of a Long Story.*

104 he had stopped breathing before the ambulance arrived. Ibid.

104 they apparently pronounced the death as due to "chronic endocarditis." Ken Cobb, former director of the NY City Archives, & A/BG interviews with DD & Romany Marie, & *Part of a Long Story.*

104 The police, arriving a short time later, accepted that finding. Ken Cobb, former director of the NY City Archives.

105 Christine Ell wept unstoppably. *A Victorian in the Modern World.*

105 "We were very happy and very young." A/BG interviews with DD.

106 "He didn't need any urging." Ibid.

106 possessing scant knowledge of the tenets of Catholicism, she would kneel during early-morning Mass. Ibid.

106 attempting to kiss it with the reverence tendered a saint. A/BG interviews with clients of the mission house.

107 "I pray that Gene turns to the light." Early in 2000, Dorothy Day was pronounced a candidate for canonization by the Vatican. She had died in 1980, by which time EO had been among the departed for a quarter of a century. But if, as Day believed, there was "no time with God," she and EO, on March 17, 2000, shared an ironic chuckle over the chance that the youthful, devil-may-care sinner they both tenderly remembered might one day transmogrify into Saint Dorothy. (According to Church authorities, candidacy for sainthood calls for a process of investigation that can take decades to complete.)

CHAPTER TEN

108 never had she "seen or touched such beautiful hair." *Part of a Long Story.*

108 Francis threw in the adjacent studio at no extra cost. letter from Francis to EO, 1/18/18, LS collection, Conn. College.

109 "As for my little girl," recalled Agnes, "so preposterous would have been the idea of my poet-genius with a child around that I don't think the idea even occurred to me." *Part of a Long Story.*

109 He didn't understand children and couldn't relate to them, he said. Ibid.

109 told a friend who asked if they planned to have children that probably all they would have was a book. A/BG interview with JR.

110 understand that he was attempting to create "a simon-pure uncompromising American tragedy?" letter, EO to R. W. Cottingham, 5/12/44, Yale, SL.

110 summarized *Beyond* as "the tragedy of the man who looks over the horizon, who longs with his whole soul to depart on the quest, but whom destiny confines to a place and a task that are not his." Olin Downes, Boston *Sunday Post*, 8/29/20.

112 "Robert Mayo was born, and developed from that beginning," as was Ruth and the rest of the play's characters, and "finally the complete play." "A Letter From O'Neill," NYT, 3/1/20.

113 Louise wrote she'd "crossed three thousand miles of frozen steppes to come back to her lover." *Part of a Long Story.*

113 "See her!" Agnes retorted in disbelief. Ibid.

114 O'Neill's vision of the "mythical symbol of the great old and mystic Irish legends." Ibid.

114 letters he knew risked the wreckage of his romance with Agnes. Bryant preserved the letters, which did not surface until Jan. 2004. Her daughter Anne Moen Bullitt gave them to the Sterling Memorial Library, Yale.

114 "I might die . . . and I want you to have everything I've got." LB's unpublished memoir, Granville Hicks Collection, George Arents Research Library, Syracuse University.

116 He drank and drank in order to drug himself into "an indifferent apathy." Ibid.

117 "I stand condemned to love you forever—and hate you for what you have done to my life." Ibid.

117 the satisfaction of being able to summarily bring O'Neill to heel. *Part of a Long Story.*

118 "And so at the crossroads I salute you as we pass: 'Adios, Stranger!'" Ibid.

118 the ramshackle studios Agnes and O'Neill occupied. A/BG interviews with Woods & her son Allen Ullman.

118 at the melting snow in a bare, brown orchard, he made no comment. Ibid.

119 the most tempestuously romantic couple outside the pages of a book. A/BG interview with Allen Ullman.

119 since the expense of operating the Playwrights' Theatre was barely covered by ticket sales. Considered not experimental enough for the Playwrights' Theatre, *In the Zone* was first produced Oct. 31, 1917, by the more flexible off-Broadway troupe, the Washington Square Players. O'Neill at first rejected the offer of a vaudeville tour as degrading, but changed his mind when he was guaranteed a twenty-five- to forty-week run on the Orpheum vaudeville circuit. In later years he disparaged *In the Zone* as "too facile in its conventional technique, too full of clever theatrical tricks," saying the play "in no way represents the true me or what I desire to express." Letter, EO to Barrett H. Clark, 5/18/19, Yale, SL.

119 forgot to alert either O'Neill or Agnes to the visit. A/BG interviews with Woods.

120 O'Neill would be finished working by two, and blandly offered to return at half past four. *Part of a Long Story.*

120 "Believe me," he wrote to Moise, "from line to line, the poor wretch can never tell whether the play is farce or tragedy—so perverse a spirit is his star." 4/9/18, Yale, SL.

120 resolved not to let the threat of Louise hinder her happiness. A/BG interviews with NM.

CHAPTER ELEVEN

123 **"Then he laughed, his mouth distorted with an ironic grin."** *Part of a Long Story,* & A/BG interviews with Teddy Ballantine & his wife, Stella.

123 **"I can remember my horrible astonishment and despair at this performance, along with a crazy dazed feeling that it just couldn't be true—it couldn't have happened."** *Part of a Long Story.*

124 **advising her to give O'Neill time to cool down.** A/BG interview with SB.

124 **"You and I always. Us always!"** *Part of a Long Story.*

124 **re-embracing her lapsed Catholic faith and concurrently conquering her morphine habit.** see LWMC.

126 **Madden, who predeceased O'Neill, remained his agent until death.** A/BG interviews with Mrs. Madden.

126 **widely quoted view that "the greatest right in the world is the right to be wrong."** The quotation continues: "If the Government or majorities think an individual is right, no one will interfere with him; but when agitators talk against the things considered holy, or when radicals criticize, or satirize the political gods, or question the justice of our laws and institutions, or pacifists talk against the war, how the old inquisition awakens, and ostracism, the excommunication of the church, the prison, the wheel, the torture-chamber, the mob, are called to suppress the free expression of thought."

127 **already a successful novelist, was among the hopeful playwrights he was guiding, along with O'Neill, at the Playwrights' Theatre.** see LWMC.

128 **work in the local hardware store to help pay for his family's rented cottage.** Sometime between late Nov. and mid-Dec. 1918, EO wrote yet another one-act play, *Honor Among the Bradleys,* never published or produced. GJN read it and chided him for writing it and EO promptly tore it up, later acknowledging to GJN that it was "a very false and feeble piece of work." Letter, EO to GJN, 6/20/20, Cornell, SL.

129 ***The Moon of the Caribbees,* the first of three one-act plays (the last two by other authors).** *Tickless Time* by SG and GCC, and *The Rescue* by Rita Creighton Smith.

129 **At his feet lay a large white dog.** *Part of a Long Story.*

129 **while she and O'Neill continued on to the station.** Ibid.

130 **"I could only stay a few minutes for I knew Gene would be restless at home," Agnes wrote in her memoir,** Ibid.

132 **His second reaction was "silence."** Ibid.

132 **pregnancy was due to an episode of heedless passion fueled by alcohol.** Judging by some expository dialogue EO later slipped into *Strange Interlude,* that might be what he came to believe. Except for the dialect, this could be Agnes talking: "We'd swore we'd never have children, we never forgot to be careful for two whole years. Then one night we'd both gone to a dance, we'd both had a little punch to drink, just enough—to forget—driving home in the moonlight—that moonlight!—such little things at the back of big things!" That is Nina Leeds's mother-in-law, Mrs. Evans, explaining the unwanted birth of her son Sam (not, in her case, because she and her husband chose to be childless, but because of a family history of insanity).

135 **"Sphinxes muffled in their yellow robes with paws deep in the sea."** "Eugene O'Neill," by Pierre Loving, *The Bookman,* Aug. 1921.

135 **"How I love to reveal my nakedness to the sun on solitary beaches!"** The ms. of the complete poem is at Beinecke. It continues: "How I love to play unconsciously, dancing like another heat-wave to its own rhythm, freed from the fretting, lukewarm glance of yielding kinship of sand which molds my own image, to relax and drown in my silent depths deep in the heart of steadfast, simple tides flowing from eternity to eternity as the cloud shadows march across the world from mystery to mystery."

135 **(Even with her mother's supervision, Agnes forgot to buy a crib.)** *Part of a Long Story.*

136 **and not a little impressed that he was the son of a famous actor.** A/BG interviews with KJP.

136 **believing, as did her mother, that O'Neill wanted to marry her.** Ibid.

137 **they were secretly married in Hoboken Trinity Church in New Jersey.** A/BG interviews with KJP, & Division of Vital Statistics & Administration, NJ State Dept. of Health; see LWMC.

137 **"We could never have made a go of it," she subsequently conceded.** A/BG interview with KJP.

CHAPTER TWELVE

138 **he'd had "a sudden clear vision of the day at the Happy Home when Shane was born, of my holding your hand, remember?"** 4/8/28, Harvard, SL.

139 **"Oceans of love to Agnes, baby, and the biggest baby of the three *You*."** dated "Sunday," probably 11/1/19, Yale.

139 **an aging woman, "who can taunt with a biting cruelty, as if suddenly poisoned by an alien demon."** O'Neill's notes, Beinecke.

140 **"His voice already carries further than the Old Man's."** 11/1/19, Princeton.

140 **O'Neill handed over *Exorcism* for production on March 26, 1920.** A/BG interview with JL.

141 **he was served with the divorce papers.** details of the divorce proceedings, from Westchester County Archives—Supreme Court, White Plains, NY, File #1673 (1912), County Clerk's office.

141 **production had opened in New Orleans on January 22.** It was reviewed 1/23/12 in the New Orleans *Times-Picayune*.

141 **told a writer researching his father's career many years later.** letter, 1/15/40, to Lawrence Estavan, of the Writers' Program of the WPA in Northern California, published in *San Francisco Theater Research*, Vol. 20, James O'Neill (1942).

141 **Eugene slunk back to Jimmy the Priest's.** A/BG interviews with NW, RC, & JMcC, among others, to whom O'Neill told versions of this story.

142 **He was, in his own words, "sick in body, brain and soul."** O'Neill's autobiographical short story, "Tomorrow."

142 **he had changed his mind about wanting to die** A/BG interview with LB.

142 **a gesture aimed largely at his father.** Among the differing versions of this story was the one published in George Jean Nathan's *The Intimate Notebooks* (Knopf, NY, 1932). In Nathan's version an unconscious O'Neill was sped by ambulance to Bellevue, worked over by two interns, and revived three hours later. Nathan ended the story with Eugene's

friends rushing to James O'Neill and returning four hours later with part of the $50 they had received from him for medical expenses; they divided what was left with O'Neill.

144 **O'Neill and his brother were fond of quoting** EO to AB, 11/30?/19, Harvard, SL.

144 **more substantial and sympathetic woman than the self-portrait she inadvertently draws in her memoir.** Most of the letters written by EO to AB did not see print until 2000. Her memoir does make use of information gleaned from some of O'Neill's letters, which she kept despite his demand that she return them to him. O'Neill's own letters were not published collectively until 1988 (*Selected Letters of Eugene O'Neill*, Yale University Press, New Haven, CT, edited by Travis Bogard and Jackson R. Bryer) although A/BG managed to gather many of them in time to quote from or paraphrase them for their previous biography, *O'Neill* (Harper & Bros., NY, 1962).

144 **"The feeling of emptiness you speak of nearly drove me crazy this afternoon—before I got your letter."** 12/1?/19, Harvard, "Wind."

145 **he bought a hat and shoes.** EO to AB, 12/2/19, Harvard, SL.

145 **planned to spend the rest of his time in the city "right under their wing."** letter, 12/1/19, Harvard, SL.

145 **assured her he was being "a good, good boy."** Ibid.

145 **"Believe me, Prohibition is very much of a fact."** letter, 12/2/1919, Harvard, SL.

145 **misdeeds that she actually "knew were not true," and asked his forgiveness.** letter, AB to EO, Tuesday, 12/2/19, Harvard, "Wind."

145 **"There was just enough kick in the wine to make everyone feel jovial and that's all," he reported to Agnes.** Tuesday a.m., 12/2?/19, Harvard, SL.

147 **Ruth Atkins, the girl both brothers fancy.** Lesser roles in *Beyond* were filled by Louise Closser Hale, Mary Jeffery, and George Rodell of the cast of *For the Defense*.

148 ***Beyond*, she wrote him, "is nearer to me, somehow, than anything you have done."** 1/14/20, Harvard, "Wind."

148 **"I get a great deal of pleasure and excitement myself out of imagining you at all your interviews and appointments."** 1/15/20, Harvard, "Wind."

148 **"Good advice, maybe," wailed O'Neill to Agnes, "but how the hell can I keep it at this stage of the game?"** letter to AB, 1/14/20, Harvard, SL.

149 **"However, I feel so keyed up I could work 24 hours a day without eating, I think."** 1/15/20, Harvard, SL.

149 **"I knew I was going to like you from the first moment we met," he told Bennett.** letter, EO to AB, 1/17/20, Harvard, SL (misdated 1919).

149 **"We were both dead."** Ibid.

149 **he went to bed and slept all day.** Ibid.

150 **"Everyone I'm associated with does—Tyler, Williams, Bennett . . . and they'd simply think me a prig if I didn't."** Ibid.

150 **deliberately put himself "in the way of this happening."** 1/21/20, Harvard, "Wind."

150 **that slave "has something actuating him that they can never understand."** 1/22/20, Harvard, SL.

150 **"You always have kicked me when I was down—do you realize that?—you did not mean to, of course, but you always have."** 1/25/20, Harvard, "Wind."

151 "I tried my best, and I'm no director, God knows, and whether my talking will result in any improvement I don't know." 1/27/20, Harvard, "Wind."

151 "I have a dreadful feeling that when the inevitable success does come there will be something to spoil it all for us." 1/31/20, Harvard, "Wind."

152 "To my eye they are the last word in everything they shouldn't be." 2/2/20, Harvard, "Wind."

152 insisted he sit beside him in the orchestra. EO to AB, 2/4/20, Harvard, SL.

152 watched as his father, in his box, "wept his eyes out." EO told this to numerous friends and later to CM.

152 "hell," he reported to Agnes the following day. 2/4/20, Harvard, SL.

152 "What are you trying to do—send them home to commit suicide?" *The New Yorker*, Hamilton Basso, Profiles, Part I, 2/28/48.

152 "All the same, I think he was pleased." Ibid.

152 play was "a flivver" artistically and "every other way." letter, EO to AB, 2/4/20, Harvard, SL.

153 "No one was more surprised than was I when I saw the morning papers and came to the conclusion that the sad expressions on the playgoers' faces were caused by their feeling the tragedy I had written." NY *Tribune*, Philip Mindil, 2/22/20.

154 "Whatever it may or may not do in a financial way, it has done all I ever expected of it already—and more." letter, 2/4/20, SL.

CHAPTER THIRTEEN

155 "Oh, My Own, My Darling Agnes, My Own Little Wife, I want you, and need you, and love you so!" 2/4/20, Harvard, SL.

155 "You are my life!" Ibid.

156 "I'm in such a funny, vibrating physical state, it almost frightens me." 2/2/20, Harvard, "Wind."

156 knew it would quickly fade and become, as she put it, "an empty bauble." 2/6/20, Harvard, "Wind."

156 "I want no other religion, no other belief, it is all there in you—in us." 2/7/20, Harvard, "Wind."

156 any chances, "for my sake, and poor Shane's, for I swear if anything happens to you I will not live in this world without you—I simply couldn't." 2/11/20, Harvard, "Wind."

157 make their home "the most beautiful place in this world—in a spiritual sense." Ibid.

157 "Success has meant to me the meaningless futility I always knew it would—only more so." 2/12/20, Harvard, "Wind."

157 "It would all be so simple, if Shane were not in our midst, or if you only had him weaned." 2/15/20, Harvard, "Wind."

157 "It's all so impossible." 2/16/20, Harvard, SL.

158 "I'm really in awfully bad shape—and can't seem to pick up." 2/19/20, Harvard, "Wind."

158 mutter about "doing as his father did, deserting family, going back to Ireland to die." self-analytical document written by O'Neill during his psychoanalysis in 1925.

158 returned to Ireland, where, soon after, he died of poison under suspicious circumstances. see LWMC.

158 "I'm all broken up and begin to cry every time the meaning of it all dawns on me." 4/1/20, Harvard, SL.

159 lengthy rewrite of a crucial scene. letter to Tyler, 3/10/20, Princeton, SL.

159 he again lied to Tyler. 3/14/20, Princeton.

159 Agnes was "quite herself again." to Pauline Turkel, 3/14/20.

159 complete such a rewrite until the following fall. letter to Tyler, 3/17/20, Princeton, SL.

160 dust jackets containing a blurb from Alexander Woollcott. March 1920, first edition. Liveright had become a publisher after failing as a manufacturer of toilet paper (marketed as "Pick Quick Papers"). After splitting with Boni he acquired—as Horace Liveright, Inc.—an author list including Hemingway, Faulkner, T. S. Eliot, and Freud.

160 "In memory of the wonderful moment when first in your eyes I saw the promise of a land more beautiful than any I had ever known, a land of which I had dreamed only hopelessly, a land beyond my horizon." *The Curse of the Misbegotten* by Croswell Bowen (McGraw-Hill Book Co., New York, Toronto, and London, 1959).

160 kitchen sink (in which she also washed his diapers). letter to EO, 4/25/20, Harvard, "Wind."

160 both his parents "were smitten with Shane." 4/24/20, Harvard, "Wind."

160 if he couldn't get director Williams to make some improvements. 4/27/20, Harvard, "Wind."

161 (The prize was withheld in 1917 and 1919.) In the category of the novel, Ernest Poole won in 1918 for *His Family*, and Booth Tarkington won in 1919 for *The Magnificent Ambersons*. No award was made to a novel in 1920.

161 "Can you imagine me at the point where Columbia University actually confers one of its biggest blue ribbons on me?" letter, 8/29/20, Yale, SL.

161 "It was the most astoundingly pleasant surprise I've ever had in my life, I think." letter, EO to R. W. Cottingham, 5/12/44, Yale, SL.

162 he "really believed the end was at hand, and Ma was on the verge of a breakdown, staying up purely on her nerve." 5/21/21, Yale.

162 chiding him for not sending any news of his father. 7/12 & 7/13/20, Harvard, "Wind."

163 "When he was only ten years old he had to start working in a machine shop for fifty cents a week." EO responding, 1/15/40, to Lawrence Estavan, who was preparing a monograph: *History of the San Francisco Theater*, Vol. 20, James O'Neill, SL.

164 "My father, somehow, managed to believe in me." *The New Yorker*, Profiles, Part I, Hamilton Basso, Profiles, Part I, 2/28/48.

164 "own flesh and blood were an incongruous and puzzling spectacle." 7/29?/ Harvard, SL.

165 "Then why should he suffer so—when murderers are granted the blessing of electric chairs." Ibid.

165 Eugene later told Agnes, "like a dying dialogue in a play I might have written." Ibid.

166 "What queer things for him to say, eh?" Ibid.

167 father's dying words, O'Neill said, were "seared on my brain—a warning from the Beyond to remain true to the best that is in me though the heavens fall." 12/9/20, Princeton, SL.

CHAPTER FOURTEEN

169 "He with the spiritual guerdon of a hope in hopelessness is nearest to the stars and the rainbow's foot." The Credo, published 2/13/21, was part of a written statement by O'Neill pegged to the 12/27/20 production of his play *Diff'rent*.

170 "But he never went into anything so heavily it could ruin him." letter to Lawrence Estavan, 11/15/40, SL.

171 "Under her hand, I honestly have a hunch that some dividends may finally accrue from the junk buried on the island of M[onte]C[risto]." 12/9/20, Princeton, SL.

171 and set off by train for Denver. A/BG interview with CM.

172 accused Jamie of having deliberately infected Edmund. O'Neill's Self Analytical Notes (see LWMC); early draft of LDJIN, Acts III & V, Beinecke; & Edmund's death certificate, Dept. of Records, Municipal Archives.

172 rented winterized house in the village of Provincetown, letter, EO to Tyler, 11/28/20, Princeton, SL.

172 "To my Mother from Eugene" (adding nothing more than "Provincetown, Mass, Thanksgiving"). Beinecke.

173 "The great dramatist is the dramatist who sees drama as life." letter, EO to GJN, 6/20/20, Cornell, SL.

173 express his "real significant bit of truth" and thereby "merit victory." Ibid.

174 wrote both *Diff'rent* and *The Emperor Jones* during the fall of 1920. letter to the critic Richard Dana Skinner, July(?) 1934, Yale, SL.

175 eight scenes onto three sheets of standard typewriter paper. Ms. is in Princeton Library; the play was labeled "expressionistic" when produced in Germany, much to O'Neill's annoyance. He felt he was being accused of imitating the contemporary German dramatists. "As a matter of fact," he said, "I had never heard of expressionism until long after the play was written. Its technique grew naturally out of my own problems." Interview with Malcolm Cowley, Brentano's Book Chat, July/Aug. 1926.

176 "How would this sort of thing work on an audience in a theater?" NY *World*, Charles P. Sweeney, "Back to the Source of Plays," 11/9/21, & *New York Sun*, "A Eugene O'Neill Miscellany," 1/12/28.

176 "I'm a very religious man, but after Sunday I lay my Jesus on the shelf." A/BG interviews with EK & AMcG.

177 left the production entirely in his hands. A/G interview with JL.

177 theater company in New York had taken such a bold step. The cast included Harold Simmelkjaer as "Dreamy" and Ruth Anderson as his grandmother.

177 cost of the production, cyclorama and all, was $502.28. NY *Daily News* series, 1/24 to 1/30/32.

178 "Where do I go from here?" A/BG interview with KM based on a scrapbook clipping.

179 compared with the previous year's three hundred. A/BG interview with KM.

179 "I'm going to beat you up." Ibid.

179 "I'm 'off' him and the result is he will get no chance to do it in London." (May? 1923), Dartmouth, SL.

179 not someone who would "lose his head if he makes a hit—as he surely will." Ibid.

180 "That actor was Charles Gilpin the Pullman porter in *The Emperor Jones*." NYT *Magazine*, 9/15/46; Gilpin's drinking led to his losing his voice and his career; he died at fifty-one on 5/6/30.

182 it was a flop. *The First Man* was produced at the Neighborhood Playhouse by Augustus Duncan, 3/4/22.

182 (But to what?) *The First Man* was not produced until March 1922.

182 during the two weeks it would take to do the job. letter, A/B to EO, 5/4/21, Harvard, "Wind."

183 "I want to lay my head on your breast for comfort, as always when in trouble or pain." 4/21/21, Harvard, SL.

183 pining love letter O'Neill expected. (probably April 22), 1921, Harvard, "Wind."

183 "I have a poignant pain of emptiness inside." 4/22/21, Harvard, "Wind."

183 "Good night my own dearest thing, I love you so—and miss you so," she wrote in her next letter. 4/24/21, Harvard, "Wind."

184 he'd "destroy" that play, claiming it had been too hastily written. *New York Sun*, 5/14/30.

185 "That was when," according to Given, "he grabbed her by the hair and tried to drag her off. She yelled, but no one interfered." A/BG interviews with EG.

CHAPTER FIFTEEN

186 "Your happiness means mine," he assured her. 8/8/21, Harvard, "Wind."

186 Shane, who "performed no end of antics and extemporized dances in honor of the sun and sea." 8/9/21, Harvard, "Wind."

187 "They are nice girls and it's rather refreshing—the chatter of youth about the place—when one is lonely." 8/11/21, Harvard, "Wind."

188 abscess in her arm that was causing her severe pain. 8/11/21, Harvard, "Wind."

188 "He knows there is no home without you." 8/12 & 8/13/21, Harvard, "Wind."

188 "You know," Agnes wrote back, "that beneath it all, we do deeply, and eternally love one another—so let's forget and forgive the silly bickering . . . and start again." 1921, Harvard, "Wind."

188 "These days crawl sufferingly like futile purgatories." 8/21/21, Harvard, "Wind."

188 she'd finally had to "go and pay $15 to get my arm operated on . . . it nearly killed me—I wept—but I'm glad, as for the first time in two weeks I've been without pain." 8/25/21, Harvard, "Wind."

189 "I don't think he spoke to any member of the cast," she said, "but I do recall his dramatic brooding face." A/BG interview with Gillmore.

189 described by Elizabeth Shepley Sergeant as "betrayal, rather than portrayal." "Portrait of Pauline Lord," *Fire Under the Andes*.

190 plot of a new play he was calling *The Hairy Ape*. A/BG interviews with Kennedy.

190 calling it "a play written with that abundant imagination, that fresh and venturesome mind and that sure instinct for the theater which set this young author apart . . . from a lot of funny little holiday workers in cardboard and tinsel." NYT, 11/3/21.

190 a bigoted egomaniac eaten by ulcers. A/BG interview with BA.

190 "If the gloomy trademark of Eugene O'Neill's depressing product has kept you hitherto away from his plays, disregard it for an hour or so and go to see *Anna Christie*."
Tribune, 11/3/21.

190 remarked that "the happy ending" worried him. Louisville, Kentucky, *Courier-
Journal*.

190 "It is the acceptance of suffering and happiness lived out into a new life." *Globe*,
11/3/21.

190 "I love every bone in their heads." In the Gelbs' 1962 *O'Neill*, the quote appeared as "I
hate every bone in their heads"; this was challenged by several of EO's close friends,
including KM and JL, who said the quote should have read "love," not "hate"—which of
course is funnier—and we have now corrected it.

191 "(In fact, I once thought of calling the play 'Comma')." *The Theater of George Jean
Nathan*, by Isaac Goldberg (Simon & Schuster, New York, 1926).

191 found it "sufficiently dramatic and in harmony with any deep rhythm of life." EO to
Malcolm Mollan (Dec.?) 1921, Conn. College, SL. Mollan, who had befriended O'Neill
during his brief stint as a reporter on the New London *Telegraph* in summer of 1912, had
sent him a list of questions, preparing for an article published in the Philadelphia *Public
Ledger* Sunday Magazine, 1/22/22.

191 "A work of art is always happy; all else is unhappy." Ibid.

192 he confessed to the writer Malcolm Cowley. Brentano's Book Chat, July/Aug. 1926.

192 with the proviso that *Anna Christie* not be one of them. AG conversation with JWK, 1962.

193 "We shall live in hopes that it may not recur." letter from Dr. John Aspell to James
O'Neill, & Dept. of Pathology, St. Vincent's Hospital records.

193 "I believe you are going to be very much interested in this play, whatever your verdict
may be." 1/2/22, Cornell, SL.

193 those two plays, said O'Neill, were "certainly two of my finest, while [Nathan] did like
Gold and *The Fountain* (two of my worst)." letter, EO to Richard Madden, 3/11/29,
Yale, SL.

193 "Think I have got the swing of what I want to catch and, if I have, I ought to tear
through it like a dose of salts." 12/10/21 (private), SL.

193 aboard the luxury liner S.S. *Philadelphia*. EO's Shipping Articles, S.S. *Philadelphia*,
lists E.G. O'Neil [(sic)], "AB," as one of two crewmen transferred from the S.S. *New York*
on 8/19/11. His wages "per month" were $27.50.

194 rare look into the fearsome life of the coal stoker. Driscoll was listed as J. Driscoll on
Shipping Articles Public Record Office, Kew, Richmond, Surrey, England; and General
Register Office of Shipping and Seamen, Cardiff, Wales.

194 "It seemed to give him mental poise to be able to dominate the stokehole, do more
work than any of his mates." NYT, LK (aka Louis Kalonyme), 12/21/24. The same
quotation (unattributed) appeared in *New Yorker*, Profiles, Part II, Hamilton Basso, Profiles, Part II, 3/6/48.

194 O'Neill learned, "by jumping off a liner in mid-ocean to the bewilderment of everyone who knew him, for there never lived a more self-assured, self-contented guy,
seemingly." letter, EO to Ralph E. Whitney (private), SL, 3/11/41.

194 "He chose to write about the hairy stoker, victim of modern industry, a man far removed from [O'Neill] himself in actual circumstance," reported Sergeant, "in order to voice through Yank that social rebellion and sense of buffeted frustration which was his philosophic message at the time." portrait of O'Neill, *Fire Under the Andes.*

195 was again "about to have the ghastly joy of attending two sets of rehearsals at the same time." 9/23/22, Yale, "TTWWF."

196 Wolheim, according to Kennedy, "roared his profane affirmative." A/BG interviews with Charles O'Brien Kennedy.

196 marked too many of his earlier efforts. letter, 1/2/22, Cornell, SL.

CHAPTER SIXTEEN

197 "My mother got him to go on the wagon and stick—and he has stuck." letter to Harold de Polo, 1/10/22, Virginia University, SL.

198 had suffered a slight stroke. letter from Libbie Drummer to her friend, a Mrs. Phillips, undated, c. 3/20/22, is among the files of Hull, McGuire, Hull, the New London law firm that handled the O'Neill estate; in LS collection, Conn. College.

198 doctor confirmed she'd had a stroke. Ibid., & Ella O'Neill death certificate signed by Dr. Hunter & filed in Bureau of Vital Statistics, California State Board of Health.

198 intimately involved with Ella during her illness. letter from Libbie Drummer to her friend, a Mrs. Phillips, undated, c. 3/20/22, is among the legal files of Hull, McGuire, Hull.

198 mutual friend of hers and Ella O'Neill's who lived on the East Coast. Ibid.

199 "She did not like it one bit that I was there, and let me see it," Drummer later wrote to Mrs. Phillips, "but I stayed for a few hours as Mrs. O'Neill wished me to." Ibid.

199 "I did not like her and could see through her from the first moment I met her." Ibid.

200 for which he was doing most of the directing. letter, EO to SC, *"Love and Admiration and Respect."*

200 later told she'd had a brain tumor. A/BG interviews with Sheridan & Brennan family members.

201 "It was the saddest closing chapter of any story I have ever read." letter, Drummer to Phillips, undated, c. 3/20/22, Hull, McGuire, Hull files.

201 "Her body arrived the day the play opened." letter to Milton Salsbury, 5/17/22 (private), SL.

202 edited by Commins's wife, Dorothy Berliner Commins. *"Love and Admiration and Respect."*

202 hurried back to the hotel and called him from the lobby. Ibid.

202 his earlier "gruesome search in the dark cellars of Grand Central Station" for his mother's casket. Ibid.

202 where "he promptly passed out on Gene's bed." SC's typed manuscript of the memorandum.

203 scold him for his dereliction. *O'Neill, Son and Artist,* by LS (Little, Brown and Company, New York, 1973).

203 "though Agnes and Saxe never knew it, O'Neill had not gone to the railway station." *"Love and Admiration and Respect."*

205 she was fifteen and "not a chaste and virtuous woman." divorce petition by Nettie O'Neill, Supreme Court Chicago, 9/7/1877; *Chicago Tribune*, 3/7/1874; *Chicago Chronicle*, 2/26/1894; interviews with Brendan & Sheridan families; records Circuit of Court Chicago (#25927-1263) and NYT, 9/8/1877; *Chicago Tribune*, 9/8 & 9/16/1877; Chicago *Inter-Ocean*, 10/24/1877; and see LWMC.

206 learned to conceal the unsavory aspects of his personal life. Ibid.

207 devoted to each other and to their son, Jim Jr. (as he was then called). Robins diaries & letters, Fales; & see LWMC.

208 in a way, she was like the Mummy. A/BG interviews with ESS.

208 could not reconcile that face with his mother's. interviews with CM.

208 to which he'd been sent after his seventh birthday. The school's formal name was St. Aloysius Academy for Boys. See LWMC.

209 "I did not know if Jamie would ever reach New York alive." letter, Drummer to Phillips, undated, c. 3/20/22; files of Hull, McGuire, Hull.

209 "I was just beginning to enjoy her." A/BG interviews with Bessie Sheridan & Agnes Brennan.

CHAPTER SEVENTEEN

211 "Usually they don't take that much trouble." letter to Marjorie Greiser, 5/5/22, SL.

212 "'Yank is my own self!'" Mary B. Mullett, *American Magazine*, Nov. 1922.

212 his play was "propaganda in the sense that it was a symbol of man, who has lost his old harmony with nature . . . the struggle used to be with the gods, but is now with himself, his own past, his attempt 'to belong.'" *New York Herald Tribune*, 11/16/24.

212 "not luxurious enough" for uptown audiences. A/BG interviews with KM.

212 (whose recollection thirty-five years later of her first encounter with O'Neill will become legend). A/BG interviews with CM.

212 "'You mean the author of this play?'" Ibid.

213 "He hadn't even had the courtesy to thank me for taking over the part on a moment's notice." Ibid.

213 he doesn't think much of her acting ability. A/BG interviews with JL.

213 "He would tease me by calling me that when he thought I was putting on airs." A/BG interviews with CM.

213 Eugene Jr. the education he deserves. A/BG interviews with KJP.

213 taught the boy to think well of him. Ibid.

214 he consents to a meeting. A/BG interviews with LK.

214 he has decided he will finance his education. A/BG interviews with KM & JL.

214 her son returns "glowing from the meeting." A/BG interview with KJP.

214 "The woman I gave the most trouble to has given me the least." quoted by CM in interviews with A/BG.

214 school was the place where he lived. A/BG interviews with Frank & Elsie Meyers.

215 he and his brother "emphatically do not desire the settling of the estate to drag on one second longer than is absolutely necessary." letter, 5/12/22; Hull, McGuire, Hull papers, Conn. College.

215 in a letter to the critic Oliver Saylor. 5/25/22 (private), SL.

216 "Gene would sneak a view of the boy and tug at one end of his mustache, which was a habit of his." A/BG interviews with EG.

216 "Once they got into the ocean," Light recalled, "the awkwardness between them disappeared." A/BG interviews with JL.

216 constant companions, "lived in the ocean." letter from Barbara Burton to AG, c. 1960.

217 "would have wonderful evening picnics and invite friends from town." Ibid.

218 read *Miss Julie* aloud to her, "losing himself in the sound of the words and their haunted meaning." *Part of a Long Story.*

219 completing his first draft of *Welded* the following spring. 4/16/23 (private), SL.

220 little more than "some very third-rate Strindberg." *The World of George Jean Nathan* (Alfred A. Knopf, New York, 1952), section "Eugene O'Neill."

220 Nathan said, "put on his hat, walked out and didn't let me hear from him for two months." Ibid.

CHAPTER EIGHTEEN

221 while they retreated to Peaked Hill Bars. A/BG interviews with EG, who occasionally accompanied AB & EO in house-hunting.

222 doctor's advice to switch to country air. A/BG interviews with EG & JL.

222 two with fireplaces, and the servants' quarters. A/BG interviews with KM, EG, & Bernard Simon.

222 he was "a person to whom Rolls-Royces and similar titillations mean less than nothing, and who desires no greater extravagance than food." Philadelphia *Public Ledger*, 1/2/22.

223 got on his nerves. A/BG interview with KM.

223 Kantor believed, "on the question of equality." A/BG interviews with EG, LK, & BB.

224 "My dear dearest, I want to write my soul out for you, telling the way I feel about you." Autumn 1922?, Harvard, "Wind."

224 "So what can I do?" to C. Hadley Hull, 12/13/22, Conn. College.

224 "NEW LONDON WILL HAVE MY FULL APPROVAL" to C. Hadley Hull, 12/17/22, Conn. College.

225 "He does not like the place, the food is wretched, and he cannot sleep during the night." 7/18/23, Beinecke, and A/BG interview with Cadenaz.

226 "I'm sure a letter from you would be very bracing," she prodded gently. Ibid.

226 "He'll only get drunk, I guess, after he gets out and then he'll be all blind." 8/7/23 (private), SL.

226 Death came on November 8, 1923. A/BG interviews with members of Sheridan family.

226 "He and I were terribly close to each other." 2/18/31, Dartmouth, SL.

227 "And so he lived on cursing & drinking, being slapped on the back and no one ever caught him." Beinecke.

228 long-dead brother who had once been his hero. Some of this material has been extracted from an article by BG, NYT, 3/19/2000.

230 giving up "self & the world to worship of God." Beinecke.

230 **anything but the rosiest of futures for him.** "School Days at Notre Dame," Vol. 4, Charles Warren Stoddard, 1936. University of Notre Dame archives; *Eugene O'Neill Review*, Vol. 15, No. 2, articles by Edward L. Shaughnessy; Hessbergh Memorial Library archives, University of Notre Dame.

231 **decline from which he would never spring back.** A/BG interviews with AMcG, PS, & St. John's (now Fordham University) archives.

CHAPTER NINETEEN

232 **"It makes me feel old and weary sometimes."** 5/28/24, letter copied with permission of Clarke.

233 **"—those vulgar speeches, God!"** A/BG interview with Young; and Young's "From My Journal," *Harper's* magazine, June 1957. The article consists of "entries" dated from 1924 to 1946; Young later admitted he did not actually keep a journal but reconstructed the entries from memory.

234 **"I'm still ashamed of myself for letting Doris Keane play the role," he later confessed.** A/BG interview with Young.

234 **all concerned "had been breaking their necks to keep him sober."** A/BG interview with Ben-Ami.

236 **"There is no temptation for me to compromise."** magazine, Philadelphia *Public Ledger*, 1/2/22.

236 **"Being a just God, and a Great Producer, he will no doubt spare the two of us; and we can then rehearse this dialog on Mount Ararat as a first step toward the Theater of the Future."** *Shadowland*, April 1922, "The Artist of the Theater: A Colloquy Between Eugene O'Neill and Oliver M. Sayler."

236 **and even Arthur Hopkins.** In a sentimental reversal at the end of his writing career, O'Neill wrote to Hopkins about his "deep gratitude for all you did for me. That, believe me, I have never forgotten nor ever can forget." EO to Hopkins, 6/5/44, Yale, SL.

237 **"Our richest, like our poorest, have desired most not to give life but to have it given them."** interview with Edna Kenton, who permitted A/BG to copy the letter.

237 **"I'll have to help create a new outlet—or remain gagged."** EO to GJN, Sunday (Dec. 1923), Cornell University, *As Ever, Gene*.

237 **along with fresh new American work.** A/BG interviews with KM & Edna Kenton.

237 **"Whenever I think of him it is with the most self-condemning remorse."** 5/26/24, Virginia, SL.

238 **"It's hard to say how much we owe him."** *The New Yorker*, Profiles, Part I, Hamilton Basso, Profiles, Part I, 2/28/45.

240 **from the loss of an infant.** Three years after the play's production, the psychoanalyst Dr. Louis Bisch, who had befriended O'Neill and was sometimes the recipient of his confidences, informally deduced that O'Neill was "emotionally starved." After O'Neill's death in 1953, and the publication three years later of *Long Day's Journey Into Night*, Dr. Bisch posited (in an interview with the authors) that many of his plays "showed an antagonism toward women, stemming from a deep antagonism toward his mother." Somewhat glibly, Bisch concluded that while O'Neill loved his father, he hated his mother, and because his mother had failed him, all women would fail him.

240 "But the sets which I described in my stage directions were so 'natural' that they inevitably conjured up all the unimportant paraphernalia of living, daily existence, to stand between the life of my characters and the lives in the audience." "O'Neill Defends His Play of Negro," NYT, 5/11/24.

241 ("That's no realistic goal for a nigger!") quoted by David Remnick, in *The New Yorker*, 4/25/2011.

241 "The present arrangement, I think, has a tendency to break down social barriers which are better left untouched." 2/25/24, *Brooklyn Eagle*.

244 "Indignation, right or wrong, that's the good old stuff!" NYT, 3/19/24, *American Magazine*, et al.

245 "—not to speak of the anonymous letters which ranged from those of infuriated Irish Catholics who threatened to pull my ears off as a disgrace to their race and religion, to those of equally infuriated Nordic Kluxers who knew that I had Negro blood, or else was a Jewish pervert masquerading under a Christian name in order to do subversive propaganda for the Pope!" letter, EO to Carol Bird in "Fifteen-Year Record of Class of Princeton University," 1925.

245 "We didn't let any of this interfere with our plans, but there was a lot of tension all around." A/BG interviews with JL.

245 a radical who could bear watching. Bruce J. Mann, *The Eugene O'Neill Review*, Vol. 15, No. 1, Spring 1991; Mann resourcefully dug up the document by invoking the Freedom of Information Act.

246 "What is the theater for if not to show man's struggle, whether he is black, green, orange or white, to conquer life; his effort to give it meaning?" "O'Neill Defends His Play of Negro," NYT.

246 according to O'Neill, "really a most ludicrous episode—not so ludicrous for me, however, since it put the whole theme of the play on a false basis and thereby threw our whole intent in the production into the discard." letter, EO to Bird in "Fifteen-Year Record of Class of Princeton University."

247 "Life is hard and bitter enough without, in addition, burdening ourselves with prejudices." Carol Bird, *Theater* magazine, June 1924.

CHAPTER TWENTY

248 dreamed a new play in its entirety. WD, 1/1/24.

248 a plot had come to him so easily. EO to Walter Huston (who starred in *Desire*) confirmed in A/BG interview with Huston's son John; and EO to the critic, Richard Watts Jr., *New York Herald Tribune*, 9/9/33.

248 writing dialogue, "as if I'd pondered over this play for months." EO to a "Mr. Maxwell," 5/8/45, Yale, SL.

249 a fully realized script. WD, 5/16/24.

250 wanted to "express what they felt subconsciously." Brentano's Book Chat, July/Aug. 1926, "Eugene O'Neill: Writer of Synthetic Drama" by Malcolm Cowley.

251 part of a freezing January and February in 1909. A/BG interviews with EK. He and Bellows turned out forty paintings between them and O'Neill wrote a series of sonnets

(later deriding them as "bad imitations of Dante Gabriel Rosetti") during their five-week stay. (Also see LWMC.) Reminiscing about the farm more than thirty years later to his son Shane, O'Neill wrote, "My father took it over in payment of debt he couldn't collect. Bellows and EK and I did our own cooking and everything, and damned near froze to death." (letter, 1/18/40, University of Virginia, SL.)

251 was "a tragedy of the possessive—the pitiful longing of man to build his own heaven here on earth by glutting his sense of power with ownership of land, people, money—but principally the land." EO to Grace Dupree Hills, 3/21/25, Berg Collection, NY Public Library, SL.

252 where farming was less of a struggle. A/BG interview with Bernard Simon.

252 attempted to "give an epic tinge to New England's life-lust, to make its inexpressiveness poetically expressive, to release it," EO to GJN, 3/26/25, Cornell, *As Ever, Gene.*

253 "The proprietor confessed to her that Gene had sat in the back room and drunk himself into a coma." A/BG interview with Cowley, and his article in *The Reporter* magazine, 9/5/57.

253 "And," she added, "this would almost always be when he had come to a stopping point in his work." *Part of a Long Story.*

255 and "might almost be given in the list of characters." Brentano's Book Chat, July/Aug. 1926, "Eugene O'Neill: Writer of Synthetic Drama" by Malcolm Cowley.

257 he'd been "a sucker ever to go in for playwriting, mating and begetting sons, houses and lots, and all similar snares of the property game." EO to KM, 8/19/24, Yale, SL.

257 Wilbur Daniel Steele, in Nantucket. WD.

258 "From the real critics I have always had a feeling that they saw what I was trying to do and whether they praised or blamed, they caught the point." *New York Sun,* 1/12/28.

259 he was "acutely conscious of the Force behind—(Fate, God, our biological past creating our present, whatever one calls it—Mystery, certainly)—and of the one eternal tragedy of Man in his glorious, self-destructive struggle to make the Force express him instead of being, as an animal is, an infinitesimal incident in its expression." EO to Quinn, 4/3/25, University of Pennsylvania, SL. Quinn's article appeared in *Scribner's,* Oct. 1926: "Eugene O'Neill: Poet and Mystic."

260 would like "ten walled acres in Siberia with a flock of Siberian wolfhounds to guard them, and broken glass on the walls." A/BG interviews with KM.

260 Arthur Hopkins, John Barrymore, and Mabel Dodge. A/BG interviews with Belinda Jelliffe.

260 therapeutic help for "a variety of specific problems." Ibid.

261 "At the hotel, we scratched around in bureau drawers and I guess we found the tickets, because I remember later saying good-bye to them all as they left for the pier." Ibid.

CHAPTER TWENTY-ONE

262 a truly singular document, The 1925 Scribbling Diary would never have come to light if not for a series of events beyond O'Neill's control. Shortly before eloping with Carlotta in 1928, O'Neill had sent his attorney, Harry Weinberger, to Bermuda to retrieve all of his playscripts, notes, and diaries. The Scribbling Diary for 1925 was not among

the papers Agnes surrendered and O'Neill believed she had hidden it. Carlotta, soon after marrying O'Neill, browsing through his diaries (with his permission), grew perturbed by the many intimate references to his life with Agnes. Aware that O'Neill intended eventually to place these records, along with his other papers, in the archives of a university, she asked him to expunge the offending entries.

Accordingly, to oblige his beloved new wife, he sanitized all the diaries he had in hand and—for the missing 1925 diary—he created, from memory and scattered notes, a cursory substitute in which no reference was made to his life with Agnes or his struggles with alcohol. At Carlotta's urging, he then transcribed all the sanitized diaries into the handsomely bound notebooks she provided, renaming the material Work Diaries, after which he destroyed the originals.

When illness ended his writing career, O'Neill deposited his Work Diaries from 1924 through 1943 into his vast collection of papers at Yale's Beinecke Library; he appended a curt introduction stating the original 1925 diary had "been stolen and sold by former wife."

Carlotta had once again triumphed over Agnes—or so it seemed at the time. In fact, her victory was trumped by Agnes (albeit after her death), when the original 1925 Scribbling Diary (with all its intimate details of her relationship with O'Neill) was found among her papers in 1968.

The unexpurgated 1925 Scribbling Diary was purchased from her estate by Yale in 1970 and was published along with the ersatz diary by the Yale Library in 1981. Just one more irony for O'Neill's ghost to chuckle over.

263   **shaky stretch of sobriety.** SD.

264   **side by side for almost a third of a mile.** Ibid.

264   **a moonlight walk on the beach.** Ibid.

264   **"You, the sun, & sea, Trinity! Sweet spirit, pass on / Keep the dream / Beauty / Into infinity.")** *Eugene O'Neill Poems 1912–1944*, DG ed. (Ticknor & Fields, New Haven, CT, and New York. 1980).

264   **at the next was barely aware of her presence.** It's true that Agnes, with O'Neill's encouragement, had at one point written a play, *The Guilty One*, based on a lame scenario of his own called "The Reckoning," which he'd abandoned in 1917. O'Neill had even helped her "reconstruct" it, but it was never produced.

265   **O'Neill wrote in his diary.** WD.

266   **"he is thus more willing than the chronic alcoholist to accept treatment for his malady."** "Alcohol and the Nervous System" published Oct. 1924 in the British medical journal, the *Practitioner*. Found among O'Neill's papers at Yale.

267   **"There is so much of the secret me in it."** 12/10/26, Yale, SL.

268   **believed people "did recognize, from their knowledge of the new psychology, that everyone wears a mask—I don't mean only one, but thousands of them."** interview with Ernest K. Lindley, *New York Herald Tribune*, 5/22/31.

268   **O'Neill once crowed to Dr. Bisch.** A/BG interview with Bisch.

269   **his "pet of all of the published plays"** letter, 12/10/26, Yale, SL.

269   **gratefully noted in his Work Diary.** 2/25/25.

CHAPTER TWENTY-TWO

271 **long-delayed liquidation of Jamie's estate.** It was not until two months later that the estate was finally liquidated, according to an item in the NYT, 4/2/25.

271 **Shane (nearly five and a half years earlier) was born.** 2/18/25.

271 **William A. Brady's** *A Good Bad Woman.* The first and second were, respectively, by Milton Herbert Gropper & Avery Hopwood; the third was a revival of a 1919 play based on a book by William J. McNally.

272 **"Fancy that, with infanticide," he quipped to Macgowan.** A/BG interview with KM.

272 **"to get 'my back up' really—it isn't so much being out of touch as the fact that I'm so chuck full of** *Brown* **that** *Desire* **seems out of my range of worry."** letter, 3/1/25, "TTWWF."

273 **appearing daily until nearly the end of April.** SD, 4/3 to 4/25/25.

273 **a similar hurt on his own child.** interviews with KJP.

274 **experiencing "couvade," he joked to Macgowan.** EO to KM, 5/1/25, "TTWWF."

274 **"Agnes and baby all serene."** EO to KM, 5/14/25; copied from KM's personal collection.

274 **"We suggested Oona, the Irish translation of Agnes," Colum later recalled.** A/BG interview with Padraic Colum.

274 **O'Neill's problem with drinking (among other concerns)** SD, 6/6/25.

274 **"I asked why he didn't just ignore those letters; he said he couldn't, that he just had to answer his mail."** A/BG interviews with Bisch.

275 **"mostly in bed reading."** 1925 Scribbling Diary.

275 **"You were as kind as you could be and I shall never forget it."** EO to KM and his wife, 7/31/25, "TTWWF."

275 **he was "very much on the old cart again, and feel as well now as I ever did, what with swimming, boating and the rest of it."** EO to KM, 7/31/25, "TTWWF."

275 **"But not serious."** SD, 8/2/25.

276 **"The sun was coming up as they headed in to shore."** A/BG interview with EK.

276 **check for her daughter's expenses.** letter, 9/8/25, Hammerman, eOneill.com.

277 **give Shane "an hour's lesson every day, take him for a walk, see to dressing & undressing him (which is not so much, as he does it himself now) and in fact, do what a governess does."** Ibid.

277 **"Gene thinks this would work out very well, too."** Ibid.

277 **and recording, "Fight with Agnes."** SD, 1925.

278 **he remained "disorganized mentally."** SD, 10/12/25.

278 **"Bisch came out—much talk about divorce."** SD, 10/16/25.

278 **began "to feel fine again."** SD, 10/22/25.

278 **death from old age several years later.** A/BG interviews with KJP.

279 **looked "wobbly."** SD, 11/2/25.

279 **"Dull as Hell."** 12/9/25.

280 **"I said it would probably enhance, rather than repress, his genius."** A/BG interviews with Bisch & KM.

280 **"sick & melancholia."** SD.

281 "Took veronal . . . very good sleep." Beinecke, Agnes Boulton Collection of Eugene O'Neill, Box 5, Folder 1925, diary notes.

281 a book called *What Is Wrong With Marriage?* Albert and Charles Boni, New York, 1929.

281 after learning of the appointment with Hamilton. 12/27/25.

281 Dr. Hamilton's book, *A Research in Marriage*, published in 1929. A & C Boni, New York.

282 O'Neill who checked the last? *A Research in Marriage*, A & C Boni, New York, 1929.

282 until, hours later, he staggered to bed. A/BG interview with KM; also Agnes Boulton Collection of Eugene O'Neill, Boxes 4 and 5, Agnes's notes and diary entries 1919 to 1925, Beinecke.

282 and only one on the thirtieth. SD.

282 "*Must* get in shape." Ibid.

CHAPTER TWENTY-THREE

284 leather couch in traditional Freudian style. A/BG interview with KM.

284 suffering from an Oedipus complex. Ibid.

284 "I am enormously interested to see what will emerge as science out of all these theories.") letter, 7/15/27/, Yale, SL.

285 this paralleled "discovery of Mother's inadequacy." diagram is at Beinecke.

285 (including his "38 days not drinking [during] rehearsals *Desire*"). Beinecke, Agnes Boulton Collection of Eugene O'Neill, Box 4, Folder 149, labeled "Eugene's Drinking": "notes put down in pencil on stationary of Gilbert Van Tassel Hamilton 'Bureau of Social Hygiene,' at 47 East 61 St, NY," where he was director of Psychobiological Research; & A/BG interview with KM.

286 "Life since then has lacked the uproarious but I must admit I feel better." letter to Frank Shay, 10/3/30, Dartmouth, SL.

286 "He'll probably never write a good play again." A/BG interview with LL.

287 "Christianity, once heroic in martyrs for its intense faith now pleading weakly for its intense belief in anything, even Godhead itself." *The Evening Post*, 2/13/26, & NYT, 2/14/26.

287 "But where an open-faced avowal by the play itself of the abstract theme underlying it is made impossible by the very nature of that hidden theme, then perhaps it is justifiable for the author to confess the mystical pattern which manifests itself as an overtone in *The Great God Brown*, dimly behind and beyond the words and actions of the characters." Ibid.

288 "lots of room—beautiful grounds, private beach [and] all at a big bargain price." EO to KM, 3/12/26, Yale, "TTWWF."

288 "It really has the feeling of home to me who usually feels in most houses like a Samoan in an igloo." copied from a letter in LK's possession & A/BG interview with him.

288 "Jesus Wept" story of the Gospel. *Fire Under the Andes.*

289 had not yet received his first royalty check. 3/12/26, Yale, "TTWWF."

290 where he could canoe, fish, and play tennis. letter, EO to KM, 4/4/26, Yale, "TTWWF."

290 "I can least afford to play philanthropist just now when I'm making my first determined effort to get my own affairs stabilized so I can work steadily ahead for the next
few years in peace." 4/28/26, Yale, "TTWWF."

290 found a property they loved. WD.

291 first draft of *Lazarus Laughed* on May 11. WD.

291 proved to be eminently producible on Broadway. WD & letter, EO to KM, 5/14/26,
Yale, "TTWWF."

291 his *Group Psychology and the Analysis of the Ego*. SD, 1/21 & 3/10/25.

291 served as a sounding board. A/BG interviews with KM.

291 before escaping Bermuda's summer heat. letter, EO to KM, 5/28/26, "TTWWF."

292 "I was his best known pupil," O'Neill later told a friend, "and Yale was really honoring him through me." letter to Saxe Commins, 2/24/43, Princeton, *"Love and Admiration and Respect."*

292 Agnes "was amused to discover that he became so interested in the spectacle that he
did finally enjoy his own part in it, and instead of dying of stage-fright 'took a bow'
on the applause." *Fire Under the Andes.*

292 unable to specify just what else it was that gnawed at him. A/BG interview with KM.

293 "madly in love" with sixteen-year-old Eugene. A/BG interview with Barbara Burton.

293 "This, after living in 'Bellevue' all winter, makes me suspect God is becoming a symbolist or something." 7/9/26, Yale, SL.

CHAPTER TWENTY-FOUR

294 lived across the lake from the O'Neill campsite. WD.

294 taking her in for the summer. A/BG interview with RC.

296 "It was an awful tea." Interview with CM by *Times* writer Seymour Peck on 10/2/56
(with A/BG and BA present and recorded by A/BG as part of their research); as a former
actress, CM had a rehearsed repertory about many aspects of her life with O'Neill, and
she often repeated the same descriptions and bits of dialogue over and over; her various
descriptions to Peck were later repeated word for word in a long interview on 4/24/57
with A/BG, as were numerous other details, in many interviews with CM. Excerpts
from interviews with CM that were included in the 1962 *O'Neill* (when CM was still
alive) have now been considerably expanded.

296 "He couldn't relate that face to his mother, and he'd been terribly upset he met me."
Ibid.

297 "It was most indecent." Ibid.

297 in his diary the following week. WD, 7/23/26.

297 before their next flirtatious encounter. WD, 8/17/26.

297 "I am miserable and hopeless and weep." 6/26/26, Yale, Beinecke. (If CM's letters to
RB are extant, they have not yet surfaced.)

298 "I love you." 7/14/26, Yale, Beinecke.

298 he would sail home on September 15. Yale, Beinecke.

298 no longer felt any urgency to reclaim her. Ibid.

298 "Florence Reed [the actress] just a quarter mile away and Carlotta Monterey, the
famous beauty (she played in my *Hairy Ape* in New York at the Plymouth Theater)

visiting not far away." letter, EO to Dolly and Jessica Rippin, 8/18/26; letter loaned to A/BG by Dolly Rippin.

301 **"Marbury, by the way, was very fond of Agnes and though she liked Carlotta, too, she was distressed when she realized that Gene seemed to be interested in Carlotta."** A/BG interview with Reed.

301 **"Toward the very end I felt the presence of some sadness which I had never felt in the O'Neill household."** letter from BB to AG.

301 **remembered the summer as "wonderful and happy."** "More of a Long Story," by SO (Shane's daughter), published by eO'Neill.com, St. Louis, 2008.

301 *"Like them—"* Theater Scrapbooks of Carlotta Monterey, Chamberlain and Lyman Brown Agency, Billy Rose Collection, NY Public Library for the Performing Arts.

302 **could "do with more real friends to talk with."** letter, EO to KM, 8/7/26, Yale, "TTWWF."

302 **asked Gaga to see her home.** letter from BB to AG.

302 **"I hope it will be O.K."** Harley Hammerman collection.

303 **contentedly back at work on *Strange Interlude*.** WD, 9/26/26.

303 **"we get it all fixed the way we want it."** AB to Edward Boulton, 10/7/26, Hammerman collection, eOneill.com.

303 **"There's no one to confide in now."** Harvard, "Wind."

303 **earnestly confiding in Carlotta Monterey.** WD, 10/17/26.

CHAPTER TWENTY-FIVE

305 **"He began with his birth, with his earliest memories of babyhood."** Material taken partly from interview, "A Talk with Mrs. O'Neill," by Seymour Peck, NYT, 11/4/56, and recorded by the authors of this biography. The interview took place at the *Times* shortly before the posthumous premiere of *Long Day's Journey Into Night*; it was attended by Brooks Atkinson, as well as the authors, and at its conclusion BA persuaded CM to agree to an open-ended series of interviews with the authors that continued over the next four years.

308 **not parting from her until 2:30 a.m.** WD.

308 **"If I could only kiss you again, Carlotta."** 11/27/26, Yale, SL.

309 **assuring him "everything will come out as we wish it."** Ibid.

309 **"Do not forget me!"** Ibid.

309 **"This Lover of mine is also my child."** letter to Saxe Commins, 1928.

309 **vividly reflected in his "lady play."** WD.

309 **even before completing *The Great God Brown*** WD, 3/8/25.

309 **"speech-thought method," he called it.** WD, 9/5 to 9/13/25 & 5/17/26.

310 **less easily satisfied with what he used to dash off.** 8/7/26, "TTWWF."

310 **the game his friend was playing.** A/BG interview with KM.

310 **also enclosing "to get to her on Christmas a.m."** 12/7/26, "TTWWF."

311 **had even offered to set him free.** 12/15/26, Yale, SL.

311 **"After all, we've got to remember I'm in the 'show business' and a good subject to hang any rag of scandal upon."** 4/16/27, Harvard, SL.

311 "When work wouldn't come I had to escape via masks of solitude, alcoholic and otherwise, provided only they were excessive." 12/10/26, Yale, SL.

312 he couldn't bear to lose her love. 12/29/26, Yale, SL.

312 "Haven't you an answer, Dear One?" Ibid.

312 "I am going to drink fifty lime squashes watching the new year in." "TTWWF," Beinecke.

CHAPTER TWENTY-SIX

313 he told Kenneth Macgowan in mid-January, letter, 1/12/27, "TTWWF," Beinecke.

313 for time to finish his life's work. notebook at Beinecke entitled "Eugene G. O'Neill, Old Peaked Hill Bar, Mass." The notebook is in YCAL MSS 123, Box 77, Folder 1426: (Ideas, scenarios, & notes for plays), holograph, in notebook, 1920s–30s.

314 bring him around to committing himself to her. letter, EO to CM, 2/10/27, Yale, SL.

314 "but now Carlotta leaves me and becomes a dream." Ibid.

314 "all caved in as if some vampire had been 'scoffing' my life up!" 3/4/27, Yale, SL.

314 "He is my sort." 3/27/27, Yale, SL.

315 Agnes had "gone off somewhere." A/BG interviews with the Lights.

315 "that gave people the impression he may not have been paying attention to his children, but actually he was terribly attached to them." A/BG interview with Breuer.

315 "He was delighted." A/BG interviews with ESS.

315 when a truck crashed into her taxi. O'Neill had been so much moved by ESS's intuitive portrait of him in "Man with a Mask" that—after warning she must "never write or tell anyone about it"—he confided what he called "the whole story" of his mother's drug addiction and its effect on his life.

315 she enjoyed going to cocktail parties, Ibid.

316 Agnes was "foolishly overconfident of him." Ibid.

316 "I judged it one of the greatest plays of all time." *The Magic Curtain*, and A/BG interview with LL.

316 (Cornell subsequently did turn it down.) WD, 3/23/27, & interviews with LL.

317 he was "in a bad way with no prospects." 3/24/27, "TTWWF."

317 she "simply couldn't stand any more talk about the theater." A/BG interviews with ESS.

317 "I would have liked to let this play rest for a couple of months more at least and then go over it before submitting it to anyone, but as you told me you are now in the midst of plans for next season, I am taking a chance on its present form." 4/4/26, copy of letter, Tao House Library.

317 others felt it needed serious cutting. A/BG interview with LL.

318 "If we fail to do this great experiment, if we lack the courage and the vision, then we should forever hang our heads in shame." *The Magic Curtain*.

318 her father, now dying of tuberculosis. EO to GJN, 4/24/27, *As Ever, Gene*.

318 than ever before in their married life. 4/15/27, Yale, SL.

319 she wanted "no more the responsibility of the home." 4/30/27, Henry E. Huntington Library, San Marino, CA.

319   "'Dead for a Ducat, dead!' as Hamlet says." 4/16, 4/17, & 4/18/27, Harvard, SL.

320   "so I could tell you how much I love you!" 4/17/27, Harvard, "Wind."

320   "Your financial status will pick up about October." 4/21/27, Harvard "Wind."

321   until she came home and life got back to normal. 4/22/27, Harvard, SL.

321   might copy the technique before *Interlude* opened. 5/1/27, Yale, SL.

321   "I love you and I don't love anyone else and that's all there is to it." 5/15/27, Harvard, "Wind."

322   for dinner as well. WD, 5/17 to 5/23/27.

322   "what lay behind the apparent simplicity of that amazing flight, behind its clean-cut success, its almost poetic precision." A/BG interview with Theresa Helburn, and *The Saturday Review of Literature*, Nov. 1927.

322   "I have often thought that Gene is a good deal of a lone eagle in his chosen field—daring new and, God knows, long enough flights on his dramatic Pegasus." Ibid.

CHAPTER TWENTY-SEVEN

323   ready to pronounce it "finally finished." WD.

323   "It is such a tepid, lukewarm ocean now, there is no life or sting to it." EO to CM, 7/15/27, Yale, SL.

324   making that novel-play seem "a mere shallow episode!" letter to GJN, 8/26/28, *As Ever, Gene.*

324   he said, "it will be just that." 4/27/28, "TTWWF."

324   to "give up the comfort of the return to Mother Death." Notebook at Beinecke entitled "Eugene G. O'Neill, Old Peaked Hill Bar, Mass." The notebook is in YCAL MSS 123, Box 77, Folder 1426: (Ideas, scenarios, & notes for plays), holograph, in notebook, 1920s–30s.

324   "The sea is a woman to me . . . pagan and physically exultant." 12/29/26, Yale, SL.

325   for the far-off autobiographical *Long Day's Journey Into Night.* a typed transcript of the penciled diagram is in Beinecke.

325   of O'Neill's journey into night. Like the 1925 Scribbling Diary, the document was among the papers O'Neill left behind in Bermuda when he parted from Agnes, and (along with the SD) either overlooked by the lawyer sent by O'Neill to retrieve them, or deliberately withheld by Agnes. After her death in 1968, the document was loaned by her daughter, Oona O'Neill Chaplin, to O'Neill biographer Louis Sheaffer. In a letter from LS to Oona, 9/27/84, he states he has sold the document (presumably with her approval) to the prominent private collector, Dr. Harley J. Hammerman of St. Louis, who provided a copy to A/BG.

327   "It was right after that Papa and Jamie decided they couldn't hide it from me any more." A/BG interviews with CM & ESS, to whom EO told the story; and A/BG interview with JQ to whom CM relayed additional details.

327   believing him too young to be told the truth. Ibid.

328   why impose it on him? Ibid.

328   on the stone plaza fronting the house. "The Wind Is Rising," edited by William Davies King (Fairleigh Dickinson University Press; London: Associated University Presses, 2000).

329 "The alcoholic days were much pleasanter!" 8/29/27, Harvard, "Wind."

330 would also have to wait for a January opening. letter, EO to AB, 9/4/27, Harvard, "Wind."

330 advised her not to "worry about anything!" Harvard, SL, & WD.

331 signing himself "Your Gene." 9/11/27, Harvard, SL.

331 "This does not mean I am trying to force you into a love affair!" 9/9?/27, Harvard, "Wind."

331 "God damn it," she fumed, "if you knew how damned bored and lonely I was here— never mind, I think I'll pack up & arrive in New York, kids & all—then we'll see how that will work." 9/13?/27, Harvard, "Wind."

331 "(Love not drink)." Ibid.

332 "Damn you anyhow Gene—something must be all wrong for you to say such things." Ibid.

332 Carlotta, she wrote, "is certainly much more beautiful than I am." Ibid.

332 circulated for years among island contemporaries of the O'Neills. *Eugene O'Neill and Family, The Bermuda Interlude* (University of Toronto Press, Inc., 1992).

332 putting her on the next boat out of Bermuda. Ibid.

332 thus "wounding an old woman who has been a good friend to us, if there ever was one." c. 4/8/28, Harvard, SL.

333 succumbed to the handsome Spithead carpenter. AB mentioned various negotiations with Johnston in several of her letters to O'Neill during Sept. and Oct. 1927.

333 enabling him to celebrate the occasion with Carlotta. miscellaneous letters and cables exchanged between EO and AB, 9/29 to 10/12/27, Virginia, Harvard, Yale, SL, and "Wind."

CHAPTER TWENTY-EIGHT

334 "But it wasn't until later that year, in November or December during rehearsals of *Marco Millions* and *Strange Interlude*, that he talked to me about divorcing Agnes." A/BG interview with LL.

334 he returned to Bermuda on October 19. letter, EO to CM, 10/24/27, Yale, SL.

334 he had said "nothing at all" to Agnes. letter, 10/24/27, Yale, SL.

335 awake and "able to see the room, and Gene all the time." letter, winter 1927, Harley Hammerman, eOneill.com collection.

335 get rid of it "even at a loss." 11/27?/27, Harvard, SL.

336 convinced the set was complete. 12/2?/27, Harvard, SL.

336 pursue her life "in whatever freedom you desire as I am with mine." 12/9/27, Harvard, "Wind."

337 "You haven't for a long time." 12/20/27, Harvard, SL.

337 live with Agnes even were she willing. 12/26/27, Harvard, SL.

337 if their roles were reversed. 12/26/27, Harvard, SL.

338 "no love, however strong, can continue to endure and live." Ibid.

338 when next she came to New York. Ibid.

339 claimed it "seemed impossible for the kids to be left here alone" letter, 9/4?/27, Harvard, "Wind."

339 help O'Neill keep his balance. A/BG interview with KM.

339 found it expedient to forgive him. A/BG interviews with CM & KM.

339 it could not possibly be with his child. letter, EO to Weinberger, 4/22/28, Yale, SL.

339 "I think he kissed me goodbye, too," said Barbara. letter to AG from BB.

339 during her final two days at the Wentworth. letter, 1/19/27, Harvard, SL.

340 "and the neighbor had instructed his butler to shoot the dog." BB letter to AG, and *Eugene O'Neill and Family, The Bermuda Interlude.*

340 attributing this incident to her father's depressive personality. "More of a Long Story," and A/BG interviews with SO.

340 "He left us all for that woman he met in Maine." Ibid.

340 "You'll get to be such a good swimmer that one of these days I expect you'll turn into one of 'them yaller grunts' yourself and swim out and leave us, and then we'll have to set the fish pot to catch you and bring you home again!" Sept.? 1927, Harvard, SL.

341 to get her "put safely away." letter, early Feb. 1928, Yale, "Wind."

341 "Jimmy told me once that Agnes was the most beautiful woman he had ever seen," said Murray. A/BG interview with Murray.

341 "He was a very charming man." A/BG interviews with Ullman.

341 in his phrase, be "caught in flagrante." letter, 7/2/28, Yale, SL.

341 each consented "to live as though unmarried." 2/17/29, NY *American Magazine.*

341 Agnes entrained for Reno. NYT, 3/12/29.

342 had not yet begun writing her memoir. Wylie's notes are at the Howard Gottlieb Archival Research Center, Boston University. He declined to share these notes with A/BG until after Agnes's death in 1968, and at that time, in discussions at his apartment with A/BG, he reiterated their accuracy.

343 for his novel *Trouble in the Flesh.* (Doubleday & Co., Garden City, NY, 1959).

PART III: MISTRESS, SECRETARY, WIFE, AND MOTHER

CHAPTER TWENTY-NINE

348 "We can't believe we are free." CM diary, 7/3/29.

348 egotistical nature "couldn't stand the idea of her marrying someone even more celebrated than himself." A/BG interviews with CVV.

348 asking them to "give Carlotta my love." Ibid.

349 "I told him I couldn't go to a man's house as a guest and hand his wife a love letter from another man." A/BG interview with Gish.

349 leave them "in peace & ignorance of *her* existence, *her* plans or *her* life!" CM to SC, postmarked "July 13, 1929."

349 "Don't forget me." 3/14/29, University of Virginia, SL.

350 trying out for the freshman crew at Yale." Ibid.

350 "Life laughs with love!" CM diary, 7/22/29.

350 "You are my laughter—and I am yours." CM diary, 7/16/38.

350 "Mr. and Mrs. Eugene O'Neill at home." 7/23/29.

350 *"Thank God!"* CM diary, 7/20/29.

351 "America has had a bellyful of my stuff for a while," he told friends. A/BG interviews with JL, KM, & BDC, and article by Ward Morehouse, *New York Sun*, 5/14/30.

352 until he was forgotten. 5/13/29, Texas University, SL.

352 to achieve "a more mature outlook as an artist." Ibid.

352 "I've everything to back me up now," he concluded, "love of the kind I've always wanted, security and peace." Ibid.

352 "Virtually decide on *Mourning Becomes Electra* as title—trilogy—with separate subtitle each play." WD, 5/18/29.

352 "But where to find that language?" 7/27/29, Library of Congress, SL.

353 "So I'm going to do a lot more of tentative feeling out and testing before I start." letter, 8/31/29, *As Ever, Gene*.

353 two weeks in late August and early September. WD.

353 "So all's well." 8/31/29, *As Ever, Gene*.

354 Carlotta once protested. letter to DG, 5/23/59, Beinecke.

354 and with it, she hoped, "the old parasites!" letters, 7/27 & 8/30/29, Princeton, *"Love and Admiration and Respect."*

354 board "so arranged that it can be maneuvered in front of him and on it he rests his pad." *The Intimate Notebooks of George Jean Nathan.*

355 "I bought him various styles of each—but it was wasted money." *What Mad Pursuits!* The pad was deposited by Carlotta in the O'Neill Collection at Yale shortly after O'Neill's death.

356 "All this in the pouring rain—we were really quite cut up about it," Carlotta said. letter to SC, 6/9/29, Princeton, *"Love and Admiration and Respect."*

356 She knows well the effect it has on him and quietly lays in a constantly replenished wardrobe for him." *The Intimate Notebooks of George Jean Nathan.*

356 "Blue ones." Ibid.

356 "There was never anything casual." A/BG interviews with LG.

357 advise both O'Neill and Carlotta by letter and cable after the crash. CM diary.

357 in charge of the O'Neill collection at Yale. *Pigeons on the Granite.*

358 "I leave about 12:30." CVV, "Daybook," 9/29/25, NY Public Library.

359 "I think of a thousand beautifully mad things concerning you & me,—and get wild with excitement to get back to you." 12/4/29, Yale.

359 none other than Kenneth Macgowan. letter from CM to SC, reproduced in *"Love and Admiration and Respect"*; dated c. 11/15/29, but probably written Oct.

360 necessitating a three-week stay in Paris, WD.

360 "It should come with a rush from now on." 11/12/29, SL.

CHAPTER THIRTY

361 outlined his blueprint for *Mourning Becomes Electra*. CM diary, 5/11/29.

361 "I have hopes, damn it!" 7/27/29, Library of Congress, SL.

362 the "best possible dramatically for Greek plot of crime and retribution chain of fate—Puritan conviction of man born to sin and punishment." MBE diary, April 1929, plus diary and other notes at Beinecke; the diary, from when EO began writing the play in "Spring, 1926" was published in its entirety in the limited edition of the play by

Horace Liveright, Inc. Excerpts appeared in *New York Herald Tribune*, 11/8/31. The diary and other relevant material at Yale were later minutely recorded by Virginia Floyd in *Eugene O'Neill at Work*.

362 **"this fits in well and absolutely justifiable, not forced Greek similarity," he noted.** Ibid.

362 **in the center of New London.** research by Sally Pavetti and Lois MacDonald, curators of restored Monte Cristo Cottage.

363 **"[Agamemnon's] Puritan sense of guilt turning love to lust."** Ibid.

363 **Greek Electra was "the most interesting of all women in drama."** letter, EO to Robert Sisk, 8/28/30, Yale, SL.

364 **Such a character contained too much tragic fate within her soul to permit this—why should Furies have let Electra escape unpunished?"** MBE Work Diary, Beinecke, Nov. 1928.

364 **"It befits—it becomes Electra to mourn—(it is her fate)—also, in usual sense (made ironical here), mourning (black) is becoming to her—it is the only color that becomes her destiny—"** *Electra* MBE Work Diary.

365 **spiritually as well as physically, mourning had "suited" her.** MBE Work Diary, 1926–1931, published by Horace Liveright, Inc. in the limited edition of the play and excerpted by the *New York Herald Tribune*, 11/8/31.

365 **"Even history of comparatively recent crimes (where they happen among people supposedly respectable), shows rural authorities easily hoodwinked—poisoning of Mannon . . . would probably never be suspected (under same circumstances) even in New England town of today, let alone 1865."** Ibid.

365 **"partly a copper brown, partly a bronze gold, each shade distinct and yet blending with the other, beautiful hair that hangs down to her knees."** A/BG interview with CM.

366 **involved "a lot of hard labor—more than there was in *Interlude*."** 12/4/29, SL.

366 **"Not a gentleman's idea of a welcome!" Carlotta quipped.** CM diary.

367 **back home with his head down.** A/BG interview with CM.

367 **"he behaved exactly as though he were worn out with having performed the duties of a good host."** A/BG interview with LG.

367 **"And I find I can get everything said about these characters' souls, hearts, and loins that can be said."** 1/7/30, *As Ever, Gene*.

368 **realized that they, too, must go.** WD.

368 **use of half masks must also be eliminated.** WD.

368 **"He always has told me he lives through everything he writes—all his strength goes into work—which leaves him physically and emotionally exhausted."** CM diary.

368 **"with all my deepest love and gratitude for all you have meant to me!—and all your help!"** *Inscriptions*.

368 **"It's a beautiful country, but a terrible climate."** 5/22/31.

369 **"This love of mine is tortured by his search for peace—rest—!"** CM diary, 1/18/30.

369 **"He wrote the plays, I did everything else."** A/BG interviews with CM & SP, NYT.

369 **was "all washed up and in need of a change of scene."** 3/28/30, "TTWWF," Beinecke.

369 **about $82,000 in today's currency.** CM diary, 5/11/30.

370 her "duty & happiness to help him." A/BG interviews with CM, & CM diary entries.

370 "—they'll last him forever!" CM diary, 3/10/30.

370 "very correct!" CM diary, 5/30/30.

370 "He had a complete wardrobe and he was so pleased." CM interview with SP, BA, & A/BG at NYT, 10/2/56.

370 "And we feel perfect fools—but continue to laugh!" CM diary, 5/24/30.

370 "I feel as if I wasn't a total loss as an American delegate at large of the arts." letter, EO to Madeleine Boyd, 5/19/30.

371 "I would answer without hesitation: O'Neill." NYT morgue, undated clipping.

371 "If we were in the Tropics I would think it a poisonous snake!" she wrote in her diary. 5/30/30.

371 with other cast members, for a festive supper. WD, 5/31/30.

371 "New men get a chance and new ideas are tried out, and the box office does not play the leading part." "O'Neill Plots a New Course for the Drama," by S. J. Woolf, NYT *Magazine*, 10/4/31.

372 once declared, "become parts of my life." "Playwright Finds His Inspiration . . ." by Olin Downes, Boston *Sunday Post*, 8/29/20.

372 calling him, in a letter to Sinclair Lewis, "the top of all living writers." 11/25/36, Yale, SL.

372 no such praise was forthcoming. A/BG interviews with CM & LG.

372 "faith—loyalty—love—God!" CM diary, 6/7/30.

CHAPTER THIRTY-ONE

373 had been swept into the sea. cable from Susan Glaspell in Provincetown.

373 diagnosed with "anemia, very low blood pressure, kidney and gall bladder upset." WD, 1/9/31.

373 ordered a three-week hospital stay. CM diary, 1/13/31.

373 offerings of flowers and other gifts. CM miscellaneous diary entries.

374 her income nor O'Neill's was seriously threatened. CM diary.

374 was, after all, "a well known international banker." 9/15/30, Theater Scrapbooks of Carlotta Monterey.

374 the Canary Islands to recuperate. WD, 1/22/31.

374 "a desolate, ugly place." CM diary, 2/28/31.

374 "sun child" as she called him, letter to LG, 3/23/31, Theater Scrapbooks of Carlotta Monterey.

374 going over it with him scene by scene. CM diary, 3/22/31.

374 "Gene discusses 'baby'!!!?"—in her diary a year earlier. 2/7/30.

375 asking about "the baby." CM diary.

375 "Between us we have four children already and find they are expensive and we are not such gluttons for punishment that we want to take on any more of these responsibilities—in bringing into the world fresh victims for the new poison gases which the lads are preparing for our children." 2/4/31, "TTWWF."

375 foundation of their new home in America. CM diary.

375 copy of the completed *Electra* script to the Theatre Guild. WD.

375 "To get enough of Clytemnestra into Christine, of Electra in Lavinia, of Orestes in Orin, etc. and yet keep them American primarily; to conjure a Greek fate out of the Mannons themselves (without calling in the aid of even a Puritan Old Testament God) that would convince a modern audience without religion or moral ethics; to prevent the surface melodrama of the play from overwhelming the real drama; to contrive murders that escape cops and courtroom scenes." 4/7/31, *As Ever, Gene.*

376 "I must always be there to help, to understand, to comfort,—*no matter what!*" CM diary, 4/11/31.

376 Komroff wrote a reminiscence (never published) about that visit. article by Richard Eaton and Madeline Smith in *The Eugene O'Neill Review*, Vol. 26, 2004.

376 without social polish or pretense, and something of a Marxist. A/BG interviews with Komroff.

376 "I don't feel comfortable with this type of man." CM diary, 4/19/31.

376 "she knew how to write a graceful 'thank you note,' and how to keep sightseers and boring acquaintances away from Gene so that he had free mornings for his work." article, Richard Eaton and Madeline Smith.

376 making him uncomfortable to be drinking alone. Ibid.

377 give the public "a chance to see how the other fellow lives . . . his sufferings, his handicaps . . . to see the sort of life which their brothers far down the social scale must face each day." A/BG interview with Komroff, and "Eugene O'Neill—The Inner Man" by Carol Bird, *Theater* magazine, June 1924 (quote also referred to in Chapter 1).

378 "Collaborator, I love you!" *Inscriptions*, 4/23/31.

378 accepting *Mourning Becomes Electra* for production. WD, 4/24/31.

378 only Blemie with them to New York. CM, 4/28/31.

379 "(That is, never disappointed in it as a work of art, aspects of its teaching I no longer concede.)" letter to BDC, 6/22/27.

380 not in the heart, but through the right temple. facts gathered 5/20/31 by the Associated Press and a team of NYT reporters from police, hotel employees, and friends and relatives of RB, and published NYT, 5/21/31.

380 called Carlotta at once, hoping to cushion the shock. CM diary.

381 "She said she couldn't understand this horrible thing—that Barton wasn't in love with her." A/BG interview with CVV.

381 the only reference made to the subject. A/BG interview with Bio De Casseres.

381 "After dinner I almost pass out—Gene is gentle and sweet." CM diary, 5/20/31.

382 "I love you, my dear lost angel." *The Last Dandy Ralph Barton*, by Bruce Kellner (University of Missouri Press, Columbia and London, 1991).

382 "They all promised," Heidt recalled. A/BG interviews with Heidt.

382 would be "like walking into hell," Carlotta predicted. CM diary, 5/20/31.

382 Chapman was selected by his peers to be that one. A/BG interviews with John Chapman, NY *Daily News*, and Sam Zolotow, NYT.

383 O'Neill thankfully agreed. A/BG interview with Joe Heidt.

384 no use waiting, because O'Neill had left. Ibid.

384 "They never did find out where O'Neill was staying." Ibid.

CHAPTER THIRTY-TWO

385 "I wonder if he will live in it!" 6/25/31.

385 "It's the place for ideas!" *The Intimate Notebooks of George Jean Nathan.*

386 "disappointed" in the choice he'd made. CM diary, 6/1/31.

386 O'Neill told Lillian Gish with a wistful smile after one of his son's visits. A/BG interview with LG.

386 they could have the whole day to become reacquainted. CM diary.

386 she was evidently content to wait until Christmas for her mother to bring Cynthia from California for a visit. CM diary, 8/12/31.

387 a nonchalant "Au revoir to Shane." 8/18/31.

387 unsuited to the role of his hard-bitten, ruthless Lavinia. WD, 8/20/31.

387 "But it was a tough job for me!" letter, 8/20/31, Yale, SL.

388 "Lavinia was *not* the 'little flower'—the 'tender virgin!'" CM diary, 8/20/31.

388 "It has a tremendous sort of abstract excitement for me." unsourced clipping, NYT morgue.

388 needed no urging from O'Neill to wire Brooks Atkinson an invitation to Beacon Farm. CM diary, 8/21/31.

389 recognized O'Neill as a giant of the American theater. A/BG interviews with BA.

389 read the trilogy and was somewhat disappointed. Ibid.

389 would find the third better than the second. Ibid.

389 meeting in New York during which they could "argue a bit." letter, 6/19/31, Lincoln Center, SL.

389 "The more of the inner workings and background of the writing of the trilogy I can set before you . . . the better for me in the sense of my getting more value out of your criticism, for or against." 8/16/31, Lincoln Center, SL.

389 "That's one of many reasons," he explained, "why I'm always glad to have any critic (whose opinion I respect, and whose right to criticize the drama I admit) read my scripts before the openings." Ibid.

390 "We were both enchanted," he said, "when a Boston steamer, headed for New York, passed by." A/BG interviews with BA.

390 sit behind her husband and take notes. CM diary, 8/30/31.

391 "It was wonderful." A/BG interviews with CM.

391 even the faint pouches under his eyes to be visible. A/BG interviews with Ann and Ben Pinchot.

391 "Sammy should know better." AG/BG interviews with CM.

392 "A.N. has 'Odessa Vapours,' (as Gene puts it!)," Carlotta once observed. CM diary, 10/21/31.

392 "I saw a different play from the one I thought I had written." interview with S. J. Woolf, NYT *Magazine,* 9/15/46.

392 she "wouldn't go through it again for anything in the world." unsourced clipping, NYT morgue.

392 "Farewell (for me), to the Mannons!" WD, 10/25/321.

395 "Sunk—worn out—depressed," he wrote in his Work Diary. 10/28/31.

396 the play from which he had derived "the most personal satisfaction." Ibid.

CHAPTER THIRTY-THREE

397 "Three skins for the Trilogy." CM diary, 11/6/31.

398 "always got me the classiest rowboat to be had, and we sported the first Packard car in our section of Connecticut." letter to BA, 8/16/31, Lincoln Center, SL.

398 "Of course I do!" CM diary, 11/26/31.

398 to be their "home until the end!" CM diary, 4/25/32.

399 protagonist-self as tethered to "the rational world of fact—but always fighting against his deeply religious pull." O'Neill's notes, Beinecke.

399 as represented by two separately acted selves. letter to KM, 6/14/29, "TTWWF."

399 who, in his search for truth, "is forced back to his old God and thereby regains his lost soul." letter, EO to KM, 10/16/33, Yale, SL, & letter, EO to Leon Mirlas, 12/19/34, private, SL.

399 O'Neill himself ultimately acknowledged "it wasn't any good." as quoted in *Total Recall* (Doubleday, Garden City, NY, 1960).

402 "It is an awful job—but *worth* it, if you know what you want & get it!" CM diary, 11/28/31.

403 O'Neill ordered a $2,500 motorboat. WD, 1/11 & 1/12/32.

403 she "*must* keep Cyn here for at least six months no matter what!" CM diary, 1/5/32.

403 a family luncheon, to which O'Neill lent his presence. WD, 1/6, 1/7, & 1/8/32, & CM diary, 1/7/32.

404 Cynthia's new boarding school in Washington, Connecticut. WD.

404 "Clean her up—give her tea and send them home." CM diary, 2/6/32.

404 he was proud to be her stepfather. letter, 5/16/32, Yale, SL.

404 holding him through the night, she succeeded in calming him. CM diary, 3/15/32.

405 "I am trying to make it a perfect house." CM diary, 4/25/32.

405 read his first draft of *Without Endings of Days* to Carlotta. WD, 5/12/32.

405 "I miss her like hell!" 5/22/32, "*Love and Admiration and Respect.*"

405 "When the lease is over," she complained, "it will mean about $10,000 down the drain!" CM diary, 9/2/32.

406 "Mother, you are my lost way refound, my end and my beginning, the hand I reach out for in my lonely night, from my ghost-haunted inner dark, and on your soft breasts there is a peace for me that is beyond death!" 5/25/32, Yale, SL.

406 went to her husband's bedroom and "slept in Gene's arms." CM diary, 5/29 & 5/30/32.

407 on the walls hung old icons and the masks from *The Great God Brown*. A/BG interview with Ann Pinchot, & CM diary, 10/5/32.

407 he had "gone stale on work—thrown off stride by moving and so many distractions." WD, 6/29/32.

408 found the house "quiet and exquisitely clean, with special boxes and bags to keep the mildew out of things and with little colored maids polishing like Dutchmen." IC, *Past Imperfect.*

408 so damp "that special bronze had to be used for all the window hardware, for ordinary metal would rust away." A/BG interview with LL, & *The Magic Curtain.*

409 adding that Fania, "who hated snakes even more than I did, trod very gingerly around the countryside after this, and I was never quite at ease either." Ibid.

409 told O'Neill he had forgotten to duck. A/BG interview with Dempsey.

410 he "secretly cherished the thought that Eugene O'Neill is greater than even Shakespeare." NYT, 4/30/28.

410 "Give it to her!" recorded interview with Herbert Freeman, Tao House Library, Danville, California.

411 "But she's just a titless wonder." Ibid.

411 "She was a good cook . . . but [after that] she didn't like me no more." Ibid.

411 "We went!" CM diary, 8/13/32.

411 he gave in: "no flow—sunk!" WD.

412 surely "the last play they would ever suspect me of writing." 1/14/33, Yale, SL.

412 That past, he said, "possessed a lot which we badly need today to steady us." letter, 5/13/33, Yale, SL.

413 he noted, "revisit Pequot Ave. old time haunts." WD.

414 "I don't want to look at it." CM interview with SP, BA, & A/BG at NYT, 10/2/56.

414 anything from a new pet canary to a brilliant sunrise, or a love letter. CM diary.

414 had known in the 1920s, she added, "could not have written this!" CM diary, 9/29/32.

414 "Great affection for this one," he had noted. WD, 9/29/32.

414 worried that the play was causing "torment and battle with himself." CM diary.

414 Poor darling, he *must always* be *tormented*!" CM diary.

414 "I hope he does not change it." CM diary, 11/6/32.

415 "He sounds more honest than Roosevelt—not so much the slick politician," she remarked to her diary. 10/22/32.

415 "I doubt if the substitution of Democratic crooks and windbags for the Republican brand will put any chicken in anyone's pot." 11/11/32, Yale, SL.

415 "Roosevelt, whatever mistakes he may make, is a man with guts who is honestly facing the facts and acting upon them—no flabby, spineless Hoover!" he wrote to his son. 5/13/33, Yale, SL.

415 "Anything with Yeats, Shaw, A.E. [George William Russell], O'Casey, Flaherty, Robinson in it is good enough for me." Ibid.

415 "but once in a hundred years it comes damn near it—unless *one is blind*." CM diary, 11/12/32.

416 seemed to him "a horrid mess." 11/28/32, *As Ever, Gene.*

416 what he described as a "lovely Christmas with Carlotta." WD.

416 O'Neill was fretting over "something fundamentally wrong" Ibid.

416 decided to abandon it "until, if ever, the right solution of problem dawns—no good thinking any more—pass buck to unconscious—a little inspiration called for here." Ibid.

CHAPTER THIRTY-FOUR

417 (in early April 1933, he had renamed it *An End of Days*.") WD 4/4/33.

417 feared another crack-up. CM diary, 4/6/33.

417 but also as the secular meaning of "without goal." Travis Bogard, an O'Neill scholar, expounds on this wordplay in his *Contour in Time* (Oxford University Press, New York, 1972).

417 "I mean the mystic faith of Catholicism whose symbols seem to me to approach closer than any other symbols to the apprehension of a hidden spiritual significance in human life." 5/1/34, Tao House Collection.

418 all of O'Neill's plays combined had thus far sold 700,000 copies. NY *Daily News* series, 1/24 to 1/30/32.

418 any play following his popular *Electra* was "in a bad spot, no matter how good" it was. letter, 8/8/33, Yale, SL.

418 seriously considering "the advisability of not producing either of the plays." CM diary.

419 before confronting audiences with his dark (and often baffling) religious meditation. 8/7/33, Yale, SL.

419 and strongly influenced by New York. 8/19/33, Texas, SL.

420 any resemblance between his adolescent protagonist and himself, for they were "exact" opposites. letter, Mr. Maxwell, 5/8/45/ Yale, SL.

420 O'Neill substituted "*Ah*" for "*Oh*" because the former sounded more nostalgic. letter, 12/15/33 to AMcG, who gave copy to A/BG.

421 All his characters were, he said, "general types true for any large-small town." Ibid.

421 The play, he later said, "was a sort of wishing out loud." PM, Croswell Bowen, 11/3/46.

421 "The truth," he insisted on more than one occasion, "is that I had no youth." Hamilton Basso, Profiles, Part II, *The New Yorker.*

422 "With deep gratitude and appreciation for all your grand portrayal of Nat Miller has meant to this play—and with the real friendship of one (I hope) regular guy for another!" Notes given to A/BG by RC.

422 "Perhaps it is because I am growing old," he said, "that I begin to look back fondly on my youthful days in a part of the country that was my one real home in those times." *New York Herald Tribune*, 9/9/33.

422 no need for him to "watch a sticky audience react!" A/BG interview with RC.

424 Metro-Goldwyn-Mayer bought the film rights for $75,000. In the film version released by MGM in 1935, Lionel Barrymore was cast as Nat Miller and Essie Miller's wayward bachelor brother Sid was played by Wallace Beery.

424 the most agreeable interview he'd ever conducted. A/BG interview with BA.

426 taken O'Neill to see it a few days after the opening of *Ah, Wilderness!* Ibid.

426 "There sure must have been an artist soul lost to the world in the New Orleans honkey-tonk—or bordello—she came from." 10/18/37, Yale, SL.

426 O'Neill danced her "gaily up and down the long hall of Casa Genotta with a 'bunny hug'—& enjoys himself no end!" CM diary, 10/17/33.

426 "I could have photographed Gene all day if I'd wanted to," said Van Vechten. A/BG interview with CVV.

426 "He'd drop a nickel in the slot and listen blissfully to the damn thing tinkle." A/BG interview with Robert Sisk.

426 "They were no Ezio Pinzas," she said, "but it was amusing to listen to them." A/BG interview with LG.

427 "He couldn't make up his mind whether or not to have the man go back to the Church." A/BG interviews with CM.

427 "He will either reach a big 'Yes'—or go to a much firmer 'NO'!" CM diary, 10/25/33.

427 "It was the Jesuits," said Carlotta, "who finally persuaded him to end the play with the protagonist going back to the Church." A/BG interview with CM.

428 But he must not be forced. notes dated Boston, 1/1/34 copied by A/BG with PM's permission.

428 "He wanted to go that way and find a happiness which apparently he hadn't got and which obviously this perfect marriage doesn't seem to bring him." Ibid.

428 "Gene wrote *Days Without End* because he'd swallowed this guff about love after death." A/BG interview with LL.

428 "And ours has, hasn't it, Darling One!" *Inscriptions.*

429 "I don't say she's divorced, in so many words—and I won't say the husband died; let them draw their own conclusions." A/BG interview with RC, reading from his diary notes.

429 moved to write a staunch endorsement of the play in the Catholic publication *America.* 1/13/34.

430 "Also my play treats adultery seriously—as a sin against love—and how could the first-night intelligentsia of New York countenance that!" to SW, 5/1/34, Tao House Collection.

430 *Days Without End* was his "last flirtation" with Catholicism. A/BG interview with CM.

430 taking pains to point out that all of his past plays, "even when most materialistic," were "in their spiritual implications a search and a cry in the Wilderness protesting against the fate of our own faithlessness." to William E. Brooks, 3/5/34 (private), SL.

430 "Again my gratitude to you all." 1/9/34, NY Public Library, SL.

431 "He equated O'Neill's 'fall' with the fall of Lucifer." A/BG interview with BDC.

431 The two men never spoke again. According to A/BG interview with BDC, two weeks before her husband died in 1945, he told her, "I'm sorry I wrote that about O'Neill."

431 "If a poet like Yeats sees what is in it," said O'Neill, "all my hard work on it is more than justified." A/BG interview with Munsell. *Days Without End* was subsequently produced with considerable success not only in Ireland but also in Holland and Sweden.

431 "The critics didn't understand it and it wasn't any good." as quoted in *Total Recall.*

431 would take up when he did start writing again. A/BG interview with RC.

PART IV: "TIME'S WINGED CHARIOT"

CHAPTER THIRTY-FIVE

435 Blemie, who all but sang with joy on seeing them. CM diary, 1/14, 1/15, 1/19, 1/23 & 1/30/34.

435 and his weight was down to 137 pounds. WD, 2/28 & 3/23/34.

435 she brooded about the "torture of being no longer young." CM diary, 2/11/34.

436 by mid-May, he'd gained fourteen pounds. WD, 5/13/34.

436 he was happy, now, to "forget about work for a time." probably May 1934, Yale, SL.

436 but found "no impulse" to work. WD, 8/10/34.

436 1928, the year the Abbey Theatre rejected his play *The Silver Tassie*. The Abbey finally produced it in 1935.

436 "He and I fell for each other at once—at least I know I fell for him, and I believe he fell for me," O'Casey later said. O'Casey letter to AG.

437 throwing O'Casey and Nathan into gales of laughter. *Redbook*, Aug. 1935.

437 telling him jokes "only two Irishmen can share." O'Casey letter to AG.

437 impressed by the way that O'Neill had finessed his way "back to the Greeks" in *Mourning Becomes Electra*. Ibid.

437 "Gene was so pleased he didn't know what to do." CM interview with SP, NYT.

437 "English critics didn't care for his work; but then they are, I fear, nearsighted, looking at the playfulness of the magpies, but with eyes too weak to watch the soar of an eagle in the upper skies." letters to AG; in 1959, O'Casey responded to BA request for a tribute when a Broadway theater was named in O'Neill's honor. "I am glad," wrote O'Casey, "that in his American soul there was, not only the touch of a poet, but also the touch of an Irishman, for the O'Neills had their origin in Ireland. This great Dramatist of America and the world tells me again that our Shamrock twines a leaf or two around every flower symbolizing each State of O'Neill's great and urgent Country. The Shamrock is an unassuming and humble plant, but it is always there."

438 had been given "everything, more than any other country." excerpt from EO interview published in *PM* and other newspapers, 9/3/46.

439 "The sentence? 'For what shall it profit a man if he shall gain the whole world and lose his own soul?'" *The New Yorker*, Hamilton Basso, Profiles, Part III, 3/13/48.

439 *The Sea-Mother's Son* (that autobiographical saga of the middle-aged man, supine on his deathbed, pondering his origin). O'Neill Collection, Beinecke.

440 who made their often illicit billions in banking, railroading, shipping, and politics. Among O'Neill's research was the recently republished *The Robber Barons—The Great American Capitalists 1861–1901* by Matthew Josephson.

441 Ethan, a sailor, is *Dream of the West*'s first mate. *Calms of Capricorn.*

441 the owner fires him—after which he and Nancy commit suicide. Ibid.

442 "But until you do this," warned O'Neill, "don't expect anything from me except the usual birthday and Christmas presents or you will be disappointed." 6/12/34, Yale, SL.

442 "It is all right for Shane to visit here in the summer, because he is so much more grown than you," O'Neill had written to his eight-year-old daughter in the summer of 1933, "but I am afraid the sudden change to this climate would not be a good thing for you until you are a little older." 6/9/33, SL.

442 while in New York for rehearsals of *Ah, Wilderness!* WD, 9/25/33.

442 would not see her father again for nearly five more years. Herbert Freeman, whose memory was not always reliable, "remembered" a visit from Oona in Sea Island that did not take place, probably confusing it with a visit to the O'Neills' later home in California.

443 "All I can say is both Mr. and Mrs. O'Neill were good to me, as if they'd been my own parents—even better." recorded interview with Freeman, Tao House Library.

443 sought to convince him that his father was not a rich man. CM diary, 1/2/35.

443 "Fine kid!" he commented in his Work Diary. 1/4/35.

443 "How (between us) we could have spent $70,000 this past year!" CM diary, 1/6 & 1/7/35.

443 "He would work on one until he felt he was stuck, get a thought about another one, and work on that." Ibid.

444 writer Sherwood Anderson and his wife, Eleanor. WD, 4/16/35.

444 "You have always been a man I have looked up to as one of the few great figures of the time and I am sorry that I cannot see more of you." 4/24/35, *Letters of Sherwood Anderson*, edited by Howard Mumford Jones and Walter B. Rideout, 1953.

444 "Certainly she is not one of the women who make a house warm." Ibid.

444 "I felt him clinging to me rather pitifully." Ibid.

445 "I've a hunch he is just now a down pin." *Letters of Sherwood Anderson*.

445 "I love him so deeply I pray I can be of some help & comfort to him." CM diary, 5/23/35.

445 on a huge folded bath towel, perspiring into its four thick layers. CM diary, 7/29/35.

445 "Two of the plays take place in New England," he elaborated, "one almost entirely on a clipper ship, one on the Coast, one around Washington [D.C.] principally, one in New York, one in the Middle West." letter, 7/3/35, Yale, SL.

446 until he had completed three plays and written first drafts of the rest. Ibid.

446 "If you keep on going back," Carlotta chided her husband, "you'll get to Adam and Eve." A/BG interview with CM.

CHAPTER THIRTY-SIX

447 she confided to her diary, "though beginning with simple beer . . . step by step, it will reach *Bourbon* & then, *God help Gene—& me!*" CM diary, 7/7/35.

448 "I *want* to believe this." CM diary, 7/8/35.

449 "He sounds either *crazy* or drunk." CM diary.

449 "What, in the name of God, is the matter with the man?" Ibid.

449 "Perhaps I shouldn't have done it!" CM diary, 8/24/35.

449 "Did he want what I had NOW?" Ibid.

450 martyred Agnes in the days when she nursed the hungover O'Neill after drinking binges. CM diary, 8/25/35.

450 "I must have been crazy—but Weinberger keeps hammering at me!" CM diary, 8/30/35.

451 pain that had been troubling him for the past two months, and which he thought originated in his liver. WD, 10/3/35.

451 prayed his discomfort was not being caused by hard liquor. CM diary.

451 a home in Georgia, he had come to hate that as well. 10/29/35.

451 point of not speaking to Carlotta during meals. CM diary, 11/1/35.

451 "I become so self-conscious when these silent moods are on!" CM diary, 11/2/35.

451 noted, three days later, that it needed "to be reconceived." WD.

452   could not bring himself to work for such "an uninteresting, stupid" organization. CM diary, 11/11/35.

452   "He used to say, 'Oh, God, if only some Good Fairy would give me some money, so I'd never have to produce a play, and I could just write, write, write and never go near a theater!" A/BG interview with CM.

452   "It sounds too good to be true!" CM diary, 11/14/35.

452   found her husband sunk in "complete mental lethargy." WD.

453   hosts to the writer Somerset Maugham and his secretary-lover, Gerald Haxton. Ibid.

453   "I didn't see another soul while I was there, but he constantly complained and said he must leave the island because it was so thronged with people." A/BG interview with SNB.

453   found him drinking whiskey out of a bottle. CM diary.

453   had known O'Neill was surreptitiously drinking hard liquor. CM diary, 12/24/35.

454   and repeated the routine the following day. CM diary, 12/25 & 12/26/35.

454   "To Carlotta—on this, her eighth birthday since our elopement—with, again, as ever, my amazed wonder at her forbearance with my blunders and weaknesses, my wondering amazement at her patience with my lost preoccupations and forgetfulness— and last and warmest, my heart's and soul's gratitude for her love, which is this Stranger's only home on this earth!" *Inscriptions.*

454   he had decided to return to a diet of "just wine and beer." CM diary.

455   as keepsakes. O'Neill apparently decided a single braid was souvenir enough. After his death, Carlotta sorted through the contents of a Chinese lacquer box, preparing to send it to the O'Neill Collection at Yale. Among the treasured letters and other memorabilia in the box, she found the single braid. By then she'd forgotten all about her 1936 diary entry describing the impulsive cutting off of the two braids, and felt compelled to invent a story to go with the single braid; it was a tale in which, typically, O'Neill's ardor for her glamorous self was the focal point. She wrote to the curator of the O'Neill collection to describe how one hot day she and O'Neill were gardening on their patio at Casa Genotta, and, when her long hair kept falling in her face, she "pulled it down & made it into a braid—& the braid kept falling into my face! I was *so* annoyed I took the garden shears and *sawed* my braid off close to my head! I was a *sight*! And Gene was *furious*! He flew at me and grabbed what was left of the poor braid." She said he didn't speak to her for twenty-four hours, and then berated her for cutting her hair, which he "had always loved," without consulting him.

456   "Mother of God—now what?" she exclaimed to herself. CM diary, 1/27/36.

456   unable to comb his hair or knot his tie. CM diary.

456   "I am frantic with fear & heartache," scribbled Carlotta. Ibid.

457   the next morning she had herself a haircut, wave, and shampoo. CM diary.

457   found he was "no longer interested, anyway," and "that was finally that." late Dec. 1937, Tao House Library.

458   "Getting nowhere," he recorded on May 31. WD.

458   now looked "as if there would have to be still another play—a ninth which will carry me back to 1770." letter, 6/20/36, Yale, SL.

458   accepting the "slavery of agricultural life" in America. Profiles, Part III, 3/13/48.

458 "I mean," he explained, "I'm not giving a damn whether the dramatic event of each play has any significance in the growth of the country or not, as long as it is significant in the spiritual and psychological history of the American family in the plays." letter, 8/12/36, Yale, SL.

459 "A lady bearing quintuplets is having a debonair, carefree time of it by comparison." Ibid.

459 let it "rest as is" for the time being. WD, 8/21/36.

462 "If a playwright doesn't work up entrances fifteen minutes long for them and have all the other characters describe them in advance as something pretty elegant, noble, chivalrous and handsome, the audiences wouldn't be able to accept them for much more than third assistant barkeeps, if that." *New York Journal-American*, 8/26/46.

CHAPTER THIRTY-SEVEN

466 Winther had published the laudatory work *Eugene O'Neill: A Critical Study* two years earlier, Random House, New York, 1934.

466 asked the Winthers to find them a furnished house. CM diary, 7/15/36, & Sophus Winther Collection, Eugene O'Neill Foundation Research Library at Tao House.

466 after which she fell into a fit of weeping. CM diary, 9/9/36.

466 he grumbled: "Will be glad leave this place—hope we can sell it soon—climate no good for work half of year—and feel am jinxed here." 10/4/36.

466 advised "absolute change—rest—forget work." WD, 10/24/36.

467 administering a series of injections to bolster her weakened condition. CM diary, 10/11 & 10/13/36.

467 O'Neill was already looking and feeling much better. CM diary, 10/31/36.

467 describing it as "comfortable" with "beautiful grounds." WD, 11/3/36.

467 staffed with a housekeeper, cook, and maid. A/BG interview with Eline Winther.

467 President Roosevelt had easily won a second term. CM diary, 11/3/36.

468 didn't care either way, as the prize was "a jinx for [the] middle-aged." WD, 10/27/34.

468 "It isn't easy to protect Gene from all these people." CM diary, 11/12/36.

469 "They'll never want to see another play." interview, *Seattle Daily Times*, 11/12/36.

469 "I thought that wonderful of him considering all the excitement." CM diary, 11/12/36.

470 "He deserves it." AG interview with BA.

470 "In fact, so far, I'm like an ancient cab horse that has had a blue ribbon pinned on his tail—too physically weary to turn round and find out if it's good to eat, or what." "TTWWF."

471 he vilified them as mostly "cheap shit-heels!" 11/25/36, Yale, SL.

471 asserting the award was largely due to O'Neill's "prestige and publicity," which neither the critics nor the public dared to dispute. *Saturday Review of Literature*, 11/21/36.

472 "Who in hell is De Voto?" 12/3/36.

472 "But, we'll just look everywhere and be very sure." *The Magic Curtain*.

473 noted that she was "deeply moved" by her return. 12/18/36.

473 who had removed her appendix seventeen years earlier. letter, CM to KM, 12/31/36, "TTWWF."

473 "A fine pair we are!" sighed O'Neill. WD.

473 once again frantic with worry. letter, CM to KM, 1/20/37, "TTWWF."

474 "This prostate has been kicking up for years." Ibid.

474 O'Neill told Macgowan, "and I want so much to get back on the job." letter, 3/30/37, "TTWWF."

474 that "an abscess in my inside burst and so poisoned me that they had to inject everything but TNT to keep me from passing out for good." 9/14/37, Yale, SL.

474 calculated they were (as always) taking a substantial loss. CM diary.

476 on the final leg of her trip to San Francisco. Wire, 3/1/37, Yale, SL.

476 "Have arranged all for honeymoon at Fairmont including double-bed!" warbled a rejuvenated O'Neill. WD, 2/27/37.

476 "*I am not complete without him!*" CM diary (at stop in Utah), 3/1/37.

476 checked herself into the same hospital for a week's "rest cure." WD, 3/6/37.

477 across the small orchard-filled San Ramon Valley. The house and land are now the Eugene O'Neill National Historic Site, administered by the National Park Service of the U.S. Department of the Interior.

477 eventually exceeded something more than $70,000. according to notes appended to CM diary 1937.

477 looking after him in a San Francisco hotel near the Fairmont. WD, 3/17/37.

477 opium couch. After being sold back to Gump's by the O'Neills when they evacuated Tao House, it was returned as a gift—at the urging of Katharine Hepburn—when Tao House became the Eugene O'Neill National Historic Site.

477 "I wanted to build a Chinese house," Carlotta once explained, "but I didn't have the money, so I built a sort of pseudo-Chinese house." CM interview with A/BG.

478 pain from his prostate condition was sometimes incapacitating. CM diary, 4/30/37.

478 took up his cycle, neglected for the past eight months, as per Dr. Dukes's orders. WD, 6/20/37.

478 "I knew a lot about vaudeville, but he knew more." A/BG interview with SNB.

478 he (at twenty-two) and Jamie, "were drunk all the time because their roles in the production of *The Count of Monte Cristo* were so ridiculous." Ibid.

479 son Eugene's achievement as a Greek scholar at Yale. A/BG interviews with SNB, & SNB diary, 6/27/37.

479 "He made a great impression on me—I loved him." Ibid.

479 "I'll get it this time!" WD, 7/3 & 7/12/37.

479 "Moreover, the climate is one I know I can work and keep healthy in." 9/14/37, Yale, SL.

479 "I go along, hand in hand with Gene—drunk with happiness!" CM diary, 10/6/37.

480 "tao" meaning in Chinese "the right way of life." CM diary, 10/27/37.

480 "The O'Neills had a naive, romantic idea of China—the wisdom, the pageantry and so forth were superficially conceived and romanticized by them." A/BG interview with Mai-mai Sze.

480 for his senior year, in a preparatory school in Colorado that O'Neill deemed pretentious. letter, HW, 9/24/37, Yale, SL.

481 should be attending "a good strict college prep school of the more democratic sort where they expect you to study seriously and fire you if you don't." Ibid.

481 "After that, I am through—and when I say through, I mean through," O'Neill blustered to his lawyer. Ibid.

481 "There is too much greedy parasitic Boulton in their blood—I am afraid—not to add Boulton stupidity in their brains!" Ibid.

482 "During all that time I did not receive one damned line from either you or Oona." (early Oct.?) 1937, Yale, SL.

483 he closed with his own and Carlotta's love. Ibid.

483 during his next spring vacation (almost a year distant). c. 10/16/37, Yale, SL.

483 "We are so tired at bed time we hardly have the strength to crawl up into our beautiful Chinese beds!" noted Carlotta. CM diary.

483 "Gene tells me he loves me & couldn't live without me!!" CM diary, 12/30 & 12/31/37.

CHAPTER THIRTY-EIGHT

484 "Dear God, let this be our real & final home!" 12/28/37, 1/2/38, & 1/12/38.

484 once they were settled and he'd fully regained his health. WD, 1/9/38.

484 if he could manage it "without winding up in the poorhouse." 2/13/38, Yale, SL.

484 seizure of neuritis that rendered his writing arm "practically useless." WD, 1/8 & 1/12/38.

485 she was at a loss for how to help him. CM diary, 2/14 & 1/26/38.

485 ("Hitler raising hell in Europe," Carlotta had exclaimed in her diary a few weeks after moving into Tao House.) CM diary, 2/21/38.

485 "I haven't yet learned to take that extra punishment and go on regardless." letter, 9/27/37, Yale, SL.

486 had him eating corn out of his hand A/BG interview with Charles O'Brien Kennedy.

486 enjoyed playing the old pianoforte in their New London home. Barrett H. Clark, *Eugene O'Neill: The Man and His Plays* (Robert McBride, New York, 1929).

487 turned, in something of a panic, to Harry Weinberger. 9/27/37, Yale, SL.

487 to the cemetery to assess the situation. Ibid.

487 O'Neill's father, who had bought the plot in 1882. 10/21/37, Yale.

487 prices in writing, before ordering the stones? 10/24/37, Yale, Beinecke.

487 stones and installation to total "within five hundred dollars." 11/6/37, Yale, Beinecke.

488 price different grades of granite. 11/15/37, Yale.

488 "It simply follows [the] pattern of [a] cast of characters in a play, which is absolutely appropriate for an actor's family." 3/8/38, Yale, SL.

489 O'Neill disparaged as his "ranch school in Colorado." WD.

489 "What he will eventually do, God knows, but for once in his life he's genuinely self-confident and enthusiastic—about horses and stock-raising, not scholastic pursuits, I might add." letter, April 1938, Yale, SL.

490 "Gene feels better—his brain full of work—thank God." CM diary.

490 pool, which was built into the side of their hill. WD, 5/12/38.

490 "I am no longer silent!" WD, 5/12/38.

490 "[Blemie] says he can't understand it, that something he drank must have disagreed with him." 5/29/38, letter to GJN, *As Ever, Gene.*

491 "Deborah fights Sara for her son's love with charm and subtlety, while Sara fights with her body." A/BG interview with CM.

491 the play was "full of evil." A/BG interview.

491 whispering in his ear, "*You shall not finish this play.*" CM diary, 7/5/38.

491 "Holds me close in his arms—while I weep my heart out." CM diary, 7/14/38.

492 "God give Cyn the strength and the courage to face life with this new burden," Carlotta prayed. CM diary, 7/15/38.

492 "His work eats into him—life itself seems to absorb him." CM diary, 7/27/38.

492 expected to finish a first draft "in another month or two." letter, 8/2/38, California, Yale, SL.

492 wouldn't be "nailed for alimony at the last moment." 4/22/38, Yale, SL.

492 "The look on Gene's face!" she exclaimed. CM diary, 8/18 & 8/20/38.

492 O'Neill characterized "the Communist Party in this country as a foreign-controlled, traitor organization." letter to HW, Yale, SL.

493 "And to an ex-house painter!" CM diary, 9/1/38.

493 "Oh, Politesse! Shame!" noted the old Tory. CM diary, 9/22/38.

493 noting it was "as long as *Strange Interlude!*—but don't think will be able to cut length much." WD, 9/8/38.

493 "*It is frightening!*" CM diary, 9/25/38.

493 "the Hitler jitters" were affecting him. 9/5/38, *As Ever, Gene.*

493 a "sinking spell & flare-up of same old infection—pains in back, fever." WD, 10/12/38.

493 inform her that "all the leg, arm & back pains are caused from the infection in the prostate." CM diary, 10/15/38.

493 "the painful disease can affect the physiological functioning of the penis, and lead to erectile dysfunction." Dr. Katz, author of *Guide to Prostate Health,* is the chairman of urology at Winthrop University on Long Island, where he continues his two decades of research into prostate disease and cure, begun in 1993 at Columbia University's New York–Presbyterian Hospital.

494 work in spurts on *More Stately Mansions.* WD, 10/16/38.

494 "I didn't feel a bit older than that, either." letter shown to A/BG by CVV.

494 "But I *do* know I love this mad Irishman!" CM diary, 12/31/38.

494 it was "psychologically extremely involved and hard to keep from running wild and boiling over." 12/28/38, "TTWWF."

496 "He had made my beauty grotesquely ugly by his presence." Act III, Scene II.

496 "How I prayed that you would die." Act IV, Scene II.

497 began making revisions on the typed manuscript. WD.

499 ("They began operating when I was 5") CM diary, 1/30/39.

499 "He would change a few words and add a few commas and make me type the page over again," she said. A/BG interview with CM.

499 January 30, he accompanied Carlotta to a specialist WD.

499 "He detests being put in any position where *he* must make a *decision* or shoulder any responsibility—*outside his work*!" CM diary, 1/31/39.

499 he had been profoundly worried about her. 2/27/39, *As Ever, Gene.*

500 "God help me!" CM diary, 3/19/39.

500 "I'm struck dumb with surprise and happiness!" CM diary, 3/29/39.

500 "We stood them as long as we could take it, on the theory that bad is better than none, for it isn't so easy to get anyone to work in the country here." 10/5/38, letter to GJN, *As Ever, Gene.*

CHAPTER THIRTY-NINE

501 he yearned for a respite. June 1939, Yale, SL.

501 "I may try writing a single play which is quite outside [the cycle's] orbit." Ibid.

501 "Feel fed up and stale on Cycle after 4½ years of not thinking of any other work," he jotted in his Work Diary. "Will do me good lay on shelf and forget it for a while—do a play which has nothing to do with it." 6/5/39.

501 second play—to be set in New London—he described in his notes as "N. L. family one." WD, 6/6/39.

502 made him feel "there was not enough recognizable future in sight to go on with something that might take four or five more years." letter, 3/25/41, copied from from Mrs. Hamilton's collection.

502 ideas for both plays had been brewing "for years." letter, 10/13/40, Beinecke.

504 "The dump in the play," he once confided to Kenneth Macgowan, was "no one place, but a combination of three in which I once hung out." letter, 12/15/40, "TTWWF."

505 Gorky's inn, in *A Night's Lodging*, was "an ice cream parlor." New York *World*, 11/9/24, by Charles P. Sweeney.

505 the building "was almost coming down, and the principal house-wreckers were vermin." NYT, 12/21/24, by LK.

505 "The realization of this should exalt, not depress." *Theater*, June 1924, "Eugene O'Neill—The Inner Man," by Carol Bird.

506 "An ache in our hearts for things we can't escape!" CM diary.

506 outline of *Long Day's Journey Into Night* in just one week. WD, 7/3/39.

506 day before O'Neill began developing his *Iceman* characters. CM diary, 7/10/39.

506 "Thank God, Gene *didn't* start *drinking again*!" CM diary.

506 "If you and I could only go to sleep together and *never* wake up." CM diary, 7/12/39.

506 began writing the dialogue for Act I of *Iceman*. WD, 7/13/39.

507 "Nor as a son." letter to HW, 2/27/39.

507 "You will be what you make yourself and you have got to do that job absolutely alone and on your own." 7/18/39, Yale, SL.

507 written to Shane without "the usual fatherly crap." Virginia, 7/22/39, SL.

508 "Elizabeth the *first* was a nice girl! I hope Sally the *third* will last!" CM diary, 6/8/39.

508 disparaged her as "a stalwart stout young woman" of "an all-too-familiar Connecticut small-city type." 9/10/39, Yale, SL.

508 "With a baby, no money & no profession!" CM diary, 8/25/39.

509 cursed him in disgust as "a ham actor!" WD.

509 had "a queer feeling that all this is really the beginning of the end of all happiness for me!" CM diary.

509 "No sleep." 9/2/39.

509 Oona joined her, looking "very much amused," as Carlotta later reported their conversation. CM diary, & A/BG interview with CM.

509 "She is 14!" Ibid.

509 "I'm going to marry a rich man.'" A/BG interviews with CM.

510 "Spengler was right." WD, 9/3/39.

510 "Oona's visit disturbed him because he felt (as a dramatist!) she had been rehearsed in how she was to act with him—she was not herself!" CM diary, 9/3/39.

510 not only intelligent, but "really a charming girl, both in looks and in manners." 9/10/39, Yale, SL.

510 found Shane's sister "loveable." Ibid.

510 "now a patriarch of twelve but still going strong." 10/1/39, Cornell, SL.

511 "Every time I think of making that trip East to face casting, rehearsals and all the rest of the game, I feel a great bored weariness and reluctance, as if I'd had quite enough of that for one life." Ibid.

511 it had "flowed right along, page after page," as he later told an interviewer for *The New York Times*. interview with Karl Schriftgiesser, 10/6/46.

511 smashed her knee in an auto accident. WD, & CM diary, 10/20/39.

511 would be hospitalized for many weeks and would "probably be lame." CM diary, 10/20 & 10/30/39.

511 a symbol she continued to draw from time to time during the next several years. CM diary.

512 after a session of pillow talk, he "remains all night!" CM diary, 11/17/39.

512 declaring it "one of [the] best plays I've ever written!" WD.

512 "I couldn't let this play be done without being there every minute, and I simply don't feel up to that ordeal now." letter, 10/16/41, Tao House Library.

512 happy reminder to them both of a brief remission from prostatitis. envelope and note reproduced in *Inscriptions*.

513 likened the play's lunges into the labyrinthine dark to "getting in an elevator and going down to the basement, thinking that's as far as you can go, and then one night you get in and see there are three more buttons leading to sublevels you hadn't seen before." NYT, 6/17/12.

514 modeled (in part) on Jimmy the Priest's. WD, 5/7/39.

514 "But never until a year or so ago, did it take definite line and form as a play in my mind, its many life histories interwoven around a central theme." 2/8/40, Cornell, *As Ever, Gene*.

515 all of them were "drawn from life, more or less." Ibid.

515 "All these people I have written about I once knew." EO interview with Karl Schriftgiesser, NYT, 10/6/46.

515 they were "free of social hypocrisy." interview with Mary B. Mullett, *The American Magazine*, Nov. 1922.

CHAPTER FORTY

517 "The actor playing Hickey is pure gold." AG, at that time a member of Atkinson's staff, was present.

519 who used to "make that typical drummer crack about the iceman, and wept maudlinly over his wife's photograph, and in other moods, boozily harped on the slogan that honesty is the best policy." letter, 2/8/40, Cornell, SL.

520 "He is all of them, you might say, and none of them." letter, 12/20/40, "TTWWF."

520 not to mention Hickman's first name, Theodore. "The 'Genius' as Iceman: Eugene O'Neill's Portrayal of Theodore Dreiser," *American Literary Realism*, Winter 2002, by Brenda Murphy, professor of English at Connecticut University.

521 she had "nagged him to death and he was relieved when she died." Beinecke.

524 Parritt, like Hickey, has his "background of fact," as O'Neill once explained in an interview in *The New York Times*. 10/6/46.

525 whom Goldman pitied for having raised "that cur." Emma Goldman's monthly magazine *Mother Earth*, Jan. 1916, "Donald Vose: The Accursed."

526 a tribute to Carlin, who died in 1934. letter, CM to KM, 2/14/34, "TTWWF."

526 exorcising O'Neill's DTs. A/BG interviews with CM & various Village friends, including JL & JJM.

528 "My private office in the shop was stocked with wines and imported cigarettes: but I was not so well off as in my happy slum." *An Anarchist Woman*. (Duffield, New York, 1909).

528 he had never met a man he could not teach, he told Kirkman. Ibid.

529 "I hire no spiritual nurse," said Jim. Ibid.

530 "It takes an eagle to soar with a heavy weight in its grasp." Ibid.

530 desperate woman friend who was weighing the choice between domestic drudgery and street walking. Ibid.

CHAPTER FORTY-ONE

532 apt to announce Polly's customers as "bourgeois pigs." A/BG interview with JL.

533 "hot" diamonds, which she pawned whenever she and Joe were hard up. A/BG interviews with NW, JL, & JJM.

533 jotted an idea for a one-acter—"Pig of the Hell Hole play." O'Neill notebook entry, 2/3/42, Beinecke.

535 tickets to Broadway performances of plays by Yeats, Synge, Lady Gregory, and Lennox Robinson. The six-month tour began 11/20/11 at Maxine Elliott Theater, West 35th St., with cast led by Sara Algood, Maire O'Neill, Cathleen Nesbitt, Arthur Sinclair, and J. M. Kerrigan.

535 "I thought then and I still think that they demonstrated the possibilities of naturalistic acting better than any other company." Charles Merrill, Boston *Sunday Globe*, 7/8/23.

537 native exhibitionist had plagued a friend's nursemaid on the same beach where Shane swam. SD 1925.

538 analyses of the play was provided by Dudley Nichols in a letter to Irving Hoffman, letter copied by Hoffman for A/BG.

538 "'No, but he's breathin' hard.'" Ibid.

539 "So, when he finally had to kill her, knowing he had to be true to his own nature and go off to Harry's saloon for a shot of Hope, a big drunk and a week with the tarts and bums, he first had to cook another pill of opium and grab the beautiful pipe dream that he was killing her for love—so she wouldn't suffer any longer from his incurable debauchery." Ibid.

540 "No one has even penetrated what reality is." Ibid.

540 Professor Day notes, "the three whores correspond in number to the three Marys, and sympathize with Hickey as the three Marys sympathize with Christ." *Modern Drama*, May 1958; Day was Professor of English at the University of Delaware.

540 "for example, the emphasis on midnight (see Matthew 25:5–6) as the hour appointed for Harry Hope's party, and the unnecessarily large number of derelicts in Hope's saloon." Ibid.

541 "You would find if I did not build up the complete picture of the group as it now is in the first part—the atmosphere of the place, the humor and friendship and human warmth and deep inner contentment of the bottom—you would not be so interested in these people and you would find the impact of what follows a lot less profoundly disturbing." 12/30/40, "TTWWF."

542 "repetition to reveal progressively more of his characters and situations." A/BG interviews with JQ.

542 "There's no life or kick in it now." Harry Hope, p. 678; Hope, p. 680; Chuck, p. 682; Rocky, p. 684; Hope p. 689; Hope, p. 691; Hope, p. 692 (page numbers, *Complete Plays— 1932–1943*, Library of America).

542 "O'Neill was too dedicated an artist with too great a sense of purity to use anything, including repetition, as a meaningless mechanical device." A/BG interviews with JQ.

CHAPTER FORTY-TWO

543 hang over his head and fill him with dread. CM diary, 1/1/40.

543 it would "have to be written in blood." 1/5/40.

543 overwhelmed by the burden of work it still demanded, he let it go; WD, 1/6/40.

544 "(I'm enjoying one right now—am writing this in bed)." 2/8/40, Cornell, *As Ever, Gene.*

544 he was "too low physically now for long stretch work." WD, 3/3/40.

544 had no choice but to succumb to his ailing body. WD, 3/8/40.

544 adapted from *S.S. Glencairn*, and that he was calling *The Long Voyage Home*, WD, 4/7/40.

544 "Like them both a lot." 2/12/40.

545 "Go on and make a fine picture if you're that nuts!" Yale, SL.

545 confessing he had "no ambition for work" WD, 5/8/40.

545 doctors advised a "stronger schedule of shots, one a day for 3 weeks, give it real try-out." WD, 5/17/40.

546 "This war is hitting us where we belong, so to speak." 6/15/40, Cornell, SL.

546 "Well, although I hate Nazism as bitterly as anyone, I can never do that in my work." Ibid.

546 "If it cannot exist as the unique whole I conceived, then I don't want it to exist at all."
     Ibid.

547 recognized the futility of brooding about "the future of individual freedom." WD, &
     CM diary.

547 he reread his first draft of Act I. WD, 6/25 & 6/26/40.

547 "At the final curtain, there they still are, trapped within each other by the past, each
     guilty and at the same time innocent, scorning, loving, pitying each other, under-
     standing and yet not understanding at all, forgiving but still doomed never to be able
     to forget." 6/15/40, *As Ever, Gene.*

547 almost nonstop for the next four months. WD, & A/BG interviews with CM.

548 *"He can turn on the charm* as he can turn on the sadistic cruelty—he recognizes no law,
     no God, and doesn't know what 'playing the game' means—unfortunately he hurts
     himself more than others!" 7/17/40.

548 "There is love that does not die, and there is your [inked silhouette of a pussycat]
     which is the most beautiful [silhouette of pussycat] in the world—so what the hell!"
     7/22/40, *Inscriptions.*

548 dealing with the "present world collapse & dictatorships," which would be "timely
     but timeless spiritually." WD, 8/15/40.

548 he described as a "timeless, timely ventriloquist play." WD, 8/17/40, & Memoranda ff
     8/31/40 entry.

548 a "duality of Man play—Good—Evil, Christ—Devil—begins Temptation on Mount—
     through to Crucifixion—Devil a modern power realist—symbolical spiritual con-
     flict today and in all times." WD, 8/30/40.

549 his real family, tracing, as she recalled, "their true relationships one to the other,"
     scrutinizing "their idiosyncrasies & disloyalties!" CM diary, 8/25/40.

549 what it had cost him "in strength & emotion to write it!" WD, 9/20/40 & CM diary,
     9/20/40.

549 had definitely decided to expand to eleven plays. WD, 10/18/40 to 10/31/40.

549 "I rate myself the most fortunate of men." letter, 10/29/40, Yale, SL.

550 "is a type of Broadway sport I and my brother used to know by the dozen in far-off
     days." letter, EO to GJN, 6/19/42, *As Ever, Gene.*

551 "She would tell Gene stories and gossip, and Gene would encourage her to talk."
     A/BG interviews with CM.

551 performed the play (in his words) "on and off everywhere for thirty-two years." A/BG
     interview with Robards.

551 "Poor Darling—no proper upbringing, no love, no tenderness, no discipline, no real
     care of any kind—oh, I can understand so many things now!" CM diary, 10/24 &
     11/18/40, & interview with A/BG.

551 "I have *never* been so disturbed by any piece of writing before! . . ." CM diary, 11/20 &
     11/21/40.

551 "*Long Day's Journey Into Night* absorbing all of my thought—& what an insight into
     the very soul of Gene!" CM diary, 11/23 & 11/24/40.

551 "I take blankets & lie on the floor with him—Give him aspirin—." CM diary, 11/19/40.

552 "He sleeps—which allows me to." CM diary.

552 "I have tried all my known remedies." Ibid.

552 I think it is thro' terror that *'Mama' isn't there to give him care* & protection!" CM diary, 12/7/40.

552 she added, "it more than 'upsets' me!" 12/16/40.

552 found him, in the early morning, sunk into a coma. CM diary, 12/17/40.

553 "—loved him for 11 years—a finer friend than most friends!" WD, 12/17/40.

553 Carlotta and O'Neill planned a headstone. CM diary, 12/18/40.

554 "It was *Blemie* we loved, not the *dog*!" Carlotta once pronounced. 3/2/41, Theater Scrapbooks of Carlotta Monterey.

554 "Never have written about Italian-Americans although in past have known many of them as close friends." WD, 1/26 & 2/11/41.

554 two earlier concepts, "Time Grandfather Was Dead," WD, 1/20, 2/15, & 2/16/41.

554 along with "The Thirteenth Apostle." WD, 2/5 & 2/7/41.

555 "Like this play better than any I have written—does most with the least—a quiet play—and a great one, I believe," 3/30/41.

555 "'I fell in love with James Tyrone and was so happy for a time.'" SW letter to Travis Bogard, 3/14/80, Tao House Library.

555 "He tells me why he hated his brother in his later years!" CM diary, 5/18/41.

556 "the 'inscription' showed what his mood was when writing it—and what hell he went through!" 11/6/55, Yale.

557 "This is the real story," A/BG interview with ESS.

558 ongoing warm friendship (recorded in letters and diaries) with the young actress Elizabeth Robins. Robins's diary & letters, Fales.

559 "I was glad when he died." 1939 draft, Beinecke.

559 changing into "an alien demon." EO's notes, Beinecke.

CHAPTER FORTY-THREE

561 "My heart aches so I can hardly breathe!" 5/2/41.

562 recalling Shane's visit in 1940. 1/23/45, Yale, SL.

562 couldn't even support himself, let alone a wife. CM diary, 5/20/40.

562 "You have got to go it alone, without help, or it won't mean anything to you." 10/25/40, Virginia, SL.

563 done so little to make himself independent. 4/18/41, Yale, SL.

564 seek out and marry rich and/or famous older men. A/BG interviews with Gloria Vanderbilt & Carol Marcus.

564 blamed her "damned N.Y. school—or maybe she's just at silly age." WD, 7/18/41.

564 clipping sent him by Harry Weinberger. CM diary, 5/9/42.

565 no wish to see or hear from her "until she has proved she has come out of this silly, brainless stage." letter, EO to HW, 5/12/42, Yale, SL.

566 too weak "to face the world and the war—or, for that matter, to face oneself in any world of decent values—in short, pure Boultonism." letter, 9/28/42, Yale, SL.

566 "considering sickness & war strain," WD, 11/13/42.

566 despite his disapproval of its contents. *Thirst* was published by Gorham Press, Boston, Aug. 1914.

567 It could, wrote O'Neill, "be strange combination comic-tragic—am enthused about it." WD, 10/28 & 10/29/41.

567 "He can never be replaced!" CM diary, 11/1/41.

568 "I never in my long and varied experience, have come across such tactless, thick skinned people." 4/24/30, "TTWWF."

568 insisting she was "a woman of no morals." A/BG interview with RR.

569 used the word *Eskimo* as code for *Jew*. A/BG interview with Carmen Capalbo, who directed the premier on Broadway of *A Moon for the Misbegotten*, in 1957; also SC & KM.

569 "This may sound mean, Mr. Francis," wrote O'Neill, "but I have had too many dealings with Jews, and millionaire Jews, too, in the theatrical business not to trust one of them any farther than I could throw your store with my little finger." 3/8/19, Conn. College.

569 "All he sent was a lousy $200—which is no way to treat me even if he is a Jew." 2/6/25.

569 "Kahn, I think, is a two-faced tin-horn Kike whom you can trust not to double cross you about as far as a worm can walk on its hands." letter to KM, 4/28/26, "TTWWF."

569 an agent "has a rich Jew in tow who seems to mean business." 9/8/37, Harvard, SL.

569 "the damned Jew changed his mind." 9/13/27, Harvard, "*Wind.*"

570 "When you live through the play you write, you have to have a lot of reserve life on tap." 4/28/41, Yale, SL.

570 the addition of "A" and "for" rendered the title "much more to [the] point." WD, 11/3 & 11/12/41.

571 "It was terrible to see him come out of his study, shaken and miserable," Carlotta later recalled. A/BG interviews with CM.

571 convinced it was "unnecessary to rub it in." Ibid.

571 "We talked and talked for the rest of the night." Ibid.

572 "I couldn't stand to see my child so miserable." interview with CM at NYT with SP, BA, & AG.

572 "Maybe not physically—but all the best of me that loves you—and that you love." CM diary, 12/20/41.

572 "Parkinson's very bad," he wrote in his Work Diary. "Can't control pencil this a.m.—also [tremor] in upper arm & shoulder—not so good, this progress!" 12/30/41.

573 made it "impossible for him to write 85% of the time." CM diary, 12/31/41.

573 "This man beside me, my husband & my child!" Ibid.

574 "But I better stop or I'll be writing you a brand new farce." 8/24/41, SL.

574 that they would have to leave Tao House. CM diary, 3/11/42.

574 "*We are now alone!*" CM diary.

574 declared himself ready to "hop right out of my skin." WD, 12/28 & 12/30/42.

CHAPTER FORTY-FOUR

575 after he was drafted into the army in 1942. A/BG interview with Elizabeth Murray.

576 was put off with an excuse by Carlotta. A/BG interviews with Carol Marcus.

576 answered his daughter with a letter designed "to knock her ears down." 12/3/42, Yale, SL.

577 "If I am right, you will sometime see the point in this letter and be grateful—in which case, au revoir." 11/19/42, Conn. College.

577 was to be no au revoir. A/BG interview with Carol Marcus.

577 "If she has any latent guts or pride, it may have a good effect in the long run when she eventually realizes what a nitwit public nuisance she has been." letter, 12/3/42, Yale, SL.

578 Carol feared she couldn't meet his literary standards. Ibid.

578 "But I knew that Bill hated liars more than anything else," recalled Carol, "so I didn't tell him." Ibid.

579 Chaplin understood. A/BG interview with JL.

579 agreed with Carlotta, who remarked, "They must be up to no good!" CM diary, 1/25/43.

580 friend "told us stuff he knew from a friend who had an apartment right under the one A. had rented in her name where Chaplin hid out—drunken parties, etc. . . . a nice thoroughly Hollywood affair!" 6/30/43, *"Love and Admiration and Respect."*

580 such a fool as "to give up her father's love and friendship—for the cheapness & vulgarity she looks upon as glamour & worldliness!" CM diary, 6/10/43.

581 "God—what a life!" CM diary.

581 You could have cut the gloom with a knife," he recalled. "The End of a Long Journey," unpublished ms. by Thalia Brewer.

581 were "filled with usual filth & nonsense." CM diary, 6/17/43.

582 "Enough is enough!" 6/19/43, Yale, SL.

582 "Nor do I—of course." CM diary, 6/27/43.

582 "We hold tight and weep—like two sick and frightened children!" CM diary, 6/28/43.

582 predicted an "Oona Chaplin divorce." 1/23/45, Yale, SL.

585 she "does the cooking, and I wipe the dishes." WD, 4/21 & 4/25/43. A copy of "Mrs. O'Neill's Book" was presented to the grateful authors by Diane Schinnerer, who played a major role in the creation of the Tao House Library.

585 "We are both *terrified* of the future!" CM diary.

585 "Dear God, if I am ever able to get all the responsibilities & hard labor of this place off my shoulders—I'll be a new human being." CM diary, 1/10/43.

586 one page during three hours of writing before "fading out." WD, 1/31/43.

586 it was "no go . . . would ask any Jap to kill me, and many thanks for the favor." WD.

586 "Eager but little done because nerves jumping out of hands, arms, can't control." Ibid.

586 "Five rooms—none for servants—just Freeman—no ground other than a pool for Gene, easy to keep up—small expense—!" CM diary, 3/30/43.

586 "He should have warmth, ocean and sand (!), doctors and good nourishment." Theresa Helburn quoting (to A/BG) from CM letter.

586 "Even *he* can't re-read it!" Carlotta exclaimed. CM diary, 5/25/43.

587 found her husband "in his study doubled up in his work chair—his tremor ghastly & he is weeping!" CM diary, 8/8/43.

587 broke down again, weeping and shaking. 8/24/43.

587 herself close to collapse. CM diary, 8/25/43.

587 to a sleeping medicine called hyoscine. CM diary, 10/7/43.

587 "You can have no idea what a loathsome beverage this is . . . you may get a grin from the picture of me absorbing salt water highballs." letter, 9/25/43, *As Ever, Gene*.

587 "I tell him we both love each other—so we must work *together* to *protect that love* and keep it." CM diary, 10/6/43.

587 "So that I could feel *he was there*, behind me—as I have always been with him." CM diary, 10/17/43.

588 "she could always jolly him in various ways." A/BG interviews with JC.

588 "We must get *back* . . . into a living life . . . here, with no help—so many worries—ill health—everything wrong—it is like waiting for death!" CM diary, 10/24/43.

588 revisions to Cynthia, who obediently typed them. CM diary, 11/30/43.

588 "We had luck—found a buyer quickly—got out at a good price—what we put into it," O'Neill reported to Nathan. letter, 3/6/44, *As Ever, Gene*. The price of $80,000 is confirmed by a note appended to CM diary 1944.

589 more than seven thousand books. CM diary, 2/10/44.

589 "because our Chinese beds are gone!" CM diary, 2/16/44.

589 "Every time I void I pass blood—the pain is *horrible*." 2/19/44.

589 in such pain she could eat no dinner. CM diary.

CHAPTER FORTY-FIVE

590 has to be nursed by the faithful Kaye Albertoni. CM diary, 2/26, 3/3, & 3/4/44.

590 "I only hope he knew the depth of my affection for him—and I feel sure he did." letter, 3/6/44 (begun 3/5/44), *As Ever, Gene*.

590 notes that he is "in a shocking state." CM diary, 3/5/44.

591 feel "all over your body until even your brain seems to do the shimmy." 5/13/44, Yale, SL.

591 "It really was quite a moment of strange drama." Ibid.

592 no other process by which he can write. A/BG interview with CM.

592 failed to regain her strength by the end of March. CM diary, 3/25/44.

592 "Keeping up the ridiculous fantasy that this is a home!" CM diary, 4/1, 4/18, 4/29, & 5/10/44.

594 three months before the Allied invasion of Normandy. letter, 3/6/44, *As Ever, Gene*.

595 she does not have "a good feeling, watching them." A/BG interview with KA.

595 exaggerates his illness to keep people away from him. Ibid., & interview with JC for Ric Burns documentary, *O'Neill*, cowritten by Burns and A/BG.

595 might have been "a forerunner of what was going to come." interview with JC for *O'Neill*.

595 "You are a good child—and I love you!" copy of snapshot given to A/BG by JC.

596 sung "with upturned eyes by a well-stewed waiter endowed with the proper adenoids, it positively wrung you to pieces!" 5/20/45, SL.

596 "And I laugh and laugh—I bend over with laughter." interview with JC for *O'Neill*.

596 "If my mother senses it, Carlotta should; but she doesn't." A/BG interviews with JC, & Ibid.

597 "large bedroom" that she never enters "unless asked." CM diary, 5/20/44.

597 work "is his *love*, his *passion*, his *integrity*, his *joy*, his *achievement!*" CM diary, 5/21/44.

597 "God, I wish I could drink a bottle of 'Old Taylor.'" CM diary, 8/6/44.

597 accuses her of "not being interested in his work." CM diary, 8/29/44.

598 "his hands are so unsteady that he writes the inscriptions with one hand helping the other to hold the pen." A/BG interview with KM.

598 Gotham Hotel on Fifth Avenue in Manhattan for November 14. CM, 7/31 & 9/16/44.

598 "Has even mentioned South Africa—& Mexico!" CM diary.

598 We can't go East until spring," a resigned Carlotta tells her diary, "winter too danger-ous for us." 10/8/44.

599 next pet bird would be a buzzard. letter, 10/19/44, Yale, SL.

599 "Nor would any woman be—" CM diary, 10/24 & 10/25/44.

599 accompany them to Georgia after his discharge from the Marines. CM diary, 11/17 & 11/28/44.

600 "Only fools with more money than brains ever live in resorts." 9/8/36, Eugene O'Neill Foundation, Tao House Library.

600 "It's an exhausted, horrible apathy." 12/4/44, Yale, SL.

600 emphatically plump pussycat at the bottom of her diary entry. *Inscriptions*, & CM diary, 12/28/44.

601 regarding both Janie and Myrtle. In 1951, two years before O'Neill's death, Carlotta had sent all her unedited diaries to Donald C. Gallup, curator of The Yale Collection of American Literature, who read and catalogued them; Carlotta asked for them back in 1954, telling Gallup she wished to copy them in "eternal" black ink on rag paper. Read-ing the rewritten diaries after Carlotta returned them five years later to Yale's Beinecke Rare Book and Manuscript Library, Gallup found that the only "substantial changes" she'd made were in the omissions of "an occasional comment on their love-making ses-sions." (*Pigeons on the Granite*.)

Her diary for 1944 turned up among the papers that Gallup bequeathed to the Beinecke on his death in 2000 (and made available by Yale to the authors in 2012).

There's a mystery about the years beyond 1944. According to Yale, there are no Car-lotta Monterey diaries at the Beinecke for the six turmoil-rocked years of 1945 through 1950 (except for a fragmentary diary Carlotta kept in 1948); there are, however, diaries for 1951 (the most horrendous year of the O'Neill marriage) and 1953 (the year of O'Neill's death)—but no diary for 1952.

Perhaps only Gallup knew the answer to the mystery of the absent diaries; his ambig-uous relationship with Carlotta, evolving over the years, was cemented when she became O'Neill's facilitator in all transactions between himself and Yale. Gallup assumed the role of Carlotta's liaison, guardian, adviser, and protector in her dealings with the Beinecke; he so ingratiated himself with her that she ultimately permitted him to partic-ipate in the "completion" of two of O'Neill's cycle plays, and he made use of her intimate revelations over the years in several books he wrote after her death.

For reasons known only to Carlotta herself (and possibly to Gallup), she gave in to his personal care—rather than to the Beinecke—her diaries for 1944, 1951, and 1953, and the partial diary for 1948. "I am glad you mentioned the diaries which you entrusted to me personally," Gallup wrote to Carlotta on Dec. 22, 1960, making no reference to why she had done so. "I think it will be best if I send you a note of their dates and then you write me saying that they are to be in my custody; then there'll be no problem so far as the Library is concerned." He added that he had the diaries "locked up in a steel filing cabinet" in his apartment. (Donald C. Gallup Archive, The Beinecke Rare Book and Manuscript Library, Yale University, 1988.)

Following Gallup's instructions, Carlotta signed the note he'd written for her, in which she declared she was entrusting the diaries to "the personal custody of Donald C. Gallup" and stating he was aware of her "wishes concerning them and is solely responsible for their eventual disposition." (*Pigeons on the Granite*, etc.) The note is typewritten, but there can be no doubt about the unmistakable flourishes of Carlotta's trademark signature; it is, however, significant to note that during that same year she was hospitalized with a nervous breakdown. Gallup attached the note to the diaries, which ultimately found their way into the Beinecke's archives.

A cursory examination of the hodgepodge of often illegible notes and letters in Gallup's archives concerning Carlotta provides no clue to the absence of diaries for the years 1945, 1946, 1947, 1949, 1950, or 1952; and according to Yale University's librarian, Susan Gibbons, there's no recorded explanation in any of their archives for the missing diaries.

The question is, did Carlotta not keep diaries during those years? If not, why? Or, did she keep and then destroy them? It would be premature to conclude they're nonexistent, for they might exist among someone's private papers and will come tumbling out of an attic one day, as did the long "lost" O'Neill one-act *Exorcism* in 2012.

601 **"Of life's forgotten mystery."** The thirty-five-line poem, entitled "To a Stolen Moment" and dated June 29, 1945, ends: "The magic of love was there / For me / And you / Standing there . . . With the sea and sky in your eyes, / And the sun and wind in your hair."

602 **"If the ocean washes us away right now, it would be okay," she remembers thinking.** A/BG interview with JC.

602 **"If I'd known how to handle it, I might've—I don't know what I would've done—I didn't want—he was older, he was older, he was older—"** Ibid.

602 **"It doesn't mean anything."** A/BG interview with JC.

602 **"I couldn't take care of him; I mean, I wasn't about to."** Ibid.

602 **"His eyes, and the beauty of speech he had—his laughter, his dancing, I loved to dance with him."** Ibid.

603 **but only to run down Janie.** A/BG interview with JC.

603 **she herself never called O'Neill by his first name.** A/BG interview with KA.

603 **later notices O'Neill's slightly puffy right hand.** Ibid.

604 **"He told me I needn't be sorry, he had a hundred people waiting for the canceled space."** A/BG interviews with CM, & SP interview.

605 **"I have to fake an interest."** 9/16/45, *As Ever, Gene*, SL.

605 **Carlotta can't wait to get back.** A/BG interviews with CM.

PART V: UNRAVELING

CHAPTER FORTY-SIX

609 Greeks and Elizabethans, who "saw their lives ennobled" by the tragic. EO to Malcolm Mollan (probably Dec.), 1921, Conn. College, SL.

610 "On the contrary, in spite of my scars, I'm tickled to death with life!" letter to Mary Clark, EO's Gaylord nurse, 8/5/23, Yale, SL.

610 "If he ever thinks for a moment that he is a success then he is finished." Flora Merrill, NY *World*, 7/19/25.

610 "If a person is to get the meaning of life, he must learn to like the facts about himself—ugly as they may seem to his sentimental vanity—before he can lay hold on the truth behind the facts; and that truth is never ugly!" Mary B. Mullett, *The American Magazine*, 1922.

610 "doing wonders in bringing him back" to physical and spiritual health. A/BG interview with LL.

611 and also "*rent a small* place in Sea Island or wherever Gene wants to go." 12/18/45, Eugene O'Neill Foundation, Tao House Library.

611 to be followed at the beginning of 1947 by either *A Moon for the Misbegotten* or *A Touch of the Poet.* 1/1/46, "TTWWF."

612 "There is only empty air now where I came into this world," he quipped. PM, John S. Wilson, 9/3/46.

612 "Once in a while," Aronberg recalls, "Gene will take a sip of a drink just for appearances." A/BG interview with Winfield Aronberg.

612 O'Neill does not contradict him. Ibid.

612 ignoring his own virtual abandonment of his son. 5/7/45, Yale, SL.

613 "A typical pure Irish family." Ibid.

613 "He has a background all torn apart, without inner or outer decency." Ibid.

613 O'Neill responds, "Tell Shane to call me, I'd like to see him." *The Curse of the Misbegotten.*

614 she visits the King Street flat, bringing a complete layette for the baby. Ibid.

614 "None of us commented much on her views of jazz." Ibid.

615 to assist him with cash and legal help. A/BG interview with CM.

615 "And I have always felt that we should be, and would be friends—(not that you haven't proved very much of a friend already as far as my work is concerned!)—if my good fortune should ever be to meet you." 2/21/26, Harvard, SL.

616 compensate just a bit for their still painful loss of Blemie. A/BG interviews with CM, Eline Winther, SW, & other friends.

616 demands that the set be removed the next day. A/BG interview with SWL.

616 "Here's for a new beginning!" *Inscriptions*, 7/22/46.

617 "We'll have to wait until they bury this fellow and the world gets more back on keel before I'll allow this play to be done." Dowling's Oral History, Columbia University.

618 "I'll tell you, Eddie, when I need you." Ibid.

620 the real bums lunch along with the actors as O'Neill's guests. A/BG interviews with Dowling.

621 warmth and admiration for his accomplishments as a scholar. Ibid.

621 "He changed suddenly; he grew a beard, a fat belly from drinking and became a Communist," she later recalled. A/BG interviews with CM.

621 tried to get into the OSS (predecessor of the CIA) but was rejected. A/BG interview with Frank Meyer.

622 "What would have interested me would have been to show the importance of Oratory in Cicero's time and the period in our history when the orations, not speeches, of our Senators had a comparable importance—the pre–Civil War period of Webster, Hayne, Calhoun, etc." 8/13/44, Yale, SL.

622 "'Why don't you go into the bedroom?'" A/BG interview with CM.

623 "We might not make any money, considering that most of our friends would open charge accounts and lovably forget them, but it would be a great sensation again to eat up the free lunch." *New York Journal-American*, 8/26/46.

625 despite his "great good fortune to earn over two million dollars by dramas greater or lesser." ESS deposited her compiled observations at Beinecke, labeling them "Casual Notes on O'Neill the Writer."

CHAPTER FORTY-SEVEN

629 entertained a crowd of friends in his dressing room instead of resting. A/BG interview with LL, & *The Magic Curtain*.

629 "To Lawrence Langner, The hell with your cuts!" Ibid.

631 "The truth is, about *The Iceman Cometh*, all kinds of things are happening all the time, but you have to listen and watch, and you hear repetition because that is the way O'Neill planned it, so that you cannot miss his meaning, and the emotions generated by his drama." copy of undated letter from Nichols to his friend Irving Hoffman of the *Hollywood Reporter*, given to A/BG.

632 soon "became aware that its length was indispensable to its power, its fullness of passion." A/BG interview with Tennessee Williams, and "Founding Father: O'Neill's Correspondence with Arthur Miller and Tennessee Williams" by Dan Isaacs, *The Eugene O'Neill Review*, Spring/Fall 1993 (Isaacs credits an article, "Concerning Eugene O'Neill," published in Souvenir Program for first production of *More Stately Mansions* at Center Theater Group, L.A., Sept. 1967).

632 "O'Neill gave birth to the American theater and died for it." A/BG interview with Tennessee Williams. The *Times* reporter was Arthur Gelb, then chief cultural reporter for the *Times* and at the time researching the 1962 biography *O'Neill*.

632 slate-gray dress "much like that of a very proper housemaid," noted Eline; Winther collection, Tao House Library.

633 "'What happened?' I asked." Ibid.

634 "Well, I hope you enjoy yourself." Ibid.

636 suspects that Carlotta did sleep with Freeman. Ibid.

638 the confidential story Carlotta has confided. Eugene O'Neill Foundation, Tao House Library.

638 he will ask the Berlins to come after dinner. A/BG interview with RC.

638 thanking him for "making Gene so happy." Ibid.

639 "His 'off the record' songs are all right for *old* gentlemen—but for a mixed party of so-called respectable folk—a bit misplaced & embarrassing! . . . personally, I am not old enough, nor young enough, to be excited by ribald songs." 3/11/47, O'Neill Foundation, Tao House Library.

639 "There we were, at opposite ends of the room, Carlotta sedately reading a book, and my face buried in a newspaper." A/BG interview with JL.

640 didn't make an issue of Carlotta's assumed amnesia. A/BG interview with BC, & BC interview for Columbia University Oral History. It must be noted that Cerf was frequently inaccurate in presenting his observations about both O'Neills.

640 "Chorus kids keep coming in for autographs and Gene has a wonderful time," says Crouse. A/BG interview with RC.

641 "I love you!" *Inscriptions*, Dec. 1946.

CHAPTER FORTY-EIGHT

642 "We just killed ourselves trying to find Irish actors," Langner later recalled. A/BG interview with LL.

642 "I signed the contract to play Josie," remembered Mary Welch, "with the added, unusual clause, 'The artist agrees to gain the necessary weight required for the role.'" A/BG interview with Welch, & *Theatre Arts*.

643 "I felt that [Gene] had idealized his brother and would never be able to accept any actor in the part." Ibid.

644 "He mentioned other words which, he said, should not be used on the stage." *The Magic Curtain*, & A/BG interviews with Marshall.

645 the producers will delete eight words. Ibid.

645 "Gene asked us to defer this until he was feeling better and he also asked us to postpone the production of *A Touch of the Poet* for the same reason." A/BG interview with LL, & *The Magic Curtain*.

646 never saw O'Neill again after she left for Hollywood. A/BG interview with Patricia Neal.

647 when it was time for her to make her excuses and leave. A/BG interview with Bergman & CM.

647 Bergman took her departure. Ibid., & *The Eugene O'Neill Newsletter*, May 1979.

647 "He said that the O'Neills felt I hadn't developed enough as an actress to play Abbie." A/BG interview with Neal.

648 "Gene is exhausted—his tremor much worse" and "more depressed than usual." letter, 3/11/47, Sophus Winther Collection, Eugene O'Neill Foundation Research Library at Tao House.

648 they are having to budget their money. Ibid.

648 "who can keep an Irishman from stepping over a cliff?" 6/8/47, A/BG interview with Kennedy, who gave the authors a copy of the letter.

649 now that his "ability to write in long hand has has improved." Aug. 1947, Yale, SL.

649 "I'm going to catch hell for this." A/BG interview with SW.

649 of his escapade and of Carlotta's disapproval. A/BG interview with Weeks.

650 expresses her disapproval of the book and of Sherlee's interest in it. A/BG interview with SW.

650 "I love you, Carlotta, as I have loved you, as I always will!" *Inscriptions.*

651 embarrassed to be a witness to their quarrel, he excuses himself and goes home. A/BG interview with SC, & *"Love and Admiration and Respect."*

652 asks him to come to the penthouse. A/BG interviews with SC.

652 Commins dared to set down his version. *"Love and Admiration and Respect."*

652 "made a melodramatic exit, swearing she would never return." Ibid.

652 removing her clothes and some of her other possessions from the penthouse. CM diary, 1/17/48.

653 asking his help in "getting Gene into a sanatorium." CM diary.

653 only too happy to move in with O'Neill. A/BG interview with Agnes Casey (Walter Casey's sister) & SC.

653 "I felt as though I was alone, in a nightmare." A/BG interview with SWL.

654 Fisk orders O'Neill into Doctors Hospital A/BG interview with SW, SC, & Dr. Shirley Fisk. (This account differs somewhat from what SC later wrote in his book.)

654 "He always managed a smile at the end of our meeting, even when he was uncomfortable." A/BG interviews with Fisk & Patterson.

655 "Where can I take up life at 60?" CM diary, 2/5 & 2/7/48.

655 knows she will always regard him as a villain. A/BG interview with Fisk.

655 describes him in her diary as "stupid, insensitive, trouble-making." 2/4/48.

656 her head in "a whirl." CM diary.

656 to sue for a separation. 3/3/48.

657 safely stored in the trunk where he kept it. *"Love and Admiration and Respect."*

658 to "punish him for reasons totally obscure to him." Ibid.

658 "We had a lovely visit." Dowling's Columbia University Oral History.

658 called his father at the hospital "and told him to leave the old Tory and come and live with him." A/BG interview with CM.

659 the hat he chose was the one she wore to bury her husband. NYT *Magazine,* 5/1/88.

659 "A great many people thought he could, but Carl and I knew they needed each other, and would always go back together." A/BG interview with FM.

660 probably got wind of the proceedings and reported to O'Neill. A/BG interview with SWL.

660 misremembered certain details when interviewed some years later. A/BG interview with JLP.

661 "In a case like this, I don't see how anyone ever understands any of the true issues." 4/9/48, Columbia, SL.

661 "Poor soul, he is as baffled as I am," writes Carlotta, "his faithfulness to the Master is thrown into gutter [together] with my 20 yrs service & love & loyalty." CM diary.

661 only too happy to return to California. Tao House Oral History.

661 to what Dr. Patterson considers "the tops in orthopedic circles." A/BG interview with Dr. Robert Lee Patterson.

662 "The shock to my already sick body and nerves almost ends me." CM diary.

662   "Quit shaking and write me." A/BG interview with Patterson.

662   "Mrs. O'Neill and I are together again with hope and love and a future!" letter
      (undated) shown to A/BG by Patterson.

CHAPTER FORTY-NINE

663   (At least for the moment.) letter, EO to Melville Cane, 6/6/48, Columbia University
      Libraries.

663   "When that was gone there was nothing but disappointment and despair between us."
      JQ, NYT *Magazine*, 5/1/88.

664   "And why complain when the world itself is one vast tremor." letter, 7/26/48, private, SL.

664   that "this letter is being written legibly, without medication." 12/3/48, *As Ever,
      Gene.*

664   new medical research under way into the cause of Parkinsonian tremors. 12/4/48,
      Yale, SL.

664   "I will never write another play and there is no use kidding myself that I will," he
      writes soon after to Aronberg. 2/4/49, Yale, SL.

655   to reaffirm that each is the other's sole beneficiary. CM diary, 5/31/48.

655   house perched on a cliff overlooking the Atlantic CM diary.

666   "The house was so much on the water," Carlotta once recalled, "that it was tied to
      rocks by steel cables and when the storms came up they came right up over our
      heads—we expected to go out to sea at any moment." interview with SP recorded by
      A/BG.

666   "Sweetheart, all my love and all of me." *Inscriptions.*

667   "for your happiness is my happiness!" *Inscriptions*, 7/22/48.

667   paid for the house "out of her reserve fund." 7/26/48, private, SL.

667   supplemented by an additional $25,000 of O'Neill's. 9/12/48, letter to Aronberg,
      Yale, SL.

668   "Gene does *not* in any way deserve this last heartache," she deplores to her diary.
      8/16/48.

668   "I don't fancy 'accusations' beginning again—an unhealthy sign." CM diary, 8/19/48.

668   "His whole body needs extra sedatives . . . watch him all night." CM diary, 9/3/48.

668   "we can't even afford a car!" Yale, SL.

668   "There is peace here for me, and for Carlotta too." 12/4/48, Yale, SL.

669   "the saddest moment of all the years I had known O'Neill," recalled Winther. Sophus
      Winther Collection.

669   "I don't need you anymore." Ibid.

669   "seemed to be filled with a longing for his ancestors." Ibid.

670   whether all tremors are in fact Parkinsonian and, ipso facto, incurable. letter, late
      Dec. 1948 or early Jan. 1949, Yale, SL.

670   "It is not only a matter of hand, but of mind—I just feel there is nothing more I want
      to say." 8/27/49.

671   "Gene's gramophone & records to be stored." CM diary, 6/18 & 6/25/48.

672   so she can keep an eye on him from her bed. A/BG interview with Mai-mai Sze, in
      whom CM confided during a visit to Marblehead Neck.

672 from the nearby town of Salem to prepare and serve their meals. A/BG interview with CM.

672 "At everything in the theatre except being tragic and being comic he is a success . . . the good clean fun of a Hitchcock movie is better." *The Playwright as Thinker: A Study of Drama in Modern Times* (University of Minnesota Press, Minneapolis, 1946).

673 Bentley regretted, "came out too late to be of any use to you." Harcourt, Brace, New York, 1962.

673 labels him a playwright who cannot write. *Paris Review*, Nov.–Dec. 1946.

675 "I don't believe I could live through a production," he tells Langner. A/BG interview with LL.

676 issued his invitation as "probably more a salute than anything else," and also "as a sort of refusal to recognize the reality." letter from Miller to Jackson Bryer, 3/7/89, published in *The Eugene O'Neill Review*, Vol. 17, Nos. 1 & 2, Spring/Fall 1993.

676 despite, as he later wrote, "that first awful production." Ibid.

677 add his "cheers to all the others." 4/29/49, Texas, private.

678 "Young Gene has just committed suicide." *"Love and Admiration and Respect."*

678 in a voice "blazing with anger." Ibid.

678 O'Neill "lapsed into silence and he never mentioned Eugene again." A/BG interview with CM (slightly augmented by SP interview).

679 no such meeting took place. 2/25/50, Yale, SL.

679 unfaithful to her and occasionally struck her. A/BG interview with RL.

680 "He told me he had tried to kill himself once, in New Haven." Ibid.

680 "He also started drinking heavily, more than I realized at first—although I never saw him really drunk." A/BG interview with FM.

680 "He told me we'd have a baby, and I could leave my hair blond, although he preferred me as a brunette," Ruth said. A/BG interview with RL.

680 "I can't get back." A/BG interview with FM.

680 "There was insanity in his eyes." A/BG interview with RL.

683 "I told her Gene had killed himself. Ibid.

684 he paid all the expenses. letter, CM to Winfield Aronberg, 10/26/50, Yale, SL.

684 asked if he could forward it to him in Marblehead. A/BG interview with FM.

684 asking that it be sent to him. 11/20/50, Yale, SL.

685 had "caused more than normal distress in the father, whose own mother had been addicted to drugs and whose tragedy had inspired what many believe to be O'Neill's greatest drama, *Long Day's Journey Into Night*." NYT, 12/7/77.

CHAPTER FIFTY

686 would instinctively try to save himself. A/BG interview with LL.

687 listening to the pounding surf, especially during stormy weather. A/BG interview with Snow.

687 violently allergic and—although she doesn't realize it—it is having a toxic effect. copy of CM's medical history at McLean, where she was confined from 2/7 to 3/29/51, in FM files.

687 unable to write a check legibly. Ibid.

688 a woman "lacking insight and judgment." Ibid.

688 legendary and often-retold events of O'Neill's life. first described in *O'Neill.*

688 dressed only in slacks and a wool shirt. A/BG interview with FM.

688 he lies in the snow. Ibid.

689 "I thought it was very strange he should arrive, when neither of us had telephoned for him to come." interview with CM, tape-recorded by AG, 11/26/61.

689 about 10:00 p.m. when he turns his car into their driveway. A/BG interview with FM.

689 "The doctor took O'Neill's arms and shoulders, and I took his legs very carefully, and we carried him inside." interview with CM, tape-recorded by AG, 11/26/61.

690 "I helped the doctor put him into the ambulance, and off he went to the hospital." Ibid.

690 look of despair that distorted O'Neill's ashen face. A/BG interview with FM.

691 an eye on the forlorn figure standing in the street. A/BG interview with Snow.

691 Snow telephones Dr. Mayo. Ibid.

691 "Then I went out like a light." interview with CM, tape-recorded by AG, 11/26/61.

691 staff psychiatrist to examine her early the following morning. Police and Salem Hospital records indicate it was 9:45 p.m. Tuesday, February 6, when CM was admitted to the hospital.

692 barely coherent and "sounded drunk." A/BG interview with Armina Marshall Langner.

692 makes plans to visit Carlotta. Ibid.

692 to be "in need of immediate care and treatment." Salem Hospital records.

692 Carlotta is taken away. A/BG interview with FM.

693 as she was wheeled into McLean. interview with CM, tape-recorded by AG, 11/26/61.

693 "You shouldn't be here, you should never have been sent here." Ibid.

693 "With all my love, [signed in a hand indisputably his own] Gene." letter dated 2/6/51.

694 when he has occasional drug-induced hallucinations. A/BG interviews with Bird.

694 "He never mentioned his daughter directly," says Bird, "but he gave the impression, in his ramblings, that his entire family had gone wrong." Ibid.

695 thirty-five dollars with which to "buy an Easter bonnet." Ibid.

695 "He just let anyone do what they wanted with him." Ibid.

696 "There's nothing wrong with you, you're putting on an act." A/BG interview with FM.

697 confined to a mental hospital or be placed under the care of a legal guardian. letter, 3/19/51, in FM's files.

697 one of them remained in the room while Moore interviewed her. interview with CM, tape-recorded by AG, 11/26/61.

697 "I couldn't imagine how a stranger *dare* tell me I must give up my husband." CM diary, 3/22/51.

698 "I walked the floor all night," she says. Ibid.

698 appears "perfectly aware of what he is doing." A/BG interview with Farley.

699 prognosis, as described in the "Discharge Summary," signed by William H. Horwitz, MD, is "good." copy of Discharge Summary, dated 3/29/51, in FM files.

CHAPTER FIFTY-ONE

700 "The clearing of my name begins." CM diary, 3/29/51.

700 April 23—is the same as that of O'Neill's lawsuit. records, Probate Court of County Essex Probate Court, in Salem.

701 he might have a hard time eliciting sympathy. A/BG interview with LL.

701 "I felt the transfer would be in his best interests." Ibid.

701 "But, even on the day he was supposed to leave, I thought he might change his mind." A/BG interview with Clare Bird.

701 O'Neill sinks into a fretful sleep. Ibid.

702 he weighs only ninety pounds. A/BG interview with Fisk.

703 early in his hospital stay. A/BG interview with RC.

703 "I stayed a long time." KA interviewed on film for Tao House archives.

704 O'Neill "could no longer arouse her romantic interest in him, so he had to do something else to get some sort of a passionate response." *Time* magazine archives.

705 "Thank God, McLean's is of the honest brand—(there are few these days)." letter, Eugene O'Neill Foundation, Tao House Library.

706 been warned "since '45" (during the production of *The Iceman Cometh*) to be on her guard. Ibid.

706 come to Marblehead and to bring some cash. A/BG interview with Sze.

706 "She talked about how Gene always had to dramatize everything; she said, 'He'll be back, he'll come crawling to me on his knees.'" Ibid.

706 withdrawn his petition for guardianship over her. document filed in Essex County Probate Court, 4/23/51.

706 withdraws her countersuit for separate maintenance. Ibid.

707 "Wicked, wicked man—always choosing unscrupulous persons as your friends and advisers!" CM diary.

707 "'Back' to *what*?" Ibid.

707 "I know that I'm going to die." A/BG interview with Winfield Aronberg.

707 the O'Neills will patch up their differences. A/BG interviews with Charles O'Brien Kennedy & GJN.

707 of course, Carlotta must take him back. A/BG interview with Armina Marshall.

708 "I felt very strongly that he was not going back to her." A/BG interview with KM.

708 overwrought (and sometimes egregiously misinformed) in his later published narrative of their reunion. *"Love and Admiration and Respect."*

708 "all too manifest" that Carlotta is "regaining control." Ibid.

709 "Together they might help each other; apart there could only be even greater torture and then dissolution." Ibid.

709 she improvises answers as best she can. A/BG interview with SW.

709 the return to Carlotta "was never weighed against any other possibility." Ibid.

710 last days alone in an apartment with a male nurse. Ibid.

711 his imminent visit with O'Neill in New York. CM diary.

712 propels her on a fresh rant of fury and resentment. Ibid.

712 reported this to O'Neill, who (Kozol tells Carlotta) believed it. A/BG interview with Dr. Harry L. Kozol.

712 she notes that she feels better. CM diary.

712 "Gene very gay and reports he and Carlotta will live in a hotel opposite Dr. Kozol's office which is good." A/BG interview with Crouse.

713 dresses altered to accommodate her newer, thirty-pounds-lighter figure. CM diary, 5/15/51.

713 asks God for "the strength to nurse Gene & make him feel secure." Ibid.

713 he pronounces, "she is trapped by her own nature and from that there is no escape." Ibid.

714 "He only seems interested in being with her again." Ibid.

715 "was only waiting to get a little stronger." A/BG interview with Joe Heidt.

715 "The next day, he left for Carlotta, instead." A/BG interview with BC.

715 "He said he always made the wrong decision when it came to money." A/BG interview with BA.

715 now Lady Chaplin, set about drinking herself to death. A/BG interviews with Carol Marcus, Phyllis Newman, & others.

716 Dorothy left the room, weeping. A/BG interview with Dorothy Commins.

716 rather than live with him and Dorothy. Commins was wounded to such a degree that, sometime later, he confided his distress to Albert Einstein, a fellow resident at Princeton and a close friend. Einstein was very much interested in O'Neill's relationship with Carlotta. He tried to comfort Commins, but the paradoxes and complexities of the black Irishman's temperament were out of Einstein's sphere and he couldn't give Commins a satisfactory answer.

717 doesn't want a dramatic farewell scene; he has already played too many. A/BG interview with SWL.

718 Patterson leaves the cramped roomette with a cheery wave. A/BG interview with Patterson.

CHAPTER FIFTY-TWO

719 "I can't believe Gene has finally come home." CM diary.

719 "And that was that." A/BG interview with CM.

720 "To Carlotta, my beloved wife, whose love I could not possibly live without, in a spirit of the humblest gratitude for her love which has forgiven my recent shameful conduct toward her." *Inscriptions*, 6/3/51.

721 nor any data "as formerly," about his income for tax returns. 5/26/51, Columbia University Library.

721 "Farewell to crooks!" CM diary, 6/26/51.

722 he and O'Neill discuss the play. CM diary, 8/21/51.

722 is not, as they first feared, cancerous. CM diary, 6/26/51.

723 "Find Gene taking Elixir—again—it is hopeless!" CM diary.

723 again sneaking Elixir (and childishly watering down the medicine bottle's contents). CM diary, 7/29/51.

725 "He had one or two falls getting out of bed, and joked about them to me." A/BG interview with Dr. W. Richard Ohler.

725 "He was reading it for the second time—when he died." Letter, CM to Donald Gallup, 7/24/54, *What Mad Pursuits!*

725 all of which aggravate his tremor. A/BG interviews with Dr. Ohler, & CM diary.

726 "I have loved you for 23 years now, Darling, and now that I am old and can work no more, I love you more than ever!" *Inscriptions.*

727 promise never again to have him hospitalized. CM diary.

728 "My income was getting low, Gene's was getting low, and I was very worried." A/BG interviews with Francis Wylie & CM.

728 "If things get worse, we will publish it." A/BG interview with CM.

729 "I am old and would be sick of life, were it not that you, Sweetheart, are here, as deep and understanding in your love as ever—and I as deep in my love for you as when we stood in Paris, Premier Arrondissement on July 22, 1929, and both said faintly 'Oui!'" *Inscriptions.*

729 "It isn't that I don't trust you, Carlotta," he says, "but you might get run over and I don't want anybody else working on these plays." A/BG interview with CM.

730 "I thought I would die—& he looked as if he had!" letter to Dale Fern, 3/4/54.

730 "It was like tearing up children." A/BG interview with CM. Carlotta, in that interview, claimed she burned the torn pages in the living room fireplace of her suite at the Shelton, a detail described in the authors' 1962 biography, *O'Neill*, but it turned out there was no such fireplace. The Shelton, by then, had been sold to Boston University and had been converted into a women's dormitory, a fact noted by Nicholas Gage, then a student at Boston U, who was the editor of his college paper and a theater fan, when he read the book. With a reporter's curiosity, he visited the reconstructed suite and was surprised to find no fireplace; he confirmed his discovery by checking the architect's blueprints at City Hall. Then he wrote about the error in our book for the Boston University *News*; the story was picked up by the AP, where it came to Arthur Gelb's attention. Gage, responding to a phone call from Gelb asking him to pursue the story, found an employee at the women's dorm who had worked as a maid when it was the Shelton Hotel; she recalled helping Mrs. O'Neill take the bundle of torn papers to the hotel engineer to incinerate in the hotel basement. Carlotta admitted to the authors that she had misspoken, and the error was corrected in a subsequent printing of *O'Neill*. Gage was later hired by Gelb, then the *Times* Metropolitan editor. Gage had a distinguished career as an investigative reporter in New York and later as chief of the *Times* Athens bureau.

730 "No one could get very far trying to persuade him to do anything." SP interview.

730 despair that death would not come. Ibid.

730 recited a poem by the mid-nineteenth-century English poet Austin Dobson, "In After Days": letter to Dale Fern, 4/19/53; researched by Virginia Floyd.

731 "If there is a God and I meet Him, we'll talk things over personally, man to man." A/BG interview with CM.

732 "The Church is a fraud." SW, Tao House Library.

732 "He wanted no one but us to see him when he was dead." CM diary, 12/27/52.

732 last recorded words are a letter to Bennett Cerf, signed by him (as dictated to Carlotta) on June 13, 1951. Columbia University, SL.

733 They carry O'Neil to his bed. CM diary.

733 "He had great trouble moving, and even talking," she recalled. A/BG interview with CM.

733 He was given antibiotics, but the heart was too weak to rally, and there seemed to be no will to live." CM letter to BA, 12/?/53.

734 "Gene wanted no religious service," noted Carlotta, and "a private burial with only Dr. Kozol, Mrs. Welton & I [sic] at his grave." CM diary, 12/27/52.

734 "But, thank God, he is at rest, no one can harm him now." CM diary ?

EPILOGUE

735 "He never had Parkinson's disease. Never." A/BG interview with CM(?).

735 performed on November 28 "at 9 a.m., 16 hours post mortem." see earlier ref. to autopsy report.

735 "perhaps familial, although the family history was never clear as to details." a photostat of "Necropsy No. 16,697" was given to A/BG by CM.

736 Gierow points out, "from top to toe the body loses all control; a helpless wreck, a foundering ship, a hull without a helm." A/BG interview with Gierow.

736 "The being without him is at times almost more than I can bear." letter dated 12/12/53; NY Public Library, Locke Collection, Carlotta Monterey Papers.

737 (In his will, O'Neill had written: "I desire to be buried in a burial lot with my wife and I authorize my Executrix to purchase such a lot and erect a simple stone thereon.") interview by SP recorded by A/BG.

738 "I planted laurel around the headstone, like the laurel wreaths of the Greek heroes." Ibid.

738 she destroys the diaries she kept for 1946 and 1947. CM diary.

740 "Will I ever be able to free myself from this man—and the love I felt for him!" 11/27/55.

740 "I hope you understand." copy of letter given to A/BG by Cohen.

742 gazing into their future, idyllic life. Carlotta signed a copy of the photo to Arthur Gelb during a period in the Gelbs' research when Barbara—who has indiscreetly inquired about an episode involving O'Neill's second wife, Agnes—is temporarily out of favor.

744 "I saw to it that he was able to work." A/BG interview with Capalbo.

744 and Betty Field as Deborah Harford. *A Moon for the Misbegotten*, unlike the still-under-rated *A Touch of the Poet*, was finally recognized for its tragic grandeur years after O'Neill's death, when, on Dec. 29, 1973, it was resurrected on Broadway by Jose Quintero. He had the glittering assistance not only of Jason Robards as the dying Jamie Tyrone, but also of Colleen Dewhurst, who made the role of the oversized Josie Hogan her own and whose Tony Award–winning performance has thus far never been topped.

745 Regent Hospital, a small private facility on East Sixty-first Street. A/BG interview with Dr. Cherrick.

746 "She had a tongue that could cut." A/BG interview with JQ.

747 peering through the magnifying glass she'd used to decipher O'Neill's handwriting. A/BG interview with RC.

748 a buffer between Carlotta and her dwindling social and business obligations. A/BG interviews with JR & Dr. Cherrick.

748 collating the material in the vast O'Neill collection. A/BG interviews with DG.

750 privately printing five hundred copies of the volume she has entitled *Inscriptions: Eugene O'Neill to Carlotta Monterey O'Neill*. In a handwritten letter accompanying a copy of *Inscriptions*, sent by Carlotta to the authors of this biography on May 5, 1960, she wrote, "Now that you have *Inscriptions*, there can be no question as to who wrote them!"

751 "Not that Gene, in spite of all his dedications and little notes swearing love and begging for forgiveness, didn't also hate me." "Carlotta and the Master" by JQ, NYT *Magazine*, 5/1/88.

751 she is in the early stages of senile dementia. A/BG interview with JR.

752 "It was very plain that she needed care," he explained. A/BG interview with DG.

752 realizes it is "clearly hopeless" for Carlotta to return to the Carlton House. A/BG interviews with JR.

752 "She would wander in the halls, and go down to the desk and complain that people were spying on her." A/BG interviews with JR & GRC.

753 "we wanted to avoid publicity, we wanted Carlotta somewhere she would not be known." A/BG interview with JR.

753 "At St. Luke's," concluded Cherrick, "Mrs. O'Neill was very attentively looked after by the staff, and she could not have had better treatment in any other hospital." A/BG interview with GRC.

754 given custodial care and treated with Thorazine, a strong tranquilizer. Ibid.

754 "'Pay no attention, she's a loony.'" A/BG interviews with DG.

755 "She said she didn't need much." A/BG interview with JQ.

756 He never sees Carlotta again. A/BG interviews with JQ.

757 he professes his concern. Ibid., & interview with GRC.

757 "she got back to the state she had been in before coming to St. Luke's." A/BG interview with GRC.

757 Carlotta would "ruminate about O'Neill, and often about her own early life." Ibid.

757 "There was really nothing I could do for her anymore." A/BG interview with JR.

757 "She visited Carlotta twice a week." A/BG interview with Crockett.

758 she is transferred there in July. A/BG interview with RC.

758 "It was not a place you'd choose to give a party," says Crockett, somewhat defensively, "but for a nursing home, it was pleasant." Ibid.

758 she is in good health and might live to be one hundred. A/BG interviews with Crockett & DG.

758 her heart has worn out. A/BG interview with RC.

759 no one to plant laurel for Carlotta. Parts of this epilogue were published in a 1972 "enlarged" edition of *O'Neill*.

PHOTO CREDITS

Page 18: Courtesy of Tao House

Page 19: Courtesy of National Parks Service

Page 20, all photos: Copyright © George Karger-Pix

Page 22, top: Courtesy of Yale University Press

Page 22, bottom: Courtesy of Beinecke Library Collection, Yale University

Page 24: Courtesy of Beinecke Library Collection, Yale University

INDEX